SHIPBUILDERS
TO THE WORLD

SHIPBUILDERS TO THE WORLD

125 years of Harland and Wolff, Belfast
1861-1986

Michael Moss and John R. Hume

THE
BLACKSTAFF
PRESS
BELFAST AND WOLFEBORO, NEW HAMPSHIRE

First published in 1986
by The Blackstaff Press
3 Galway Park, Dundonald, Belfast BT16 0AN, Northern Ireland
and
27 South Main Street, Wolfeboro, New Hampshire 03894 USA

Typeset by The Brown Fox
Printed in Northern Ireland
by The Universities Press Limited

British Library Cataloguing in Publication Data
Moss, Michael S.
Shipbuilders to the world: 125 years of Harland and Wolff,
Belfast, 1861-1986.
1. Harland and Wolff Limited — History
I. Title   II. Hume, John R.
338.7'62382'0094167   VM301.H3

Library of Congress Cataloging-in-Publication Data
Moss, Michael S.
Shipbuilders to the world.
Bibliography: p.
Includes indexes.
1. Harland and Wolff—History. 2. Shipbuilding—Northern
Ireland—Belfast—History. 3. Belfast—History, Naval.
I. Hume, John R. II. Title.
VM301.H3M67   1986   338.7'62382'094167   85-28632
ISBN   0 85640 343   1

CONTENTS

LIST OF TABLES

FOREWORD

It is a great honour to have been invited by the board of Harland and Wolff to write a foreword to the Company's history. I recognised from the start that it would be no easy task, but, as one who was proud to have been its chairman in the early 1970s, I hope I have been able to capture something of the atmosphere of this truly remarkable company. Like many of its own great ships, it has, in its 125 years, undoubtedly encountered frequent rough passages, but it has come through. That surely shows the mettle from which it draws its strength.

Over many years I have been involved with a wide variety of different industries: one common experience which stands out in my mind, and which is a cause for serious concern, is a too frequent failure to safeguard the records of our great industrial past, before they are lost or dispersed beyond easy collection and analysis. Histories like this one represent so much of the real life of our nation during the last century or two. There may be accounts of wars, histories of imperial growth and decline, of burning political and other issues, biographies of great statesmen and public figures, but at the end of the day how many successful nations, governments or rulers did not depend on the contribution of industry, its leaders, its designers and its workforce, with all their varying skills? Together they provided the foundations without which so much else could not have been built.

During my years as chairman of Harland and Wolff I do not recall any project such as this history even having been contemplated. Perhaps we were mesmerised by the day-to-day problems and were not sufficiently far sighted, but, whatever the excuse, I can hardly imagine that today's problems are any less absorbing that those we had to deal with. So at the outset let me pay a humble tribute to the wisdom of the present board of directors for commissioning this book.

It is Lord Byron of Rochdale – the poet – who is recorded as saying that 'truth is stranger than fiction'. Certainly, as I read through the draft pages of *Shipbuilders to the World*, not only did I learn much of the past of which, to my shame, I was unaware, but I realised that here was an extraordinary, and in some ways unique, industrial saga, clearly of great importance.

I have been particularly impressed by the way in which the authors have described the varying fortunes and vicissitudes of the Company, in no way in isolation but rather against the backcloth of the wider and often turbulent events of the day. I have in mind such matters as the vexed issue of Home Rule, sectarian controversy, the disruptive, and at times devastating, effect of two world wars, the swing from boom to depression and recovery, the technological explosion, the decline of traditional shipping and its traumatic effect on shipbuilding worldwide, to say nothing of the surge of competition from overseas, particularly from the Third World. All this suggests a daunting sequence of events that could not fail to make an indelible mark on the fortunes and morale of any company. Harland and Wolff has been no exception. Such an account as this must surely appeal not only to those particularly interested in the shipbuilding industry but to a far wider readership in many fields.

ix

There can be no more telling examples of change than to point to the ships themselves: from a mere 500-ton vessel built when Edward Harland first arrived in Belfast at the end of 1854, to the 330,000-tonne-deadweight crude oil carriers which were building when I left the Company; from ships of wood to vessels of iron and steel; from sail to steam and diesel; from riveting to welding. The authors highlight many such vivid comparisons. Perhaps, however, the most striking phenomenon described is the staggering growth from what started as a small partnership, almost a family undertaking, to the 'most powerful shipbuilding and shipping group in the world' (Chapter 6).

How did all this come about? Undoubtedly the life of the Company has spanned a period of great opportunity, both technologically and commercially, but opportunities are not always clearly seen, nor their potential appreciated: there is not always the vision or indeed the will to risk incursion into the unknown. Yet it is just such vision and will that the following pages disclose.

At times of great opportunity leaders of stature and imagination are needed at the helm, people who can see and take full advantage of the situation whether in peace or in war – and Harland and Wolff had the leaders it needed. Sir Edward Harland, Gustav Wolff, Lord Pirrie and Sir Frederick Rebbeck stand out, but there were others in more recent years who have made notable contributions and who are to be found in the text. Also well recorded is the magnificent response to challenge which has been made on many occasions by the Company's management and the workforce at large.

Of course there were mistakes, of course there were failures, misjudgements and lost opportunities, but considering the periodic storms and changes of direction that had to be mastered – never more so than in the many years of recurring financial crises – the final judgement on the Company must surely be that its achievements were remarkable.

So what were some of the strong points that made these achievements possible? I will mention four: determined pioneering on new and advanced technical methods and designs; bold investment to meet growing and changing demands wherever they might be foreseen; constant attention to technical excellence and the unshakeable conviction that what was worth doing was worth doing well; and, perhaps above all, good and understanding industrial management. These were some of the qualities for which Harland and Wolff earned a well deserved reputation.

But what of the weaknesses? I will mention one. In every walk of life there is too often a tendency for great men to have difficulty in realising when it is time for them to hand over to the next generation who must inevitably succeed and hopefully surpass them. Herein lies danger and, whilst readers will judge for themselves, it seems to me a danger which Harland and Wolff has not always managed to avoid.

As they move into the last lap of the story in Chapter 14, readers will realise that here was a period of confusion for the shipbuilding industry – internationally, nationally, commercially, and, at times perhaps, politically. Certainly it is an era that offers endless scope for discussion and argument, but as it was the period which included the years of my own chairmanship, it would be improper for me to enter into the ring. I would merely say that the account of this time set out in the text is, I believe, correct and fair.

In the final chapter, 'The way ahead', we see a Company smaller, indeed, in size but firmly established as an advanced shipbuilder, with strong and determined leadership committed to innovation and rapid and informed decision-making. It can be likened to some 'splendid ship' – to quote Robert Bridges – 'that fearest nor sea rising, nor sky clouding', sailing around the world and flying the flag of Queen's Island, Belfast. Here surely is a picture of which Edward Harland and Gustav Wolff could well be proud.

I regard the effort put into this book as an immensely valuable investment, I congratulate the authors on a complex task well done, and I commend their work for reading.

Rochdale

House of Lords
Westminster
1986

INTRODUCTION

BENEATH TWO YELLOW GANTRIES

The skyline of Belfast today is dominated by two enormous yellow gantries that tower over the port. Named Samson and Goliath, they can be seen right across the city. Only those visitors with no imagination or curiosity can fail to pause and wonder at their size and stark beauty. The people of Belfast will tell you that they mark the site of Harland & Wolff's shipyard on Queen's Island. They will speak with fierce pride of its achievements, the magnificence of its transatlantic liners, the tragedy of the *Titanic*, the yard's vital role in two world wars, its colossal oil tankers and its recent success in winning business. They could tell of the unlikely partnership between a Yorkshireman, Edward Harland, and a Hamburg Jew, Gustav Wolff; of the triumph of Lord Pirrie; of the courageous deeds of Sir Frederick Rebbeck and of the confidence instilled by John Parker. Everyone in Belfast has their own history of the yard, since few families have not been touched by the scale of its enterprise.

The inquisitive visitor who is drawn to the two yellow gantries will find a vast complex of engineering shops and shipyard buildings. A walk through Queen's Island is an awe-inspiring experience. Curiously, perhaps because of its size, the full history of the 'Island' and its shipyards has never been written. This book is an attempt to compensate in part for this omission. It has been published to mark two anniversaries: the 125th anniversary, in 1986, of the formation of the original partnership between Edward Harland and Gustav Wolff; and the centenary, in December 1985, of the limited company. In the chapters which follow we have told the exciting, and at times incredible, story of the growth and development of Harland & Wolff from its origins in the mid-nineteenth century up to the present. In writing this history we have guarded against the ever present temptation to tell too much about the wonderful ships the firm has built. This would take several volumes. We have included illustrations of many of the vessels, and a list of ships built appears at the end of the book. The berths in the Company's yards were periodically renumbered and, to reduce confusion, we have included plans in appropriate places. We make no apologies for the complexity of the story, for to over-simplify would merely be to understate the achievements of those who created, managed and worked for Harland & Wolff.

To help readers we have adopted some conventions. The firm as a partnership between Edward Harland and G.W. Wolff is referred to as Harland and Wolff. The limited company is referred to as Harland & Wolff or the Company (although in fact the current style of the name is Harland and Wolff plc). When writing about the Royal Mail Shipping Group as a whole, in Chapters 7, 8 and 9, we have referred to it as the Royal Mail Group or simply the Group. Capital letters have generally been avoided in referring to the Company's branches, plant and executives. In following the story it should be noted that the firm's financial year coincided with the calendar year until 1885. From 1885 the financial year began on 1 July and ended on 30 June. After 1924 the financial year again followed the calendar year until 1981 when it was changed to match the fiscal year from 1 April to 31 March. Information in the tables is based on the internal financial records of the Company which are described in the introduction to the reference section, on page 494. Readers should note that the names of shipowning companies given in the ship list and sometimes referred to in the text are not necessarily the names of the lines which operated the vessels. For example, the *Titanic*, ship no. 401, a White Star liner, was owned by the Oceanic Steam Navigation Company. Where the story parallels that told in the book by Edwin Green and Michael Moss *A Business of National Importance – The Royal Mail Shipping Group, 1902–1937* we have either adapted or précised the account to be found there. We realise that in attempting to record a history as monumental as that of Harland & Wolff we will have made mistakes. For these we beg your forgiveness. We hope they will not mar your enjoyment of a story which we have found compelling and fascinating to research and write from the moment we first stood underneath the two yellow gantries.

ACKNOWLEDGEMENTS

We are most grateful to the chairman and directors of Harland and Wolff plc for inviting us to write the history of their business. We have greatly enjoyed the task. We would like to thank all the staff of the Company and the former employees who have helped us and made our visits to Belfast pleasurable. Their kindness and enthusiasm was often overwhelming. They are too numerous to name individually and we ask their pardon if we mention only a few whose contribution has gone beyond the call of duty. Although the project was conceived under the chairmanship of Dr Vivian Wadsworth, John Parker from his appointment has been a fervent supporter, continuously seeking out people who could offer us insights into the Company's history. We are thankful to him and to his predecessors Dr Denis Rebbeck, Sir John Mallabar, Alan Watt, the Viscount Rochdale, Sir Brian Morton and Alec Cooke, all of whom have given their views freely and frankly. We are bound to mention John S. Baillie, who joined the Company in 1913: he has an uncanny memory and without his sage counsel this book would have been the poorer. He recalls events with startling precision and with a wit which illuminates the humanity of those who directed the Company's fortunes. Ronald Punt, a former managing director, and Douglas Cooper, the present deputy managing director, gave us valuable insights into the recent history of the Company, as did four of the present directors, Bert Harkness, Eric Hellström, Stewart Tennant and David Tinkler, on their respective areas of responsibility. Past director Herbert Crossey shared his memories of his active and varied career at Queen's Island. We are deeply indebted to other former employees: D.H. Alexander, formerly principal of Belfast College of Technology, for his recollections of the Company from his childhood; Carl Beck who shared with us his researches into the Company's aircraft production; and Helen W. Taylor who worked in the London office in Lord Pirrie's time.

In our quest into the history of the Company, which has been such a major force in British business, we have consulted the records of customers, finance houses, banks, government and many individuals. We would like to thank in particular the following people: Lord Aberconway; the late 4th Duke of Abercorn; the late Rt. Hon. Sir John Andrews and Thomas Andrews, formerly of Ardara, for permission to consult the Andrews family papers; A.P. Armitage of Liverpool; the Governor and Court of the Bank of England; the Bank of Ireland and J.F. Rudd, secretary; Belfast

City Council, particularly the Town Clerk's and Parks Departments; Belfast Harbour Commissioners for permission to consult their records, and C. Nimmons, E. Menelly and E. Finlay; Tom Boyd; Belfast Steamship Company; the British & Commonwealth Shipping Company, its subsidiaries Clan Line Steamers, King Line and Union-Castle Mail Shipping Company, its chairman Lord Cayzer, K.W. Donald and Charles Lemon; John Brown & Company; Rowland Brown for his researches in Liverpool; Bibby Brothers & Company, Derek Bibby, chairman, and J.E. Roberts, secretary; Brown, Picton and Hamly Libraries, Liverpool; David Burrell; Dr Ian Buxton; Dr Stanley Chapman of the University of Nottingham for kindly showing us his notes on the Schwabe family's textile interests; Bruce Ismay Cheape for permission to consult the Ismay family papers; Colonel John Christie Miller; Dr Tom R. Craig, formerly chairman of Colvilles Limited, for permission to consult his father's papers and for his own recollections; J.P. Corry & Company and Roger Corry; H.M. Customs & Excise, Belfast, for permission to consult the register of ships for the port; the Imperial War Museum and Paul J. Kemp, Department of Photographs; Dr Peter Davies, head of the Department of Economic History, University of Liverpool; Dr D.S. Johnson, the Queen's University of Belfast; Lord Kennet; the Linen Hall Library, Belfast, and John Gray, the librarian; Sir William Lithgow for permission to consult his father's papers and for his own recollections; Alan McLintock for permission to consult the papers of the Royal Mail voting trustees; M.A.N.-B&W Diesel A/S, Copenhagen, and Bo Haarmark; Colonel Terence Maxwell for permission to consult the papers of the Royal Mail voting trustees and those of his father; the Midland Bank; the National Maritime Museum, Dr Roger Knight and Campbell McMurray; Pat Newman; the County Archives Department, North Yorkshire County Council; the Northern Bank; the Northern Ireland Office, and the Rt. Hon. James Prior, formerly Secretary of State; Nigel Overton, keeper of maritime and aviation history, Tudor House Museum, Southampton; Christopher Norton, the University of Ulster; Dr John Orbell of Baring Brothers, Sons & Company; Ocean Transport & Trading Limited and H.N. Smyth; the Peninsular & Oriental Steam Navigation Company, Stephen Rabson, group librarian, Amanda Gosling, public relations secretary, and Dr Freda Harcourt, of Queen Mary College London, who is writing a history of the formative years of that company; Dr G.D. Pirrie, of Eastbourne, and other members of his family; Price Waterhouse and Anthony Wilson, formerly senior partner; the Public Record Office; the Public Record Office of Northern Ireland; Ian Ramsay of Langbank; Gordon Reid, Merseyside County Archive Service; Viscount Runciman of Doxford for his recollections of the events of 1931; J. Henry Schroder Wagg & Company and Dr R. Roberts; H.B.T. Schwabe; Anthony Slaven, professor in business history at the University of Glasgow, for kindly making available his notes on the records of National Shipbuilders Securities Limited; the late Michael Babington Smith for permission to consult the papers of the Royal Mail voting trustees and for his graphic recollections of his period of service as personal assistant to Brigadier-General Sir Arthur Maxwell; Staatsarchiv, Senat der Freien – und Hansestadt Hamburg; Cecil Slator; Tyne and Wear Archives Department; the Ulster Bank and C. Colthurst, secretary; the Ulster Folk and Transport Museum and Michael McCaughan; the Ulster Museum; the Ulster Steamship Company Limited, and M.W.S. MacLaren, J.C. Walsh and C. McAuley; the Union Discount Company of London and G.T. Cleaver; Andrew Weir & Company and the late Lord Inverforth, Captain F.B. Rodgers and Brian Lucy; West Yorkshire Archive Service; and Hugh Peebles of the University of Stirling.

In navigating a course through the Company's history we have been fortunate to be able to call on the advice of a number of 'pilots'. Outside the Company, Douglas Carson has read the text and has supplied valuable comment, additional information and insight. He has also allowed us to see the results of his investigations into the history of his family and to publish the family tree which appears on pages 94 and 95. We thank him for his companionship and enthusiasm and we extend our thanks also to his colleague Victor Kelly, of the East Belfast Historical Society, for allowing us to tap his deep knowledge of the past. Robin Sweetnam has generously given us the benefit of his research of a lifetime into the history of Belfast harbour and shipbuilding on the Lagan, correcting and illuminating many of our assumptions. William Lind, with customary zeal, has unearthed a great deal of information relating to the Company and has cheerfully loaned us books from his extensive library. Edwin Green of the Midland Bank, who wrote *A Business of National Importance — The Royal Mail Shipping Group, 1902-1937* with Michael Moss, has proved a tower of strength, as both a critic and a friend. Robert Blunden, who has compiled an exhaustive record of ships built by the Company, has cast his searching gaze over the ship list which begins on page 506. Trevor Parkhill, at the Public Record Office of Northern Ireland, has encouraged us with his good humour, provided a mass of information, read the manuscript with a cautious eye, and cheerfully listed piles of the Company's records—now transferred to his safekeeping. In this he was ably assisted by Patricia Kernaghan.

Inside the Company, David Geary, the former Company secretary, introduced us to all those he thought might help and was always ready with kindly advice along the course. At the special request of the board, his predecessor, Ewart Murphy, read the bulk of the text and gave us the benefit of his knowledge of the workings of the Company. The assistant secretary, Trevor Neill, and Alan Hedgley, the former publicity officer, were constant sources of information. Eric Patton, of the finance department, produced like a magician a bewildering store of financial records which he cheerfully copied for us. Former Queen's Island men Billy Baxter, Alan Brew, Angus Carrick, David Comeskey, Jack Kirkpatrick, Francis Lowry, Douglas Liddell, Norman McArthur, Sam McCabe, Malcolm Mackenzie, James Magee, Edward Moller, Jimmy Salmon, Johnny Simpson, John Tyack and Stanley Watson contributed memories of their times with the Company; and present employees Robin Cameron, Edward Greer, Bill Harrison, Maurice McKeown and Jim Smith have all given freely of their expert knowledge. In the detailed preparation and checking of the ship list, Gordon Lindsay's dedicated efforts were particularly valuable, while John Bedford, William Gilles, John McNally, Joe Vance and Elizabeth Childs contributed to first-class teamwork. We are also indebted to the office-bearers of the H & W Staff Sports & Recreation Association Limited and the H & W Welders Social & Football Club, not only for information, but also for their warm welcome. The fine plan drawings that illustrate the book were prepared by Isaac Busby, assisted by Keith Whitelaw and Derek Menice of the Company's facilities department drawing office. Bertie Traynor, assisted by May Gilliland, has given us the run of his 'Aladdin's cave' of photographic negatives, skilfully and uncomplainingly printing those that took our fancy. In the selection of photographs, John Rankin's assistance has been invaluable, as has that of Tommy McCluskie in searches for archival drawings. Dr Maria Moloney, the public relations manager, has worked closely with the publishers to produce this beautiful volume. We gratefully acknowledge the contribution of Steven Thom in the text-checking process.

Our greatest debt is to Rodney McCullough who has devoted his time and energies to our needs, guided us through vast storerooms filled with records, been our host and friend, masterminded the typing of the text and eased our burden with countless kindnesses. Behind every good man it is said there is a woman but in this case there were six – all skilled word-processor operators attached to the Company secretary's office. Recognising the magnitude of their task, it would be an omission not to mention them by name – Effie Cairns, Laura Edgar, Alison Graham, Sylvia Kinkead, Rose Lynch and Ann Marshall.

Michael Moss
John R. Hume
1986

1
THE LAGAN WATERWAY

Ships and seafaring are part of the fabric of Ulster life. Boats have been built commercially on the shores of Belfast Lough for at least 300 years. A list of ships owned by Belfast merchants in 1663 includes two vessels of between 30 and 40 tons, a barque of 25 tons, a ketch of 50 tons and eleven gabbards (small trading vessels) that had been constructed locally.[1] These craft were probably built by groups of itinerant ships' carpenters, whose main trade would have been in repairs.

For much of the eighteenth century the Lagan was a narrow twisting river where navigation was hazardous. As Belfast grew in importance as a trading centre so pressure increased for improvements in the waterway. During 1729 the Irish Parliament passed an 'Act for cleansing the Ports, Harbours and Rivers of the City of Cork, and of the Towns of Gallway, Sligoe, Drogheda and Belfast, and for erecting a Ballast-Office in the said City and each of the said Towns'. Belfast Corporation was to control the Ballast Office which was to have a monopoly over the supply of ballast, and power to impose dues to pay for the maintenance of the harbour. Ballast could be taken only from the river bottom and not from the banks. This legislation was largely ineffective and in 1785 a new Act was passed, forming 'The Corporation for preserving and improving the Port and Harbour of Belfast', better known as the 'Ballast Board'. It had wide powers which included 'building and erecting such ballast wharfs and such wet and dry docks for shipping as the said Corporation shall judge requisite and proper'.[2]

The members of the new Ballast Board, most of whom were merchants in the town, were determined to make reforms: buoys and perches were constructed to mark the channel, and land leased to form new quays. In 1791 their activity attracted the attention of William Ritchie, a shipbuilder from Saltcoats on the Ayrshire coast. He had opened a yard there in 1775 and catered for demand from west-of-Scotland shipowners who, as a result of war, could no longer obtain new tonnage from America. Using timber imported from south Wales, his business flourished and was shortly joined by two others. Between 1775 and 1790 the three yards built sixty-four vessels, a total tonnage of 7,095, some of which were for Belfast owners. Their trade was depressed in 1790/91 and William Ritchie was keen to explore opportunities elsewhere.[3] He visited Belfast in March 1791 at the invitation of some of the local merchants to discover that there were only six jobbing ships' carpenters, who, lacking direction, were not in regular employment. As an inducement to Ritchie to set up in Belfast, the Ballast Board agreed to build a 'graving platform' on which vessels could be beached for careening and repair. He returned to the city on 3 July with ten men and a quantity of shipbuilding apparatus and materials and set up in business, in partnership with his brother Hugh, at the Old Lime Kiln dock. This was situated on the Co. Antrim side of the Lagan at the foot of the Fore Plantation,[4] where Corporation Street now runs. Ritchies' first ship, the *Hibernian*, of 300 tons, was launched on 7 July 1792, reportedly 'the only vessel of any burthen which for many years had been built in the port'.[5]

William Ritchie, a
shipbuilder from Saltcoats
in Ayrshire, who moved to
Belfast in 1791 and opened
a shipyard at the Old Lime
Kiln dock. (*William Ritchie*,
by Thomas Robinson,
courtesy of the Belfast
Harbour Commissioners)

So successful were the Ritchie brothers that three years later they leased from the Marquess of Donegall additional sloblands to the north of their yard. The following year, 1796, the Ballast Board commissioned the Ritchies to build a graving dock on Corporation ground immediately adjacent to this new addition to their yard, at a cost of £7,684. The dock (named 'Clarendon dock no. 1' some forty years later) could accommodate two vessels of 300-ton burthen and was completed in November 1800.[6] During the course of its construction in 1798 Hugh Ritchie left the firm to open another shipyard on slobland to the north of the new dock. His elder brother carried on the original business, William Ritchie & Company, at the Old Lime Kiln dock, now named Ritchie's dock. Hugh Ritchie died in January 1807 and was succeeded by his eldest brother, John, who had continued as a shipbuilder in Saltcoats. Four years later he took another Scotsman, Alexander McLaine, into partnership to form the firm Ritchie & McLaine. Later Alexander McLaine married John Ritchie's daughter, Martha.[7] William Ritchie launched the *James*, of 400 tons, in 1810, the largest ship constructed in Belfast up to that time. By 1812 he was able to record:

> Since the commencement I have built thirty two vessels, and my brother eight, besides several lighters and small ones. The vessels I have built were from 50 to 450 tons burthen, the greatest part about 220 tons . . . since I came here, I have brought from Scotland several ship-joiners, block-makers, and blacksmiths. In my blacksmith's shop all kinds of ship-work are done in the best manner, also anchors of all sizes to fourteen hundredweight. There are now employed in the two shipyards forty four journeymen carpenters; fifty five apprentices; seven pairs of sawyers; twelve blacksmiths and several joiners.[8]

William Ritchie was an adventurous and innovative shipbuilder. The *Belfast News-Letter* noted in March 1818:

> On Tuesday next there will be launched from the dockyard of William Ritchie & Co a new schooner of about 60 tons burthen, built for the purpose of displaying a new system of naval architecture. She is constructed without frame timber, beams or knees, and without any metal below water, except a few bolts in her keel and rudder brace. The advantages presumed in this method are saving in price of shipbuilding, strength, duration, capacity, tightness, buoyancy, sailing and safety.

Called the *New System*, she was launched with her crew and provisions on board and her sails fitted. Six years before, in 1812, Henry Bell, of Helensburgh on the Clyde, had had built for him the first commercially successful steam boat, the *Comet*. Very quickly his example was copied by shipbuilders and marine engineers elsewhere in the United Kingdom. The first steam-boat hull to be constructed in Ireland seems to have been the *City of Cork*, built by Andrew and Michael Hennesey, of Passage, Co. Cork, in 1816. During that year the first steam boat appeared on the Lagan, the luggage boat *Greenock*, of 98 tons, which came across from the Clyde. It was not until 1819 that the first passenger steam boat is reported to have docked at Belfast; this was the *Rob Roy* built by William Denny, of Dumbarton on the Clyde, and designed by the celebrated marine engineer David Napier. During March of the following year Ritchie & McLaine launched the hull of the steam boat *Belfast* for George Langtry, a Belfast shipowner – 'The day was extremely fine and the novelty of the sight attracted a great concourse of spectators, many of whom had come from distant parts of the country.' The ship was 115 feet long, of 200 tons and powered by two 70-horse-power engines, supplied by the Lagan Foundry of Coates & Young.

3

This concern, which had been established in 1799, manufactured textile machinery and steam engines.[9]

William Ritchie retired in 1820 at the age of sixty and entrusted the management of his yard to a fellow Scot, Charles Connell, whom he had employed since 1818. Connell, like Ritchie, enjoyed the confidence of the Ballast Board. Shortly after taking the reins he was instructed by the Board to remove the sloop *John and Mary* which had foundered at the mouth of the channel and blocked it. Instead of using salvage equipment he persuaded the commander of the Belfast garrison to lend him all his available troops. Next morning before high tide they assembled on the strand and bodily hauled the vessel out of the waterway. During 1824 Charles Connell purchased Ritchie's business and renamed it Charles Connell & Sons. The first ship to be built by the new firm, the schooner *Jane*, was launched in June 1825. The following year the Ballast Board completed a second graving dock, which had been under construction spasmodically for ten years.[10]

John Ritchie died on 4 April 1828 at the age of seventy-seven. His Pilot Street shipyard became the property of his son-in-law, Alexander McLaine, who, following Connell's lead, took his sons into partnership and formed a new business, Alexander McLaine & Sons. The two yards would seem to have continued the pattern of activity set by their founders, with Connell building more and larger vessels than McLaine. In 1832 Connell launched the *Fairy*, of 310 tons, which was the first ship to bring tea direct from Canton to Belfast. This was followed in the next year by the 500-ton ship *Penington* for John Harrison of Belfast. Both firms built steam-boat hulls. Connell launched the hull of the steam ship *Aurora*, of 700 tons, on 9 October 1838. Since she was the largest vessel built in Ireland up to that time, large crowds gathered to see her slip down the ways.[11] So as to sustain their enterprises, both concerns signed on apprentices to learn the shipbuilder's craft. The apprentice's indentures left him in no doubt of what was expected. He swore that he:

> shall not reveal any of his Master's secrets, nor conceal his loss or prejudice when known to him, but shall in due time discover and do his utmost to prevent the same. He shall not be guilty of drinking, nor accessory to any riots or tumults on the street, nor haunt idle or debauched company. He shall not walk in processions. He shall not commit fornication, nor contract Matrimony within the said Term . . . but shall in all respects promote his Master's interests, and behave and acquit himself as becomes a faithful and diligent apprentice,

Two views of William Ritchie's yard in Belfast in 1812. In both views the same ship is depicted on the ways ready for launching. On the left a vessel has been canted to have her bottom cleaned. (Painting by D. Stewart, courtesy of the Ulster Museum)

and shall, during the whole Term aforesaid, provide all the Tools and Implements necessary for learning and practising his said Trade.[12]

By 1838 there was a third shipyard, opened by Kirwan & McCune at Dunbar's dock, which had recently been constructed on the same bank further down the river from the two dry docks. The yard launched its vessels into the Lagan and not the dock. During the year it constructed the *William and Mary*, a 114-ton schooner.[13]

While the foundations of the Belfast shipbuilding industry had been laid in the fifty years since 1791, every major port in the United Kindom had experienced similar developments. The Thames shipbuilders led the industry, hotly pursued by those on the Tyne and Wear. The techniques of iron shipbuilding were pioneered in England by the Horseley Ironworks, of Staffordshire, which built the first all-iron vessel, *Aaron Manby*, in 1822. The Birkenhead shipbuilders Lairds were building in iron by 1829, and in the early 1830s the leading London builders Maudslay Sons & Field, of Lambeth, and William Fairbairn, of Millwall, followed suit. During 1838 William Fairbairn constructed the first iron ship classed A1 in *Lloyd's Register*. In that year Coates & Young, whose Lagan Foundry had become the principal marine engine works in Ireland, diversified into iron shipbuilding when they launched the *Countess of Caledon* for the Ulster Steam Navigation Company. The *Belfast News-Letter* recorded that 'the craft glided majestically into the water, amidst the firing of ordnance and the hearty cheering of a large number of spectators'.[14] The vessel was to be employed in towing lighters on Lough Neagh. None of the other Belfast shipbuilders followed this example.

The emergence of the shipbuilding industry on the Lagan during the opening decade of the nineteenth century was a reflection of the sharp rise in Belfast's trade as the town became an important centre of linen manufacture, exporting worldwide. Towards the end of the Napoleonic Wars Belfast merchants were becoming concerned about the difficulty of navigating the channel from the Pool of Garmoyle at the head of the lough to the docks in the town centre. The channel was so shallow that many vessels had to anchor three miles from the quays and have their cargoes and passengers taken in by light craft. The Ballast Board and the local collector for the Commissioners of Customs for Ireland investigated various schemes for improving the waterway. In 1821 the famous civil engineer John Rennie proposed that the harbour should be converted into a wet dock, with a ship canal running down to the Pool of Garmoyle. The enormous cost of this scheme, estimated at £250,000,

Captain William Pirrie, who was a member of the Ballast Board and later a Harbour Commissioner, was responsible for improvements in the Lagan waterway in the 1830s and 1840s. He was grandfather of Lord Pirrie, chairman of Harland & Wolff. (*Captain William Pirrie*, artist unknown, courtesy of the Belfast Harbour Commissioners)

hindered progress.[15] Meanwhile trade continued to expand.

The growing prosperity of Belfast attracted new settlers from rural Ireland, Scotland and Merseyside. Between 1800 and 1832 the population grew from 20,000 to 50,000. Amongst the new arrivals was a middle-aged sea captain, William Perrie, or Pirrie, who seems to have crossed from the west coast of Scotland in about 1820. He seems to have come to Belfast to represent the coastal shipping interests of his father, William Perrie senior, of Port William, Wigtonshire, on the Scottish shore of Solway Firth. Captain William Pirrie had had a colourful career, being captured by the French during the Napoleonic Wars and escaping across the English Channel in an open boat. By the time of his arrival in Belfast he already had strong links with Ulster. In 1810 he had married Elizabeth Morison, daughter of William Morison of Sandyland: the Morisons were related to the Blackwoods of Clandeboye and lived near the Blackwood estate at Conlig, north Down. Pirrie had not been long in Belfast before he became a vigorous advocate for improvements in the channel and this won him nomination to the Ballast Board in 1827.[16]

During 1829 and 1830 the Board called for fresh reports. One of these proposed that the twisting old channel should be straightened by making two new cuts to be maintained by using the recently developed steam dredger. The harbour was to be deepened and the private docks on the Co. Antrim shore purchased by the Ballast

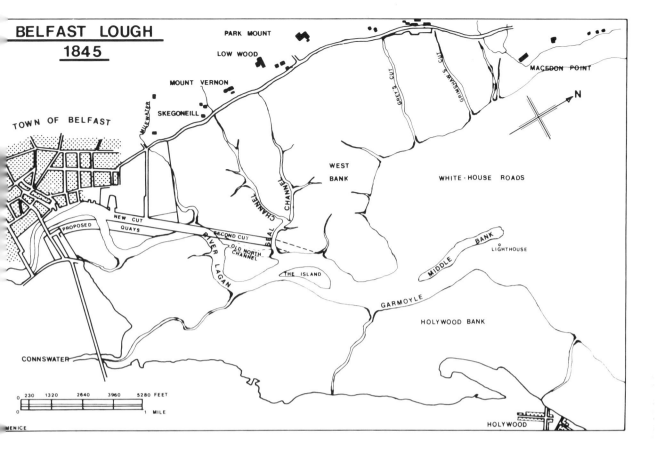

BELFAST LOUGH
1845

PARK MOUNT

LOW WOOD

MACEDON POINT

MOUNT VERNON

SKEGONEILL

TOWN OF BELFAST

MILEWATER

GREY'S CUT

GRIMSHAW'S CUT

WEST BANK

WHITE-HOUSE ROADS

N

BELFAST CHANNEL

CHANNEL

NEW CUT

QUAYS

PROPOSED

SECOND CUT

OLD NORTH CHANNEL

RIVER LAGAN

THE ISLAND

MIDDLE BANK

LIGHTHOUSE

GARMOYLE

HOLYWOOD BANK

CONNSWATER

0 230 1320 2640 3960 5280 FEET
0   1 MILE

HOLYWOOD

MENICE

Belfast Lough in 1845 showing the two cuts made in the 1830s and 1840s to straighten the Lagan and allow ships access to Belfast harbour.

Board for use as public trading docks. This plan, which was to be carried out in stages, avoided the necessity of building a wet dock with a tidal lock at the entrance. When a Bill was introduced into Parliament to give the Ballast Board powers to undertake the project, it was opposed by the Marquess of Donegall, probably in an effort to raise the compensation he would receive. The Belfast merchants, led by Captain Pirrie, counterattacked and in 1837 a settlement was reached. The Treasury advanced the Ballast Board £25,000 to help meet the cost of making the first cut, and more funds were raised by public subscription. In April 1839 the contractor David Logan was commissioned to carry out the work, but died before the job could start. He was replaced by William Dargan, probably the only man in Ireland capable of tackling such a massive enterprise. He had been responsible for constructing the Grand Canal and the Ulster Canal, and several railway lines. As excavation progressed the spoil was dumped on the Co. Down side of the river to form a seventeen-acre island, nicknamed 'Dargan's Island'. The first cut was opened in January 1841 by Captain William Pirrie.[17] By this time Belfast was Ireland's major port in terms of the value of its exports.

By 1845 the Ballast Board had purchased all the private docks and quays in the harbour, including the shipyards of Charles Connell & Sons, Kirwan & McCune (by then Thompson & Kirwan) and part of the yard of Alexander McLaine & Sons. Proposed improvements to the quayside would leave only McLaines' yard with access to the river and, even in their case, facilities for launching ships would be much restricted. At first the Board was reluctant to make any provision for the displaced shipbuilders. They turned down applications to rent land on Dargan's Island, explaining obscurely that it was 'not advised under present circumstances'. Before further development could happen the Ballast Board needed additional powers. Fresh legislation was passed in 1847 which vested the management of Belfast harbour in

7

the hands of Harbour Commissioners. The membership of seventeen Commissioners was identical to that of the Ballast Board and included Captain William Pirrie. Although he was not appointed chairman, it was his influence that persuaded the new Commissioners to press ahead with the second cut. William Dargan again carried out the work. The waterway was inaugurated on 10 July 1849 by Pirrie himself who christened it the Victoria channel by pouring a bottle of whiskey onto the water.[18] In March Dargan's Island had been renamed Queen's Island in honour of Queen Victoria who was to visit Belfast that August.

With the channel complete down to the Pool of Garmoyle, the Commissioners pushed ahead with improvements to the docks. Ritchie's dock was filled up and, with Connells' yard, formed the site of the new Harbour Commissioners' Office. On the east side of Queen's Island in 1846 a timber pond for seasoning shipbuilding timber had been staked out, capable of taking 2,000 logs. Before the appointment of the Harbour Commissioners it had been decided to build a 'patent slip' on the south side of the island, to replace some of the ship-repair facilities that the shipbuilders had previously enjoyed on the Co. Antrim shore of the river. This device, which had been recently developed by Morton & Company of Leith near Edinburgh, allowed ships to be drawn out of the water on a cradle mounted on tracks and powered by a steam-driven hauling engine. The slip, supplied by Mortons, was 550 feet long, with a capacity of 1,000 tons, and driven by a 20-horse-power engine. By the end of 1848

The opening of the Victoria channel (the second cut) on 10 July 1849 by Captain William Pirrie. (*View of Belfast harbour from the Custom House taken on the day of the opening of the new channel*, lithograph from drawing by James Howard Burgess, 1849, courtesy of the Ulster Museum)

the Commissioners were able to report that the slip was nearing completion and that – 'It was expected to afford, at a very moderate expense, compared to a Graving Dock of the same capacity, a great relief to the Shipping Trade of a Port, where so many large vessels require, during the year, to be repaired.'[19] Presumably Connell and McLaine were to be allowed access to the slip as the need arose, in much the same way as they used the Clarendon graving docks. The slip opened in 1849, and during that year the Harbour Commissioners agreed to build a small shipyard immediately to the east of the slip, beside the entrance to the timber pond, for Thompson & Kirwan who moved there during 1851. At the same time a new slipway was laid down for Charles Connell between Clarendon dock no. 2 and McLaines' yard; but Connell soon gave up shipbuilding in favour of the more lucrative ship-repair business. The north part of Queen's Island was made into a public park with a bathing pool at the end of the timber pond. The Victoria Fete Committee constructed a 'crystal palace' in the centre, containing a winter garden and a small zoo. Trees were planted and flower gardens and lawns laid out. During the summer months a regular ferry service ran across to the island from the Co. Antrim shore. It was said that a visit 'combined the excitement of a sea voyage with a rest afterwards on one of the garden seats in the cool shade of trees'. At the north end of the island was a battery of cannon for firing salutes.[20]

In the sixty years between William Ritchie's arrival in Belfast and the closure of

An emigrant vessel leaving Belfast in about 1850 with Queen's Island in the distance. On the left of the land is the Crystal Palace, and on the right the brick building is the engine house of the patent slip. (*The emigrant ship leaving Belfast, 1852,* by John Glen Wilson, courtesy of the Ulster Museum)

his dock, the shipbuilding industry on the Lagan had taken root. When compared with the almost meteoric rise of shipbuilding on the Thames, Tyne, Wear and Clyde, the achievements of the Lagan were scarcely significant. In the last five years further development on the Co. Antrim shore had been stifled by the necessary improvements to the quayside. The Harbour Commissioners hoped that others would follow Thompson & Kirwan's lead by establishing yards on Queen's Island with their help. The only iron shipbuilding firm on the Lagan, Coates & Young, showed no indication of doing so, preferring, whenever they won a contract, to lease parts of the Corporation's ground for short periods. The three existing firms of shipbuilders clearly calculated that their future lay in the profitable trade of ship-repair. The future of the Belfast shipbuilding industry was at a crossroads.

2
APPRENTICES AND RELATIVES
1853–74

By the late 1840s several firms that had won reputations in the previous thirty years for iron-working or marine engineering had diversified into iron shipbuilding. For example, in 1841 Robert Napier, the father of Clyde marine engineering and shipbuilding, opened an iron shipyard at Govan to complement his renowned Lancefield Engine Works on the opposite side of the river. Although iron ships accounted for less than a fifth of all tonnage constructed in the United Kingdom in 1852, many firms were entering the trade on the crest of the early 1850s boom. On the Clyde in 1851 brothers James and George Thomson (who had worked for Robert Napier before setting up their own marine engineering business) laid out an iron shipyard in Govan, while on the Tyne Andrew Leslie, a Scottish engineer, began an iron shipbuilding business at Hebburn in 1853. On 6 September of the same year the Belfast Harbour Commissioners agreed to lay out an iron shipyard on Queen's Island for Robert Hickson, who had just taken over as proprietor of the Belfast Iron Works in Eliza Street. The new yard, like that of Thompson & Kirwan, was to be directly alongside the patent slip, but to the west of it. It was agreed that Hickson should be allowed the use of the steam engine that served the slip. The Harbour Commissioners' decision was the outcome of more than a year's deliberation.[1]

The Belfast Iron Works had been opened in November 1851 by Robert Pace, an engineer and son of a Liverpool shipowner, and Thomas Nugent Gladstone, an ironmonger from the same place. The works had taken almost two years to build and cost the large sum of £25,000, partly raised by mortgaging the premises to the Ulster Banking Company. The *Belfast News-Letter* of 22 October had reported enthusiastically:

> During the past two years, the attentive observer of the manufacturing progress of our town must have been struck with the gradual growth of a huge establishment in Eliza Street, occupying a site upon what previously had been an unprofitable swamp on the North side of the River between the Lagan and Connare bridges. Within the enclosure, a forest of tall and graceful chimney stalks, cylindrical in shape, and symmetrical in architectural elegance, slowly rear their towering points over an extensive area for the most part occupied by handsome sheds, supported by metal columns and girders and by all the usual but in this place novel accessories of a first rate wrought-iron foundry.

The works was equipped with 'four steam engines and boilers, puddled iron mill and squeezer, plate and angle iron mills, a tilt hammer, roll turning lathes, shears, drilling and screwing machines, large wooden cranes, a large number of cast metal rolls, and many tools'. The business was inaugurated by the 4th Marquess of Downshire who personally rolled the first boiler plate to be produced, and seems to have been a willing supporter of the venture. Pace and Gladstone were almost certainly attracted to Belfast in the expectation that workable deposits of coal and ironstone would shortly be discovered on the Downshire estate and elsewhere in the north of Ireland. In this

11

they were to be disappointed. As early as February 1852 Pace was already complaining: 'All my means are locked up in the Belfast Iron Works, which are now in the hands of the mortgagers.' Gladstone was probably looking for a way out of the firm's difficulties when he suggested to the Harbour Commissioners in June 1852 that they should establish an iron shipyard on Queen's Island.[2]

The Commissioners appointed a committee under the chairmanship of Captain William Pirrie to investigate the proposal. Pirrie was enthusiastic about the prospect for iron shipbuilding in Belfast and persuaded his fellow Commissioners to back Gladstone's plan. In October advertisements were placed in the English and Scottish newspapers, offering ground for shipbuilding yards. Early in 1853 Pace and Gladstone decided to withdraw from the ironworks and leased it to another Liverpool engineer, Robert Hickson. At the end of March Gladstone introduced Hickson to the Harbour Commissioners with a warm recommendation. During the autumn of 1853 the new yard on Queen's Island was fitted up by the Commissioners, at a cost of £1,116.17s.6d., with one launching way and the equipment needed to shape and bore the iron plates and angles. Early in 1854 Hickson leased an additional plot to the south west of the yard, for the formation of another berth to cost not more than £393.2s.9d.[3]

Robert Hickson received his first contract, for a wooden sailing ship of 1,289 tons, from Edward Bates & Sons, the Liverpool firm of shipowners. This vessel, the *Silistria*, was launched in September 1854. Her hull was immediately towed to Liverpool to be fitted out as a fast clipper for the Indian trade. It is not known why Bates chose to give Robert Hickson his first order. It may be that he knew of Hickson's Liverpool connections. Before the launch of the *Silistria* the hull of a large steam ship, the *Khersonese*, had been laid down on the new second berth, for two Belfast merchants, Frederick Lewis and Edward Geoghegan, who were financed by four Liverpool shipowners. Recognising his lack of shipbuilding experience, Robert Hickson had engaged J. Jordan as manager to oversee the new yard. However, Jordan was summarily dismissed before the launch of the *Silistria*. Hickson at once advertised for a replacement, and at Christmas 1854 Edward James Harland arrived from the Tyne to take up the post.[4]

Edward Harland had been born in May 1831 at Scarborough, the sixth child of Dr William Harland, who had a successful practice in the town, associated with the Spa. Apart from being a medical man, Dr Harland was an enthusiastic amateur engineer and scientist. In 1827 he had invented and patented a steam carriage 'embracing a multi-tubular boiler for quickly raising high pressure steam';[5] and he dabbled with electricity and experimented in the use of organic fertilisers. He was a close friend of the famous engineer George Stephenson. Dr Harland seems to have passed on his enthusiasm for mechanical invention to his sons. Although the eldest, William, became a doctor, he was, by the time he entered Edinburgh University, 'an excellent mechanic', proficient in making models of machines and buildings. Edward attended the local grammar school where, by his own admission, he neglected his studies, 'preferring to watch and assist workmen when I had the opportunity of doing so . . . thus I got to know every workshop and workman in the town'. During these early years he regularly frequented the large wooden shipbuilding yard of William and Robert Tindall, who also had a big London-based shipowning concern. At the age of twelve, in 1843, Edward was sent to Edinburgh Academy to receive a classical education, since his father wished him to become a barrister. Edward was determined to be an engineer and persuaded his brother William, who was then in his final year

12

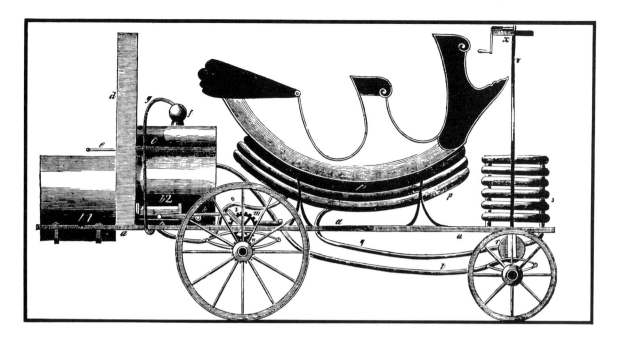

The design drawing of Dr William Harland's steam carriage, 'embracing a multi-tubular boiler for quickly raising high pressure steam', which he submitted as part of his patent application.

at university, to teach him mathematics and train him to build engineering models. During 1844, following his mother's death, Edward returned to Scarborough and went back to the grammar school for two years. Dr Harland abandoned his legal ambitions for Edward and secured, through his friend George Stephenson, an apprenticeship for him at the engineering works of Robert Stephenson & Company of Newcastle upon Tyne.[6]

On his fifteenth birthday, in 1846, Edward Harland commenced his five year indenture:

> I was now in my element. The working hours it is true were very long, – being from six in the morning until 8.15 at night, excepting Saturday, when we knocked off at four. However all this gave me so much the more experience, and, taking advantage of it, I found that, when I had reached the age of eighteen, I was entrusted with the full charge of erecting one side of a locomotive . . . I afterwards went through the machine-shop. I was fortunate enough to get charge of the best screw-cutting and brass turning lathe in the shop . . . After my four years had been completed, I went into the drawing office, to which I had looked forward with pleasure, and, having before practised lined as well as free-board drawing, I soon succeeded in getting good and difficult designs to work out, and eventually finished drawings of engines.[7]

It was during these years that Edward Harland first became interested in the design of sea-going vessels. Appalled, like many of his contemporaries, at the terrible loss of life at sea following the frequent foundering of sailing vessels, he began, during his holidays at Scarborough, to investigate with his father's help the design of lifeboats. He came to 'the conclusion that the cylindrico-conical form, with the frames to be carried completely round and forming beams as well, and the two screws, one at each end, worked off the same power, by which one or other of them would always be immersed, was worth registering in the Patent Office'. Harland built a 32-inch working model and conducted sea trials which, he reckoned, proved the effectiveness of his design. In the summer of 1850 he entered the model for a competition, sponsored by the Duke of Northumberland, for the best new lifeboat. To his lasting disappointment, he failed to secure the prize. At the same time Robert Stephenson & Company contracted to build three iron caissons for the Keyham docks and, 'as these were very similar in construction to that of an ordinary iron ship, draughtsmen conversant with that class of work were specially engaged to superintend it'. Harland was appointed assistant on the project and so quickly mastered the technique of laying down the lines that he was soon able to improve it.[8]

On his twentieth birthday, in May 1851, Edward Harland completed his apprenticeship with Robert Stephenson & Company. He was 'at once entered on the books as journeyman, on the "big" wage of twenty shillings a week'. However, business was poor and Harland quickly resigned his position so that he could spend time in London marvelling at the wonders of the Great Exhibition. He was so enthralled by 'the works of art and mechanics' on display that he remained in London for two months. By the time he returned home to Scarborough, his future employment was assured.[9]

During his apprenticeship Edward Harland had become friendly, through his uncle Dr Thomas Harland, with Gustav Christian Schwabe. Thomas Harland had graduated in medicine from the University of Edinburgh in 1822 and had subsequently practised in Salford. In 1842 he had married Mary Dugdale, niece of John Dugdale of Dovecot, a powerful Liverpool and Manchester merchant. Some years later Gustav Schwabe had married John Dugdale's daughter, Helen. Gustav had been born in Hamburg in 1813, the son of Philipp Benjamin Schwabe, a wealthy Jewish merchant. During June 1819, along with the rest of his family, Gustav was baptised into the Lutheran church.[10] In the 1820s many members of the Jewish community in Hamburg established businesses in Britain where trading conditions were more liberal than in Germany. The Schwabe family participated in this trend. Salis Schwabe, Gustav's uncle, set up a calico printing business in Manchester and cousins M.M. and H.L. Schwabe opened a merchant house with a branch in Glasgow.[11] During 1832 Gustav Schwabe's elder sister, Fanny Maria Schwabe, married another Hamburg Jewish merchant, Moritz Wolff. Like his father-in-law, Moritz Wolff was a respected member of the Jewish community in Hamburg, friendly with the Jaffe, Ellerman and Ballin families. Fanny and Moritz had two sons, Gustav Wilhelm, born in 1834, and George Moritz Otto, born in 1840.[12]

It is not known when Gustav Christian Schwabe went to Liverpool. In 1838 he was in partnership with Edward Little in a firm of commission agents. When Little died the following year, Schwabe seems to have acquired his house and business interests. Later he became involved with the East Indies shipping firm of J.S. de Wolf & Company, investing in their ships and learning the business of ship management in the Far Eastern and Australian trade. By the early 1840s he had established the merchant house of Sykes Schwabe & Company in partnership with Adam Sykes, Benjamin Rutter, and his father-in-law, John Dugdale of Dovecot.[13] In 1844 the firm was reported to be 'doing a very respectable business' with Manila and Singapore and by 1849 its capital had reached £50,000.[14] It seems to have been involved in the merchanting of printed calico goods, produced by Schwabe's uncle and other Lancashire firms, and in importing raw cotton and silk. In 1856 the company sent out a silk-buyer to China. This import/export business had naturally led G.C. Schwabe to maintain and extend his shipping investments. During the 1840s he had become a junior partner in John Bibby & Sons, the Liverpool shipping concern established in 1805.[15] The Bibby family quickly became friendly with Schwabe's Dugdale and Harland relatives.

During 1850 John Bibby & Sons began to switch from sailing ships to iron screw steamers. Edward Harland, through Gustav Schwabe, advised the company on the acquisition of the first screw steam vessel in which they held shares, the *Rattler*, built at Cork in 1846. Their first two new steam vessels were constructed in 1851 by John Reid of Port Glasgow, with engines supplied by J. & G. Thomson's Clydebank Foundry in Glasgow, established in 1847. These were followed the next year by an order for three ships, of roughly 800 gross tons, to be built at the recently opened shipyard of J. & G. Thomson at Govan on the Upper Clyde, and engined at the Clydebank Foundry. G.C. Schwabe, knowing Edward Harland's interest in marine engineering and shipbuilding, arranged for him to be employed as a journeyman by Thomsons on the same terms as he had been at Stephensons. Dr William Harland, himself a prophet of the future of the iron ship, must have been delighted at his son's good fortune. Edward Harland rapidly proved his abilities as a shipbuilder. After Thomsons appointed an experienced naval draughtsman, Harland 'was "told off"' [sent] wherever he needed assistance'. When the draughtsman left the yard for a post on the Tyne, Harland was named as his successor: – 'I was placed in the drawing office as head draughtsman. At the same time I had no rise of wages, but still went on enjoying my twenty shillings a week.' In the autumn of 1853, shortly after being offered a higher salary and a long-term contract, Harland resigned to become manager at Thomas Toward's shipyard at St Peter's, Newcastle upon Tyne, on the recommendation of Robert Stephenson & Company. Harland had used his two years on the Clyde profitably, visiting most of the shipyards and marine engineering works on the river and scrutinising their technique.[16] He had participated at Thomson's yard in the design and construction of eleven iron steamers and the whole range of marine engineering products.

When Edward Harland arrived at Toward's yard, he later recalled:

> I found the work, as practised there, rough and ready; but by steady attention to all the details, and by careful inspection when passing the 'piece work' . . . I contrived to raise the standard of excellence, without a corresponding increase in price . . . I observed that quality was a very important element in all commercial success.

He stayed only a year with Thomas Toward. Although he was left more or less in sole charge of the business and had done much to improve it, by early 1854 he was keen to leave 'as there did not appear to be a satisfactory prospect'. In the summer, still aged only twenty-three, he was appointed to the post of manager of Robert Hickson's shipyard in Belfast, no doubt encouraged by his friend, Gustav Schwabe. When Harland arrived at Queen's Island there was a large ship on order, the *Khersonese* which 'was partly in frame'. Harland's efforts to drive ahead with this contract were not welcomed by the workforce. His predecessor had paid wages above the going rate and the craftsmanship had been shoddy. Harland at once struggled to improve quality, as he had done on the Tyne.[17] He cut wages and imposed a ban on smoking during working hours. He prowled constantly round the yard with a lump of chalk and an ivory rule in his pockets, measuring pieces of work and marking every defect with a circle. He quickly became notorious for his keen powers of observation:

> He had an all-smelling nose as well as an all-seeing eye. One day he was walking rapidly along, and suddenly he stopped dead and sniffed at a saw-pit. In a flash

An advertisement in the
Belfast News-Letter offering
for sale the plant of the
Belfast Iron Works in
Eliza Street.

the trapdoor was lifted, and there squatting in the sawdust was a wizened little man, puffing at a little clay pipe.[18]

The workforce of some fifty craftsmen did not take kindly to this stern treatment and went on strike. Harland replied by recruiting fresh hands from the Clyde, but, by his account, they were 'intimidated, or enticed, or feasted, and sent home again'.[19] However, his tactics eventually eroded the strike.

Early in 1855 Harland's difficulties were compounded by the failure of Hickson's Belfast business when the Ulster Banking Company foreclosed. Edward Harland was forced to meet the expenses of the shipyard out of his own pocket, pending a settlement with the creditors. This resulted in the closure of the Eliza Street Iron Works and an agreement to allow Hickson to retain control of the Queen's Island yard.[20] At the same time Harland's sacked predecessor, J. Jordan, acquired the lease of Thompson & Kirwan's old yard on the Co. Antrim shore, with permission to launch across Prince's dock quay. He immediately began iron shipbuilding in competition to Hickson, recruiting workmen dissatisfied with Harland's strict discipline.[21] Undaunted, Harland persevered as 'there was a prospect of profit from the work in hand'. In the midst of these difficulties a friend counselled that he should try his luck elsewhere. Harland rejoined: 'Having mounted a restive horse, I would ride him into the stable.'[22] During the summer relief came unexpectedly when, following the death of Thomas Toward, 'his head foreman William Houston, and a number of leading hands' moved to Queen's Island. Harland later reflected: 'From that time forward the works went apace; and we finished the ships in hand to the perfect satisfaction of the owners.'[23]

The *Khersonese* (1,273 tons) was launched on 5 October, 1855. It stuck on the ways, but 'Mr Harland . . . immediately discovered the cause, and effected the remedy before the ground sank beneath the enormous weight which pressed upon it.'[24] Early in the following year the screw steamer *Circassian*, of 1,387 tons, was completed for the North Atlantic Steam Navigation Company, promoted by the owners of the *Khersonese*. This was the largest vessel to be built in Ireland up to that time, and two years after her delivery won praise for her builders when she made the passage from Galway to Newfoundland in six days and one hour.[25] The *Khersonese* was recalled to Queen's Island to be refitted and re-engined 'to bring speed and accommodation' into line with the *Circassian*. In the summer of 1857 the *Dewa*

16

Gunghadur, an iron sailing ship, was completed for Edward Bates, followed later in the year by the *Mayola* for William Porter of Liverpool. Like other shipbuilders, the yard supplemented its business by 'lifting and repairing wrecked ships', using the Harbour Commissioners' adjacent slip for this purpose.[26]

During 1857 Edward Harland engaged Gustav Schwabe's nephew, Gustav Wilhelm Wolff, as a personal assistant. Wolff had left Hamburg in 1849, at the age of fourteen, for his uncle's home to attend Liverpool College. He had then been apprenticed for five years to the well known Manchester engineering firm of Joseph Whitworth & Company. He had represented the company at the Paris Exhibition of 1855, before joining B. Goodfellow Limited, of Hyde on the outskirts of Manchester, as a draughtsman.[27] When he arrived in Belfast he was welcomed by a friend of his family from Hamburg, Daniel Joseph Jaffe, who had come to Belfast to establish a linen mill. In the same year the brothers Walter Henry and Alexander Basil Wilson were indentured to Robert Hickson & Company as the first 'gentlemen apprentices' – usually the sons of wealthy families, who wished to learn a business which they hoped eventually to direct. They were well connected, coming from a family with long associations in the Ulster linen industry. Walter, 'Wattie', had been born in 1839 and had 'early exhibited his taste for engineering, for as a boy he was keenly interested in making model engines from scraps of metal'. Alexander completed his training at the marine engine-builders MacNab & Company of Greenock.[28]

By this time Harland was anxious to open his own business. He was now an experienced shipbuilder and, through his family connections, could almost certainly draw on sufficient capital and orders to start a viable concern. Accordingly, late in

1857 Edward Harland, no doubt encouraged by Schwabe, applied to Liverpool City Council for ground to open a yard at Garstang. This application was rejected, 'youth and inexperience being assigned as one of the main refusal reasons'. With similar lack of success he 'made inquiries at Birkenhead and other places'. Thwarted in these ambitions, he encouraged Wolff to leave Belfast to gain further marine engineering experience at sea, probably on board one of his uncle's steamers.[29]

In February 1858 the iron sailing ship *Norah Graeme* (1,001 tons) was launched for Edward Bates, 'everything being in excellent order on the vessel, and the vessel gliding down into the water without shock or disturbance'. This was followed by the tug *Adjutant* for Liverpool owners. During the year the economy dipped sharply and Hickson seems to have been left with the *Oceola* (sister ship of the *Mayola*) on his hands. So as to keep the yard open, Robert Hickson turned to the well tried technique of completing the vessel to his own account. This venture would seem to have overstretched his fragile resources, for on 21 September 1858 he wrote to Harland:

> I offer you my interest and goodwill in the shipyard at the Queen's Island, Belfast, together with Steam engine Boiler Plant tools, machinery and other appliances for shipbuilding as now is used by me, for the sum of five thousand pounds.

His only condition was that he should be able to complete the iron ship *Oceola*, renamed *Bebington*, which he was now building for himself, and to finish some repair work to the steamer *Rose*. Edward Harland accepted this offer with effect from 1 November 1858 when the firm's name was changed to Edward James Harland & Company. Wolff was at once recalled from sea to take charge of the drawing office.[30]

Table 2.1

Ships built at Queen's Island by Robert Hickson 1854-9

Date	Name	Owner
1854	*Silistria*	Edward Bates, Liverpool
1855	*Khersonese*	Frederick Lewis and Edward Geoghegan, Belfast
1857	*Circassian*	North Atlantic Steam Navigation Company
1857	*Dewa Gunghadur*	Edward Bates, Liverpool
1857	*Mayola*	William Porter, Liverpool
1858	*Norah Graeme*	Edward Bates, Liverpool
1858	*Adjutant*	Liverpool owner, name unknown
1859	*Oceola* renamed *Bebington*	R. Hickson & Company, Liverpool

Harland's decision to acquire the lease of the Queen's Island yard was almost certainly taken on Schwabe's advice and promise of financial support, for immediately John Bibby & Sons placed an order for three 1,500-gross-ton iron steamers. These were to be equipped with 'lifting screws' to be disconnected and raised when the vessel was running before the wind, thus preventing drag. The engines were subcontracted to MacNab & Company of Greenock, and the cranes to Harland's previous employers, J. & G. Thomson, who with no ill feeling offered the new firm a generous discount.[31] The partners in both these firms of suppliers were presumably inspired by the belief that there was more than enough demand for the shipbuilding and marine engineering industry to welcome newcomers.

As Hickson's yard was not large enough to handle such a big contract, Harland purchased the small semi-derelict yard of Thompson & Kirwan's Belfast Shipbuilding Company on the other side of the patent slip. This business, which had moved to Queen's Island in 1851, had constructed wooden ships mostly for local owners. Harland seems to have completed the ship on the stock, the *Esmak* for R. Megaw of Belfast and Liverpool. The two yards had to be combined and 'required many additions to the machinery, plant and tools, including the installation of two steam engines to drive the punching, drilling, shearing and shaping machinery . . .' A sailmakers' loft was constructed since Harland believed sail design was an essential ingredient in the success of even a steam vessel.[32] In 1859, their first full year in business, Harland and Wolff completed the *Bebington* and also the *Venetian*, the first of the Bibby boats.

Harland recollected, 'In the midst of all my engagements, I found time to woo and win the hand of Miss Rosa Wann of Veremont [Old Malone Road], Belfast, to whom I was married on the 26 January of 1860.' Her father, Thomas Wann, was a well-to-do Belfast stockbroker and insurance agent, related to the powerful Gallaher tobacco family.[33] As a result Edward Harland quickly found himself welcomed into Belfast society.

The other two Bibby ships were delivered in 1859 and 1860, along with three smaller sailing craft for local customers, including the *Jane Porter*, the first iron sailing ship owned by J.P. Corry & Company of Belfast. All these vessels were fitted with a new type of iron deck invented by Harland and patented during the year – 'filling in the spaces between frames, etc. with Portland cement, instead of chocks of wood, and covering the iron plates with cement and tiles'. This immediately became standard practice at Queen's Island and was copied elsewhere. The yard was now so busy that Harland found it necessary 'to employ about one thousand workmen in the various branches of the fast extending business', some of whom were working night shift.[34] From the outset, the workforce was predominantly Protestant. There were reasons for this which had nothing to do with sectarianism. In the first place, the shipyard required skilled tradesmen from Britain and most of these were Presbyterians (like the elder Pirrie), Episcopalians or Anglicans (like the converted Wolff). In the second place, Belfast itself was approximately two-thirds Protestant and the shipyard was to draw heavily on the Protestant populations of the city and the north Down countryside.

Bibbys were so pleased with their new ships that during 1860 they placed orders for a further six vessels of almost 2,000 gross tons. In designing the first two of these ships, completed in 1861, Harland put into practice a theory developed since his time with J. & G. Thomson:

> of the greater carrying power and accommodaton, both for cargo and passengers, that would be gained by constructing the new vessels of increased length, without any increase in the beam . . . The result was, that I was allowed to settle the dimensions; and the following were then decided upon: length, 310 feet; beam, 34 feet; depth of hold, 24 feet 9 inches; all of which were fully compensated for by making the upper deck entirely of iron . . . In this way, the hull of the ship was converted into a box girder of immensely increased strength.

19

Edward Harland, a portrait painted in 1884.

Their rigging was equally novel, with pole masts, a fore and aft rig, and the use of steam winches and braces for all the heavy lifts so as to reduce the size of the crew. Their engines incorporated an improved version of Hall's surface condenser, which used sea water to condense the exhausted steam from the cylinders, so preserving the pure water for reuse, thus saving fuel and expensive repairs caused by salt corrosion. Harland had first seen such a condenser discarded in a Clyde yard because the lack of suitable packing had caused it to leak badly. In the improved model, fitted on these Bibby ships and 'patented by Spenser', rubber rings were used to pack the tubes to prevent any leaks.[35]

So successful were these innovations that the last four vessels, completed between 1861 and 1863, were lengthened to 331 feet. The vessels had a 'flatness of bottom and squareness of bilge', which became known by Liverpool shipowners as the 'Belfast bottom'. These new 'long ships' were nicknamed 'Bibby coffins', because of their long box-like appearance.[36] During 1862 two smaller vessels of similar design were delivered to Bibbys for use in their Spanish trade. The year before, Harland had also lengthened by over 90 feet Bibby's *Tiber* and *Calpe* which had been built in 1851 by John Reid & Company, of Port Glasgow, and engined by J. & G. Thomson. This work was almost certainly carried out on the patent slip. Lengthening ships was, at the time, a popular method of increasing the carrying capacity of a fleet without incurring the expense of new construction.

On 11 April 1861 Edward Harland and Gustav Wilhelm Wolff formally entered into partnership for eight years. The deed of agreement of partnership contained twenty-one clauses including provisions for all eventualities:

Second – That the said Edward James Harland and Gustav Wilhelm Wolff do now become and continue partners until January first, one thousand eight hundred and sixty nine in the trade or business of building and repairing Iron ships and Engines and doing all work connected with said trade or otherwise which the partners may from time to time undertake.

Third – That the business of the Partnership shall be carried on as heretofore under the name and style of 'Edward James Harland' until the said Gustav Wilhelm Wolff shall desire to have his name added when the style of the partnership shall be changed to 'Harland and Wolff' . . .

Ninth – That the said Edward James Harland shall be at liberty to draw out of the partnership funds in each year the sum of seven hundred pounds sterling and the said Gustav Wilhelm Wolff the sum of five hundred pounds sterling for their private use respectively and in addition to the annual sum of five hundred pounds the said Gustav Wilhelm Wolff may in the event of his being married or of his requiring to furnish a house draw out of the partnership funds the sum of eight hundred pounds . . .

Thirteenth – That each of the partners shall devote his entire time to the business of the partnership and neither of the partners shall without the consent of the other being first obtained in writing act as trustee, executor, assignee or agent for any person or become security or guarantee for any person or persons for any purpose whatsoever . . .

The signatures of the two partners were witnessed by John Bailey, Edward Harland's clerk and book-keeper, who was to keep the books of the new firm.[37]

Despite its detail, the agreement gave no indication of how Edward Harland and Gustav Wolff planned to share the workload of the business. From later evidence it is almost certain that Harland was to be the practical shipbuilder and spokesman for the firm, whereas Wolff was to provide engineering skill and manage the yard, with the help of William Houston, in his partner's absences on visits to owners. In addition he was to place at the disposal of the firm the financial expertise and resources of his wealthy family. The capital of the partnership was to be £2,416, of which Harland was to subscribe £1,916 and Wolff £500. This was a tiny capital for a new concern with such large commitments. It was less than half the price that Harland had paid for Hickson's business alone. So as to cover the balance of the purchase price of the two yards and the cost of new plant, the partners had been generously lent money by Gustav Schwabe and his sister Fanny, Wolff's mother. It is likely that these loans amounted to about £12,000. They were to be repaid with interest out of the profits of the new firm. However, neither Schwabe nor Fanny Wolff was entitled to share in the net profit or loss of the business, which was to be divided between the partners in the proportion of three to one. James Bibby and James Dugdale, a relation of the family into which the Harlands and Schwabes had married, were appointed as arbitrators in the event of any dispute between the partners.

With the approaching completion of the large Bibby contracts that had so successfully launched the business, the partners had to seek other work. Despite the severe recession in the United Kingdom economy, caused by the American Civil War, demand for shipping was strong, buoyed up by the Confederate States' purchase of fast steam tonnage to act as blockade runners. As a result Harland and Wolff had no difficulty in winning contracts, launching sixteen further vessels in the years 1862 to 1864. The first contract was for four 1,000-ton sailing ships, *Star of Erin, Star of Denmark, Star of Scotia* and *Star of Albion*, to form the Star line of J.P. Corry & Company, for whom the partners had already built a vessel. Corry also ordered a steam tug, *Kitty of Coleraine*, for service on the River Bann navigation with the Lower

Table 2.2

Capital 1863-75

| | LOAN CAPITAL | | | | PARTNERS' CAPITAL | | |
| | F. M. Wolff | G.C.Schwabe | J. Bailey | James Bibby | E. J. Harland | G. W. Wolff | Total |
	£	£	£	£	£	£	£
1863	1,012	8,000	—	—	9,404	4,504	22,920
1864	1,020	6,180	—	—	12,702	7,038	26,940
1865	1,025	6,150	—	—	15,773	8,793	31,741
1866	1,025	6,000	—	—	11,433	6,636	25,094
1867	1,000	6,000	—	—	17,680	9,891	34,571
1868	1,000	6,000	—	—	21,251	11,778	40,029
1869	1,025	6,117	—	—	21,836	12,446	41,424
1870	—	—	—	—	36,279	19,579	55,858
1871	—	5,212	115	1,798	42,203	18,979	68,307
1872	—	4,200	59	1,695	48,780	23,808	78,542
1873	—	3,626	—	—	64,194	28,641	96,461
1874	—	2,513	—	—	59,717	25,276	87,506
1875	—	—	—	—	55,453	23,200	78,653

Note
The accounts of the partnership were balanced twice a year on 30 June and 31 December. The figure for 31 December has been used.

Bann Steamboat Company. Harland was able to put his misspent schooldays to good advantage by gaining an order from W.H. Tindall & Company, who had recently given up shipbuilding at Scarborough. Similarly the partners were contracted to build two 1,300-ton ships for T. & J. Brocklebank who had just closed their Whitehaven shipyard in Cumbria and shifted to Liverpool. The links between the yard and the Mersey were strengthened during 1864 when the partners obtained orders from the Liverpool firms of James Moss & Company and British Shipowners Limited.

These early contracts brought good returns. The first balance sheet of the partnership, dated 1863, shows that Edward Harland's share in the business had more than trebled in two years, from £2,416 to £9,404, and Wolff's had more than quadrupled, to £4,504. This would have been achieved by ploughing back the bulk of the profits into the partnership. In 1863 the value of the plant stood at a little over £8,379, suggesting that its original cost had been almost £10,000 (allowing for a 9 per cent depreciation). Profits in 1863 and 1864 were strong, at 24 per cent of the combined loan and partners' capital. Although part of G.C. Schwabe's loan was repaid, most of the income was needed to finance the large volume of work in progress.

The first vessel for which costs survive is ship no. 24, the *Star of Scotia*, completed for J.P. Corry in 1864. This 1,000-ton sailing ship was priced at £14,498 and earned the firm £350 in profit, less than 2 per cent. Unlike most of the early contracts, this ship was paid for by means of bills of exchange 'drawn on' Harland and Wolff and accepted by J.P. Corry, which in effect gave J.P. Corry credit for a fixed period of time at a specified rate of interest. Throughout the second half of the nineteenth century these 'negotiable instruments' were a popular method of paying for a variety of merchandise, particularly large fixed assets such as ships. They were accepted for settlement, with interest usually at least 1 per cent above bank rate, after the expiry

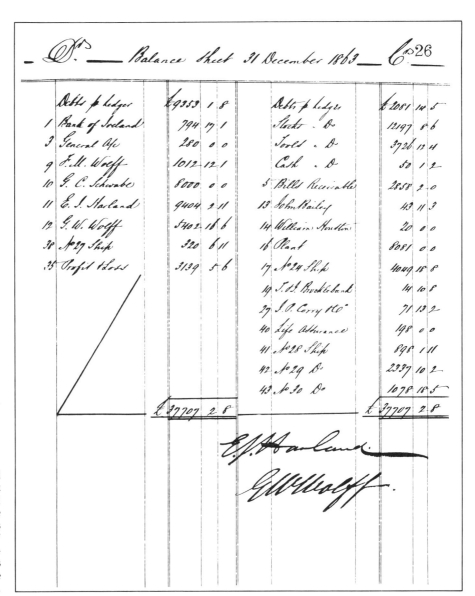

Debts p ledger	£9353	1	8		Debts p ledger	£2081	14	5
1 Bank of Ireland	794	17	1		Stocks Do	12197	8	6
3 General A/c	280	0	0		Tools Do	3726	12	4
9 F.M. Wolff	1012	12	1		Cash Do	50	1	2
10 G.C. Schwabe	8000	0	0	5	Bills Receivable	2858	2	0
11 E.J. Harland	9404	2	11	13	John Bailey	43	11	3
12 G.W. Wolff	5402	18	6	14	William Houston	20	0	0
38 No.27 Ship	320	6	11	16	Plant	8081	0	0
35 Profit & Loss	3139	5	6	17	No.24 Ship	4009	18	8
				19	J.S. Brocklebank	14	10	8
				27	J.P. Corry & Co	71	13	2
				40	Life Assurance	198	0	0
				41	No.28 Ship	898	1	11
				42	No.29 Do	2337	10	2
				43	No.30 Do	1078	18	5
	£37707	2	8			£37707	2	8

Dr. — Balance Sheet 31 December 1863 — C.26

Balance sheet of Harland and Wolff for the six months ending 31 December 1863. On the left-hand side the liabilities include the partners' capital and on the right-hand side the assets include the valuation of the plant and stock.

of a fixed term, normally six months but sometimes longer, up to seven or eight years. They could be held by the original drawer (in this case Harland and Wolff) until expiry or discounted at less than their face value through the London money market, using one of the discount houses. Bills of exchange were often used by shipbuilders as a means of providing security for short-term loans made to customers, since they were secured as a first charge over a ship. Consequently shipbuilders only discounted such bills if strapped for cash, preferring to let them run to maturity. At the end of 1863 Harland and Wolff had drawn a total of £2,858 in bills of exchange, which rose to £4,429 the following year. These seem to have been short-term bills of between three and ten months. Most of the first ships were paid for in cash. Whatever the method of payment, accounts were rendered in instalments as work progressed, usually after the laying of the keel, when the framing was complete, when the hull had been plated, after the launch and on delivery.

The success of the new firm had attracted the attention of William James Pirrie,

Table 2.3

Capital, profit, plant and depreciation 1863-75

	Capital[1]	Profit[2] (loss)	Profit (loss) as percentage of capital	Plant[1]	Depreciation[2]	Depreciation as percentage of plant
	£	£	%	£	£	%
1863	22,920	5,693	24	—	—	—
1864	26,940	6,636	24	8,379	836	9
1865	31,741	(1,878)	(5)	8,012	787	9
1866	25,094	1,776	7	9,513	791	8
1867	34,571	21,940	63	9,340	947	10
1868	40,029	(5,327)	(13)	9,465	929	9
1869	41,424	7,366	17	10,067	891	8
1870	55,858	37,090	66	17,385	583	3
1871	68,307	16,975	24	19,289	2,687	13
1872	78,542	25,386	32	20,290	1,947	9
1873	96,461	20,802	21	24,769	2,265	9
1874	87,506	9,098	10	23,236	2,338	10
1875	78,653	(2,101)	(2)	31,118[3]	1,115	3

Notes
1   As at 31 December
2   Calculated by adding the figures at each balance in the year
3   Transferred to new firm

a schoolboy at the Royal Belfast Academical Institution. He had persuaded his mother to arrange for him to become a gentleman apprentice in succession to Alexander Wilson, who would complete his time in 1862. As a result, on 23 June of that year, Pirrie had begun his apprenticeship at Queen's Island. He had been born on 24 May 1847 in Quebec. His father James Alexander Pirrie had been sent to Canada in 1844 to enter the timber trade. James Alexander was the son of Captain William Pirrie, of Belfast, who had recently formed a new firm in partnership with his eldest son, William, connected by marriage to the influential Barbour family, owners of a large linen thread business. The new concern, named William Pirrie Junior & Company, was to act as a commission agency, arranging cargoes and insurance for shipowners.

Shortly after his arrival in Canada, James Pirrie married Eliza Swan Montgomery, daughter of Alexander Montgomery of Dundesart, Co. Antrim. During January 1847, in partnership with James, Captain William Pirrie purchased the brig *James* which had been built in New Brunswick in 1825. After James Pirrie's death in 1849 his wife brought the young William James and his sister, Eliza, back to their paternal grandfather's home at Conlig, Co. Down. Over the next ten years his grandfather showed a keen interest in William James's upbringing and education.[38] It was natural that Captain Pirrie, who died on 8 June 1858, should have encouraged his grandson to choose a career connected with ships. After the Captain's death the chairman of the Harbour Commissioners moved a vote of condolence: 'During his thirty years' service in the Board ... a tortuous and shallow stream had been succeeded by a deep direct channel navigable at every period of the tide. Than Captain Pirrie to no Commissioner is Belfast more indebted for these improvements.'[39]

Just one month before his grandfather's death, William James Pirrie had been enrolled as a pupil at the Royal Belfast Academical Institution. A year before he left the school his uncle, John Carlisle, husband of his mother's sister, Catherine Montgomery, was appointed head of the English department and soon became virtual headmaster of the school. Pirrie had grown up surrounded by relations who were involved in trade or shipowning. One of his aunts, Eliza Pirrie, was married to John Sinclair, whose son, William Pirrie Sinclair, had established a shipping business in Belfast and moved to Liverpool. Another aunt, Letitia, was married to the Chevalier Gustavus Heyn who had come from the Baltic port of Danzig and established himself as a shipping and marine insurance agent in Belfast. His uncle William had moved to Rockferry, Liverpool, in 1848 where he continued his business as a commission agent and insurance broker. When in 1851 J.P. Corry sought insurance cover for the vessel *Hercules*, William Pirrie arranged it. Another uncle, Washington Pirrie, was in partnership with William Pirrie Sinclair in his Liverpool shipping venture. Like many business families of the time, the young William James Pirrie's family were shifting their political affiliations towards the Liberal Party, with its commitment to free trade. William's uncle, John Carlisle, was an articulate exponent and supporter of such policies.[40]

The influence of these relatives over the young man was slight in comparison to that of his mother. Like the rest of her family, she had a strong personality and a staunch Presbyterian faith. When he started work at Queen's Island, his mother gave him a little book of maxims to guide him through the world of business. These included:

> You have your own way to make. It depends on your exertions whether you starve or not.
> Accuracy also is of much importance and an invariable mark of good training in a man – accuracy in observation, accuracy in speech, accuracy in the transaction of affairs.
> What is done in business must be well done; for it is better to accomplish perfectly a small amount of work than half do ten times as much.
> Method is essential and enables a large amount of work to be got through with satisfaction.[41]

Pirrie himself was a small neat man, with sparkling eyes and a smiling face which gave little hint of his enormous energy and intelligence.

Despite the strong order book, William J. Pirrie's first year at Queen's Island was a traumatic one for the business. Early in 1863 Edward Harland and G.W. Wolff became locked in a violent public debate about the location of the proposed new graving dock to be built by the Harbour Commissioners. It had been intended in 1847 to build the dock on the Co. Antrim side of the Lagan. In November 1862 the Commissioners changed their minds and chose the Co. Down side, but without naming a site. The Belfast Shipwrights Society objected: 'The risk to life, owing to crossing the river (often in crowded boats before and after daylight), and the enormous evils attendant upon lost time and hasty meals, would make us better satisfied with considerably less wages on the Belfast side than the Ballymacarrett.' This complaint fell on the ears of sympathetic electors in the forthcoming ballot for members of the Commission. Harland and Wolff, on the other hand, pointed out that a graving dock adjacent to their works would encourage their trade and might stimulate others to set up iron shipbuilding businesses. They countered the proposal that the Commissioners remove the yard to the Co. Antrim side, by suggesting that they would prefer to shift to Liverpool in that eventuality. The argument raged throughout January 1864 up to the election day, 5 February. Although those in favour of the Co. Down side for the graving dock won a majority, the quarrel continued. It was not resolved until 6 April when the Commissioners agreed to build a large floating dock on the Co. Antrim side of the river (the Dufferin and Spencer docks) and a graving dock and service basin on the Co. Down side at the south end of Queen's Island. The Hamilton graving dock was to be constructed on the site of the timber pond, and the Abercorn basin created out of the open water facing the Harland and Wolff berths.[42]

Work began almost at once. It involved a large number of Catholic navvies from other parts of Ireland where industrial employment was rare and men from the large rural population were attracted by the wages offered to unskilled labourers on building projects throughout the United Kingdom. Tensions quickly developed between the Protestant community and the incomers. On Monday 8 August a large party of Catholics returned to Belfast after attending a ceremony in Dublin to unveil a statue to Daniel O'Connell. The Protestants, infuriated that such a demonstration could take place at a time when Orange marches were banned under the controversial Party Processions Act, retaliated by burning a giant effigy of O'Connell. Rioting continued throughout the week. Shipwrights, including those from the Harland and Wolff yard, marched into the town centre on Tuesday 16 August. They broke into shops, stealing guns to attack St Peter's Pro-Cathedral, though fortunately their intention was frustrated by the military. The following day the shipwrights trapped the navvies at work, leaving them no way of escape except into the water or across the mud flats. At Harland and Wolff the Protestant workforce determined to evict the small number of Catholic employees. The shipwrights went on strike, demanding the dismissal of Catholics alleged to be informing on workers involved in the riots. Edward Harland reacted swiftly, putting notices up throughout the works stating that if any Catholics were turned out the yard would close until they were permitted to return. It was rumoured that he had 'a telescope at his house through which on one occasion he detected an Orangeman dropping a hammer on a Papist'. The stern warning, combined with heavy rain, brought the rioting to an end.[43]

In 1865, partly because of the American Civil War, the shipbuilding industry went into a sharp recession which lasted until 1867. On the Clyde the large business of Scott & Company, of Greenock, was forced to suspend payments in December 1866. Harland and Wolff also found the going tough: contracts were hard to come by and sometimes had to be taken at a loss. Of the nine vessels completed in 1865 and 1866 for which prices survive, six were built at a loss. These reverses resulted in a total loss for 1865 of £1,878, the partnership's first setback. Apart from writing off this sum, the partners, prudently, reduced their investment in the firm during the following year, Harland taking out about £3,500, and Wolff roughly £1,500. Nevertheless, by the spring of 1866 they could look forward with confidence to the coming year, as John Bibby & Sons placed an order for three new 'coffin' steamers of almost 3,000 gross tons and nearly 400 feet long. Before work could begin on this contract the ways had to be lengthened and strengthened and new equipment installed at a cost of nearly £1,500. The small profit in 1866, when only three ships were completed, resulted from good returns on two vessels ordered by T. & J. Brocklebank, the *Candahar* and the *Tenasserim* . However, the partners were dealt a blow during the year when a barque (ship no. 44) was left on their hands halfway through construction.

26

The completion of the Bibby contracts in 1867, with a total return of over £24,000, contributed towards profits of nearly £22,000, or 63 per cent of the reduced loan and partners' capital. Early in the year the partners successfully raised the steamer *Earl of Dublin* which had foundered on the rocks at Ballyhalbert, Co. Down, and been written off by her underwriters. Harland and Wolff at once began to repair and lengthen her at their own expense. While this task was in progress William Houston resigned. Some of his duties were taken by Samuel Dunlop who was appointed to the new post of cashier. At the same time the business, now known as Harland and Wolff, was approved by the Admiralty for naval construction and an order was placed for the gunboat HMS *Lynx*.[44] During 1867 the facilities at Queen's Island were greatly improved by the opening of the Harbour Commissioners' Abercorn basin and Hamilton graving dock. The Abercorn basin had a water area of 12½ acres, and the Hamilton dock was 450 feet long. Their inauguration attracted a potential competitor to Queen's Island, MacIlwaine & Lewis, a local firm of engineers, established in 1863, who built an engineering works at the south-east corner of the Abercorn basin. John H. MacIlwaine had been trained by Hickson and Harland before being appointed draughtsman to John Elder & Company of Glasgow.[45]

Harland and Wolff's first Admiralty order, completed in 1868, proved a doubtful blessing, resulting in a loss of nearly £5,000, almost half the contract price. Contemporary reports suggest that many shipbuilders were prepared to build at a loss one of the eight Admiralty vessels ordered from private contractors in 1867, in the hope of winning business from foreign governments who refused to deal with firms that had no experience of working for the British Navy.[46] This loss, along with the cost of lengthening the *Earl of Dublin* (renamed *Duke of Edinburgh*),

amounting to nearly £16,000, pushed Harland and Wolff firmly back into the red. The result might have been worse had not G.C. Schwabe again come to the rescue by securing a purchaser for ship no. 44 which the partners had completed at their own expense. During the year a young Liverpool shipowner, Thomas Henry Ismay, acquired, with Schwabe's help, the bankrupt White Star line which had been founded to provide services from Liverpool to Australia on the back of the gold rush. Ismay needed new tonnage to maintain the service and Schwabe arranged for him to take over ship no. 44, named *Broughton* (after Schwabe's Liverpool home, Broughton Hall), on the understanding that, through Harland and Wolff, Schwabe would provide a quarter of the finance.[47]

During 1868 Harland and Wolff received widespread publicity as a result of the raising of G. & J. Burns's paddle steamer *Wolf* which had been run down the previous autumn in Belfast Lough by the steamer *Prince Arthur*. Edward Harland would have been well known to the Burns brothers from his time at J. & G. Thomson and they probably had no hesitation in asking him to attempt lifting the *Wolf*. This difficult and novel operation was achieved by using a raft of air tanks and powerful lifting screws. It took eight days to bring the vessel up and manoeuvre her into the Hamilton graving dock. Harland later recalled that 'at the end of the docking our friends scarcely recognised us for we had neither undressed nor shaved during that anxious time'.[48]

By this time William J. Pirrie had finished his apprenticeship and been appointed draughtsman in the place of Walter Wilson who had been promoted to be manager of the yard in succession to William Houston. As part of his training, Pirrie had spent some time learning the techniques of marine engine building with the Greenock firms of MacNab & Company and Caird & Company. He had shown that he not only had a talent for ship design and construction, but was equally fascinated by finance, keen to learn all that Wolff and John Bailey, the firm's clerk and book-keeper, could teach him.[49]

Early in 1869 the partners again found themselves with a vessel on their hands, ship no. 60, *Lady Cairns*, which had been built at a cost of almost £17,000. Unable to find a buyer, they decided to own and operate this sailing vessel themselves. This was an isolated setback. In the spring succour came again from Schwabe with an order for three 400-foot vessels from John Bibby & Sons. The first of these ships, the *Bavarian*, was completed before the end of the year, bringing a return of £8,553 on a price of £51,663. This more than covered the loss on the *Lady Cairns* and lifted the business strongly back to profitability in the second half of the year. By the time the accounts had been made up, the partners had concluded a momentous agreement, with Schwabe's help. During the autumn he had put an ambitious proposal to them for the formation of a new shipping line to compete with the Cunard and Inman lines on the North Atlantic. After the American Civil War there was a rapid development of the Atlantic trade routes, based on expanding commerce and on massive emigration from Europe. Tradition has it that the project for the new line originated over an after-dinner game of billiards at Schwabe's home. He is reported to have suggested to his opponent, Thomas Ismay, that if Harland and Wolff built the ships for the new concern he would mobilise the finance. Ismay, a director of the Liverpool-based National line since its formation in 1864, was no stranger to North Atlantic shipping and quickly agreed to relinquish his Australian business. Accordingly, on 6 September 1869 the Oceanic Steam Navigation Company was registered to acquire the White Star line with the public intention of improving its Australian service. The

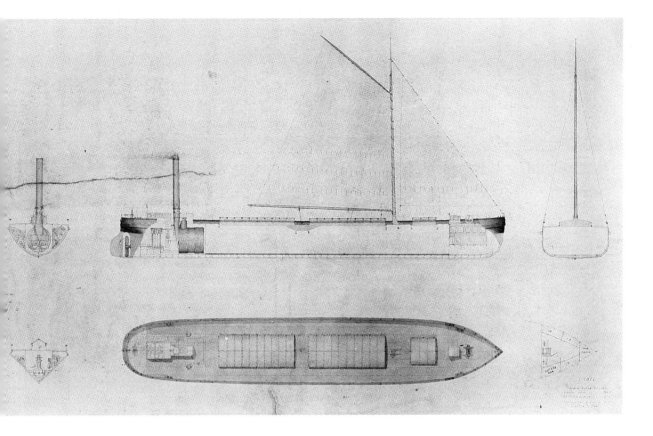

new line was to be managed by Thomas Ismay and his partner, William Imrie, through their firm Ismay, Imrie & Company.[50]

An order for five 420-foot steamers of just under 4,000 gross tons, at a price of over £110,000 each, was immediately placed with Harland and Wolff. Both the partners invested in the new company, Edward Harland purchasing twelve shares, costing £1,750 each.[51] Such investments by shipbuilders were not uncommon. Robert Napier had helped finance Samuel Cunard's business in exchange for the contract to build his first four ships. Where Harland and Wolff's understanding with the new line differed was in an agreement to build the vessels and subsequent orders at cost plus 4 per cent commission on the first cost of the ship. This cost included material and direct labour charges, but no allowance for overheads. There appear to have been penalties for late delivery. This type of contract was a novel and imaginative arrangement.

Before work could begin on this massive order the yard needed to be totally re-equipped and modernised. Four new berths were constructed in the south-west part of the yard, facing into the Abercorn basin. The land behind the patent slip was taken over from the Commissioners and the two yards knocked into one. A new platers' shop and smithy were built. At the same time the small 269-ton steamer *Camel* (ship no. 78) was constructed on the partners' own account. This vessel was fitted with very big hatchways and specially strengthened to carry the iron and machinery which needed to be brought from Britain for the order. As an experiment Harland fitted direct-acting spring safety valves to the *Camel*'s boilers, rather than the Board-of-Trade-approved counter-weight type, in an effort to economise in the use of steam. The trials were successful and the valves were adopted in the new White Star vessels.[52] These projects cost the partners nearly £30,000 between 1869 and 1872, all paid for out of profits.

29

The new investment was complemented by the Harbour Commissioners, who during 1871 installed a large pair of 50-ton masting shears (built by Courtenay Stephen & Company of Dublin) on the east side of the Abercorn quay, to be used not only for masting but also for engining vessels. Relations with the Commissioners were not entirely amicable. In 1870, at the time the decision to install the masting shears was taken, Harland and Wolff were pressing for an extension of their lease to thirty-one, instead of twenty-one, years, and the rescinding of the clause that allowed the Commissioners to repossess sections of the yard for improvements to the navigation. Edward Harland was elected a Commissioner in October 1870, but resigned in December over this issue. In October 1871 the Commissioners yielded to the firm's demands.[53]

While the improvements to the yard were progressing during 1870, Alexander Montgomery Carlisle joined the firm as a premium apprentice. He was the son of William Pirrie's uncle, John Carlisle, the head of the English department at the Royal Belfast Academical Institution.[54] Apprentices bound themselves for five years to even more onerous conditions than those imposed by Charles Connell a generation before. When Lawson Albert Bell, son of a gateman of Belfast, became an ordinary apprentice in 1872, he agreed that he:

> his said Masters faithfully shall serve, their secrets keep, their lawful commands everywhere gladly do, he shall do no damage to his Masters in their goods, chattels, or estate, or know or procure any to be done by others; but when he shall know, or have any reason to suspect such intended, he shall forthwith give warning to his said Masters of the same; he shall not waste the goods of his said Masters, or give or lend them unlawfully to any, he shall not commit fornication, or contract matrimony within the said term; hurt to said Masters in their persons or families, he shall not do, cause, or procure to be done by others, he shall not play cards, dice, or any unlawful game with his own or

others' goods, whereby his said Masters may have loss, during the said term. Without license of his said Masters he shall neither buy nor sell, he shall not frequent taverns, alehouses, or playhouses, or absent himself from his said Masters' service day or night unlawfully . . .

The parents of premium apprentices like A.M. Carlisle paid a premium, normally of 100 guineas, for their child to learn a trade; while ordinary apprentices, like Lawson A. Bell, were paid a wage, starting at six shillings a week and rising to ten shillings a week in their final year.[55]

When designing the first White Star ships, Harland and Wolff adopted the hull form that they had pioneered in the successful Bibby 'coffins'. In consultation with Thomas Ismay, the partners planned totally novel passenger accommodation. The saloon ran the breadth of the ship, allowing passengers on a transatlantic liner to eat together for the first time. A built-in smoking room was provided instead of a canvas deckhouse. The cabins were almost doubled in size and fitted with larger portholes and electric bells. These elaborate interior fittings owed many of their features to observation of large hotels, made by Pirrie who had been sent on a tour of England and the Continent for this purpose.[56] When choosing the type of engine, the firm was able to take advantage of the expiry of John Elder & Company's patent over the compound engine. Alexander Wilson, the brother of the yard manager, who had trained as an engineer, was commissioned to make a number of voyages in steam vessels fitted with the best examples of compound engines. These investigations resulted in the installation of vertical overhead compound engines with five-feet stroke and oval single-end transverse boilers. One contract for three sets was placed with Maudslay Sons and Field of London, and another with George Forrester & Company of Liverpool.[57] The first ship of the class, the *Oceanic*, made her maiden voyage to New York in March 1871 and was an immediate success. The remaining three vessels, along with an order for a further two, were completed by the end of 1872. Despite the construction of these powerful competitors, Cunard & Company commissioned Harland and Wolff during 1871 to lengthen four of their steamers, *Marathon*, *Hecla*, *Olympus* and *Atlas*.

This welter of activity was reflected in the balance sheet. There was a massive jump in profits in 1870, when they reached £37,090, or 66 per cent of the loan and partners' capital which stood at about £56,000. This result owed more to returns of about 20 per cent on the Bibby contracts completed that year than to the Oceanic deal. Profits retreated in 1871 and 1872 because the large White Star boats had been built on a 4 per cent commission rather than for a straight profit, which on such large and prestigious vessels might have equalled more than 10 per cent. There may have been another explanation for the drop in profits. In 1871 the engineering trades had started a campaign, known as the 'short time movement', to reduce the working week from fifty-seven to fifty-one hours. There had been disturbances and strikes throughout the United Kingdom, and early in 1872 the employers conceded a gradual reduction over the year to fifty-one hours. Meanwhile, during August 1872 violence erupted on the streets of Belfast over the Home Rule question, and the largely Protestant Harland and Wolff workforce pitched in. On 15 August 500 men stopped work early and fought a running battle with the police. Although Edward Harland and Gustav Wolff stood out against intimidation of their Catholic employees, they could do nothing to prevent Catholics being turned out of their homes in Protestant areas of the city.

Despite these problems, however, the partners had cause to be satisfied with a total return for the two years 1871 and 1872 of over £42,000. Not all of these profits were ploughed back into the firm: the partners withdrew some of their earnings to buy stock in the Oceanic Steam Navigation Company and to make other investments. During 1872 the Belfast Ropework Company was established by W.B. Lowson, of Lowson & Smiles, commission merchants and insurance agents; John Davidson, a patent hemp and wire rope manufacturer, sailmaker and ship chandler; Samuel Wilson, of Wilson Brothers, flax spinners and merchants; and W.H. Smiles, the eldest son of the famous reformer and social theorist Samuel Smiles. Since rope was needed in quantity for rigging both sailing and steam ships, ropemakers were often closely associated with shipbuilders and were regular customers for shares in ships and shipping ventures. Gustav Wolff reversed this process in July 1873 when he became a partner in the new firm, along with Dr J.P. Hartee. Edward Harland chose to buy, for nearly £9,000, two farms at Brompton Park in Ardoyne, then an industrial village on the outskirts of Belfast.[58]

Although only the *Gaelic* and *Belgic* were delivered in 1873, profits held up, sustained by the extension of the business to include more major repairs and refits. This was a growing trade. With the introduction of iron ships, along with iron masts and wire rigging, most large repairs, which had previously been carried out on wooden vessels by the crew, had to be done in a shipyard. The Queen's Island yard was well situated to win such work, with its patent slip and adjacent Hamilton graving dock, complemented by the new masting shears at the top of the Abercorn basin. These facilities, provided by the Harbour Commissioners, were better than those available to Harland and Wolff's competitors on the Clyde and the Mersey. During 1873, apart from the completion of the lengthening of the four Cunarders, the firm finished major repairs on at least another four vessels. Early in the previous year W.H. Smiles had been invited by Harland to inspect the work in progress on the refit of the paddle steamer *Albert Edward*. He later recorded his impression of 'an immense

The White Star liner *Germanic*, sister ship of the *Britannic*, delivered in April 1875. Both vessels are typical Queen's Island 'coffin' ships with straight stems and square bottoms.

clatter of hammers!'[59]

The lack of new building in 1873 was probably caused by a further upheaval in the yard, resulting from the placing of another contract by Oceanic for two liners, the *Britannic* and *Germanic*, of 5,000 tons and 455 feet long. They were to be built to meet competition from the Inman line's *City of Chester* and *City of Richmond* which were completing on the Clyde. Before work could begin, the new berths had to be strengthened and, as the construction progressed, new plant and machinery purchased. The efficient layout of this equipment owed much to observations made by Pirrie during a visit to the United States in 1872.[60] These improvements cost some £10,000 during 1873/4. The two new vessels were priced at £200,000 and were again built for 4 per cent commission. They were delivered in 1874 and 1875. Although the tonnage completed during 1874 was far greater than the previous year, profits dwindled. This poor performance probably reflected a rise in material prices and wages as the boom in shipbuilding peaked. (The *Star of Bengal*, delivered to J.P. Corry in March, recorded a loss of nearly £2,000.) It may, also, have resulted from offers to other owners to build on a cost-plus basis. Two ships on the stocks in 1874, the *Star of Russia* for J.P. Corry & Company and the *Majestic* for T. & J. Brocklebank, were both constructed on 4 per cent commission. These deals with established customers were presumably struck on the understanding that future contracts and repair work would be placed with the yard.

During the summer of 1874 it was decided to reconstruct the partnership to embrace Walter H. Wilson, the yard manager; his brother, Alexander B. Wilson, who was in charge of engine design and installation; and the chief draughtsman, William J. Pirrie. In the absence of evidence it is only possible to guess at the motives of Edward

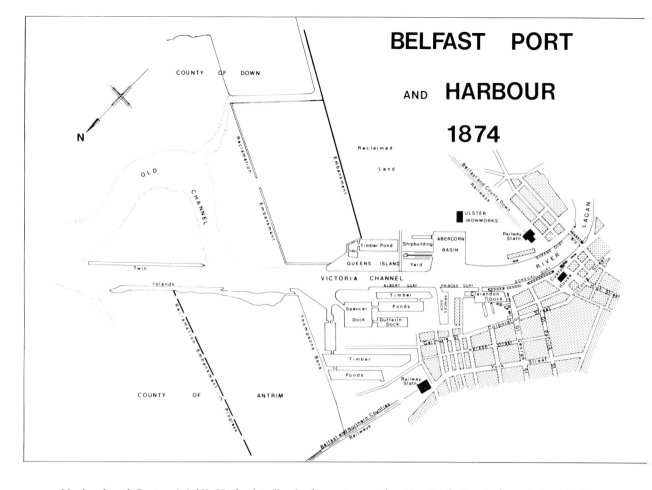

Harland and Gustav Wolff. Undoubtedly the largest consideration in their minds was the disposal in 1873 of the Bibby fleet to one of its partners, Frederick Leyland, and Schwabe's withdrawal from the business.[61] Although Leyland had become a close friend of both Harland and Wolff since 1858, his commitments to his commercial supporters would prevent him ordering any new vessels for some time. This uncertainty coincided with a desire by both Harland and Wolff to pursue other interests which would take them away from the yard. In April Harland had been elected to the onerous post of chairman of the Belfast Harbour Commissioners, where he would be well placed to help the yard but would have less time to share in its direction. Wolff was becoming increasingly involved in the affairs of the ropeworks. The partners almost certainly could not rely on either the Wilson brothers or William Pirrie to stay with the firm unless they were admitted to the partnership. All three were relatively well-off and, like Harland and Wolff themselves a generation earlier, were probably keen to own their own business. Both Harland and Wolff could afford to be generous. Since 1863 their share in the firm had increased sixfold with no additional injections of capital from outside. They had also drawn considerable sums from the firm. In June 1875 Harland calculated that his fortune, including his share in the business, totalled almost £125,000.

On the termination of the first partnership in the autumn of 1875 the business was just twenty-two years old. It had grown from a tiny works with one berth, employing forty-eight men, to a large yard with six slips and a workforce of over 1,000. It had turned out nearly 100 vessels with an aggregate gross tonnage of over 100,000 tons. These ships bore the traffic of a worldwide empire – emigrants, armies, administrators, raw materials from the ends of the earth. This trade, in turn, was

A plan of Belfast port and harbour in 1874 showing, on the County Down shore, the site of the Harland and Wolff yard on Queen's Island, with the timber pond and the pleasure ground behind.

34

The platers' shed built in 1874 to upgrade the facilities at Queen's Island. In the foreground is a punching and shearing machine.

part of a wider phenomenon – the increasing domination of Europe in the markets of the world and the expansion of European influence into Asia and Africa. The success of the firm was due in large measure to the confidence of Gustav Christian Schwabe and his partners, John S. Bibby and Thomas Ismay, in the ability of Harland and Wolff to design and construct new, technically advanced tonnage, which would prove commercially viable. Harland and Wolff had more than justified this faith. They had shown themselves to be remarkably effective partners. Their talents and personalities were complementary. Wolff's good humour and wit were an excellent foil for Harland's stern fastidiousness. They had both become enthusiastic Ulstermen and admirers of Belfast. Wolff lived at Strandtown, calling his house 'The Den', and despite the fact that all his life he retained his German accent, he felt sufficiently at home to write:

> You may talk of your Edinburgh and the beauties of Perth,
> And all the large cities famed on the earth,
> But give me my house though it may be a garrett
> In the pleasant surroundings of Ballymacarrett.[62]

The workforce responded to this commitment with intense loyalty and pride in working on Queen's Island. They soon saw themselves as a race apart, earning the nickname 'Islandmen'.

35

3
H & W
ALIAS PIRRIE AND WILSON
1874–85

The mid-1870s was not a propitious time for new recruits to become partners in a shipbuilding enterprise. A serious depression persisted, with only a slight upturn, until 1880. Demand for quality, and therefore highly priced, passenger ships was severely dented. At the other end of the market, orders for large, technically advanced, bulk-carrying sailing vessels could be received but often only at the expense of profit, and by drawing long-dated bills on their customers by way of payment. Winning business in such difficult trading conditions tested the financial skill and technical experience of all shipbuilding concerns. So as to keep the greatly enlarged Queen's Island yard in business, the members of the new partnership would have to look to a wider clientele for their tonnage. They could no longer rely on the Bibbys for help at times of crisis and the Oceanic Steam Navigation Company's White Star line had enough tonnage to meet its needs in a slack market. It was Edward Harland and Gustav Wolff's intention that their new partners should share in the difficult task of broadening the yard's custom, reaping both the gains and losses.

There is no record of how the partners planned to divide their responsibilities. Pirrie, with his great personal charm and close relations in the shipping world, was the natural leader of the young men. He had already travelled widely on the firm's behalf and had a firm grasp of all aspects of the business. He enjoyed the contacts he made with leading industrialists on his travels and revelled in publicity. He was immensely hard-working and emulated Edward Harland in his attention to detail and firm discipline. The Wilson brothers worked no less hard, but were shy, preferring to grapple with technical problems than with men and money.

When the new firm was inaugurated at the end of August 1874 the partners' capital stood at £76,250, of which Edward Harland held £31,500, Gustav Wolff £15,750, William James Pirrie £13,000, Walter H. Wilson £10,000, and his brother Alexander B. Wilson £6,000. Although Pirrie and the Wilson brothers must have been well paid as managers in the old firm, it is improbable that they had been able to amass such fortunes. It is more likely that the cash to pay for their shares came from their families. The new firm was loaned £73,369 by the old partnership which remained in being until the loan had been repaid in the autumn of 1875. The order book was weak. Like Russell & Company, which had just been formed to acquire a shipyard at Port Glasgow on the lower Clyde, the new firm of Harland and Wolff had to accept whatever contracts could be found. The vessels ordered after the formation of the new firm were small by the previous standards of the yard. The largest were two 1,400-gross-ton sailing ships, *Fiji* and *Pizarro*, for W.J. Myers of Liverpool. The smallest were little 105-foot barges for use on the Nile. All but the *Fiji* and *Pizarro* were built at a loss, and these yielded only 2½ per cent on their contract price. In 1875 the new partnership recorded a small profit of £1,343, which was more than cancelled by the old partnership's loss of £2,101.

Faced with these difficulties the partners looked for orders principally among shipowners in the north west of England and in Ireland, where they already had

Table 3.1

Capital 1874-85[1]

PARTNERS' CAPITAL

	E. J. Harland	G. W. Wolff	W. H. Wilson	W. J. Pirrie	A. B. Wilson	Total
	£	£	£	£	£	£
1874	31,500	15,750	10,000	13,000	6,000	76,250
1875	31,100	15,550	10,200	13,250	6,150	76,250
1876	27,420	13,710	18,400	16,720	—	76,250
1877	24,920	12,460	19,300	19,570	—	76,250
1878	20,820	10,410	22,375	22,645	—	76,250
1879	32,260	16,130	28,795	29,065	—	106,250
1880	27,860	13,930	28,195	36,265	—	106,250
1881	26,860	13,430	31,345	34,615	—	106,250
1882	18,120	9,060	37,900	41,170	—	106,250
1883	12,620	6,310	42,025	45,295	—	106,250
1884	—	—	51,490	54,760	—	106,250
1885[2]	—	—	51,490	54,760	—	106,250

LOAN CAPITAL

	Harland and Wolff (old partnership)	E. J. Harland	G. W. Wolff	G. C. Schwabe	Sundry small loans	Bank of Ireland	Total[3]
	£	£	£	£	£	£	£
1874	73,369	—	—	—	2,474	4,524	80,367
1875	44,913	—	—	—	10,447	—	55,360
1876	—	23,497	9,336	—	2,171	—	35,004
1877	—	5,512	289	—	3,483	1,148	10,432
1878	—	10,106	3,178	—	9,526	2,905	25,715
1879	—	16,141	3,435	—	13,074	1,676	34,326
1880	—	35,638	18,587	14,000	3,560	28,340	100,125
1881	—	42,386	24,824	14,000	20,709	26,266	128,185
1882	—	60,541	34,452	14,000	16,374	3,739	129,106
1883	—	58,061	27,844	14,000	39,859	10,933	150,697
1884	—	80,383	38,725	14,000	13,404	1,347	147,859
1885[2]	—	79,192	41,075	14,000	—	—	—

Notes

1 The accounts of the partnership were balanced twice a year on 30 June and 31 December. The figure for 31 December has been used.

2 As at 30 June 1885

3 Total column appears in the private ledger as 'Loans bearing Interest': the loans itemised above are included in this total, together with various other small loans and other interest-bearing amounts totalled under the heading 'Sundry small loans'.

strong links. No doubt this policy enabled them, like shipbuilders in other parts of the United Kingdom, to assist in mobilising finance. G.W. Wolff's partnership in the Belfast Ropework Company gave them access to low-priced rope and sailcloth, providing a further inducement to owners. During the period from November, 1875 to March, 1877, the firm launched eleven vessels of which just two were steamers – the paddle steamer *Princess Beatrice*, for the Larne & Stranraer Steam Packet Company, and *Thursby* for W. Thursby of Fleetwood. For some now unknown

reason the *Thursby* was constructed at 4 per cent commission. The other vessels included a barge for the Cork Harbour Commissioners, five sailing ships, two of which were almost 1,750 tons, the *Slieve More* and the *Slieve Bawn*. These vessels were ordered by none other than Pirrie's cousin, William Pirrie Sinclair, whose shipping business was now based in Liverpool. So as to secure the contract the partners used the well tried technique of agreeing to participate in the ownership of both vessels. E.J. Harland took a share in each at a cost of just over £3,200. At the same time he purchased £1,000 of shares in the State Steamship Company, whose steamers called at Larne, in exchange for a slice of its repair business. Despite these initiatives, profits remained under severe pressure, falling to a mere £221. During 1875 A.B. Wilson withdrew from the business to become managing director of John Rowan & Sons, who were general and marine engineers in Belfast. It is likely that A.B. Wilson was appointed to protect Harland and Wolff's interest in this business, particularly as it had the contract for building the engines for the *Thursby*. Edward Harland and possibly his other partners were shareholders.[1] A.B. Wilson's share in Harland and Wolff was taken over by his brother, W.H. Wilson. During the year E.J. Harland and G.W. Wolff reduced their commitments to the partnership, while Wilson and Pirrie invested more capital. By the end of the year G.W. Wolff was the junior partner.

The four partners in Harland and Wolff from 1876–85: (left to right) G.W. Wolff, W.H. Wilson, W.J. Pirrie and Edward J. Harland.

38

Table 3.2
Profit and shipping investments 1874-85

	Partners' capital[1]	Profit (loss)[2]	Profit as percentage of partners' capital	Investments in shipping
	£	£	%	£
1874	76,250	2,533[4]	3	—
1875	76,250	1,343	2	—
1876	76,250	221	—	—
1877	76,250	6,709	8	3,775
1878	76,250	32,391	42	5,779
1879	106,250	12,860	12	21,847
1880	106,250	8,239	7	26,329
1881	106,250	10,414	9	23,301
1882	106,250	27,566	25	4,826
1883	106,250	51,076	48	—
1884	106,250	49,724	46	2,713
1885[3]	106,250	17,682[4]	16	10,328

Notes
1 As at 31 December
2 After charging interest and depreciation
3 As at 30 June 1885
4 Half year only

Table 3.3
Plant and depreciation 1874-85

	Shipyard plant	Shipyard plant, tools and stock	Engine works plant	Engine works plant, tools and stock	Dufferin dock	Total plant	Depreciation	Depreciation as percentage of total plant
	£	£	£	£	£	£	£	%
1874	30,112	74,584	—	—	—	30,112	n/a	—
1875	28,250	68,472	—	—	—	28,250	n/a	—
1876	26,274	68,370	—	—	—	26,274	n/a	—
1877	25,864	61,915	—	—	—	25,864	n/a	—
1878	26,475	64,521	—	—	—	26,475	n/a	—
1879	29,491	78,115	7,089	7,089	643	37,223	n/a	—
1880	39,503	95,436	58,649	62,708	1,236	99,388	n/a	—
1881	44,608	110,425	63,526	71,501	802	108,936	n/a	—
1882	45,461	130,099	66,680	77,002	1,182	113,323	n/a	—
1883	49,539	121,357	73,190	83,362	n/a	122,729	8,935	7
1884	53,393	116,379	73,853	83,337	n/a	127,246	9,522	7
1885[1]	51,983	108,367	74,534	84,239	n/a	126,517	4,960	3
1885[2]	72,803	—	93,877	—	—	—	—	—

Notes
1 At 30 June 1885 for the partnership
2 At 30 June 1885 value of assets transferred to Queen's Island Shipbuilding & Engineering Company. The discrepancy
   between the figures is explained by the cancellation of all the depreciation on the fixed assets.
n/a = Not available

Table 3.4 (cont. on p.41)

Edward James Harland's personal shipping investments 1875-84[1]

	Camel $\frac{42^2}{64}$	Broughton $\frac{22^2}{64}$	Worral $\frac{22^2}{64}$	Oceanic Steam Navigation Co.	Asiatic Steam Navigation Co.	African Steamship Co.
	£	£	£	£	£	£
1875	7,668	2,169	1,751	29,000	—	—
1876	6,826	2,880	2,209	39,410	—	—
1877	6,826	—	1,948	21,000	—	—
1878	5,578	—	1,948	21,000	3,000	—
1879	—	—	1,948	21,000	5,000	—
1880	—	—	1,751	21,000	5,000	514
1881	—	—	1,751	21,000	5,000	3,661
1882	—	—	1,751	21,000	5,000	4,314
1883	—	—	1,914	21,000	5,000	5,897
1884	—	—	—	—	—	—

Notes

1 Abstracted from E. J. Harland's private ledger 1875-84 in possession of the Company. They represent his private investment in ships built by the Company and in shipping companies with which Harland and Wolff were associated.

2 Shares in ships owned as partnerships were normally divided into sixty-fourths.

The next year, 1877, brought no relief. Only three sailing ships were launched for two Belfast firms – two for J.P. Corry & Company, and one for R. Neill & Sons. The two Corry ships, *Star of Italy* and *Star of France*, were fast clippers for the Far East trade, unlike the slab-sided vessels built for W.P. Sinclair, designed for carrying heavy, bulky cargoes rather than for speed. One sailing ship (ship no. 103) was left on the partners' hands and remained in the yard. During the year the firm purchased shares totalling £3,775 in two vessels, the sailing ship *Blair Athole* owned by Thomson & Gray of Glasgow and built in 1875 and the steamer *Irishman* previously owned by A.P. Laird of Glasgow and built in 1854. It is likely that these investments were made as a condition of contracts to refit both ships. This work helped to lift profits to almost 8 per cent of the partners' capital. W.H. Wilson and Pirrie again raised their stake in the business, presumably by drawing on the resources of their families. Roughly £29,000 of the loan made to the new firm by E.J. Harland and G.W. Wolff was repaid.

Since the spring of 1877 the outlook had been improving. The Admiralty had awarded a contract for the 3,360-ton store and torpedo ship HMS *Hecla*. This contract, completed in 1878, earned the firm a profit of £17,439, or 14 per cent on the contract price of £117,947. Simultaneously further business was received from the Liverpool-based British Shipowners Limited for the construction of the steamer *British Empire* and the lengthening of the sailing ship, *British Peer*. The layout of the *British Empire*, of 3,361 tons, was based on that of the White Star liner *Britannic* 'but fuller, being intended for cargo'.[2] The *British Peer* had thirty feet added amidship, raising her tonnage from 1,230 gross tons to 1,478 gross tons and increasing her speed and performance. So successful was this that in one subsequent voyage she sailed from Calcutta to within 1,000 miles of London in eighty-five days.[3] Early in 1878 an order was placed for a 2,000-gross-ton steamer, the *Nubia*, by the African

Table 3.4 (cont.)

Edward James Harland's personal shipping investments 1875-84[1]

Lord Cairns	Slieve More $\frac{52}{64}$	Slieve Bawn	Slieve Roe	State Steamship Co.	Belfast Steamship Co.	Total
£	£	£	£	£	£	£
—	—	—	—	—	5,003	45,591
—	2,372	791	—	800	5,003	60,291
—	3,229	3,262	1,896	1,000	5,003	44,164
3,423	3,117	3,262	3,199	1,044	5,003	50,574
3,535	3,117	3,262	3,040	—	5,003	45,905
3,449	3,117	3,124	2,922	—	5,003	45,880
2,951	2,817	2,890	2,780	—	2,378	45,228
2,648	2,817	2,801	2,747	—	2,378	45,456
—	2,611	2,663	2,546	—	—	41,631
—	—	2,596	—	—	—	2,596

Steamship Company of Liverpool. Around the same time Edward Harland embarked on a more ambitious venture with Thomas Ismay and William Imrie, promoting the Liverpool-based Asiatic Steam Navigation Company in March 1878.[4] The new company's first four 1,600-ton steamers were to be built at Queen's Island more or less at cost. The first steamer was launched before the end of the year. One sailing ship was also completed in 1878, the *G.W. Wolff* (1,700 tons) for Samuel Lawther of Belfast, and ship no. 103, *Lord Cairns*, which had been left on the partners' hands was sold to Thomas Dixon Hughes & Company, also of Belfast, with the partners agreeing to participate in its ownership. In designing these large sailing craft it would seem that the partners followed the fashion set by two Clyde yards, Russell & Company of Port Glasgow and Charles Connell & Company of Whiteinch, of using standard layouts modified to the requirements of each owner.

This revival in 1878 was reflected in a large advance in profits to £32,391. After they had been distributed between the partners, Wilson and Pirrie emerged as the senior partners, since both Harland and Wolff preferred once more to reduce their commitment to the business. This was confirmed at the end of the year when the steamer *Camel* was sold to the firm by Edward Harland and G.W. Wolff, who loaned the money for the purchase. It is only possible to guess at their motive, but it looks as if they were preparing to retire, especially as Alexander Montgomery Carlisle, who had shown himself to be skilled both as a shipbuilder and book-keeper during his apprenticeship, was appointed shipyard manager at the end of the year. If retirement was their intention, it was to be frustrated.

From its establishment the firm had relied for the supply of engines on a number of independent marine engine-builders. Harland and Wolff had done business with at least a dozen different firms, including John Rowan & Sons of Belfast; James Jack & Rollo of Liverpool; MacNab & Company of Greenock; G.K. Stothert & Company of Bristol; and Maudslay Sons & Field of London. They had not built up a special relationship with any of these concerns, preferring to place contracts with the firm whose expertise best matched the type of engine to be supplied. The only company in which the partners had a direct involvement was John Rowan & Sons of Belfast and this seems to have been to secure supplies of the countless small pieces of

machinery required in all vessels whether sail or steam. By the late 1870s most yards that built a similar mix of ships to Queen's Island had invested in their own engine works, probably because margins on engines tended to be higher than those on hulls, and it was becoming increasingly difficult to subcontract technically advanced engines to independent builders. For example, during 1872 Alexander Stephen & Sons added an engine works to their new shipyard at Linthouse on the upper Clyde.

Late in 1878 Harland and Wolff followed suit by acquiring the engineering, shipbuilding and ship-repairing business of Alexander McLaine & Sons for almost £7,000. This firm, whose roots stretched back to Ritchie's yard, had works on the other side of the river, and a repair facility at the Dufferin dock. Alexander McLaine, the firm's senior partner, died in 1878 at the age of seventy-three, and his son, John, the following year. His other son, Alexander, was Board of Trade surveyor in Belfast:

A group of apprentices around 1890. G.W. Wolf nephew, Fred May (back row, first left), is standing beside Lord Pirrie's nephew, Thomas Andrews (back row, second left).

he also had a naval architect's practice and made a hobby of experimenting with the design of iron gun boats.[5] He had no interest in carrying on the family business and was happy to sell out. Harland and Wolff took over the last ship on McLaine's order book, the 283-ton schooner *Ulster*. At the same time the partners leased from the Harbour Commissioners property on the other side of Queen's Road from the shipyard.

They were spurred into this expansion by the entry of the Ulster Iron Works, owned by McIlwaine & Lewis, into shipbuilding. This firm, since its removal to the Abercorn basin in 1868, had gained a reputation for marine engineering.[6] An equal anxiety to the Harland and Wolff partners must have been the construction, which was in progress, of a shipyard across the river to the north of Milewater basin. This yard was being built by the new firm of Workman Clark & Company whose founders, Frank Workman and George Clark, had both served their time as premium apprentices at Harland and Wolff and graduated to junior management positions. They were well known to the Harland and Wolff customers and, through their family links, were in a strong position to capture some of the business of their former employers. The Workman family had many connections with shipowning both in Scotland and Ireland, while the Clarks were deeply enmeshed in the Scottish and Ulster textile industry. George Clark's father was senior partner in one of the largest thread spinning businesses in Britain, based in Paisley. Already the new firm of Workman Clark had taken the repair and new construction work for J.P. Corry & Company. Corry family tradition has it that this switch in allegiance came about because Edward Harland, while at the family home, had deeply offended the young William Corry by putting a piece of coal in his bedtime glass of milk when he was a little boy. It is likely that the reason was more prosaic; the Workman, Clark and Corry families were closely related.[7]

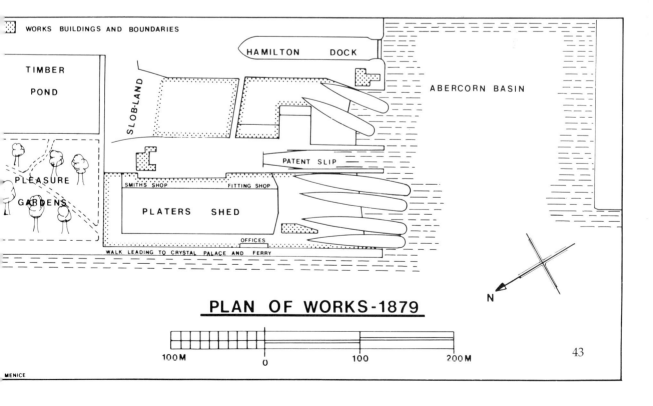

PLAN OF WORKS - 1879

43

MENICE

Between the autumn of 1879 and the end of the following year the Harland and Wolff partners spent nearly £60,000 on the new engine and boiler works, roughly a third as much again as the value of the shipyard plant. As originally planned, the works consisted of a boiler shop alongside Queen's Road, with iron and brass foundries behind, and a two-bay erecting shop facing onto the road. As part of this development, tramlines were laid along Queen's Road to the head of the Abercorn basin, where the masting shears were strengthened at the firm's expense.[8] In the expectation of an upturn in business, it was planned to lay out a new shipyard on the old pleasure gardens to the north of the existing yard. During the previous two years the firm had leased two and half acres of this ground for storing materials. In 1879 the rest of the site was leased from the Harbour Commissioners with permission to build a new shipyard. Work began in 1880 but was quickly abandoned, probably because all the firm's available resources were being devoted to the engine works. Since A.B. Wilson was no longer a partner, the firm lacked an experienced senior marine engineer capable of managing the new works. The partners recruited, as engine works manager, W.J. Pratten, who had occupied a similar position with Earle's shipbuilding yard at Hull. Born in 1854, he had trained at the Royal School of Naval Architects and Woolwich Dockyard, before joining the Royal Navy.[9]

The massive investment in the engine works was financed partly by raising the capital of the partnership to £106,250 and partly by a package of loans. Edward Harland resumed the position of senior partner by reinvesting £12,000 in the firm, while Wolff, Wilson and Pirrie contributed £6,000 each. In addition E.J. Harland lent the firm £20,000, G.W. Wolff £15,000, G.C. Schwabe (who had not been an investor in the firm since the dissolution of the first partnership) £14,000, and the Bank of Ireland almost £30,000, the largest single contribution.

Despite these bold initiatives, 1879 offered the partners little cause for optimism. The three remaining at-cost Asiatic ships returned a small loss, because Thomas Ismay, despite the fact that Edward Harland had helped to promote his company, refused to meet all the claims submitted by Harland and Wolff for extras. Although he admitted that the vessels were 'admirably suited for the India trade', he pointed out that the performance of the vessels did – 'not come up to the Builder's guarantee in load capacity nor in speed nor in economy of fuel. So far as could be ascertained

Margaret Pirrie, née Margaret Montgomery Carlisle, who married William James Pirrie on 17 April 1879.

the deadweight left was full 130 tons below guarantee, the speed about half a knot below guarantee and the consumption something like three tons in excess of guarantee.'[10] The steamer *Fair Head*, delivered to the Ulster Steamship Company, returned a loss of 12 per cent on a contract price of £20,000. This was probably partly intentional as this company was owned by Pirrie's Heyn cousins from whom he might expect further orders. The two highlights of the year were a repeat order from British Shipowners Limited for another 3,400-ton steamer, *British Crown*, bringing profits of just over £11,300 on a contract price of £74,000, and a further contract from Thomas Dixon for a 1,700-ton sailing ship, *Lord Dufferin*, producing a profit of 6 per cent on a price of £20,728. The overall profit of the firm retreated sharply. During September 1879 the *Ulster* was completed at the old McLaine yard and was acquired by Harland and Wolff, presumably because no purchaser could be found. At the same time an order was placed by the American-owned Red Star line for the lengthening and refitting of the ex-Cunarder *Russia* which was to be renamed *Waesland* and to continue as a passenger liner. This was the first major overseas contract to be won by the firm.

Amidst these difficulties William James Pirrie found time to marry his cousin, Margaret Carlisle, on 17 April. She was born in 1857 and, like her brothers Alexander, John and Henry, received an excellent education from her father. She was strikingly good-looking and, like all the members of her family, she had a forceful and dynamic personality. Unusually for a woman at the time, she was deeply interested in business. From the beginning of their marriage she made it plain that she wished to share fully her husband's business life. He soon made no secret of his respect for her judgement and advice. She did not always agree with him. Legend

45

has it that shortly after their marriage she arrived at Queen's Island demanding that part of their capital be withdrawn from the firm. Her husband agreed and took her into the yard and showed her a large machine which he was willing to let her have if she could arrange to take it away. From her first visit she took a keen interest in the welfare of the workforce, accompanying her husband on tours of the yard and asking after the men's wives and families. It may have been on her initiative that, at about this time, Harland and Wolff purchased an ambulance to convey injured workmen to the Belfast Royal Hospital.[11] It is self-evident that shipbuilding was a dangerous occupation: the risk of injury or death was always there for the workmen, whose image was in some ways comparable to that of miners. It has been suggested that the eminence of the medical school in Belfast, like that in Glasgow, was linked with the development of shipbuilding, and that local surgeons refined their skills in coping with casualties from the shipyards.

Profits remained under severe pressure throughout the next two years, dwindling to just over £8,200 in 1880 and recovering modestly to £10,414 in 1881. The partners were again obliged to build a vessel to their own account, the sailing ship *Dawpool*, launched in January 1880. This ship was sold at a loss of £1,400 to Ismay, Imrie & Company, who managed the Oceanic Steam Navigation Company, with Harland and Wolff retaining a quarter share. It was placed in the ownership of the North Western Shipping Company, which controlled all of Ismay, Imrie & Company's sailing ships. More ambitiously, the partners invested on their own account in the African Steamship Company and agreed, through the firm, to help finance the construction of two 1,400-ton steamers, *Akassa* and *Winnebah* (delivered in 1881). During 1880 the gun boat HMS *Algerine* was completed, and the 3,500-ton passenger liner *Rosetta* for P & O. Both these contracts had been won against stiff competition; no less than ten yards had tendered for the P & O boats.[12] In the face of such opposition the partners cut their price to less than cost, possibly in the hope that further business might follow. As a result HMS *Algerine* returned a loss of £2,129, or 8 per cent of the contract price of £84,961. Similarly the *White Head* and *Black Head*, two 1,200-ton steamers for the Heyns' Ulster Steamship Company were constructed deliberately at a loss of 13 per cent to provide business for the yard. Although the *British Merchant*, a 1,700-ton sailing ship for British Shipowners Limited, was built at a loss of 7 per cent, two further 3,500-ton steam ships for the same company brought modest returns. When the White Star line once more gave succour with orders for two 4,400-ton intermediate cargo liners, the *Arabic* and *Coptic*, designed particularly for the transatlantic live cattle trade, these were again built on commission, this time of 4½ per cent.

These two ships along with the two 3,500-ton British Shipowners vessels, *British Queen* and *British King*, were the first steel vessels to be constructed at Queen's Island. Shipbuilders had experimented in the use of Bessemer steel for parts or for whole vessels since the late 1850s. Edward Harland tested it sometime before 1869 but discovered it too brittle to be serviceable. With the development of open-hearth steel-making in the late 1870s, steel shipbuilding became technically possible. In 1877 *Lloyd's Register* published rules for building in steel. After a few small craft had demonstrated the utility of open-hearth steel, William Denny & Brothers, of Dumbarton on the Clyde, constructed in 1879 the first ocean-going steel ship, *Rotomahana*. At the same time a number of iron-making firms, which had supplied the shipbuilding industry, began to invest in open-hearth steel-making plant. The new steel plates and angles were larger than those of iron; and since steel was tougher than iron it did not need to be so thick. This required those shipbuilders who were intending to adopt steel in place of iron to re-equip their shipyards with larger bending rolls, cranes, and other bending equipment.[13] Between 1880 and 1881 Harland and Wolff invested almost £15,000 in the shipyard for this purpose, financed, like the engine works, by further loans from Edward Harland and G.W. Wolff. In the early spring of 1881 the engine works completed its first set of engines for the African Steamship Company's *Winnebah*. These were compound inverted two-cylinder engines of 27 inches and 52 inches by 36-inch stroke, producing 120 horse power. Although engines would no longer need to be imported from mainland Britain, the firm's specially strengthened steamer, *Camel*, was still required to import iron and steel plates and angles, pig iron, and heavy forgings, particularly from the Clyde.

Between 1882 and 1884 shipbuilding boomed and the partners were able to reap the rewards of their courageous investments. During these years the yard turned out a mix of vessels. The links that the partners had fostered, and built up during the long depression since the formation of the new partnership, bore fruit. Two further 'intermediate' (middle-sized) cargo/passenger liners, *Ionic* and *Doric*, were built for White Star; a 3,300-ton steamer for G.H. Fletcher & Company (who had been associated with the formation of White Star); three 2,000-ton steamers for the African Steamship Company; two 3,000-ton vessels for the Asiatic Steam Navigation Company; and a 4,000-ton steam ship for British Shipowners Limited. The firm won some new customers, notably the West India & Pacific Steam Navigation Company, which ordered three steam ships. This company had been established in 1863 by the Liverpool firm of Leech, Harrison and Forwood, who still managed it, and, as it was deeply involved in the raw cotton trade, it is likely that Gustav Schwabe had a hand in placing these contracts with Harland and Wolff.

By this time Pirrie's charm and love of travel had made him the natural choice as the partners' principal salesman. Mrs Harland later commented, 'My husband builds the ships, but Mr Pirrie gets the orders for them.' His powers of persuasion were uncanny. Legend has it that 'one day on the Liverpool Exchange a shipowner was seen looking very melancholy. "What is the matter?", asked a friend. "Pirrie", he replied, "has just persuaded me to order a ship and I don't know what the deuce I'll do with it." '[14]

In designing the steamers built in these years, the partners simply adapted the features that had proved so successful in the first Bibby and White Star ships. Walter Wilson, the partner responsible for design, had improved on the coffin shape and in 1882 patented, through the firm, his upgraded steering gear. This invention markedly reduced vibrations from the rudder by 'applying springs to the arms spokes or other parts of the steering tiller, yoke or quadrant so that there will be an elastic medium between the rudder head and the steering chains, ropes or rods'. It was quickly recognised as one of the best systems. Four years before, in collaboration with Edward Harland, he had discovered that the corrosion of propellers by electrolytic action could be prevented by covering the steel plates near the propeller with zinc plates, which reversed the electric current.[15] In the construction of sailing ships the partners combined steel with iron 'to give them great carrying capacity and fair speed, with economy of working'. In common with other builders they introduced other novel labour-saving devices, notably steam donkey engines for hoisting sails, raising anchors, and working pumps. During 1882 and 1883 the firm delivered five very large sailing ships of 2,500 tons – *Walter H. Wilson* and *W.J. Pirrie* for Samuel Lawther, *Fingal* for R. Martin & Company of Belfast, *Lord*

Downshire for T. Dixon & Sons and *Lord Wolseley* for Irish Shipowners Company. Writing at the time, Edward Harland was convinced of the future these developments would give to sail 'notwithstanding the recent development of steam power':

> Sailing ships can still hold their own, especially in the transport of heavy merchandise for great distances. They can be built more cheaply than steamers, they can be worked more economically, because they require no expenditure on coal, nor on wages of engineers, besides the space occupied in steamers by machinery is entirely occupied by merchandise, all of which pays its quota of freight.[16]

The large volume of business in the years 1882/4 yielded vast profits, equalling more than the partners' capital. In 1883 and 1884 they exceeded 45 per cent of the capital. Edward Harland and G.W. Wolff, encouraged by this success, withdrew from active involvement in the firm to pursue their interests in other businesses and in politics. They had reduced their commitment in 1880/81 and by 1884 had ceased to be partners who shared in the management of the business and thus its profits and losses. Instead they preferred to make loans to the firm. By 1884 Edward Harland had advanced £80,383 and G.W. Wolff £38,725, partly to meet the cost of fixed capital projects and partly to help finance work in progress. Thirty years later Walter Wilson's son, Alec, recalled the relationship of the remaining partners: 'My father was the practical naval architect, ready to take any step as soon as he could make sure of it, but no sooner; and Mr. Pirrie . . . was the businessman, the captain of industry upon the largest scale.'[17]

Despite the boom in demand, Pirrie and Wilson found that much of their business could be won only by offering attractive financial terms. This was only twice provided by taking a direct interest in vessels. During 1883 they were left with two 900-gross-ton steamers on their hands, *Dundela* and *Dunluce*. These were acquired through the firm by the partners and their friends, including members of the Schwabe family, and placed under the management of A.M. Carlisle's brothers, John and Henry, who had established a London shipping agency. Although the income passed

The large four-masted barque *Lord Downshire*, built for T. Dixon & Sons o Belfast in 1882. Edward Harland was convinced that there was a future fo sail 'notwithstanding the recent developments of steam power'.

48

through the books, no shares in these vessels were held by the partnership as such, almost certainly because of the strains placed on the firm's finances by the big investment programme and the large volume of work. In fact the partners sold off the firm's shipping investments during 1882 and 1883. The *Camel* and the *Irishman* were transferred to Wolff, Pirrie and Wilson and were likewise managed by John and Henry Carlisle. This manoeuvre was almost certainly to take advantage of 'wear and tear' allowances which became allowable against personal income tax in 1878.

The cash released by these sales supplemented the loans made by Edward Harland and G.W. Wolff and allowed the partners to make large advances to customers. The African Steamship Company was loaned over £40,000 to finance ships under construction and the refit of the *Ambriz* and the *Whydah*. On their own account the partners, along with Edward Harland and G.W. Wolff, raised their investment in the company. Edward Harland purchased an additional £3,000 of stock during 1882.[18] The Oceanic Steam Navigation Company and its sister business, the Asiatic Steam Navigation Company, were regularly given temporary facilities. The practice of building on 4 or 5 per cent commission for Oceanic was extended to Asiatic ships. In October 1883 Harland and Wolff wrote to the Asiatic Company explaining the terms of the arrangement:

> We shall build for the Asiatic Steam Navigation Co two screw steamers on the same terms as those on which we have built for the White Star line (Oceanic Steam Navigation Co Ltd.) viz: that we shall be paid the actual first cost of the said steamers including their due proportion of fixed expenses and establishment charges also five per cent commission of the said first cost as remuneration for our services in the transaction. Payments to be made in cash in such sums as we require during the building and on the completion of the steamers . . .[19]

Short-term loans on a smaller scale, of between six months and a year, were provided on many contracts. These sometimes exceeded £10,000.

By 1884 the shipbuilding industry was again moving sharply into recession. At the end of 1882 freight rates had collapsed and they remained under severe pressure for the next four years. Owners of tramp steam ships, who had both higher initiation and operating costs than their sail competitors, were forced to lay up tonnage. It has been estimated that as much as a third of the steam vessels registered at Liverpool had been taken off the market by 1886.[20] Shipbuilders with the large fixed capital commitments found they could remain in business only by resorting to the proven techniques of building at cost, integrating more deeply into shipowning, and cutting wages. On the Clyde John Elder & Company and Russell & Company adopted these policies with success. Harland and Wolff forced riveters and platers to accept a cut in wages in January 1884. In March the boilermakers struck against a 10 per cent wage reduction and during the summer the firm locked out 900 riveters and helpers for a month. In an effort to win business, the partners intensified their relations with those shipping concerns which were either established customers or in which the partners held shares. In late 1883 the firm was awarded a contract from the Oceanic Steam Navigation Company, at 4 per cent commission, for four ships for completion early in 1885. During 1884 the partners secured an order for the steam ship *Elmina* from the African Steamship Company by extending a loan of £30,000 secured as a charge on the vessel. They won orders for one steam ship each from the West India & Pacific Steam Navigation Company and from Edward Bates & Son by agreeing to build at only 1½ per cent above cost. They struck a deal with T. & J. Brocklebank to construct at cost two 2,000-gross-ton sailing ships to the same designs as those built in 1882/3. They agreed to build two 900-ton steamers for the Belfast Steamship Company to be paid for partly in shares.

In completing these ships, the partners were helped by the Harbour Commissioners' decision to construct two fitting-out jetties in the Abercorn basin at a cost of £12,171. Since the spring of 1881 Harland and Wolff had petitioned the Commissioners for additional fitting-out facilities. At first they had responded by laying additional moorings in the Abercorn basin, but these had proved less than satisfactory. The *British King* (completed in 1881) had lifted her mooring and damaged other vessels fitting out. No. 1 jetty, 350 feet long, was opened in 1884 and no. 2 jetty, 317 feet long, the following year. At the same time there had been agitation for better dry-dock provision. In February 1881 'Lawther, Browne, Coates, Samuel Wilson, A.B. Wilson, Feary, Workman, Wright, and Munster' presented a petition to the Commissioners for the construction of a new graving dock. A subsequent inquiry recommended a site at the north end of Queen's Island, which was accepted. Early the following year Lawther and Workman tried to have the decision rescinded. Their motion was resoundingly defeated; nevertheless it was not until the spring of 1884 that the design and dimensions of the dock were settled after visits had been made to Glasgow and Liverpool to inspect facilities there.[21] The following year Princess Alexandra cut the first sod and gave her name to the new dock. At the same time the Harbour Commissioners decided to lay out two additional shipyards on Queen's Island, on either side of the graving dock. The one to the south was taken by MacIlwaine & Lewis, of the Ulster Iron Works, who changed their name during the year to MacIlwaine & MacColl. The yard to the north was provisionally booked by Workman Clark, but never constructed. It was subsequently used by John McCausland, a boat-builder.[22]

Harland and Wolff, in common with other shipbuilders, sought a way out of the depression through the economies offered by the newly developed triple-expansion engine. From the early days of the steam engine it was known that improvements in efficiency could be obtained by increasing steam pressure but development was restricted by the quality first of iron and then of steel available for boilers. As the quality of metal improved, the steam pressures rose and, to attain even further improvements, the steam was passed through two cylinders in succession, in the form of the compound engine. In the early 1860s it was proposed that three cylinders be used and in the 1870s John Elder & Company on the Clyde pioneered this development. It was not until 1881 however, when open-hearth steel became available, that Robert Napier & Sons was able to demonstrate the savings to be had from combining high pressure and triple expansion. These engines quickly became popular and United Kingdom builders, Harland and Wolff among them, produced eighty-seven sets of triple-expansion engines in 1885. In the autumn of 1884 the firm acquired the *Chilean* from the West India & Pacific Steam Navigation Company, in part payment for the *Texan* and *Floridan*. This vessel had been built in 1871 by the London & Glasgow Engineering and Iron Shipbuilding Company at Govan on the Clyde and fitted with compound engines. Harland and Wolff rebuilt the engines as triples and installed new boilers. The re-equipped *Chilean* was placed under the management of John and Henry Carlisle, presumably so that the partners could monitor the performance of the new engine in normal working conditions.[23] This experiment was successful. Almost overnight the firm ceased building compounds.

50

The Abercorn basin around 1900, showing the two fitting-out quays built by the Harbour Commissioners for the use of Harland and Wolff in 1884 and 1885.

Construction work in progress on the Alexandra graving dock around 1885. The rail lines, in the centre, were used for hauling the spoil out of the bottom of the dock, which had all to be excavated by hand.

The first three steam ships launched in 1886 were all fitted with triple-expansion engines, the *Iran* for Edward Bates & Son, the *Saint Fillans* for Rankin, Gilmour & Company of Liverpool and the *Inishowen Head* for the Ulster Steamship Company.

The firm's success in meeting the adversities of the 1885 recession was tempered by a serious deterioration in the political situation in Ireland. During the early 1880s, at a time of severe agricultural decline due to a combination of bad weather and cheap imports, demands for Home Rule had grown louder. The Third Reform Act, which was passed between December 1884 and June 1885, offered the Home Rulers, under the leadership of Charles Stewart Parnell, the chance of victory at the polls in Ireland. Protestants were alarmed. An Ulster Unionist movement began to emerge, with the active support of the Conservative Party and of Liberal Unionists. The Orange Order, which had been gathering support since the mid-1860s, found its membership swelling. The Protestants in the Ulster counties, who formed the majority of the population, felt themselves threatened. The partners in Harland and Wolff were apprehensive. They could foresee the inevitable consequences of Home Rule to their enterprise, which depended for its success on orders from Britain. There were fears for the long-term future of Admiralty contracts. Moreover they had a duty to their workforce, many of whom had come from shipyards and marine engineering works on the mainland. Those who had been laid off as a result of the depression, or who were dissatisfied with wage cuts, were already flocking back across the Irish Sea.

During 1885 Edward Harland, in addition to his duties as chairman of the Harbour Commissioners, became Mayor of Belfast. In these twin capacities he welcomed the Prince and Princess of Wales to the city in April to open the Donegall quay and to cut the first sod of a new graving dock in Queen's Road alongside the yard of MacIlwaine & MacColl. The Protestants responded enthusiastically to the visit, while the Catholics remained lukewarm, if not hostile. The warmth of the loyalist welcome owed much to careful preparations by Harland who is reported to have spent £18,000 of his own money on the visit. However, the Protestants remained uneasy about much of the tour, especially in Dublin, and suspected it was designed to curry favour with Nationalists. In May Harland was deeply offended to be offered only a knighthood, rather than the customary baronetcy, for his services as Mayor. Ulstermen, outraged at this apparent sop to Home Rule opinion, bestowed on him the highest honour they could provide, a safe Belfast seat in Parliament as a Unionist. Their action prompted an offer, later in the year, of a baronetcy which Harland readily accepted.[24]

Despite the opposition of the partners in Harland and Wolff to Home Rule, they were sufficiently realistic to recognise the strength of Parnell's position. They therefore made secret preparations to withdraw to mainland Britain if the situation became intolerable. In June 1885 the firm commenced the lengthy process of selling the works to a new limited company, Queen's Island Shipbuilding & Engineering Company Limited, officially registered on 22 December. The memorandum of association gave the company wide powers, not only to build and repair ships, but also to own and charter vessels, to take over other businesses with related interests, 'to enter partnership or into any arrangement for sharing profits, union of interests, co-operation, first adventure, reciprocal concession, or otherwise, with any person or company with similar objectives, and to lend money to customers'. The promoters were Sir Edward Harland, G.W. Wolff, Walter Wilson, W.J. Pirrie, Lady Harland, Mrs Wilson and Mrs Pirrie.[25] It is not known how the shares were distributed in the new company; but it would seem that Sir Edward Harland was the biggest holder,

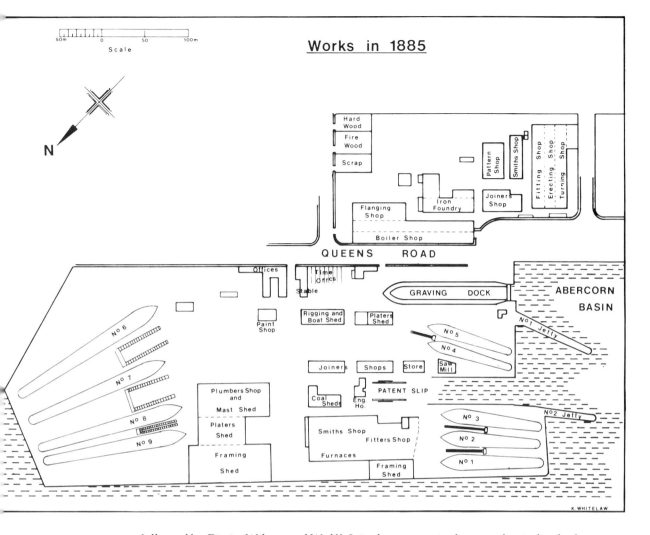

followed by Pirrie, Wilson and Wolff. It is almost certain that no other individuals, except the promoters, participated. Limited liability had been available to promoters of business since 1854, but few took advantage of the protection it offered. However, during the depressed trading conditions of the mid-1880s many firms registered as limited liability companies. In shipbuilding John Elder & Company was converted into the Fairfield Shipbuilding & Engineering Company Limited in 1885, followed by Hawthorn Leslie the next year.

For the partners in Harland and Wolff, limited liability was a convenient device should it have proved necessary to sell the Queen's Island establishment. The new company took over the works, the contracts in progress and the *Chilean*. The shipyard was valued at £72,803 and the engine works at £93,877, cancelling all the depreciation of the previous two years. The new company had 350 shares of £850 totalling £297,500, plus loans from the former partners, G.C. Schwabe and senior employees, amounting to £22,432. Following the example of shipowning, where fleets were owned by limited companies and managed by partnerships, the Harland and Wolff partnership of Wilson and Pirrie remained in being to manage the shipyard. It also retained the linkages with Ismay, Imrie & Company and its associates, the Oceanic and Asiatic Steam Navigation Companies. The partnership immediately opened negotiations for the purchase of the Liverpool marine engineering business of James Jack & Rollo, proprietors of the Victoria Engine Works. This firm, with which the partners had done business since 1867, had opened a shipyard at Seacombe

53

on the Mersey in 1884. With the onset of the depression this proved a disastrous investment. Under the strain, James Jack junior, the sole partner, became seriously ill and the business closed.[26] In an emergency the Seacombe yard would have provided an ideal refuge for Harland and Wolff, but no decision was taken until the political outlook became more certain.

Although Gladstone's second Liberal Government was defeated in June 1885, the election was delayed while the provisions of the Third Reform Act were implemented. In November the partners' worst fears seemed confirmed when Home Rule candidates won eighty-five of the 103 Irish seats, including seventeen of the thirty-three in Ulster, and thus held the balance of power in the new Parliament.

By the time the Queen's Island works was sold to the new limited company, the second partnership had survived ten turbulent years. It had boldly invested in a new engine works and re-equipped the shipyard to handle the new steel plates, without losing its reputation for quality and reliability. It had enlarged its clientele, building strong links with the African Steamship Company and the West India & Pacific Steam Navigation Company. It had maintained and strengthened its close relations with Thomas Ismay. It had switched, in the van of fashion, to the construction of triple-expansion engines. Its success had been reflected in a rising tide of profits between 1882 and 1884. These were maintained in the first six months of 1885 despite the recession. At the peak of their achievement the partners and their supporters were faced with a political crisis that threatened the continued existence of the business in Belfast. The coming year would test the resolution of Pirrie and Wilson, who had come to control the firm's fortunes. There is no doubt that Pirrie, with his strong family links to Liverpool shipping, would have been prepared to move to the Mersey. The threat of their withdrawal made the future of the Queen's Island works very uncertain. In the circumstances it would have been difficult to find a tenant – and impossible to get anyone with the contacts necessary to win custom at the level Harland and Wolff had done.

4
CORPORATE MAN
1885–98

When the Queen's Island Shipbuilding and Engineering Company Limited was formally registered at the end of December 1885, the outlook was bleak. Demand for new tonnage was still slackening and, worse still, only five days earlier the press had leaked the news that Gladstone had changed his attitude towards Home Rule. In February 1886 Gladstone's third ministry took office, committed to immediate legislation to grant Irish Home Rule. The battle that followed was traumatic, splitting the Liberal Party and dividing public opinion. Although the Bill provided for devolution rather than separation, the Unionists and the Orange Order were convinced that Charles Stewart Parnell and his supporters would simply use the legislation as a stepping-stone towards full independence. During February 1886 Lord Randolph Churchill addressed a meeting in Belfast's Ulster Hall, coining the slogan of those opposed to Home Rule – 'Ulster will fight; Ulster will be right.' As Mayor of Belfast, Sir Edward Harland plunged into co-ordinating the campaign against the measure. William Pirrie had no compunction in announcing that should Home Rule be granted Harland and Wolff would move to the Clyde; but he did not explain that preparations were well advanced to find a haven on the Mersey. At the lunch hour on 4 June shipwrights from Queen's Island, armed with nuts and bolts, marched on navvies working at the Alexandra dock site at the bottom of Queen's Road, who the day before had expelled a Protestant. In the ensuing skirmish eighteen-year-old James Curran drowned while trying to swim across the Lagan and ten Catholics were taken to hospital.[1]

On 8 June the Bill was defeated when ninety-three Liberals voted against. The Government collapsed. The consequent general election in July affirmed public support for the Unionist cause, with the Conservatives and Liberal Unionists winning a huge majority. This did little to ease the tension in Belfast. Rioting continued up until mid-September when, as in 1864, the equinoctial storms dampened down the situation. During the riots shipwrights and carpenters made regular sorties into the city armed with bolts and rovings (small pieces of scrap metal), sinisterly nicknamed 'Queen's Island confetti'. At Harland and Wolff 190 of the 225 Catholics employed in the works left, fearing for their safety. Although Catholics represented less than 10 per cent of the total workforce of 3,000 men, Sir Edward Harland was adamant that the firm's policy had always been non-sectarian. 'Some of our best men – some of the men who are paid the best – are Catholics and some of the men who are paid the lowest are Catholics.' By early 1887 only seventy-seven of the Catholics had returned to work.[2]

Sir Edward Harland, as Mayor, was a key witness in a Parliamentary inquiry into the disturbances. He was closely cross-examined about the failure of his firm to censure the workforce by threatening closure and to prosecute those who removed bolts and rovings. His replies were guarded. He made no reference to plans to shift to the mainland and excused himself by stating, 'For the last few years I have really dropped out of the immediate direction of the business.'[3] In all probability the partners were powerless to intervene if they wished to retain even a core of skilled men. The weak order book, combined with the Home Rule threat, sapped the commitment of the Protestant workforce to Queen's Island. Demoralised, they followed the partners' example in looking for safe moorings on the mainland. The Amalgamated Society of Engineers' Belfast branch reported during 1886 that 'vast numbers of skilled artisans have emigrated',[4] and closure of the works would have almost certainly accelerated the trend, making reopening doubtful. With the disturbances at an end and a Conservative Government in office, the political outlook for the new Queen's Island Shipbuilding and Engineering Company was assured at least in the short term.

Against this very uncertain background trading proved difficult. Perhaps as an attempt to reassure the Ulster community and Sir Edward Harland, the Government, through the Admiralty, placed contracts with the firm for two gun boats, HMS *Lizard* and HMS *Bramble*. These two vessels were to be built for materials' and wages' cost and 'other direct expenses with a due proportion of the fixed and trade expenses and 5 per cent commission'.[5] In fact they yielded profits of only 4 per cent. At the same time engines were constructed for HMS *Serpent* and HMS *Racoon*. The nine vessels completed in 1886 were relatively small: the *Iran*, *Optic*, *Saint Fillans*, *Inishowen*

Table 4.1
Capital of Queen's Island Shipbuilding & Engineering Company, later Harland & Wolff Limited, 1885-99

Date at start of financial year[1]	SHARE CAPITAL	LOAN CAPITAL							
		G. C. Schwabe	G. W. Wolff	E. J. Harland	W. H. Wilson	W. J. Pirrie	A. M. Carlisle	W. J. Pratten	J. Bailey
	£	£	£	£	£	£	£	£	£
1885	297,500	14,000	1,549	140	1,900	—	—	—	—
1886	297,500	14,000	7,430	(1,605)	1,421	(1,149)	—	—	—
1887	297,500	14,000	2,020	(2,141)	3,141	200	—	—	—
1888	297,500	14,000	3,476	436	3,207	4,005	—	—	—
1889	297,500	14,000	4,643	1,165	4,729	1,072	—	—	—
1890	297,500	14,000	7,125	(8,166)	10,907	289	—	—	—
1891	297,500	14,000	4,565	4,618	7,535	2,946	—	—	—
1892	309,500	14,000	8,042	25,424	13,899	12,630	—	—	—
1893	309,500	—	19,995	34,997	21,865	25,713	—	—	—
1894	446,000	—	(473)	6	(1,608)	339	—	—	—
1895	446,000	—	—	249 [3]	601	1,975	3,696	15,624	4,315
1896	446,000	—	—	(11,490)[2]	3,146	649	6,695	17,860	4,847
1897	446,000	—	1,183	2,740 [3]	4,985	428	5,791	20,612	5,556
1898	446,000	—	2,451	5,909 [3]	2,608	519	8,949	23,641	6,178
1899	446,000	—	(2,009)	(2,420)[3]	397	478	12,586	24,585	7,068

Notes
1   1 July-30 June
2   Executors of E. J. Harland
3   Lady Harland
( ) = Debit balances

Head, a dredger, and four sailing ships of 1,800–3,200 gross tons apiece. The years 1885/6 marked the last peak in the construction of sailing vessels, which in times of recession were the choice of tramp-ship owners since they were cheaper to build and operate. During the year the new Company also re-engined the *Africa* for the African Steamship Company.

The formation of the Company brought a change in the financial year, which now ran from July to June instead of the calendar year. John Bailey, the book-keeper to both partnerships, was to keep the accounts and, as was customary at the time, to audit them on behalf of the shareholders. During the first year to 30 June 1886 profits, after paying dividends of £15,750 and management fees to the partnership of £3,000, were £16,334. Although down on the total for the last full year of trading of the partnership, this was in the circumstances a creditable result. Understandably no major investments were made in either the shipyard or the engine works. A modest £7,166 was spent on new machinery which, no doubt, could be moved to Liverpool if necessary. This sum, probably more by design than coincidence, almost exactly cancelled the depreciation. However, the Company acquired a £15,000 equity stake in the City of Liverpool Steam Navigation Company (controlled by D.&C. MacIver and providing transatlantic services) in return for a contract for two 2,100-net-ton steamers, on the understanding that the partnership would provide a short-term loan to D.&C. MacIver of £20,000. It seems likely that this deal formed part of the negotiations to buy the Liverpool business of James Jack & Rollo.

By the autumn of 1886, with the immediate danger of Home Rule safely out of the

Table 4.2
Profit and loss 1885-99

Date at start of financial year (1 July)	Declared profit[1]	Balance carried to following year	Dividends	Profit before transfer to reserves
	£	£	£	£
1885	32,084	16,334[2]	15,750	32,084
1886	21,194	13,756	21,437	18,859
1887	18,851	13,601	15,750	15,595
1888	50,071	34,321	28,350	49,070
1889	58,048	42,298	45,500	53,477
1890	85,627	61,127	65,500	84,329
1891	90,444	64,955	79,488	83,316
1892	25,418	10,853	70,258	16,156
1893	31,966	20,816	18,792	28,755
1894	42,423	31,273	26,760	37,217
1895	57,740	46,590	33,450	48,767[3]
1896	46,079	34,929	48,450	36,789
1897	92,511	81,361	35,680	82,112
1898	98,829	76,529	85,750	80,918
1899	91,361	80,211	69,600	73,282

Notes
1 Including balance brought down from previous year, before payment of interim dividend
2 This figure has been used for comparison with 1885-6 as the partnership profits were declared after paying interest on capital.
3 Includes transfer of £32,130 from the finance account (see Table 4.4, p. 70)

Table 4.3
Fixed assets, tools and stock 1885-99

Date at start of financial year[1]	SHIPYARD			ENGINE WORKS		
	Plant	Tools	Stock	Plant	Tools	Stock
	£	£	£	£	£	£
1885	72,803	24,786	41,453	93,877	—	9,704
1886	74,642	23,330	43,736	93,027	—	10,692
1887	81,558	22,705	40,988	102,652	—	12,326
1888	90,383	24,145	42,462	115,973	—	16,291
1889	89,935	26,029	43,792	104,975	11,919	19,083
1890	99,777	26,647	47,927	113,847	12,841	21,077
1891	113,979	26,826	49,725	127,551	14,266	20,727
1892	121,349	27,144	56,095	145,237	14,621	20,044
1893	139,467	31,340	48,296	161,968	16,300	20,977
1894	135,325	30,206	56,099	156,779	16,553	20,272
1895	133,224	31,831	60,914	153,955	16,125	20,846
1896	129,812	30,853	64,562	150,667	17,145	20,391
1897	140,334	32,218	78,580	163,607	18,219	26,393
1898	162,998	37,922	125,725	167,258	18,939	30,316
1899	Buildings, plant and tools £365,307; shipyard and engine works stock £141,385[2]					

Notes

1 1 July-30 June
2 The ledger for 1899 does not provide the same detail as that for the previous year. After 1900 stocks were no longer included in fixed assets and this explains the difference in the totals for 1899 and 1900 (see Table 5.3).

way, the partners were able to take stock for the future. The Queen's Island Company had secured a contract from P & O for two large liners of 6,362 gross tons, 468 feet long, the largest vessels yet to be constructed at the yard. Similarly, George Warren & Company of Liverpool had placed orders on behalf of American owners for two cargo liners of 3,200 gross tons and 5,000 gross tons. At the same time the partners were negotiating with White Star to build two giant liners, of almost 10,000 gross tons and 565 feet in length, to replace the *Britannic* and *Germanic*, now twelve years old, along with two 4,600-gross-ton intermediate cargo liners. Meanwhile, the British Government was concerned to maintain a fleet which would sustain the needs of a worldwide empire, and was already anxious about the intentions of imperial Germany. It was searching for tonnage which could quickly be converted for troop-carrying at times of war and Ismay proposed that the Admiralty should meet some of the cost of construction, so that the vessels could be strengthened to support gun mountings and have their engines and steering positions placed below the waterline. This suggestion was adopted without hesitation as the Admiralty had experienced great difficulty in chartering troop transport during the Egyptian campaign that followed Gordon's death at Khartoum in 1885.[6]

The upturn in business coincided with an increase in the size of steel plates as new mills came into production. This required shipbuilders to install new machine tools and handling equipment. The partners had no option but to initiate immediately a programme for enlarging and re-equipping the shipyard if they were to be able to build this next generation of liners. It was planned to recommence the laying-out of a new north yard with four 550-foot berths and platers' sheds behind,[7] on the site of the old pleasure gardens to the north of the works, which had been leased from the Harbour Commissioners between 1877 and 1879. New offices were to be constructed facing onto Queen's Road. Between July 1886 and June 1888 over £20,000 was spent on this development. During the spring of 1888 the partners abandoned their bid for the engineering works and shipyard of James Jack & Rollo and instead decided to 'extend the Company's own engineering establishment at a cost not exceeding £30,000'.

During July 1888 the Institute of Mechanical Engineers held its annual meeting in Dublin and members travelled north to inspect various works in Belfast, particularly the Queen's Island shipyard and engineering works, where the two massive White Star boats were on the ways. Both the magazines *Engineer* and *Engineering* carried long descriptive articles about the Company following this visit.[8] These are the first detailed descriptions of the yard to survive. The magazine *Engineering* commented:

> The well-known Belfast shipyard has been doubtless the chief object to attract mechanical engineers to the Northern Irish city . . . Those who extend their trip to the final day will not regret doing so as the Queen's Island works are alone well worth a visit . . . The building slips, it will be seen, are situated at each end of the premises, and there is plenty of room for launching the largest vessels . . . The workshops are situated between the two ranges of slips . . . The machine tools placed in them are of a description that becomes the work turned out in this yard, and are necessarily of great size and power in order to deal with the big work and notably the extra long plates used in the construction of the two big vessels. There are several heavy punching and shearing machines and double punches, the largest capable of punching a 1½ inch hole in the middle of a plate 7 feet broad and 1½ inch thick. There are also shearing and punching machines with 3 feet 6 inch gaps. These tools are by James Bennie & Company of Glasgow. The next machine is a shear punch of the same size, which has attached to it a second punch for making limber holes, or for punching 5 inch squares for centre plates where the frame goes through. There is one of Davis and Primrose's angle-iron levelling machines placed on rails conveniently between the angle-iron furnaces and the frame bending slabs. Beyond are two large radial drills with jointed radial arms, which have a range of about 10 feet radius, and near here is a large plate edge planer by Smith Brothers and Company of Glasgow, which will take a cut of 27 feet, and a still larger machine, a side end planer by Hetherington and Company of Manchester, which will plane 28 feet 6 inch in the length of the plate and 7 feet across. The most notable features in this part of the works, however, are the very massive plate rolls by Messrs T. Shanks and Company of Johnstone. They have recently been lengthened in order to take the extra long plates now used.

As part of the improvements a telephone system had been installed linking 'all the departments . . . with the main office and with one another'. The whole of the shipyard had also been fitted with electric light, replacing gas mantles:

> In the electric light department there are twelve dynamos on different systems. They are driven by a pair of horizontal engines by Tangyes of Birmingham, having cylinders 15 inches in diameter by 24 inches stroke.

The engine works was described with equal care:

> The chief building comprises the erecting shop, fitting shop, and machine shop, the whole being on one floor, and covered by a roof of three spans, so that a bay is set apart for each purpose. The centre portion is where the erecting is done and here are two erecting pits 45 feet by 30 feet . . .
>
> Amongst the heavy machine tools in the department may be noticed the following: a large horizontal slotting and planing machine by Smith, Beacock, and Tannett, which will plane 21 feet and slot 15½ feet . . . On the opposite side is a somewhat smaller, but more modern machine of the same class, made by T. Shanks and Company of Johnstone. This will take a 12 feet cut both ways. Near here was a great pile of castings, standards, and other parts waiting for their turn at the tools. There is a double-pillar horizontal drilling machine by Smith, Beacock, and Tannett, with a 10 feet vertical range of saddles and a horizontal traverse of the pillars of 15 feet. Next to this is a six-spindle drill for condenser tube-plates, made by Buckton of Leeds . . . The surface table which stands by is 15 feet by 10 feet.

The south-west bay of the engine works in the late 1880s, with an engine be[d] plate suspended from the overhead crane. On the right-hand side are two face-plate lathes and a shaft lathe, and on the le[ft] hand side a cylinder-boring machine.

The article continued with a description of the rest of the drilling and slotting machines and resumed:

> Passing now to the south-west bay we find the lathes and some more fine machine tools. The first is a treble-geared face-plate lathe by Buckton. It has two slide rests, a 7 feet face-plate, and is 4 feet between centres. It will take 10 feet diameter in the pit, and in the bed can be extended to 22 feet. Next to this is a long shaft lathe, with double headstock by Smith, Beacock, and Tannett. It will turn a shaft 56 feet long. Each headstock has two slide rests and the leading screw is down the centre of the bed . . .
> The next department is the engine works smithy where there are three steam hammers by Davis and Primrose and twenty-two fires . . . The foundry is a large building and has three cupolas, like all marine engineering foundries it is no doubt interesting chiefly for the size of the castings turned out . . . The boiler shops are a fine range of buildings . . . There are some fine tools, including two hydraulic shell riveters, one with an 8 feet gap by Fielding and Platt and another one with a 10 feet gap by H. Smith and Company. There are also two hydraulic riveters by the same firms . . . There is a fine four-column shell drilling machine by Smith, Beacock, and Tannett . . . There are five radial pillar drills by T. Shanks and Company, two tube-plate hole-cutting machines . . . There is a large manhole cutter by Embleton and Company of Leeds, which will cut a round or oval hole up to 4 feet. There is a plate edge planer by Hetherington and Company of Manchester, which will plane 28 feet by 8 feet on two edges at once. There is a second smaller machine to take 10 feet by T. Shanks and Company. The rolling is done by a large pair of vertical rolls also supplied by T. Shanks and Company.

During 1889 these massive investments were complemented by the opening of the Alexandra graving dock and its associated facilities. It was inaugurated by the newly completed White Star liner *Teutonic*. The dock was 830 feet long with a jetty built parallel to the Alexandra wharf to form a fitting-out basin. On the wharf was installed a steam crane 'capable of lifting loads of 100 tons at a radius of 50 feet, 80 tons at a radius of 60 feet, and 60 tons at a radius of 70 feet'. It was designed 'for the shipment of heavy machinery and boilers' and was reputedly 'one of the finest and largest derrick cranes in the United Kingdom'.[9]

Despite the enormous disruption during the building of the extensions to the shipyard and engine works, the Company delivered fifteen vessels – five sailing ships, a dredger, two gun boats and seven steamers – in the financial years 1886 and 1887. However, many of these contracts had been secured at the bottom of the trough, more or less at cost. Two 1,800-ton iron barques, *Stanmore* and *Swanmore* for W. J. Myers Son & Company of Liverpool, both yielded losses of over £2,300 on contract prices of about £18,500. The *Hercules*, an 800-gross-ton dredger, for the Londonderry Harbour Commissioners, produced an equally disappointing result. The two ships constructed for D.&C. MacIver's City of Liverpool Steam Navigation Company were built on the customary 4 per cent commission. Low returns on new building could not be cancelled, as before, by profitable repair work. At the general meeting in 1887 the directors complained that there had been a general falling off in repair work. The profits of the Company fell sharply to an estimated £15,595 for the financial year ending in June 1888 and rose the following year to £49,070, of which a quarter was contributed by profits of £12,000 on the P & O contract. At the end

of the financial year in June 1889 there was a little over £34,000 at the credit of the profit and loss account to help towards the finance of the extension programme.

Since neither the issued capital of the Company nor its loan capital increased during these years, the finance for the extension programme had to be found mainly by slashing the Company's financial support for its customers, and persuading owners to make payments on account, which would bear interest, in return for cut-priced vessels. At the end of the Company's first year in business almost £130,000 was laid out on work in progress, with only £31,000 held on account. By June 1888 the gap had narrowed to £55,000, with £76,600 advanced and £21,700 held on account. Moreover, of the £76,600, £13,700 was in receivable bills which could be converted into cash at a discount if the need arose. These bills had been drawn on behalf of the American-owned passenger shipping firm Baltimore Storage & Lighterage Company as part of a package of finance for Williams, Torrey & Feild's cargo liner *Minnesota* and the White Diamond's *Michigan*. This was the first time the firm had used long-term bills. Until then the Company and the partners had used three to twelve-month bills when they had occasion to resort to bills rather than receiving payment in cash (see page 22). For the Queen's Island Shipbuilding and Engineering Company,

The White Star liner *Teutonic* in the Alexand graving dock shortly af the dock's inauguratio The reception marquee be seen in the distance the right. The propeller have been dismantled f inspection and are resti on the dock floor.

Ormiston House in lower
Castlereagh, Belfast, the
home of Sir Edward
Harland and later owned
by William Pirrie, who laid
out the grounds as they
appear here.

discounting such long-term bills could provide only a partial solution to the finance of the business at a time when margins were slim.

By June 1888 there was no longer the same compelling reason as there had been two years before for the partnership to continue in being. Indeed, it was advisable that it should be wound up, since in 1887 Sir Edward Harland, on standing down as Mayor of Belfast, had become the Parliamentary candidate for North Belfast and it was considered unethical under the rules of the House for Members to benefit directly from Government contracts. Ostensibly for this reason John Elder & Company had been converted into the Fairfield Shipbuilding and Engineering Company in 1885 when its senior partner, William Pearce, had been elected to Parliament. On 5 June 1888 the name of the Queen's Island Shipbuilding and Engineering Company was changed to Harland & Wolff, Limited and at the end of the financial year 'all assets and liabilities' of the partnership were transferred to the limited Company. The management of the Company, instead of resting in the partnership, was entrusted to the principals, Walter H. Wilson and William Pirrie, at a princely salary totalling £4,500 'for their joint service'. Even before the formal alteration in the firm's title, revised instructions were issued by Harland & Wolff to the workforce, laying down the conditions of employment.[10]

Although Sir Edward Harland and G.W. Wolff were named as principals, they played little active part in the business. Harland was preoccupied with his other investments and his political affairs. He was elected to Parliament as the Unionist Member for North Belfast in 1887 and removed to London to live next door to his long-standing collaborator G.C. Schwabe in Kensington Palace Gardens. He made his Irish home at Glengorme Hall, Co. Leitrim. His Belfast house, Ormiston in lower Castlereagh, was acquired by his partner, William Pirrie, who extended and improved it, installing a nine-hole golf course in the grounds.[11] Wolff was still at the helm of the expanding Belfast Ropework Company, which was challenging the dominance of the Gourock Ropework Company in the United Kingdom market. In this capacity he not only continued to supply the shipyard with rope and twine at a discount, but also provided an important source of employment for the wives and daughters of men who worked at Harland & Wolff. He was able to abandon even the ropeworks for long periods. During 1887/8, in company with Thomas Ismay and his wife, he made an extensive tour of India, probably negotiating for supplies of jute and sisal. At Cawnpore, ever on his guard against sharp dealing, he complained about the price of his ticket on the overnight sleeper to Allahabad. The railway staff responded by uncoupling his coach, leaving him stranded at Cawnpore. Throughout the trip, Ismay was constantly asked: 'When are you going to start a White Star service to India?' He replied: 'The freights are much too low, but if you care to start a company of your own, my friend Mr Wolff will build you some very fine steamers.'[12]

During 1889 and 1890 shipbuilding boomed. As in the upturn earlier in the decade, several established customers, following White Star's lead, placed orders with the Company. White Star's sister business, the Asiatic Steam Navigation Company, contracted for three 3,000-gross-ton steamers to be built once again on a 5 per cent commission, with the added proviso: 'expenditure on the ships while building in advance of payments from you to bear interest at 5 per cent per annum, and payment made by you in advance of expenditure to bear interest at the same rate'.[13] The Ismay-managed North Western Shipping Company ordered the *California*, a 3,000-gross-ton, four-masted barque 318 feet long. T. & J. Brocklebank, taking advantage of an offer to build on commission, ordered two 4,000-gross-ton cargo liners at cost plus 3 per cent. The Bibby family, which had resumed its direct shipowning interests through a new concern, Bibby Brothers & Company and its subsidiary, the Bibby Steamship Company, placed an order for two similar vessels, *Lancashire* and *Yorkshire*, to form the first components of its fleet. These were built at cost, in the expectation of further business. At the same time Frederick Leyland, who managed the old Bibby fleet, ordered two 5,000-gross-ton steamers. Rankin,

An artist's impression of the vast Belfast ropewo... which claimed to be the largest in the world. G.W. Wolff was a founding partner and la... chairman of this busine... (Courtesy of the Public Record Office of Northe... Ireland)

rtists at work at Queen's
land, painting panels for
e interior decoration of a
White Star liner in 1899.
The notice at the back
of the shop was for
the launching ceremony
of the *Teutonic* on
19 January 1889.

Gilmour & Company, Edward Bates, Elder Dempster and the African Steamship Company all ordered a steamer apiece. In securing this business from long-standing customers, Wilson and Pirrie kept their profit margins low in the recognition that the enlarged plant could pay its overheads, and therefore make a profit, only if throughput was high. Although the firm had more or less given up direct involvement in shipowning as a means of winning custom (leaving the former partners, Pirrie, Wilson, Wolff and Harland to invest on their own account for this purpose), the Company in 1890 acquired £20,000 of stock in the Baltimore Storage & Lighterage Company as part of a deal to finance the building of two cargo liners.

The *Teutonic* and *Majestic*, the flagships not only of White Star but also of Harland & Wolff's extension programme, were delivered during 1889 and 1890. The members of the Institute of Mechanical Engineers had marvelled at the technical skill in their design and construction when they had visited the works in July 1888. Like other observers, they were struck by the ingenuity of the overlapped plating which gave the hull great structural strength and had been used to form the bosses for the twin screws, doing away with the need for a heavy cast-steel stern-frame.[14] The two ships quickly came to dominate the premier Atlantic passenger trade. Their interiors were sumptuous, benefiting in their design from Pirrie's visits to continental hotels. One commentator declared:

> The fittings throughout are really superb, and the decorations highly artistic, indeed, they must be seen to be fully appreciated. In each ship the midship-saloon is 60 × 57 feet, the full width of the ship, 10 feet in height, with a crystal dome in the roof. The decorations in this splendid banqueting hall are in the

65

Renaissance style. Bas-relief figures of tritons and nymphs in gold and ivory gambol around, and the ceiling is decorated in a corresponding style . . . The smoking-room is a cosy and handsome apartment. The woodwork is of dark mahogany; the walls are covered with embossed leather of the same tone, richly gilt. The panels are oil-paintings representing the ships of the Middle Ages . . . On the promenade deck and upper decks there are a number of spacious state-rooms, luxuriously fitted up, some of them have double bedsteads, wardrobes, armchairs, writing tables, and couches . . . There are numerous bathrooms and lavatories in the charge of special attendants, and a barber's shop fitted with electric motors to drive revolving hairbrushes.[15]

Each vessel could accommodate 855 'fore cabin' (steerage) passengers, 175 second class and 300 in 'the saloon'. Despite being on commission, the contract for the two ships yielded a loss of almost £9,000, probably because Harland & Wolff incurred penalties on the late delivery of the *Teutonic*. The intermediate cargo liners *Cufic* and *Runic* were handed over to White Star in the same financial year.

The acceleration in business was rewarded by a swift rise in profits, which totalled almost £140,000 for the two years 1889 and 1890. The programme of investment in new plant continued. During 1890 the berths in the south yard were extended and strengthened and the patent slip, now forty years old, was demolished.[16] The berths were serviced by 'a complete hydraulic plant for riveting, punching, channel bar shearing and keel plate bending' installed by Hugh Smith & Sons of Glasgow. A small pneumatic riveting system, powered by a 20-horsepower Crossley gas engine, was also purchased. The engineers' shop in the shipyard was demolished and replaced with 'a new shop with all the most recent machines'. This equipment, along with additional heavy machine tools for the engine works, cost over £35,000. The finance was provided by cancelling the gap between the loans to customers and the cash held on account for customers. In the financial year ending June 1890 advances to the Oceanic Steam Navigation Company were slashed by almost £80,000.

During the following year, one of international financial uncertainty, the shipbuilding industry turned down. The Company's principals, led it would seem by Pirrie, responded by radically changing the financial structure of the business when they decided boldly to extend the practice of building on fixed commission to the majority of their established customers. Pirrie's brother-in-law, Alexander Carlisle, the general manager of the yard, collaborated with John Bailey, the chief accountant, to devise a system for allocating material and labour costs to each contract, which would be acceptable to any customer as the basis for calculating commission. Such an offer was hard for a shipowner to refuse, since it allowed tonnage to be acquired much more cheaply than from other yards either in the United Kingdom or overseas. As an extra inducement Harland & Wolff offered always to have a berth available for such privileged customers. In return, owners agreed to place their United Kingdom repair work with Harland & Wolff, again on commission, and where possible to pay in cash in advance rather than by long-dated bills. The risks of this scheme were enormous, if sufficient companies could not be enrolled at a time when the market was showing signs of giving way. Any anxieties the principals may have had were groundless. By the end of the year the original group of favoured clients (White Star, Asiatic, Brocklebank and MacIver) had been joined by the Baltimore Storage & Lighterage Company, G.H. Fletcher & Company of Liverpool, the Dominion Steamship Company, Elder Dempster, the African Steamship

Company, the Bibby line and Edward Bates. By October 1890 the offer had yielded orders for twenty-five steamers, which would not be completed before the end of 1893 when the market could be expected to recover. The principals must have been delighted with the almost unbelievable success of their plan.

The Company's triumph in winning this volume of business at a time of uncertainty perplexed its competitors. During the autumn of 1890 J. & G. Thomson Limited, the Clyde shipbuilding firm, sent two of its managers to inspect the Queen's Island works. Alexander Carlisle gave them a conducted tour. They were struck by the lavishness and sometimes wasteful layout of the plant. In the joiners' department they noted:

> At the present time they have 1,000 joiners employed. A considerable number of men must necessarily be employed doing work by hand which ought to be done by machines had they been properly placed and in sufficient number.

In the sawmill department they observed:

> The only thing worthy of consideration which they have is a patent drying store for timber which enables them to cut pine decks and have them ready for laying in three weeks. There can be no doubt that being enabled to have decks seasoned in such a short time ought to be a great advantage in the matter of holding small stocks. Judging, however, from the enormous stock of timber which we saw piled up they do not seem to desire that benefit.

They commented on the shipyard generally:

> The order and general tidiness of the yard is very marked and they have a special staff employed whose duty it is to keep the works clean and in good order . . .

They formed similar impressions of the engine and boiler works. Although willing to discuss the layout of the works and its management, Carlisle, understandably, did not show much inclination to go into the system of book-keeping. He explained in general terms that 'heads of departments know that whenever the costs were completed they would require to appear and explain any excess cost, the foremen were consequently compelled never to overlook that only economical production would pass unchallenged'. In reporting their findings to J. & G. Thomson, the two managers concluded:

> From the general information obtained, and considering the somewhat extravagant expenditure in many of the departments compared with what it is here, it does appear somewhat curious how they can work so cheaply as to procure such an enormous amount of freight-carrying tonnage, as, with the exception of their iron department, we consider that your establishment is all over as well equipped as theirs and in many respects superior.[17]

Since membership of the club of favoured customers was secret and almost certainly known only to the directors of the companies concerned, there was no way in which this curiosity could be satisfied.

In the financial years 1890/91 to 1893/4 the business boomed. In each of these years the Company headed the list for the largest number of vessels constructed by any shipyard in the United Kingdom. Over fifty vessels were delivered, totalling almost 250,000 gross tons. The majority of these were twin-screwed, triple-expansion-engined cargo and passenger liners of between 5,000 and 6,000 gross tons. There were exceptions like the *California*, a 3,000 gross-ton, four-master sailing ship for Ismay,

Company. Since Harland had left the Commission six years before, the shipbuilding firm of Workman Clark had grown into a strong competitor for the land and services provided by the Commission. Since its formation in 1879 this firm had expanded its shipyard on the Co. Antrim side of the Lagan. It had leased all the available newly reclaimed ground to the north of the original berths. By the mid-1890s the firm had laid out in this Co. Antrim yard seven slips. Two of these were as long as the large ways in the Harland & Wolff north yard. During 1891, following Harland & Wolff's example, Workman Clark leased from the Harbour Commissioners a large, recently reclaimed site in Queen's Road for the construction of an engine and boiler works, named Victoria Engine Works. This was situated immediately to the north of the Harland & Wolff engine works and was of an equivalent scale. During 1893 Workman Clark took over the shipbuilding yard of MacIlwaine & MacColl, which was opposite its new engine works, and at once began to reconstruct the yard to provide five berths.[24] With this work in progress, Pirrie's membership of the Harbour Commission would be vital for the defence of Harland & Wolff's right of access to the facilities provided on the Co. Down side of the river.

Although some of the vessels delivered in 1894/5 recorded substantial losses, profits continued to recover, reaching £37,217. This healthy return disguised a serious deterioration in the Company's prospects. Several of the vessels delivered in the second half of the year recorded losses which were taken into the accounts the following year, the *Oropesa* and the *Orissa* for the Pacific Steam Navigation Company yielding in total a loss of nearly £20,000 on a contract price of £244,303. At least one of the contracts, the *Marino* for the firm's established Belfast customer Thomas Dixon & Sons, was undertaken on the understanding that Harland & Wolff, through Ocean Transport Company, would subscribe half the shares in the vessel at a cost of £35,000. Towards the end of the financial year, in April, the Company had sustained a serious setback when the timber yard was almost totally destroyed by fire, resulting in the loss of £10,000 of stock.

By the beginning of the financial year in July 1895, like other shipbuilders, Harland & Wolff found its problems compounded by a strike over wage rates. The Amalgamated Society of Engineers nationally demanded a 10 per cent rise across the board and a minimum hourly wage of 7½d. (3p). This was to compensate for a

Table 4.8

Shareholders in Harland & Wolff Limited in December 1894

Name	Shares (at £1,000 each)
E. J. Harland	139
Lady Harland	1
G. W. Wolff	70
W. H. Wilson	99
Sarah E. Wilson	1
W. J. Pirrie	99
Margaret M. Pirrie	1
Total	410

Note

This is the only extant list of shareholders in the Company's archives from this period. The total of 410 shares does not agree with the total of 446 shares for 1894 in Table 4.1 because the capital was raised in two stages during the year.

reduction in rates made during depressed trading in 1893. Harland & Wolff, who were paying craftsmen higher rates than most of their competitors so as to attract labour, refused to accede to this demand. The principals could not look for support to non-union labour as the Company had always operated a closed shop for skilled workers. On the other hand they were not keen to impose a lockout for fear that their pool of skilled labour would drain away to the Clyde. Consequently Harland & Wolff, in conjunction with Workman Clark, came to an agreement whereby the Clyde shipbuilders would 'suspend from work 25 per cent of their men per week during the continuance of the Irish Strike, or until the whole of the shops and yards of the Clyde have been brought to a standstill owing to depletion'. In mid-October the Belfast engineers came out on strike and in the first week of November 25 per cent of the engineers on the Clyde were locked out. Both the Lord Mayor of Belfast and the Lord Provost of Glasgow tried unsuccessfully to arbitrate. By mid-November engineers on the Clyde had also withdrawn their labour. The dispute dragged on until Christmas, when an offer to the Belfast men of 1s. (5p) a week was rejected by the unions. The Belfast shipbuilding and engineering firms responded by opening the works and inviting those who wished to return to work to do so. Over the holidays Harland & Wolff fitted up dormitories for those men who feared to go home. The strike collapsed.[25] This seems to have been the first major industrial dispute in the firm's history.

Although the strike caused 'great delay in the completion of the machinery for the various vessels', the Company's output was sustained. Thirteen ships were completed, one more than the year before. Only one was loss making, the *American* for the West India & Pacific Steam Navigation Company, yielding the slight deficit of £392.

This was more than offset by profits on the other contracts, including the White Star liner *Georgic* and the *Cestrian* for F. Leyland & Company, but these could not cover the large losses incurred the year before. Profits slumped to a little under £16,500. This bad result was disguised in the balance sheet presented to the annual general meeting, which purported to show a profit of £57,740. This declared profit included over £30,000 brought forward from the previous year. In addition the principals had transferred £32,000 from the finance account, almost certainly to match depreciation allocations. Not everyone was deceived; the agent for the London house Baring Brothers noted in January 1895 that there were a large number of the Company's bills in circulation making them 'virtual owners of tonnage of enormous amount'.[26] In effect, as long as the bills were not redeemed by the customers, Harland & Wolff owned the ships, since they could possess them as security if they themselves were required to redeem the bills. (Records do not survive of the quantity of bills at discount.) This situation reflected a sharp decline in commission earnings, since most of the vessels completed during the year were for customers who did not belong to the club, but had been offered attractive financial deals, normally in the shape of loans underwritten by bills. The security for such loans had been greatly improved by the Merchant Shipping Act of 1894 which specified that mortgages over shares in British ships should specifically secure either the principal sum and interest of a loan or a current account. The poor return for the year 1895/6 was a prelude to worse fortune. On the evening of Sunday 26 July 1896, only a month into the new financial year, came a fresh blow: a disastrous fire which devastated a great part of the south yard and most of Workman Clark's engine works and yard. Like the fire the previous April, it originated in the woodworking area of the yard. Great crowds gathered on both sides of the river to watch the blaze and

the following morning the *Belfast News-Letter* carried the headline:

The launch of the *China* P & O on 13 June 1896.

GREAT FIRE IN BELFAST.

TWO SHIPYARDS BURNT DOWN.

TREMENDOUS BLAZE.

QUEEN'S ISLAND IN FLAMES.

EXCITING SCENES.

THE FIRE DEMON HOLDS COMPLETE ASCENDANCY.

GALLANT WORK BY THE FIRE BRIGADE.

HAIRBREADTH ESCAPES OF FIREMEN.

THE LORD MAYOR PRESENT.

VAST CROWDS OF SPECTATORS.

ENORMOUS LOSS OF PROPERTY.

BRILLIANT SCENE FROM THE RIVER.

FIRE STILL RAGING.

It was estimated that the total loss to the insurers on Harland & Wolff was £42,024 and on Workman Clark £24,620. At Harland & Wolff the joiners' shop, sawmill and mould loft, along with almost 100 machines, were destroyed and the timber yard was only saved by workmen hauling planks and baulks of wood to safety. With characteristic resilience, the yard was operational again within a week. In taking stock for the future after the fire, the principals could afford to be ambitious in their plans for reconstructing the works.[27]

By the summer of 1896 the political outlook for the Company was more certain. In June 1895 the Liberal Government had resigned. The ensuing election campaign was intense with Ulster Unionists determined to defeat the Liberals and the Home Rulers. Pirrie is reported to have financed two Unionist candidates in Scotland. The election result was a landslide victory for the Conservatives and their Unionist allies. Both Sir Edward Harland and G.W. Wolff were returned unopposed.

Harland enjoyed his third term as a member for only six months. On Christmas Eve 1895 he died quietly during the night at his Irish home, Glengorme Hall, Co. Leitrim. Since 1889 he had gradually withdrawn from the firm and even from Ireland, making his home in London. His funeral in Belfast on Saturday 28 December was enormous. Flags on public buildings and ships in the port were at half mast, and the bell of the Albert Memorial was tolled for the duration of the service. Despite the strike, 'the cortege was headed by some five hundred of the employees of Messrs Harland & Wolff Limited walking four abreast, and representing practically every department, a pleasing proof that the unhappy dispute still existing in the shipbuilding trade had not embittered the personal relations between the workmen and the late head of the great establishment which had so much to do with the prosperity of Belfast'. The procession to the City Cemetery included 'men of all shades of politics and thought, of all religious beliefs, the representatives of all our public bodies, businessmen and artisans, and even the humble labourer'.[28] Harland's shareholding in the firm was divided between his wife and his brother, the Reverend Albert Augustus Harland.

Early in 1896 Pirrie assumed Edward Harland's mantle as leader not only of the firm, by becoming its first chairman, but also of the Ulster community when he was elected Lord Mayor of Belfast. As Lord Mayor, Pirrie disappointed loyalist opinion by his immediate renunciation of his political affiliations, and his proposals for some measure of representation for the Nationalist and Labour parties. One of his last official engagements in 1898 was to preside at a large Roman Catholic bazaar.[29] This softening of his opinion against the background of a strong Tory Government was entirely in character. He and his wife had been influenced by the Liberal attitudes of their family since childhood. His growing Liberalism had the advantage of easing sectarian tensions, which could only damage the Ulster business community. With Pirrie preoccupied by his mayoral duties and Harland dead, G.W. Wolff had to devote more of his time to assisting W.H. Wilson, A.M. Carlisle and John Bailey in the direction of the business. Not long before Sir Edward Harland's death Wolff had commented wittily: 'Sir Edward Harland builds the ships for our firm; Mr Pirrie makes the speeches; and, as for me, I smoke the cigars for our firm.'[30] This was far from the truth. Although he had withdrawn from the day-to-day management, he had continued to contribute his ideas on financial policy. He, it would seem, had encouraged Pirrie to extend the commission club and he provided the personal bond with Thomas Ismay. At the end of his period of office as Lord Mayor in 1898 Pirrie was made the first Freeman of the City of Belfast, followed the next year as second

Freeman by Thomas Ismay in recognition of his contribution to the success of Harland & Wolff.

The passing of anxieties about Home Rule was not the only cause for the principals to be optimistic in the summer of 1896, for the order book was swelling fast. In October 1895 the Hamburg Amerika line had offered the Company two of its old steamers, *Rugia* and *Rhaetia* (built in 1883), in part exchange for one new liner of almost 13,000 gross tons and two intermediate vessels of 5,000 gross tons. Shortly after Harland's death, his friend Thomas Ismay had placed orders for three new vessels. Two of these were to be of over 17,000 tons and almost 700 feet long, 'the largest and most elaborately and luxuriously furnished vessels in the world'. At the same time one of the commission club's newest recruits, the Union Steamship Company, contracted for three 6,300-ton intermediate vessels and invited the firm to lengthen the *Scot*. As well, the Dominion line ordered a 9,000-gross-ton liner. This line had recently been acquired by Richard Mills's British & North American Steam Navigation Company, based in Liverpool.

It would seem likely that, even before the fire, the principals had decided to embark on major improvements to accommodate the two large White Star liners. The fire gave them an excuse to undertake a massive reorganisation programme over the next three years. The building berths, which had previously been numbered from south to north, were renumbered from north to south. During 1897 the new no. 2 berth

The smoking room on the *Briton*. Built in 1897 for the Union Steamship Company, this vessel set new standards in the South African trade.

A newly installed hydraulic riveting machine at work on the keel of the *Oceanic* on 1 October 1898. The man on the platform controlled the hydraulic crane that positioned the machine. The boy who heated the rivets is in the distance on the right.

was reconstructed to allow a ship 700 feet by 70 feet to be built, with a cofferdam to enable work at the stern to proceed at all states of the tide. The berth was covered with a gigantic gantry, carrying mobile, hydraulically-operated cranes to lift the hydraulic riveting machines for riveting the double bottoms and tank tops. Pirrie, who greatly admired American production techniques, probably borrowed the design from the Newport News yard. In 1898 and 1899 the gantry was enlarged to cover the two adjacent berths, nos 1 and 3, which were also repiled. The gantry, a novelty in a United Kingdom shipyard, attracted much comment in the technical press:

> Each gantry consists of vertical legs on each side of the berth travelling on six pair of wheels, the clear space between the legs being 95 feet, and the clear height from rail level to the under side of the cross girders, 98 feet 6 inch to 111 feet. Each has four jib cranes, one on each of the four corners of the structure, lifting power being 4 tons, through a height of 80 feet, with a radius of 40 feet. Each jib circles through an angle of 180 degrees, and this covers a space of about 80 feet at each side of the centre line of the ship. The hydraulic cylinders and valves for activating each respective crane are placed near the ground, on the leg of the gantry on which the crane is mounted . . . On the cross girders there are three hydraulic travelling cranes, two on the upper beam and one on the lower

The re-equipped south yard facing the Abercorn basin around 1903. The engine works can be seen in the background.

beam, to enable them to work closely together. These are controlled by hand from the level at which the riveters are worked, and are used for supporting the riveting machines carried upon hydraulic lifts suspended from the travelling carriages of the cranes, and for putting the large shell plates in position.[31]

This ingenious contraption was supplied by Fielding & Platt of Gloucester.

At the top corner of the south yard the old nos 1, 2 and 3 berths were reconstructed and extended out into the Abercorn basin along the line of no. 2 jetty 'to form two good slips suitable for the long ships required by our shipbuilding friends'. These new berths, nos 5 and 6, were fitted with 'a large steel derrick with hydraulic hoisting gear', along with the derricks that were no longer required on the three berths covered by the gantry. A new berth no. 7 was built on the site of the patent slip which had been scrapped in 1890. Old berths nos 4 and 5 (renumbered 8 and 9) beside the Hamilton graving dock were reconstructed, 'so as to admit ships 500 feet × 60 feet being laid down'. These three berths were built partly on the site of buildings destroyed in the fire. The whole shipyard was equipped with powerful electric arc lights.

A new joiners' shop, sawmill and mould loft were put up at the junction of Queen's Road and Victoria Road at the top of the north yard. Timber drying sheds and a boat shed were erected beside the engine works, parallel to Hamilton Road. Down Queen's Road, opposite the Alexandra dock, additional land was leased from the Harbour Commissioners to accommodate a two-bay building of 300 feet by 60 feet. Fitted with shipyard and engine works tools, it housed a new repair department and was named the Alexandra Dock Works. This building also contained mock-ups of staterooms for passenger liners to allow owners to select their preferred design and layout. A storage shed was put up along the side of Harland Road. During 1898/9 the boatyard of John McCausland, which stood on the opposite side of Harland Road, was taken over and converted into stabling for the horses needed to supplement the tramway system in moving material around the works. All these new buildings were equipped with insulated walls and doors to prevent a fire from spreading. The engine works was extended at the top of Abercorn Street by placing a new building, 205 feet long by 80 feet wide, across the existing bays. The capacity of the boiler shop and new foundry were similarly enlarged.

The engine and boiler works were extensively re-equipped. In 1896/7 alone the Company purchased 'a wall engine, two shafting lathes, six screw-cutting, sliding and surfacing lathes, seven brass finishers and hollow spindle lathes, two large table planing machines, three horizontal boring, drilling and tapping machines, one horizontal milling machine, one brass finishing machine, one special slotting machine for crankwebs, one 15-inch slotting machine, six swing cranes, one boiler shell drilling and tapping machine, one Barrows and two ordinary screw machines, one large double-headed boring, drilling and tapping machine, two radial drilling machines, and two pillar drilling machines'. Two years later 'several American labour-saving tools' were installed, including five turret lathes, three milling machines and two grinders for milling cutters. These extensions to the engine and boiler works, together with the construction of the adjacent timber sheds and other buildings to the north east, required the lease of further land from the Harbour Commissioners. The whole improvement programme took nearly three years to complete and cost almost £100,000 (over and above the £42,000 recovered from insurance after the fire). This was financed in the first instance by a loan of exactly this amount from Ismay, Imrie & Company.

At the same time the Harbour Commissioners also embarked on an equally massive dock extension scheme. During 1897 the Commissioners began to frame plans for a new wet dock and graving dock. Just as in 1863, the Commissioners were sharply divided over the choice of a site, between the Antrim or Down side of the river. By November it looked as if Co. Antrim had emerged triumphant. The draft legislation excluded any reference to a graving dock, first proposing a wet dock on the Co. Antrim shore. Pirrie, as a Commissioner, was outraged. After an intense campaign, the Commissioners, under the leadership of their chairman Sir James Musgrave, changed their mind, agreeing to the opening of a new 'channel to run from the east side of the Victoria channel, with a sweep in a south-easterly direction to the reclaimed lands on the east side of the Harbour'. The Victoria channel had been formed between 1886 and 1891 seaward of the Pool of Garmoyle. At the top of the new channel, immediately behind the engine works of Harland & Wolff and Workman Clark, three fitting-out quays were to be constructed. The new graving dock was to be parallel to the Alexandra dock. The Bill was presented to the House of Lords in the spring of 1898, despite protests from the Belfast Corporation. Pirrie's successor as Lord Mayor, Sir James Henderson, with representatives of the council, twice appeared at the bar of the House of Lords to object to the legislation, only to be told by the Lord Chancellor that they had no competence in the matter. The nature of the criticisms, orchestrated by the Irish Nationalist John Redmond, had as much to do with the narrow franchise of the Commission – similar to that used in Parliamentary elections – as with the choice of site. Membership of the Commission

was restricted to those with qualifications as shipowners, occupiers of property, or with personal or real estate of a specified amount. With the passing of the Act in July 1898, work began at once to deepen the Victoria channel by three feet. The following year excavation started to form the new 'Musgrave channel'.[32]

By this time Harland & Wolff was locked in an intense dispute with the Commissioners over an application to lease all the land between the new Alexandra Dock Works and the Musgrave channel for the construction of a large repair works to service both the Alexandra dock and the proposed new dock. The Commissioners refused and the application was withdrawn. It was reported at the time that the Commissioners' attitude was coloured by Pirrie's growing estrangement from the Unionist Party. Pirrie immediately began to look for a new location for the Company's repair business. He made overtures to the recently reconstructed Dublin Port and Docks Board and visited possible sites in England and Wales. These manoeuvres were clearly designed to frighten the Commissioners into giving way, and the tactic succeeded. Speaking in Montreal in September 1899 Pirrie declared:

> We asked the Belfast Harbour Commissioners for a piece of ground, which was refused . . . In the meantime we have had a great deal of correspondence with corporations in England and Scotland. Indeed the correspondence has pursued

The completed boilers of the *Oceanic*, in the boiler shop awaiting installation in the spring of 1899.

(opposite)
The triple-expansion engines of the *Oceanic* under trial erection in the engine works in 1898. These massive engines were designed to give the ship a regular speed of 20 knots.

82

me, as you may see [holding up a number of bulky documents], asking us not to remove any portion of our works to another part of Ireland, but to use facilities which they [the Belfast Harbour Commissioners] are ready to place at our disposal. The matter awaits final decision.

The frames of the *Oceanic* in November 1897.

Speculation continued in the press for the next two months. Montrose, Stranraer, Kircaldy and Cork were all rumoured to be contenders. Later in October Harland & Wolff was reported to have turned away fitting-out work on four vessels for lack of adequate facilities in Belfast. Settlement was finally reached with the Harbour Commissioners early in the New Year.[33]

Despite the inevitable disruption after the fire and during the improvements to the yard and the waterway, the output of the firm was prodigious. In the financial years 1897/9 twenty-six steamers were delivered, of a total of 206,323 tons. These included several notable vessels. The *Pennsylvania* of 13,726 gross tons, for the Hamburg Amerika line, was the first of her class and the first ship built by Harland & Wolff to be equipped with quadruple-expansion engines. Their specification in the contract was almost certainly to allow German engineers to observe this novel machinery in

action and to copy it in the three sister ships to be built in their own country. The
Briton (10,248 gross tons) for the Union line was, when delivered, the largest liner
afloat not on the transatlantic run. The *Oceanic* (17,274 gross tons and 685 feet in
length), for the White Star line, was the first vessel launched from the rebuilt no. 2
berth and was at the time the largest vessel ever to have been built. Her launch, on
14 January 1899, was a gala day for Queen's Island. Visitors came from Britain,
America and Germany; special excursion trains brought sightseers from all over
Ireland; and estimates of the numbers present ranged from 25,000 to 150,000. Money,
raised from the sale of tickets to a specially constructed stand, was donated to the
Royal Victoria Hospital. Even the Kaiser was impressed by the ship's beauty – 'a
marvel of perfection in building and fittings'.[34] The *Rotterdam* (8,301 gross tons)
and the *Statendam* (10,319 gross tons) represented a new departure for the Holland-
America line (Nederlandsch-Amerikaansche Stoomvart Maatschappij). Such was
the pressure of orders that three of the ships ordered from Queen's Island in these
years (*Imani*, *Monmouth*, and *Manhattan*) were subcontracted.

    Repair business burgeoned. Apart from minor repairs, at least twenty major refits

were carried out. These included some remarkable achievements. During 1896 the
Union line's unsuccessful *Scot*, built by William Denny & Brothers of Dumbarton,
was lengthened by 54 feet. This operation, undertaken in the Alexandra graving dock,
attracted considerable attention from the technical press for its ingenuity. After the
vessel had been docked, launching ways were constructed under the fore half, which
was supported by a cradle. The ship was then cut in half amidships. The bow section
was dragged forward, using 'massive chains' and 'a pair of powerful steam winches
of the latest type'. 'So carefully had everything been planned and carried out that,
when tests were applied afterwards, it was found that there had not been the slightest
deviation either horizontally or vertically in the part moved, as compared with the
stern portion.' The following year the *Auguste Victoria* of the Hamburg Amerika
line was lengthened using the same technique. Perhaps the most brilliant repair was
the complete rebuilding of the bow and much of the bottom of P & O's *China*, which
had run aground in March 1898 at Perim, an island in the Red Sea, on passage from
Sydney. It took Harland & Wolff six months to salvage the vessel and bring it back
to Belfast.[35]

The high throughput of 1897/9 yielded profits approaching £240,000, of which
the bulk was earned as commission. Almost £140,000 was distributed in dividends.
The 'Reserve' was raised from £25,000 to £58,485 and the 'Finance account' from
£19,220 to £42,825. At the end of the 1898/9 financial year the plant was revalued
by Wheatley Kirk, Price & Goultly of London, who reckoned it was over-valued by
some £60,000. This figure, which was charged against the profit and loss account,
was largely offset by cancelling the 'Finance account'. The book value of the plant
was entered at £365,307. The enlarged reserve was supported in part by big external
investments. During 1898 the Company acquired a very modest stake in the National
Steamship Company, no doubt to help B.N. Baker of the Baltimore Storage &
Lighterage Company. During the year Baker took over this firm and the goodwill

86

of the Atlantic line, whose ships had been purchased by the American Government to provide transport for the war with Spanish America. Late in 1898 these three businesses were amalgamated to form the Atlantic Transport Company, in which Harland & Wolff had a stake of £34,659; the Ocean Transport Company held a further 500 shares of $100 and £25,000 of debentures in the National Steamship Company.[36] As part of this deal, C.F. Torrey, one of the British directors of the new company, joined the board of the Ocean Transport Company, and the new concern, like its predecessor the Baltimore Company, was to enjoy specially favoured status at Queen's Island. At the end of the 1899 financial year £80,211 stood at the balance of the Harland & Wolff profit and loss account. Together with a loan of £85,000 from the Ocean Transport Company and an overdraft of almost £20,000 from the Bank of Ireland, this more than replaced the advance of £100,000 from Ismay, Imrie & Company which was withdrawn towards the end of the year. This was almost certainly because Thomas Ismay had become seriously ill shortly after the launch

The new dining saloon installed in the extended section of the *Scot*. The sumptuous fittings were based on William Pirrie's studies of first-class hotels on the Continent and in America.

The 'black squad' of
[wor]kmen who undertook
[heavy?] and unpleasant tasks
photographed in 1898
[be]low the gaping hole in
China, which had been
[b]rought back to Belfast
[aft]er running aground in
the Red Sea.

of the *Oceanic*. He would seem to have made urgent preparations to leave his son, J. Bruce Ismay, with sufficient cash to meet death-duty payments (introduced in 1894) in event of his sudden death. As a result, the proposed sister ship to the *Oceanic*, the *Olympic*, was cancelled.[37]

In achieving such spectacular success in the late 1890s Harland & Wolff became estranged from the rest of the shipbuilding industry. After the strike of 1895 the principals were cautious about becoming involved in any industry-wide action which might result in confrontation with the unions. This was almost certainly because the Company's commission arrangements and expansion programme made it impossible to contemplate a lockout or prolonged strike. During 1897 the shipbuilding industry was crippled by a serious dispute with the engineering unions over two unrelated issues, the ratio of skilled journeymen to apprentices and the eight-hour day. The employers imposed a national lockout which lasted for nearly six months. The principals of Harland & Wolff refused to participate, considering 'the lockout of men

89

being uncalled for'. Instead Pirrie, who believed passionately in plant negotiations rather than national agreements, conceded a shorter working day in exchange for an American-style three-shift system.[38] The improved electric lighting and fittings in the shipyard would allow night work all the year round, weather permitting. This deal, combined with the commission club, gave the yard an unassailable advantage over its competitors. It also won the principals the admiration of the workforce. During the summer of 1898 Pirrie and his wife were guests of the annual outing of the Loyal Order of Ancient Shepherds, whose membership was dominated by Harland & Wolff workers. On returning to York Street station, Belfast, 'the party formed themselves into lines facing one another and, crossing sticks and umbrellas which did service upon the occasion for crooks, cheered lustily as Mr and Mrs Pirrie passed beneath this improvised canopy'. When the Shipbuilders' Employers' Federation was formed in 1899 Harland & Wolff, along with Workman Clark, refused to join.

The expansion of the two Belfast shipyards had accelerated the growth of east Belfast. It had led, in particular, to a rapid colonisation of Ballymacarrett. The process was reflected in the development of the local parish church: Christ Church (later St Patrick's) became 'the Shipyard Church', and the building was successively enlarged

The *Oceanic*, the most luxurious liner on the Atlantic at the time, waiting to leave Que[e] Island on her maiden voyage in August 189[9]

to accommodate worshippers from the 'boom town' which grew around it. There was a similar expansion of the Presbyterian community, and by the 1890s there were vigorous 'free' churches – among them Methodists, Salvationists and Brethren. Ballymacarrett became a very self-conscious community, intensely proud of its achievements and itself. It was only semi-urbanised, with green fields and cottages; but it contained the biggest ropeworks and the biggest shipyard in the world. Unlike some British shipbuilders, Harland & Wolff did not invest in housing for its workforce, preferring to allow private developers to build the two-storey brick houses so characteristic of the area. Most of the people who lived there were rural – the sons and daughters of farming people from north Down or the Lagan valley; but they knew their work and their workmanship was second to none. To the east the informal boundary of Ballymacarrett was the railway bridge locally known as 'the Arches'. It was something of a social, as well as a territorial frontier: beyond the Arches were the houses of the wealthy, the solid Victorian villas of Sydenham and Strandtown. By the end of the century, however, colonists from Ballymacarrett were intruding on the green fields of the Holywood Road and developers were building 'parlour houses' for the accommodation of clerks and upwardly-mobile artisans.

Since the formation of the limited company in 1885, Harland & Wolff had

conquered the shipbuilding industry in the United Kingdom by a combination of technical excellence, ingenious financial packaging, bold investment in new plant and good internal management. The Company had seen three of its principal competitors, the Barrow Shipbuilding Company, J. & G. Thomson of Clydebank, and Robert Napier & Sons, driven into amalgamations with steel or armaments concerns in the closing years of the century. Nevertheless Pirrie and his colleagues could not afford to view the future with equanimity. The American economy was slipping rapidly into recession and there were proposals to provide subsidies to United States shipping, clouding the prospects for the North Atlantic passenger trade, the Company's most important market. Thomas Ismay, who more than any other customer had provided the motive and sometimes the finance for the expansion of the business over the previous thirty years, lay dying at his home outside Liverpool. Gustav Schwabe, the *éminence gris* behind the formation of Harland & Wolff and the establishment of the White Star line, had died the year before. To add to the uncertainty there were reports of takeover bids for some of the members of Harland & Wolff's commission club. Pirrie, knowing that the continued prosperity of the Company depended on a high throughput of quality passenger tonnage, which could be best assured by retaining the custom of club members, shifted his headquarters to London where he would be better placed to defend his market.

By this time Pirrie was not only the undisputed chief of Harland & Wolff, but also the leading shipbuilder in the world. His eyes still sparkled and he still carried his mother's book of maxims in his pocket. His charming open manner, combined with a soft Belfast accent, often deceived the less wary. His wife accompanied him wherever he travelled. He discussed all his business plans with her and in return she gave him 'sound, shrewd advice'.[39] He revelled in the success of their partnership, often boasting that his achievement could be largely attributed to his wife. There is little doubt that many of his colleagues at Belfast and his contacts in the world of business were in awe of him. His presence was electrifying and his skill as a negotiator formidable. He believed that it was always essential to take the initiative to secure victory, often quoting the proverb 'An ounce of pluck is worth a ton of luck.' It was in this fighting spirit that he and his wife made their glittering debut into London society during 1898 when they rented the magnificent Downshire House in Belgrave Square.

The *Venetian*, the first s built by Edward James Harland & Company a Queen's Island. Delive to J. Bibby Sons & Company in August 18 her design and engine power greatly enhance her performance in comparison to previous Bibby ships. (Painting William Clark, courtesy Bibby Brothers & Company)

The *Istrian*, built in 1867 J. Bibby Sons & Compa one of the earliest 'coffi steamers, so-called because of their long, narrow, box-like appearance. (Painting b Samuel Walters, courte of Bibby Brothers & Company)

The *Oceanic* (ship no. 73), pioneer vessel
of the White Star line, launched in
August 1870. Revolutionary in the
luxury of her accommodation, she was
also faster than any passenger steamship
afloat. The innovative placing of the
saloon amidships greatly increased the
comforts of a long ocean voyage.
(*Oceanic,* by W.L. Wyllie, 1895, courtesy
of the Ulster Folk & Transport Museum)

(below)
The *Oceanic* (ship no. 317) launched for
the White Star line on 14 January 1899,
and the best appointed twin-screw
steamship of her time. One of the most
elegant vessels ever built by Harland &
Wolff, she won the reputation of
crossing the Atlantic with the
punctuality of an express train. (*Oceanic,*
by J.F. Carvill, 1908, courtesy of the
Ulster Folk & Transport Museum)

THE SHIPYARD FAMILY

(Family tree overleaf)

Harland and Wolff's Queen's Island shipyard was a family firm. It grew out of a family, and a family grew round it.

The story started in Germany where Philipp Benjamin Schwabe was the head of a Jewish family in business in Hamburg. In 1819 he and his children were baptised into the Lutheran Church. His son, Gustav Christian Schwabe, moved to England where he became a financier in Liverpool and married Helen Dugdale, daughter of a family of wealth and position. One of Helen's cousins, Mary Dugdale, was married to a member of the Harland family – an uncle of Edward James Harland, the shipbuilder. The Schwabes had another important connection through Gustav's sister, Fanny Schwabe, who married Moritz Wolff of Hamburg, and by him became the mother of Gustav Wilhelm Wolff.

The scene was set for a historic partnership, which grew out of the Schwabe business interests. These extended into transatlantic trade and Gustav Schwabe was a major promoter of the Bibby and White Star lines. He wanted a shipyard to support the lines, so he turned to the young engineer Edward Harland. Schwabe provided Harland with finance, with customers and with his partner.

Meanwhile, about ten miles up the Lagan from Harland and Wolff's yard, another family had been growing and spreading, headed by Robert Carson of Drumbo. His eldest child, Jane Carson, born in 1782, married Samuel Kennedy, a Lisburn miller. Their eldest child, Eliza Kennedy, born in 1800, married William Barbour, who built up a massive threadworks at Hilden.

The Barbours were related to the Pirrie family, headed by Captain William Pirrie, from Port William in Dumfriesshire. He married a descendant of the Hamiltons of Claneboye, and two of his sons married nieces of William Barbour. Another Pirrie married the Chevalier Gustavus Heyn, whose family created the Ulster Steamship Company; and the Pirries were the ancestors of William Pirrie Sinclair who built up a shipping business in Liverpool.

An elaborate network of family connections was exploited by the Captain's grandson, William James Pirrie, later Viscount Pirrie of Belfast, who became the leading figure in British shipbuilding after 1900. He married a first cousin, Margaret Montgomery Carlisle. Her brothers, John and Henry Carlisle, set up their Blue Star line of ships in London; another brother, Alexander Carlisle, became a managing director of Harland & Wolff; and a sister, Agnes Montgomery Carlisle, was also much involved in the family business.

Lord Pirrie had no children to succeed him, but his sister married and brought up a family. One of her sons was John Miller Andrews, the second Prime Minister of Northern Ireland; another was Thomas Andrews who helped to design the *Titanic*. Thomas Andrews was widely expected to succeed his uncle as head of the shipyard – Pirrie, however, never committed himself.

In 1908 Thomas Andrews married Helen Reilly Barbour, a great-great-granddaughter of Robert Carson of Drumbo. She was a sister of (Sir) John Milne Barbour, Deputy Prime Minister of Northern Ireland.

Thomas Andrews died on the *Titanic*, and in 1917 his widow married again. Her first husband had been a nephew of Lord Pirrie; her second, Henry Peirson Harland, was a nephew of Sir Edward Harland.

The family had come full circle, and in less than half a century it had changed Ireland. It had created the biggest threadworks, the biggest ropeworks, the biggest shipyard and the biggest ships in the world.

Douglas D.P. Carson

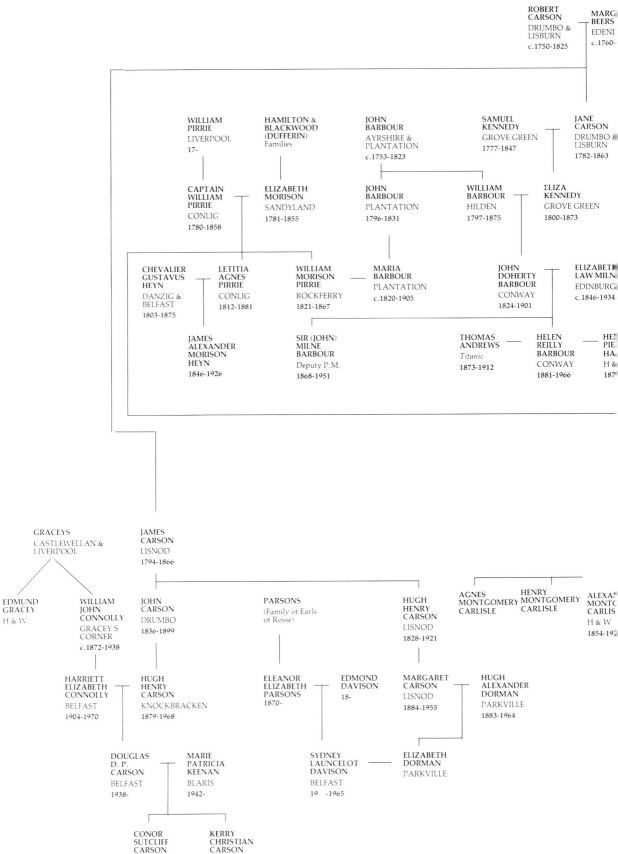

ROBERT
CARSON
DRUMBO &
LISBURN
c.1750-1825

MARG
BEERS
EDENI
c.1760-

WILLIAM
PIRRIE
LIVERPOOL
17-

HAMILTON &
BLACKWOOD
(DUFFERIN)
Families

JOHN
BARBOUR
AYRSHIRE &
PLANTATION
c.1753-1823

SAMUEL
KENNEDY
GROVE GREEN
1777-1847

JANE
CARSON
DRUMBO &
LISBURN
1782-1863

CAPTAIN
WILLIAM
PIRRIE
CONLIG
1780-1858

ELIZABETH
MORISON
SANDYLAND
1781-1855

JOHN
BARBOUR
PLANTATION
1796-1831

WILLIAM
BARBOUR
HILDEN
1797-1875

ELIZA
KENNEDY
GROVE GREEN
1800-1873

CHEVALIER
GUSTAVUS
HEYN
DANZIG &
BELFAST
1803-1875

LETITIA
AGNES
PIRRIE
CONLIG
1812-1881

WILLIAM
MORISON
PIRRIE
ROCKFERRY
1821-1867

MARIA
BARBOUR
PLANTATION
c.1820-1905

JOHN
DOHERTY
BARBOUR
CONWAY
1824-1901

ELIZABETH
LAW MILN
EDINBURG
c.1846-1934

JAMES
ALEXANDER
MORISON
HEYN
1846-1926

SIR (JOHN)
MILNE
BARBOUR
Deputy P.M.
1868-1951

THOMAS
ANDREWS
Titanic
1873-1912

HELEN
REILLY
BARBOUR
CONWAY
1881-1966

HEL
PIE
HA
H &
187

GRACEYS
CASTLEWELLAN &
LIVERPOOL

JAMES
CARSON
LISNOD
1794-1866

EDMUND
GRACEY
H & W

WILLIAM
JOHN
CONNOLLY
GRACEY'S
CORNER
c.1872-1938

JOHN
CARSON
DRUMBO
1836-1899

PARSONS
(Family of Earls
of Rosse)

HUGH
HENRY
CARSON
LISNOD
1828-1921

AGNES
MONTGOMERY
CARLISLE

HENRY
MONTGOMERY
CARLISLE

ALEXAN
MONTG
CARLIS
H & W
1854-192

HARRIETT
ELIZABETH
CONNOLLY
BELFAST
1904-1970

HUGH
HENRY
CARSON
KNOCKBRACKEN
1879-1968

ELEANOR
ELIZABETH
PARSONS
1870-

EDMOND
DAVISON
18-

MARGARET
CARSON
LISNOD
1884-1955

HUGH
ALEXANDER
DORMAN
PARKVILLE
1883-1964

DOUGLAS
D. P.
CARSON
BELFAST
1938-

MARIE
PATRICIA
KEENAN
BLARIS
1942-

SYDNEY
LAUNCELOT
DAVISON
BELFAST
19 -1965

ELIZABETH
DORMAN
PARKVILLE

CONOR
SUTCLIFF
CARSON
BELFAST
1976-

KERRY
CHRISTIAN
CARSON
BELFAST
1973-

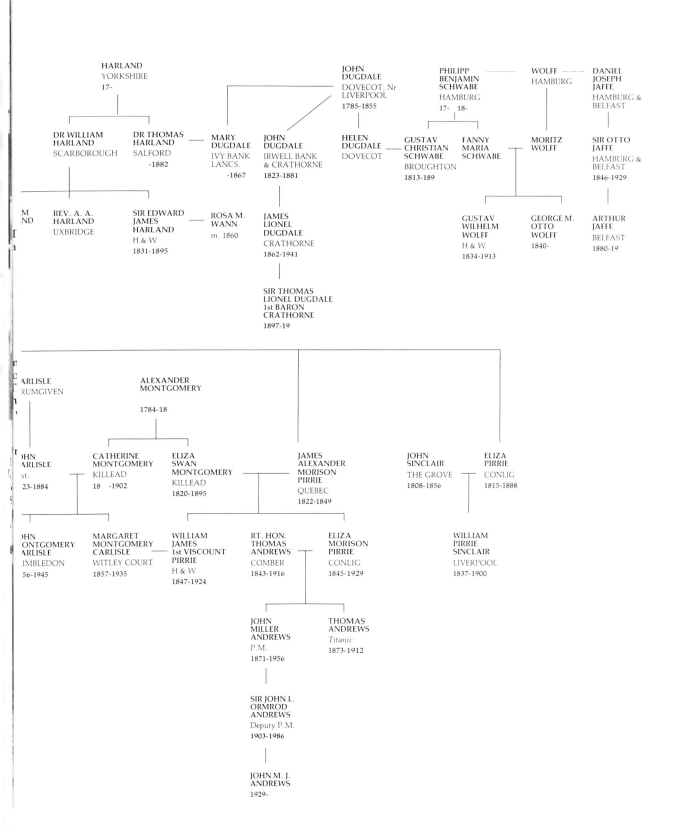

HARLAND
YORKSHIRE
17-

JOHN
DUGDALE
DOVECOT, Nr
LIVERPOOL
1785-1855

PHILIPP
BENJAMIN
SCHWABE
HAMBURG
17-   18-

WOLFF ———
HAMBURG

DANIEL
JOSEPH
JAFFE
HAMBURG &
BELFAST

DR WILLIAM
HARLAND
SCARBOROUGH

DR THOMAS
HARLAND
SALFORD
-1882

MARY
DUGDALE
IVY BANK
LANCS.
-1867

JOHN
DUGDALE
IRWELL BANK
& CRATHORNE
1823-1881

HELEN
DUGDALE
DOVECOT

GUSTAV
CHRISTIAN
SCHWABE
BROUGHTON
1813-189

FANNY
MARIA
SCHWABE

MORITZ
WOLFF

SIR OTTO
JAFFE
HAMBURG &
BELFAST
1846-1929

M
ND

REV. A. A.
HARLAND
UXBRIDGE

SIR EDWARD
JAMES
HARLAND
H & W
1831-1895

ROSA M.
WANN
m. 1860

JAMES
LIONEL
DUGDALE
CRATHORNE
1862-1941

GUSTAV
WILHELM
WOLFF
H & W
1834-1913

GEORGE M.
OTTO
WOLFF
1840-

ARTHUR
JAFFE
BELFAST
1880-19

SIR THOMAS
LIONEL DUGDALE
1st BARON
CRATHORNE
1897-19

ARLISLE
RUMGIVEN

ALEXANDER
MONTGOMERY

1784-18

OHN
ARLISLE
st.
23-1884

CATHERINE
MONTGOMERY
KILLEAD
18 -1902

ELIZA
SWAN
MONTGOMERY
KILLEAD
1820-1895

JAMES
ALEXANDER
MORISON
PIRRIE
QUEBEC
1822-1849

JOHN
SINCLAIR
THE GROVE
1808-1856

ELIZA
PIRRIE
CONLIG
1815-1888

OHN
ONTGOMERY
ARLISLE
IMBLEDON
56-1945

MARGARET
MONTGOMERY
CARLISLE
WITLEY COURT
1857-1935

WILLIAM
JAMES
1st VISCOUNT
PIRRIE
H & W
1847-1924

RT. HON.
THOMAS
ANDREWS
COMBER
1843-1916

ELIZA
MORISON
PIRRIE
CONLIG
1845-1929

WILLIAM
PIRRIE
SINCLAIR
LIVERPOOL
1837-1900

JOHN
MILLER
ANDREWS
P.M.
1871-1956

THOMAS
ANDREWS
Titanic
1873-1912

SIR JOHN L.
ORMROD
ANDREWS
Deputy P.M.
1903-1986

JOHN M. J.
ANDREWS
1929-

The luxurious first-class saloon of the P & O liner *Marmora*, delivered in November 1903.

This volume of orders yielded combined profits in the financial years 1901/2 and 1902/3 of over £230,000 with 86 per cent being earned in commissions. As in previous years, not all the profits were distributed to the shareholders. The 'Reserve' was raised to £161,328 and the 'Finance account' to £74,733. In June 1902 two new reserves were opened, 'Reserve against losses on contracts' and 'Reserve for expenditure on additions and alterations'. By 1903 they were credited with almost £70,000. Although their titles may have reflected the principals' pious intentions, they had no legal validity. Like the 'Finance account', they were not itemised in the balance sheet presented to the shareholders, but included under the title 'Sundry accounts in suspense', nor were they supported on the other side of the balance sheet by cash or easily convertible securities.

W.H. Wilson retired from his position as a principal at the end of 1901 to grow orchids. Since 1894 he had ceased to provide additional funds for the firm beyond his shareholding. He died in May 1904 and Pirrie was appointed as executor to administer his estate.[25] John Bailey, who had been responsible for keeping the firm's books from its foundation, died in July 1902. Wilson's retirement and Bailey's death allowed Pirrie to reallocate their responsibilities. Wilson's position as overseer of the yard and engine works was partly taken by John Westbeck Kempster, an electrical

engineer with an interest in economics, who was recruited as manager of the new electrical department from W.H. Allen & Sons of Bedford, a firm of electrical contractors which had close contacts with Harland & Wolff.[26] A.M. Carlisle continued as general manager, while the book-keeping was entrusted to William Tawse, who was appointed the accountant. He had been trained by Harland & Wolff's auditor, Price Waterhouse, and had joined the Company the year before to understudy John Bailey, who was already ill. At the same time Samuel Dunlop, who had joined the yard on the day it first opened, stood down as cashier and was replaced by Duncan McNeill. William Bailey was appointed Company secretary, based in London. Saxon Payne, who had accompanied Pirrie in all the IMM negotiations, was placed in charge of the Belfast office. The Company's private ledger, which contained all the information Pirrie needed to control the business, was to be made up in London by Tawse from notes taken in Belfast. All the completed private ledgers and balance sheets from the firm's foundation in 1860 were also transferred to London. Saxon Payne was instructed to forward to London for scrutiny copies of all letters sent out from the shipyard. Pirrie and his wife expected these men to live in a style befitting their positions and to give them their unswerving loyalty.[27] It is doubtful whether they were allowed to give the only remaining principal, G.W. Wolff,

111

or the general manager, A.M. Carlisle, unrestricted access to confidential information.

The resources retained in the Company by the new reserve provisions, along with their predecessors (the 'Reserve' and 'Finance account') and a balance at the credit of the profit and loss account in 1902/3 of £100,000, were deployed as a contribution to the financing of the purchase of the IMM securities and in an accelerated modernisation programme for the yard. The projected gantry over nos 5 and 6 berths, which was expected to cost £75,000 was ordered from the Brown Hoisting Machine Company, of Cleveland, USA. This structure differed from that on nos 1, 2 and 3 berths. It was of lattice girder construction, 185 feet high supported on steel columns. On the top rested a massive mobile cantilever crane 'of a total length of 230 feet, with a span on each side of the gantry of 102 feet in order to serve the berths on either side'. Between the upper and lower booms of the gantry girders were independent cantilever cranes of a similar reach 'for carrying hydraulic riveters and lifting the heaviest gear on board'. Another paddle tug, the *Despatch*, was purchased in 1902 to assist in the shipyard and to act as a ferry for workmen to vessels on trial. A new brass foundry, consisting of seven bays 50 feet wide and 150 feet long, was built between the iron foundry and the Musgrave channel, which was nearing completion. The boilershop was upgraded by the installation of a huge hydraulic bending machine for working plates 12 feet wide, and a hydraulic riveter with a gap of 1½ feet to facilitate the

112

The newly completed gantry over nos 5 and 6 berths facing into the Abercorn basin in 1903. This was supplied by the Brown Hoisting Machine Company of Cleveland, USA. In the distance on the left, the hull of the *Baltic* can be seen under the existing gantry.

construction of the 'heaviest boiler up to 12 feet 3 inches long in one circumferential strake of plating instead of in two strakes, so saving one seam of treble rivets'. A new sawmill, to replace the one in the north yard converted into a platers' shop, was constructed at the Alexandra Dock Works. The most ambitious project, however, was the conversion of the plant to electric drive to improve efficiency. This was to be carried out piecemeal. For example, in 1902 all the machines in the north yard, the two 20-ton cranes in the turning shop and the two 30-ton cranes in the erecting shop were fitted with electric motors. During the year work began on a large electric generating station, built parallel to the boiler shop, to cost over £150,000. It was to be equipped with three Sulzer engines and five Lahmeyer generators. Cables were laid under Queen's Road to the shipyard and the Alexandra Dock Works. The total cost of all this refurbishment in 1902 and 1903 was over £150,000.

The Belfast Harbour Commissioners complemented it, as they had often done with similar developments in the past, by opening the Musgrave channel in 1903 and undertaking the new graving dock, which was to be the largest in the world, at an estimated cost of over £300,000. Nevertheless, when Pirrie asked for additional land for a new yard at the head of the Musgrave channel, this was refused even though the sloblands had been reclaimed for this purpose.[28] The Company and the Commissioners had no choice but to make these investments since, on the mainland, port facilities and the bigger yards which specialised in naval work and large passenger liners were being similarly upgraded. The most spectacular example of this trend was probably the building, at a cost of well over £1 million, of the Dalmuir Naval Construction Works on the Clyde, by William Beardmore & Company Limited, forgemasters and armour-plate-makers of Glasgow.

It was left to Pirrie to muster the funds needed to finance these capital additions and the massive holding in IMM. G.W. Wolff was in no position to supply funds, as during 1902 he borrowed £42,525 from the Company, for investment in other activities. Pirrie looked to the band of lenders to provide some of the capital. Total loans were increased by around £½ million. James Dugdale raised his commitment from £2,000 to £30,000 and Lady Harland advanced a further £60,000. The most spectacular contribution was from Pirrie himself, who credited more than £423,000 to his account with the Company in 1903. It is not known how he was able to mobilise such an immense sum at a time when the financial institutions had little sympathy with his lack of patriotism in joining in the promotion of IMM. It is possible it represented the cash he received for his own shareholding in White Star. The attitude of the London City & Midland Bank, with which Harland & Wolff had opened an account in 1892, was typical. Edward Holden, the bank's managing director, cautioned Pirrie that 'having regard to the temper of my Board the business had better pass us'.[29] Nevertheless he was prepared to make an overdraft of £50,000 available to Harland & Wolff which was matched by a £70,000 facility from the Bank of Ireland. P & O also advanced £100,000 on account of the two steamers under construction (ships no. 351 and 355). On the other side of the balance sheet the loans that had been outstanding to the British & North American Steam Navigation Company and the Atlantic Transport Company were reduced by almost £350,000, presumably by converting this amount into IMM stock. This was more than offset by short-term commitments of almost £600,000 to IMM members for work in progress (notably the *Baltic*) for which bill finance was unobtainable as the finance houses had doubts about IMM's reliability. As a result, at the end of the 1902/3 financial year Harland & Wolff's finances were at full stretch, with reserves and the

balance in the profit and loss account deployed to support the modernisation programme.

Pirrie betrayed no anxieties about the Company's commitments at the general meeting in October 1903, held at his London house for the second consecutive year. In the report the modernisation of the Queen's Island works was painstakingly reviewed, while the investment in IMM, which had been mentioned the previous year, was not referred to, even though this was the first time it appeared in the balance sheet. Pirrie's lack of concern may have resulted from his success in stalking a new and promising candidate for the commission club, Owen Cosby Philipps, the recently elected chairman of the Royal Mail Steam Packet Company. Owen Philipps, with the support of his brother John, had boldly snatched control of the moribund Royal Mail Steam Packet Company earlier in 1903. Neither Owen nor John had any experience of operating passenger liner services. Owen's background lay in tramp shipping and his own successful King line of steamers. John was a financier who had links with South America through directorships of the Costa Rica Railway Company and the Buenos Aires & Pacific Railway Company.[30] It is not known how Pirrie and the Philippses came into contact. The coincidence of a railway investor acquiring a shipping line must have struck a live nerve with Pirrie, who had all too recently witnessed how Morgan had exploited this advantage in promoting the IMM merger. Equally Owen Philipps must have been aware of the reputation of Harland & Wolff for building quality intermediate liners. What he would not have known of was the

The steamer *Pardo*, the fir vessel to be built by Harland & Wolff for Ow Philipps's Royal Mail Steam Packet Company.

A steerage-class cabin or the Royal Mail steamer *Aragon*, delivered on 22 June 1905. This very basic accommodation wa designed for emigrants. The iron beds could be dismantled to provide cargo space for the return journey.

114

existence of the commission club. In the late spring of 1902 Pirrie had offered to build two cargo liners of 4,300 gross tons at 13 per cent less than cost for the previous management of the Royal Mail Steam Packet Company, and this had been accepted. Pirrie's motive may have been to bring Royal Mail into the IMM combine. If this was so, it had been frustrated first by Sir Christopher Furness and then by the Philipps brothers. The discovery that Harland & Wolff was building on such generous terms for Royal Mail must have thrown the Philipps brothers into a dilemma. Part of their appeal to the ordinary shareholders of Royal Mail had been Owen's strongly worded denouncement of foreign investment in British shipping. However, the line, as Pirrie knew, was in desperate need of new tonnage. As soon as the brothers had won control, Pirrie proposed the construction of two passenger liners of a quality unfamiliar in the River Plate trade, to be built . . .

> on their usual commission terms, that is that the builders should render the [Royal Mail Steam Packet] company a monthly statement of their expenditure on the ship, plus five per cent for profit and the company pay in cash or by bills at 3, 4 and 6 months after date equal to cash. Messrs Harland and Wolff's books to be open to inspection of a verification by any persons appointed for this purpose by the Royal Mail Steam Packet Co.

The steerage-class dinir room on the *Baltic*, delivered in June 1904. This room could hold ov 1,000 passengers, mostl emigrants from central Europe.

Owen Philipps could not afford to look such a gift horse in the mouth and Royal Mail was enrolled into the club, on the understanding that all new building and repair would be placed with Harland & Wolff.[31] The first vessel to be built under the arrangement was the *Aragon*, of 9,441 gross tons. In designing this liner Pirrie introduced a standard of fittings novel to the South American trade, imitating his success on South African routes. With 305 luxurious first-class berths, the vessel gave Royal Mail an instant advantage over its competitors. Philipps was delighted and placed orders for two more liners, the *Amazon* and the *Avon*.

During the autumn of 1903 Pirrie began to doubt the wisdom of his participation in IMM, particularly when it was suggested that Harland & Wolff might meet the cost of completing the White Star liner *Baltic* (ship no. 352). This, as Pirrie later admitted to Bruce Ismay, the Company was in no position to do – 'It must . . . be borne in mind that neither my own resources nor those of my firm are inexhaustible, and, as a matter of fact they are exhausted at the present moment . . . This is not a pleasant confession for one who has so long been accustomed to conduct his legitimate business on a ready cash basis.'[32] Pirrie was convinced that IMM needed stronger management with practical shipping experience. He proposed, with the support of the British directors, that Ismay should replace the ailing Clement A. Griscom as president of the line. In making his decision to accept the appointment Ismay discovered the perilous financial situation of the concern, despite its vast capitalisation. He was equally unimpressed with the quality of the shipping services. When he left Boston on 15 February 1904 on the *Republic* (completed as the *Columbus* but renamed when it was transferred from the Dominion line to White Star) he noted: 'Her departure was most unsatisfactory and most discreditable to all concerned. There was no one from the office to see her away: in fact, the whole thing was as bad as it could well be.' After intense discussion, in which Morgan undertook to 'make good any deficiencies for a term of three years' in IMM or its subsidiaries, Ismay accepted the post in March.[33] Pirrie's relief could not be disguised, particularly since his friend Ismay had persuaded Morgan to allow Harland & Wolff's claims on IMM to rank in front of those of the Morgan bank. The *Baltic* was delivered in June and Harland & Wolff were relieved of the short-term financial obligations that had been so burdensome the previous year.

In the financial year 1903/4 most of the remaining IMM vessels that had been on order for constituent companies at the time of formation were delivered. As a result commission earnings remained high at £88,783 and estimated profits were over £114,000. Not all the profits were distributed. Of the amount at the credit of the profit and loss account (including the balance of £100,000 from the year before), £65,000 was transferred to the 'Reserve for additions' and almost £33,000 was credited to the 'Reserve'. These provisions were almost certainly to help meet the cost of the capital additions programme. During the year £140,000 was spent on new plant and equipment, including the following: accommodation for 320 additional joiners, provided by constructing a second floor with an area of over 30,000 square feet in the mast shed and a portion of the old sawmill; the continuation of the electric conversion programme; the erection of another wood store; the building of a new stable block; and the completion of the generating station. Morgan's commitment to underwrite IMM and its subsidiaries allowed Harland & Wolff to finance its advances to IMM and the Atlantic Transport Company by means of bills, thus reducing its obligation from nearly £556,000 to under £111,500. This permitted the hard-pressed Pirrie to withdraw the loan made the previous year and the Company

The beautiful yacht HM
Enchantress, delivered to
the Admiralty in June 19

to repay nearly £60,000 of its overdrafts. These were partly replaced by raising the capital by a further £100,000 to £600,000 (with Pirrie taking all but six of the new £1,000 shares) and by an advance from G.W. Wolff of £35,000.

Over the previous five years Pirrie had succeeded in defending the Company's tied market by courageously participating in the formation of IMM. Without yielding one inch of control of Harland & Wolff, he had moulded Morgan's far-reaching scheme to his own ends. When IMM appeared to have failed he had propelled Bruce Ismay into the presidency. Despite the scale of his commitment to the combine, he had been aware from the outset that it alone could not generate sufficient orders to fill all the berths at Queen's Island. With this in mind he had maintained the Company's friendship with those members of the commission club who remained outside IMM. In his ambitions for Harland & Wolff he had found unlikely and potentially powerful allies in Owen Philipps and his brother. In five years he had walked confidently onto the international business stage, brilliantly spotlighted by his seemingly unpatriotic behaviour. Nevertheless, the harshness of the press scrutiny had failed to reveal Pirrie's motive of maintaining Harland & Wolff as the leading shipyard in the world. Socially the price of success had been high for him and his wife. Their apparent lack of patriotism and showy lifestyle had turned London society against them, much to Margaret Pirrie's bitter disappointment.[34]

Table 5.1

Capital 1900-1904

Date at start of financial year[1]	1900	1901	1902	1903	1904
	£	£	£	£	£
Ordinary shares	446,000	500,000	500,000	500,000	600,000
Loan capital	46,943	214,449	181,862	662,294	282,816
Major loans					
James Dugdale	—	2,000	5,000	30,000	30,000
Lady Harland	—	978	3,033	63,000	74,968
A. M. Carlisle	18,527	18,855	21,727	23,827	25,531
Lord Pirrie	478	599	3,119	426,167	764
G. W. Wolff	985	1,359	(42,525)	(7,148)	35,704
Ocean Transport Co.	—	102,698	68,310	4,935	11,430
W. J. Pratten	26,953	27,742	31,261	39,184	33,075
Robert Tennant	—	—	9,200	9,200	9,200
J. Bailey	—	—	—	23,079	—

Notes

1   1 July-30 June
( ) = Debit balance

Table 5.2

Profit 1900-1904

Date at start of financial year[1]	Profit[2]	Commission earnings	Balance-sheet profit[3]
	£	£	£
1900	92,711	81,000	80,211
1901	89,269	70,036	80,269
1902	108,873	52,158	80,498
1903	123,175	97,616	83,181
1904	114,245	88,783	89,245

Notes

1   1 July-30 June
2   Before making transfer to hidden reserves, but after paying interest on loans and depreciation provision
3   Not including balance brought forward from previous year, and before payment of dividends and transfer to the 'Reserve'. This was not the figure that appeared in the balance sheet circulated to shareholders, which included the balance brought down after the payment of the previous year's final dividend, transfers to 'Reserve' and bonus to the chairman.

Table 5.3

Fixed assets 1900-1904[1]

Date at start of financial year[2]	Additions	Depreciation	Total
	£	£	£
1900	—	—	346,963
1901	19,898	34,143	332,718
1902	38,032	33,214	337,536
1903	115,094	33,795	418,835
1904	139,973	38,756	520,052

Notes

1   See Table 4.3, Note 2
2   1 July-30 June

Table 5.4
Reserves 1900-1904

Date at start of financial year[1]	'Reserve'[2]	Finance account	Reserve against losses on contracts	Reserve for expenditure on additions and alterations
	£	£	£	£
1900	82,652	—	—	—
1901	106,714	36,279	—	—
1902	130,412	52,540	13,404	15,000
1903	161,328	74,733	14,083	55,759
1904	194,029	87,151	14,798	83,590

Notes

1 1 July-30 June
2 Transfers to this account were made out of the balance brought forward on the balance-sheet profit.

Table 5.5
Bank balances 1900-1904

Date at start of financial year[1]	London City & Midland Bank	Bank of Ireland	Union Discount Co.	Total
	£	£	£	£
1900	13,714	8,121	813	6,406
1901	(7,142)	(6,842)	(130)	(14,114)
1902	(23,167)	(4,833)	(145)	(28,145)
1903	(48,891)	(67,143)	(417)	(116,451)
1904	(36,979)	(19,911)	(454)	(57,344)

Notes

1   1 July-30 June
( ) = Debit balance

Table 5.6
Bills receivable discounted 1900-1904

Date at start of financial year[1]	£
1901	277,142
1902	545,000
1903	678,000
1904	813,500

Note

1   1 July-30 June

Table 5.7

Shipping investments 1900-1904

Date at start of financial year[1]	Ocean Transport Co.	Atlantic Transport Co.	International Mercantile Marine preference stocks	Navigation Syndicate (IMM)
	£	£	£	£
1900	—	—	—	—
1901	47,805	31,775	—	—
1902	45,577	31,240	—	—
1903	43,245	31,905	26,504	615,438
1904	42,336	—	27,849	676,663

Note

1   1 July-30 June

6
PIRRIE UNLIMITED
1904–14

Despite the defensive action taken by many companies in the opening years of the twentieth century to protect their markets by merger and price-fixing arrangements, the outlook for much of British industry in 1904 remained very uncertain. Alterations, however massive, in the organisational structure of British business could only provide a framework for future competitive action. It was for the architects of such changes to prove that they were not merely contrivances to disguise weakness but could be made to work effectively and profitably. In many cases this was not easy. The new combines were overburdened with large boards of directors and too much capital, which would defy the most talented executives. International Mercantile Marine, as Pirrie had come to realise, suffered more than most from such problems. Pirrie realised that the immediate future of Harland & Wolff would depend on his skill as a business manager. In an unpredictable market, where forward planning was impossible, he recognised that survival would require courage and audacity. Pirrie was well endowed with these two virtues.

Although Bruce Ismay's appointment to the presidency of IMM relieved Harland & Wolff of its enormous short-term commitments to the combine, Pirrie knew that it would do nothing to bring business to Queen's Island in the months ahead. Ismay was determined to strengthen the management and regroup the combine's finances to compete with Cunard, which Morgan had failed to capture. In the winter of 1904 Pirrie's worst fears were confirmed when the capital of IMM was reorganised. The participants in the syndicate were issued with gold bonds, secured by Morgan, to replace their original shareholdings, and faced further calls on their investment. (Harland & Wolff's commitment rose over the next year from £676,603 to £1,019,401.) At the same time, as part of Bruce Ismay's economy drive, work on two ships was suspended after they had been launched. These were the *Servian* (ship no. 353), and *Scotian* (ship no. 354) for Frederick Leyland & Company (1900) Limited, a participant in IMM. The projected White Star liner *Adriatic* (ship no. 358) – a sister ship to the *Baltic* which had been delivered in June – was postponed and it was unlikely that IMM would place any new contracts in the foreseeable future. There were only two large liners left on the ways for companies associated with IMM, the *Amerika*, of 22,724 gross tons, for the Hamburg Amerika line and the *Nieuw Amsterdam*, of 16,913 gross tons, for the Holland-America line.

Pirrie had no alternative but to respond vigorously to the crisis. With shipbuilding depressed by low freight rates, it was doubtful if any new members could be recruited to the commission club. Instead Pirrie chose to save the business, as had been done before, by accepting orders at or below cost and by building vessels for which the firm would not normally have tendered. He agreed to construct two small coastal steamers for the London & North Western Railway, *Slievemore* and *Slieve Bawn*, at 30 per cent below cost. An order was negotiated with the Pacific Steam Navigation Company for two cargo liners, *Ortega* and *Oronsa*, at a loss of over 10 per cent. T. & J. Brocklebank placed an order for four cargo boats of 7,600 gross tons at cost.

Excavation in progress on the site of the Thompson graving dock in 1905. The soil is being removed by steam navvies and carried away by rail to be used to reclaim further slobland at the north of Queen's Island.

Of the twenty vessels delivered in the financial years 1904 and 1905, nine yielded a loss. Output, when measured by total tonnage, slumped from 73,264 gross tons in 1903 to 48,404 gross tons in 1904, and workers were laid off. The lack of new orders from IMM in these two years was in part offset by an increase in refit work. Contracts were placed for new boilers for three of the combine's ships, and seven of its liners were sent to Belfast for major overhauls to their engines and extensive alterations to their accommodation. Harland & Wolff was also fortunate to win orders from the Admiralty for the engines of the battleship HMS *Hibernia* and the cruiser HMS *Minotaur*. During the summer of 1905 the Company's repair business suffered a severe setback when the west wall of the Alexandra graving dock gave way as a result of excavation work to form the new Thompson dock. No sooner had rebuilding begun than another subsidence occurred, leaving the dock 'practically in ruins'. Consequently Harland & Wolff had to repair the White Star liner *Georgic* at Liverpool and lost the contract for the reconditioning of Hamburg Amerika's *Deutschland*.

Despite the Company's difficulties, the modernisation programme was not interrupted. A bewildering number of new tools was installed throughout the works. It would have been difficult to postpone the electrification of all the tools, which was completed during 1905, following the full commissioning of the new generating station on 24 October 1904, when the supply of current from Belfast Corporation ceased. The engine shops were extended out to the edge of Queen's Road; and the paddle tug *Despatch* was replaced by the ex-Admiralty screw tug *Jackal*. Finally, in the summer of 1906 it was decided to raise the height of the gantries over nos 1, 2 and 3 slips so that they could accommodate even bigger vessels.

These large capital additions cost about £80,000 during 1906. Although they were itemised in the chairman's annual report, they appeared to have cost only £16,777 according to the accounts circulated at the annual general meeting, in an effort to disguise the Company's difficulties. This was achieved by reallocating part of the expenditure to the following year and transferring £50,000 from the undisclosed 'Reserve for expenditure on additions' (see page 127). Since this reserve was not supported by cash, the transfer and therefore the additions were met by increased advances: £31,000 from Lady Harland, £22,000 from G.W. Wolff, and £32,000 from the Ocean Transport Company. At the same time the 'Finance account' was closed and transferred to the other side of the balance sheet to form a new secret 'Reserve against interests in IMM' which was simply subtracted from the value of the Company's investment. Profits were under pressure. In 1904/5 they fell back to an estimated £71,000 and the following year retreated steeply to £45,844. However, the accounts presented at the annual general meeting in 1906 showed profits of £93,076,

The collapsed wall of the Alexandra graving dock. The wall gave way as a result of work on the new dock alongside in 1905.

Table 6.1
Capital 1905-14

Date at start of financial year[1]	1905	1906	1907	1908	1909	1910	1911	1912	1913	1914
	£	£	£	£	£	£	£	£	£	£
Ordinary shares	600,000	600,000	600,000	600,000	600,000	600,000	600,000	600,000	600,000	600,000
Preference shares	—	—	—	—	—	—	—	—	79,965	164,890
Loan capital	337,550	447,896	422,222	516,473	695,692	692,642	429,600	597,042	394,808	549,368
Major loans[2]										
James Dugdale	30,000	30,000	30,000	30,000	30,000	30,000	30,000	30,000	30,000	30,000
Lady Harland	105,128	74,543	83,106	82,574	90,085	107,256	107,256	34,657[3]	47,602[3]	43,590[3]
A. M. Carlisle	22,797	27,817	31,264	35,682	53,579	50,233	31,340	39,199	10,809	12,060
Lord Pirrie	2,584	17,446	4,647	85,370	184,682	39,755	116	37,415	(2,736)	—
G. W. Wolff	57,678	46,694	38,927	37,813	45,560	51,792	47,612	40,022	37,077[3]	28,980[3]
J. P. Morgan & Co.	—	150,000	150,000	150,000	150,000	151,849	—	—	—	—
IMM	—	—	—	—	45,000	160,000	40,000	—	—	—
African Steamship Co.	—	—	—	—	—	—	18,304	—	—	—
Ocean Transport Co.	43,354	26,935	879	—	—	—	—	34,585	60,969	74,084
International Navigation Co.	—	—	—	—	—	—	—	60,000	—	—
W. J. Pratten	36,124	30,700	29,412	28,767	28,806	28,694	23,046	19,496	15,976	12,443
Morgan Grenfell & Co.	—	—	—	—	—	—	—	148,003	—	—
R. Crighton	—	—	3,935	5,561	6,484	7,557	8,607	10,266	8,689	10,182
Sir William Arrol & Co.	—	—	—	—	—	—	—	—	—	28,000
Union-Castle	—	—	—	—	—	—	—	—	—	50,616

Notes

1 1 July-30 June
2 Included in loan capital
3 Trustees of
( ) = Debit balance

Table 6.2
Profit 1905-14

Date at start of financial year[1]	Balance brought down from previous year[2]	Dividends, transfers to 'Reserve' and bonuses to chairman	Balance-sheet profit[3]	Profit earned as commission	Profit before transfer from reserves
	£	£	£	£	£
1905	65,447	90,000	71,781	45,636	71,780
1906	47,228	75,000	93,077	103,188	45,849
1907	65,304	90,000	91,226	77,852	85,921
1908	66,530	90,000	84,422	53,210	85,421
1909	61,952	90,000	84,208	89,725	84,207
1910	56,160	60,000	67,292	40,086	67,291
1911	58,452	80,000	109,959	93,906	109,959
1912	88,411	109,000	124,319	96,203	124,319
1913	103,730	129,000	94,216	128,264	95,598
1914	68,946	96,739	105,960	207,360	105,960

Notes

1 1 July-30 June
2 From which have been deducted the final dividends, transfers to 'Reserve' and bonus to the chairman
3 Not including balance brought down from previous year and before payment of dividends and transfers to the 'Reserve'. This was not the figure that appeared in the balance sheet circulated to shareholders, which included the balance brought down after deductions (see Note 2).

Table 6.3
Fixed assets 1905-14

Date at start of financial year[1]	Additions	Depreciation	Total
	£	£	£
1905	11,089	43,470	487,671
1906	41,147	48,857	479,961
1907	70,783	47,602	503,142
1908	163,685	48,824	618,003
1909	44,063	52,708	609,358
1910	(35,277)	56,045	518,035
1911	93,715	51,275	560,475
1912	122,256	56,403	626,328
1913	316,876	62,812	880,392
1914	304,476	90,501	1,094,367

Note

1 1 July-30 June

Table 6.4
Reserves 1905-14

Date at start of financial year[1]	'Reserve'[2]	Reserve against losses on contracts	Reserve for expenditure on additions and alterations	Reserve against interests in IMM
	£	£	£	£
1905	228,538	15,547	46,829	113,703
1906	249,935	16,334	—	128,882
1907	287,167	17,161	13,422	80,693
1908	184,749	18,032	14,104	87,133
1909	208,499	18,032	14,104	223,387
1910	208,499	18,032	14,104	242,387
1911	208,499	18,032	14,104	242,387
1912	217,916	18,032	14,104	242,387
1913	241,457	18,032	14,104	282,387
1914	210,000	18,032	14,104	347,846

Notes

1   1 July-30 June
2   Transfers to this public account were made out of the balance brought forward on the balance-sheet profit.

which included the transfer of the balance in the 'Reserve for expenditure on additions' to meet the depreciation allocation. The use of 'hidden' or 'secret' reserves for this purpose was not only legal but was widely practised as a means of ironing out the adverse effects of the trade cycle. During the year Pirrie's importance as a business leader in Ireland and as a bank customer was recognised when he was appointed a director of the London City & Midland Bank.

In the midst of the economic chill, the political environment in the north of Ireland, which had been relatively stable since 1895, became very unsettled following the landslide Liberal victory early in 1906. However, since the Liberals did not need the support of the Irish Nationalists to hold office, Home Rule was low on their list of priorities. By this time Pirrie and his wife had distanced themselves from the Unionist cause. They supported some measure of Home Rule for Ireland and had joined the ranks of the Liberal Party where their sympathies had lain since childhood. Support for the Liberals had cost Pirrie a seat in Parliament in 1902: he had been nominated as Unionist candidate for South Belfast but, since he was a Liberal, the Conservative Association had selected an alternative Unionist to represent them, Charles Dunbar-Buller. An unpopular choice, he was challenged at the polls by the nominee of the Belfast Protestant Association, its leader Thomas Sloan, a semi-skilled worker at Harland & Wolff where he held evangelical meetings in the platers' shed during the lunch breaks. He was a staunch Presbyterian and denounced Roman Catholicism and ritualism in the Church of Ireland. The Conservative Unionists were convinced that Pirrie, in a fit of pique, was the 'cloven foot' financing Sloan. Although many of Pirrie's Liberal Unionist supporters switched their allegiance, including his brother-in-law Alexander Carlisle, it is doubtful if Sloan's narrow sectarian platform found any sympathy with Pirrie himself. Much to the anger of Conservatives and Orangemen, Sloan won the election,[1] which led to a far-reaching split in the Orange movement. The denial of a seat in Parliament was a bitter blow to Pirrie who had repeatedly hinted publicly that he would shortly be entering the House.

The following year, 1903, Pirrie's breach with Ulster Protestant opinion had led to a disgraceful incident at the opening of the Belfast Royal Victoria Hospital by King Edward VII. Mrs Pirrie had raised most of the funds, some £100,000, for the building, with Harland & Wolff and her husband donating £5,000 apiece. Probably Pirrie's contribution was partly in memory of his uncle, Dr J.M. Pirrie, who had been a consultant physician at the hospital. On being introduced to Pirrie, the King observed: 'And so Mr Pirrie, this magnificent hospital is your great work.' Pirrie bowed, but before he could reply another guest interjected: 'Yes, his wife collected the money.' During the 1906 election campaign Pirrie helped finance Liberal candidates in Ulster. His motive may not have been entirely honest.[2] His new-found business friends, the Philipps brothers, were active Liberals and keen Home Rulers. They also held the keys to London society where the Pirries longed for acceptance. The new Liberal Government was not slow to recognise the value of Pirrie's support and in the Birthday Honours list he was created a peer.

By the time the announcement was made on 29 June, the new Viscount Pirrie had other reasons to congratulate himself. G.W. Wolff had intimated his retirement from his post as principal at the end of the month and had sold Pirrie his shareholding.

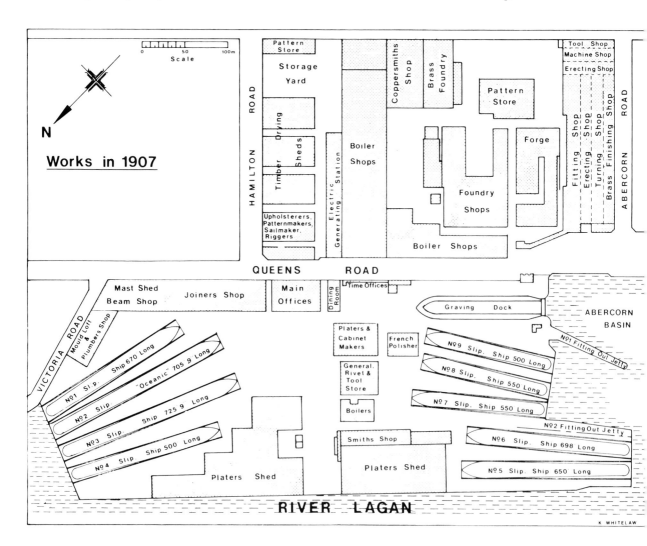

He died ten years later on 17 April 1913 at the age of seventy-nine. Pirrie's changed political views, combined with his growing autocracy, prevented him from nominating as principals either of the managers to whom he was related, Carlisle and Andrews, both of whom were more committed to the Unionist cause. Instead he chose the recently appointed J.W. Kempster, an agreeable academic man who could be relied on to obey orders. Kempster was not offered a shareholding in the Company. The new Lord Pirrie could now regard Harland & Wolff more or less as his personal fiefdom. His friend Albert Ballin, of the Hamburg Amerika line, was negotiating an order for two liners, *Europa* (ship no. 391) and *Alberta* (ship no. 394), of about the same dimensions as White Star's *Baltic* and *Adriatic*. No sooner had work begun than Bruce Ismay sold the two unfinished Leyland boats to Hamburg Amerika. They were completed at Queen's Island during 1907 and renamed *President Lincoln* and *President Grant*. The contract for the *Europa* and *Alberta* was cancelled and replaced by an order for two smaller, 15,000-gross-ton liners, the *Laurentic* (ship no. 394) and *Megantic* (ship no. 399) for White Star. At the same time Ismay informed Pirrie that White Star was about to enter the market for two gigantic 46,000-gross-ton liners to compete with Cunard's *Lusitania* and *Mauretania*, then under construction.

Before vessels of this size could be laid down extensive alterations had to be made to the berths in the north yard and this was done over the next two years. It involved taking down the gantry over nos 2 and 3 slips and rebuilding it to form a single gantry over no. 1 slip. Nos 2, 3 and 4 slips were then converted into two berths, covered by a new gantry supplied by Sir William Arrol & Company of Glasgow at a cost of some £100,000. This was a massive structure 840 feet long, 270 feet wide and 230 feet high. On the top was a cantilever revolving crane . . .

> capable of lifting a load of 3 tons at an outreach of 135 feet and 5 tons at 65 feet. As it traverses the whole length of the berth, it can lift loads to a height of about 180 feet from the ground at any point within an area of 1,070 feet long by 285 feet wide . . . On each berth there are three overhead travellers with two 10 ton trucks on each. These travellers consist of a framework built up of lattice bracing and mounted on four two-wheeled swivelling bogies. Upon this framework are two 10 ton electric travellers. The two cranes nearest the water have two lifting-eyes for lifting 40 tons, so that they may deal with heavy stern-frames and propeller brackets. There are, at a still lower level, side walking-cranes – five for each berth. These have jibs of 53 feet 3 inches radius and each carries 5 tons . . . [There are] also two electric elevators on each slip for the use of workmen, enabling them to get on board quickly.[3]

So as to accommodate the new berths, the platers' sheds in the north yard had to be demolished and replaced. Since the existing harbour crane on the Alexandra wharf was inadequate for lifting the heavy machinery onto these giant ships, a floating crane, with revolving jib capable of lifting 150 tons to 134 feet and 75 feet outreach, was ordered from the German Benrather Company at a cost of £30,000, for delivery in 1908. It was reckoned that it would be 'the largest floating crane in existence'.

During 1906 White Star took the bold decision to move the home port for its liners engaged in the New York mail service from Liverpool to Southampton, chiefly because the dock facilities at Southampton were superior to those in Liverpool. This presented the line with servicing problems. Since its formation it had maintained a workshop at Liverpool for minor repairs and maintenance. Harland & Wolff was conveniently near, just across the Irish Sea, for any major item. Southampton was too far from the Lagan for anything but extensive refits. As an alternative to building its own works at Southampton, White Star invited Harland & Wolff to develop repair facilities there. Pirrie was attracted by the proposal, particularly as there was no immediate prospect of either the reopening of the Alexandra graving dock or the new Thompson dock alongside. In March 1907 Harland & Wolff leased a Southampton site at the head of the London & South Western Railway's Trafalgar graving dock, which was almost the same size as the Alexandra dock. The site was at once let to the Southampton shipbuilders J.I. Thornycroft & Company for one year. Robert Crighton, the superintendent engineer of the IMM Red Star line, was recruited as manager. The new plant, which was constructed by the Waring White Building Company during the ensuing twelve months, covered two acres and comprised platers' shed, boiler shop, fitting and turning shop, smithy, brass foundry, coppersmiths', plumbers', tinsmiths', joiners', cabinetmakers', pattern-makers', french polishers', painters', riggers' and electricians' shops, general store and offices for the manager and his assistants, clerks and draughtsmen.

The shops were well equipped. Among the largest machine tools was 'a massive 32-inch centre double-bed quadruple-geared shafting lathe . . . capable of taking shafts up to 55 feet long', built by Thomas Shanks & Company of Johnstone. In the yard there was a gigantic set of plate-bending rolls built by James Bennie & Sons to take plates 33 feet 6 inches long by 1½ inches thick.[4] The floor above the platers' shed was leased to White Star for use as a laundry. The whole works was powered

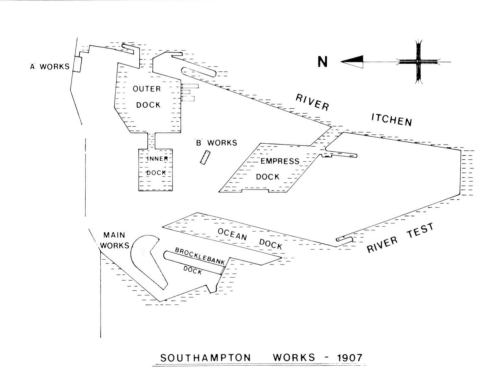

SOUTHAMPTON WORKS - 1907

The gigantic gantry over
os 2 and 3 slips, nearing
completion early in 1909
efore work began on the
Olympic and *Titanic*. The
mplex steel lattice-work
ructure was supplied by
the Glasgow structural
gineering concern of Sir
lliam Arrol & Company.

by electricity and cost almost £40,000 to build and equip. One of the first major repairs to be carried out by Thornycroft at the new works was the remarkable reconstruction of the White Star liner *Suevic*, which stranded at the Lizard in March 1907. Three-quarters of her hull was rescued by the Liverpool Salvage Company and towed to Southampton. A new bow section was built at Belfast and, after launching in September 1907, was taken to Southampton to be joined to the remains of the original hull in the Trafalgar dock.[5]

The decision to build the Southampton works and the long periods Pirrie needed to spend in London negotiating for new business were the preludes to a radical reconstruction of the Company's management, which took place in March 1907. The administrative headquarters was transferred to a new London office at 1A Cockspur Street, the head office of the Oceanic Steam Navigation Company. Pirrie removed the all-important private ledgers and internal balance sheets from his London house, which had served as an office, to the new premises. After he moved in Pirrie quickly formed the habit of arriving by nine in the morning and working often as late as seven and sometimes nine at night. Lady Pirrie arrived every night at six in a chauffeur-driven Rolls-Royce and helped her husband finish the business of the day, before taking him home.[6] Under the new arrangements, J.W. Kempster, the only other principal, was to divide his time between London and Belfast. Despite his position

SHIPBUILDING & ENGINEERING

he was not allowed access to those records which contained the central financial information that Pirrie needed to give him mastery of his business empire. The only man who could consult them was the chief accountant, William Tawse, who compiled them. The privilege was subsequently extended to William Bailey who, in addition to his duties as Company secretary, acted more or less as Pirrie's personal assistant in the London office.

The day-to-day management of the Company was devolved onto a committee of newly appointed managing directors: A.M. Carlisle; W.J. Pratten (just retired as engine works manager); J.W. Kempster; Thomas Andrews (appointed chief designer in 1903); George Cuming (one of Pratten's apprentices and recently appointed engine works manager); and Robert Crighton. A.M. Carlisle was named as chairman of the managing directors, perhaps as compensation for not being appointed a principal four years before. These were Lord Pirrie's 'splendid men' who could be relied on for their technical skill and the devotion of their service. All of them, with the exception of Carlisle, owed their promotion to him and would never have dared question his decisions.[7] Pirrie reserved the right to sanction any 'addition or alteration to the Company's building or plant' and to approve any 'change . . . in the existing administrative system and policy of the Company'. The new managing directors were given only the barest financial information and were not to be told

132

The newly completed Harland & Wolff Southampton works in 1908 with, in the distance the *Philadelphian*, in the Trafalgar graving dock. This ship had been reconstructed at Belfast years earlier for the Inman International line.

The badly damaged White
Star liner *Suevic* entering
the Trafalgar graving dock
at Southampton on
4 April 1907.

of the basis on which contracts were accepted. They were cautioned to exercise great care in their dealings with the trade unions. Monthly statements were to be prepared of the number of men employed and the incidence of industrial accidents and absenteeism. The initial roll call for December 1907 showed that 7,045 men were on the payroll of the shipyard and 2,429 on that of the engine works. One of the first actions of the committee of managing directors was to establish a contracts-buying department which was to supervise the procurement of all materials.

In accepting the contract for the White Star liner *Laurentic*, Pirrie committed Harland & Wolff to learning the new and complex skill of building and fitting marine turbines. Since 1905 Pirrie, like most of his competitors, had been alive to the challenge posed by the recently developed marine turbine to existing reciprocating engine technology.[8] The marine turbine had been invented by Charles Parsons in 1894 and its potential effectively demonstrated in his experimental craft *Turbina* at Queen Victoria's Diamond Jubilee naval review in 1897. The Admiralty showed cautious interest, but it was not until the new-generation battleship *Dreadnought* was ordered in 1905 that turbines were generally accepted. Cunard investigated their application in large liners, and tested their performance and reliability in the *Carmania* against that of her sister *Caronia*, fitted with quadruple-expansion engines. Both liners were built at John Brown's Clydebank yard in 1904/5. The success of the *Carmania* persuaded Cunard to adopt turbines for the *Lusitania* and *Mauretania*. Harland & Wolff, unlike John Brown, lacked a customer for the new technology and had no immediate incentive to invest in the expensive machinery needed to

133

manufacture and position turbine blades. Nevertheless Pirrie himself visited the Berlin works of the Allgemeine Company early in 1905 to observe the practicalities of turbine construction. He made a trip on the Hamburg Amerika liner *Kaiser* which had been fitted with Allgemeine turbines. On his return, W.J. Pratten was recalled

The new bow section of t Suevic leaving the Lagan under tow for Southampton. This remarkable engineering feat won Harland & Wo high praise in the technical press.

Table 6.5

Ordinary shareholders in Harland & Wolff Limited 1907

Name	Shares (at £1,000 each)
Lady Harland	12
Mrs S. E. Wilson	1
Lady Pirrie	1
Rev. A. A. Harland	19
H. S. Metcalfe and two others	80
John Kinahan and another	80
J. W. Kempster	10
John Brown & Co.	310
Lord Pirrie	87
Total	600

from retirement and sent to the United States to inspect the more robust and simpler Curtis turbine. In November, at the same time as John Brown, Harland & Wolff took out a licence to build Parsons turbines. It was agreed not to power the *Laurentic* solely with turbines, but instead to drive two shafts with triple-expansion engines and a third shaft with a Parsons turbine using the exhausted steam from the two sets of reciprocating engines. With the Company only just emerging from its difficulties and committed to taking a bigger share in IMM, building the two giant slips and the Southampton works, Pirrie could not afford to shoulder the additional burden of investing in turbine-manufacturing plant.

This handicap coincided with a serious threat to Harland & Wolff's sources of supply of heavy forgings.[9] Since the opening of the engine works, forgings had been purchased from a number of suppliers including William Beardmore & Company of Glasgow and Thomas Firth & Sons of Sheffield, which had merged with John Brown in 1902. Since the turn of the century the five largest forgemasters, with the equipment to make the massive crank and tail shafts needed for the new generation of marine engines, had all acquired shipyard and marine engine works, chiefly to control the market for armour plate. During 1905 the Fairfield Shipbuilding & Engineering Company, which lacked such links but also built warships, joined in an alliance, called the Coventry Syndicate, between John Brown and the recently formed Cammell-Laird (an amalgamation of the Sheffield steelmakers Charles Cammell and Lairds, the Liverpool shipbuilders), to tender for foreign naval orders and secure supplies of armour plate and forgings. Such arrangements could be adapted, particularly during depressions, to disadvantage Harland & Wolff. In purchasing supplies of materials the Company had used the size of its requirements to drive down prices. Huge orders, of over 25,000 tons of steel plates at a time, were placed with David Colville & Sons, Guest Keen & Company and the South Durham Steel Company at prices well below the market rate. It was not a big step to move from cut-price bulk purchase to a commission system of procurement from tied suppliers. With this in view and with the need for turbine capacity in mind, Pirrie approached John Brown in May 1907 with the offer of a merger. John Brown was quick to accept and in June purchased from Pirrie a majority stake in Harland & Wolff of 310 £1,000 ordinary shares for £1,500 each. In return Pirrie was allotted 100,000 £1 ordinary shares in John Brown & Company, 6,000 £10 preference shares and £219,000 in cash. As part of the agreement it was understood that within five years Pirrie was to buy personally £250,000 of the IMM bonds held by Harland & Wolff in his name. (Evidence does not survive to show why the Company held these bonds on Pirrie's behalf.) John Brown undertook to share its turbine technology with Harland & Wolff, dividing any profits equally, and to supply, on commission as far as possible, all the Company's requirements for 'steel shaftings, flues, castings, and forgings'. The Parsons low-pressure turbines for the *Laurentic* were immediately subcontracted on commission to Clydebank. In reporting the deal to the John Brown shareholders, that company's chairman was evasive:

> Now gentlemen, in matters of business the less said the better. Details that many of you might like to hear are also heard by others whom we don't want to tell them to.[10]

In the financial years 1906/7 and 1907/8 the last of the contracts placed during the depression were completed. These included in 1906/7 the *Oronsa*, an 8,000-ton liner for the Pacific Steam Navigation Company, and the *Avon*, an improved version

(overleaf)
e gigantic low-pressure
rbine for the White Star
liner *Laurentic*, under
construction at the
ydebank works of John
Brown & Company in
07. It was partly to gain
ccess to this technology
at Pirrie had sought an
iance with John Brown
earlier in the year.

135

of the *Aragon*, for Royal Mail. Four small vessels all of the same class were delivered to Elder Dempster, financed by an additional loan from Harland & Wolff, supported as before by means of bills. Under the terms of its membership of the commission club, Royal Mail sent two of its older steamers, *Orotova* and *Oruba*, to Queen's Island for refit. Of the eight vessels delivered, five yielded a loss. The *Oronsa* returned a loss of £20,390 on a contract price of £180,000 and the *Rohilla*, for P & O's sister company British India Steam Navigation Company, £16,440 on a contract price of £213,741. Since provision for most of these losses had been made the previous year, profits for 1906/7 recovered sharply to just under £86,000. The order book swelled. Apart from the two White Star liners, IMM companies placed orders for four new vessels. The advances to members of the combine were phased out during the year, presumably being replaced by gold bonds. As a contribution to the cost of the new capital projects, J.P. Morgan & Company loaned Harland & Wolff £150,000. The new financial year opened auspiciously with the confirmation of the order from White Star at a cost of over £3,000,000 for the two giant liners *Olympic* and *Titanic*, ships nos 400 and 401. At 46,328 gross tons, the *Titanic* was to be slightly larger than her sister ship and was hailed as the largest ship in the world: she measured 882½ feet in length and 92½ feet in breadth. On 1 January 1908 Harland & Wolff took back the new Southampton works from J.I. Thornycroft & Company, employing there 1,400 men on average over the next six months.

Table 6.6

Bank balances 1905-14

Date at start of financial year[1]	London City & Midland Bank	Lloyds Bank	Bank of Ireland	National Bank of Scotland	Total	Union Discount Co.[3]
	£	£	£	£	£	£
1905	(19,542)	—	(10,726)	—	(30,268)	—
1906	(14,019)	—	(43,903)	—	(57,922)	(50,000)
1907	(5,037)	—	(1,690)	—	(6,723)	(30,000)
1908	(87,129)	—	(54,118)	—	(114,247)	—
1909	10,095	—	3,349	—	13,444	—
1910	(16,482)	—	(10,531)	—	(27,013)	—
1911	(16,289)	—	5,132 [3]	—	(11,157)	—
1912	(26,200)	—	4,668 [3]	—	(21,532)	(100,000)
1913	(119,671)	—	(14,772)	(63,035)	(197,478)	—
1914	(143,186)[3]	5,056	(41,263)[3]	(42,349)	(221,742)	—

Notes

1   1 July–30 June
2   Although the Union Discount Co. was a discount company and not a bank, these advances were essentially overdrafts.
3   Includes cash in hand
( )   = Debit balance

Table 6.7
Bills receivable discounted 1905-14

Date at start of financial year	£
1905	690,927
1906	585,564
1907	633,300
1908	891,600
1909	957,526
1910	595,500
1911	950,000
1912	1,535,000
1913	1,424,500
1914	2,227,500

Note

1   1 July-30 June

Table 6.8
Investments 1905-14

Date at start of financial year[1]	Ocean Transport Co.	Navigation bonds	IMM bonds, common and preference stock	IMM common stock	SS *Pericles*	SS *Demosthenes*	Belfast Steamship Co.	London & Glasgow Engineering & Iron Shipbuilding Co.	Burmeister & Wain
	£	£	£	£	£	£	£	£	£
1905	41,376	381,922	172,982	17,262	—	—	—	—	—
1906	35,172	—	108,960	27,300	—	—	—	—	—
1907	32,562	—	1,001,029	27,300	—	—	—	—	—
1908	28,816	—	1,001,192	27,300	—	—	—	—	—
1909	26,938	—	1,001,359	24,921	91,356	—	—	—	—
1910	23,907	—	996,028	23,817	—	—	—	—	—
1911	19,287	—	996,028	23,817	—	—	—	—	—
1912	14,430	—	996,028	23,817	—	109,208	16,428	218,142	32,500
1913	8,698	—	996,028	23,817	—	103,557	—	218,142	66,125
1914	3,319	—	996,028	23,817	—	38,203	—	—	—

Note

1   1 July-30 June

Table 6.9 (cont. on p. 141)
Loans to shipping companies and subsidiaries 1901-1914

Date at start of financial year[1]	Elder Dempster & Co.	British & North Atlantic Shipping Co.	Atlantic Transport Co.	IMM loans
	£	£	£	£
1901	70,000 (44,375)	297,963	319,000	—
1902	102,504 (3,371)	117,861	437,565	—
1903	82,149 (2,562)	26,939	179,617	—
1904	52,413 (2,278)	48,944	223,633 (39,145)	332,351 (72,253)
1905	18,222 (2,278)	322,275 (95,638)	234,991 (92,610)	—
1906	72,809 (2,108)	—	—	—
1907	57,784 (1,998)	—	—	—
1908	159,339 (5,015)	—	—	—
1909	134,539 (3,960)	—	—	—
1910	44,729 (7,074)	—	—	—
1911	—	—	—	—
1912	—	—	—	—
1913	—	—	—	—
1914	—	—	—	—

Notes
1 1 July-30 June
( ) = Balance after deducting the value of discounted bills

During the year 1907/8 eight vessels, totalling 82,729 tons, were delivered to their owners. Amongst these were the *Rotterdam*, of 24,000 gross tons, for the Holland-America line and two novel bulk oil-carriers for the Anglo-American Oil Company. One of the carriers, the steamer *Iroquois*, of 9,200 gross tons, was designed to tow the other, the *Navahoe*, which was a remarkable six-masted 'east coast' schooner of 7,700 gross tons. As three of the vessels recorded together a loss of almost £10,000, profits remained level. To help pay for the capital additions and work in progress, overdrafts were increased to £100,000, and loans to the Company were raised by over £100,000, with Pirrie contributing the lion's share, £80,000. The public reserves were reduced by £102,000 and this was transferred to the 'Reserve against interests in IMM', which was not referred to in the balance sheet circulated to shareholders. Nor was mention of this transaction made at the annual meeting. During the year Pirrie was appointed for a two-year stint as Comptroller of the Viceregal Household in Ireland: when on duty, he managed the Company's business by telephone from Dublin Castle. The Pirries revelled in this mark of social acceptance after the reverses following the IMM deal, but Dublin society was not London society.[11]

Output in the 1908/9 financial year retreated to six vessels of 72,000 tons, because of the disruption caused by the installation of the new gantry and the laying down of the *Olympic* and *Titanic*. To help finance the work, Pirrie advanced a further £100,000 to the Company and IMM loaned £45,000 in addition to the £150,000 contributed by J.P. Morgan & Company. The Benrather floating crane was delivered in October and immediately commissioned to lift the 'turbine and other machinery into the *Laurentic*'. The *Laurentic* and *Megantic* were both handed over during the year, along with the 18,000-gross-ton Red Star liner *Lapland*. In November 1908 the

Table 6.9 (cont.)

Loans to shipping companies and subsidiaries 1901-1914

Oceanic Steam Navigation Co.		Frederick Leyland & Co. (1900) Ltd		African Steamship Co.		London & Glasgow Engineering & Iron Shipbuilding Co.	
£		£		£		£	
—		—		—		—	
—		—		—		—	
—		—		—		—	
75,565		—		—		—	
		15,995		—		—	
—		—		—		—	
—		—		—		—	
—		—		—		—	
—		—		—		132,463	(4,961)
—		—		107,892	(34,283)	—	
—		—		—		33,388	
—		—		—		130,448	
—		—		—		—	
—		—		—		—	

Compagne Belge Maritime du Congo, an Elder Dempster associate, took delivery of the large liner *Leopoldville*, financed by a loan of £132,000 from Harland & Wolff; like the Elder Dempster loan, this was supported by bills. Despite the fall in production, profits remained steady at just over £84,000, largely because the bulk of the work in hand was on commission. The order book continued to grow, with contracts for seven new vessels, including two for Royal Mail, one for the Bibby Steamship Company, and one for Union-Castle, the latest recruit to the commission club. Pirrie was appointed a Knight of the Order of St Patrick at the end of his tenure as Comptroller of the Viceregal Household in February 1909. In keeping with his growing status and his wife's social ambitions, Pirrie purchased during May, for a reported £200,000, the Witley Court estate at Godalming, Surrey. This was a bargain as the previous owner, the fraudulent company promoter Whitaker Wright, had spent about £700,000 on the property.[12] He had planned the house extravagantly, with large public apartments and a crystal-domed room under a pond on the terrace. The estate extended to about 2,800 acres, the house and park alone covering some 500 acres. Pirrie came to enjoy weekends at Witley Court, but his wife hated the place.

Just as Harland & Wolff appeared to have recovered from the depression that followed the IMM deal, disaster struck in December 1909 when Sir Alfred Jones, the owner of Elder Dempster, died suddenly. Since his appointment as chairman of the African Steamship Company in 1901, Pirrie had participated in the ownership and management of the shipping enterprises that Jones had built up under the Elder Dempster umbrella. Pirrie was personally the owner of a large stake in African Steamship. Harland & Wolff held as collateral 6,050 £20 ordinary African shares, 8,000 £10 ordinary shares in the British & African Steam Navigation Company and

141

7,000 £10 ordinary shares in Elder Line Limited. Of immediate concern to Pirrie was the loan of £267,000 for which these shares formed the security. Recognising that he was in a strong position to influence the future of the business, he formed an informal partnership to bid for control with Owen Philipps, the Royal Mail chairman, who had been knighted during the year. Pirrie had, no doubt, built up considerable respect for Philipps's skill in shipping management and finance. Since Royal Mail had joined the commission club in 1904, Harland & Wolff had constructed six ships for the line, aggregating 47,308 gross tons. Philipps had been impressed by the attention Pirrie had given to the pioneer *Aragon* and, as a member of the Royal Commission on Shipping Rings, had been struck by Jones's methods. By January 1910 the partners had been granted an option over the entire shipping and commercial interests of the Jones estate, at the apparently knock-down sum of £500,000. These assets were to be transferred to a new company, Elder Dempster & Company Limited, which was to be controlled through management shares by Royal Mail. The low price almost certainly reflected the size of Pirrie's own investment in African Steamship and the debts due to Harland & Wolff. Harland & Wolff did not itself subscribe for shares in the new company as it had done with IMM eight years before. Fuelled by success, Philipps went on in the summer of 1910 to acquire, through Royal Mail, another member of the Harland & Wolff commission club, the Pacific Steam Navigation Company.[13]

The liner *Rotterdam* leav the Lagan in March 190 Built for the Holland-America line she was on of the finest ships in the world in her day.

The curious six-masted 'east coast' schooner *Navahoe*. This oil-carrying vessel for the Anglo-American Oil Company was designed to be towed by her sister ship, *Iroquois*, pictured here lying directly behind her.

Sir Owen Philipps was now Pirrie's closest business confidant. He was the only man who was allowed to walk straight into Pirrie's private office unannounced. Sixteen years his junior, Philipps was as tall and arrogant as Pirrie was small and homely. Despite their physical dissimilarities, they had much in common. They had both been brought up with strong Christian values which gave them a deep sense of their own mission in life and their duty to work hard and long. Pirrie, as a Presbyterian, and Philipps, as an Anglo-Catholic, had both been led by their faith to adopt liberal politics. Like Pirrie, Philipps was a master of finance and had an astonishing grasp of the detail of the financial structure of the businesses he controlled. He shared Pirrie's love of grand designs and giant enterprises conceived with great stealth and secrecy. They both revelled in opulence at the office and in the home. They both had commanding personalities and deeply loyal wives. Despite their intimate working relationship, however, they rarely met socially. Lady Pirrie, the only other person who shared Pirrie's confidence, disliked Philipps intensely, possibly she was jealous of him. Philipps had succeeded in London society, entertaining royalty in his fabulous Chelsea House, whereas the Pirries, with equally luxurious homes, had failed to gain admission to the charmed circle.[14]

In the 1909/10 financial year, work on the *Olympic* and *Titanic*, which were urgently required by White Star to match competition from the new Cunarders, hampered progress on the other vessels on order. Although six vessels were turned

143

out, they totalled only some 40,000 gross tons. Since fewer men engaged in the finishing trade were required, the number of men working in the yard fell back by about one-third. So as to secure access to the skilled interior decorators who would be needed for the fitting out of the two giant liners, the well-known London firm of Aldam Heaton was taken over by the Ocean Transport Company. The managing directors at Queen's Island were so concerned about the jam in production that in July 1909 they resolved to exclude all visitors to the works 'owing to the time lost by our employees and the risk of accident'. The following June members of staff were forbidden to take time off to witness a launch 'unless he has an actual duty to perform . . . Any violation of this rule will mean dismissal.' The yard was so hard pressed that during the year the Company was obliged to subcontract to John Brown at Clydebank the *Preussen* (ship no. 417C), one of an order of three 8,000-gross-ton liners for Hamburg Amerika. The fall in output was, however, compensated for by an upturn in repair business following the restoration of the Alexandra graving dock at the beginning of 1909. During the year the first-class saloon of the *Nieuw Amsterdam* was enlarged and extensive repairs carried out on the Royal Mail's *Trent* and the Elder Dempster boats *Port Henderson* and *Leopoldville*. At Southampton, apart from minor repairs, the bottom of Atlantic Transport's *Minnehaha* was rebuilt after she had stranded on the Scillies. The Southampton works was extended to provide space for an iron foundry and the repair of Admiralty steam launches and pinnaces. Overall profits dipped to £67,000, reflecting losses on three of the vessels completed during the year, probably caused by time penalties incurred due to the backlog of orders. In reviewing the investment in Harland & Wolff in 1910 the chairman of John Brown & Company observed:

> Under the hypnotic influence of Lord Pirrie, Messrs Harland & Wolff, I am glad to say, have been full of work. Lord Pirrie has a sort of magic by which I think he charms orders for ships out of his customers.[15]

This admiration did not prevent John Brown from seeking to share in the overall management of the Company, probably because turbine capacity was being installed at Queen's Island to build the low-pressure turbines for the two giant liners. In April 1909 John Brown nominated two of its directors, Charles Ellis and John Sampson, as principals for election at Harland & Wolff's annual meeting. At the same time Charles Payne, the assistant shipyard manager (no relation to Saxon Payne), was appointed a managing director. He was a showman with social ambitions that appealed to Pirrie. Almost at once the turbines for the dreadnought HMS *Neptune* (building at Portsmouth) were subcontracted by John Brown to Harland & Wolff, as an educational exercise.

Amid a glare of publicity the first of the giant liners, the *Olympic*, was launched on 20 October 1910. Tickets were sold to spectators and the £456 raised was donated to the Royal Victoria Hospital in Belfast. Try as they might, the press were unable to persuade either White Star or Harland & Wolff to divulge detailed technical data about the design of the ship and her sister.[16] Even before the launch, in anticipation of the extensive fitting-out, the number of men at work in the yard had begun to rise. By the end of the year there were almost twice as many employees (11,389) at Queen's Island as there had been the year before (5,785), contributing to a boom in Belfast's prosperity. The task of engining and fitting out the *Olympic* proceeded at breakneck pace throughout the autumn and into the spring of 1911. By the end of March the liner was almost completed. On 1 April she inaugurated the new Thompson graving

One of the enormous fo cylinder, triple-expansi steam-reciprocating engines for the *Olympic* under trial erection in th engine works at Belfast I in 1910.

144

dock.[17] At the same time equal efforts had been made to complete the hull of the *Titanic*. In a magnificent ceremony on 31 May, attended by Bruce Ismay and J. Pierpoint Morgan, the *Titanic* was launched and the *Olympic* left the Lagan with the principal guests for her maiden voyage. The fittings of the *Olympic* dazzled reporters:

The *Titanic*, the largest sh in the world, painted an ready for launching in May 1911.

> The accommodation for first class passengers was placed amidships, and extended over five decks, access from one to the other being obtained via two grand staircases and other smaller stairways, and there were three electric elevators. The first class public rooms included the dining room, reception room, restaurant, lounge, reading and writing rooms, smoking room and the verandah cafes and palm courts; other novel features were the gymnasium, squash racket court, Turkish and electric baths, and the swimming bath. Magnificent suites of rooms, and cabins of size and style sufficiently diverse to suit the likes and dislikes of any passenger were provided. There was a barber's shop, a dark room for photographers; a clothes pressing room; a special dining room for maids and valets; a lending library, a telephone system and a wireless telegraphy installation. All with an effort to equalize a first class hotel.[18]

Bruce Ismay, always fastidious, could find little to complain of during the maiden voyage. He wired for a potato peeler for the crew's galley, arranged for cigar and cigarette holders to be fitted in the WCs and noted:

146

A drawing of the
sumptuous first-class
bathrooms on the *Titanic*.

The only trouble of any consequence on board the ship arose from the springs
of the beds being too 'springy'; this, in conjunction with the spring mattresses,
accentuated the pulsation in the ship to such an extent as to seriously interfere
with passengers sleeping.[19]

may have been that he disliked the dictatorial ways of his brother-in-law, Lord Pirrie.
Like his sister, Lady Pirrie, he was endowed with a strong and determined personality
which must at times have clashed with that of Lord Pirrie. He moved to London to
be near her and his brothers, John and Henry, who had sold their shipping
business.[20]. Carlisle was succeeded as chairman of the committee of managing
directors by J.W. Kempster. At the same time Saxon Payne became responsible for
supervising the complexities of the Company's growing bill business and for liaising
between the management and the unions. There was now no managing director with
sufficient strength of character to stand up to Pirrie. Only the two principals
nominated by John Brown could check his actions.

The strong order book allowed Pirrie to embark on new capital projects at Belfast.
Apart from the purchase of turbine machinery, the old offices were replaced by 'a
well appointed three storey building', the boiler shop was extended by 112 feet, a
new smiths' shop, 296 feet by 100 feet, was constructed, and the iron foundry and
boilershop yards were roofed over. Plans were prepared for the extension of the iron
foundry by the addition of two new bays 260 feet long. Orders were placed for the
new generation of tower cranes for the berths in the south yard, to replace the 'existing
hydraulic derricks, which are unsuitable for the higher ships now being built on these

he generating station at
Queen's Island,
commissioned on 24
Dctober 1904 as the final
ige in the programme to
ctrify all the tools in the
works. It was equipped
with large gas engines.

(overleaf)
Part of the re-equipped
complex of the platers'
ed in the north yard, laid
out to service nos 2 and 3
oerths for the *Titanic* and
Olympic, 1911.

slips'. The berths there, apart from nos 4 and 5 (formerly 5 and 6), were to be strengthened to take heavier vessels. All this work took two years to complete and cost almost £250,000. So as to avoid being forced to subcontract orders, Pirrie was also anxious to increase the Company's shipbuilding capacity. It is uncertain if he planned to achieve this on the Lagan.

During November 1909 the United Kingdom had been plunged into a constitutional crisis following the rejection by the House of Lords of the Liberal Government's budget. In the ensuing general election campaign Asquith, who had succeeded Campbell-Bannerman as Prime Minister in 1908, assured the Irish Nationalists of Liberal commitment to Home Rule. Although the Liberals won the election, the Irish Nationalists held the balance of power. Ulster Unionists, thoroughly alarmed at the real prospect of Home Rule, grouped themselves under the leadership of Sir Edward Carson. Pirrie publicly declared in favour of Home Rule.[21] In October 1911 he used this platform to launch a vicious and unwarranted attack on the Belfast Harbour Commissioners, accusing them unfairly of hampering the operations of the Company and refusing to lease additional land because he supported Home Rule. In April of that year the Company had asked for a small piece of land at the Hamilton graving dock, for a canteen, and had rejected an offer on the grounds that the proposed rent

151

was excessive. It emerged, however, that Pirrie was referring to the bid for land at the head of the Musgrave channel which he had been refused as long ago as 1903. Pirrie was clearly trying, as he had done in 1899, to bully the Commissioners into submission. He repeated his tactics by opening negotiations with the Dublin Port and Docks Board who, at once, began to seek the necessary permissions for Harland & Wolff to open a works on the Liffey.[22]

Simultaneously Bruce Ismay suggested to Pirrie that, following the success of the Southampton works, Harland & Wolff should take over and enlarge the White Star and Leyland repair and maintenance shops in Liverpool. Pirrie was attracted by this proposal, which would allow Harland & Wolff to fulfil its obligations not only to IMM but also to the fast-expanding Royal Mail Group. A four-acre site alongside the new Brocklebank graving dock was leased early in 1912 from Mersey Docks and Harbour Board for a period of sixty years. The existing Atlantic Engine Works of the Leyland line was to be converted into iron and brass foundries.[23] The contract for building the new works and the conversion, which it was estimated would take about eighteen months, was awarded to Sir William Arrol & Company of Glasgow. The whole project cost about £90,000 and was opened in the spring of 1913. The first thirty-six workers were recruited in January 1913. The number of employees rose swiftly to almost 4,800 by the end of the year. It is difficult to tell how many of these men had been attracted from Belfast to Liverpool by the more secure political environment.

Pirrie's much-publicised attack on the Belfast Harbour Commissioners alerted other shipbuilders to Harland & Wolff's need for additional capacity. By 1911 the experience of the long depression at the beginning of the century and the need to reinvest continually to remain competitive had persuaded the owners of a number of medium sized shipyards that the time had come to withdraw from the industry. The news that Pirrie was in the market for a shipyard caused Caird & Company of Greenock and the London & Glasgow Engineering and Iron Shipbuilding Company, with a yard at Govan on the upper Clyde, to offer him their businesses. There were also reports, later denied, that Harland & Wolff was keen to sell out. Although these rumours may have originated with Pirrie, he subsequently refuted them. An agreement was struck with Hawthorn Leslie, of Newcastle upon Tyne, whereby it would build for Harland & Wolff if Queen's Island was fully booked,[24] and early in the new year Pirrie opted to acquire the London & Glasgow business for £218,000. This was £100,000 below the value placed on the yard. The company, which had been formed in 1864 to operate the Middleton Shipyard in Govan, had failed to pay a dividend since the completion of an extensive modernisation programme in 1910. After William Beardmore & Company had acquired the business of Robert Napier & Sons in 1900 and transferred the shipyard and engine works from central Glasgow down the Clyde to Dalmuir in 1905, London & Glasgow had taken over the old Napier yard, next door to its own yard in Govan, and the celebrated Lancefield Engine Works across the river in Finnieston. The two yards and engine works had been amalgamated and re-equipped,[25] and the company had for some time built a mix of intermediate passenger vessels and naval ships. Harland & Wolff took over the six vessels that were under construction (London & Glasgow's ships nos 355, 358, 363, 364, 366 and 367), comprising three 'K'-class destroyers, the torpedo depot ship HMS *Woolwich*, the auxiliary cruiser HMS *Sydney* and a passenger vessel, *Evangeline*, for the Plant line. The decision to invest on the Clyde was not due primarily to the reluctance of the Harbour Commissioners to lease more land on the

Lagan, but to a shortage of skilled men in Belfast. Early in 1911 the Company had to fight off attempts by Vickers and Cammell-Laird to recruit in Belfast.

The reason why Pirrie needed so much additional capacity emerged during the autumn of 1911, when there was speculation that he and Sir Owen Philipps were preparing a gigantic offer for Union-Castle. This was confirmed in mid-December when they announced that Royal Mail and Elder Dempster were making a joint offer of £5.48 million. Sir Donald Currie, the architect of Union-Castle, had died in 1909 and, like Sir Alfred Jones, had left no obvious successor. As in the case of Elder Dempster, Pirrie was well placed to learn of the progress of events within Union-Castle, since G.W. Wolff was still a large shareholder and remained a director. The offer was accepted in April 1912. Pirrie and Philipps had won control of a massive fleet of forty-four vessels, a total of 319,514 gross tons.[26]

If this welter of dealing was not enough, Pirrie was also locked in negotiations for a licence to build diesel engines. The heavy oil engine had been invented in the 1890s by Dr Rudolph Diesel, who gave it his name. A marine version had been developed by two established marine engine-builders, Burmeister & Wain, of Copenhagen, and Sulzer Brothers, of Winterthur in Switzerland. In November 1910 the Clyde firm Barclay Curle & Company acquired the licence to build Burmeister & Wain engines. Early in 1911 Pirrie secured the British Empire patent rights from Dr Diesel's own firm, Maschinenfabrik Augsburg Nuremburg (MAN). So as to test the engine, he purchased for £16,632 the steam yacht *Valiant*, which had been built in 1893 for the American millionaire W.K. Vanderbilt. The transaction was undertaken through the Ocean Transport Company. This plan was abandoned during the summer when Barclay Curle proposed that Harland & Wolff 'should join with them in laying down

special works for the manufacture of oil engines'. Pirrie rejected this overture and Barclay Curle turned to the Tyne shipbuilders Swan Hunter & Wigham Richardson Limited, who were licensed by Burmeister & Wain in October 1911. The two companies planned to amalgamate and, in collaboration with Burmeister & Wain, promote a new company, the Burmeister & Wain (Diesel System) Oil Engine Company. This was to be owned two-thirds by Burmeister & Wain and one-third by Barclay Curle and Swan Hunter. Pirrie applied directly to Ivar Knudsen of Burmeister & Wain with the offer of the existing Lancefield Engine Works on condition that Harland & Wolff could become sole licensee in the United Kingdom. He was too late to prevent the flotation of the new company in April 1912, but when the issue of preference shares failed, Knudsen accepted Pirrie's offer the following month. Barclay Curle and Swan Hunter reluctantly sold their one-third interest to Harland & Wolff. In July 1912 the new company formally purchased the Lancefield Works. The brilliant young engineer Frederick Rebbeck was appointed works manager. Born in Wiltshire in 1877, he had served an apprenticeship with the Metropolitan Amalgamated Railway Carriage & Wagon Company before coming to Belfast to gain experience with Harland & Wolff and the engineering firm Victor Coates & Company. He had become manager of the engine works' drawing office at Queen's Island, but had left about 1907 to work for the British Westinghouse Company in Manchester.[27]

By this time the success of the *Selandia*, the first ocean-going, oil-engined ship,

Lord Pirrie (centre) wi[th] Ivar Knudsen (second right) inspecting the Govan yard in 1912 sh[ortly] after the formation of t[he] Burmeister & Wain (D[iesel] System) Oil Engine Company whose work[s] were situated at Finnie[ston] on the other side of th[e] Clyde. (Courtesy of M[...] B & W Diesel A/S, Bo[...] Haarmark, Copenhage[n])

had earned Burmeister & Wain, who had built the propelling machinery, a great reputation. Winston Churchill, the First Lord of the Admiralty, described the vessel as 'the most perfect maritime masterpiece of the century'.[28] Pirrie at once plunged into negotiations with Andrew Weir, the founder of the successful Bank line of steamers and reputedly the largest private shipowner in the United Kingdom, for the purchase of an option of a controlling interest on stock of the Union Oil Company of California. These resulted in July 1914 in the formation of the British Union Oil Company. The proximity of war prevented the successful issue of the shares and the option was abandoned, with considerable loss to Weir, Pirrie and the other sponsors, the Earl Grey and Thomas Royden of the Cunard Company.[29]

During the early weeks of 1912 the political atmosphere in Ulster had become increasingly tense. Pirrie stood against the tide of Protestant opinion which had been mobilised by Carson and his supporters. Although he had shown leanings towards Home Rule, he had never been a militant supporter, but the Home Rule cause was fashionable in London and Lord and Lady Pirrie were determined not to be condemned as a dyed-in-the-wool Ulster couple, and to show their commitment to the Liberalism of their childhood. In the first week of 1912 it became known that Pirrie had booked Belfast's Ulster Hall for a meeting to be held on 8 February, addressed by Winston Churchill and John Redmond, leader of the Irish Nationalist Party. The Unionists, incensed, booked the hall for the evening before so that they would have to be ejected before the meeting took place. The venue for Pirrie's meeting was changed to a large marquee in Celtic Park. He took the chair and inveighed against what he regarded as the bigoted attitudes of the Unionists – 'Was loyalty to mean steadfastness to inherited phrases, and any evolution either in religion or politics to be regarded as lacking reverence to their ancestors?' The meeting passed off with little incident, but when Pirrie boarded the steamer at Larne four days later he was pelted with rotten eggs, flour and herring, and called 'a traitor and a turncoat'.[30] Within a week, at the height of the political uproar in Ulster and as the negotiations to acquire London & Glasgow were nearing completion, Pirrie was lying gravely ill in hospital in London suffering from an enlarged prostate gland. He underwent surgery on 20 February. At the time this was a most dangerous procedure with a high mortality rate. Bulletins concerning his health appeared in *The Times* for the following fortnight and there was speculation that he might not make a full recovery.[31] Now aged almost sixty-five, he was ordered by his doctors to rest until the autumn. He recuperated by taking an extended cruise to the Baltic in the *Valiant*, which he bought personally from the Ocean Transport Company. He attended the Kiel Regatta in July where he entertained Albert Ballin, and together they inspected the new diesel-engined ship *Fionia*. Pirrie was enthusiastic, summing his impressions up in a simple phrase: 'The future!'[32]

At Queen's Island early in 1912 the fitting-out work on the *Titanic* was nearing completion. White Star, pleased with the performance of the *Olympic*, had ordered another ship of the same class, *Britannic*, to be laid down as soon as the *Titanic* was handed over. On 2 April, rather than the proposed but inauspicious 1 April, the *Titanic* left the Lagan for Southampton to make her maiden voyage. Thomas Andrews, Pirrie's nephew, was on board as representative of the builders. In October 1910 it had been decided, on his uncle's authority, that he 'should be present on board all steamers built by us while undergoing their trials and accompany them on the run round to the cross-channel or other port to which they are ordered from Belfast'. For some unrecorded reason Andrews was to accompany the vessel on the whole voyage,

157

probably because Pirrie was forbidden by his doctors to go. With Andrews were eight Harland & Wolff workmen, four of them apprentices. Bruce Ismay joined the liner at Southampton. On 10 April she set sail with no ceremony and by the time she left Queenstown, outside Cork, on the following day she was carrying 2,224 passengers and crew.

At almost midnight on Sunday 14 April in mid-Atlantic the *Titanic* struck an iceberg which sliced a 300-foot gash in her hull from just forward of the foremast to no. 5 boiler room. The watertight doors were closed at once, but so extensive was the damage that she sank within two-and-a-quarter hours. Throughout that time Thomas Andrews behaved with exemplary courage. He was last seen throwing deck chairs to survivors in the water. Seven other Island men died: William Parr, assistant manager of the electrical department; Roderick Chisholm, ships' draughtsman; Anthony Frost, foreman engineer; Robert Knight, leading hand engineer; William Campbell, apprentice joiner; Frank Parkes, apprentice plumber; and apprentice electrician Ennis Watson. Some time later it was learned that apprentice fitter Alfred Cunningham, also believed dead, had been picked up by the *Carpathia* and taken to America, where he was to get a job and settle down in New York. Also among the survivors was Bruce Ismay.[33] After the tragedy he bought a property in the west of Ireland which he continued to own until his death twenty-five years later.

Altogether 1,513 people lost their lives on the *Titanic* and the news of the worst disaster in maritime history stunned the world. In the ensuing inquiry the Master, Captain Smith, who had lost his life, was blamed for driving his vessel too fast in an area where ice was known to be present. The Board of Trade was severely censured

160

Thomas Andrews, Lord Pirrie's nephew and chief designer at Harland & Wolff, who lost his life in the *Titanic* disaster.

The patent 'Macfarlane' watertight door developed by Harland & Wolff after the loss of the *Titanic*. The door was to be fitted in the *Britannic*, her sister ship.

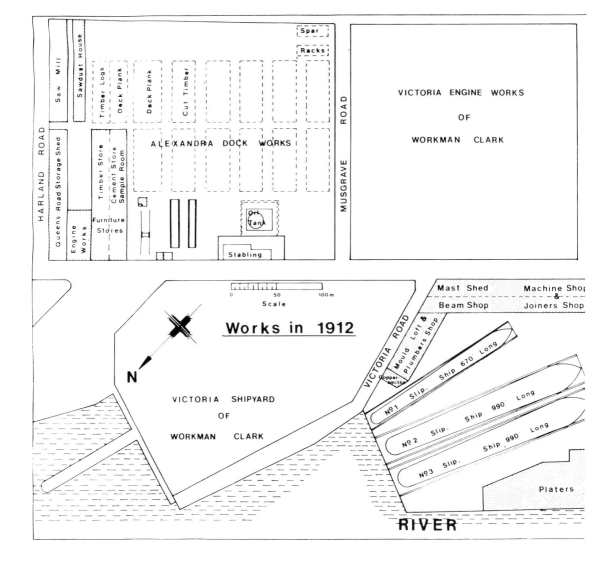

Works in 1912

for its failure to update its regulations for large liners, particularly regarding the watertight subdivision of hulls and the provision of lifeboats. Harland & Wolff was exonerated and the quality of its workmanship praised. Some questioned whether the watertight bulkheads should have been extended up to the highest continuous deck, which was thirty feet above the water line, rather than to the deck eleven feet above.[34] At Queen's Island Thomas Andrews's successor as chief designer, Edward Wilding, threw himself into an investigation of methods of improving the safety of large passenger liners. This he was well placed to do as he had been trained by Andrews and worked closely with him in designing the *Titanic*. Over the next three years Harland & Wolff patented new designs for systems of lowering and raising lifeboats, working watertight doors and keeping bulkhead doors open in an emergency.[35] In late 1912 the *Olympic* was sent to Belfast to have an inner skin fitted and the bulkheads heightened and strengthened.

It is difficult to know how Pirrie was affected by the death of his nephew and the loss of the *Titanic*. Photographs taken at her commissioning show a man who had aged out of all recognition since his illness. His face was drawn and his hair had turned snow white. The shock of the *Titanic* tragedy further prolonged his recovery, and there were rumours in the press that he intended to retire. Pirrie denied these; but

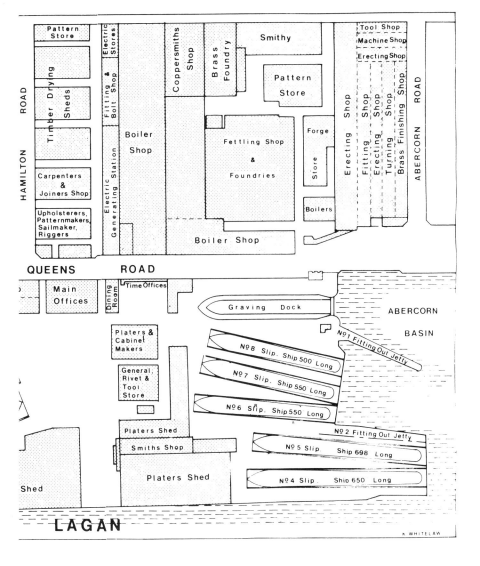

he does appear to have turned his mind to the succession should he die prematurely. There is nothing to suggest that he ever planned to nominate Thomas Andrews as chairman. In 1907 he had not made him a principal nor had he offered him a share in the Company. Instead he had chosen J.W. Kempster, an outsider, and had sold a majority stake in Harland & Wolff to John Brown & Company. Later in life, after her husband's death, Lady Pirrie wistfully reflected on what might have been had Thomas Andrews lived, and slowly a myth grew up. Pirrie was not completely fit until the end of 1912.

Apart from the *Titanic*, seven other vessels were completed in the 1911/12 financial year, including the Royal Mail liner *Arlanza*, the first of a new class of 'A steamers', and the P & O vessel *Maloja*, which was fitted out for her maiden voyage as a royal yacht to carry King George V and Queen Mary to the Durbar in India, for the coronation of the King Emperor. The *Demosthenes* was handed over to George Thompson & Company, owned since 1905 jointly by White Star and Shaw Savill. This was the first intermediate liner to be fitted with low-pressure turbines, made by John Brown at Clydebank. Four major repairs were carried out at Belfast, including that of the *Olympic* which had been seriously damaged in a collision with the cruiser HMS *Hawke* in Southampton Water on 20 September 1911. Three refits

163

were undertaken at Southampton. By the end of the financial year the Company held orders for no fewer than fifteen vessels.

Although losses totalling almost £87,000 were recorded on four of the vessels delivered during the year, the profit for the year rose to £124,319, due largely to the commission paid on the *Titanic* and work in progress. The Company's need for funds to finance the programme of capital additions and acquisitions helped push its contingent liabilities for discounted bills receivable to over £1,500,000. The loans to the Company were increased to almost £600,000, with new advances of nearly £150,000 from Morgan Grenfell & Company (J.P. Morgan & Company's London representatives) and £100,000 from Union Discount Company (curiously classified as an overdraft in the accounts). Overdrafts almost doubled to £21,000, all provided by the London City & Midland Bank. At the annual meeting it was resolved to increase the share capital by creating £600,000 of preference stock. Pirrie explained to his managing directors that these new shares were being created specifically to allow them to participate in the ownership of the Company. However, since the preference shares carried no voting rights, the move gave them no more right to comment on the direction of the Company than if they had continued simply to lend money. It seems likely that the issue was connected with secret preparations Pirrie was making for the settlement of his estate after his death, whereby the preference shareholders would benefit from the income of trust funds. Sir Edward Holden, managing director of the London City & Midland Bank, now seriously worried about Pirrie's reliance on heavy borrowing, summoned him to discuss the Company's liabilities, particularly the volume of bills. Pirrie explained that White Star had credit of over £1.2 million and that Elder Dempster, Royal Mail and Union-Castle (the Royal Mail Group) had a balance 'after all transactions of £1,625,000'. Holden was not to be confused by this smoke screen:

> I then pointed out that, having regard to the fact that Harland & Wolff would be doing the extended business of these companies, one must of necessity look to the available resources of that Company.

Despite Pirrie's resistance, Holden insisted that Harland & Wolff should pay an extra ½ per cent for the privilege of placing their bills with his bank.[36]

During the second half of 1912 Pirrie framed his plans for the Govan yard, against a background of growing unrest in Belfast as the Home Rule Bill made its way through Parliament. He was worried that it might prove necessary to close Queen's Island if civil war broke out in Ulster. Although the Lancefield Engine Works had been sold to Burmeister & Wain, so that all Govan's requirements for steam engines could be met from Queen's Island, he prudently decided to build a new engine works at Govan and to rebuild the yard completely with new platers' sheds and framing shops, strengthened berths and a new fitting-out basin. So as to accommodate the framing shop, a row of seventeenth-century cottages, 'Water Row' beside Govan ferry, was demolished. On 23 November Harland & Wolff came to an understanding with Mackie & Thomson, which owned the adjoining yard but had recently moved to Irvine on the Ayrshire coast. Under the terms of the agreement, to relieve pressure on the Harland & Wolff order book, Mackie & Thomson was to build the hulls of ships nos 448I *Maryland*, 449I *Missouri*, 451I *Falstria*, and 452I *Lalandia*; in return Harland & Wolff acquired the site of the yard. Henry P. Harland, the nephew of Sir Edward Harland, was sent to Govan to supervise the construction of the sub-contracted vessels. At the same time Pirrie asked Alexander Stephen & Sons, of

(overleaf)
A hydraulic riveting machine at work on the *tannic* being constructed in no. 2 berth in the north yard just before the First World War.

The steamer *Alcantara,* one of the three 'A' steamers built by Harland & Wolff for the Royal Mail Steam Packet Company between 1913 and 1920. This vessel was converted to an armed merchant cruiser and was sunk by the German commerce raider *Greif* on 29 February 1916.

Linthouse, if they would be willing to build hulls for Harland & Wolff should the need arise.[37] By early 1913 Pirrie was planning the total reconstruction of the berths at Govan, with new slips extending out into the river, protected by a moveable caisson. All these investments at Govan were to cost an estimated £300,000 over the next financial year. They were to be supervised by the new general manager, J.P. Dickinson, who had previously been manager of the ships' finishing department at Belfast. He was instructed to introduce 'Belfast practice' at Govan, including the long-standing 'no smoking' rule during working hours. He was made a managing director of the Company and quickly joined the ranks of Pirrie's 'splendid men'.

Throughout the 1912/13 and 1913/14 financial years contracts continued to flood in. The order book was dominated by the Royal Mail Group, with contracts for fifteen liners, and IMM companies with ten. During the two years Harland & Wolff, either at Queen's Island or Govan or through subcontractors, delivered twenty-four vessels of an aggregate 193,000 gross tons. These included, for the Royal Mail Group, the five 'D'-class intermediate liners of 11,500 gross tons each and two second generation 'A'-class vessels, the *Andes* and *Alcantara,* and the new style Elder Dempster liners *Abosso* and *Appam*. Following the report of the *Titanic* inquiry in the autumn of 1912, the Company was inundated with repair work from all the lines with which it had commission arrangements, to make their ships comply with new safety regulations. By the close of the 1913/14 financial year the Company had

contracts for thirty steamers of almost 450,000 gross tons. A quarter of this total was made up of the White Star liners *Britannic* (48,158 gross tons) and *Ceric*, the replacement for the *Titanic*, of a projected 60,000 gross tons. The *Ceric* was allocated ship no. 391, previously reserved for the cancelled Hamburg Amerika liner *Europa*. On 1 January 1914 Edward Wilding, who had already made designs for this massive vessel, was appointed a managing director of the Company.

So as to maximise production, Pirrie resolved to improve the machinery for dealing with demarcation disputes. The Company's industrial relations had been remarkably good since the 1895 strike. There had only been a handful of trivial disputes since the formation of the committee of managing directors in 1907. Pirrie had gone out of his way to win the confidence of the representatives of the numerous trades employed at Queen's Island and at the new works on the mainland. He insisted that, wherever possible, demarcation disputes should be settled amicably between the unions involved, with the management acting as referee. He had made it a rule that his managers, and more recently his managing directors, should always be prepared to negotiate with union delegates. When five electricians at the Liverpool works withdrew their labour in December 1912 as part of a wider dispute, Kempster immediately acceded to their demands and wrote to the Electrical Trades Union in Manchester . . .

An unusual photograp the engines of the *Brit* being erected in the er room. Unlike many ot shipbuilders, Harland Wolff installed most machinery prior to launching so as to avo lengthy periods at the fitting-out wharfs for which it had to pay fee the Harbour Commissioners.

Queen's Road at close of work in the summer of 1912 with the Harland & Wolff engine works behind, and, in the distance on the right, the Victoria Engine Works of Workman Clark.

from the information we obtained we think that the question of the rate was a very fair one for your members to raise and we should have been quite prepared, as we are at all times, to discuss it on its merits. We think therefore you should have no hesitation in persuading the men to return and discuss the matter with us in the usual way, when, should a satisfactory settlement be arrived on the basis of an increase, the arrangement would be retrospective, so that the men would lose nothing, but on the contrary would gain by the procedure.[38]

Early in the year William Walker, the Belfast district delegate of the Amalgamated and General Union Society of Carpenters and Joiners, had resigned. His letter informing Harland & Wolff that he was standing down bears testimony to the rapport between management and unions:

I desire before closing finally my trade union activity to express to your firm my deep indebtedness for the many courtesies extended to me and for the fair and generous way in which on all occasions my advocacy of the workman's claims have been met by those of your firm with whom I came into contact.[39]

Such close bonds worked to the Company's advantage. When James Freeland, the Belfast secretary of the Amalgamated Society of Engineers, met the assistant secretary of Harland & Wolff, Saxon Payne, in October 1913, he explained that he had only

169

small matters to discuss, but 'he thought it would be in the interest of the firm to get them settled as they were being regularly brought up by his members and he was anxious to avoid any friction or complication'.[40] Occasionally the unions looked to the Company for help. In May 1914 senior officials of the Shipwrights' Society met the managing directors to express their concern about James McWhirter, the society's local secretary and an employee of Harland & Wolff, who had dislocated his hand in an industrial accident:

> Mr Crawford (Assistant General Secretary) stated that they felt that owing to Mr McWhirter having nothing to do (being in receipt of an allowance from the firm for compensation) it gave him opportunities for interfering and making trouble and if the firm could possibly see their way to give him some job of a suitable kind he considered it would not only be to the Society's interest but to the firm's.[41]

The managing directors were happy to oblige.

Although the Company had remained outside the Shipbuilders' Employers' Federation, Pirrie had maintained close contact with it and its sister organisations, the Clyde Shipbuilders' Association and the North West Engineering Trades' Employers' Association. When the Shipbuilders' Employers' Federation concluded a general demarcation agreement with the shipyard unions in 1912, Harland & Wolff considered following suit, but finally preferred to make more formal the existing system of persuading unions to settle demarcation disputes between themselves. The Company was probably deterred by the failure of the Boilermakers to ratify the general agreement.[42] However, during 1913 there was mounting pressure from the other unions for Harland & Wolff to draw up a demarcation list with external arbitrators. As a consequence of the agreement of the Shipbuilders' Employers' Federation the managing directors found themselves having to adjudicate in an increasing number of arguments between trades, which not only hindered output but also occupied a great deal of their time. In December 1913, for example, they

The front page of the booklet issued to every member of the staff and manual workforce in 1914, detailing demarcation procedures.

had to settle a contest between the fitters and boilermakers over the facing of boiler manholes and mudhole doors. By this time negotiations were in progress with the various trades to agree a demarcation list. These were concluded with the unanimous support of every trade in July 1914, and shortly after the outbreak of war the Board of Trade appointed its three surveyors at Belfast as referees, with a supplementary panel of 'several gentlemen in Great Britain'. Under the terms of the agreement, issued on the very day war was declared, the twenty-two trades represented among the workforce accepted the following conditions:

1 If any disputed question arises regarding demarcation of work between different trades employed by Harland & Wolff Limited, the men affected shall report such in writing to the management, through the foreman, and the management will immediately communicate with the trades affected, and endeavour to arrange matters satisfactorily between the parties.

2 In case of failure to do so when the preliminaries mentioned in clause 3 have been complied with, the question shall be brought before a Committee, consisting of three representatives of each of the trades involved in the dispute and three representatives of the firm, and also an impartial referee. Not more than three witnesses on each side to be called.

3 The preliminary method of procedure shall be as follows: – Each of the trades claiming the work shall make a formal application to the firm on an agreed form, describing the work in dispute, the nature and grounds of the claim and all relevant particulars within two days. The firm shall, immediately on receipt of both claims, submit them to the referee, with their written comments thereon.

4 The Committee shall sit at the works where the question has arisen within three days of the papers being submitted to the referee, at a time to be mutually agreed upon, when all correspondence shall be read.

5 The two trades shall be at liberty to state their respective cases to the referee, who shall also take the opinion of the firm's representatives at the same time.

6 If, after discussion, an agreement between the two trades is not reached, the question shall be decided within three days by the referee, who shall be one of the Shipbuilding and Engineering Board of Trade representatives. The method of choosing such referee shall be decided after consultation with the Board of Trade, say by rota, from a panel consisting of the said Board of Trade representatives.

7 In cases where work is in dispute, Harland & Wolff Limited shall continue to employ the same trade on such work as has previously been customary in the works where the dispute has arisen, until such time as a settlement is arrived at.

8 If in the absence of custom or precedent, due to the work being of a novel character, uncertainty exists as to which trade shall do the work, or, for the same reason, the interpretation of a clause in an existing demarcation agreement is in the opinion of the firm, open to reasonable doubt, the management shall be entitled to either give a temporary decision, which shall not be adduced in evidence or prejudice the ultimate settlement, or may, if time permits, stop the work until the referee has given his decision.[43]

The agreement was signed on behalf of the following trade unions: the Associated Blacksmiths and Iron Workers' Society; the Boilermakers, Iron and Steel Ship

Builders' Society; the Brassfounders, Turners, Fitters, Finishers and Coppersmiths' Association of Great Britain and Ireland; the West of Scotland Brass Turners, Fitters, Finishers and Instrument Makers; the Scottish Brassmoulders' Union; the Amalgamated Union of Cabinetmakers; the Amalgamated and General Union Society of Carpenters and Joiners; the National Society of Coppersmiths, Braziers and Metal Workers; the Electrical Trades Union; the Belfast District Committee of the Amalgamated Society of Engineers; the National Amalgamated Society of Painters and Decorators; the United Patternmakers' Association; the United Operative Plumbers' Association of Great Britain and Ireland; the National Amalgamated Sheet Metal Workers and Braziers; the Sheet Iron Workers and Light Platers' Society; the Shipconstructors and Shipwrights' Association; the National United Smiths and Hammermen; the Steam Engine Makers' Society and the Amalgamated Society of Woodcutting Machinists.

Profits, before making provisions, remained level at an estimated £130,000 in 1913 and £140,000 in 1914. The massive volume of business, along with the re-equipment of Govan, was to be financed by discounting bills which in June 1914 had reached the colossal total of £2,227,500, approaching four times the nominal value of the Company's ordinary share capital. Two-thirds of these bills were drawn on companies in the Royal Mail Group. Although the loans to the Company fell back in 1913 as the preference shares were issued, they rose again in 1914. Overdrafts jumped to £221,742 in June 1914, with the London City & Midland Bank contributing over 60 per cent. As a result of the takeover of London & Glasgow, Harland & Wolff had acquired an account with the National Bank of Scotland, which was also overdrawn.

This growing burden of debt deeply troubled Holden at the London City & Midland Bank. In the week before Christmas 1913 Pirrie was again interviewed about the Company's escalating overdraft and volume of bills. Holden found Pirrie evasive when questioned about the balance sheet circulated at the annual meeting. He noted: 'It is impossible to ascertain from the balance sheet what the profits of Harland & Wolff are, as they are so much hidden up in depreciations before the declaration of profits.' Pirrie spun Holden a yarn about the heading in the balance sheet 'Sundry contingency accounts and amounts in suspense', not daring to explain that these contained hidden reserves. Holden quizzed Pirrie with an equal lack of success about Burmeister & Wain and the joint ventures with Philipps. For his pains he was told: 'I would not advise you to irritate Philipps because if I died he would be absolute master of everything.' Holden did, however, wheedle out of Pirrie the way in which bills were used by the Company:

> When he contracts to build a ship as soon as he has put into that ship a certain amount he draws a bill on the firm, negotiates it, and the proceeds are used to pay off the expenditure incurred on the ship . . . Some of the bills are drawn before any money is expended at all, but these bills are discounted and the money is used to commence building the ship.

Holden, who felt he could push Pirrie no further 'without breaking with him', cautioned . . .

> that the time would come when profits would all come tumbling down and when he would get no dividend out of Elder Dempster and it would be everything he could do to pay his preference dividend.[44]

Thoroughly disconcerted, Pirrie hurried off to open an account with Lloyds Bank, in which he placed £5,000 on deposit. Holden's prophecy was only too accurate. Even before the loss of the *Titanic*, Bruce Ismay had decided to give up the presidency of IMM. He was replaced briefly by H.A. Sandersen, a director of White Star, and then by the American P.A.S. Franklin. By 1914 IMM was in serious financial straits and having difficulties in meeting its bills of £585,000 drawn by Harland & Wolff.[45] There were rumours of impending failure at a time when the international bill market was confused and dislocated by the approach of hostilities in Europe. This placed enormous strain on Harland & Wolff's resources. In the middle of this crisis William Bailey, the Company secretary, died on 8 April. Both William Tawse and Saxon Payne had hopes of the succession. Instead Pirrie chose to bring in an outsider, John Philp, who had been trained by Price Waterhouse and had been secretary to the Argyle Motor Company, of Glasgow, which had recently become bankrupt. Saxon Payne, whose skill in managing Harland & Wolff's bill business was vital in the uncertain financial conditions that lay ahead, was promoted to the new position of financial secretary.[46] At the annual general meeting in September 1914 Pirrie asked the ordinary and preference shareholders to lend their dividends back to the Company 'owing to the present state of financial affairs'. By the time this appeal was made the Company had been overwhelmed by the declaration of war on 4 August.

In the ten years since Pirrie had persuaded Bruce Ismay to accept the leadership of the troubled IMM combine, he had welded Harland & Wolff into the most powerful shipbuilding and shipping group in the world. With great determination he had seized every opportunity that had come along during a period characterised by the unexpected. He had become a business dictator on a gigantic scale, and no-one within the Company was able to challenge his authority and skill. He would not countenance any failure, however human. Consequently his staff were terrified of him. In later life R.S. Johnson, by then managing director of Cammell-Laird, the Liverpool shipbuilders, recalled that while working in the design office at Queen's Island he had been summoned at a few hours' notice to join Lord and Lady Pirrie on a voyage to New York. He crossed to Liverpool that night taking with him the design drawings of a new IMM liner, which were only half complete. On arriving at Liverpool he went straight to Lime Street Hotel. Lord and Lady Pirrie and her sister, Agnes Carlisle, were waiting in the foyer. There was a delay in the arrival of the carriage to take them to the landing stage. Pirrie became fussed and the young man was sent out to find the transport. They eventually got away; but as the ship departed R.S. Johnson realised that in the confusion he had left the drawings behind in the hotel. Too petrified to tell Lord Pirrie, he confided in Agnes Carlisle who, in turn, immediately told her sister, Lady Pirrie. Pirrie instructed the pilot, who was still on board, to have the drawings collected and sent by another steamer which would arrive before them in New York. Unnerved by the experience, R.S. Johnson looked elsewhere for employment.[47] On the other hand, to those loyal and efficient servants, Lord and Lady Pirrie could be immensely kind, bringing them presents from their travels and sending Christmas gifts. These included woollen pullovers knitted by Lady Pirrie and her sister for the senior staff, to keep them warm on their trips across the Irish Sea.[48]

Pirrie had learned more quickly than most of his British contemporaries how to manage large enterprises employing many thousands of people by using financial information and other statistics which were fed to him every month by his chief accountant, William Tawse, and his managing directors. These men were responsible for the details of production, cost control and labour relations, but were never given access to the central accounts, which were kept by Pirrie in London. They did not know which ships were built on commission or at a loss. Pirrie told them only what he wished to, which, apart from the news of the developing public crisis in IMM, was very little. Like Andrew Carnegie, the American steel baron, Pirrie understood that the cost of new labour-saving plant was irrelevant if a high level of throughput was assured. To this end he had used his connection with Sir Owen Philipps to fill the gap left by his former IMM customers, winning control of a large slice of the British premier shipping market. In attaining this goal he had not been forced to share the direction of Harland & Wolff with Philipps, even though he was his nominated successor. Despite the sale of a majority of the shareholding to John Brown, Pirrie was left in undisputed control of the business. Yet as Holden had rightly divined, Harland & Wolff was vulnerable, depending, like all its sisters in the Royal Mail Group, on too much loan capital. It was equally at the mercy of civil unrest in Ulster, and this was almost certain to be the consequence of Home Rule, which passed through Parliament in September 1914 on the understanding that it would not become law until the end of hostilities. The outbreak of war temporarily drove all these problems beneath Pirrie's horizon.

7
MONITORS AND A MODERN NOAH
1914-18

When war was declared on 4 August 1914, it was assumed that the hostilities would be shortlived. No preparations had been made for a long campaign. There were no detailed plans for the procurement of war material and little consideration had been given to the effect war would have on commerce and industry. Merchant shipbuilding firms, like Harland & Wolff, which had no Admiralty work on hand, were immediately disadvantaged as supplies were diverted to yards with naval vessels under construction. Lack of materials caused production to slow down or even halt, and that in turn led many men to enlist, in the belief that their civilian skills would not be required in the war effort.

In the first week of the war Pirrie shared this view, suggesting that work on several contracts should be suspended and all the yards placed on half-time working. His managing directors did not agree, preferring a progressive reduction in the number of men rather than half-time working which they feared would result in the loss of men 'whom it is important for us to keep'. Night shifts at Belfast and Glasgow were stopped at once. J.W. Kempster, as chairman of the managing directors, urgently reviewed progress on all the contracts on the order book. The Company's ability to proceed with work was made more difficult by its commitments to the troubled IMM. Pirrie, on 13 August, imposed tight cash limits on new building work and halted the ambitious scheme for reconstructing the Govan yard, with the exception of work on the new framing shop in Water Row, which was allowed to continue. Nevertheless, Kempster and his colleagues were determined to maintain the building programme at as high a level as possible in an attempt to keep as many men employed as they could. At their meeting on 2 September the managing directors, in Pirrie's presence, approved a scheme for continuing work on all thirty-two vessels under construction at either Belfast or Govan or subcontracted to Barclay Curle, a total which included nine vessels for IMM. This brave decision succeeded in preserving the Harland & Wolff workforce almost intact. At the end of July 1914 the Company employed a total of 24,425 people throughout the organisation. By the end of October this figure had only fallen to 18,412. Some of its competitors had lost almost half their workforce in the first weeks of the war. All those who joined the forces and found themselves less well off as a result were to have their wages made up by the Company for the duration of hostilities.

During the first three months of the war the Admiralty concentrated on the completion of the contracts placed in the previous three years with established naval builders. There was no attempt to award business to yards that had little experience of building naval vessels. Although Harland & Wolff owned the London & Glasgow yard at Govan, which had constructed light cruisers and destroyers for several years, no orders were placed with the Company. However, in October Harland & Wolff was given the unusual task of converting ten cargo liners into dummy battleships for the Special Service Squadron. This enterprise was the product of the fertile mind of the First Lord of the Admiralty, Winston Churchill, who hoped the dummies could

be used to deceive the enemy about the strength and the whereabouts of the Grand Fleet. Pirrie welcomed the challenge. He deployed 2,000 shipwrights and other skilled men on the tasks which involved the construction of wood and canvas dummy superstructures and the installation of false gun turrets. The artificial funnels were made to appear realistic by the installation of small hearths to produce smoke, and false stems and sterns had to be contrived – a difficult operation. So that the freeboard of the vessels would seem realistic, 34,000 tons of stone and iron ballast had to be loaded into their holds.

The first vessel for conversion, the Ellerman liner *City of Oxford*, arrived at Queen's Island on 30 October to be transformed into the battleship HMS *St Vincent*. She was followed on 3 November by the Royal Mail's *Oruba*, to be converted into a replica of the battleship HMS *Orion*. By 5 November seven vessels were in the course of conversion. On 3 November Harland & Wolff received its first war casualty, the *Olympic*, which had been damaged the week before in an unsuccessful attempt to tow the stricken battleship HMS *Audacious* to Belfast. The liner was taken out of service and requisitioned for conversion into a troopship. Her fittings were removed and stored at Belfast. Churchill instructed that the loss of HMS *Audacious* should remain a secret and it was announced that she had arrived at Queen's Island for repair. So as to convince the enemy of the truth of this statement, the *Mountclan* was to be mocked up as HMS *Audacious*. Later in the month four more vessels were requisitioned for conversion. These included the American line's *Merion* which was to become the battle cruiser HMS *Tiger*. The first dummies were ready for service in the first week of December. They were to be formed into a squadron under the command of Commodore Herbert Haddock, the erstwhile master of the *Olympic*.[1]

One of the passengers on the *Olympic* had been Charles M. Schwab, president of the Bethlehem Steel Corporation of Pennsylvania, who was on his way to the Admiralty with an offer to place at its disposal his firm's skill in building submarines. His arrival coincided with the resignation of Prince Louis of Battenberg as First Sea Lord and the reappointment of Lord Fisher.

It was already evident that the war would last much longer than anticipated and that many new naval vessels of all types would be required to achieve victory. Fisher at once embarked on a massive building programme. Schwab was invited to build twenty submarines, and quizzed about other resources Bethlehem might have. He offered four twin 14-inch turrets that were nearing completion for a Greek battle cruiser under construction in Germany. Since Britain's gun-making and mounting capacity was at full stretch, Fisher accepted with alacrity. He planned to employ the guns in a novel type of vessel, christened a 'monitor', to be used to bombard the enemy coastline in support of a seaborne invasion. Rough design drawings had been prepared by 6 November and by the third week of the month Pirrie had agreed to build the first three vessels, which were to be given priority over all merchant work and delivered within five months.[2] On 1 December the keel of the first monitor (ship no. 476G/B) was laid at Govan. The other two were to be constructed at Queen's Island on berth no. 2, taking the place of the Red Star liner *Nederland* (ship no. 469). Since the outbreak of war only a minimum amount of work had been undertaken on the Red Star contract, with the exception of making frames 'in the shed to keep furnaces going'. The slip was cleared at great speed and the keels of the monitors laid on 12 December. The engines for the two Belfast monitors were to be constructed by Harland & Wolff, while the order for those for the Govan vessel was awarded to Mackie & Baxter, the Govan marine engineering firm. Two days later the light

The White Star liner *Olympic*, fitted out as a troopship. The large number of lifeboats was fitted to improve safety standards following the *Titanic* inquiry.

cruiser HMS *Venus* came in for repairs. This sudden influx of urgent Admiralty work placed great strain on the workforce. More men had to be recruited and by the end of the year the number employed had recovered to over 20,000. Overtime and weekend working were restored. At Pirrie's insistence the men were rested in batches on alternate weekends.

No sooner had work begun on these vessels than Fisher and the First Lord of the Admiralty, Winston Churchill, began enthusiastically to explore their use in a variety of theatres, particularly against the new enemy, Turkey. After feverish discussion during early December, it was decided to proceed with the construction of eight 12-inch-gun monitors. Pirrie volunteered to build five of these vessels (four at Belfast and one at Govan) and to manufacture specially designed twin-screw, triple-expansion sets of engines. The order for the engines of the Govan monitor was also transferred to Queen's Island. The keels of all five 12-inch-gun monitors were laid between 9 January and 1 February 1915.[3] At the same time a contract was placed for the 15-inch-gun light battle cruiser HMS *Glorious* of 22,354 displacement tons, the first of her class, which was to succeed the first two monitors on berth no. 2 at Belfast. Three ship numbers (482-4) were allocated to this vessel in an attempt to confuse the enemy as to its size. As if all this new construction work was not sufficient, the Company undertook early in January to overhaul and repair 'practically the whole of the Patrol squadron on the Irish coast'. The following month the first of four of the dummy battleships was returned for conversion, over the next sixteen months, into a special troop transport for the Dardanelles campaign.

Despite this growing weight of Admiralty contracts, work continued on those merchant vessels that were well advanced at the outbreak of war, partly to make space on the ways for the monitors. The *Mississippi*, for the Atlantic Transport Company, was delivered on 5 November 1914; the *Falstria*, for the East Asiatic Company, on 31 March 1915; and the *Apapa*, for the African Steamship Company, on 4 March 1915 – all from Govan. The *Mississippi* and the *Falstria* were the first ships completed by the Company to be fitted with oil engines, constructed at the Finnieston works of Burmeister & Wain. The *Almanzora* was launched from Belfast on 19 November 1914 and was followed by the *Belgenland*, renamed, less Germanically, *Belgic*, on the last day of the year. At Govan the *Bostonian*, renamed *Glengyle*, went down the ways on 19 January, with the *Montezuma*, renamed *Glenartney*, coming after on 14 April. Nothing is known of the work undertaken at Liverpool during the first six months of the war, but, since the number of people employed remained at just over 4,000, it can be safely assumed that the works was fully occupied with repair business. Although the workforce at Southampton fell from 1,800 to 1,300, it remained constant thereafter, presumably because the plant was heavily engaged in building naval pinnaces and carrying out repairs to the Channel flotillas.

From the beginning of 1915 many firms engaged in the construction of naval vessels and the manufacture of monitors encountered growing friction with their skilled employees over wage rates and the introduction of semi-skilled or unskilled workers to replace those who had joined the services. These difficulties, which were worst on Clydeside, passed Harland & Wolff by, almost certainly because of the wise tactics of the managers in retaining the skilled labour force in the early days of the war. The Company's traditions of a closed shop, of regular consultation between the managers and shop stewards and of better wages and conditions of service than many of its competitors made for an easy transition to the urgency of wartime production. In

The hull of HMS *Sir Thomas Picton*, a 12-inch-gun monitor under construction on no. 1 slip at Queen's Island in the spring of 1915.

179

mid-November the usual demarcation between the joiners and shipwrights was temporarily cancelled 'in connection with emergency Admiralty work on hand'. The managing directors constantly reviewed wage rates and hours, offering extra holidays 'to those who have had a specially arduous time'. On 17 February 1915, the day after serious labour unrest including strikes and demonstrations had broken out on the Clyde, it was decided to increase wages across the board by 10 per cent to reflect 'the extra cost of living', and to prevent any sympathy action, particularly at Govan. Rates for apprentices were raised correspondingly. The platers and riveters working on the monitors were awarded an extra 10 per cent as a productivity incentive. The following month generous bonuses were introduced for good time-keeping:

Piecework Platers, Riveters and Caulkers	2/6 per day
Holders-up	2/- per day
Boys	1/- per day
Helpers	1/3 per day

Towards the end of May all these bonuses were replaced by an across-the-board 7 per cent wage increase throughout the Company's works.

By this time the workforce was working incredibly long hours. In the week ending 27 April two shipwrights and three boilermakers worked over eighty-five hours each; twenty-nine shipwrights and forty-one boilermakers over eighty hours; and 893 shipwrights and 271 boilermakers between sixty and eighty hours. The managing directors, with the blessing of the Admiralty, looked to the union officials to help them recruit additional skilled labour for Admiralty work. In March the Belfast district delegate of the Boilermakers Society was asked by Harland & Wolff to find out 'what men Messrs Workman Clark & Company had at present on merchant work, as we should require suitable men to be transferred to us for Government work'. The Boilermakers Society was more than enthusiastic in enlisting additional workers. In May Harland & Wolff received a complaint from the Belfast works of Brunner Mond & Company to the effect that the shipyard had stolen twenty of that firm's boilermakers.

Although the strike on the Clyde in February had been decisively defeated by the end of the month, it had made the Government determined to bring the firms engaged on war work directly under its control. During March, Walter Runciman, the President of the Board of Trade, reached an agreement with fourteen armaments, shipbuilding, and engineering firms, including Harland & Wolff, 'for the limitation of excess profits'. This agreement was to provide the basis for the financial control exercised by the Government for the rest of the war. Runciman and Lloyd George held parallel discussions with the trade unions, who were persuaded to relax restrictive practices during the war, provided profits were curbed. After some delay, due to the necessity of getting the budget through Parliament and the formation of the coalition Government, the Ministry of Munitions was established on 26 May to oversee war production for military purposes and on 2 July the Munitions of War Act was passed.[4] Under its terms the Harland & Wolff works at Belfast, Glasgow, Liverpool and Southampton were declared 'controlled establishments'. The Ministry had wide powers over labour practices in such establishments and could, through local Munitions Councils, order men who misbehaved to the front. It had authority to raise from the owning companies an excess profits tax, assessed on the basis of the profits earned in the two years prior to the war. There were certain allowances, notably on capital projects expenditure, which could be set against the tax. Final

HMS *Sir Thomas Picton*
ready for launching on
30 September 1915.

settlement was to be made after the war. The management of 'controlled establishments' was left undisturbed but their actions were severely circumscribed. No longer could Harland & Wolff set its own wage rates or hours: these were to be fixed according to nationally agreed scales.

Meanwhile the Harland & Wolff workforce had responded magnificently to the challenge presented by the very short construction time allowed for the monitors. The first 14-inch-gun monitor was launched from Queen's Island on 25 April, followed by the other two on 29 April. Fisher was delighted and wrote to congratulate Pirrie. Already the First Sea Lord had been planning and ordering yet more monitors carrying 15-inch and 9.2-inch guns. Early in March 1915 a supply of ten 6-inch turrets became available when the secondary armour of the 'Queen Elizabeth'-class battleships was relocated. A new small monitor was designed at once and five vessels of the class were ordered, all from Harland & Wolff. Pirrie instructed his managers to lay down all five vessels on no. 5 slip, on either side of the keel of the P & O liner *Narkunda* (ship no. 471). In the event Pirrie contracted out two of the vessels and their machinery, ships nos 488WC and 489WC, to Workman Clark. The keels of

181

HMS *Earl of Peterborou[g]*
on the day of her launc[h]
26 August 1915. The ve[ssel]
was delivered a month
later on 23 September.

the remaining three were laid on 23 March, only a week after the yard had received notice of the order.[5] Early in April the Admiralty took over the Pacific Steam Navigation Company's *Orduna* (ship no. 440) and the Royal Mail's *Almanzora* (ship no. 441) for conversion into armed merchant cruisers. Later in the month orders for two fast anti-submarine patrol boats were allocated to the Govan yard. On 18 May a contract was placed with the same yard for two 15-inch-gun monitors. The first keel (ship no. 492G/B) was laid on 5 June; but on 10 June the order was cancelled as the turret was required for the battleship HMS *Royal Oak*.[6] The first 14-inch-gun monitor, HMS *Admiral Farragut* (later *Abercrombie*), was delivered on 29 May, less than six months after the keel was laid. By the end of June all three 14-inch-gun monitors had been handed over. By mid-July three of the 12-inch-gun monitors had been launched and one, HMS *Lord Clive,* completed. By the end of the month all five 6-inch-gun monitors had been commissioned. The other four 12-inch-gun monitors were delivered between August and mid-November 1915.[7] This staggering achievement left Queen's Island short of Admiralty contracts in the autumn and allowed work to be resumed on some of the merchant hulls awaiting completion, including the *Britannic* for White Star.

The avalanche of naval orders, which were paid for in advance on a cost-plus or commission basis, brought welcome relief to Harland & Wolff's strained finances. At the end of the financial year the problems which Sir Edward Holden, the managing

Table 7.1
Capital 1915-18

	1915	1916	1917	1918
	£	£	£	£
Ordinary shares	600,000	600,000	600,000	1,000,000
Preference shares	177,511	195,011	270,456	281,074
Loans and deposits bearing interest	549,334	509,571	593,089	961,607
Loans over £10,000				
African Steamship Co.	—	—	—	25,890
Sir William Arrol & Co.	89,568	—	—	—
John Brown & Co.	14,579	—	—	—
Caird & Co.	—	—	100,000	74,763
A.M. Carlisle	12,963	2,723	—	—
James Dugdale	30,604	—	—	—
Thomas Firth & Sons	—	—	150,000	—
Gallaher Ltd	40,000	—	—	—
Mrs L.E. Harland	—	11,000	12,000	10,000
Executors of Lady Harland	34,940	39,640	34,014	27,362
Johnston Hughes	10,125	10,125	10,125	10,125
A&J Inglis	—	—	—	30,540
Ocean Transport Co.	69,077	197,975	197,400	200,293
H&W Nelson	—	—	—	500,000
W.J. Pratten	10,814	9,122	—	5,305
Mary K. Purcell	—	10,383	10,159	7,804
Executors of G.W. Wolff	27,846	—	—	—
R. Crighton	11,115	6,946	8,881	8,878
Union Discount Co.	100,000	—	—	—
Elder Dempster	—	152,102	—	—

Table 7.2
Profit and loss 1915-18

	Gross profit/(loss) for year before tax and depreciation	Net profit/(loss) per published accounts after tax and depreciation	Distribution (transfers to/from reserves and dividends)	Balance carried to following year
	£	£	£	£
1915	298,167	193,911	60,288	211,790
1916	520,578	111,256	178,376	144,670
1917	529,051	154,930	163,980	135,620
1918	930,818	236,916	170,761	201,775

Table 7.3
Fixed assets 1915-18

	Additions	Depreciation	Total
	£	£	£
1915	143,181	100,308	1,137,240
1916	102,777	163,874	1,076,142
1917	645,533	109,518	1,612,158
1918	1,088,742	128,289	2,572,611

Table 7.4
Reserves 1915-18

	1915	1916	1917	1918
	£	£	£	£
Reserve[1]	210,000	280,000	365,000	650,000
Reserve against losses on contracts	18,032	18,032	18,032	18,032
Reserve for expenditure on additions	14,104	14,104	14,104	14,104
Reserve for repairs etc. at Southampton	1,068	1,253	1,447	1,652
Reserve for investment in IMM (Investment reserve account)	371,392	451,064	451,064	460,837
Depreciation reserve	—	54,723	54,723	54,723
Income tax account reserve for excess profits tax	—	—	264,603	547,177

Note
1 Transfers to this account were made out of the balance brought forward on the balance-sheet profit.

Table 7.5
Bank balances 1915-18

	London City & Midland Bank[1]	Belfast Banking Co.[1]	Clydesdale Bank[1]	Lloyds Bank	Bank of Ireland	National Bank of Scotland
	£	£	£	£	£	£
1915	4,965	—	—	5,027	(87,027)	(54,902)
1916	150,196	—	—	27	(2,011)	28,778
1917	(401,453)	(188,853)	—	27	(41,970)	(60,549)
1918	(463,047)	(141,194)	(43,172)	27	(223,396)	(14,297)

Notes
1 In 1917 the London City & Midland Bank acquired the Belfast Banking Co. and the Clydesdale Bank and changed its name to Midland Bank Ltd.
( ) = Debit balance

Table 7.6
Bills receivable discounted 1915-18

	£
1915	755,000
1916	25,000
1917	—
1918	—

director of the London City & Midland Bank, had forcibly called to Pirrie's attention eighteen months before, were, for the moment, things of the past. The overdrafts had been slashed from almost £231,500 to just under £142,000. Frightened by Holden's onslaught, Pirrie had taken care to keep his London City & Midland account in the black, leaving his indebtedness with the Bank of Ireland and the National Bank of Scotland. The contingent liability on discounted bills receivable had fallen by two-thirds to £756,000. All the outstanding bills were now drawn on associated companies. The loans to the Company remained level, and profits almost doubled to reach a record £193,910. Despite the disruption caused by the outbreak of war, over £143,000 was spent on capital additions during the year, principally in extending the generating station at Queen's Island and on completing the large Water Row framing shop at Govan, which cost nearly £76,000. By the time the results were made known to the shareholders at the annual general meeting on 30 October, Pirrie had even better news. Earlier in the year IMM had been placed in receivership under the supervision of a committee of bond-holders. Their stewardship, fortified by unprecedented wartime demand for tonnage, rapidly restored IMM to health. In August the committee was able to place before the bond-holders proposals for reorganising the combine.[8] These were adopted and the bonds once more became marketable at a price above their entry in the Harland & Wolff balance sheet. On 11 November the principals of Harland & Wolff, Pirrie, J.W. Kempster, John Sampson and Lord Aberconway (who had just replaced Charles Ellis as the other John Brown representative), decided to sell the whole of the Company's stake in the combine as soon as possible.

The respite in Admiralty work was only temporary. During August a contract for two 'R'-class destroyers was placed at Govan, with the machinery being supplied from Belfast. The keels of both ships were laid on F slip before the end of the month. At the end of August three more of the dummy battleships arrived at Belfast to be dismantled and converted into water-carriers. On 29 September the order for the two 15-inch-gun monitors with Govan, which had been cancelled in June, was revived, but to altered designs. Instead of both vessels being built at Govan, one was to be laid down at Belfast and all the machinery was to be constructed there. In October the Admiralty requisitioned the *Britannic* for conversion as a hospital ship. This work was completed by 8 December, when she left Belfast to be turned into a troopship. Towards the end of the year four additional 'R'-class destroyers were allocated to Govan. The machinery of these vessels, along with that for the cruiser HMS *Effingham*, building at the Royal Naval Dockyard in Devonport, was to be manufactured at Queen's Island. At the same time four 50-foot steam launches were ordered. Early in 1916 the machinery for another cruiser, HMS *Curacao*, was ordered from Belfast. This was followed in the spring by a contract for the hull and machinery of the light cruiser HMS *Cavendish* to be built at Belfast on no. 2 slip, from which HMS *Glorious* was launched on 20 April. At about the same time another patrol boat was allotted to Govan, and instructions were received to complete the Holland-America liner *Statendam* as a troopship. On 18 May 1916 the *Britannic* returned to Queen's Island to be converted back into a hospital ship over the next three months. Apart from the *Britannic*, three diesel-engined vessels were delivered during the 1915/16 financial year to make way for naval contracts: the *Lalandia*, renamed the *Kangaroo*, for the Western Australian Government and the *Glengyle* and the *Glenartney*, both for the Glen line.

While the Company was shouldering this additional burden of national service,

many of the armaments concerns and shipbuilding firms were finding it hard to fulfil their wartime obligations due to a combination of restrictive practices and shortages of skilled labour. Throughout the second half of 1915, attempts by the Ministry of Munitions to enforce the dilution of labour – admitting unskilled workers to trades – were resisted, particularly on the Clyde where there was the added problem of serious disruption due to widespread agitation over increases in house rents. As earlier in the year, these problems scarcely affected Harland & Wolff. Unlike some other employers, Lord Pirrie was much too experienced a manager of labour to seek open confrontation with the unions. Having retained its labour pool in the first weeks of the war, Harland & Wolff suffered no sudden addition to its workforce of large numbers of men with no experience of shipbuilding. Between January and December 1915 the number of people employed by the Company as a whole rose only from 20,632 to 22,379. Following the declaration of the Company's works as controlled establishments, the managers rejected the Ministry's pressure to railroad the unions into accepting the relaxation of demarcation, and the dilution of trades. Early in August there were complaints because the management assumed that the agreement to waive demarcation between the joiners and shipwrights on Admiralty work (made the previous year) could be extended, without consultation, to new contracts.

Although 'it was realised that, notwithstanding all that had transpired during the war, it was still difficult to get the trades to work together', compulsion was not considered; instead the managers promised 'that in any future arrangement it would be well to submit the proposals to both Societies before confirming the settlement'. The Company, on Pirrie's instructions, responded sensitively to demands for increases in wages due to the rise in the cost of living, which could not be met without permission from the Ministry. By the end of the year they had hammered out settlements with all the trades, which were presented as a package to the Ministry.

These harmonious relations contrasted strongly with other firms. Towards the end of the year, in response to the protest against dilution, the Government reached an agreement with the unions which was put into effect in January 1916. Some employers, like Sir William Beardmore, saw the agreement as a chance to undermine the authority of the shop stewards. During the last week in March strikes against the forcible implementation of dilution broke out in several Clyde shops. These collapsed, but not before the men's leaders were arrested. Harland & Wolff's Govan works was not affected. On 1 February the manager reported that 'he had already four handymen working as fitters and receiving the full rate'. The Company as a whole refused to be rushed, preferring to confirm the agreement with its own union representatives. The managers firmly rejected proposals that dilution should include women, and even wrung from the Ministry the concession that 'We need not put the dilution scheme into force so long as we could get a reasonably sufficient supply of men.' These patient tactics were rewarded. The manager of the Govan works observed, 'We had 120 joiners doing shipwrights' work at Govan and no difficulties arose.' In the first week of June J.W. Kempster noted that, at Belfast, dilution of labour had been applied in the following trades, to the extent indicated:

For shipwrights' work – 67 joiners and cabinetmakers
For caulkers' work – 35 platers and a few riveters
For shipyard fitters' drilling work – 14 joiners

During the early months of 1916 Pirrie shifted his sights from the welter of Admiralty work towards the construction of new merchant vessels. It was now nearly two years since the outbreak of war, when merchant shipbuilding had come almost to a standstill. Pirrie, as a shipowner as well as a shipbuilder, realised that wartime sinkings, the requisitioning of ships for military purposes, and heavy use of vessels would result in a shortage of ships by the end of 1917, whether the war continued or not. He was convinced that the diesel engine had many advantages over steam-reciprocating engines, declaring that 'in no. 466G (*Glengyle*) the freedom from oil smell and vibration pointed to the possibility of adopting diesel engines in passenger ships as well as cargo boats'. In June he contracted with his friend Sir Owen Philipps to build no less than fifteen diesel-engined cargo boats for companies in the Royal Mail Group. He also secured an order for one vessel from the Bibby Steamship Company and one from G. & J. Burns. Seven of the seventeen ships were to be of a standard class (485 feet × 62.2 feet × 39.5 feet); three were smaller (482 feet × 58 feet × 38.3 feet); and two were larger (630 feet × 78.5 feet × 32 feet). The majority were to be built at Govan with engines supplied by Burmeister & Wain. Two of the hulls were subcontracted to John Brown's Clydebank yard, and two to the Pointhouse yard of A. & J. Inglis at the mouth of the river Kelvin on the upper Clyde. In addition, Pirrie arranged for two hulls for Lamport & Holt, another Group member, to be constructed by D. & W. Henderson's Meadowside yard, which was opposite Inglis across the Kelvin. He was also looking ahead to the postwar needs of the members of the commission club. He concluded a building agreement with P & O and its subsidiary, British India Steam Navigation Company. He reached a tentative treaty with the newly reconstructed IMM to build 'three vessels of 10,000 tons each, 16 knots speed for the Montreal trade; two Australian boats, something between "Ceramic" and "Afric" class; and a new *Norseman* and a new *Englishman* – all the foregoing to be steamships'. He persuaded IMM to allow him to convert the *Minnekahda* (ship no. 446), building for the Atlantic Transport Company, into a troopship. At the same time, in conjunction with John Brown and the Fairfield Shipbuilding & Engineering Company, Harland & Wolff's neighbours in Govan, he concluded a similar understanding with Canadian Pacific, obtaining permission from IMM for this agreement. The first in this massive programme of merchant ships was to be laid down as soon as possible, and the Company obtained permission from the Board of Trade to have them all classified as munitions work.

Pirrie was aware that there would be little possibility of completing the new merchant orders and fulfilling the commitments to Canadian Pacific and P & O, as well as the Admiralty and merchant contracts in progress, without increasing the capacity of the Belfast and Govan yards. After the inconclusive Battle of Jutland on 31 May 1916, the Ministry of Munitions had become sensitive to the Admiralty's urgent need for new tonnage and was prepared to make machinery and materials available for shipyard extensions. In April Pirrie had agreed a modest capital expenditure for the coming financial year; but early in June he announced the revival of the original scheme for the reconstruction of the Govan yard, which he hoped would be completed within a year. The yard was to be 'laid out for building ships suitable for diesel engines'. The following month he leased a large piece of ground on the east side of the Musgrave channel, adjacent to the Queen's Island yard, to provide additional storage. By September, with Admiralty approval, he was finalising plans for big extensions at all the Company's works. These included new buildings at both Southampton and Liverpool; a new timber shed and insulating department at the Alexandra Dock Works at Belfast; and an enormous new joiners' shop. As part of this work the berths at Belfast were numbered in reverse order and likewise the Govan slips, which had previously been referred to by letter, were numbered; G becoming no. 1 and A no. 7.

In October Pirrie found a more immediate way of enlarging the Company's capacity by purchasing for cash all the share capital of the Greenock firm, Caird & Company, which he had first been offered in 1911. Cairds had been established in the late eighteenth century, and enjoyed a special relationship with P & O for whom, like Harland & Wolff, they built on commission. Before making a formal bid, Pirrie 'had consulted Lord Inchcape and Sir Thomas Sutherland of the P & O Co', and was able to report that 'they looked favourably on the deal'. He also obtained permission from his majority shareholders, John Brown & Company, whose board he had recently joined. He offered them the opportunity to participate in the future direction of the yard, which they declined. J.W. Kempster was appointed managing director of the company which, like London & Glasgow, was to become a division of Harland & Wolff, using its ship numbers and being subject to Belfast practice with the 'no smoking' rule during working hours. The purchase price was £432,493. At the same time Pirrie persuaded Burmeister & Wain to sell Harland & Wolff its stake in Burmeister & Wain (Diesel System) Oil Engine Company for £100,000. This concern

ing out the light cruiser HMS *Glorious* (ship no. 82/3/4 – three numbers were allocated to this vessel in an attempt to disguise its size), in the autumn of 1916. The gantic Benrather crane, delivered in 1908 and able of lifting 150 tons, is alongside.

had been formed in 1912 to acquire the Lancefield Engine Works from the London & Glasgow Engineering & Iron Shipbuilding Company: this transaction had never been settled (see page 156). The purchase allowed Harland & Wolff to cancel this debt, which was secured by a bill of £25,000 – the only outstanding contingent liability at the end of the 1915/16 financial year. Pirrie financed these acquisitions out of the funds released by the sale of the IMM bonds, which had been completed by the end of May.

In presenting the accounts to the annual general meeting at the end of October 1916, Pirrie gave no hint of the underlying financial strength of the Company as a result of the removal of the burden of the IMM shareholding. Instead he asked the meeting to sanction the issue of a further £200,000 of preference shares, and simply stated that there was almost £175,000 at the credit of the profit and loss account. Despite his reticence, Pirrie must have been cock-a-hoop at the improvement in the Company's financial condition over the previous eighteen months. The overdrafts had been cancelled, with £150,000 at the credit of the London City & Midland account, and nearly £29,000 on deposit with the National Bank of Scotland. Only the Bank of Ireland account remained overdrawn, but for the tiny sum of £2,011. Apart from the normal 10 per cent depreciation, the Government had allowed an extra 5 per cent (nearly £55,000) to take account of the additional wear and tear on the plant caused by the high wartime turnover.

The reserve had been bolstered by £70,000, and the reserve for investment in IMM, no longer needed for the purpose for which it had been created, had increased to £451,064. Although the loans to the Company had fallen by only £40,000 to just under £510,000, their composition had changed. Many of the small lenders had either switched their investments to preference shares or been paid out. James Dugdale, who had been a lender since loans were first raised, had died, and his heir had withdrawn his £30,000, which had been advanced as long ago as 1903. Likewise, G.W. Wolff's executors had ceased to be lenders. Since the bill market had been diverted to financing the Government's wartime expenditure, Union Discount had taken out its £100,000 loan as Harland & Wolff wound up its outstanding bills. Their place had been taken by big advances from associated companies – nearly £129,000 from the Ocean Transport Company and £152,102 from Elder Dempster. Despite the cutback in the re-equipment programme made at the beginning of the war, over £100,000 had been spent on new additions during the year, of which £42,500 had been laid out on equipping the Water Row framing shop and £19,000 on machines for the engine works at Belfast that were urgently needed for the war effort.

Pirrie's motive in underplaying the Company's strong cash position and raising additional capital was not hard to find. On 1 December 1916 he informed his colleagues on the John Brown board that he planned to buy the Motherwell steel company of David Colville & Sons, which supplied Harland & Wolff with the bulk of its ship plates. The bid failed, due to a difference of opinion over the valuation of the plant with the energetic young managing director, John Craig, who had recently taken command following the sudden deaths of two members of the Colville family.[9] However, there were other firms on Pirrie's shopping list. Early in 1917 he told his fellow principals that he had purchased for £397,466 all the ordinary shares of the two Clyde shipbuilding firms to which he had subcontracted merchant contracts the previous year – A. & J. Inglis, of Pointhouse, and D. & W. Henderson, of Meadowside. For the time being both companies were to remain independent, using their own hull numbers. These takeovers, which were to remain confidential, were to be financed immediately from Harland & Wolff's cash resources, but in the long run by raising the ordinary share capital from £600,000 to £1,000,000 at the annual meeting in October. This further slice of capacity was to be deployed, like the Caird yard, in supporting Pirrie's ambitious programme of merchant shipbuilding. However, by the time the bids were agreed the Government had assumed direct control of all new merchant construction through the Ministry of Shipping established on 19 December 1916.

From midsummer there had been mounting criticism of existing provision for building new merchant ships. There was growing support in the shipping and shipbuilding industry and in Parliament for accelerating output by the construction of a fleet of standard ships with interchangeable parts. In July some shipowners were so exasperated with the failure of the Government to respond to this pressure that they planned a shipyard at Chepstow to construct nothing but standard vessels. Pressure for standard shipbuilding was fuelled by the increased deployment of U-boats against merchant ships in the last three months of the year. Sinkings more than doubled, from 80,000 tons a month to 175,000 tons. By December, when Sir Joseph MacLay, a partner in the Glasgow shipping firm of MacLay & McIntyre, was appointed Shipping Controller, the situation was critical. He at once initiated a massive scheme for the construction of standard ships for the Government. Work on all existing merchant contracts was suspended, with the exception of tankers and meat ships, and new contracts from private owners were prohibited for the duration

of hostilities.[10] It was natural that MacLay should look to Pirrie for help. Harland & Wolff and its new subsidiary, D. & W. Henderson, worked at incredible speed to design the first two standard class vessels, 'A' and 'B'. Both types were 400 feet × 52 feet × 31 feet, and of 3,030 gross tons. The only difference was that class 'A' was a single-decked freighter while class 'B' had a second deck.[11] By the third week of January 1917, Pirrie was making preparations to lay down three of the vessels at Belfast, two at Greenock, and two at Govan. The keels of the first two ships were laid during February.

Eleven merchant ships on order from Harland & Wolff escaped the Shipping Controller's embargo: five from Belfast; three from Govan; two subcontracted to Barclay Curle; and one to A. & J. Inglis. Most of these were requisitioned by the Admiralty as troopships, and had to be completed to clear the berths for standard ships. The other outstanding orders were laid aside until the end of hostilities. Pirrie, anxious to secure Harland & Wolff's position after the war, continued negotiations with his shipowning friends. The shipowners, forbidden to place new orders and with most of their tonnage either requisitioned or engaged in arduous war service, were troubled by rumours of nationalisation or the continued operation by the Government of its new fleet of standard ships after the emergency was past. In the circumstances, Pirrie's offer of long-term building agreements and continued membership of the commission club was very welcome news. The agreement with Canadian Pacific was completed during March. John Brown, Fairfield and Harland & Wolff were 'to undertake all their building work . . . excepting as regards two small boats built at Denny's, which under certain circumstances may be repeated'. Simultaneously the understanding with P & O was extended to include the Greenock yard. P & O reserved the right to place, through Pirrie, one contract at a time with William Denny & Brothers of Dumbarton. Lord Pirrie explained to his managing directors on 12 March: 'At present the contract was to have two ships always building with Harland & Wolff Ltd, but now that we have taken Cairds, the contract will be changed so that they would keep Cairds fully occupied.' He added almost as an afterthought:

> A few days before leaving London [I] had concluded important arrangements with Sir Owen Philipps, who had entered into a contract with us for ten years (with five years' notice of termination) on behalf of the companies of which he is Chairman or with which he is associated, including Royal Mail, Lamport & Holt, Elder Dempster, Union-Castle and others, to place all their building with us.

He was able to tell the meeting that the Royal Mail Group had 'within the last fortnight' formed a new constituent company, Coast Lines Limited, to provide local connections with the main ocean lines. With such a store of work, Pirrie was able to dispel any doubts his senior management may have had about the need to extend the business.

Pirrie recognised that the management structure which had served so well since 1907 was no longer suitable if he was to hold the Company's seven works on a tight rein. At the same meeting that he told his managing directors of the new building agreements, he announced a new management structure. Three new works' committees were to be formed 'to meet the developments of the different establishments' at Belfast, the Clyde district, and at Liverpool and Southampton. They were to be chaired either by Pirrie or by a resident principal. The loyal Kempster, as managing director of Cairds, was to take command of the Clyde district; George Cuming was promoted to be principal, taking Kempster's place at Belfast; and Robert Crighton was made principal in charge of Liverpool and Southampton. The committee of managing directors was to continue, with Pirrie as chairman. He would call meetings, when necessary, 'to discuss general questions of policy, works developments, organisation or other matters affecting any of the works'. Pirrie made it clear that no capital expenditure could be made without his approval, and ordered that all purchases be made through the central contracts and buying department in Belfast. In April, when these changes were ratified, Pirrie thanked his managing directors for their loyal support; but he drew their attention to an extract from a recent speech by Sir William Robertson, Chief of the Imperial General Staff, which he considered 'appropriate to the circumstances of a concern like Harland & Wolff'. He even had it recorded in the minutes, so that the managing directors could remind themselves of its contents:

> On taking up a staff appointment your first object must be to obtain the confidence of your chief and you might do worse than begin by remembering

that you yourself are not the chief but the chief's agent and assistant. The extent to which he will entrust you depends largely upon yourself . . . Learn to take 'No' for an answer. The business of a staff officer is to put a case as it arises fully before his General and to make appropriate and practical suggestions for dealing with it. The General then decides, and when he has done that it is for the staff officer whole-heartedly to devote his efforts to carrying out the decisions whether it is in accordance with his suggestions or is opposed to them.

At the end of this homily, Kempster expressed his and his colleagues' pleasure at 'working under Lord Pirrie's guidance and their feeling that no arrangement could be more happily conceived in the interest of the Company than that which now formally recorded his Lordship's position at the head of every phase of its activities'.

While Pirrie had been shaping the framework for the Company's postwar order book and management, the development of unrestricted U-boat warfare on 1 February had taken a heavy toll of British and allied shipping. The losses for April, the peak of the campaign, totalled 555,056 gross tons, while new production was only 69,711 gross tons. Britain was in danger of being starved into submission. The Royal Navy, which since the outbreak of war had steadfastly set its face against organising convoys of merchant ships, reluctantly changed its mind. As the sinkings mounted, the Admiralty belatedly took action to accelerate the building programme. On 20 April all shipbuilders were wired:

> Assuming you got all materials you require for present commitments, what is maximum number of men you could employ . . .? Assuming materials available and with Admiralty demands continuing as now to what extent could you increase your present output of merchant work?

Pirrie was equal to the challenge, estimating that output could be raised by a half. The Belfast works' committee wired back:

> We could take additional 1,000 men in shipyard and 300 in engine works . . . Shipyard could increase forty per cent taking additional 5,000 men to fully man up continuous night shift. Engine works could keep pace with additional 1,500 men. Additional machines and extensions of shops would be necessary in both departments.

Early in May the Government Department of Deputy Controller for Auxiliary Shipbuilding was formed to take control of all merchant shipbuilding and repair. The young Lt. Colonel James Lithgow, whose family business Russell & Company had been building standard ships at Port Glasgow on the lower Clyde since the late 1870s, was appointed Director of Merchant Shipbuilding. He at once announced a massive increase in the standard-ship programme, with a production target for the forthcoming year of a staggering 3 million tons, rising to 4 million the year after.[12] Taking Pirrie at more than his word, orders for sixteen more 'A' and 'B'-class and two 'D'-class standard ships were allocated to Harland & Wolff. The first keels of this second contract were laid out at Belfast on 26 May. In the midst of the crisis, on 21 June, the first standard ship to be built by any shipyard in the United Kingdom was launched from the Belfast yard, ship no. 520, *War Shamrock*.[13]

There were many obstacles in the way of the management's efforts to raise production. There had already been short stoppages at Govan over some of the pay rates for work on standard ships. These skirmishes continued, symptomatic of more

general unease on the Clyde. Although there were no strikes at Belfast, arbitrators had to be called in to adjudicate in demarcation quarrels, and on rates. In the spring of 1916 it had taken almost six months and several mass meetings to conclude a dilution contract with the shipwrights on the understanding that 'no shipwright would be paid off, if his work and conduct were satisfactory, for twelve months after the last man who had been brought in from any other trade for shipwrights' work had been paid off'. Throughout 1917 the management had constantly to make small concessions to hold the confidence of the workforce. For example, in July E.J. Harrison, the Belfast secretary of the Federation of Sailmakers of Great Britain and Ireland, complained:

> If you could only see some of the jobs that is given to your sailmakers such as repairing coal bags that has been used coaling ships and dirt bags for shipyard use canvas slings full of filth and tarpaulin that is almost rotten and your old office mats full of dust we don't grumble at any of this and we understand there is no allowance for it that it is all shipyard expense.

George Cuming at once agreed an allowance of a halfpenny per hour dirt money.[14]

The launch of the first standard merchant ship *War Shamrock*, from Queen's Island on 21 June 1917.

HMS *Cavendish*, a cruiser, later renamed HMS *Vindictive* and commissioned as a seaplane carrier, shortly before her launch on January 1918 from no. 2 at Queen's Island. The flight deck is being constructed towards the aft of the ship.

The Company's good relations with its workforce were disturbed in the late summer of 1917 by the Government's newly formed Shipyard Labour Department. The formation of this department encouraged the unions to push the shipbuilders into making concessions. In September such advice caused a strike of plumbers at Queen's Island. The management remained emphatic that they could not go beyond an award made by an arbitrator, nor could they 'dismiss the Head Foreman over an incident that occurred two years ago without any complaint having been lodged'. The men accepted this decision and dismissed their branch secretary. The *Queen's Island Annual*, published at Christmas 1917, testified to the good-humoured way in which the staff and workforce had accepted the ever increasing burden during the year:

THINGS WE WOULD LIKE TO KNOW
How the devil a fellow can do double the work of pre-wartime in half the time allowed then?
Suggestions and advice will be gratefully received by the H & W (Harrassed & Worried) Time Office Staff.

The Admiralty had led the Company to believe that extra labour would be directed to its yards for merchant work; but, on receiving the additional orders, Pirrie was told that he would have to recruit the men required himself. This blow was not as heavy as it might have been, as the Company had been building up its workforce steadily since the beginning of the year. Almost 2,000 new workers had been enlisted and more skilled men were being released from the colours to join them. A more serious threat to the production schedule was the Admiralty's decision to transform ship no. 500, HMS *Cavendish*, into a seaplane carrier, necessitating alterations to the hull to give greater stability, which would delay the launch from Queen's Island no. 2 berth for three months. This berth, covered by the most recent and efficient gantry, was urgently needed for the standard ships on order.

The conversion of HMS *Cavendish* reflected the increasing use of aircraft in the war. The night bombing of England, which began in the early summer of 1917, forced the Government to strengthen air protection. Pirrie once more answered the emergency call, volunteering to open an aeroplane works at Belfast. Within a few days the old model office had become an aircraft drawing office, the ships' electric store had 'been cleared entirely and was available for erecting fuselages', and the joiners' shop had started work on a batch of de Havilland 6 machines. The works' joint committee of the Furniture Trades Union was drawing up lists of its members

196

in Belfast who could be employed on the first contract, which was to be completed in six to eight weeks. Pirrie reckoned that building aircraft would encourage 'the standardisation of fittings and joinery work in other directions'. This was not the only fresh burden that the Company shouldered in the summer of 1917. Shortage of aircraft was paralleled by an equivalent lack of submarines, needed to attack German coastal shipping. In carrying the war almost to the enemy's shores many vessels were badly damaged, and Pirrie agreed to provide a rapid reconditioning service at Belfast. By the end of October eight submarines had arrived for major repairs.

At the end of the financial year the Company's vast new commitments had consumed all its liquidity. The overdrafts totalled almost £693,000. The largest advance was one of £401,453 on the Company's London City & Midland Bank 'War Loan and Special Account', to meet the cost of purchasing A. & J. Inglis and D. & W. Henderson. This advance was made on the understanding that the Company cancel its joint subscription with John Brown for £3 million of war loan. In addition the Company's ordinary account with the Midland was overdrawn by £190,000. This was entered in the ledger under the heading 'Cinnabar', the London City & Midland's telegraphic address, because it had been arranged that, when payments in excess of £100,000 were cleared, Belfast was to be notified by cable. Although the issued preference share capital had been raised by £75,000, the loans to the Company had advanced by nearly £85,000. The advance from Elder Dempster had been replaced by a loan of £150,000 from John Brown's associate company Thomas Firth & Sons, and Caird & Company had made £100,000 available to its parent. Nevertheless, the Company's financial health was still good. The record declared that profits for the year of £154,408 had been calculated, after £90,000 had been set aside for excess profits tax. £85,000 from the profits was credited to the reserve and, presumably, deployed to fund capital projects. £645,533 had been laid out on capital additions during the year, more than half the book value of the existing plant. The biggest item of expenditure had been the re-equipment of the Govan works. At the annual meeting it was agreed to raise the ordinary share capital to £1 million worth of £1,000 shares. John Brown & Company volunteered to subscribe half of the additional capital, so as to maintain its majority shareholding.

On 20 August 1917 the first standard ship to enter service, the *War Shamrock*, was delivered by Harland & Wolff to the operating Company, Thomas Dixon & Sons of Belfast. The King wired Sir Joseph MacLay:

> Heartily congratulate you and Harland & Wolff that the first standard ship has been completed and gone to sea. I trust that she will arrive safely at her destination and be followed by many others.

By the end of the year four standard ships had been completed at Queen's Island and one at Govan. Shortly after the formation of the Department of Deputy Controller of Auxiliary Shipbuilding, it became obvious that the production targets could be achieved only by an enormous increase in capacity. Every shipbuilding firm in the country was invited to make proposals for investment to be paid for by grants representing the difference between the prewar price and wartime price for the work. Bridge builders and structural engineers with no shipbuilding experience were called on to build prefabricated sections for a new no. 2 standard design. The embryo Chepstow yard was taken over in September to become the first National Shipyard, which was followed almost at once by two more on the Severn.[15] The Deputy

The 'A'-type standard s...
War Clover, on trials in
September 1917.

Controller of Auxiliary Shipbuilding, Major General Collard, by threatening to form
such yards in other parts of the country, forced the shipbuilders to embark on massive
extensions. He told Pirrie that unless he built a new yard at Belfast the Government
would have to open one of its own in Ulster. Pirrie characteristically obliged. By
2 October forty-one acres had been leased from the Harbour Commissioners on the
east side of the Musgrave channel (originally intended for a new Corporation power
station), and plans had been prepared for a six-berth east yard to cost almost
£600,000. This was to be complemented by a new fitting-out quay to the north east
of the Thompson dock, built by the Harbour Commissioners. At the same time the
Govan reconstruction scheme was extended. Additional ground was acquired so that
the south platers' shed could be enlarged and a building put up to accommodate
women workers who had been recruited to carry out light duties in the workshops.
Women had been employed from about 1900 as secretaries and 'female tracers' in
the drawing office. The Finnieston Engine Works, which had been switched to the
construction of standard steam-reciprocating engines, was to be extended to match
Govan's increased capacity. At Liverpool more land was purchased for a

The massive new joiners' shop being built at Belfast in 1918.

boatbuilding yard to cost £83,000, and at Southampton new buildings, including a canteen for women workers, were authorised at a cost of £74,000.[16] Simultaneously Pirrie, with his friend Sir Owen Philipps, purchased the Dumbarton shipyard of Archibald MacMillan & Son, through Lamport & Holt (a Royal Mail Group member). Pirrie was appointed managing director and the management of the yard was entrusted to Harland & Wolff.

The pressure on the Company to build the east yard was followed a month later by an urgent order from the Air Board to provide facilities for building the new Handley Page V/1500 heavy bomber which was to be used in retaliatory raids on Berlin. The first three were to be constructed under the personal supervision of Handley Page, the founder of the company which bore his name. Another new joiners' workshop, 595 feet long with two 120-foot bays, was constructed with a view to beginning mass production by March 1918. Since the Government agreed to meet the whole cost of the plant and machinery, Pirrie could not refuse. In February 1918 the Company was instructed to stop building de Havilland 6 types after a hundred planes had been delivered, and to concentrate on an order for 300 Avros and 20

V/1500 aircraft. Pirrie was told to acquire land for an aerodrome to used as an 'acceptance port' for these planes. Accordingly he and George Cuming purchased the 170-acre Aldergrove farm in Co. Antrim to the north of Belfast. This site had first been reconnoitred by Sholto Douglas, who had been sent to Ireland in the summer of 1917 to find suitable locations for aerodromes.[17] The enthusiastic response of the Company to the challenge of air-frame manufacture earned the admiration of the newly appointed Secretary of State for Air, Sir William Weir, and of Handley Page.

Late in 1917 the Government took a bold initiative to solve its shortage of tonnage by offering to purchase all the British ships in the IMM combine. In December Pirrie and Philipps were commissioned to make an offer. On 10 January 1918, through the Royal Mail's London solicitors, Ashurst Morris & Crisp, they bid the vast sum of £27 million. Before the deal could proceed it was squashed by the United States Government, on the grounds that it was contrary to the US national interest.[18] By this time most of the ships that were under construction at Belfast and Govan when the standard-ship programme commenced had been cleared from the ways. HMS *Cavendish* was launched on 17 January, freeing no. 2 slip, and the Government ordered that work on the vessel was only to proceed 'as may suit the Company's merchant shipbuilding'. Nearly all the unfinished merchant hulls on the Company's books were completed for the Admiralty, providing much-needed transport for American servicemen. The Dominion line's *Regina* (ship no. 454G/B) and the Canadian Pacific liners *Melita* and *Minnedosa* (ships nos 463BC and 464BC) were fitted out at Queen's Island as troopships.

The Company was now free to concentrate solely on building standard ships. By the end of March 1918 two more vessels had been delivered and six launched. During October and November orders had been placed for an additional eleven standard vessels; five 'A' or 'B' types; three 'G' types; and four prefabricated 'N' (no. 2) types. The keel of the first of this batch (ship no. 540) was laid on Belfast no. 1 slip on 22 November. Despite efforts to reduce the amount of repair work undertaken at Belfast, production was interrupted by a continuous stream of Admiralty vessels arriving for overhaul. In the first three months of 1918 six destroyers and a submarine were sent to the yard for refit. In common with other shipyards, the Company found itself short of shipwrights and platers. Efforts were made to persuade the shipwrights and joiners to relax once again the demarcation between the two trades, and caulkers were used for some plating jobs. As far as possible the managers resisted attempts by the Shipyard Labour Department to enforce further dilution, preferring, as before, to negotiate with the unions for the relaxation of demarcation. In March thirty-nine cabinet makers and six drillers were allowed to perform on the standard ships tasks normally reserved for shipwrights. Relations with the trades were improved by the formation on 1 April of a pension fund open to foremen after twenty years' service and to leading hands after thirty years. Although the entry qualifications appeared arduous, a large proportion of the workforce was entitled to join.

During March, following the German offensive and the failure of the standard ship programme to achieve its target, Lloyd George invited Pirrie to accept the newly created post of Controller General of Merchant Shipbuilding. Pirrie agreed, provided he could continue as chairman of Harland & Wolff and hold his other directorships in the Royal Mail Group. He was the natural choice. He commanded the respect of both the shipbuilding and shipping industries, and Harland & Wolff had already built more standard ships than any other concern. He could give authority to the well laid plans of James Lithgow and allay the shipbuilders' anxiety about the postwar use of the National Shipyards. On his appointment Pirrie was asked what staff he would need. He informed the astonished First Lord of the Admiralty that all he required was Iris Edmiston, his secretary, who had been with him for some years.[19] Nevertheless he was allocated, as his ADC, Captain A.T. Marshall, who before joining the army had worked in the secretarial division of the Mersey Port and Docks Board. By this time Pirrie liked to conduct most of his business either sitting on an easy chair or lying on a large *chaise longue* with his papers spread about him. He reportedly disliked formal offices with desks and straight-back chairs, preferring a more relaxed atmosphere.[20] On his appointment as Controller, Pirrie was forced to delegate some of his responsibilities at Belfast. He chose to appoint George Cuming, the engine works manager, as deputy chairman and to replace him with Frederick Rebbeck, manager of the Burmeister & Wain engine works at Finnieston. Henry P. Harland was transferred from Govan to the London office as the chairman's personal assistant. However, Cuming, like Kempster before him, was not given access to the private ledger containing the essential financial information for the overall management of the business. This ledger continued to be made up by the chief accountant, William Tawse, and was kept in the chairman's London office.

Pirrie's priority was to involve the shipbuilding trade unions, as well as the shipyard management, in monitoring productivity. To this end he established joint

Handley Page V/1500
ber after a test flight at
Aldergrove in 1918.

district and national output committees between the Shipbuilders' Employers' Federation and the Shipyard Trade Unions Joint Committee. He made certain these committees were working efficiently by regularly touring the yards. He exhausted his staff on these expeditions, inspecting four or five shipyards a day. The shortage of skilled men persuaded him to place the introduction of labour-saving equipment, particularly pneumatic riveting plant, ahead of a shipyard extension scheme. In July capital grants were discontinued, except for machinery that would raise productivity. Pirrie remained uneasy about the dilution proposals made by the Shipyard Labour Department, preferring the policy, pursued by Harland & Wolff, of negotiating the relaxation of demarcation agreements between the skilled trades. In managing the 260 berths for which he was responsible, he demanded better statistics and financial information, modelled on the system which he had evolved for controlling Harland & Wolff. Using this information he streamlined the allocation of contracts, making each yard concentrate on one single standard ship design rather than a mix. From his observations he insisted that steel and other materials should be delivered only when they were required, and not stockpiled; and that the construction of hulls and engines should be synchronised so as to reduce fitting-out times. He seconded Charles Payne from Queen's Island to manage the National Shipyards, with a commission to bring them into production swiftly. He devoted some of his attention to improving the prefabricated 'N' ship, switching the design work and supply of templates from Swan Hunter to his own Company. Edward Wilding took charge of this project with

Lord Pirrie, Controlle. General of Merchant Shipbuilding, and Lo MacLay, Minister of Shipping, with their s at the National Shipya Chepstow in 1918.

cartoon by E.T. Gracey, from the *Queen's Island Annual* of 1917.

enthusiasm, quickly working out more effective and imaginative designs.

As Controller, Pirrie had his critics, who had hoped that his appointment would result in the cancellation of the standard-ship programme in favour of other designs. In effect it led to its ruthless imposition, along with technical change and better relations with the trade unions. However, by the end of the war he had gained the

The site of the new east
yard at Belfast, with wo
in progress during 1918

grudging respect of the whole shipbuilding and shipping industry for his achievement
in raising output by nearly 50 per cent during the last eight months of hostilities. By
the end of December 1918, 181 standard ships had been delivered.[21]

The two Belfast shipbuilders, Harland & Wolff and Workman Clark, were in the
van of this achievement. Harland & Wolff provided more standard ships than any
other company. Between April and the end of the year, Harland & Wolff delivered
ten vessels from Belfast, and six from Govan. The average construction time was about
nine months. Workman Clark, whose reputation for breaking riveting records was
unchallenged, set an incredible example. One of their standard ships was launched
from Queen's Island on the morning of Tuesday 10 September, and by nightfall the
engines and boilers had been placed on board and secured. Mooring trials were
conducted on Friday 13 September, and the vessel was ready for sea by nine o'clock
the following evening.[22] Apart from the prodigious output of standard ships,
Harland & Wolff found the resources to complete six of the liners that had been
requisitioned as troopships, as well as the seaplane carrier HMS *Cavendish*
(commissioned as HMS *Vindictive*). The new aircraft factory had also completed
the order for 300 Avros and assembled seven V/1500 bombers. Pirrie and his
lieutenants did not allow such swift completion times and high output to erode the

The *Andes*, built in 1939 to celebrate Royal Mail's centenary, and intended for the South American service. Completed with magnificence furnishings, she was converted into a troopship just after the outbreak of war and was not returned to passenger service until January 1948.

The innovative Shaw
Savill liner *Southern Cross*,
with her propelling
machinery aft, delivered in
February 1955.

The *Canberra*, at 45,2[...]
gross tons and with [...]
speed of 26.5 knots, t[...]
largest liner built in t[...]
United Kingdom since t[...]
Queen Elizabeth. H[...]
beautiful design still loo[...]
modern in the 1980s. T[...]
launch of this vessel, [...]
P & O, on 16 March 19[...]
marked the end of Harla[...]
& Wolff's long tradition [...]
a builder of passeng[...]
line[...]

exacting standards of the Company. Errors continued to be severely censured. In the *Queen's Island Annual* of 1917 a light-hearted cartoon showed the chairman telling an unfortunate manager who had made a mistake, 'You know Mr — this is the second time this has happened in the last 15 years.'

The work on the new plant sanctioned in 1917 proceeded rapidly. During the financial year £1,087,720 was spent on new additions. Almost £58,000 was laid out on the joiners' shop and other plant at the Alexandra Dock Works; £42,000 on new machinery and tools for the existing yards at Queen's Island; nearly £350,000 on the reorganisation of the Govan yard, including the purchase of additional land at Broomloan; £180,000 on the Lancefield engine shop; and £200,000 on the new east yard. At the annual meeting in November Pirrie was able to announce that the east yard was nearing completion, presently being fitted with tower cranes which were much more flexible than the gantries in the north and south yards. He reported that the work of remodelling the Govan works was finished, and that the Lancefield Engine Works had been enlarged to allow for the production of twenty-four sets of diesel engines a year. He observed that the extensions at Liverpool and Southampton were progressing, and hinted that plans were being prepared for large extensions at the Greenock yard. At the end of the financial year the Company's plant was valued at nearly £2,600,000, more than double its value at the outbreak of war.

Harland & Wolff was well rewarded for its national service in the financial year 1917/18, with profits jumping to a little over £235,000, after no less than £428,691 had been set aside for income tax and excess profits liabilities. The reserve had been raised to £650,000 by transferring £85,000 from the profit and loss account and £200,000 in premiums on the ordinary shares issued during the year. The income tax account reserve had climbed to over £500,000. None of the reserves were supported by cash, since all the Company's available resources had been deployed to meet the cost of the extensions to the plant. In financing these, the loans to the Company were almost doubled, with A. & J. Inglis contributing £50,000 and H. & W. Nelson (a member of the Royal Mail Group) £500,000. In addition Burmeister & Wain made another £200,000 available through the Company's 'special ledger'. This massive support was not sufficient to meet the Company's needs and bank overdrafts jumped by nearly £200,000 to just under £900,000.

The structure of bank lending had changed. During the year the Belfast Banking Company and the Clydesdale Bank had become subsidiaries of the London City & Midland Bank, which was renamed the Midland Bank. Accounts were opened with both subsidiaries to provide for current services for Belfast and the Clyde district, while a special account was maintained at the London head office. The Company's total overdraft with the Midland and its subsidiaries was about £650,000. The accounts with the Bank of Ireland and the National Bank of Scotland were also overdrawn. Pirrie was nervous about the size of the loans and overdrafts, which totalled half as much again as the issued ordinary and preference share capital. At the annual meeting an extra 500 £1,000 ordinary shares were created to be issued to companies in the Royal Mail Group, 'cementing the building agreement'. This manoeuvre had the advantage of wresting voting control of the Company from John Brown & Company, and entrusting it to Pirrie and Sir Owen Philipps. John Brown did not object, on the understanding that 'it would not interfere with their working relationship'.[23]

When the armistice was declared on the morning of 11 November 1918, the workforce spontaneously downed tools and took a week's holiday to celebrate.

Within a week the Admiralty instructed the Company to halt work on the conversion of the P & O liner *Narkunda* into an armoured merchant cruiser, and announced that no more naval vessels would be sent to the Company for refit. On Monday 18 November Pirrie was issuing instructions for the resumption of work on the twenty-one merchant contracts which had been placed before the Ministry of Shipping's embargo. He was also making preparations for a flood of vessels to be reconstructed as they were released from war service. Every spare storeroom at Queen's Island was crammed with furniture and fittings of liners that had been requisitioned as troop or hospital ships. The week before the end of hostilities the hospital ship *Asturias* (previously a Royal Mail liner), which had been severely damaged by torpedoes in March 1917, was towed to Queen's Island to be rebuilt as the cruise ship *Arcadian*. As a shipowner, Pirrie was only too conscious of the need for British companies to rebuild their fleets as soon after the war as possible, so as to match competition from neutral countries and America. At the end of armistice week he issued a manifesto to shipyard workers and marine engineers:

> The War is over in the Fields, but not in the Shipyards, Germany is beaten, but she cannot give us back all the shipping she has destroyed.
>
> The British Mercantile Marine has been one of the most decisive factors in bringing the war to a successful conclusion, but even now there must be no slackening of effort in shipbuilding as ships are as vitally necessary today as at any period in the history of this country . . .
>
> The Prime Minister in December 1917 stated, 'Victory is now a question of Tonnage and Tonnage is Victory', and to this I might now add, 'Peace is a question of Tonnage and Tonnage is Prosperity'.[24]

On 8 January 1919 he told shipowners that they were now free to place new orders with shipbuilders. Pirrie turned his wartime office to the advantage of the Company. Even before the armistice he had recruited his ADC, Captain A.T. Marshall, for the secretary's office at Queen's Island.

The contribution of Harland & Wolff to the war effort had been staggering. According to the official returns from the Controller General of Merchant Shipbuilding (Pirrie), during 1918 alone the Company had completed 201,070 gross tons of merchant vessels, 120,000 gross tons more than their nearest rivals. As Controller, Pirrie's achievement earned him the nickname 'a modern Noah'. During the war Pirrie's political outlook had changed. The Easter Rising in Dublin in 1916 was to bring about the rapid destruction of the Irish Home Rule movement, which was replaced by a militant republican separatism. The separatists appealed for German help, and their policies alarmed many Liberals. As a leading figure in the British war effort, it was inevitable that Pirrie would revise his political opinions. He became a unionist in the sense that partition, as provided for in 1914, appeared to him to be the only workable solution.

Pirrie had willingly volunteered for the arduous post of Controller General because he was concerned about the demands from some sections of the Liberal Party for the nationalisation of the shipping and shipbuilding industry. In office he had resolutely defended the free enterprise of the private shipbuilders and shipowners, pushing the Government into a rapid return to unrestricted competition. His friend Sir Owen Philipps had crossed to the Conservative Party, being elected to Parliament as Unionist member for Chester, where he was a stern critic of state intervention. Pirrie could afford to take only fleeting pride in his Company's wartime achievement, because he had to turn the building agreements urgently into firm contracts to show that those who championed state intervention were wrong-headed. Although he was now seventy-one, he did not believe that his old skill, charm and energy could desert him at the moment of his triumph. He still possessed the vitality and zest for business that had been the hallmark of his career. James Douglas, a journalist with the *Strand Magazine*, recounted an interview with him at this time:

> A little spectacled old man jumps out of his chair at a desk and with a brisk, light step and a jolly smile hastens to shake your hand . . . His close-clipped hair and moustache and beard are white; he ought to be tired and feeble and weary of the world; but you discover in two minutes that he is not tired or feeble or weary of the world . . . He chuckles like a happy schoolboy as he talks airily about his twelve-hour day and almost suggests that a twenty-four-hour day would afford him a chance of getting through some work . . . 'Work,' he earnestly assured me, 'is my pleasure. There is no pleasure like work. I am never idle. I work all day.'[25]

8
PIRRIE'S VICTORY
1918–24

Lord Pirrie and his ally, Sir Owen Philipps, as they stood at the helm of their massive shipbuilding and shipping enterprise in 1918, were not as confident as many of their contemporaries that the waters lying ahead held no hazards to navigation. In his manifesto to shipyard workers, Pirrie had already warned that victory in the field was only a prelude to a peacetime campaign of equal intensity to restore commercial prosperity. In his speech to the Lamport & Holt shareholders in April 1919, Philipps declared, 'We may find it by no means easy fully to re-establish ourselves in our ordinary sphere of operations', and concluded that unless the Government speedily dismantled wartime controls 'the working men of this country will have to face a period of leanness and unemployment'.[1] Whatever his fears for the future, Philipps had no alternative but to begin rebuilding the shattered fleets of the Royal Mail Group as fast as possible, and Pirrie had the tools for the job.

At the armistice every berth in the Harland & Wolff group was occupied with standard ships at various stages of construction. Although the design of standard ships had been criticised during the war by shipowners and shipbuilders, it was found that 'in service they proved a good, serviceable cargo boat, seaworthy, moderately fast, handy to work and reasonably economical'.[2] Even before he became Controller General, Pirrie had been convinced of the benefits of standardisation. From his experience of working alongside Lt. Colonel James Lithgow, who had more knowledge of standard ship construction than other builders, he had learned a great deal about the practicalities of standardisation. In developing the prefabricated 'N' ship, he had borrowed American techniques of building modules in covered sheds for later assembly on the building bays. He was determined that these lessons, which had helped raise productivity in wartime, should not be lost in the peace. Instead of abandoning the standard ship contracts that had only recently been laid down, Pirrie, unlike most builders, pressed ahead with the whole programme, modifying the designs to suit peacetime conditions. He insisted that the sections used in the main framing of hulls should be standardised 'to save time in the delivery of materials'. He urged Rebbeck to work up standard designs of diesel engines, which he believed passionately would emerge as more economic than either steam-reciprocating or turbine engines. Pirrie's commitment to the standard ships probably influenced Philipps and Inchcape, chairman of P & O, in their decision in mid-January 1919 to take over the 137 standard ships under construction in United Kingdom yards.[3] Out of that total, no fewer than thirty-six vessels were on the ways in the Harland & Wolff yards.

While Pirrie was making these radical preparations for the future design and construction of ships by Harland & Wolff, his hopes that the workforce throughout the industry would co-operate in a smooth transfer to peacetime working were dashed. Throughout 1918 there had been rumblings in all sections of the trade-union movement about a shorter working week. The concessions that Pirrie had made in 1897 had been eroded under the exigencies of wartime working. As long as the works

'N'-type standard ship *War Vision*, renamed *Jasmyth* and delivered to the Liverpool Brazil & River Plate Steam Navigation Company in May 1919. Unlike most shipbuilders, Harland & Wolff completed all the standard ships which were under construction in their yard at the time of the armistice.

was controlled by the Ministry of Munitions, there was nothing the Company could do. As soon as the war was over George Cuming, the deputy chairman, offered to restore the forty-seven-hour week. This proposal was rejected and on Saturday 25 January 1919 the whole of the workforce went on strike. Other discontented unions also took action and a wide range of industries was involved. The effect was devastating, the streets of Belfast were without trams and light, and gas was cut off. Supplies of food and fuel were threatened. The Harland & Wolff head office in Queen's Road was besieged by pickets. Access was possible only in armed vehicles. The management was forced to retreat to the offices of the Belfast and County Down Railway at the Station Street terminus. Cuming, concerned at the effect a long stoppage would have on production, threw himself into intense negotiations to solve the dispute. This anxiety, on top of the enormous strain of the last four years, was too great and on 1 February he died unexpectedly of pneumonia at the early age of forty-four. This was a heavy blow for Pirrie. Since he had no children, he had looked increasingly to Cuming to carry out the day-to-day administration of the Company and its subsidiaries, grooming him to take over as chief executive, rather than the previously favoured J.W. Kempster.

Pirrie had no time to mourn. On board the Stranraer–Larne ferry on his way to attend the funeral, he was approached by members of the strike committee who were travelling back from a meeting in London. They requested an interview, as they had become troubled by the militant socialist views of some of the strikers, notably Jack O'Hagan who had condemned Pirrie as an enemy of the proletariat. Pirrie, speaking as Controller General of Merchant Shipbuilding, demanded the immediate restoration of public services affected by the strike, and repeated the offer of a forty-seven-hour week rather than the forty-four-hour week demanded by the unions. He at once ordered new machinery for Harland & Wolff, which would raise productivity to compensate for the cut in the working week. After intense heart-searching and

RULES

To be observed in these Works and subject to which all persons employed are engaged.

1. Ordinary working hours from 6.20 till 8.20 o'clock; from 9 till 1 o'clock; and from 2 till 5.30 o'clock. On Saturdays work will cease at 1.30 o'clock, but without interval for dinner. Wages will be paid by the hour; and only the number of hours actually worked will be paid for. Any workman commencing work and absenting himself without leave until the termination of the ordinary working day, will not be entitled to payment for any time he may have worked on the day in question.

2. The first two hours of Overtime, Saturdays included, to be paid for as time and a quarter, and further Overtime to count as time and a half; but no time will be counted as Overtime until the ordinary number of hours for the day has been completed. Sunday work, when absolutely necessary, will be paid for as double ordinary time.

3. Workmen on the night shift to start work at 5.30 p.m., and continue until 6.20 o'clock the next morning; intervals for meals from 9 till 9.25 p m., and 1.35 till 2 o'clock a.m. For the hours worked on the night shift, time and a quarter will be paid.

4. Wages will be paid fortnightly on each alternate Saturday, at 1.30 o'clock - to be counted up to the previous Thursday night, and from it the amount of any fines, debts, or damages will be deducted. Men off work on the pay day will not be paid until after those working have received their wages.

5. All hands will enter the Works through the Time Offices at starting time, and also on resuming work after breakfast and dinner. Each workman to draw his Time Board on commencing work; and on resuming work after breakfast and dinner, must, as he enters the Works, take his Token off the Board and put it into the receiving slot. On leaving work each workman to pass out through the Time Offices and hand in his Time Board, with the amount of time worked and for what purpose written thereon, and on each Thursday evening the total amount of the previous week's time to be written thereon. Any breach of this Rule will subject him to a fine, and any workman not delivering his Token or Time Board personally at the times mentioned will forfeit all claim to wages for that day. All workmen passing through the gates during working hours must show their Time Boards to the Gatekeeper and give any explanation that may be demanded as to their business; non-compliance with this will forfeit wages for the day and subject the offender to fine or dismissal.

6. Those provided with Tool Boxes or Lockers to leave the key thereof at the Office or Store before quitting work, if so ordered.

7. Any one causing disturbance in the Works, neglecting the orders of his Foreman, avoidably absent for more than one day without the leave of his Foreman, bringing spirituous liquors into the Works, or appearing here in a state of intoxication, will be subject to fine or dismissal.

8. Any one carelessly or maliciously breaking, injuring, or defacing any Machine or Tool, altering any Template, removing Shores without leave, or committing any other mischief, to pay the cost of repairing the same, or, in the option of the Employers, to be fined.

9. Those provided with Tools must satisfactorily account for the same before leaving the employment, or the value of any that may be missing will be deducted from the wages due.

10. Any one entering or leaving the Works except by the appointed gates, or carrying out material to ships without having it charged by the Storekeeper and also giving account of same to the Gateman, will be subject to fine or dismissal.

11. No person is allowed to take strangers into any portion of the Works without first having obtained an authorized pass.

12. Any one stopping work, or preparing to stop work before the appointed time, will be fined or dismissed.

13. Any one wasting, injuring, or destroying Oil, Pitch, Tar, Oakum, Paint, Candles, Nails, or any other material, to pay the cost thereof.

14. Any one smoking, or preparing food during working hours, or smoking at any other time near combustile material, will be fined or dismissed.

15. Any one leaving a candle, lamp, or fire burning after use, will be fined.

16. In the event of work being spoiled by the carelessness of workmen, the labour expended thereon will not be paid for, and those in fault will be held responsible for the loss of the material.

We reserve to ourselves the right of fining for any irregularity or offence not specially mentioned in the foregoing Rules.

HARLAND & WOLFF.

The Harland & Wolff rules for employees introduced in 1888 and extended to all the new works on the mainland. The fifty-four-hour week specified had been reduced in 1897, but was reintroduced during the war.

under the threat of military intervention, the unions conceded and work resumed on 20 February.[4]

Cuming's post of deputy chairman was given to Robert Crighton, but not one of the other managing directors was invited to be a principal. Frederick Rebbeck succeeded Cuming as managing director of the engine works at Belfast, which he was to combine with his existing duties as managing director of the diesel engine works.

Pirrie could not afford to allow either Cuming's tragic death or the strike to stand in the way of his plans. New orders were flooding in. By the end of April contracts for twenty-two vessels had been placed, comprising two from the Bibby Steamship Company, five from P & O, one from the Holland-America line and fourteen from the Royal Mail Group. In July the annual meeting was told that the Company had orders for seventy-two vessels totalling almost 500,000 tons and contracts for twenty-three sets of machinery for vessels under construction either by subsidiaries or associate companies. Pirrie knew the Royal Mail Group was so big that it would be impossible for even the enlarged Harland & Wolff to satisfy anything approaching the whole of its demand for new tonnage unless the extension plans sanctioned during the war were completed. The construction of the new east yard at Queen's Island continued as quickly as possible. A plan to rebuild the Greenock yard, which had not progressed much beyond the drawing board before the armistice, was put into action. The Greenock Corporation and Greenock Harbour Trust agreed in August to lease the Company the West Harbour, which was to be filled in. The North Parish Church, whose graveyard contained the tombs of James Watt's father and Robert Burns's Highland Mary, was to be moved to another site to make way for six building berths, two of which were to be over 750 feet long.[5] It was anticipated that the number of employees at Cairds would jump from 2,000 to 9,000. Across the Clyde in Dumbarton Pirrie launched an equally bold scheme to reconstruct the yard of Archibald MacMillan & Son, owned by Lamport & Holt, a member of the Royal Mail Group. This was to involve the removal of the town gasworks.[6] In earnest of the undertaking made the previous year, when John Brown relinquished control of Harland & Wolff, Pirrie booked for the Royal Mail Group over the next five years one of the large berths in the east yard at Clydebank and three berths in the new west yard built during the war.[7] He fulfilled the building agreement with P & O by reserving one slip at the Dumbarton yard of William Denny & Brothers, with which John Brown was associated through its subsidiary Thomas Firth & Sons. In a heady moment he offered to rent the now-disused Govan Burgh Hall as a head office for the Clyde area of Harland & Wolff.

Pirrie conceived a most ambitious project to supply diesel engines to the yards of the Company and its associates on the Clyde. He calculated there would be demand for engine installation on eighteen ships a year, or thirty-six engines, which could be satisfied by the enlarged Finnieston works. Work on the extension, which had commenced the year before, was hurried on and Frederick Rebbeck ordered new machinery for building diesels. On Friday 13 June he reported to his fellow managing directors that nine-tenths of the machinery was now in commission. The large projected output of diesel engines would require a continuous supply of big high-quality steel castings of major components. In the autumn of 1917 Pirrie and George Cuming had selected a site for a new steel foundry in Helen Street, Govan. The purchase was delayed by the exigencies of the accelerated standard ship programme and was not concluded until early 1919. Rebbeck at once prepared plans for a huge building, designed to be the biggest foundry in the United Kingdom. In the interval before this new works was completed, all the castings required by the Finnieston engine works were to be subcontracted to the Paisley ironfounders Fullerton Hodgart & Barclay. The rationalisation of engine-building at Finnieston meant that it was no longer necessary to proceed with the Govan engine works, mooted before the war, and that Caird's engine works at Greenock could be closed. On 1 January Caird's engine works was sold for £210,000 to the neighbouring Scotts' Shipbuilding & Engineering Company.

While these preparations for the future were being made, construction of the standard ships continued as quickly as interruptions, caused by the strikes for the shorter working week, would allow. In the last six months of the 1918/19 financial year ten standard ships were completed at Belfast, with two launched awaiting completion, and one delivered and one launched from Greenock. Substantial progress was made on the merchant contracts left over from the war. At Belfast the *Arundel Castle* (ship no. 455) was almost ready to be launched, the fitting out of the *Narkunda* (ship no. 471) was in progress, and more impressively the Bibby

passenger/cargo liner *Yorkshire* (ship no. 509) was launched on 29 May. Work had been resumed shortly after the war on ship no. 470 for the White Star line. This ship, previously named *Germanic*, was rechristened *Homeric* and redesigned as a 40,000-gross-ton-liner to replace the *Britannic*, lost during the war. The keel was laid in June 1919. At Govan all four of the motor ships (511G-514G) – ordered by Elder Dempster in mid-1916 and since transferred to the Glen line – were in progress. The first vessel, *Glenade*, was launched on 15 April and delivered on 16 July. Although seven liners that had been requisitioned for war service had arrived at Queen's Island for major refits by the end of June, most of the repair work was diverted to Liverpool and Southampton.

The gross profits for the year were almost £600,000, just £65,000 less than the record of the previous year. Only a little over £100,000 was distributed in dividends; £303,000 was transferred to the income tax reserve; and the residue was left at the credit of the profit and loss account. During the year the reserve had jumped from £650,000 to £1,175,000, largely through crediting £425,000 premiums on the 500 shares issued to the Royal Mail Group. Although these additional provisions, totalling nearly £1,075,000, were deployed to meet the cost of new plant, they covered only half the total capital expenditure of £2,005,631 incurred during the war. The biggest outlays were £275,000 on machine tools to raise productivity at Belfast; £160,000 on the improvements to the Alexandra Dock Works; £520,000 on the east yard at Belfast; £100,000 on improvements at Southampton; £315,000 on the

The *Arundel Castle*, a 19,500-ton liner deliver to Union-Castle on 8 April 1921. She was t last of the four-funnel 'Olympic'-type liners t built at Belfast. Her sist ship, the *Windsor Castle* was completed at Clydebank in 1922.

212

reconstruction of the Govan yard; and £240,000 on the Lancefield Engine Works. The remaining £1,000,000 of these outlays was more than offset by the increased share capital, by additional overdrafts of £100,000, and by loans totalling £949,312 from Shaw Savill & Albion (the shipping company controlled by Sir John Ellerman), Sir William Arrol & Company, Burmeister & Wain, and London & Glasgow. The balance of these funds, along with advances of £450,000 from customers, was needed to finance work in progress while the bill market readjusted to peacetime conditions. At the end of the financial year the Company had contingent liabilities on bills discounted of nearly £400,000 for bills drawn on P & O and on itself for Elder Dempster. As Pirrie must have been aware, Harland & Wolff was very exposed: there was no cash to meet even the wartime tax liabilities, and the current commitments to plant extensions were estimated at a colossal £10,000,000. However, with such a big order book, he was confident that the policies which had proved so successful before the war would not fail him now that he was at the peak of his power as a shipbuilder.

Pirrie had good reason to be optimistic. Contracts continued to flow in. By the end of 1919 another sixteen orders had been placed, twelve for members of the Royal Mail Group and four from IMM companies. On 12 August the *Olympic* had arrived to be reconditioned and refitted for her peacetime duties. During the summer of 1919 Pirrie had revived his plan to secure oil supplies for the diesel-engined ships he was building for the Royal Mail Group. Along with his partners in the unsuccessful British

Table 8.1
Capital 1919-24

	1919	1920	1921	1922	1923	1924[3]
	£	£	£	£	£	£
Ordinary shares	1,500,000	2,000,000	3,000,000	3,000,000	3,000,000	3,000,000
Preference shares	531,074	1,993,594	3,094,094	3,094,094	3,094,094	3,095,094
'A' preference shares	—	—	18,300	20,300	20,300	20,300
Loan capital	1,951,401	3,415,830	3,294,166	3,312,177	3,588,591	3,493,857
Loans over £10,000						
Atlantic Transport Co.	—	—	504,938	531,542	558,452	335,466
African Steamship Co.	27,200	535,912	101,010	212,287	224,131	234,928
Sir William Arrol & Co.[1]	186,952	—	27,390	33,447	—	—
J.M. Barbour & J. Andrews	—	9,378	9,776	10,198	10,627	11,042
John Brown & Co.	—	—	—	200,000	250,253	252,225
Burmeister & Wain[1]	126,554	220,666	282,603	153,909	114,869	128,612
Caird & Co.	354,951	295,107	—	103,532	57,187	—
David Colville & Sons						
J.A. Spens and 5 others	—	218,997	170,331	121,665	72,999	24,333
J.A. Spens and 4 others	—	230,994	179,662	128,330	76,998	25,666
John Colville	—	110,403	85,869	61,335	36,801	12,267
G.G. Napier	—	18,000	30,800	22,600	14,400	6,200
Mrs Isabella Napier	—	—	16,800	12,600	8,400	4,200
J.B. Hope Robertson	—	18,288	14,224	10,160	6,096	2,032
D.M. McLay	—	15,300	11,900	8,500	5,100	1,700
J.B. Allan	—	12,600	9,800	7,000	4,200	1,400
David Colville	—	10,800	8,400	6,000	3,600	1,200
J.A. Bilsland	—	16,272	12,656	9,040	5,424	1,808
James Russell	—	42,876	33,348	23,820	14,292	4,764
W. Russell	—	59,571	46,333	33,095	19,857	6,619
Jackson Russell	—	59,571	46,333	33,095	19,857	6,619
G.H. Russell	—	16,695	12,985	9,275	5,565	1,855
Coventry Ordnance Works[2]	—	325,000	—	—	—	—
R. Crighton	10,236	11,230	5,426	6,021	3,601	595
David Colville & Sons Ltd	—	—	818,806	334,918	9,007	72,537
Dinnington & Mail Coal Co.	—	30,000	—	—	—	—
Elder Dempster	—	17,895	—	105,158	111,025	—
Thomas Firth & Sons	200,000	200,000	—	—	—	—
Mrs L.E. Harland	11,800	11,800	11,800	11,800	11,800	17,800
Executors of Lady Harland	20,358	4,113	4,036	4,581	3,324	1,548
Johnston Hughes	10,125	10,125	10,125	10,125	10,125	10,125
D.&W. Henderson	—	80,000	250,000	385,000	421,000	363,000
A.&J. Inglis	50,000	44,875	119,000	25,146	—	—
George Lambert	—	30,000	30,000	30,000	20,000	—
London & Glasgow Engineering and Iron Shipbuilding Co.[1]	154,737	340,423	592,114	306,901	88,256	88,124
H.&W. Nelson	500,000	350,000	350,000	285,000	285,000	250,000
Ocean Transport Co.	195,030	192,933	196,100	196,107	35,807	33,290
Royal Mail	—	643,750	100,986	212,312	224,157	198,505
Shaw Savill & Albion	501,164	—	—	—	—	—
Sheepbridge Coal & Iron Co.	—	30,000	30,000	20,000	20,000	20,000
Mary K. Purcell	—	13,912	14,279	10,459	7,625	10,501

214

Table 8.1 (cont.)

	1919	1920	1921	1922	1923	1924[3]
	£	£	£	£	£	£
Laurence Scott & Co.	—	—	—	—	25,000	15,000
British Mexican	—	—	—	—	200,000	13,324
Wagon Finance Corporation	—	—	—	100,000	—	—
F. Leyland & Co. (1900) Ltd	—	—	—	—	122,886	129,124
Government TFA and NGA loans	—	—	—	80,297	686,706	1,382,349

Notes
1 Not classified as loans
2 Balance of purchase price of Scotstoun works
3 At 30 June 1924

Table 8.2
Profit and loss 1919-23[1]

	Gross profit/(loss) for year before tax and depreciation	Net profit/(loss) per published accounts after tax and depreciation	Distribution (Transfers to/from reserves and dividends)	Balance carried to following year
	£	£	£	£
1919	1,361,776	321,224	272,531	250,468
1920	1,282,447	433,820	425,008	259,280
1921	125,691	420,585	525,306	154,559
1922	1,144,845	341,347	415,925	79,981
1923	1,225,726	335,112	336,864	78,229

Note
1 For 1924 see Table 9.2, p. 255

Table 8.3
Fixed assets 1919-24

	Additions	Depreciation	Total
	£	£	£
1919	2,005,631	190,551	4,387,691
1920	2,101,301	431,126	6,057,866
1921	1,980,059	548,009	7,489,916
1922	653,595	40,000[1]	8,103,511
1923	811,980	150,000[2]	8,765,492
1924[3]	623,884	75,000[4]	9,314,376

Notes
1 £266,028 deferred
2 £153,328 deferred
3 At 30 June 1924
4 £224,013 deferred

Table 8.4
Reserves 1919-24

	1919	1920	1921	1922	1923	1924[2]
	£	£	£	£	£	£
Reserve[1]	1,175,000	1,725,000	2,325,000	2,325,000	2,325,000	1,525,000
Reserve against losses on contracts	18,032	18,032	18,032	18,032	18,032	435,922
Reserve for expenditure on additions	14,104	14,104	14,104	14,104	14,104	14,104
Income tax account	850,000	417,500	—	—	—	—
Investment reserve	460,837	460,837	460,837	460,837	460,837	460,837

Notes
1 Transfers to this account were made out of the balance brought forward on the balance-sheet profit.
2 At 30 June 1924

Table 8.5
Bank balances 1919-24

	1919	1920	1921	1922	1923	1924[1]
	£	£	£	£	£	£
Midland Bank	(558,238)	(802,182)	(750,750)	(764,747)	(1,247,401)	(1,423,756)
Bank of Ireland	(247,456)	(560,610)	(205,647)	(397,026)	(513,656)	(538,937)
Belfast Banking Co.	(96,318)	(158,928)	(63,437)	(193,819)	(249,532)	(249,629)
Clydesdale Bank	(49,660)	(336,464)	(225,882)	(246,013)	(283,681)	(329,998)
National Bank of Scotland	(84,097)	(209,851)	(113,278)	(212,107)	(174,122)	(196,993)
Union Discount Co.	—	(37,230)	8,592	(11,983)	(30,307)	(20,606)
Lloyds Bank	27	5,027	5,027	5,027	5,027	5,027
P&O Banking Corporation	—	—	—	12,835	9,965	18,921
Royal Bank of Scotland	—	—	(193,432)	(184,252)	(135,236)	(233,274)
Total	(1,035,742)	(2,100,238)	(1,538,807)	(1,992,085)	(2,618,943)	(2,969,245)

Notes
1 At 30 June 1924
( ) = Debit balance

Table 8.6
Bills receivable discounted 1919-24

	£
1919	398,572
1920	3,030,300
1921	9,174,000
1922	12,311,386
1923	10,235,783
1924[1]	9,447,084

Note
1 At 30 June 1924

216

Table 8.7
Investments 1919-24

	£
1919	774,712
1920	3,620,535
1921	4,800,621
1922	4,614,174
1923	4,534,937
1924[1]	4,535,719

Note
1 At 30 June 1924

Table 8.8
Shareholders in Harland & Wolff Limited in 1921

Name	Shares (at £1,000 each)
Mrs S.E. Wilson	1
Lady Pirrie	1
Captain W. Harland	10
Albert Harland	10
Gowan Harland	4
H.P. Harland	10
Neville Harland	10
Captain Charles C. Harland	10
John Kinahan and another	40
J.W. Kempster	10
John Brown & Co.	560
Viscount Pirrie	507
Executor of Miss E.A. Harland	6
Mrs E.E. Duckworth	6
Rev. W.H. Metcalfe	12
Miss M.J. Metcalfe	5
Miss E.A. Metcalfe	5
Mrs E.N. Eggar	3
Ronald Halley	1
Mrs E. Watson	3
Miss E.M. Halley	2
William Halley	3
Mrs Annie Low	4
William Harland	1
British & African Steam Navigation Co.	175
African Steamship Co.	175
Imperial Direct Line	88
Elder Line Ltd	88
Elder Dempster & Co.	350
Union-Castle	375
Royal Mail Steam Packet Co.	525
Total	3,000

Union Oil Company, Pirrie approached an American oil tycoon, E.L. Doheney, who had massive interests in the Mexican oilfields through the Mexican Petroleum Company. In July they formed the British Mexican Petroleum Company which Doheney agreed to supply with all the oil it required at a fixed price for twenty-five years. The new company's affairs were to be managed by Andrew Weir & Company, whose founder had recently been created Lord Inverforth in recognition of his wartime service, most recently as Minister of Munitions. As part of the promotion, the British Mexican Petroleum Company agreed to order all its tankers and barges from Harland & Wolff on a 10 per cent commission basis.[8] British Mexican's initial needs were to be supplied more or less at cost. Towards the end of the year Lord Inverforth ordered seven barges and two lighters (ships nos 617-25) and took over seven vessels under construction for members of the Royal Mail Group. These were to be converted into oil tankers by the construction of six circular oil tanks in the hold spaces. Four of these ships (nos 589-91 and 609) were prefabricated 'N'-type standard ships. At the end of the financial year contracts had been received for a further thirty-one vessels of all types, ranging from more barges for British Mexican, to a cable-laying ship for the Western Telegraph Company, two ferries for the Clyde Navigation Trust and two large passenger liners for the Holland-America line. During

Small oil tankers under construction at Queen's Island for the British Mexican Oil Company. These vessels were designed with a shallow draft to allow them to enter Lake Maracaibo in Venezuela. In the background (at the right centre), at the Thompson wharf, can be seen the *Olympic* (left), undergoing major refurbishment after war service, and the *Arundel Castle*, at the fitting-out stage.

John Craig,
managing director of
David Colville & Sons,
the Scottish steelmakers,
which was acquired by
Harland & Wolff in 1920.

the financial year orders for MacMillans, Inglises and Hendersons were, for the first time, allocated Harland & Wolff ship numbers.

With such a colossal volume of business on the books, Pirrie was anxious that nothing should hinder production. Since the failure of his merger bid for the west-of-Scotland steelmakers David Colville & Sons in 1917, Pirrie had continued desultory negotiations with the chairman, John Craig. These were intensified early in 1919 and on 14 May it was agreed that Harland & Wolff be allocated 15,000 ordinary shares in Colvilles in exchange for 300,000 6 per cent, £1 preference shares in Harland & Wolff, 'thus sealing a long friendship and close working connection of many years'. This transaction was merely a prelude to the purchase of Colvilles in March 1920 by Harland & Wolff and 'various steamship companies represented by Sir Owen Philipps' for £5,250,000, paid partly in cash and partly by an exchange of shares. In acquiring Colvilles, Harland & Wolff and the Royal Mail Group had won control of a group of companies which could melt 800,000 tons of steel ingots a year, turn out 80,000 tons of pig iron and nine million tons of coal, and make every conceivable type of steel product. Its more important subsidiaries (all bought out in 1916) were the Clydebridge Steel Company, the Glengarnock steelworks, and Archibald Russell Limited, coal owners and quarry masters.[9] When Pirrie told his

managing directors of the takeover, he cautioned them that he expected 'never to hear of our being delayed through lack of material, as only the exercise of foresight in anticipating our requirements should be necessary to ensure the supplies as required and at the proper time'. John Brown agreed to participate in the deal, to secure supplies for its Clydebank shipyard, by making advances to both Harland & Wolff and Colvilles. John Brown, along with its subsidiary, Thomas Firth & Sons, reaffirmed its willingness to supply the Harland & Wolff yards with steel forgings, used to manufacture moving parts in engines and other machinery. These were to be shipped in advance, to be paid for only as required.

In the meantime Pirrie was driving ahead with his expansion plans. On 27 November 1919 the new east yard at Belfast was officially inaugurated with the launch of the first vessel, the *Maine* (ship no. 565, an 'N'-type standard ship) for the Atlantic Transport Company. The six berths (of which only two were complete) would give Harland & Wolff more space for large vessels than the combined capacity of the two existing north and south shipyards. The berths were fitted with portable cofferdams to exclude the sea during construction, and between each berth were concrete causeways housing 'salt water and cofferdam pumps, hydraulic, pneumatic, fresh and salt water pipes and electric cables'. Along the top of the causeways were roadways for electrically driven ten-ton tower cranes. Behind the slips was a massive platers' shed, planned for efficient materials-handling. Instead of being fitted with a system of rails and bogies for moving plates, frames and other components out to the berths, it was equipped with novel electric trolleys for carrying the large
220

Diesel engines under construction at the Finnieston engine work The two engines on the are the port and starboa engines for the *Glenogle* These massive direct-acting diesel engines we difficult to build, requir machining to very high tolerances.

(above, opposite)
Harland & Wolff's diese engine works at Finnies in the 1920s.

(opposite)
The Harland & Wolff Scotstoun works on the north bank of the Clyde This plant was built bef the First World War for construction of gun mountings. It was acquired by Harland & Wolff in 1919.

prefabricated sections.[10] Two fitting-out wharfs were to be constructed by the Harbour Commissioners in the Musgrave channel alongside the yard.

By the time the east yard opened, Pirrie was becoming concerned about the capacity of Finnieston Engine Works. Throughout the year Rebbeck had been signalling that it would be realistically possible to produce only twenty-four engines a year, compared with Pirrie's optimistic forecast of thirty-six engines. This was a serious blow, as it meant that the Company could not supply diesel engines for all the ships under construction in its yards or those of its subcontractors in the Clyde area. Rebbeck encouraged Pirrie to purchase the Scotstoun factory of the Coventry Ordnance Works, which had been constructed in 1910 to manufacture gun mountings for the Fairfield and Clydebank shipyards. The Coventry Ordnance Works owed its origins to a syndicate formed in 1905/6, by John Brown & Company, Fairfield Shipbuilding & Engineering Company and Cammell-Laird, to secure supplies of naval ordnance. Its principal factory was in Coventry. During the war the works had built up considerable expertise in electrical engineering. With the coming of peace the biggest shareholder, John Brown & Company, decided to amalgamate the works with other electrical contractors to form the English Electric Company. Lord Aberconway explained the choice of name: 'There has been too much Hun about some of the electric companies so we were determined that we would keep ourselves a British concern.'[11] The Scotstoun works was superfluous to English Electric's requirements and Pirrie's offer of £475,000 for it, made early in 1920, was quickly accepted on condition that Harland & Wolff would still manufacture gun mountings for John Brown and for Fairfield. The factory, which was already well equipped, was converted for diesel-engine manufacture.

Pirrie and Rebbeck were also worried at the total lack of progress on the Helen Street, Govan foundry, partly because of delays in obtaining permission from Glasgow Corporation to close streets and partly because the contractor, Sir William Arrol & Company, was concentrating its efforts on reconstructing the Greenock and Dumbarton yards. A strike of iron-moulders in the autumn of 1919 had cut off supplies from Fullerton Hodgart & Barclay, of Paisley, and Rebbeck doubted if he would have sufficient casting to build all the diesel engines required in 1920. Early in May Pirrie called a crisis meeting at Belfast of the managing directors and senior management. He announced a ruthless plan to ensure the completion of the foundry, which he christened the Clyde Foundry:

> Recognising the prime necessity of devoting money to and proceeding at the utmost speed with the new Foundry at Helen Street, it is decided to subordinate everything in the shipyards and engine works to this consideration, and at Belfast, Govan and Greenock capital expenditure is to be curtailed as much as possible, and projected schemes of development deferred in the meantime. This applies to the additional Smiths' Shop and new Brass Foundry and two bays of the Platers' Sheds at Belfast, the completion of the Greenock scheme, development work at MacMillans, Dumbarton, Govan, Finnieston and Scotstoun, so that the Contractors (Sir Wm Arrol & Co Ltd) may concentrate with all their available men and material on the construction of the Clyde Foundry, from which . . . we may get some castings by Christmas and be almost in full swing a year hence.

The only plants exempt from this embargo were Southampton and Liverpool, where new facilities were required to fulfil an agreement made at the beginning of the year

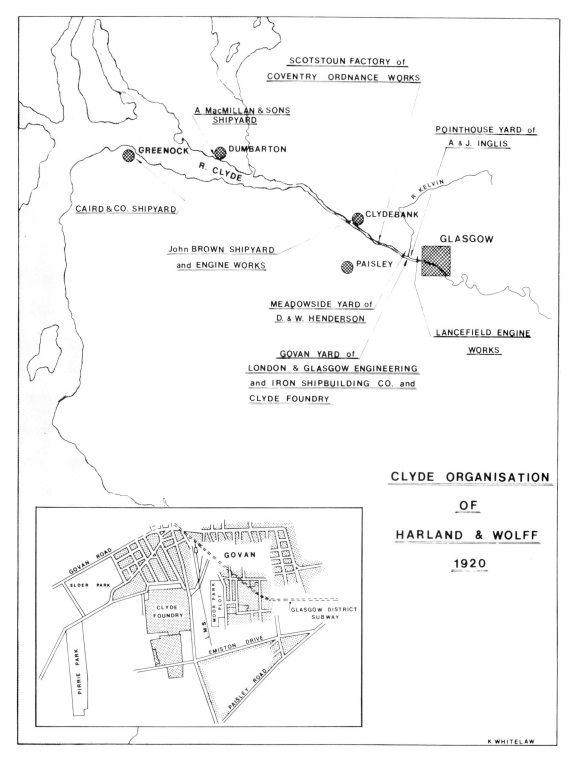

SCOTSTOUN FACTORY of
COVENTRY ORDNANCE WORKS

A MacMILLAN & SONS
SHIPYARD

POINTHOUSE YARD of
A & J. INGLIS

GREENOCK   DUMBARTON

R. CLYDE

R. KELVIN

CAIRD & CO. SHIPYARD

CLYDEBANK

GLASGOW

John BROWN SHIPYARD
and ENGINE WORKS

PAISLEY

MEADOWSIDE YARD of
D. & W. HENDERSON

LANCEFIELD ENGINE
WORKS

GOVAN YARD of
LONDON & GLASGOW ENGINEERING
and IRON SHIPBUILDING CO. and
CLYDE FOUNDRY

CLYDE ORGANISATION

OF

HARLAND & WOLFF

1920

GOVAN ROAD

GOVAN

ELDER PARK

CLYDE
FOUNDRY

MOOR PARK
PLOT

GLASGOW DISTRICT
SUBWAY

L
M
S

PIRRIE PARK

EMISTON DRIVE

PAISLEY ROAD

K WHITELAW

to take over the repair establishments and works of Union-Castle and the Royal Mail Steam Packet Company. The opportunity was taken at the crisis meeting to confirm the plan for the foundry, which Pirrie reckoned would cost almost £1,000,000 and be capable of producing between 20,000 and 25,000 tons of castings a year.

223

Pirrie's motive in buying the Scotstoun works and driving ahead with the Clyde Foundry does not seem to have been simply anxiety about diesel-engine production for the Clyde area of Harland & Wolff. It was uncharacteristic of Pirrie to have overestimated the capacity of the Finnieston works. As Controller General he had shown his uncanny talent for forecasting very accurately the output of each firm under his authority. There was also something contrived about the crisis meeting at Belfast in May. The conference lasted three days from Tuesday 4 to Thursday 6 May. The first day was occupied with an elaborate tour of Queen's Island, during which Pirrie continually pointed out facilities such as the chemistry and photographic departments which could be called on by all the works. When Pirrie dropped his bombshell the next day he went to great lengths to emphasise that the embargo was to apply to all the shipyards. This careful stage management was almost certainly designed to disguise Pirrie's grave concern about the future of the Queen's Island yard at a time of increasing political tension. Since the Easter Rising of 1916 the Home Rule movement had been eclipsed by the meteoric rise of Sinn Fein which would accept nothing other than the formation of a republic. The Irish Republican Army (IRA) was reorganised in 1919 and at once opened a brutal campaign against the Unionists, particularly those in the south. The British Government responded with equal violence, raising the infamous special force known as the 'Black and Tans'. By April 1920 feeling in Ulster was running high, and Unionists were particularly concerned about the boundaries of the proposed new state of Northern Ireland. When Pirrie led his senior managers around the Queen's Island yard in the first week of May, the outlook was grim. During the war the Conservatives had lost their enthusiasm for the Orange cause. Pirrie must have been deeply concerned. As the largest employer

The massive Clyde Foundry built after the First World War for making precision casti for diesel engines constructed at the Finnieston engine wor The foundry cost over £1 million and never operated at full capaci

224

in Ulster, his works would be a natural target for sectarian trouble. From its foundation the firm had tried never to discriminate between Protestants and Catholics, but, inevitably in east Belfast, a majority of employees were Protestant and Unionist. Moreover, many of the workforce were only recent arrivals in the Province from either Scotland or the north of England. The engine works, staffed by a great many Englishmen, was nicknamed the 'English Shop'. It was probably this British orientation of the firm, more than anything else, that persuaded Pirrie to buy Scotstoun and build the Clyde Foundry. As on other occasions in the past when there was a threat of strife in Belfast, the Company was making contingency plans for moving to the mainland.

Any secret fears that Pirrie may have had early in 1920 were confirmed with the onset of summer. In June rioting broke out in Londonderry and quickly spread to Belfast, where there were three nights of continuous disturbances at the end of the month. The Belfast riots were fuelled by the decision of the Belfast Protestant Association to expel all Catholic workers from the city's factories.[12] It is not known where the idea originated but by 5 July Harland & Wolff had been told by the joiners' shipyard delegate that 'all men starting must have a card from the District Delegate'. Although the management was resolved to ignore this instruction, its effect quickly became apparent at the end of the annual fortnight's holiday in July. On 21 July the apprentices and rivet boys from Workman Clark's south yard marched through the Harland & Wolff works demanding the expulsion of all Catholics and of Protestants with socialist sympathies. During the following week loyalist meetings were held throughout the Company's works and employees passed resolutions refusing to work with anyone 'in alliance or sympathy with the Sinn Fein party or policy and the red flag of mad revolution'. The repair department reported on 2 August that it had lost 'men, particularly joiners'. In the middle of the month the works' committee agreed to pay up to the end of July the wages of all those expelled from Queen's Island and was confronted with 'applications from our Works Apprentices absent on account of the disturbances and requesting transfer to our other branches'. Although these were at first resisted by the management, some transfers subsequently seem to have taken place. The expulsions continued throughout August. The four Catholic waitresses in the staff dining room were driven out on 27 August.

During September the Government proposed a new Home Rule Bill which would partition the country, establishing parliaments in North and South. The Ulster Unionists accepted the compromise which guaranteed the six northern counties continuing membership of the United Kingdom. On the formation of the Stormont Parliament, Pirrie became a senator – public recognition of his return to the Unionist fold. Pirrie and his Belfast managers used the settlement to persuade the Federated Trades and Vigilance Committee to allow Catholics to return to work, 'putting them on their honour that they are not associated with the Sinn Fein or any other disloyal organisation'. The Harbour Police Force, under the control of the Harbour Commissioners, was strengthened, with the object of excluding sectarian outrages from Queen's Island. The militant joiners' union refused to co-operate in the reinstatement of Catholic members of their union, but the other trades consented. It took almost a year and several further outbreaks of sectarian violence for all those who had been expelled to return. The only permanent loss would seem to have been 120 apprentices.[13]

It is possible only to guess at Pirrie's attitude to these political developments. The Liberalism of his youth had become Conservatism in his old age. The attitudes that

iscount and Lady Pirrie
n the steps of Ormiston
use, their Belfast home,
on their way to the
pening of the Northern
land Parliament in 1921.
Pirrie adored the
geantry of public life. He
wearing the uniform of
n Irish Privy Councillor.

had persuaded him to support Home Rule in 1912 struck few chords with the policies of Sinn Fein. On the wider political stage he had no sympathy with those Liberals who supported nationalisation and state intervention in industry. At a personal level his close business ally Sir Owen Philipps had become a staunch Conservative and, as a result, was no longer on speaking terms with his brother, Lord St Davids, who had stood by Lloyd George. Pirrie could not afford a similar difficulty with the man nominated to succeed him at the head of the Company. Socially, Home Rule was anything but fashionable and Pirrie's war service had earned him a place in public life, if not in society. He delighted in the theatre of national service, wearing military uniform and court dress, and loved playing the squire at Witley Court. Although emotionally he and his wife were still deeply attached to Belfast, they had earned that status in British life that they had so hankered after in their youth, and nothing was going to take it from them. In the world of business Harland & Wolff was now spread throughout the United Kingdom, with links to many important British shipping lines. It would have been unthinkable for Pirrie to allow its massive Belfast shipyard to fall under the control of a new republic, even if his workforce had agreed. There was nothing to encourage Pirrie to oppose the views of the majority of Ulster people. His innate wish to help the less fortunate in the south of Ireland could find expression in the various non-political and non-sectarian initiatives by businessmen to stimulate the growing of flax and sugar beet.

The disturbances in Belfast came too late to affect production in the 1919/20 financial year. Output continued to be dominated by wartime standard ships, mostly the 'N' type. All these vessels were fitted with standard triple-expansion engines, with the exception of two ships (nos 574 and 577) which had twin turbines installed. Belfast delivered nine of these vessels, Govan three and Greenock three. The P & O liner *Narkunda*, which had been ordered before the war, was delivered from Belfast along with six British Mexican barges. All four of the Glen line motor ships were commissioned at Govan. Every berth in the Company's yards was fully occupied. On 17 June 1920, after a repetition of the two days of public viewing in aid of the Royal Victoria Hospital that had taken place at her commissioning, the *Olympic* left the Lagan for Southampton with a large party of Pirrie's guests. At a dinner held on board, H.A. Sanderson, who had succeeded Bruce Ismay as president of IMM, referred to the liner as 'the one ewe lamb of the White Star line' and stated that 'owing to world conditions he could not see such a large vessel being built for some time to come'.[14] This must have been a bitter disappointment to Pirrie, who had cherished the hope of building the *Homeric* as a replacement for the lost *Britannic*.

Profit, before allowing for excess profits duty, was a record £851,319. The excess profits duty was settled with a final payment of £417,500. Altogether the Company was allowed £439,150 against its liability for the estimated additional cost, over prewar prices, of plant installed during the war. In addition an almost equivalent sum had been received in Treasury grants for capital projects and nearly £84,000 had been allowed for extra depreciation to offset exceptional wartime wear and tear. During the financial year just over £2,100,000 had been spent on the various additions to the plant and £2,642,923 on buying 48,544 ordinary shares to give Harland & Wolff control of David Colville & Sons. These huge outlays, which totalled more than twice the Company's issued capital in 1919, were covered by the issue of a further £500,000 of ordinary shares and £1,462,520 of preference shares to Royal Mail and Union-Castle. The issue of the ordinary shares was at a premium of £450,000 which was credited to the reserve. The Colville shareholders loaned the Company £1,000,000

to be repaid over five years. As part of its contribution to the acquisition of Colvilles, John Brown advanced £60,000 through two subsidiaries, the Dinnington & Mail Coal Company and the Sheepbridge Coal & Iron Company. Harland & Wolff called for a loan of £800,000 from D. & W. Henderson, a further £90,000 from Burmeister & Wain and an extra £200,000 from London & Glasgow. Overdrafts quadrupled to over £2,100,000, with the Midland Bank group contributing more than 60 per cent. The work in progress was once more being financed by bills drawn either on customers or on Harland & Wolff on the customers' behalf. At the end of the financial year the contingent liability on bills discounted stood at £3,030,000. Almost two-thirds of these bills were for companies in the Royal Mail Group. Some clients, following the prewar practice of commission club members, placed large sums on account with Harland & Wolff against work in progress. Union-Castle had over £500,000 placed in this way and IMM £220,000. Altogether the Company held deposits of £1,223,704, which more than covered its outlays.

Although Pirrie told the annual meeting in July that ninety vessels were on order, he did not mention that there were no inquiries for any further contracts. In mid-1920 the postwar shipping boom came to a sudden end. Freight rates collapsed and the cost of second-hand tonnage spiralled downwards, due largely to the destruction of the prewar economic order. Shipowners, sensing a stormy passage ahead, quickly realised that they had been rash in acquiring tonnage at the inflated wartime prices.

Their first reaction was to review shipbuilding programmes, delaying deliveries or cancelling contracts outright. Before the war the commission club had insulated Harland & Wolff from such problems. However, so swift and widespread was the decline in freight rates in 1920 that every shipping company was forced to reduce its commitments. By the end of July Harland & Wolff had been instructed to hold up work on a number of contracts, including ships nos 516G and 518C/G for Royal Mail; nos 560, 562G and 568G for Elder Dempster; nos 575 and 576 for George Thompson & Company and nos 587 and 588, two 20,000-ton liners, for P & O. Some orders were revoked – ship no. 507 for Union-Castle (later allocated to the Royal Mail vessel, *Asturias*), and no. 518C/G for Royal Mail. So uncertain was the outlook that Pirrie had to revise the construction schedules regularly as the year drew to a close. He summoned his managing directors and senior managers to a meeting in his London office on 2 February. He opened by explaining, as reported in the minutes,

> his wishes generally regarding the revision of our programme of work with a view to realising the most economical production . . . At the present time our shipowning friends would be gratified to see that their interests were being protected by our using every means in our power to effect economy.

He ordered that berth 'no. 6 and certain other slips in the South yard' at Belfast should be closed as soon as possible, along with one slip at Govan and one at Greenock. He insisted that the managing directors should be vigilant in their stock control, demanding that material ordered for suspended contracts be transferred to ships in progress. Overtime was to be cut, bonus payments paid during the war withdrawn, wages reduced and staff and workers laid off. In the circumstances, the workforce was in no position to offer effective resistance. Early in March Pirrie was arranging for ten ships from the fleets of the Royal Mail Group to be laid up temporarily under Harland & Wolff supervision at Belfast.

Despite these difficulties nineteen vessels were delivered from the Company's yards in the 1920/21 financial year. However, since the majority of these vessels were small, the total tonnage turned out was down by a third and the total horse-power by two-thirds. The most significant liner to be commissioned was the *Arundel Castle* for Union-Castle, which had been ordered before the war. Although it was the last of the four-funnelled liners to be built at Queen's Island, it was of entirely novel design, setting new standards in accommodation for passenger liners. Bibby took delivery of three ships, the 10,000-ton passenger/cargo liner *Yorkshire*, ordered during the war, and two 'N'-type standard ships, *Dorsetshire* and *Somersetshire*. The fall in output was partly offset by a stream of repair work. Major refits were completed at Belfast on over fifteen ships, including the White Star liners *Cedric* and *Baltic* and the Pacific Steam Navigation Company's *Oropesa* and *Orduna*. Profits plunged to an estimated £300,000. The figure entered in the balance sheet was £420,584 but this included a refund of about £130,000 excess profit duty.

Pirrie's efforts during the year to concentrate on the construction of the Clyde Foundry were reflected in the accounts, in the recorded outlay of almost £1,000,000. Little investment was made at Scotstoun, probably because the danger of unrest in Belfast subsided, and instead the plant was used for civil engineering work connected with the Clyde Foundry and reconstruction work at the Govan, Greenock and Dumbarton yards. The completion of the capital projects which were too far advanced to be cancelled in May 1920 contributed another £1,000,000 to expenditure during the year. This was matched by the purchase of a further £1,000,000 of shares in David Colville & Sons. These additions and investments were paid for by issuing to members of the Royal Mail Group an additional £1,000,000 of ordinary stock and £1,100,000 of preference stock. Overdrafts were cut by £500,000 and loans to the Company remained level. These modest improvements were overshadowed by a startling increase in the Company's contingent liabilities on bills receivable but discounted, from £3,000,000 to over £9,000,000.

During the summer of 1921 IMM solved the problem of providing a sister ship for the *Olympic*, now that ship no. 470, the *Homeric*, had been cancelled. The combine finalised a deal to acquire two half-completed German liners which had become the property of the Ministry of Shipping as part of the war reparations. These were the Norddeutscher Lloyd line's *Columbus* (34,350 gross tons), which had been launched in 1913 at the Danzig yard of Schicau, and the *Bismark* (56,550 gross tons), the third of Albert Ballin's giant liners, launched in June 1914 at the Blohm and Voss yard in Hamburg. By way of recompense for the loss of ship no. 470, Harland & Wolff was entrusted with the work of completing the two liners. Pirrie consigned this task to

An aerial view of the reconstructed Govan yard of Harland & Wolff, with the realigned berths and the massive platers' shed on Govan Road. On the north bank of the Clyde the yard of D. & W. Henderson can be seen.

the managing director responsible for ship design, Edward Wilding, and to Henry Harland, who was based at the London office. Wilding was to supervise the design and details, while Harland was to chair the Hamburg committee. Work at Danzig was to be supervised by W.D. Donaldson of the White Star line. The *Columbus*, renamed *Homeric*, entered service in February 1922 and the *Bismark*, renamed *Majestic*, in May. Although Pirrie had bowed to events in helping to fit out these two liners, he regretted for the rest of his life the lost opportunity to build another sister ship for the *Olympic*. At the same time Royal Mail acquired the *Munchen*, building at Bremen. She was renamed the *Ohio* and the supervision of her fitting-out was added to Wilding's duties. These commissions were beset with problems. There were difficulties in communicating between Germany and Belfast and the rapid depreciation of the German deutschmark made costing almost impossible. Pirrie was impressed by the way in which Wilding and Harland conquered these obstacles.[15]

The shipping market and the rest of the economy slid further into recession in the autumn of 1921 and unemployment grew steadily. The Government – with only the example of the long depression that followed the Napoleonic Wars a hundred years before – became concerned that history was repeating itself. On Wednesday 19 October 1921 the Prime Minister, Lloyd George, introduced a package of measures designed to reflate the economy and, by so doing, reduce unemployment, particularly in the engineering and shipbuilding industries. Although Lloyd George demanded cuts in production costs, he stressed his Cabinet's view that many of the difficulties, for customer and supplier alike, arose from the lack of an adequate supply of capital at reasonable rates. This he proposed to remedy by making £25 million available during 1922/3 'to guarantee the payment of loans to be applied towards the carrying out of capital undertakings or in purchase of articles manufactured in the United Kingdom required for the purpose of any undertakings'. Under the scheme, loans from clearing banks, often for periods of ten years or more, would be guaranteed by the Government in case the borrower defaulted. The allocation of this fund was to be entrusted to a committee of 'men of high authority and great knowledge in financial, industrial, and economic matters', who would be instructed 'to consider each application in the light of fresh employment which the scheme proposed will bring to this country, and of the benefits by way of increased and cheapened production and transport facilities, which it will confer'. This measure, termed the Trade Facilities Bill, became law in November 1921.[16] As the Act did not apply to the new Province of Northern Ireland, separate provision was made under the Northern Ireland Loans Guarantee Act of April 1922, to be supervised by the Stormont Ministry of Finance. Pirrie could expect to be treated kindly by the Northern Ireland Government, with two of his relatives, John Milne Barbour and John Miller Andrews, as members of the Cabinet.

No sooner had Lloyd George made his statement in the House of Commons than Pirrie was proposing to the Chancellor of the Exchequer that Harland & Wolff be guaranteed a loan under the measure, to permit its programme of capital extension in mainland Britain to be resumed. Pirrie, who had been created a Viscount in the Birthday Honours list, in recognition of his war service, had several meetings with the Chancellor to discuss his application before the measure became law. His main objective was to secure finance for a new repair yard on the Thames at Tilbury, which would also be equipped to build barges and other small craft. This had first been proposed in the late summer of 1920 when Pirrie and Crighton had obtained an option on a site from the Port of London Authority for £700. The scheme had its origins in an offer made by Lord Devonport, the Port of London Authority chairman and a close friend of Pirrie's, to place all the Authority's repair work, both to its vessels and docks, with Harland & Wolff on a commission basis if the Company opened a plant in London. Lack of funds had prevented progress, but Pirrie hoped that work could begin early in 1922 with the help of a Trade Facilities Act (TFA) guaranteed loan of £1,200,000. Less ambitiously he hoped to obtain £145,000 for work at Scotstoun and the Clyde Foundry; £100,345 for rounding off a modified version of the Greenock reconstruction plan; and £48,000 to extend D. & W. Henderson's fitting-out basin at the Meadowside shipyard.

The Government was sympathetic to these requests, stipulating that the orders placed for equipping the new plant should be 'distributed so as to give work to such places as Manchester, Liverpool, Leeds, etc.'. The detail of the negotiations was left to H.G. Baird, a Treasury official, who was not so well placed as Edward Holden of the Midland Bank had been eight years earlier to assess Harland & Wolff's credit-worthiness. Baird complained, 'I found it very difficult to discuss the matter with Lord Pirrie as he talks so much himself that I do not get much opportunity of talking to him.' His repeated requests for security were brushed aside – 'Lord Pirrie stated more than once that as far as he was concerned he would prefer not to carry on the proposed works at the present moment and that he was only making these arrangements to oblige the Government and that it was contrary to his practice to create debentures.' This statement was not entirely accurate since Harland & Wolff had for years depended on a large slice of fixed-interest loans, and at the managing directors' meeting on 23 November 1921 Pirrie was enthusiastic about the possibilities of TFA guaranteed loans. Whatever misgivings Baird may have had were swept aside and the arrangement was finalised in February 1922 – the first guarantee to be sanctioned under the measure.[17]

The successful outcome of the TFA negotiations provided little practical help to the shipyards. During the late summer, as an economy measure, the diesel design department at Lancefield was closed and transferred to Belfast where it was placed directly under Rebbeck's watchful eye. In November 1921 Pirrie ordered that there was to be no new capital expenditure beyond 'what has already been authorised'. Overheads were to be cut to a minimum. For instance, the practice of photographing vessels at every stage of construction was to be abandoned and 'photographs to be generally limited to owners' requests'. By the spring of 1922 the future looked bleak. All the orders from the Royal Mail Steam Packet Company and its subsidiary, Pacific Steam, were suspended, as the conditions under which they were trading were 'the worst they had ever known'. The Holland-America line had taken similar action and it had been only with difficulty that Pirrie had persuaded IMM to proceed with the *Doric* (ship no. 573), the *Minnewaska* (ship no. 613) and the *Minnetonka* (ship no. 614). The Clyde Foundry, although complete, was not commissioned, largely because Harland & Wolff had contracts for castings, with Fullerton Hodgart & Barclay and the Sheepbridge Coal & Iron Company, which had still to expire. At the managing directors' meeting on 9 March, Pirrie issued stern instructions placing an embargo on all further capital expenditure (except that sanctioned under the TFA loan). He reiterated his demand that materials should not be ordered in advance of require-ments. He threatened that work would be awarded to the yard which had achieved the lowest cost. He ordered the Dumbarton and Pointhouse yards to be closed down as soon as the vessels under construction had been completed. This proved unnecessary in the short run as Pirrie managed to persuade the British & Irish Steam Packet

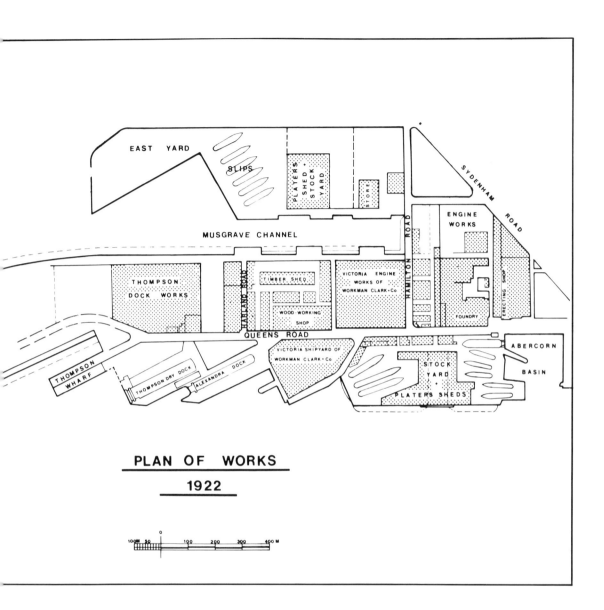

EAST YARD

SLIPS

PLATERS SHED & STOCK YARD

STORE

SYDENHAM ROAD

ENGINE WORKS

MUSGRAVE CHANNEL

THOMPSON DOCK WORKS

HARLAND ROAD

TIMBER SHED

WOOD-WORKING SHOP

VICTORIA ENGINE WORKS OF WORKMAN CLARK•Co

HAMILTON ROAD

ERECTING SHOP

FOUNDRY

QUEENS ROAD

THOMPSON WHARF

THOMPSON DRY DOCK

ALEXANDRA DOCK

VICTORIA SHIPYARD OF WORKMAN CLARK•Co

STOCK YARD

PLATERS SHEDS

ABERCORN

BASIN

PLAN OF WORKS

1922

100M 50 0   100   200   300   400 M

e Belfast works in 1922.

Company (owned by Burns & Laird) to allow work to be resumed in May on the *Ayrshire Coast* (ship no. 607P) and the *Lurcher* (ship no. 657P) and David MacIver & Company to go ahead with the *Araby* (ship no. 630D). However, the Belfast south yard was placed on a care-and-maintenance basis and the workforce dismissed.

At the general meeting in November 1922 Pirrie declared that there was 'a grave shortage of work', but that nevertheless, seventeen ships had been completed during the financial year. This statement exaggerated the Company's success in riding out the recession, since two of the vessels had been built at John Brown's Clydebank yard. The ships delivered from the Company's own yards were unexceptional and bore little comparison to the succession of quality liners built in the years before the war. Low output was anathema to Pirrie's financial strategy which depended on high productivity to achieve low prices and profits. As a consequence, by the end of the 1921/2 financial year Harland & Wolff was in serious trouble. The Scotstoun works

233

alone had lost £68,000. Pirrie announced a profit of just over £341,000, but did not explain that this had been obtained only by deferring depreciation of £266,000, and transferring £369,129 of capital expenditure to the following year. It would seem likely that the dividends and interest payments on the loans were met by increasing overdrafts to over £2,000,000. The work in progress continued to be financed by discounting bills, which totalled a staggering £12,311,386 by the end of the financial year.

During November the National Discount Company became very concerned about the volume of Harland & Wolff bills in the market, the majority of which were endorsed by the P & O Banking Corporation. The managing director made discreet requests at the Midland Bank for a sight of the Company's balance sheet. He pointed out that, since P & O's balance sheet showed contingent liabilities for bills endorsed exceeding £13,000,000, 'the value of the guarantee has entirely evaporated'. The Midland explained that Harland & Wolff had not let them see their balance sheet; but expressed 'undoubted faith in Harland and Pirrie'. It later transpired that Frederick Hyde, the Midland's new managing director, had seen the balance sheet circulated to shareholders and had no doubts. He reported that 'he had seen the figures of Harland & Wolff and their position was a very strong one indeed'. He added that 'it was a concern that was very efficiently managed'. If he had known the true situation of the Company he would have been horrified; but he was in no position to question the word or the accounts of one of his own directors and a leader in the business community.[18]

Harland & Wolff's problems, in common with those of most of the British ship-building industry, persisted throughout the summer of 1922. Eleven vessels were delivered in the last six months of the year and Pirrie continued to curb capital expenditure and unnecessary stocking. He also searched for new markets, particularly in the manufacture of land diesel-electric sets in collaboration with W.H. Allen & Company, of Bedford, winning a contract for three sets from Egypt. These were to be a new trunk-type of engine with four cylinders designed in collaboration with Burmeister & Wain. Pirrie agreed to share the development cost, contributing some £16,000. He made efforts to win structural engineering work, using the expertise that had been acquired in the various plant-reconstruction schemes.

Pirrie was very worried that the lack of new orders might weaken his authority, as managing directors tried to win business themselves. Despite the difficulties, he encouraged recreational events, especially sporting fixtures, between the various works, to instil a sense of loyalty and unity. He impressed his own personality on these activities by arranging for the Company's sports grounds at Glasgow and Liverpool to be named 'Pirrie Park', and endowing a new 'Pirrie Park' in Belfast to be opened the following year. He and his wife continued their practice of giving presents to senior staff as a token of their affection. In 1984 Cecil Slator, whose father, William, was manager of the civil engineering department, recalled the regular arrival of presents and gifts from Lady Pirrie, including aeroplane linen for his mother 'to make up into sheets or pinafores for the youngsters'.[19] Her most unusual gift was pyjamas for the managers, which she arranged for the staff at Witley Court to make when, as more often than not, she and her husband were away. Company officials visiting London were instructed, sometimes to their annoyance, to take back to Queen's Island hampers full of pyjamas for distribution. Such generosity was to be repaid by strict obedience to Pirrie's will. He forbade any individual to reply personally to correspondence and reorganised the design department to bring it more

(overleaf)
The interior of the Clyde
Foundry showing the
massive castings
manufactured in
the works.

directly under his personal control. Edward Wilding, the managing director responsible for ship design, was instructed to remain in Belfast, while one of his assistants accompanied Pirrie on visits to clients. Pirrie was determined that he should be consulted about all decisions. Later in 1922 he was furious when he discovered that the managing directors had made differing arrangements for the Christmas and New Year holidays.

He visited the yards regularly, often accompanied by Lady Pirrie. The managers dreaded these occasions. He was reputed 'to see more in an hour than an ordinary man can see in a week'. He criticised anything that deviated from his orders. After inspecting the Elder Dempster liner *Adda* (ship no. 608Gk) at Greenock, he wanted to know why the Pullman berths were the wrong height and a fraction too close, and why there were no expansion joints on the hot water pipes on C deck. When Pirrie made such expeditions in these years he took three black despatch boxes with him: one, marked RVH, holding paper relating to the Royal Victoria Hospital in Belfast and Lady Pirrie's other charitable activities; a second, marked Stormont, holding papers concerning the Northern Ireland Government; and the third, unlabelled, holding despatches relating to Harland & Wolff.[20]

At the end of 1922 there was a glimmer of hope that the worst of the recession might be over. In December the first order to be received for almost eighteen months was placed by the Japanese company Nippon Yusen Kaisha, for the diesel-engined *Asuka Maru* (ship no. 658M). This unexpected contract for one of Japan's first motor ships was an exploratory move, to give the Japanese information about the Harland & Wolff/Burmeister & Wain four-stroke oil engine. It was followed almost at once by orders from P & O for three cargo liners, from Elder Dempster for six ore-carrying barges, and from Andrew Weir & Company for three motor ships. The three Weir vessels were to be sisters of ships nos 655G and 656G, which had been suspended by British Mexican but were now to be completed for Weir. These contracts were not on commission, but on fixed prices. This was unfamiliar territory to all Harland & Wolff's senior management, who had never needed to estimate a contract price since nearly all ships had been built on commission. Although precise methods, using sophisticated calculating equipment, had been devised for allocating costs to contracts, there was no system for using this information to forecast costs with any accuracy.

The improvement in the order book was given impetus by the change of Government in November 1922 when the Conservatives took power. Lloyd George's outgoing Liberal Government did not favour extending TFA guaranteed loans to shipowners, whereas the Conservatives had no such qualms. The new Government immediately recognised the services of Pirrie's ally, Sir Owen Philipps, by creating him Baron Kylsant of Carmarthen. Pirrie and Kylsant at once took advantage of the provision of TFA loans for shipbuilding to complete some of the suspended contracts. Guaranteed loans were negotiated with either the British or Northern Ireland Governments to allow work to be resumed on seven vessels, including the *Adda* for Elder Dempster, the *Carnarvon Castle* (ship no. 595) for Union-Castle (formerly the *Glenlochy* for the Glen line), and three refrigerated cargo boats for Royal Mail. Since Harland & Wolff had helped to finance some of these vessels already by discounting its own bills and lending to the client, it was a party to most of the loans guaranteed by the Northern Ireland Government. At the same time Andrew Weir arranged a TFA loan of £1,800,000 to finance a contract for a further twelve motor ships of the same class as the five already under construction. This

235

massive order was confirmed in December 1923.[21]

The welcome relief to the beleaguered shipyards and engine works did not close Pirrie's eyes to the extent of Harland & Wolff's over-commitment. The Scotstoun works was instructed to pursue structural engineering contracts and the range of castings that could be made at the newly opened Clyde Foundry was advertised widely. Of most concern to Pirrie was the deteriorating position of David Colville & Sons. By early 1923 the prospects for the company, like the rest of the British steel industry, were dismal. However, Colvilles was not as badly placed as its Scottish competitors, particularly William Beardmore & Company. In February Lord Invernairn, the chairman of Beardmore, called a meeting of Scotland's steelmakers to discuss co-operative action to meet the industry's problems. John Craig, who had remained in command of Colvilles after the takeover, attended the meetings but was not impressed with the reaction of his colleagues to Invernairn's plea for a united front. On receiving Craig's report, Pirrie was sufficiently encouraged to pursue an ambitious merger scheme that he was discussing with Sir Robert Horne, a director of Baldwins Limited. This was to involve the flotation of a holding company, with a projected capital of £65,000,000 to acquire the assets of Baldwins, Cargo Fleet's steel interests, Dorman Long & Company, Bolckow Vaughan, William Beardmore & Company, and Colvilles. Such a proposal had obvious attractions for Pirrie, as it would relieve Harland & Wolff of the burden of deploying its fragile resources to support its ailing steel subsidiary, of which it had no further need as supplies were plentiful. After a preliminary meeting in July the well known accountant Sir William Plender, a partner in Deloitte, Plender, Griffiths & Company, was commissioned to prepare a draft scheme of amalgamation. This foundered over the difficulties of valuing the assets of the participants, and by November Pirrie had shelved it, probably in favour of a fresh plan in which John Brown & Company hoped to participate.[22]

The support afforded by the TFA guaranteed loans prevented the results of the 1922/3 financial year from being worse than those of the previous year. Output improved. The yards handed over twenty-four vessels, totalling 180,815 gross tons. These included the liner *Adda*, the second diesel-engined passenger vessel to enter Elder Dempster service, the 15,000-gross-ton liners *Volendam* and *Veendam* for the Holland-America line, and the 12,000-gross-ton *Orova* for the Pacific Steam Navigation Company. Although most of the vessels completed in 1922/3 were built on commission and yielded the customary 4 per cent on contract costs, an insufficient number of ships was finished or under construction for all the overheads to be allocated. An overall profit was only declared by once again deferring depreciation and in some cases making no provision at all. Depreciation provision for the year amounted to £303,328 (of which £153,000 was deferred) on a total fixed capital of just over £8,300,000. (A more realistic depreciation figure might have been £500,000.) Moreover, capital additions were kept to a bare minimum, even routine maintenance and repairs were cancelled. When the TFA guaranteed expenditure of £686,707 was discounted, the total outlay was a mere £112,000. In announcing a profit of £335,111, Pirrie was therefore disguising what was at best an approximate breakeven outcome. Apart from the TFA guarantees, which were classified as loans rather than overdrafts, bank overdrafts advanced by more than £600,000 to £2,633,935, of which the Midland Group had subscribed over 65 per cent. The additional facilities were needed to replace the loan of £800,000 from the shareholders in David Colville & Sons. The one indication that the market might be picking up was a drop of over £2,000,000 in the contingent liability on discounted bills. As Pirrie admitted at the general

238

meeting, the outlook was uncertain, particularly for the associated companies like John Brown and A.&J. Inglis. In May 1923 he could offer no comfort to a desperate appeal for work from the Clydebank yard: 'I know that you have not very much work at present and you can rely on me to bear you in mind if anything turns up, but I still think the time before us will be very bad.'[23]

Pirrie's biggest headache was to find work for Belfast where overheads were far higher than at either Greenock or Govan. He had always known this, but in the prewar years there had been no cause for concern so long as the commission club generated an order book crammed with high-value large passenger liners. Now he was able to obtain only a small number of contracts for quality liners from the Royal Mail Group, IMM and P & O on commission, while the rest of the orders had to be taken at a fixed price. However, he could not jettison Belfast, and by implication the new province of Northern Ireland, at a moment of intense political crisis. Matters at Queen's Island came to a head in the autumn of 1923 when an account was rendered to the International Navigation Company for the conversion of the *Belgic* from a troopship to a liner. This task had commenced in March 1922 and taken a year to complete. As was the custom, the contract was accepted on a commission basis and the owner's specification was carried out without any estimates of the final cost. When the bill was received, the International Navigation Company 'objected to the amount of the account on the grounds that the expenditure involved in their requirements had not been fully put before them for their approval'. Although much of the blame should have been ascribed to the commission system devised by Pirrie and his former partners, he censured his managing directors for failing either to maintain efficient control of the workforce or make accurate estimates of costs or completion dates. These criticisms were not fair, since the managing directors did not have access to all the information needed to estimate costs and Pirrie had repeatedly altered the work schedules without consulting them. The chief accountant, the faithful William Tawse, was censured for not rendering final accounts quickly enough.

A more serious problem arose towards the end of 1923 as a result of the reorganisation of the design office the year before. Since he moved to London at the beginning of the century, Pirrie had maintained personal control of the accounts and contracts. He had always worked out the rough designs of every vessel personally, in consultation with the owners. The final drawings were then worked up by the design office in Belfast; but until the vessel was under construction the managing director in charge of design was forbidden from dealing with the owners directly. After the war Pirrie, who was anxious to weld all the yards into one single production unit, tried to extend this system to Govan, Greenock and the associated companies. This policy would seem to have failed. In the declining market, managers, particularly of the associated companies, resented Pirrie's autocratic allocation of work, and sought to win business from long-established customers. The centralisation of the design department under Wilding in Belfast had been an attempt to counteract such independent action. The other yards hit back by complaining that the design office was inefficient, failing to supply drawings on time and so holding up production. Simultaneously Wilding used his increased responsibility to discuss directly with owners alterations and additions to designs without informing Pirrie. Unfortunately he failed to mention that changes would necessarily involve extra expenditure. Wilding, with no reason to believe to the contrary, assumed that all the vessels were being built on commission. He made the mistake of agreeing to extras on the massive Andrew Weir order, which Pirrie had accepted almost at cost. He was encouraged in this decision by John Dickinson, the managing director responsible for Govan, who gave in to all the requests of Weir's superintendent engineer, Captain McBride.[24]

When he discovered this error, Pirrie summoned Wilding to London and challenged him. Wilding, naturally highly strung, broke down completely. He was suspended for twelve months, reportedly on health grounds, and removed from his post. He was not even allowed to return to his office on Queen's Island to recover his belongings. Pirrie ordered his desk to be broken open to discover what other independent decisions he had taken. Wilding, suspecting that he would have to pay with his job, had wisely cleared his desk before departing. Walter Edmenson, an able young member of the secretary's office, was at once despatched to Govan to control the wayward Dickinson. Pirrie's harsh judgement of Wilding was out of character and can possibly be attributed to failing health. Neither he nor Lady Pirrie were well. During October he was showing some special friends over his poultry farm at Witley Court when he slipped and dislocated his left shoulder. He was confined to the house for several weeks, where he seems to have fallen prey to anxieties about the future of the Company.[25]

At the meeting of managing directors on 12 February 1924 Pirrie strengthened his control over design. He made no reference to Wilding's disappearance, but stated, as recorded in the minutes:

> Mr John Angus has been appointed to personally assist Lord Pirrie and accompany him to meetings with shipowners when plans are to be discussed. The preliminary designs will be worked out under the supervision of Mr Angus and until the official order is actually given and the question of whether the work is to be allocated to Belfast or one of the branches settled, the Managing Directors will not usually be troubled with the arrangement, but when necessary Lord Pirrie wishes Mr Angus to have the advantage of being able to consult Mr Payne and Mr Rebbeck as regards hull and machinery designs respectively to help and guide him in discussions with the Owners and to prevent mistakes.

T.C. Tobin, Wilding's assistant, was appointed head of the design department at Belfast which was placed under the control of Payne and Rebbeck. Tobin disliked Angus intensely and was unwilling to do business with him. It is almost impossible to understand how Pirrie thought this system could be successful. If the managing directors were not to be consulted at the design and estimating stage, how were accurate forecasts of costs and prices to be calculated? How could a man in his late seventies, with many other commitments and just one assistant, design anything up to twenty ships a year? Wilding was not the only managing director to be removed from office at the 12 February meeting. The faithful Kempster, without being consulted, was stripped of his duties as managing director of the Belfast electrical department, which he had retained when he moved to Greenock in 1916. He made a feeble protest, but gave way.

Pirrie's attitude throughout the meeting was dictatorial, mirroring precisely the nostrums of Sir William Robertson that he had ordered to be engrossed in the minute book in 1917. As was reflected in the minutes, Pirrie was at his most commanding when outlining, in the vaguest of terms, the programme of new building:

> **Belfast:** . . . [The Chairman] hopes that before long he will have arranged definitely for certain works such as another large passenger vessel like the *Adda*,

The North Woolwich Works, the nerve centre of Harland & Wolff's organisation on the Thames, opened in 1924.

also two large oil boats, which he thinks of laying in Belfast, all Diesel engined ships. We have not actually closed these yet, but we are in very close negotiation regarding them. His own feeling is that in two or three months' time we shall be in a better position as regards work, and meantime both the shipyard and Engine Works Departments at Belfast will have an excellent opportunity of getting everything into good shape.

Clyde [Govan]: It must be very gratifying to Mr Dickinson to have such a lot of work on hand and a keel ready to follow another as each ship is launched . . .

Greenock: We are also on the point of settling for five vessels about 400 feet long, single screw with Diesel engines of the long stroke type. One vessel might be laid down at once on No. 4 slip at Greenock and the next one on No. 3 slip when the P & O vessel (No. 659GK) is launched. Greenock would then be in a similar position to Govan of having all slips occupied . . .

Hendersons: Lord Pirrie hopes to close for a further five vessels about 400 feet long, pure cargo boats, and thinks of putting them down at Meadowside to keep Hendersons busy. Mr Crighton and he think Hendersons will be cheaper than Belfast for this class of boat and therefore it is better to reserve the Belfast slips for the larger vessels.

Inglis: Lord Pirrie is trying to obtain work for Inglis, and hopes to get four boats

241

of 250 feet long each. He is also dealing with enquiries for MacMillans Yard, we of course being interested in the supply of Diesel engines for these vessels.

Lord and Lady Pirrie attending a launch in 192? the Ardrossan Dockyard Shipbuilding Company part of the Royal Mail Group.

Pirrie gave no hint as to where all this work was to come from. Since the confirmation of the twelve-ship contract for Govan from Andrew Weir & Company in December, only three small ships had been ordered, two by J. & P. Hutchison from Pointhouse (nos 688P and 689P) and one by the Steamship Trading Company from Govan (no. 690G). There is little evidence that any of the projected orders amounted to more than tentative inquiries. The large liners for Belfast were dependent on the outcome of applications for guaranteed loans by the British & African Steam Navigation Company and the Pacific Steam Navigation Company, which would take some time to process. However, Pirrie confidently told his managing directors that he expected all the orders to be finalised by the first week in March, when he intended to leave on a visit for South America.

Although Pirrie delayed his departure until 21 March, no new orders had been placed. His purpose in visiting South America was to inspect 'the ports and facilities for shipping in that country' and to explore the possibility of launching Christmas holiday trips and summer holiday tours to Europe. He had doubts about going, and uncharacteristically consulted Crighton about the wisdom of being out of the country for so long. Crighton reassured him, 'as he felt it would be desirable for him to make the trip in the interests of the Company, as we are so deeply associated with that trade by our connection with the Royal Mail, Pacific S.N. Co., Lamport & Holt, Nelson, MacIvers & Co., RMSP Meat Transports and also Argentine Navigation Co.'. One of Pirrie's last engagements before leaving was to inspect the now-completed London works, which consisted of eleven separate units spread throughout the Port of London Authority's complex of docks. It was designed to provide a rapid repair service to the PLA and those companies for whom Harland & Wolff did such work on commission. At the Tilbury site there were facilities for building barges and other small craft. On the eve of his departure, Pirrie called on his lawyers, Ashurst Morris and Crisp, to sign his will. He had been unwell since his fall the previous October, with a recurrence of the prostate illness that had nearly killed him in 1911. There is much to suggest that he had a premonition that he would never return.

On 21 March Lord and Lady Pirrie departed for Buenos Aires on the Royal Mail liner *Arlanza* which had been built at Queen's Island in 1912. Pirrie was accompanied by A.T. Marshall, acting as his private secretary, and by his personal physician, Dr J.S. Morrow, of Belfast. He had planned to return on the *Avon* which sailed from Buenos Aires. Instead, since the trip was benefiting both his and Lady Pirrie's health, he extended his tour by rounding Cape Horn to Valparaiso. There he transferred to the *Ebro*, sailing to Autofagosta in Chile. While staying in the town he caught a chill, which rapidly developed into pneumonia. By the time the vessel reached the Panama Canal, he was beginning to convalesce. Dictatorial even on his sickbed, he insisted on being brought up on deck to view the canal. The result was fatal. Despite a gallant fight by a team of doctors and nurses who had joined the ship, he died at 11.30 in the evening on 7 June 1924, at the age of seventy-eight.[26]

Messages of sympathy poured onto the *Ebro*. When she docked in New York, Lord Inverforth, who had planned to go home with the Pirries, was waiting at the quayside. Lord Pirrie's embalmed body was placed on the *Olympic* and taken to Belfast. He was buried in Belfast City Cemetery on 23 June 1924, the sixty-second anniversary of his entry into Harland & Wolff. His obituary notices paid tribute to his colossal achievement as a shipbuilder. The magazine *Syren and Shipping Illustrated* carried the headline 'The Passing of the World's Greatest Shipbuilder'. H.M. Pollock, Minister of Finance in the Northern Ireland Government, said on hearing the news:

> A great Ulsterman has fallen today! And today more than ever we realise all his greatness as we mourn his loss. Lord Pirrie was not only a mighty architect, whose vast designs embraced the globe; he was the great master builder who carried these designs into execution, a veritable Napoleon of industry in the greatness and splendour of the schemes which had even then taken form in his mind. He had gifts of an extraordinary character. No one could withstand his enthusiasm. He carried men along with him by the very intensity and ardour of his great ideals. His death leaves a gap which our limited vision can discern but little power to fill.[27]

Like Pollock, everyone praised his qualities, extending their sympathy to Lady Pirrie whose constant support was acknowledged as a keystone in his success. A few mentioned the current lack of work in the shipyards, but since no one other than Pirrie knew how serious Harland & Wolff's position was, all had assumed that the problems were purely temporary, the solutions lying with Lord Pirrie on his return. Sadly Pirrie was never to return and, as all the Company's managing directors had realised only too well after the 12 February meeting, Pirrie alone knew the details of negotiations for new tonnage, and his secrets, if there were any, had died with him.

He had made no practical preparations for his death or retirement, which he must have known were imminent. For this negligence, despite all the glowing tributes, he must stand condemned. His ambition and dictatorial ways had blinded him to the need to educate his managers in the methods he used to control the business. He had surrounded himself with 'splendid men' who emulated his lifestyle but lacked the strength of character to stand up to him. He had promoted to senior posts weak men who would not argue with him. George Cuming had died, Edward Wilding had suffered a nervous breakdown and Robert Crighton was not well. J.W. Kempster was a kindly gentleman who would have been more at home in a university cloister than in the world of business. J.P. Dickinson at Govan was incompetent and weak and Charles Payne at Belfast was a showman, whose vanity had been encouraged by the Pirries. Of the managing directors the only one with any stamina was F.E. Rebbeck, but he, as junior, was in no position to argue with his colleagues. The two men who knew something of Pirrie's methods, William Tawse, the chief accountant, and John Philp, the Company secretary, lacked authority and had been in awe of their master, telling him what he wished to know. Harland & Wolff, the biggest shipbuilding concern in the world, was without a pilot and none of the directors had even the vaguest idea how to pass orders from the bridge to the engine room. It is doubtful if even Pirrie, when he had left for South America in March, had any clear plan for taming the leviathan he had created. There is a sense that death came as a relief in the midst of the worst tempest he had experienced in his business life.[28]

KYLSANT'S CATASTROPHE
1924-30

Ever since the managing directors had been appointed in 1907 it had been understood that when Lord Pirrie died the office of principal would cease to exist and the managing directors would assume executive control of the Company. With only sketchy knowledge of the capital structure of Harland & Wolff and the terms on which contracts were accepted, the managing directors were unprepared to assume their awesome responsibilities. Pirrie, however, did not intend that they should be left to direct the business unaided. As he had told Edward Holden ten years before, he planned that after his death Lord Kylsant 'would be absolute master of everything'. Unfortunately he had neglected to inform his deputy chairman, Robert Crighton, and his lawyer, Charles Crisp. Three days after his death the managing directors met in a state of shock and confusion at the London office. In sombre mood they solemnly recorded their tribute to Lord Pirrie, promising faithfully to cherish his memory and example. Crighton, keeping his head, recoiled from hastily accepting the chairmanship and reminded his colleagues that 'whereas hitherto they had individually approached Lord Pirrie for authority to carry out certain work, adopt a certain policy or incur expenditure, each in future would have to consult the others in view of their joint responsibility'.

Within a matter of days Kylsant had taken possession of Lord Pirrie's private office in London and installed himself as chairman. Although Lady Pirrie probably knew of her husband's intention, she did not approve. She had never liked Kylsant and had steadfastly refused to socialise with him or his wife. She found him arrogant and aloof, though this may have had more to do with his great height and stuttering speech than with any deliberate attitude towards her. He enjoyed a social acceptance which she craved. Although a baronet, Kylsant's father had been first and foremost a clergyman with strong Anglo-Catholic attitudes, establishing a convent and a training college for missionary priests in the rural Wiltshire town of Warminster. From this background, Kylsant and his brothers had come to the world of business with an almost missionary zeal. By the mid-1920s their achievements were remarkable. The eldest brother, Lord St Davids, controlled a massive group of investment trusts, known collectively as the 118 Old Broad Street Group. The second brother, Major General Sir Ivor Philipps, controlled Schweppes, the soft-drink manufacturers, and Ilford, the photographic suppliers. The youngest brother, Laurence Philipps, later Lord Milford, owned the Court line and a marine insurance company that bore his name. Their view of business was coloured by their liberal Anglo-Catholicism and they saw it as a means for employment rather than for making profit. Such an approach won them respect at a time of high unemployment.

On the way back from America on the *Olympic* Lady Pirrie had offered Lord Inverforth the post of chairman, in the mistaken belief that as a trustee of her husband's estate she automatically had voting control. This was not the case, as Kylsant's Royal Mail Group had held the controlling interest since 1919.[1] As a friendly gesture, Kylsant appointed Lady Pirrie president of the Company for life.

Her fellow trustees of the estate were three of her husband's most loyal servants, Robert Crighton, William Tawse, the Company's chief accountant, and John Philp, the Company secretary. The will was a long, complex and singular document. The principal legatee was Lady Pirrie, who was to enjoy most of the income and property of the estate for the rest of her life. There were other annuities to be paid annually; £500 to John Philp as long as he kept the accounts of the estate; £300 to Saxon Payne; £300 to Lord Pirrie's secretary, Iris Edmiston; £1,000 to his niece, Mrs Hind; and £500 to Elva Andrews, daughter of Thomas Andrews. These were to be paid out of the income on Lord Pirrie's investment in Harland & Wolff. On Lady Pirrie's death, provided Harland & Wolff was still a private company, the income and eventually the capital of the trust were to be paid into the Company's reserve, 'to be applied by it in the manner and for any purposes in and for which the reserve fund of the Company may be applied under its Articles of Association'. If Harland & Wolff became public, then Lord Pirrie's trustees were to continue to administer the estate on behalf of 'the persons or corporations registered at the date of the passing of the resolution for the conversion of the Company into a public company as holders of the ordinary and "A" preference shares'.[2].

It is not known to what extent Kylsant was aware of these arrangements. Pirrie had probably told him the outline, but had not explained in any detail the methods he employed to control the business in his iron grip. Kylsant, as one of the largest

Lord Kylsant (centre) at launch of the Royal Mail liner *Asturias*, from Queen's Island on 7 July 1925 by the Duchess of Abercorn (left). On the right are Charles Payne, the shipyard manager, a Lady Kylsant.

customers, would have been familiar with the commission arrangements and would have known something of the unusual system of loans. He would have been aware of the terms of loans under the TFA and Northern Ireland Loans Guarantee Act and of the contingent liabilities. He would have known nothing of the overall financial framework of the Company. As a shareholder, he would have been given only a very summary and misleading balance sheet at the annual meetings. Like the managing directors, he had been denied any information about the new building programme, except in so far as it involved the Royal Mail Group. Pirrie may have imagined that Kylsant could slide easily into his seat with little preparation. He had worked closely with him in the acquisition of Elder Dempster and Union-Castle and respected his consummate skill as a financier and shipping manager. As men of business they were different. Pirrie was, from first to last, a technician-turned-manufacturer. He understood better than most how to design and build ships. He used this technical knowledge to control the Company's building programme and to catch out those who had disobeyed orders. Kylsant had no such technical background; however, in one respect, the two were very much alike. To the end of his life Pirrie retained the rare gift of controlling a massive manufacturing enterprise by numbers. He endlessly compared figures, ruthlessly censuring those who were shown by their accounts to have failed in their duty. Kylsant exercised his absolute authority over the Royal Mail Group by the manipulation of capital and astute presentation of the accounts of the member companies. He grasped in his early years in business, at the end of the nineteenth century, that shipowning and management, particularly in the framework of the conferences, were matters of finance and margins. He was preoccupied with strategy, squeezing margins to the disadvantage of competitors in conference arrangements and mail agreements. The niceties of tactics bored him. When he had established the policy, he preferred to leave it to others to carry it out. Consequently he had come to rely on a faithful band of able lieutenants for the day-to-day management of the Group. Pirrie, who had dealt with these men over the details of the design of new tonnage, had no subordinates of equal calibre, with the possible exception of John Craig.

Kylsant quickly introduced a system for directing the affairs of Harland & Wolff. Since he had no private office, he was accustomed to moving, according to a set routine, from the office of one company of which he was chairman to another. Midday on Saturdays was set aside for Harland & Wolff's London head office. Insensitive to the desire of the staff to get home to their families, he would keep them in attendance until he had finished his review of the business of the week, which was often late in the afternoon. His arrival each week was reported to P.G.M. Mitchell, the general manager of the Royal Mail Steam Packet Company who knew that it was then safe to leave for the weekend.[3]

Immediately after Pirrie's death, Kylsant, Tawse and Philp began to inquire into the state of his personal affairs and those of Harland & Wolff. This task was made almost impossible by Lady Pirrie's campaign to nominate Inverforth to the chair. She sought out her husband's business friends, particularly Inchcape and Aberconway, imploring them to intervene on her side.

Meanwhile, Kylsant was stunned by the results of their investigations. It appeared that Pirrie's magnificent lifestyle had left him almost destitute. He had an overdraft from the Midland Bank, secured over the Witley Court estate, of some £325,000, and was committed to buying back personally £473,260 worth of Harland & Wolff 'A' preference shares from members of the Colville family. His principal assets were

of John Brown and a former principal. Although not named as deputy chairman, Craig was to take over all Crighton's management responsibilities, particularly the chairmanship of the all-important management committee. Kylsant also formed a new committee, comprising himself and John Craig, to control the Company's finances. In the immediate future Kylsant and Craig had little room to manoeuvre. Plant closures would necessitate the cancellation of contracts and would inevitably trigger a loss of confidence. All Kylsant and Craig could do was to reinforce Pirrie's policy of restraint and hope that the economy would improve. At the first management committee meeting Kylsant chaired, on 18 November 1924, it was decided to introduce from the New Year 'a co-ordinated system . . . to ensure the regular periodical review of expenditure and secure every possible reduction in working costs'. It was difficult to halt capital expenditure, as many of the projects in hand – like the London works and the east yard at Belfast – were being financed by Government-guaranteed loans. Some investment was needed to equip the Belfast engine works to manufacture the new generation of Burmeister & Wain long-stroke diesel engines. Reducing the workforce was equally hard, as contracts were dispersed, often at the customer's wish, throughout the yards in the Group.

Since Pirrie's death none of the catalogue of prospective contracts he had outlined at the meeting on 12 February 1924 had materialised. Kylsant had ordered two motor ships from D. & W. Henderson through the King line's new subsidiary, the British Motorship Company. The Pacific Steam Navigation Company had contracted with Govan for a lighter. At Queen's Island orders had been confirmed at the time of Crighton's death by Elder Dempster, supported by guaranteed loans, for the

9,000-gross-ton liner *Apapa*; by the Belfast Steamship Company for two 3,700-gross-ton cargo liners; and by the Lago Shipping Company (managed by Andrew Weir) for four small steam-engined oil tankers. These four vessels were specially designed to enter Lake Maracaibo in Venezuela, whose rich oil reserves were being exploited by British Mexican. With the exception of the *Apapa*, all these ships were to be built at a loss as a means of keeping the workforce in being. Towards the end of the year Kylsant instructed the Royal Mail Group members to provide some succour. The Argentine Navigation Company ordered two small craft from A. & J. Inglis, Elder Dempster six barges from Govan, and David MacIver a 5,000-gross-ton liner from MacMillans of Dumbarton.

During December Kylsant, taking up where Pirrie had left off, inquired into the big discrepancies between estimates and prices. He was especially anxious about the huge losses that were accumulating on three P & O boats completing at Greenock. These vessels, built on a normal commercial basis, were set to lose £311,256, or over 11 per cent on a total contract price of £2,672,700. The directors were ordered to carry out a detailed and urgent review of overhead charges, co-ordinated by Craig who insisted on the 'necessity of immediate and drastic retrenchment'. For the first time they were to be given access to the information contained in the private ledger. On 8, 9 and 10 January 1925 the management committee convened in Belfast, under Craig's watchful eye, to review the results of the inquiry. The meeting revealed the directors' ignorance of the way in which overheads and development charges were allocated. In answer to Kylsant's questions about the P & O boats, it emerged that Pirrie's obsession with high standards was partly to blame. J.W. Kempster, who was

BALANCE SHEET

CAPITAL AND LIABILITIES.	£	s.	d.	£	s.	
Capital :—						
Authorised :—						
4,000,000 6% First Cumulative Preference Shares of £1 each	4,000,000	0	0			
4,000,000 6% "A" Cumulative Preference Shares of £1 each	4,000,000	0	0			
100,000 "B" Preference Shares of £1 each	100,000	0	0			
4,000 Ordinary Shares of £1,000 each	4,000,000	0	0			
	12,100,000	0	0			
Issued :—						
4,000,000 6% First Cumulative Preference Shares of £1 each	4,000,000	0	0			
Less Calls in Arrear	7,370	5	0			
				3,992,629	15	
3,095,094 6% "A" Cumulative Preference Shares of £1 each				3,095,094	0	
20,300 "B" Preference Shares of £1 each				20,300	0	
3,000 Ordinary Shares of £1,000 each	3,000,000	0	0			
225 Ordinary Shares of £1,000 each (£100 paid)	22,500	0	0			
				3,022,500	0	
				10,130,523	15	
Reserve				1,300,000	0	
Pension Fund				165,030	8	
Amount at Credit of Controlled Companies				727,301	8	
Trade Facilities Act Advances repayable in five equal yearly instalments commencing 17th May, 1928				1,293,344	19	
Deposits				605,696	1	
Sundry Creditors and Credit Balances				2,656,189	8	
Receipts on Account of Work in Progress in excess of Expenditure				121,766	18	
Dividends on Preference Shares payable 1st January, 1925 (since paid)				126,601	6	
Profit and Loss Account :—						
Balance for period ended 31st December, 1924, after providing for Preference Dividends paid and accrued to 31st December, 1924, and including transfer from Reserve and balance of £3,228 14s. 3d. brought forward from last year	241,538	10	9			
Less Interim Dividend of 2½% less tax paid on Ordinary Shares	58,125	0	0			
				183,413	10	
				£17,309,867	18	
Contingent Liabilities.						
In respect of Bills discounted	£8,830,570	0	0			

responsible for Cairds, noted that Lord Inchcape had been satisfied with the quality of vessels built by Cairds before the takeover when 'Belfast practice' had been introduced. The meeting observed correctly that, since 'the Belfast yards were designed and equipped for building vessels of the large Atlantic passenger type', overheads there were necessarily very high; but they were powerless to draw the conclusion that the Queen's Island yards should be closed for the time being. All the directors could recommend was an intensive campaign to identify all unnecessary expenditure, cut salaries and wages and reduce stocks by 25 per cent in the coming year. It was also decided to appoint a general manager to take charge of the three repair works, whose individual management had been severely criticised by several shipowners since Pirrie's death.

Kylsant took great care in preparing the Harland & Wolff balance sheet for publication in March 1925 – the first time in the Company's history that it had made any disclosure other than to its very small band of ordinary shareholders and its bankers. Further huge losses in the second half of 1924, estimated at more than

The first published ba... sheet of the limited Company, drawn up Lord Kylsant and desi... to conceal more than to reveal.

ASSETS.

	£ s. d.	£ s. d.
Shipbuilding Yards at Belfast, Glasgow and Greenock		
Marine Engineering Works and Foundries at Belfast and Glasgow		
Ship and Engine Repairing Establishments at London, Liverpool and Southampton		
Freehold and Leasehold Land, Property and Buildings ; Machinery, Plant and Tools ..		12,720,399 5 4
Additions during period		727,692 17 11
		13,448,092 3 3
Less : Depreciation and amounts specially written off to 30th June, 1923 ..	3,954,906 19 7	
Depreciation for period to 31st December, 1924	107,913 7 1	
		4,062,820 6 8
		9,385,271 16 7
Investments in Steel Works and other controlled Companies at cost		4,720,334 0 5
Government and other Investments .. ¡ ..		354,510 4 2
Stock of Materials		851,630 14 0
Sundry Trade Debtors and Outstandings ..		644,058 15 3
Expenses of Issue of Preference Shares, *less* written off		33,205 4 5
Expenditure on Work in Progress in ex:ess of Receipts		1,066,567 12 11
Cash at Bankers and in Hand		254,289 10 3

KYLSANT, *Director.*

JOHN CRAIG, *Director.*

£17,309,867 18 0

£400,000, were hidden from view by transferring £225,000 from the 'Reserve' and a little more than £210,000 from the 'Reserve against losses on contracts'. These transfers appeared in the profit and loss account under the entry '£456,093 from reserve for depreciation'. In addition, special dividends were paid by the Company's wholly-owned subsidiaries Caird & Company of £120,000, and D. & W. Henderson, of £600,000. Depreciation was suspended, with the value of the fixed assets in fact being increased by £2,520. Almost certainly the preference dividend was paid out of the proceeds of the cash raised by the issue of the first cumulative preference shares. Apart from cutting the loans to the Company, the issue had allowed Kylsant to reduce the overdrafts from nearly £1,100,000 to £858,391 and hold a cash balance of £254,289. In addition the Company had purchased £100,000 of 3 per cent Government stock. None of these transactions was explained in the balance sheet published on 20 March 1925.

This was a masterly document. The liabilities' side of the balance sheet was headed by a list of the authorised capital, totalling £12,100,000, beneath which was the issued

Table 9.1
Capital 1924-30

	1924[2]	1925	1926	1927	1928	1929	1930
	£	£	£	£	£	£	£
Ordinary shares	3,022,500	3,090,000	3,090,000	3,090,000	3,090,000	3,090,000	3,090,000
First cumulative preference shares	3,992,629	4,000,000	4,000,000	4,000,000	4,000,000	4,000,000	4,000,000
'A' preference shares	3,095,094	3,095,094	3,095,094	3,095,094	3,095,094	3,095,094	3,095,094
'B' preference shares	20,300	20,300	20,300	20,300	20,300	20,300	20,300
Amount at credit of controlled companies	729,623	295,254	186,506	704,806	695,685	623,900	691,470
David Colville & Sons	62,748	65,771	10,241	10,241	8,005	5,768	11,163
D.&W. Henderson	313,000	173,000	167,650	92,650	92,650	2,650	3,916
Sir Frederick N. Henderson[1]	6,253	6,505	6,766	—	—	—	—
Ocean Transport Co.	31,432	4,429	1,847	—	465	—	—
Burmeister & Wain	97,784	33,647	(35,009)	313,997	310,476	320,298	343,782
London & Glasgow Engineering and Iron Shipbuilding Co.	90,505	—	—	—	—	—	—
Caird & Co.	116,427	—	(249,499)	289,917	284,088	295,183	306,297
Clyde Alloy Steel Co.	11,474	11,902	(11,137)	(11,137)	—	—	—
Heaton, Tabb & Co.	—	—	—	—	—	—	26,310
Deposits	605,696	377,417	378,145	371,758	375,968	237,098	40,395
Deposits over £10,000							
African Steamship Co.	40,497	—	—	—	—	—	—
J.M. Barbour and Lord Justice Andrews	11,256	11,657	11,925	12,203	12,492	12,793	—
F. Leyland & Co. (1900) Ltd	132,379	139,081	139,081	139,081	139,081	100,000	—
H.&W. Nelson	250,000	182,500	182,500	—	—	—	—
Nelson Steam Navigation Co.	—	—	—	76,500	76,500	25,003	25,000
Mary K. Purcell	13,032	13,776	13,786	12,904	19,107	—	—
Royal Mail Steam Packet Co.	107,302	—	—	—	—	—	—
White Star	—	—	—	100,000	100,000	80,000	—
Johnston Hughes	10,125	—	—	—	—	—	—

Notes
1   Sir Frederick N. Henderson was the owner of the bulk of D.&W. Henderson's preference stock.
2   At 31 December 1924
( )   =   Debit balances: these were not deducted from the amount at credit of controlled companies.

capital standing at £10,130,523 and the 'Reserve' of £1,300,000. The old heading 'Loans and deposits bearing interest' was split into three: 'Amount at credit of controlled companies' (representing loans from David Colville & Sons, D. & W. Henderson Limited, the Ocean Transport Company, Burmeister & Wain, London & Glasgow and Caird & Company); 'Trade Facilities Act advances' (repayable in five equal yearly instalments commencing 17 May 1928); 'Deposits' (representing the loans from individuals but more significantly from the members of the Royal Mail Group and Frederick Leyland & Company).

Table 9.2
Profit and loss 1924-30

	Gross profit/(loss) for year before tax and depreciation	Net profit/(loss) per published accounts after depreciation and tax	Distribution (transfers to/from reserves and dividends)	Balance carried to following year
	£	£	£	£
1924[1]	550,396	409,776	304,591	183,414
1925	559,175	200,449	248,394	135,469
1926	229,476	201,446	192,000	144,915
1927	(149,857)	(157,712)	(108,000)	95,203
1928	479,302	204,356	192,000	107,558
1929	559,258	216,749	192,000	132,307
1930	367,882	105,746	—	238,053

Note
1 Accounts for eighteen months to 31 December 1924

Table 9.3
Fixed assets 1924-30

Freehold and leasehold land, property and buildings

	1924[1]	1925	1926	1927	1928	1929	1930
	£	£	£	£	£	£	£
Additions	31,755	194,850	(3,915)	515,852	9,993	19,075	(2,849)
Depreciation and losses on sales	—	175,333[2]	—	—	1,000[2]	78,283[2]	66,890[2]
Total	5,033,543	5,053,060	5,049,143	5,564,997	5,573,990	5,514,782	5,445,043

Machinery, plant and tools

Additions	72,051	267,826	35,434	245,580	61,997	79,331	39,708
Depreciation and losses on sales	102,521[2]	170,951[2]	3,931	3,559	248,998[2]	221,715[2]	183,106[2]
Total	4,351,728	4,448,604	4,480,107	4,722,129	4,535,129	4,392,745	4,249,347

Notes
1 Half year only to 31 December 1924
2 Included in the published accounts sometimes for the succeeding year
( ) = Negative sum

Overdrafts, the 'Reserve against losses on contracts' and 'Reserve for expenditure on additions' were buried under the entry: 'Sundry creditors and credit balances'. There was only a bald profit and loss statement at the bottom of the liabilities' side. This stated that transfers had been made from reserves, but the wording was designed to suggest that these were insignificant:

Balance for period ended 31st December 1924, after providing for Preference Dividends paid and accrued to 31st December 1924, and including transfer from reserve and balance of £3,228 14s 3d brought forward from last year.

Table 9.4
Reserves 1924-30

	1924[1]	1925	1926	1927	1928	1929	1930
	£	£	£	£	£	£	£
Reserve	1,300,000	1,300,000	1,300,000	1,300,000	1,000,000[2]	1,000,000	1,000,000
Reserve against losses on contracts	221,222	228,794	16,161	16,161	6,839	6,839	26,839
Reserve for expenditure on additions	14,104	14,104	14,104	14,104	14,104	14,104	14,104
Reserve for investments	460,837	—	—	—	—	—	—
Reserve for losses of subsidiaries	—	—	134,600	—	21,437	21,437	21,437

Notes
1   At 31 December 1924
2   Transfer of £300,000 included in 1927 published balance sheet

Table 9.5
Bank balances 1924-30

	1924[1]	1925	1926	1927	1928	1929	1930
	£	£	£	£	£	£	£
Midland Bank	(718,047)	(1,010,848)	(1,062,955)	(769,123)	(872,499)	(1,145,083)	(1,162,042)
Belfast Banking Co.	1,495	(200,037)	(246,277)	212,720	(142,938)	(211,497)	(232,431)
Clydesdale Bank	(49,113)	(176,061)	112,534	(191,571)	194,899	(149,275)	(196,696)
Bank of Ireland	77,981	(277,404)	(318,136)	(258,858)	(184,246)	(223,941)	(333,096)
National Bank of Scotland	147,946	(152,546)	(88,631)	(84,541)	(91,904)	(80,804)	(96,809)
Royal Bank of Scotland	(86,852)	(208,668)	(162,597)	(160,796)	(104,988)	(110,752)	(142,616)
Union Discount Co.	(4,379)	(388)	8,719	10,035	64,213	40,408	26,711
Lloyds Bank	5,027	5,027	5,027	10,626	10,132	10,188	10,529
P&O Banking Corporation	12,476	134,171	60,617	79,686	48,289	57,446	18,178
Total	(613,466)	(1,886,754)	(1,691,699)	(1,151,822)	(1,079,042)	(1,813,310)	(2,108,272)

Notes
1   At 31 December 1924
( )   =   Debit balances

Table 9.6
Bills receivable discounted 1924-30

	£
1924[1]	8,830,570
1925	8,156,570
1926	6,511,430
1927	4,178,754
1928	4,461,810
1929	4,524,487
1930	4,257,800

Note
1   At 31 December 1924

The profit and loss account mentioned a 2½ per cent interim dividend on ordinary shares but made no reference to the payment of a final dividend which Kylsant had decided to suspend. The assets' side of the balance sheet was even more opaque. The value of the property, buildings, machinery, plant and tools was entered as a global sum of £12,720,399, to which was added £727,693 for acquisitions over an unspecified period. The total of £13,448,092 was reduced by subtracting £3,954,906 – representing, apparently, 'Depreciation and amounts specially written off to 30th June 1923'. In fact this sum was the whole of the depreciation that had been allocated since the formation of the limited company in 1885. Depreciation for the eighteen months since 1 July 1923 was entered at £107,913. Although this had been achieved entirely by making transfers from reserves, this was not mentioned. Moreover, unknown to the shareholders, Kylsant had cancelled the deferred depreciation of £643,174. Beneath the fixed assets was an entry for 'Investments in steel works and other controlled companies' of £4,720,334. Previously it had been the custom to show investments after deducting the 'Reserve for investments' but this was not done in the published account, and instead the reserve was credited to 'Sundry creditors and credit balances'. As a result, the Company's investments appeared to be worth considerably more than their market value. The investments in other companies like John Brown & Company and Royal Mail Steam Packet Company were grouped under another heading, 'Government and other investments', totalling £354,510. This was, no doubt, to give the impression that these were readily realisable assets mostly in the form of Government stock. In fact only £79,036 represented Government securities. At the foot of the assets' side was 'Cash at bankers and in hand', totalling £254,289. In the absence of any reference to bank borrowing, this reinforced the impression of healthy liquidity. Despite Kylsant's best endeavours the Company's accountant, Price Waterhouse & Company, qualified their report:

> Subject to the sufficiency of the provision for Depreciation, we are of the opinion that such Balance Sheet is properly drawn up so as to exhibit a true and correct view of the state of the Company's affairs.

At the general meeting Kylsant admitted that contracts had been accepted at a loss. Despite a few raised eyebrows at these reservations and the absence of a final ordinary share dividend, the overall reaction of the shipping and shipbuilding press was positive, allaying fears that the dividends on the new first cumulative preference shares would never be paid.

As Kylsant knew all too well, such a brilliant presentation of the Harland & Wolff balance sheet could only provide a framework for the future. It could not cut costs, reduce manpower and win new business in a difficult market. Throughout March Craig had continued his campaign to cut costs and improve efficiency. By 3 March £25,000 a year had been saved by making staff redundant at Belfast and by the decision taken to sack the inefficient and prodigal manager of the London works, replacing him with the colourful and more dynamic Robert Rainie. Early in April James Gray, the superintending engineer of Union-Castle, was recruited as general manager of the three ship-repairing establishments, with the commission to carry out a penetrating inquiry into their services. The extravagance and opulence of their management horrified him. His knowledge of the commission system quickly helped him identify one source of waste in the practice of submitting very detailed accounts for every job that was done. This custom, which had grown up to foster the loyalty of commission customers, involved the employment of great numbers of clerks and added to the overheads. Gray quickly persuaded the directors to negotiate simpler accounting procedures with commission customers. Craig, equally convinced that the commission system was at the root of the Company's problems, simultaneously encouraged the directors to conduct exercises in comparative costings between their individual yards and with competitors. John Dickinson, the manager of Govan – who, with the now departed Wilding, was largely responsible for the huge losses on the Andrew Weir order – was made to apply himself diligently to these tests. The result showed Harland & Wolff's costs to be far greater than those of its rivals. Armed with this information, Kylsant and Craig redoubled their efforts to cut overheads. They met with considerable opposition from those, like Kempster, Dickinson and Rebbeck, who had learnt their trade in the days of luxury before the First World War. These men seem at times deliberately to have contrived with the counting house at Belfast to produce favourable costs.[7]

There were some grounds for optimism during 1925. Eight ships of the loss-making twelve-ship order for Andrew Weir were completed. The *King James* and the *King Malcolm* were delivered to the British Motorship Company, a subsidiary of the King line, along with the *Temuco* to the Pacific Steam Navigation Company. These vessels, ordered after Pirrie's death, more or less broke even. The returns on the four oil tankers for Lake Maracaibo were disappointing, yielding a loss of £20,493, or 8 per cent on a contract price of £251,231. Almost certainly this contract had been accepted at a loss in the anticipation of further business. Losses on new tonnage were offset by an upturn in commissioned repair business, resulting in part from Gray's reforms. At Belfast major refits were carried out to the White Star liners *Bardic* and *Vedic*. The completion of so much loss-making tonnage, combined with the economy programme, allowed Harland & Wolff to trim its workforce. The number of men employed by the Company as a whole was reduced progressively from 40,548 in April 1925 to 35,606 the following April.

In midsummer there was good news for Belfast when White Star announced an order for a 60,000-ton liner, the *Oceanic* (ship no. 844), which was planned to be one of the most competitive liners on the North Atlantic, and the largest ship in the world. Work began at once on the design of the vessel and berth no. 14 was extended

The model of the 60,000-gross-ton turbo-electric White Star liner *Oceanic* which was ordered in 19⬚ and finally cancelled in 1930. The design is remarkably similar to tha⬚ of the *Queen Mary*.

and repiled to take the weight of the giant liner. At the same time White Star sought support under the Trade Facilities Act. In June the Oceanic Steam Navigation Company, proprietor of the White Star line, received a ten-year guarantee of £250,000 from the British Government to purchase machinery from the Lancefield Engine Works for the cabin-class steamer *Laurentic* which was to be built at Belfast. Later in the year work on the *Oceanic* was suspended because IMM could not mobilise the finance. The contract was then transferred to the *Laurentic*. Despite this setback, by December orders had been received for twenty-nine small vessels, of which thirteen were for members of the Royal Mail Group. These included four 3,800-gross-ton motor ships for the British & African Steam Navigation Company (Elder Dempster) and five ships of 1,345 gross tons for MacAndrews & Company, all financed by a guaranteed TFA loan. There was a wide spread of business, with contracts from T. & J. Harrison of Liverpool, the Government of Western Australia, the Southern Railway, and from the Lago Shipping Company for more oil tankers for Lake Maracaibo.

During 1925 Kylsant found a permanent solution to the settlement of Lord Pirrie's estate when he proposed the formation of the Pirraca Trust Limited to purchase Pirrie's shareholdings in Harland & Wolff, the Royal Mail Group companies, John Brown & Company and British Union Oil Company. The trust company was also to be responsible for collecting the subscriptions for Lady Pirrie's annuity. Before this plan could be adopted Lady Pirrie's consent had to be secured. Relations between Kylsant and herself had deteriorated further since the autumn of 1924. She rarely mentioned him by name in her letters, always referring to him simply as 'the Chairman'. Increasingly she had looked to John Craig, of Colvilles, for support and guidance. As she confided to him, she had no alternative but to agree, since she had received no income since her husband's death. Craig was in an awkward position. He liked Lady Pirrie but since her husband's death he had come to enjoy Kylsant's confidence and to respect the way he had tried to make the Harland & Wolff directors face reality. He was conciliatory, encouraging Lady Pirrie to accept the plan with good grace and to think better of her husband's successor. Under the scheme all Pirrie's remaining property was to be disposed of, including 24 Belgrave Square and his interest in Ormiston which was to become Kylsant's Belfast home. These sales, together with that of Witley Court and some other investments, yielded some £270,000 against total liabilities of £800,000. The outstanding burden of £530,000, which principally represented the obligation to buy the Harland & Wolff 'A' preference shares from Colvilles, was to be shouldered by the trust company. The Midland Bank agreed that Pirrie's overdraft could be transferred. Lady Pirrie, much to the sadness of members of the Colville family, was left to fend for herself on the generous annuity that Kylsant had collected for her.[8] She continued to live at Belgrave Square for a while and when it was sold she moved to Mount Street.

Harland & Wolff's results for 1925 must have pleased Kylsant. There was a gross profit of £569,655 before allowing for depreciation and the payment of dividends. Determined not to have the published balance sheet qualified for a second time, he made an allocation of £300,000 for depreciation. This, combined with the dividend on the first cumulative preference shares of £190,259, meant that dividends on the 'A' and 'B' preference shares as well as the ordinary shares were not paid. The balance sheet reflected the completion of capital reconstruction. The amount at credit of controlled companies was slashed from £727,000 to £295,000 and loans (deposits) fell from £605,000 to £377,000. These reductions were achieved only at the expense

The Union-Castle motor liner *Carnarvon Castle* at Queen's Island in May 1936, being fitted out with one of the large round funnels so characteristic the motor vessels design by T.C. Tobin in the 192 and 1930s.

of liquidity. Overdrafts climbed to over £2,000,000, with the Midland Group contributing an additional £600,000. This was matched by a tidying-up of the investments in steelworks and other controlled companies. During the year the London & Glasgow Engineering and Iron Shipbuilding Company, whose shares stood in Harland & Wolff's books at £456,957, was liquidated. The investment was cancelled by the abolition of the 'Reserve for investment'. The 'Government and other investments' increased by £55,000, representing the purchase of £50,000 shares in the British Motorship Company, part of the arrangement for the construction of the *King James* and *King Malcolm*. The published accounts took the same form as the previous year and again reassured the shipping press of the viability of the Company.

At the beginning of 1926 there was hope that the worst of the depression might be over. Freight rates were creeping up and shipowners were entering the market for new tonnage. Kylsant, always quick to take advantage of an upturn, negotiated a guaranteed loan from the Government of Northern Ireland to finance the construction at Belfast of three 4,500-ton and six 5,200-gross-ton motor ships. This contract ensured continuity of work after the completion of the last of the Andrew Weir twelve-ship order, in the first four months of 1926, and the deliveries of the refrigerated ship *Asturias* to the RMSP Meat Transports Company in February and the *Carnarvon Castle* for Union-Castle, due to be handed over in June. The better prospects did not cause Kylsant or Craig to relax their campaign to cut costs. Comparative statements, showing the savings that had been achieved in 1925, were circulated during March. Kylsant, dissatisfied, ordered a renewal of effort, partic-

Scene
From
the
Pirates of Penzance

ESTIMATING OFF.

PRIVATE O

ATTACK
on
HIGH COSTS.

ularly at Queen's Island. Here the root of the problem lay in the engine works where Rebbeck and his assistant, C.C. Pounder, were amassing large research and development costs in designing the new generation of diesels. They seemed impervious to the chairman's strictures.

This fresh initiative to contain costs was timely for the anticipated recovery was abruptly halted by the national lockout of the miners on 3 May which was followed by the short-lived general strike. The miners remained on strike until the winter. The coal stoppage quickly affected Harland & Wolff and on 4 May all the customers were notified that 'there may be some delay'. There was only sufficient 'steel, coal and coke in hand to last six or eight weeks'. Merely 158 tons of steel were delivered to Belfast in May, while 963 tons were taken out of the shipyard racks. Only four ships were completed in the firm's yards in the second half of the year, including the 9,300-gross-ton motor ship *Accra* for Elder Dempster, built at Belfast and owned by the British & African Steam Navigation Company. Only four vessels were launched: the *Dolores de Urquiza* from Pointhouse on 10 August; the *Apapa* (sister to the *Accra*) from Queen's Island on 26 August; the *Koolinda* from Govan on the same day; and the floating crane *London Mammoth* also from Govan on 9 September.

By the autumn the position was very serious: nearly 40 per cent of the workforce had been laid off – the total number employed fell from 35,606 in April to 21,562 in October. Kylsant, unable to cajole the directors into cutting costs further, had appointed an economy committee under Craig's chairmanship in midsummer. Its report, which was considered by the management committee on 30 September and 1 October, laid down targets for savings in overheads for each department. Kylsant ordered Craig to impress on those present 'the necessity of the Directors, with the Departmental views before them, taking a broad view of the whole subject and arriving at unity of action as Directors of the Company'. Although the meeting concluded that 'the present slack time must be utilised to cut out ruthlessly all unnecessary expenditure so as to get on the most effective basis for meeting competition', the decisions were ones of detail. The directors closed their minds to the rationalisation of the Company by closing plant, almost certainly because this would have resulted in one of them losing his kingdom. Even the loss-making and unproductive Scotstoun works was kept open in the hope that more work could be expected after the coal strike. The following month the launch of the *Laurentic* (ship no. 470) was indefinitely postponed due to the steel shortage. Schedules for repairs and refits had been totally disrupted. Owners were instructed not to send ships for refit until the supply of steel could be assured. Just one vessel, the Pacific Steam Navigation Company's liner *Orduna*, arrived for major refitting at Queen's Island after the end of June. The work on the vessel, which involved converting the boilers from coal to oil-burning, was delayed by a shortage of materials.

The dispute, however, did not sap shipowners' confidence nor the willingness of the Government to provide further guaranteed loans to support new contracts. Apart from the King line contract, Harland & Wolff received orders for a further thirty-six vessels during 1926. This total was less impressive than it appeared as twenty-five were very little craft, including fourteen tiny lighters and four Lake Maracaibo steam tankers for Andrew Weir & Company and four river boats for the Argentine Navigation Company. The remaining eleven ships were also relatively small. The largest was the 6,300-gross-ton motor ship *Saugor* for James Nourse Limited and the majority were of approximately 2,500 gross tons. Some of these orders would seem to have been taken at a loss, while contracts that were known to be in the pipeline were finalised.

In the autumn of 1926, at the very time when the shortage of materials was most serious, Harland & Wolff was dealt a heavy blow by the announcement that IMM would cancel the ship-repairing and shipbuilding contract early in the New Year. Not only had the Southampton and Liverpool works been established to meet IMM's requirements, but the repair business from the group, carried out on commission, was a major source of profit. Although work on the *Oceanic* had been suspended, the ending of the agreement would jeopardise the order for the *Laurentic* which was almost ready to be launched from Queen's Island. IMM was in serious difficulties. Sir Frederick Lewis, chairman of Furness Withy, had been negotiating to purchase the British components of the fleet (including White Star) since mid-1925. In July 1926 he withdrew his offer, as IMM was unable to show an annual return on the assets of at least 8 per cent since 1919. Kylsant immediately entered the ring and at the end of November 1926 he agreed to buy the Oceanic Steam Navigation Company (the White Star parent company) for £7,000,000. The company was to form a component in the Royal Mail Group which would find the purchase price over the next ten years. At once Kylsant began to negotiate with the Treasury and the Ministry of Finance of the Northern Ireland Government for guaranteed loans totalling £1,400,000 to finance the construction of a 27,000-gross-ton, cabin-class motor liner for the Liverpool – New York service. He also made efforts to mobilise an estimated £9,000,000 to underwrite the cost of the *Oceanic*. Design work was resumed early in 1927.[9]

Despite the serious impact of the coal strike, Harland & Wolff's published results were far better than might have been expected, showing a profit 'after making provision for losses of controlled Companies' of £201,445. The qualification was a coded way of saying that £134,600 had been transferred from the hidden 'Reserve against losses on contracts' to a new hidden 'Reserve for losses of subsidiary companies'. It is difficult to understand why Kylsant chose to create this new reserve unless it was to show that an additional £129,310 had been advanced to subsidiaries. Since nearly all the ships delivered in 1926 had either had their profits taken into the accounts in preceding years or recorded losses, the profit for the year arose largely from repair work. At Queen's Island in December 1926 the managers reflected with contentment: 'During the present year approximately seventy-five small vessels have passed through our hands for repairs and have given us our full establishment charges in addition to a reasonable profit.'

Dividends were paid on the first cumulative preference shares, but were again passed on the ordinary and 'A' and 'B' preference stock. Loans remained steady, whereas the 'Amount at credit of controlled companies' was cut by over £100,000, with the withdrawal of the whole of the Burmeister & Wain advance and £55,000 of that from David Colville & Sons, whose business was strained enormously by the coal strike. Overdrafts were reduced by some £150,000, with the Clydesdale Bank holding a credit balance of £112,534 and reductions in the commitment of the Royal and National Banks of Scotland. This may have been because these three banks were making advances directly to David Colville & Sons to keep it afloat. The contingent liabilities fell back to a safer level of £6,511,438, as more bills were retired. The published accounts were again qualified: 'No Depreciation of Plant and Machinery has been charged against the profits of the year.' Nevertheless, Kylsant looked forward at the end of 1926 to 'a revival of British trade and industry as alone can provide the wherewithal for the maintenance of a better standard of life for the workers and the means whereby the progress and development of the British Commonwealth of nations can be achieved'.

During the early months of 1927 Kylsant did his best to make the prophecy come true for Harland & Wolff by mobilising orders from the Royal Mail Group. The order for the 27,000-gross-ton cabin liner *Britannic*, for White Star, was confirmed. H. & W. Nelson, a subsidiary of the Royal Mail Steam Packet Company, placed a contract for four 14,000-gross-ton liners, three of which were to be built at Queen's Island and one at Govan. These were financed by guarantees from the Treasury and the Northern Ireland Government. Union-Castle ordered the *Winchester Castle*, a 20,000-gross-ton motor liner, the Argentine Navigation Company four river boats; David MacIver & Company (another subsidiary of the Royal Mail Steam Packet

Company) the *Brittany*, a 4,800-gross-ton cargo liner; and Elder Dempster two small tenders. Apart from the Royal Mail Group business, orders were received for fourteen other vessels. These were all small ships of under 2,400 gross tons. Andrew Weir & Company commissioned Queen's Island to build two more 2,400-gross-ton steam tankers for Lake Maracaibo. T. & J. Harrison ordered the *Designer*, a 5,900-gross-ton cargo liner, Burmah Oil, an oil barge, and the Entre Rios Railways Company (of which Kylsant's brother, Lord St Davids, was chairman) a 2,235-gross-ton railway steamer, *Delfina Mitre*. By the time the Harland & Wolff annual meeting took place in the first week of May it was clear that the six large Royal Mail Group orders would not be complemented by similar contracts from elsewhere. In his speech Kylsant was much less optimistic than he had been at the opening of the year:

> All shipbuilding undertakings have in a greater or lesser degree felt the effect of the depression in the industry. Some companies have been so gravely affected that a capital reorganization has been unavoidable. I am glad to say that so far as this company is concerned, notwithstanding a diminished volume of work, we have throughout these difficult times, always, had a nucleus of orders in hand ... The general position of shipbuilding in the country has improved much in the past year and I trust that with a continuance of co-operation between all sections of the industry and given more favourable general conditions we may look forward to further progress through a return to normal activity and prosperity.

Between the annual general meeting and the end of the year orders were placed for eleven more ships: five of these were further 2,400-gross-ton, steam-powered oil tankers for Lake Maracaibo, one was a 6,100-gross-ton tramp ship for the Hain Steamship Company and another a 5,800-gross-ton cargo liner for Raeburn & Verel.

Although the number of men employed by the Company had recovered to over 35,000 by midsummer 1927, Kylsant was deeply troubled about the future. He and Craig concluded that their effort to reduce overheads was exhausted. Instead they turned their attention to construction methods, suggesting that something less than the high standards imposed by Pirrie might be acceptable to owners. They persuaded the shipyard fitters to hand over hole-boring to machine drillers, using electric or air drills. One fitter, frightened that this was a prelude to his own redundancy, penned a lament:

> Ah, my heart is nigh broken
>   And sad is my lot,
> I must part with my ratchet,
>   My swan-neck and pot;
> I must part with my soouter,
>   My socket and drill,
> And my old can of glouter
>   No more will I fill.
>
> You kept food in my stomach
>   And clothes on my back,
> You have kept me in work
>   And evaded 'the sack'.
> Oh, I'll never get over
>   My glouter and can,
> Being taken from me
>   'Cause I bored with the hand.

My helper, I'll miss him,
  My wedges and shore,
Good-bye to my top drill,
  I'll need it no more.
My drill file, so useful,
  My angle-plate too,
Oh, it's so hard to part
  And bid you adieu.

Oh, hard is my fate,
  Which I'll ever deplore,
With my ratchet I'm finished,
  Now no march to the store.
No more wait at the gangway,
  No drawing next morn,
Ah, my heart is like lead,
  And I feel all forlorn.

Good-bye, dear old ratchet,
  The day's coming too,
When I shall be treated
  The same way as you.
But I'll just have to take it
  The best way I know,
When machines do my work,
  And hand-fitting's too slow.

I'll think of you often,
  Though now you must go,
You'll be in my dreams
  Poor old ratchet, so slow.
Oh, how woefully cruel,
  Time and progress should take
From me my old ratchet,
  My friendly 'crake crake'.

Kylsant and Craig, impervious to such sentiment, attempted to improve the cumbersome estimating procedures, appointing J.W. Kempster and John Dickinson to work out a common practice for all the shipyards. When, as might have been predicted, this failed, they ordered William Tawse, the chief accountant, to impose a new system. Towards the end of July they began belatedly to review the Company's plant requirements. The first works to be placed on care-and-maintenance was Scotstoun which had never been in full production as political unrest in Belfast in the early 1920s had not seriously disrupted output. In November it was decided to transfer to Harland & Wolff all the assets of the Burmeister & Wain (Diesel System) Oil Engine Company and of Caird & Company, and to sell A. & J. Inglis's engine works and stables.

Output for 1927 was a marked improvement on the previous year. During the year forty-nine vessels were completed, totalling 152,702 gross tons. The majority were the small craft that had been ordered in the past two years. During January the *Apapa*, sister ship of the *Accra*, was delivered to Elder Dempster, followed later in the year by three of the four 3,800-gross-ton cargo boats from the Dumbarton yard of Archibald MacMillan & Son. MacAndrews received three of the five 1,346-gross-ton cargo boats ordered from Govan. In mid-April the liner *Statendam*, for the Holland-America line, which had been launched three years before and only partly fitted out, was towed to Rotterdam for completion. In November the *Laurentic* was

handed over to White Star. Her luxurious interiors were acclaimed by the shipping press, showing that Harland & Wolff had lost none of its skill in designing and building passenger liners:

> The amenities provided for passengers are, probably, unexcelled by any steamer afloat. The public apartments comprising for cabin passengers, dining saloon, drawing room, lounge, smoking room and card room, verandah cafe, gymnasium and children's playroom, have all been designed with care in a variety of decorative styles. Thus from the Louis Seize dining saloon, which seats 310 passengers, one may pass either to the lounge, a reproduction of Italian Renaissance work – and here is a parquet floor for dancing – or to the Empire drawing room, or the oak pannelled smoking room designed on Jacobean lines. It is not inappropriate that the decorations of the card room should be reminiscent of the early French Renaissance period, remembering the close ties between France and Canada in the older days . . . The builders have had well in mind the growing popularity of democratic travel, a movement which has brought a transatlantic crossing within the means of many who have not hitherto been able to entertain it as a possible holiday, and the

The beautiful White S liner *Laurentic*, which much critical acclaim it was delivered in November 1927.

Laurentic has excellent accommodation for the increasing volume of tourist third class passengers . . . In addition to the well-furnished and airy state rooms for four and six persons, there is a number of two-berth rooms, fitted with hot and cold water, available for married couples, and friends desirous of being berthed together.[10]

Despite the slight recovery in output during 1927 the results for the year were catastrophic. The Company recorded an estimated total loss of £388,752. All the efforts of Kylsant and Craig to cut costs notwithstanding, nearly all the vessels delivered during the year lost money, irrespective of the yard in which they were built. The floating crane *London Mammoth* (ship no. 731G), built at Govan, lost £2,348 on a contract price of £40,847. The three MacAndrews's ships from the same yard lost about £12,500 on a total price of roughly £240,000. The four small oil tankers delivered from Govan to the Shell subsidiary Nederlandsch Indische Tank Stoomboot Mij lost the huge sum of £168,697 on a total price of £475,223. The *Dunkwa*, built at Dumbarton for Elder Dempster (ship no. 735D), earned the paltry profit of £50 on a contract price of £48,277. Her two sisters, *Duala* and *Daru*, yielded only £2,638 on a total price of £97,990. At Greenock the P & O's *Lahej* (ship no. 796GK), completed in October, lost £7,143 on £40,105 and the *Nimoda* (ship no. 797Gk), for the Hain Steamship Company, lost £31,105 on £118,355. All the King line ships building at Queen's Island were set to lose at least 14 per cent on the contract price. The first two delivered in 1927 lost £62,440 on a price of £283,502. The four Lake Maracaibo tankers for the Lago Shipping Company lost £14,696 on a price of £251,092. Although some of these contracts had been accepted almost at cost, many of the losses, particularly on ships built for members of the Royal Mail Group, were due, as in the past, to faulty estimating and poor cost-control. The responsibility lay with the directors, who had failed, in the three crisis-torn years since Pirrie died, to heed the urgent appeals of Kylsant and Craig to master the craft of estimating and to devise procedures to control costs. All that had been achieved were once-and-for-all cuts, rather than a system for permanent and continuous review. Only the outsider James Gray, general manager of the repair works, had matched expectations.

The internal accounts showed a loss of £154,152, before depreciation. This result had been possible only by cancelling the reserves of £134,600 for losses of subsidiary companies. The store cupboard of secret reserves was now empty, apart from £16,161 at the credit of the 'Reserve for expenditure on additions'. Any big loss could now be covered only by a transfer from the public 'Reserve'. The 1927 loss was increased to £346,152 by adding the dividend on the 6 per cent first cumulative preference shares. This had to be paid, not just to maintain confidence but also to ensure that the ordinary shareholders retained voting control. In the event of the dividend being passed, the preference shareholders, who normally had no voting right, would have been enfranchised, further complicating the Company's problems. The balance brought forward was deducted, leaving a debit balance of £201,237. No provision was made for depreciation, except for £3,559 on motor vehicles.

In the published accounts £300,000 was transferred from the 'Reserve' into the profit and loss account. Since the 'Reserve' had always been itemised in the published balance sheet, commentators were able to calculate that the Company had sustained a heavy loss, particularly as the auditor's report was once more qualified with the statement, 'No depreciation of Plant and Machinery has been charged this year.' During the year the overdrafts had again been reduced and now stood at less than £1,500,000. The credit balance with the Clydesdale Bank was replaced by an overdraft, and instead a credit balance of £212,721 was placed with its sister, the Belfast Banking Company. The overdraft with the Midland Bank was slashed from £1,060,000 to £770,000. This pruning of the overdrafts, no doubt designed to prevent criticism from the banks, was more than offset by a sharp rise in the 'Amounts at credit of the controlled companies', from £186,506 to £704,806. The loans to Burmeister & Wain and Caird & Company were cancelled and, instead, these two companies advanced Harland & Wolff over £600,000. These loans represented the transfer of £700,000 of assets to Harland & Wolff, accounting for the bulk of £761,432 capital additions during the year. The repayment of the advances made the previous year provided the cash to pay the dividend on the first cumulative preference shares.

On learning of the result, Kylsant took immediate action to reduce outgoings. Capital expenditure was restricted to essential repairs and purchases. The managing directors were instructed to be even more vigilant in preventing costs escalating and holding down levels of stocks and stores. Kylsant and Craig decided to establish an independent estimating department to improve the 'estimating system and methods'. They ordered the closure of the Greenock yard as soon as the last ship on the ways, the *Behar* (ship no. 830Gk), had been launched in the late summer. Of more immediate concern to Kylsant than the monetary losses was the Company's commitment to begin repaying its guaranteed loan, made under the Trade Facilities Act, when the first instalment of some £300,000 became due on 17 May 1928. This Harland & Wolff was in no position to do. However, Kylsant did not wish either to default or to ask the TFA committee to reschedule the debt, as this would have called into question the Royal Mail Group's ability to repay its other guaranteed loans of some £9,000,000. As a solution he instructed Union-Castle, White Star, the Argentine Navigation Company, Pacific Steam Navigation Company and British & African to advance Harland & Wolff sufficient funds against work in progress. In addition, later in the year A. & J. Inglis repaid its loan of £203,590. With this crisis safely defused, Kyslant could face the annual meeting in May 1928 with something approaching confidence. Although he was forced to admit that the year represented a 'low water mark', he had no difficulty in blaming the Company's continuing problems on the disruption caused by the 1926 coal strike. He drew comfort from the fact that for the sixth year running the Company headed the list of output from individual firms in the United Kingdom. He explained that every effort was being made to contain costs, but avoided any reference to the forthcoming closure of Greenock. The shipbuilding industry was in such disarray that the results, bad as they were, came as a relief to the financial press.

The committee that supervised the TFA loan guarantees was not so easily satisfied. On 23 April 1928 it reviewed the Company's printed accounts. Walter K. Wigham, a director of the merchant bankers Robert Fleming & Company, attacked the accounts, commenting that 'he did not understand them and he thought that Lord Kylsant did not either'. Harold Morland, who was in the unenviable position of being both a member of the committee and the auditor of Harland & Wolff and other Royal Mail Group companies, defended them. He explained that the Company had made a loss which had been met by transfer from reserves. At the end of its meeting the Committee noted that the loan, which was unsecured, could be covered by the published reserve of £1,000,000, supported by liquid assets of £408,307 (representing the 'Government and other investments') and cash in hand of £327,500. Morland, in his position of trust as auditor, could not tell his colleagues that they had been deceived by Kylsant's careful choice of headings. The 'Government and other

investments' only contained £79,036 of easily realisable Government paper; the remaining £330,000 was locked up in shares, in firms such as the Royal Mail Steam Packet Company, John Brown & Company and Laurence Scott & Company, which could not be sold for anything approaching their balance-sheet entry. Moreover, the cash in hand was more than eclipsed by the overdraft of £1,464,893 which appeared in the balance sheet under the mysterious heading 'Sundry creditors and credit balances'.[11]

During 1928 the Royal Mail Group continued to offer Harland & Wolff much-needed succour. Union-Castle, to fulfil the terms of its new mail contract, ordered another 20,000-gross-ton liner, the *Warwick Castle*, and two more 10,000-gross-ton liners, *Llangibby Castle* (11,951 gross tons) and *Dunbar Castle* (10,002 gross tons). These vessels, like their predecessors, were to be motor ships. The order for the *Oceanic* was confirmed and allocated ship no. 844. This was announced in the *Belfast Telegraph* on 18 June 1928, with the headline 'World's Biggest Liner – Laying Keel at Belfast – Lord Pirrie's Dream'. The Pacific Steam Navigation Company decided to proceed with a sumptuous new 17,700-gross-ton cruise liner, *Reina del Pacifico*, for which TFA-guaranteed loans had been made available in 1924. The British & African Steam Navigation Company placed a contract on behalf of Elder Dempster for the 9,500-gross-ton motor ship *Achimota*. All these ships were to be built on commission at Belfast, with the exception of the *Dunbar Castle* and the *Llangibby*

Castle which were allocated to Govan. For the first time since the war, Queen's Island had on its books a relatively large number of quality passenger liners, the type of vessel for which Pirrie had conceived the yard's facilities. The only other ships allocated to Belfast in 1928 were a further four Lake Maracaibo tankers for the Lago Shipping Company. Govan was awarded the 6,000-gross-ton *Bhutan*, for the Hain Steamship Company, and the 8,100-gross-ton *Westralia* for Huddart Parker Limited. A. & J. Inglis was given five small contracts; D. & W. Henderson two tramp ships, a river boat for the African Steamship Company and two railway steamers for South Indian Railways; and Archibald MacMillan & Son at Dumbarton two river steamers and a cargo liner for the Moss Steamship Company. Of the twenty-six ships ordered during the year, seventeen were for Royal Mail Group members.

Output during 1928 dropped back to 121,230 gross tons. Deliveries included from Belfast, the remaining seven loss-making King line ships and five more Lake Maracaibo tankers for the Lago Shipping Company; from Greenock, the *Saugor* for James Nourse Limited; from Dumbarton, the *Brittany* for David MacIver & Company; and, from Meadowside, the *Designer* for T. & J. Harrison. As planned, after the *Behar*, for the Hain Steamship Company, was launched from Greenock on 16 August the yard was closed and the vessel towed up to Govan for completion in early November. Although the majority of the contracts finished in the year resulted in losses, provision for most of these had been made the year before. Kylsant was able to take profits on all the vessels being built on commission for the Royal Mail Group. As a result, he was able to show a profit before depreciation of £454,355. So as to prevent the qualification of the published accounts, £250,000 was provided for depreciation. The printed accounts showed a net profit of £299,558, which, after the first cumulative preference dividend had been subtracted, left a balance of £107,558. The advances against contracts in progress had allowed Kylsant to push overdrafts down below £1,400,000 and stabilise the deposits and 'Amounts at credit of the controlled companies'.

The more pressing financial problems of Harland & Wolff and the other members of the Royal Mail Group gave Kylsant no time to prosecute his battle to reduce costs. Equally John Craig could not afford to be diverted from the mounting crisis in the Scottish steel industry. Without their firm guidance, the other directors lost interest. The management committee ceased to meet. The minutes of its last meeting on 8 May were never signed. The campaign to contain stocks petered out, largely because the volume of work in progress had increased. The total inventory of stock advanced from £542,021 in 1927 to £573,158 in 1928. The independent estimating department was not formed, possibly because the order book had filled up with vessels to be built on commission. Nevertheless, despite the healthier order book, the outlook for Harland & Wolff, in common with the rest of the British shipbuilding industry, remained bleak. During the year, Winston Churchill, as Chancellor of the Exchequer, had terminated the guarantees provided under the Trade Facilities Acts which Pirrie and Kylsant had called on so regularly to support the Company. As a special concession, the Government of Northern Ireland had been allowed to continue its separate measure. If the Company was to survive it was essential that further economies be achieved; but there was no director with sufficient breadth of vision or authority to take control of the day-to-day management of the business.

Kylsant's most urgent problem in 1929, as it had been a year before, was to locate sufficient cash to meet the next TFA loan repayment. This proved impossible. All the members of the Royal Mail Group were themselves seriously strapped for cash

270

Table 9.7
Investments 1924-30

	Investment in steel works and controlled companies £	Government and other investments £
1924[1]	4,259,496	354,510
1925	4,263,376	404,855
1926	4,263,376	408,036
1927	4,263,376	408,036
1928	4,457,880	402,153
1929	4,241,353	236,352
1930	4,271,353	206,401

Note
1   At 31 December 1924

Table 9.8
The structure of the Royal Mail Group and its principal wholly owned subsidiaries 1929-30

Royal Mail Steam Packet group

MacAndrews & Co. Ltd
David MacIver & Co. Ltd
Pacific Steam Navigation Co.
Royal Mail Steam Packet Co.

H.&W. Nelson Ltd
Nelson Steam Navigation Co.
RMSP Meat Transports Ltd

African Steamship group

African Steamship Co.
Elder Line Ltd

Interinsular Mail Steamship Co.

Argentine Navigation group

Argentine Navigation Co. (Nicholas Mihanovich) Ltd
'Sud Atlantia' Navigation Co.

Uruguayan Navigation Co. Ltd

Coast Lines group

Ardrossan Harbour Co.
Belfast Steamship Co. Ltd
British & Irish Steam Packet Co. Ltd
Burns & Laird Lines Ltd
City of Cork Steam Packet Co. Ltd
Coast Lines Ltd

Dublin General Steam Shipping Co. Ltd
Dundalk & Newry Steam Packet Co. Ltd
Michael Murphy Ltd
Tedcastle McCormick & Co. Ltd
John Westcott Ltd

Elder Dempster group

Atlantic Coaling Co. Ltd
British & African Steam Navigation Co. Ltd
Elder Dempster & Co. Ltd

Elders Insurance Co. Ltd
Imperial Direct Line Ltd
West African Lighterage & Transport Co. Ltd

Glen Line group

Glen Line Ltd
Arthur Holland & Co.

McGregor Gow & Holland Ltd

Harland & Wolff (non-shipping group)

Burmeister & Wain (Diesel System) Oil Engineering Co. Ltd
Caird & Co. Ltd
A.&J. Inglis Ltd

Harland & Wolff Ltd
D.&W. Henderson & Co. Ltd
David Colville & Sons Ltd

Lamport & Holt group

Ardrossan Dockyard & Shipbuilding Co. Ltd
Lamport & Holt Ltd
Liverpool Brazil & River Plate Steam Navigation Co. Ltd

Archibald MacMillan & Son Ltd (managed by Harland & Wolff)
United States & South American Steamship Co. Ltd

Moss group

J.&P. Hutchison Ltd
James Moss & Co. Ltd

Moss Steamship Co. Ltd

Union-Castle group

Bullard King & Co. Ltd

Union-Castle Mail Steamship Co. Ltd

White Star group

Oceanic Steam Navigation Co. Ltd
Shaw Savill & Albion Co. Ltd
White Star Line Ltd

George Thompson & Co. Ltd (Aberdeen & Commonwealth Line)

and could not advance Harland & Wolff the necessary funds. Kylsant had no alternative but to ask the Treasury for permission to extend the repayment timetable. Kylsant told John Craig, as the other member of the Harland & Wolff finance committee, and the Company secretary, John Philp, to approach the TFA committee with a request for a five-year moratorium on their outstanding guaranteed loan from the Midland Bank of £1,194,676. They saw Eric Bamford, the secretary of the committee, on 15 April and, on Kylsant's instructions, outlined the political importance of the Company and the unprofitability of the works. They excused their request on the grounds that the loan was obtained by Lord Pirrie 'as a scheme of unemployment relief, that the Company had afforded extensive employment as a consequence through the period of depression . . . and that to enforce the obligation of the loan would involve the Company in reducing stocks and consequently in reducing employment'. Despite the previous year's review of the Company's accounts, the committee and the Treasury were taken completely by surprise. They decided to dismiss the request, since it was obvious that the Company and its shareholders had benefited materially from the loan. It was agreed that if the Government was forced to give way then Harland & Wolff should suspend the preference dividend until the loan had been liquidated. On 22 April the application was formally rejected.[12]

Kylsant was prepared for this eventuality. Philp replied the following day, repeating the request and adding 'As we understand that the Government are anxious to encourage employers to keep as large a number of men as possible employed, we think this matter will receive the favourable consideration of the Treasury.' Kylsant, hoping that an extension might be granted for political reasons during the election campaign, wrote to the Prime Minister, Stanley Baldwin, and the Chancellor of the Exchequer, Winston Churchill. But they found no difficulty in refusing this request from a prominent member of their own party. Kylsant also called on the Governor of the Bank of England, Montagu Norman, who supported the TFA committee's views. Payment of the annual instalment of £298,669 fell due on 17 May. Instead of the full amount, the Midland Bank received only £100,000. Kylsant had found this sum by the simple expedient of borrowing it from the Midland Bank on his ordinary account. In so doing, Harland & Wolff's overdrafts with the Midland and its subsidiaries had reached a ceiling of £1,500,000, above which, under the terms of the TFA-guaranteed loan, it could not rise without permission from the Treasury. The Midland notified the Treasury of the receipt of the payment and the level of the overdraft, but did not formally implement the guarantee whereby the Government would be obliged to make good the shortfall.[13]

The TFA committee and the Treasury were uncertain how to proceed with Kylsant, who was one of the most respected figures in the City of London. They consulted the Company's auditor, Harold Morland, who counselled that there was no reason to grant an extension. The Treasury also asked him if the Midland Bank should be paid the outstanding £198,669 by the Government on condition that an action would be brought against Harland & Wolff. Morland, who must have known that Harland & Wolff was more or less insolvent, urged that pressure be brought on the Company to repay. In late May, following this advice and with the support of the new Labour Chancellor, Philip Snowden, the Treasury wrote to the Company demanding the money and threatening legal action. There was no reply. Another letter was sent on 17 July 1929, intimating that if the money was not paid in seven days legal proceedings would commence. There followed a series of meetings and lengthy correspondence

The novel Harland & Wolff/Burmeister & Wain airless-injection diesel engines for the *Ulster Monarch* in the process of shop erection at Queen's Island in the spring of 1929. This type of engine, which was developed by F.E. Rebbeck and C.C. Pounder, took several years to bring to perfection.

between John Craig and Sir Richard Hopkins, Controller of Finance and Supply at the Treasury. On 29 August Harland & Wolff offered to pay £100,000 on 31 October and the balance on 31 January 1930. This was accepted by the Midland Bank and the Treasury.[14] It is not clear how Kylsant proposed to find this sum. He was, more likely, simply buying time in the hope that prospects would improve following an early settlement of a strike at Belfast of joiners and polishers. This dispute, which had begun in April, had badly affected production. Although the management had taken a hard line, declaring that they were prepared to close Queen's Island if need be, in October they eventually had to concede the payment of wages for these trades in Belfast comparable to those which had recently been negotiated on the Clyde.

Despite the disruption caused by the strike, substantial progress was made during the year on the contracts in hand, with the completion of twenty-six vessels of a total of 145,000 gross tons, the highest output since Pirrie's death. Two of the 14,000-gross-ton liners built at Belfast were handed over to H. & W. Nelson and the remaining two were nearing completion at Belfast and Govan. The *Ulster Monarch*, which had been ordered as long ago as 1920 by the Belfast Steamship Company but suspended, was now completed. This vessel and her sisters, *Ulster Queen* and *Ulster Prince*, launched during the year, were intended for the Liverpool–Belfast service. Their design and appearance attracted favourable reviews, especially for the smooth operation of the novel airless-injection, ten-cylinder engines with direct reversing gear, which had been worked out in collaboration with Burmeister & Wain. Harland & Wolff designed the airless-injection fuel pumps, which were half built using detail drawings of the individual components, as the final arrangement drawings were not ready for issue.[15] The development of the engines owed much to the work of F.E. Rebbeck, Vilhelm Mickelsen, the Danish engine-designer, and C.C. Pounder, the chief draughtsman of the diesel-engine works, whose skill and turn of phrase were making him notorious. Already the *Queen's Island Annual* had published an article under the banner headline 'Take Up Pounderism', which, it was claimed, 'trains the senses and brings increased Horse-Power to the mind ... A short course in Pounderism does to the mind what a supercharger or pressure induction does to a Diesel Engine.' During the year the *Llangibby Castle* was also delivered to Union-Castle, and the *Winchester Castle* and the White Star liner *Britannic* were launched. All three of these vessels were equipped with massive double-acting, air-injection diesels. Passengers on the first voyage of the *Llangibby Castle* from Belfast to Southampton were impressed at the quiet way the new liner rode out a severe gale in the Irish Sea.[16] Such compliments did much to sustain the loyalty and pride of the workforce. A poem published in the *Queen's Island Review* in 1929 showed that the workforce had retained its confidence and sense of humour:

HOW TO BUILD THEM

Och, shure, the Queen's Island's a wonderful place,
Where the typists all type and the tracers all trace,
And the bobbed-hair brigade tabulate every day,
Never shirking their work, always earning their pay;
Where draughtsmen draw plans at the rate of a snail,
And apprentices hasten to post the last mail,
Where clerks keep the books when they're not half asleep,
And vessels from Harland's slip down to the deep.

The Union-Castle liner *Winchester Castle* on trial in 1930.

Outside in the Shipyards the platers all plate,
And the riveters toil at a terrible rate,
And smiths 'swing the hammer', with vig'rous impact,
(Most folk do the same, as a matter of fact!)
The foremen wear hard hats, some quite green with age,
When a job's in a hurry they fume and they rage.
By all of these efforts there will now and then be
A vessel from Harland's slip down to the sea.

In the Engine Works patterns are made every day,
And the sawdust flies round like a great shower of spray,
Then the moulders all cast and the fitters all fit,
Thus an engine superb is built bit by bit;
And after a test is sent out to the boat,
To propel her along when she is afloat,
And when all is completed there will proudly sweep
A vessel from Harland's out over the deep.

Meanwhile, Kylsant and the other directors scanned their stormy horizon for new tonnage. Early in the New Year of 1929 British & African and its associate company African Steamship had placed an order for three 4,000-gross-ton cargo boats. This was followed by contracts from the Royal Mail Group's latest acquisition, David MacBrayne (1928) Limited for the steamer *Lochness*, for its services up the west coast of Scotland, and from the Argentine Navigation Company for five 1,500-gross-ton motor ships and two of 900 gross tons. Andrew Weir contracted for two fast, twin-screw motor vessels of 5,582 gross tons. The Silver line, denied access to TFA finance in Britain, ordered four twin-screw motor ships with support from the Northern Ireland Government. The Compagnie Générale Transatlantique drew on the same facilities to finance six 6,000-gross-ton motor ships. Towards the end of the year the *Oceanic* (ship no. 844) was finally abandoned, after the expenditure of over £150,000, and replaced by the more modest 27,000-gross-ton liner *Georgic* (ship no. 896), designed as a sister to the *Britannic*. The last contracts to be placed during the year were for a twin-screw steamer of 6,000 gross tons, for James Nourse Limited, and a similar vessel for P & O. With the exception of the twelve ships for the Royal Mail Group that were to be built on commission, the other twenty contracts signed during the year had been accepted at a loss, in a desperate bid to keep the works employed. Even this suicidal tactic had failed to yield sufficient business.

By the autumn of 1929 the outlook, not only for Harland & Wolff but for the whole of the Royal Mail Group, was bleak. The financial press was alive with rumours about the viability of Kylsant's companies. At the end of October the Government was forced to consider how total collapse might be avoided. Sir Richard Hopkins was asked to investigate the extent and security of the loans guaranteed by the Treasury and the Northern Ireland Government. His report thoroughly alarmed Chancellor of the Exchequer Philip Snowden. Before the Government had time to work out a plan of campaign, Kylsant, on 16 October, called on Sir William Plender, chairman of the TFA committee and a distinguished accountant, requesting the postponement of some of Royal Mail's TFA-guaranteed loan repayments. He promised that he would not reopen the Harland & Wolff position, but would meet the instalment when it fell due on 31 October. Plender was unsympathetic. Disappointed, Kylsant went to see Hopkins on 28 October to be met with a similar rebuff. At the same time he approached the Ministry of Finance of Northern Ireland with a request to defer payment of bills of exchange guaranteed under the Loans

Guarantee Act – amounting to £4,100,700 – for members of the Royal Mail Group. These formed the bulk of Harland & Wolff's contingent liabilities of £4,524,487 and if the shipping companies on which they were drawn defaulted, as seemed likely, then Harland & Wolff would be obliged to meet them. The Ministry of Finance of the Province was as determined as the Treasury not to relent and rejected the appeal. After his meeting with Hopkins, Kylsant formally requested the extension of the TFA loans. He instructed Harland & Wolff not to pay the £100,000 to the Midland Bank on 31 October. It is doubtful if the Company could have completed this transaction even if it wanted to. There was no cash and the overdraft facilities had been exhausted. Instead of informing the Midland Bank, Kylsant waited to see what would happen. On 26 November Hopkins wrote to John Craig requesting the settlement of the overdue account. There was no response. Plender demanded to see a more detailed balance sheet and wanted confirmation that the Company intended to pay the dividend on the first cumulative preference stock as usual.[17]

On Friday 6 December Craig called on Hopkins and Eric Bamford, the secretary of the TFA committee, to discuss the Harland & Wolff loan. He tried to persuade them of the necessity of a further deferment and the payment of the preference dividend. He explained that 'the Government could either have the money or

276

The massive double-ac air-injection port engi the *Britannic* in the erec shop at Queen's Islanc Engines of this type w very difficult to build.

employment, whichever they wished'. Hopkins and Bamford considered the payment of the preference dividend would be foolhardy and pressed for a complete statement of the Company's borrowings, 'including bank overdrafts, creditors apart from loans, and contingent liabilities', from 1 January 1929. Bamford advised Craig that if the Company could not meet its TFA liabilities then the Government must be offered a scheme giving priority to the redemption of the TFA-guaranteed loans. The situation of the whole Royal Mail Group became more confused later in the month as further TFA-guaranteed loans fell due for payment. In his dealings with the committee Kylsant said he had been assured that unless Harland & Wolff paid the preference dividend the £4,500,000 outstanding bills would not be discounted, which would bring the Company to a standstill. He proposed to pay the dividend by increasing the Company's overdrafts. Appalled at Kylsant's inability to face up to the problems of Harland & Wolff and the rest of the Royal Mail Group, Plender recommended that Sir William McLintock be appointed to conduct an appraisal of the Group's finances. McLintock was an obvious choice. He was a brilliant accountant with long experience of dealing with large corporate enterprises. Kylsant was told of this decision on 19 December and wrote immediately to William Tawse, the Harland & Wolff chief accountant, ordering him to provide McLintock with every facility. For the first time since its foundation seventy-five years before, an outsider was to be given access to the firm's very private financial affairs, of which most of the directors were ignorant.[18]

Although more tonnage was turned out in 1929 than in any year since the Company had become public, returns were no better than in 1928. The accounts showed a profit before depreciation of £516,749 and took account of the repayment of only £150,000 of the TFA-guaranteed loans, instead of the £300,000 due. Many of the contracts completed during the year had again yielded a loss. The two Nelson liners scored a loss of £65,182 and the *Kufra* (ship no. 858G) a loss of £12,874 on a price of £21,535. The subsidiary companies returned the meagre sum of £718. The Company depended for its positive cash flow on commission earnings on the liners building for White Star and Union-Castle and on repair work carried out for the Royal Mail Group and other commission customers at Liverpool, London and Southampton. During the year Liverpool carried out 560 repairs and 144 dry-dockings. The London works extended its business beyond ship-repair and the commissioned maintenance of the Port of London Authority's installations, to highly profitable electrical contracting, particularly street-lighting projects. After the subtraction of the proposed first cumulative preference dividend of £192,000 and a notional depreciation of £300,000, the balance in the profit and loss was £132,307. The most alarming feature of the accounts was the enormous rise in the overdrafts, from just under £1,400,000 to over £1,920,000. The additional borrowing had been used to pay off part of the TFA-guaranteed loan and to finance yet more loss-making contracts that were in progress. Kylsant must have known that it would not take McLintock long to discover that the Company was more or less insolvent and that failure was only a matter of time.

McLintock pursued his investigations at breakneck speed throughout January and February 1930 against the background of escalating crisis, with Kylsant growing more and more desperate to find a way of retaining control of the Royal Mail Group. It came as no surprise that Harland & Wolff failed to pay the Midland Bank the instalments due on 31 January. The Company simply did not have the cash to meet the obligation. Moreover Kylsant decided, probably to forestall criticism from

McLintock, to abandon the system of building on commission, which had been the Company's only source of cash for the last two years. On 4 February notice was given that the building agreements with White Star and Royal Mail would be terminated on 30 June. Kylsant reported to Bamford on 13 February that the Midland Bank was prepared to extend the outstanding TFA-guaranteed loan of £1,044,000 for five years. This statement was not entirely true, as Kylsant had led Reginald McKenna, the chairman of the Midland Bank, and Frederick Hyde, its managing director, to believe that he was awaiting confirmation from the Treasury of the extension of all the TFA-guaranteed loans made to the Royal Mail Group. It is probable that by this time McKenna was encouraging Kylsant to step down as chairman of Harland & Wolff and the other Royal Mail Group companies. Kylsant responded by offering the deputy chairmanship of all his companies to Walter Runciman, a respected figure in shipping and financial circles, wartime President of the Board of Trade and chairman of the Runciman group of shipping companies. Runciman would accept nothing but executive control and Kylsant's resignation. Not surprisingly, Kylsant turned down this proposal.

McLintock completed his research at the end of the month and on Friday 7 March he delivered the preliminary results to a meeting of Montagu Norman (Governor of the Bank of England), Sir Warren Fisher (Permanent Secretary of the Treasury), Sir Richard Hopkins, Sir William Plender of the TFA committee, and John Morison (one of Sir William McLintock's senior partners). He showed that the Group had total current liabilities of a staggering £30 million. Norman had no doubt that the Government was partly responsible for this appalling state of affairs. Those present agreed that Kylsant should be forced to take action. Lt. Colonel W.B. Spender, permanent secretary of the Ministry of Finance of Northern Ireland, supported the plan and proposed that Harland & Wolff should be hived off.[19]

With no confidence in Kylsant's commitment to reform, the Treasury summoned a conference on 20 March of all the directors of the constituent companies of the Royal Mail Group, including Harland & Wolff and its subsidiaries. Fisher and Hopkins made it abundantly clear to the assembled directors that they must take steps towards reconstruction at once. Unfortunately the directors of Harland & Wolff, like most of their colleagues throughout the Royal Mail Group, lacked the financial information to make any proposals for the future. The only director at Harland & Wolff with sufficient independence and initiative to build an escape route was John Craig, the managing director of David Colville & Sons. Ever since Kylsant had taken the helm, Craig had continued to hold sporadic discussions with his fellow steelmakers in an effort to hammer out a survival plan for the industry. These negotiations, which were highly complex and often muddled, firmed up late in 1929 over a proposal to create a single Scottish steelmaking combine. Craig, with Kylsant's approval, took the lead in progressing this plan. After his dealings with the Treasury over the TFA-guaranteed loans, Craig must have been painfully aware that time was short. He returned from the meeting on 20 March determined to push ahead as fast as possible. The following day he was in touch with Sir James Lithgow, head of the lower Clyde shipbuilders that bore his name and owner of the steelmaking firm James Dunlop & Company. By mid-April an agreement had been reached to merge Dunlops and Colvilles as a step towards the total rationalisation of the Scottish industry. The new company was to be called Colvilles Limited. This deal, which needed Treasury approval, was held up by the much more serious issue of forcing Kylsant to find a solution to the problems of the Royal Mail Group as a whole.[20]

278

Unlike Craig, Kylsant failed to respond with any sense of urgency to the Treasury's call for action on 20 March. Instead he continued to nurture the belief that the Government would look favourably on his petition for the extension of the TFA loans. Plender had other ideas and, taking Runciman fully into his confidence, advised him to put pressure on Kylsant to tell the shareholders of the true position of the Royal Mail Group. This commission was made simpler for Runciman by the circulation during the first fortnight of April of a series of detailed reports on the finances and capital structure of the chief components of the Group, prepared by McLintock. The report on Harland & Wolff was completed on 4 April and concluded that the Company's grave situation stemmed from:

1   The continuation of the policy of expansion during the post war period, resulting in a large amount of capital being locked up in assets which are not meantime producing revenue.

2   The investment of a large sum at a period of high prices in the shares of David Colville & Sons on which no return has been received.

3   The losses sustained in the contract with the Bank Line Ltd.

4   The payment of dividends out of reserves when the reserves were unrepresented by liquid assets.[21]

When he addressed the Harland & Wolff annual meeting on 7 April Kylsant made no reference to these problems, but cleverly 'stressed the favourable factors'. McLintock, lest anyone should be misled, prepared a glossary on the speech:[22]

In our case large amounts have been specially written off in the past, and it is satisfactory that, in the year under review, notwithstanding the difficult conditions, we have been able to set aside the substantial sum of £300,000 for depreciation of fixed assets.

The special writings-off since 1914 total £1,000,000 which about £520,000 were from special E.P.D. allowances. These allowances are not substantial in view of the large additions made at a period of high prices.

As a result of this conservative financial policy, the book value of the shipbuilding yards, marine engine-works, foundries, and repairing establishments now represents very little more than the amount expended on enlarging and brings the works up-to-date since the war. This indicates in a striking manner the modern character of our works and equipment.

The depreciation appropriation of £300,000 must be regarded as an absolute minimum. The depreciation taken by the Company for the purposes of their own cost records in 1929 was £336,035 and this does not include depreciation on Clyde Foundry or London Repair Works, the aggregate book value of which is £2,500,000.
Book value of Fixed Assets after deducting 1929 depreciation   £9,907,528
Book value at June 1918
                    £2,572,807
Additions since 1918
                    £9,660,014

The loan of £1,500,000 advanced under the Trade Facilities Act in 1922 has now been reduced to £1,044,000.

Kylsant, rattled by Runciman and McLintock, switched his attention to the Northern Ireland Government. On 10 April 1930 he threatened to close down Harland & Wolff and its subsidiaries unless the TFA-guaranteed loans were extended. Plender assumed he was bluffing, but the Ministry of Finance of the Province could not run the risk. Fortunately Runciman, with advice from Norman, McKenna and the other clearing bankers involved, had drawn up a list of conditions under which he would be prepared to take over as deputy chairman:

1   Kylsant, chairman
2   Walter Runciman, vice-chairman (and there is only to be one)
3   Boards reconstructed
4   Finance Committee (small in number) to be set up with Walter Runciman as chairman
5   Finance overhauled along lines agreed by banks and Treasury and Price Waterhouse & Co's and Sir William McLintock's advice
6   Consequent writing down of nominal capital
7   Kylsant to give every assistance in reconstruction and to meet the annual meeting of shareholders himself
8   Management agreements to be revised
9   The Lines and companies to be free to buy stores, fuel, etc. at the lowest possible price on a competitive basis
10 The Lines and companies to repair and build on competitive tenders, but giving Harland & Wolff preference on equal terms and prices.

On 15 April Runciman sent a copy to Kylsant who was leaving for ten days' holiday in Wales, still apparently unaware that the Royal Mail Group was on the verge of collapse. He did not reply. Eventually, on 5 May, he emerged from retreat and agreed to Runciman's conditions. However, he was still not prepared to begin the process which inevitably would lead to his loss of office. Sir Warren Fisher at the Treasury was exasperated and on 14 May he managed to entice Kylsant to come to a meeting with John Craig and two of the Price Waterhouse partners. Unknown to Kylsant, Fisher had invited Hopkins, Plender, McLintock and Bamford to attend. Together they ambushed Kylsant into facing up to the gigantic difficulties of the Group and forced him to summon a meeting of the secured creditors at Royal Mail House on 19 May.[23]

The attendance at the conference reflected the gravity of the crisis. The Treasury delegation comprised Plender, McLintock and Bamford. The banks' representatives included chief executives from five of the clearing banks, three other banks and three

major discount houses. The meeting was unequivocal in its support of McLintock's findings, and agreed to appoint a committee of inquiry, comprising McLintock, Brig. General Arthur Maxwell (managing partner with the bankers Glynn Mills & Company) and Frederick Hyde (managing director of the Midland Bank). Maxwell's participation was vital; not only was he a respected figure in the City but he was also an Ulsterman with strong contacts in the Belfast business community. The committee of inquiry took immediate action. In less than a week they had adopted the principle that there were sufficient assets to meet all the Royal Mail Group's obligations, but only on condition that the Group companies were kept as going concerns. They also saw it as essential that the TFA-guaranteed loans and the Group's discount facilities should be extended by a moratorium until 31 December 1930. In return the lenders' position would be safeguarded by the appointment of voting trustees, who would be granted voting control over the finance and management of the Group companies. Each company would be asked to pass resolutions transferring all voting rights to the trustees and undertaking not to enter into capital commitments, declare

281

dividends, lend or borrow without the voting trustees' permission. Kylsant, bowing to events, accepted. After frantic activity McLintock had secured the consent of all the banks involved by 11 June. The committee was to remain in being for the rest of the year. Runciman was to be appointed deputy chairman of the Royal Mail Steam Packet Company and a director of the principal subsidiaries. The Harland & Wolff board met on 19 June and transferred voting control to the newly appointed voting trustees, McLintock, Maxwell and Runciman.[24] Two days later, amidst a blaze of publicity, the beautiful motor liner *Britannic* left the Lagan for its first cruise to Southampton. The magazine *Motor Ship* commented: 'It is scarcely possible to appreciate to the full how completely the *Britannic* reflects modern principles in every possible respect without spending hours in examining the vessel from end to end as we have done during her construction.'[25] On board were many of the directors of the Royal Mail Group. Kylsant, however, was not one of their number. Within six weeks he announced his resignation as chairman of Harland & Wolff. There was a sense of relief in the press reports, after months of speculation about the future of the Company and the rest of the Royal Mail Group:

> Lord Kylsant's resignation from the chairmanship of Messrs Harland & Wolff Ltd is perhaps the most important event in the history of the firm since the lamented death of Lord Pirrie in 1924. At that time anxiety was felt in home quarters as to the future of the concern. It was realised that Lord Pirrie was a leader with unusual qualities, and that only a man of great organizing abilities and wide experience could hope to fill his place. Happily for Belfast and the numerous cross-channel centres where Lord Pirrie had established shipbuilding yards and engineering works Lord Kylsant, who had been associated with him in the development of many great schemes and knew him intimately, consented to shoulder the responsibility that he had borne for so many years and to direct the affairs of the world's greatest shipbuilding company.[26]

It is hard to blame Kylsant alone for the catastrophe that he presided over in his six years as chairman of Harland & Wolff. Much of the responsibility belonged to Lord Pirrie, who had been the architect of the Company's downfall. Kylsant had used all his skill as a financial manager to keep the business afloat and it was a measure of his achievement that it survived as long as it did. From the outset Harland & Wolff had been a massive liability to his Royal Mail Group, draining it of cash in 1924 and colouring Kylsant's judgement over new building and the acquisition of White Star. Like Pirrie in the years just before his death, Kylsant had found it impossible to enforce financial discipline on the directors. With John Craig's able and vigorous support, he had tried his best; but there was still no adequate system for estimating prices or controlling costs. The only shred of comfort that Kylsant could take on his expulsion was that if the position of Harland & Wolff was grave it was no better elsewhere. The Company's principal competition in Belfast, Workman Clark, had been reconstituted in 1928 by William Strachan and his brother into Workman Clark (1928) Limited. Since then it had struggled with little success against the hurricane and was almost insolvent.

10
CUT DOWN ON THE WAYS
1930–39

When they agreed to take command of the salvage of the Royal Mail Group, Sir William McLintock, Frederick Hyde, Arthur Maxwell and Walter Runciman underestimated the awesome task that confronted them. Believing that voting control would give them complete authority over the Group, they failed to appreciate that such power was as nothing compared to the autocratic rule of Pirrie and Kylsant. They did not realise that the directors of the constituent companies had only the vaguest idea of the seriousness of the shipwreck and, freed of Kylsant, were anxious to steer their weatherbeaten units of the Group away from the rocks. Unwittingly the voting trustees encouraged the notion that reconstruction might be effected quickly and with little fuss. McLintock assumed that a series of swift blows with the accountant's axe could hack the Group up into manageable components. His breakneck investigation into the Group's liabilities had scarcely touched on the bewildering intricacies of its cross-shareholding structure, which were made more complex by the fact that some shares had been only partly paid up. He and his fellow salvage experts soon discovered that any proposal for one member of the Group had consequences for all the constituents. Before they had time to inform the directors of the individual member companies of their error, the tide of events had swept the trustees away from the shelter of the bankers' meetings.

The most immediate problem facing the committee of inquiry was to shore up Harland & Wolff's crumbling finances. John Craig was anxious to press ahead with the scheme which would give Colvilles the chair in the rationalisation of the Scottish steel industry. His impatience infected Frederick Rebbeck, who wished to take command of Harland & Wolff and to maintain its prestige as the largest shipbuilding company in the world. When it became clear that Kylsant would disappear from the stage, Craig and Rebbeck began to frame proposals for the reconstruction of the balance sheet. This was unwelcome news to the committee, who would have preferred the management of the Company to tackle the more urgent job of containing costs and reducing overheads. McLintock and Maxwell knew from their close contact with the Governor of the Bank of England, Montagu Norman, that Colvilles, alone in the Royal Mail Group, could be treated as a special case. Colvilles, like most of the other Scottish steelmakers, had been exposed to a searching examination of its production costs and overheads by Norman's team of industrial experts. It had emerged with a far cleaner bill of health than any of its competitors. The quality of its management had earned Craig the respect and confidence of the financial institutions. During the last fortnight in June 1930 McLintock had numerous telephone conversations and meetings with Craig. Although the voting trustees considered that the proportion of preference stock in the new company was too great and would have preferred a wider scheme, the merger was being pressed by Sir James and Henry Lithgow, the Lower Clyde shipbuilders and owners of the other party in the merger, James Dunlop & Company. Neither McLintock nor Maxwell was keen to antagonise the Lithgow brothers so soon after taking charge of Harland & Wolff,

The cover of the booklet prepared by Frederick Rebbeck in 1930 to advertise the Company's products and facilities.

and by 4 July the voting trustees had reluctantly given their consent.[1]

This was a small price to pay for the goodwill of the Lithgows – a goodwill which would be vital to the success of the trustees' mission to rationalise Harland & Wolff's resources. Two years earlier, on 1 February 1928, a meeting in Edinburgh resolved to form the Shipbuilding Conference, whereby shipbuilders throughout the UK would pool tenders and add sufficient sums to them to cover the cost of submitting an unsuccessful bid, a process which involved considerable expenditure of both time and money. Although most of the large shipbuilders had joined the Conference by early 1929, Harland & Wolff had remained apart, as it had done when the Shipbuilders' Employers' Federation was established thirty years before. Late in 1928 the Conference had appointed a subcommittee under the chairmanship of Sir James Lithgow to examine the possibility of setting up a fund to purchase redundant

284

shipyards. Within a few months, on 24 April 1929, Sir James, T.E. Thirlaway (chairman of Swan Hunter) and John Barr (until 1927 president of the Shipbuilders' Employers' Federation) had outlined to Montagu Norman a proposal 'for an association charged with the task of securing the closure of uneconomic yards which might be purchased by a holding company'. Norman had been enthusiastic and promised the Bank of England's backing for such a scheme, providing it had the support of the shipbuilding industry as a whole. After lengthy discussions, the holding company had been registered in March 1930 under the name of National Shipbuilders Security Limited (NSS). The issue of £1,000,000 of stock had been sponsored by the embryonic Bankers Industrial Development Company, a co-operative venture between the Bank of England, the major clearing banks and other financial institutions, designed to assist rationalisation projects. The shipbuilding industry had been unanimous in electing Sir James Lithgow chairman of NSS.[2]

While McLintock was making himself familiar with the details of the Colville amalgamation, the committee of inquiry's search for a new chairman for Harland & Wolff was taking equal priority. McLintock asked his great friend, the Glasgow industrialist Lord Weir, to let him know of any suitable candidates. Lady Pirrie, the Company's president, was deeply disturbed by the course of events leading up to the appointment of the voting trustees, of which she learned from her friend and confidant, John Craig. She discussed the possible appointment of Walter Runciman with her late husband's close business partner, Lord Inverforth. This confirmed her belief that Runciman would not be an asset to Harland & Wolff – a view shared by the committee of inquiry. On 18 July Frederick Hyde and McLintock canvassed Sir James Lithgow for the vacancy. Apart from his role at NSS, he was an obvious choice. He had been deputy Controller to Pirrie during the war and, as a result, knew personally many of the Harland & Wolff senior management. Hyde & McLintock were disturbed to discover that 'Sir James . . . would apparently only be interested in Harland & Wolff as a means of furthering his interests in the rationalization scheme', and withdrew the proposal. Sir James never forgave them for robbing him of this opportunity, and for the rest of his life remained bitterly critical of the Harland & Wolff management.[3]

McLintock and Maxwell had learnt from their involvement in other reconstruction schemes of the enormous difficulties entailed in recruiting chief executives with sufficient experience to direct large engineering and shipbuilding companies. In the case of the Glasgow armaments, steelmaking, shipbuilding and engineering conglomerate William Beardmore & Company, which had become more or less bankrupt in 1926, Montagu Norman had been forced to confess three years later: 'I know not where to turn for a Chairman with adequate knowledge and prestige to ensure a proper policy through proper control.'[4] The committee could not afford to embark on such a lengthy head-hunting expedition which would only serve to alert the whole industry to Harland & Wolff's predicament. Instead, on Hyde's recommendation, they decided to offer the job to F.E. Rebbeck in the hope that they could teach him how to control the business.[5] They knew that he could rely on the support and advice of the very able John Craig, who was to remain on the board after the formation of Colvilles Limited. As a test of his ability they asked him to review the Group's shipbuilding and ship-repairing capacity in conjunction with James Gray, the director responsible for ship-repair.[6]

The appointment was welcomed in Northern Ireland. David McKee, senior director of the Belfast Banking Company, told Hyde that Rebbeck had the right

Frederick Rebbeck (right)
and Henry P. Harland,
Sir Edward Harland's
grandson, on board the
Union-Castle liner
Capetown Castle, during
commissioning cruise,
1938. Frederick Rebbeck
was appointed chairman,
Harland & Wolff in
June 1930.

'ballast' for the job and was 'in the very front of marine engineers . . . the *Britannic*
has been an outstanding tribute to [his] genius'. The *Belfast News-Letter*, under the
banner headline 'NEW CHIEF FOR HARLAND AND WOLFF', commented:

> Mr Rebbeck's appointment will give great satisfaction to his many friends in
> Belfast and to the Shareholders of the Company also. He is a man of great
> experience and he has been with Messrs Harland & Wolff for more than a
> quarter of a century. In his professional career he has been in touch with all
> the latter-day developments of the engineering industry, and of course with

the developments of the motor ship. He has always devoted himself assiduously to his work, and he earned the full confidence of Lord Pirrie.[7]

Harland & Wolff occupied a disproportionate amount of the time of the committee of inquiry and the voting trustees in their first weeks in office. Early in June 1930 McLintock explained the position of the Royal Mail Group to the London discount houses, requesting them to continue their facilities in discounting the Company's shipbuilding bills of exchange, totalling some £4,800,000. The Union Discount Company and Alexanders Discount Company were agreeable but on 13 June McLintock learned that Brightwen & Company, Brocklebank, Hoare & Brown, and Smith St Aubyn would not accept any more of the Company's bills. He hurriedly persuaded the clearing banks to waive their normal reservations about lending to the discount market. This inducement proved insufficient, with the result that the burden of shipbuilding bills was left on the shoulders of Union Discount, Alexanders and the clearing banks themselves. Since the bills were spread throughout the Royal Mail Group and amongst six banks as well as the two discount houses, their renewal involved the secretariat of the voting trustees in a maze of time-consuming, and often tense, negotiations.[8]

Late in July 1930 McLintock found out that Union-Castle had ended its repair contracts with Harland & Wolff. It is probable that Runciman had encouraged this decision, as he was strongly opposed to shipowners' holding interests in shipbuilding concerns, believing it obscured commercial judgement on both sides. Throughout Rebbeck and Gray's inquiries into the Group's shipbuilding and repair facilities Runciman continually sniped at their queries about tied business. McLintock came to the brink of resignation over the issue. Reporting to Maxwell, he doubted whether Runciman appreciated that Harland & Wolff would need to call in its debts if the shipping companies severed their links with the yards: 'He has none of the daily concern which you and I have re the Harland & Wolff position.' Although at the end of August the Group's shipping companies were instructed not to transfer their repair work in this arbitrary way, shortly afterwards the Royal Mail Steam Packet Company itself rescinded its repair agreement with the Company. In despair, McLintock wrote to Runciman: 'The Harland & Wolff position is difficult enough without this constant friction between Harland & Wolff and certain of the shipping companies.' In the circumstances he was no doubt glad that there had been no question of appointing Runciman to the board.[9]

James Gray presented a report on the Company's ship-repair works on 1 August 1930. He explained how the commission system for the members of the Royal Mail Group worked and was confident that, since his last investigation for Kylsant, the three repair yards were offering the Group a competitive service. His main recommendation was that overall direction of repair work should be centralised under 'a proper manager' and that 'owners should have every means and opportunity for criticism'.[10] On 7 August, after a careful scrutiny of the order book, he and Rebbeck submitted their review of the Group's shipbuilding capacity. They recommended that no less than twelve of the Group's forty-two shipbuilding berths could be dispensed with. They proposed the sale of the two Lamport & Holt yards at Dumbarton and Ardrossan and the 'sterilisation' (permanent closure) of Cairds. These recommendations were reinforced by a further memorandum from Rebbeck on 16 August in which he pleaded that, at least for the present, the Royal Mail Group companies should not invite tenders from other shipbuilding firms. He was nervous

287

Table 10.2

Table 10.2

Profit and loss 1931-8

	Gross profit/(loss) for year before tax and depreciation	Net profit/(loss) per published accounts after tax and depreciation	Distribution (transfers to/from reserves and dividends)	Balance carried to following year
	£	£	£	£
1931	(280,917)	(280,917)	(50,000)	7,136
1932	(117,204)	(60,078)	(100,000)	47,058
1933	(161,387)	(152,777)	(150,000)	44,281
1934	(70,450)	(64,227)	(70,000)	50,054
1935	67,820	67,820	—	117,874
1936	86,007	86,007	—	203,881
1937	13,804	(186,568)[1]	—	17,312
1938	625,888	127,915	100,000	45,227

Note

1 After costs re scheme of reorganisation – £200,372

Table 10.3

Fixed assets 1931-8

Freehold and leasehold land, property and buildings

	1931	1932	1933	1934	1935	1936	1937	1938
	£	£	£	£	£	£	£	£
Additions	(16,413)	—	10,249	—	44,304	11,806	3,051	32,876
Depreciation and losses on sales	—	67,143	63,986	10,552	643,741	4,920	1,523,224[1]	350[2]
Total	5,428,628	5,361,485	5,307,745	5,297,196	4,697,759	4,704,645	3,184,471	3,216,999

Machinery, plant and tools

Additions	6,968	2,469	830	25,877	75,063	94,213	73,543	64,968
Depreciation and losses on sales	—	3,099	19,183	—	139,782	—	1,286,430[1]	9,342[2]
Total	4,255,659	4,255,030	4,236,676	4,262,555	4,197,836	4,292,049	3,079,165	3,134,791

Notes

1 Special writing-off under scheme of reorganisation
2 In addition £500,000 was allocated from the profits for depreciation

Queen's Island to identify any source of fresh cash. He returned in gloomy mood, diagnosing 'a disastrous state of affairs', with the Company needing £250,000 by the end of the month to pay for wages and materials. There was only £45,000 left in overdraft facilities and the only alternatives were to appeal to the Midland Bank for more or to call in debts from some of the equally hard-pressed shipping companies.[13]

The outlook was tempestuous. Following the Wall Street Crash in the USA in late 1929, shipping freight rates had collapsed to unprecedented levels. There was no

Table 10.4
Reserves 1931-8

	1931 £	1932 £	1933 £	1934 £	1935 £	1936 £	1937 £	1938 £
Reserve	1,000,000	900,000	750,000	680,000	680,000	680,000	—	—
Reserve against losses on contracts	26,839	26,839	26,839	17,181	4,952	3,291	307	25,251
Reserve for losses of subsidiary companies	21,437	21,437	21,437	21,437	21,437	21,437	—	—
Reserve for expenditure and additions	14,104	14,104	—	—	—	—	—	—
Reserve for interest	—	—	—	45,672	54,365	69,847	—	—
Reserve for writing down fixed assets	—	—	—	—	—	—	88,266	78,785
Reserve for bad debts	50,000	50,000	61,432	43,332	50,580	47,860	49,597	57,229

Table 10.5
Investments 1931-8

	1931 £	1932 £	1933 £	1934 £	1935 £	1936 £	1937 £	1938 £
Investment in subsidiary companies	4,271,353	4,277,553	4,282,293	4,284,493	3,990,017	2,367,917	144,037	208,924
General investments	206,451	206,520	206,520	217,225	209,725	87,492	100,575	100,575
Indebtedness in associated shipping companies discharged by deferred creditor's certificates	273,644	837,424	843,920	835,128	663,873	604,193	—[1]	—[1]

Note
1 Transferred to the voting trustees to be realised on behalf of the creditors

demand in 1930 for new tonnage. During the year Harland & Wolff received orders for only sixteen vessels. All except five were under 2,000 gross tons and the largest were two oil tankers, *Cliona* and *Conch*, for the Anglo-Saxon Petroleum Company. Apart from these two vessels, all the contracts were allocated to Meadowside, Govan and Pointhouse, and no less than nine had been delivered by the end of the year. There were scarcely any inquiries for vessels of any description. On 9 December the directors belatedly took stock. Their first resolution was that in future the board should meet at intervals of not more than seven months. They decided to abandon, for the time being, building small craft at London as they were pledged to the Port of London; to lease part of the Southampton works as a wool store; and to close Scotstoun temporarily. They discussed the rationalisation plans being pursued by

Table 10.6

Number of employees 1930-39[1]

	Belfast	Glasgow (including Greenock)	Associated companies[2]	Repair branches
1930	10,428	2,739	1,915	5,971
1931	4,477	1,579	1,317	3,816
1932	1,554	620	650	4,181
1933	2,573	1,082	615	4,132
1934	9,204	2,715	1,975	5,405
1935	14,078	2,894	670	4,928
1936	10,210	5,169	679	6,427
1937	12,569	4,966	719	6,232
1938	13,872	3,911	878	5,989
1939	17,850	5,451	1,290	8,233

Notes
1   At December in each year
2   The wholly owned subsidiaries A.&J. Inglis and D.&W. Henderson

NSS and agreed to make overtures for the sterilisation of Greenock. They considered the future of Meadowside and Pointhouse but were of the opinion that the mouth of the River Kelvin was needed for fitting-out work, as the facilities across the Clyde at Govan were inadequate. It was agreed that the workforce should be cut as contracts were completed. This was implemented, at the instance of the voting trustees, under the supervision of a 'committee of economies' – chaired by Sir Ernest Clark – which was to replace the works committees established by Pirrie partly for this purpose in 1917. Despite these initiatives, the directors, congratulating themselves on the big output for the year, had still failed to grasp the fact that the Company was insolvent. They even resolved to win orders by extending credit to owners. No mention was made of any possible source of such finance and there was no discussion of ways in which costs and overheads might be reduced to provide a little flexibility. Rebbeck and his colleagues clearly imagined that McLintock would supply the financial mattress that they had come to expect from Pirrie and Kylsant.

This assumption was not totally incorrect. McLintock, Maxwell and Hyde were very conscious that it was essential to make every effort to maintain employment at Queen's Island so as to retain the active support of the Northern Ireland Government for the whole rescue operation. The members of the Stormont Cabinet were well aware that the closure of Harland & Wolff would be a disaster for Northern Ireland. At least two members of the Cabinet had strong personal associations with the shipyard – John Miller Andrews was a nephew of Lord Pirrie, and his former brother-in-law, John Milne Barbour, was also a relation of the Pirrie family.

Throughout the autumn and winter of 1930 the voting trustees had made valiant and successful sorties to prevent the suspension or cancellation, through lack of finance, of the vessels being built by Harland & Wolff for the Royal Mail Group, notably the *Georgic*, *Winchester Castle*, and *Warwick Castle*. They had fought and won a tremendous battle to stop the creeping withdrawal of the Group's repair work from the Company. In mid-October it was learned that the Royal Mail Steam Packet Company intended, with no explanation, to transfer its 'boiler and scaling work' at Southampton to other contractors. Gray, outraged, complained to McLintock and

Maxwell who in turn challenged Runciman. They were stunned by his accusation that 'Gray's high handed attitude is the chief obstacle to the harmony of arrangements made for economical working' and his parting quip that 'we ought not to be pestered with this type of ha'penny job'. Taking the opposite view, McLintock and Maxwell managed to bypass Runciman and negotiate directly with the Royal Mail marine superintendent for the retention of the business. Since the liquidity crisis of early October the trustees' small secretariat had been forced to shoulder the additional burden of ingeniously assembling the funds required to prevent failure. Michael Babington Smith, one of the staff, and McLintock's partner Duncan McKellar devoted long hours to calculating weekly cash-flow charts to reduce the hazards of the passage.[14]

By November 1930 it was obvious to the voting trustees that there was no easy solution to the Royal Mail Group's massive difficulties. The axeman would have to give way to a painstaking surgeon. Accordingly, the banks, the Treasury and the Northern Ireland Government agreed to an extension of the moratorium on the Group's loan repayments for a further year until 31 December 1931. This arrangement necessitated the voting trustees' winning the approval of the Group's shareholders and debenture holders, who were ignorant of the extent of the breakdown earlier in the year. McLintock and Maxwell were keen to leave Harland & Wolff to last in this exercise. Its balance sheet was in an appalling mess and a simple question would easily have revealed the true position of the Company. In any case, the accounts had not normally been issued until the end of March and a few months' delay would cause little comment. During February, in a series of brilliantly conceived meetings, the grim tidings were broken gently to the shareholders. However, although they endorsed the moratorium, publication of at least some of the details of the collapse had an unforeseen consequence. It led to questions in the House of Commons about the Treasury's role and there were demands for an investigation, possibly by the police, into the affair. This was the last thing that the voting trustees would have wished for. The Attorney-General, Sir William Jowitt, had little alternative but to bow to pressure from the Commons.

On 13 May 1931 Kylsant and Harold Morland, Royal Mail's auditor, were summoned for fraud under Section 84 of the Larceny Act of 1861. They were tried at the Old Bailey between 20 and 30 July. Mercifully for the voting trustees, Kylsant was identified in the public mind with the Royal Mail Steam Packet Company and not with any of the other associated companies. The police investigation and the trial centred on Royal Mail and its own subsidiaries, and only passing reference was made to other parts of the Group. Kylsant was eventually found guilty of issuing a false prospectus, which gave erroneous information about past profit. He was imprisoned for a year. There were many who considered this sentence severe, believing that, if Kylsant was guilty, other chairmen of large companies should join him behind bars. There was some truth in this view. Although haughty in manner, Kylsant, by the standards of his time, had done little wrong, except perhaps to pilot the Royal Mail Group to bankruptcy. So convinced was he of his innocence that he had done little to prepare his defence. From the voting trustees' perspective this was probably just as well. Throughout the proceedings they had held their breath lest the prosecution or defence should unwittingly stumble on evidence relating to other constituents of the Group. The most likely candidate for a chance reference was Harland & Wolff which, in the months leading up to the appointment of the committee of inquiry and the voting trustees, Kylsant had continually used as an excuse for the Group's collapse. Investigation of the Harland & Wolff finances would have raised very damaging questions about the Company's solvency and Kylsant's business methods.[15]

In the midst of this crisis, on 12 June 1931, the Harland & Wolff accounts for 1930 were issued. In the circumstances the voting trustees adhered to the formula devised by Kylsant in 1924. The overdrafts, for example, still appeared under the confusing heading 'Sundry creditors for supplies, bank overdrafts, provision for accruing expenses, income tax and contingencies'. For the first time the shareholders were sent a printed circular explaining the accounts, which spelled out the gravity of the situation. It was made clear that £238,053 at the credit of the profit and loss account was 'not represented by liquid resources'. The shareholders were told that the directors were 'acting in co-operation with the Voting Trustees appointed by the Treasury and the Banks to control the Royal Mail Group of Shipping Companies, with which this Company is closely associated and from which a large proportion of the amounts outstanding is due in cash or under Bills and in respect of which there are contingent liabilities on bills discounted and guarantees'. The report underlined the bleak prospects: 'The Company has at the present time only three vessels on the stocks and three being fitted out.' The need to reduce the value of the fixed assets and investments was mentioned, but it was explained that capital reconstruction would have to form part of a general scheme covering the whole of the Royal Mail Group.

Since dividend on the first cumulative preference shares had not been paid, the holders of the stock acquired voting rights in the Company and the power to petition the courts for the appointment of a liquidator or receiver. On 25 June 1931 Rebbeck addressed a combined meeting of stockholders of all classes. His speech was masterly, highlighting the technical excellence of the Company and placing the blame for its difficulties on membership of the Royal Mail Group and on the general depression in shipbuilding and engineering. He lifted the shareholders' spirits by concluding:

> You have in our different establishments the best equipped shipbuilding, marine engineering and repair works to be found anywhere. The organization is in a healthy condition so far as its technical ability is concerned and is backed by a capable and willing body of hard working men . . . Optimism is not fashionable at the present time but I sincerely hope that its place will not be taken by pessimism.

Rebbeck may have been whistling in the dark, but he won the confidence of the meeting. In expansive mood he promised to consult the preference shareholders before any reconstruction scheme was implemented, and he appeared to support their request to nominate a director.

By midsummer 1931 the outlook for Harland & Wolff, in common with the rest of British shipbuilding, was atrocious. Only one vessel had been ordered since the beginning of the year, the *Highland Patriot*, of 14,156 gross tons, for the Nelson Steam Navigation Company, a member of the Royal Mail Group. The only vessels left on the Company's books were the *Georgic* for White Star, the *Achimota* for Elder Dempster, and the two tankers ordered in 1930 by Anglo-Saxon Petroleum. The large and beautiful motor liners *Warwick Castle* and *Reina del Pacifico* had been delivered earlier in the year. At the end of April the Company's overdraft had touched its limit of £2,300,000. The committee of economies redoubled its efforts to cut costs, while Rebbeck was desperately searching for new work. He published an imaginatively

designed brochure, which for the first time advertised the Company's facilities and range of expertise. In common with other builders of marine diesel engines, he sought relief in the construction of diesel locomotives. The staff at Scotstoun (foremen and office workers) agreed to take a massive cut in salary pending the outcome of negotiations with the 'Big Four' railway companies. As Armstrong Whitworth and Beardmores had already discovered, diesel-locomotive manufacture was risky and technically difficult. There were enormous problems in designing and building a tractionable engine. At their meeting on 24 June 1931 the directors agreed that they had no alternative but to sell the Greenock yard and allow NSS to sterilise the building berths. This decision was not easy to implement. It emerged that the Greenock Harbour Trust would prevent the sale of the yard to anyone other than themselves. As an alternative Rebbeck proposed that the businesses of A. & J. Inglis and D. & W. Henderson should be amalgamated and transferred to Greenock. The Pointhouse and Meadowside yards would then be sold and their berths sterilised. This scheme had its drawbacks. It would deprive the Govan yard of the essential fitting-out facilities at the mouth of the Kelvin and would also require the consent of the D. & W. Henderson preference shareholders who, following the waiving of the dividend in 1930, had voting control of that company.

By November the committee of economies had made substantial headway. The

The keels of the *Amber* and the *Guayra*, both for the Argentine Naviga Company, a member of Royal Mail Group, under construction at the Pointhouse yard of A. & J. Inglis on the C early in 1930.

wages and salary bill had been slashed by £132,102 per annum. The Liverpool South Works had been closed, yielding an annual saving of £4,470. The office staff throughout the Company had been placed on short time and their salaries cut. Piecework had been extended to include most of the workforce and the piecework pricelist had been reduced. The total annual savings were almost £200,000. Rebbeck knew that these measures would show their full effect only when the order book improved. The second half of the year had been worse than the first. Orders had been received for one tramp ship, a floating crane and three small vessels, including the Clyde steamer *Duchess of Hamilton* for the Caledonian Steam Packet Company. None of these were to be built at Queen's Island where, after the launch of the *Georgic* on 12 November 1931, just the *Highland Patriot* remained on the berths. Neverthless, the finance committee, confident that recovery would come, drafted a plan for reconstructing the Company's balance sheet. The details do not survive, but in any case the voting trustees refused to discuss any question relating to the balance sheet. Deeply troubled, the finance committee, which now included Sir Ernest Clark, agreed on 21 October that Rebbeck should discuss the Company's prospects with McLintock as soon as possible. They resolved to meet immediately Rebbeck had any news.

Terrifying as the hazards were that faced Rebbeck and his fellow directors, they paled in comparison with the monumental job of devising a scheme for dealing with all classes of the Royal Mail Group's creditors – a task which the voting trustees had undertaken to complete by the end of the year. Kylsant's trial had interrupted and frustrated this work. Immediately afterwards the voting trustees had to take urgent action to secure the survival of White Star and the finance of the *Georgic*. On 11 June 1931 Sir Ernest Clark and Rebbeck had told Hyde that Harland & Wolff required an additional £200,000 to pay the 'wages and their accounts for materials supplied', because funds to complete the *Georgic* were unavailable. Eventually the Northern Ireland Government came to the rescue with the necessary guarantees. These delays prevented the drafting of a scheme until late in the year. Towards the end of October Michael Babington Smith, of the voting trustees' secretariat, suggested to Maxwell that the shipping assets be segregated from the old companies that originally formed the Group and were now covered by the moratorium. This simple proposal was explained in a hugely complex document drafted within a week. Although Harland & Wolff was excluded from the scheme, it was implied that its creditors would be dealt with at the same time. Rebbeck's request for an early interview arrived with the voting trustees in the middle of this flurry of composition. By way of response, a copy of the scheme was sent at once to Sir Ernest Clark with permission to discuss it with the finance committee in preparation for an interview between Rebbeck and the voting trustees, arranged for the afternoon of 29 October 1931.[16]

The finance committee reconvened on the morning of this meeting. The members' main cause for concern was the lack of provision of working capital for Harland & Wolff, since overdrafts were to be frozen and debts due by the Royal Mail Group

The fabulous liner *Reina del Pacifico*, for the Pacific Steam Navigation Company, leaving the Lagan in March 1931.

were to be satisfied by the issue of deferred creditor's certificates. They could see no alternative but to accept the issue by Harland & Wolff itself of deferred creditor's certificates to the Company's creditors and the holders of the discounted bills drawn on the Royal Mail Group. They were appalled that the Company's security for discounted bills over the *Reina del Pacifico*, *Achimota*, and *Georgic* was to be cancelled. The committee members were also troubled by Rebbeck's commitment to keep the preference shareholders informed of any reconstruction proposal and felt threatened by the suggestion that the Midland Bank, as holder of the bulk of the Company's deferred creditor's certificates, would have the power to appoint the board, which was to be limited to five members. They feared that the scheme might obstruct an amalgamation with Workman Clark which was being discussed with William Strachan and NSS. The afternoon meeting, attended by all the voting trustees, overruled most of Rebbeck's objections to the scheme. They did not consider an extraordinary meeting of preference shareholders to be necessary and confirmed that amalgamation talks could proceed. It was explained that the provision of working capital for the Group members would be a matter for the holders of the deferred creditor's certificates.[17]

Disappointed, Rebbeck consulted the Northern Ireland Ministry of Finance, which in turn asked the Treasury for advice. Sir Richard Hopkins advised the Government of the Province to give its unqualified consent to the scheme. Rebbeck was full of fighting talk, suggesting that the Company's finance committee had to 'come to grips' with the Midland Bank over the question of working capital. Eventually, after days of intense negotiations, McLintock agreed to allow Harland & Wolff a working margin of £100,000 and restored the Company's security over the three liners. These amendments were incorporated in the final version of the scheme, agreed in principle at the end of the year. So as to give the voting trustees time to secure the necessary consents before going to the court for approval, the moratorium on the Royal Mail Group's debts was extended for a further three months. The Harland & Wolff finance committee was still keen to consult the holders of the first cumulative preference shares, particularly as the Midland Bank had given them no assurance about the future composition of the board. Deeply troubled by the implications of the scheme, including the possibility of liquidation, Clark and Craig urged Rebbeck to 'consider the position of the Company under the scheme over the next three years'. Clark demanded detailed budget estimates for six strategies, ranging from the complete closure of all the Company's plant to its full employment. In the knowledge that at current prices all classes of shipbuilding were unremunerative, Rebbeck assumed the worst. He discounted the complete closure of the works, reckoning that such a course would lead to the permanent break-up of Harland & Wolff. Instead he favoured the option of closing the shipyards, preserving just a nucleus of staff and carrying on the business only at the repair works at Liverpool, London and Southampton, whose custom had remained surprisingly buoyant. He forecast heavy losses, £108,000 in 1932, £137,000 in 1933 and £137,000 in 1934. On learning of this unpleasant prediction, the voting trustees vetoed the calling of a meeting of first cumulative preference stockholders.[18]

The final preparation of the scheme for submission to the courts resulted in the devastating discovery by Archibald Forbes, an assistant to McLintock, that the Harland & Wolff pension fund was invested within the Group and was in no way secured. In effect, all the employees who were members of the fund were unsecured creditors, much to the horror of the voting trustees and the Governor of the Bank of England. The trustees hurriedly consulted two counsel, E.S. Murphy MP and Gordon Brown, who confirmed that the fund was not within the scope of the moratorium. The principal creditors of the Group were called together and told of the special circumstances and, to the relief of the trustees and the secretariat, they agreed to continue the pension payments outside the scheme. At the same time the Company's cash position was eased by the announcement in March of the sale of the *Achimota* (originally intended for Elder Dempster) to the Australian firm Huddart Parker Limited.[19]

The Royal Mail scheme provisionally came into effect at the end of March and was sanctioned by the High Court on 24 June 1931, with subsidiary approval being obtained simultaneously in Northern Ireland and Scotland. Under its terms the moratorium on the Group's debts was to be extended for another three years until 31 December 1934. The Harland & Wolff articles of association were immediately amended to transfer voting control, and thus the power to appoint directors, to the holders of the new deferred creditor's certificates. Despite the fears expressed earlier in the year, no radical changes were made in the composition of the board. J.W. Kempster, who had been a director for twenty-five years, retired, along with the ineffectual John Dickinson who had been a supernumerary since the closure of the Greenock yard. The Midland Bank nominated as its representative directors Rebbeck, Craig and Henry Harland, the Treasury confirmed its selection of Sir Ernest Clark and the other creditors were to be represented by James Gray. After lengthy negotiations Charles Payne was appointed an additional director. The financial management of the Company was transfused: Pirrie's loyal servants William Tawse and Saxon Payne were pensioned off, and Frederick Spark promoted to chief accountant. Spark, who, like Tawse, had been trained by Price Waterhouse, came from the north east of England and had first joined the Company in 1910. L.V. Dunlop, a competent shipbuilder and former chief draughtsman at Cairds, was posted as general manager at Govan.

At the same time the Midland Bank offered to make fresh funds available above the £100,000 ceiling, providing they were secured by registered mortgage and the Company could show evidence of substantial reductions in expenses and a real possibility of winning business. The accounts for 1931 were not published until September 1932. They revealed the heavy loss of £283,136. This was cancelled by the credit balance of £238,053 and the transfer of £50,000 from 'Provision for contingencies not now required'. No depreciation provision was made and capital additions had been kept to a bare minimum of £24,791. The published account itemised the creditors who were to be issued with deferred creditor's certificates:

Trustees of Harland & Wolff pension fund	£276,239.4s.6d.
Amounts owing to subsidiary companies	£657,738.17s.4d.
Trade Facilities Acts advances and interest	£1,073,203.7s.11d.
Bank overdrafts, deposits and interests accrued	£2,325,508.19s.10d.
Liability as drawers of matured bills of exchange accepted by associated companies and as guarantors on behalf of associated shipping company	£3,354,886.3s.3d.
	£7,687,576.12s.10d.

This vast sum, representing roughly 75 per cent of the Company's issued capital, was only half covered by current assets of £4,196,926, whose realisation was deferred

from 31 December 1931 under the scheme. The financial press had been so buffeted by the shocks of the year that this further evidence of the tempest sweeping the engineering and shipbuilding industry aroused little comment.

Rebbeck's predictions for 1932 and 1933 proved remarkably accurate. After the launch of the *Highland Patriot* from Queen's Island on 10 December 1931 there was not another launch until the Shaw Savill cargo liner *Waiwera* on 1 May 1934. The *Georgic* was the last vessel to be completed before the order famine, leaving the Lagan on 10 June 1932. At the handing-over ceremony the following day in Liverpool Rebbeck made a heroic speech drawing attention to the liner's cost-saving features. He observed that sooner or later shipowners would need to order new ships to remain competitive, since 'one sharp knife is more use than a basketful of blunt ones'. These remarks were endorsed by McLintock and Maxwell who were both present.[20] Thereafter the Belfast yards were placed on a care-and-maintenance basis, with foremen and apprentices occupied in painting and repairing plant. Only three vessels were reconditioned at the yard in the two years. The engine works won some orders for stationary land engines and diesel locomotives. The first contract for an experimental locomotive was placed by the Belfast and County Down Railway in September 1932, followed during 1933 by orders from Iraq, the British Oxygen Corporation and the London Midland and Scottish Railway. The nucleus of staff that had been retained busied themselves in investigating hull forms and improving the design of the Harland & Wolff/Burmeister & Wain engine. At the insistence of the voting trustees, the technical staff collaborated with the accountant's office and secretary's department to devise, under the direction of John Philp and Frederick

The launch of the
Baron Dunmore for
H. Hogarth & Sons of
sgow on 9 August 1933
n the Meadowside yard
of D. & W. Henderson
on the Clyde. Two
years later the yard
was closed and the
shipbuilding rights sold
o National Shipbuilders
Securities Limited.

Spark, an improved system of cost control. After lengthy consultations and trials, regular monthly and quarterly summaries showing approximate working results began to be prepared from October 1932. The virtual closure of the Queen's Island establishment intensified unemployment in Belfast, which by 1932 had risen to 76,000 or 28 per cent of the insured workforce. Unemployment in shipbuilding and engineering alone was 64.5 per cent by the end of 1932. Thousands of Belfast people were surviving, on the verge of starvation, on Outdoor Relief payments – a miserable 16s. a week for a couple with two children. The scale of the deprivation led to protests and violence. On 3 October 1932 Outdoor Relief workers went on strike and 60,000 people, Protestants and Catholics, took part in a march to demand more aid for the destitute. In the days that followed riots flared and at least two people were killed.

The ten vessels delivered by the Company during the depression years of 1932/3 were constructed on the Clyde at Govan, Meadowside or Pointhouse. With the exception of three 4,000-gross-ton tramp steamers built by D. & W. Henderson for H. Hogarth & Sons of Glasgow, they were all small craft. The Pointhouse yard more

301

or less closed after the delivery of the *North Carr* in February 1933, but Govan and Meadowside struggled on. Such income as there was came from the repair works at Liverpool, Southampton and London.

The losses for these two crisis years were £118,177 and £164,305. They were prevented from accumulating by the time-honoured method of making transfers from reserves. There were no capital additions and every effort was made to sell unwanted fixed assets. In November 1932 Pirrie Park, the firm's sports and recreational ground in Belfast, was sold to Methodist College for £12,000. However, it proved impossible to sell the Greenock yard until the moratorium expired at the end of 1934. Despite the foul conditions, Rebbeck again inspired the annual meeting in 1933. He could not avoid saying frankly that there was 'no apparent prospect of a substantial improvement in trade at present', but he indicated that the auguries were good, emphasising the Company's technical ability to build vessels that would be very economical in service. During July Sir Ernest Clark resigned as Treasury representative on the board, on his appointment as Governor of Tasmania. He was not replaced. Released from Clark's watchful presence, Rebbeck made a rash bid for freedom, proposing a capital reorganisation and requesting additional overdraft facilities from the Midland Bank. Reginald McKenna, the bank's chairman, had no difficulty in turning down this application.[21]

Rebbeck's optimism was nevertheless justified. World trade picked up late in 1933 as confidence in the international monetary system was restored, and early the following year freight rates began to inch forward. During the summer of 1932 Shaw Savill & Albion had ordered three 10,000-gross-ton cargo liners (two to be built at Belfast and one at Govan to give relief to the acute unemployment in the Clyde area), but they had been postponed almost at once. Work was resumed in the autumn of 1933. Hard on the heels of this harbinger of better weather came orders from the Blue Star line for three 10,000-gross-ton refrigerated cargo ships; from the Anglo-Saxon Petroleum Company for an 8,000-ton tanker; from the Admiralty for a 5,000-ton light cruiser, HMS *Penelope*; and from the War Office for a large towing vessel. The order book began to fill rapidly. In the first month of 1934 the Ministry of Finance for Northern Ireland urgently began preparing a package of finance with the Midland Bank, to enable the Company to accept an order from Union-Castle for two 25,000-gross-ton liners, *Stirling Castle* and *Athlone Castle*, and for two smaller cargo boats of 7,000 gross tons, *Roslin Castle* and *Rothesay Castle*. This order was not won easily. Sir Vernon Thomson, who had recently been appointed a director of Union-Castle, insisted on regular and lengthy discussions with Rebbeck in London. By mid-1934 orders had been received for no less than twenty-four vessels, complemented by contracts to replace the diesel engines in the Royal Mail liners *Asturias* and *Alcantara* with geared turbines, and an order from the New South Wales Government for two railcar engines.

In euphoric mood the board resolved that there was no longer any need for a capital reorganisation, since Reginald McKenna, the chairman of the Midland Bank was prepared to take a long view of the Company's prospects. Rebbeck had gained this impression after a long interview with McKenna on 24 February. He claimed McKenna had answered him that . . .

> As long as Mr Rebbeck was doing as he had been doing and the staff working
> with him as they have been working, the Bank were content simply to bide the
> time and the day when Harland and Wolff could begin to pay back the debt

The keel-laying ceremony for HMS *Penelope* on 30 May 1934 in the presence of the Duke and Duchess of Kent. The laying-down of this vessel symbolised recovery from the depression.

they owed to the Bank. The Bank were not interested in what McLintock or anyone else thought about the Balance Sheet, but were very much interested in Harland and Wolff with its traditions, plant and geographical distribution of the Yards and Works. If the work Mr Rebbeck was at present getting was at a low price, he [McKenna] recommended him to get a lot of it and to grind away at it and endeavour to make a margin in that way.

If Rebbeck reported this conversation accurately, McKenna's views did not accord with those of his senior colleagues at the Midland Bank. On 11 April Frederick Hyde, the managing director of the bank, and his assistants quizzed the Company secretary, John Philp, about various items in the profit and loss account. His explanation of the system of tendering did not convince Hyde that the contracts which the bank was being asked to finance had been accepted at a profit:

When tendering for work, their prices are made up as follows:
  Costs
  Wages
  Materials and
  Direct Expenses

to which is added fifteen per cent of wages – an estimated amount of out of pocket expenses directly attributable to the job. The total equals the minimum price that they can accept. To the latter figure they add as much as they think they can to meet overheads, according to the competition for the job and other causes. In some cases, they are not able to add anything towards meeting the overheads as they feel at times it is essential to obtain the job and they can only get it by putting in a price at bare cost. On contract [commission] work, the surplus income over expenses on material and labour is taken into the profit and loss account in the year in which the work is done, but it does not necessarily follow that this is an accurate profit or loss, which cannot be definitely ascertained until the contract is completed.[22]

The Midland Bank was in a difficult position, because the upturn in Harland & Wolff's fortunes was being heralded as the first step towards a return to full employment in depressed Northern Ireland at a time of heightening political tension, marked by recurring sectarian outbreaks.

Work on the new contracts began at once, providing employment by May for some 10,000 men in Belfast. The first vessel to be launched from Queen's Island for more than two years was the *Waiwera* on 1 May 1934. Between then and the end of the year sixteen vessels went down the ways at the Company's yards and eleven were delivered. The *Waiwera* and *Waipawa* for Shaw Savill immediately made their impact, attracting high praise in the shipping press as 'probably the finest type of modern motor cargo ship in the world'. Nevertheless the Midland Bank's doubts about the profitability of these contracts was not unfounded. The *Sir Hastings Anderson*, built at Govan for the War Office, lost an amazing £80,000 on a contract price of £34,000 and the *Waiwera* and *Waipawa* together lost £18,151 on a contract price of £580,000. The Company's total loss for the year was £112,939. This was again covered by making a notional transfer from reserves and no provision was made for depreciation.

Understandably the Midland Bank was not impressed by this outcome. Hyde called for copies of the accounts for all contracts completed and in hand during 1934 so that he could investigate the Company's rules for allocating overheads to contracts. His suspicion that work had been taken on at a loss was confirmed by John Philp, the Company secretary:

> . . . under present strenuous competitive conditions it is not possible to obtain work allowing for these normal establishment charges in the tender. It is therefore necessary to take something off the normal price to obtain the work and get as much out of the contract towards the establishment charges as Harland & Wolff Ltd think the job will stand, taking into consideration for whom the work is done, what other firms are tendering and what work it will mean to the associated companies, such as Colvilles for the supply of steel. The result of this policy is that although, in the main, contracts provide something towards the establishment charges, it is far short of the amount required to put their Profit and Loss Account on the right side.

Hyde was not to be confused by this ingenuous explanation, particularly as he had heard from the Shipbuilding Conference that Harland & Wolff was thought to be tendering at less than cost. He ordered Philp to explain precisely how all the establishment charges for each works were calculated and how they were

304

group of Queen's Island stagers at the main yard in 1935.

incorporated into the estimates. From what he knew and guessed, he was not surprised to learn that . . .

> Although the accountant gives a figure of what he considers should be the Establishment charges charged to each job, the actual amount included in the contract price is considerably less and is at a figure which Mr Rebbeck considers right . . .

However he was amazed to discover that even the accountant's calculations did not cover the Company's 'general standing charges' (including rates, office overheads and staff costs), amounting to £216,000 a year, which were to be taken care of out of the profits. Hyde realised that this vestige of Pirrie's halcyon years before the First World War, when work was plentiful and overheads irrelevant, would be hard to break, especially when the bank's nominee as chairman of the Company condoned it. Rebbeck was apparently incapable of appreciating that the overheads of competitors might be less than those of Harland & Wolff. When challenged with the accusation that the Company had been tendering at less than cost he replied 'that Swan Hunter have been taking vessels at the same price as Harland & Wolff and that Hawthorn Leslie took the contract from Elder Dempster Lines which Harland & Wolff lost on the question of price'.[23]

This investigation of the internal financial management of the Company was inspired by the desire of the Northern Ireland Government to provide guaranteed loans to shipowners for the construction of new craft at Queen's Island, so as to sustain the apparent recovery. There was every indication that the spate of orders secured in the first half of 1934 would not be repeated, and no contracts were placed between June and the end of November. Relief came late in the year with an order from McIlwraith, McEachern & Company for an 11,000-gross-ton cargo vessel and

305

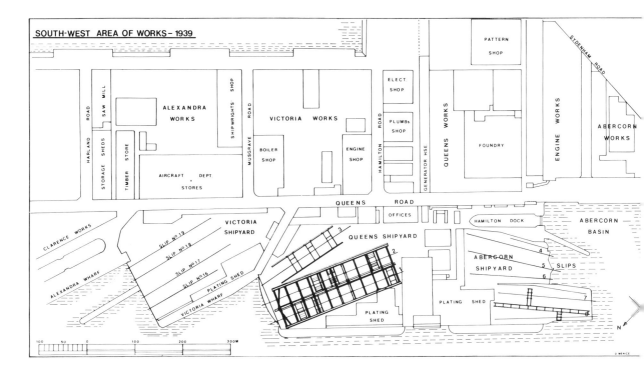

from the London & North Eastern Railway for the *Talisman*. During the first two months of 1935 Blue Star, Union-Castle and the Anglo-Saxon Petroleum Company again came to the rescue with orders supported by guaranteed loans for two 11,000-gross-ton motor cargo vessels, two 15,000-gross-ton motor liners and two 6,200-gross-ton tankers respectively. By the beginning of March orders had been received for ten ships, but there were few inquiries for further business. The darkening skies quickly became stormy when it was learned that the British Linen Bank and the Clydesdale Bank were no longer willing to finance D. & W. Henderson, owners of the Meadowside yard, and were keen that the yard be sold to NSS. There were three vessels under construction at Meadowside *Baron Renfrew* (ship no. 947M) for H. Hogarth & Sons; the *Saganaga* (ship no. 950M) for Salvesen of Leith; and the *Inventor* (ship no. 953M) for T. & J. Harrison Limited. The Harland & Wolff board did not object to the sterilisation of the berths but was determined to retain the repair works, dry dock and fitting-out facilities in the mouth of the Kelvin, in order to support Govan. Despite the efforts of Harland & Wolff, D. & W. Henderson was placed into liquidation on 4 April 1935 and Andrew McHarg, Sir James Lithgow's accountant and financial adviser, was appointed liquidator. To the relief of Harland & Wolff, McHarg agreed to complete the vessels under construction, while a deal was worked out with NSS on the sterilisation of the Meadowside yard and the future of the Belfast business of Workman Clark.[24]

Desultory negotiations had continued between Harland & Wolff and Workman Clark since William Strachan's approach in 1930 shortly after the appointment of the Royal Mail committee of inquiry. In 1931 Workman Clark had concentrated production in its north yard, and its Victoria yard on Queen's Island had more or less been dismantled. Only two tankers, totalling 33,300 gross tons, for Anglo-Saxon Petroleum, had been completed during the year. Workman Clark's position had deteriorated badly during 1932 and 1933. Just one vessel, the *Erin*, had been delivered in 1932 and no further orders were received until August 1933. The last contract had been placed in November by Anglo-Saxon Petroleum for the tanker *Acavus*. During

306

most of 1934 the yard had survived on repair work. At the end of February 1935 the staff were sacked and re-engaged on a day-to-day basis. Late in April it became known that NSS had purchased the business and that Harland & Wolff was to acquire the firm's Victoria Shipyard and Engine Works in exchange for its shareholding in D. & W. Henderson. This was a logical rationalisation, giving Harland & Wolff control of most of Queen's Island. Workman Clark's Victoria Engine Works stood between Harland & Wolff's Abercorn Engine Works and the Alexandra Dock Works, beyond which were Workman Clark's Thompson Works and King's Works. Moreover, on the corner of Sydenham Road at the head of the Abercorn basin Workman Clark had a small ship repair works, the former engine works of MacIlwaine & MacColl.[25]

The deal was finalised in June 1935 and all the works and shipyards were renamed. The south yard became the Abercorn Shipyard, the north yard became Queen's Shipyard, the Workman Clark south yard was to be the Victoria Shipyard and the east yard became the Musgrave Shipyard. The Harland & Wolff Engine Works was renamed Queen's Works, while the old name Abercorn Works was reserved for the small works at the corner of Sydenham Road and Queen's Road . As part of the transaction the Greenock yard of Caird & Company passed to NSS and, at Rebbeck's suggestion, William Strachan junior became a director of Harland & Wolff. He was immediately thrust into the firing line by being placed in overall control of estimating. At the same time James Gray resigned as director responsible for ship repair, to return to Union-Castle as engineering director. He was replaced by F.G. 'Stick Face' Dunlop, who had entered the Queen's Island drawing office thirty-nine years earlier. He was the son of Samuel Dunlop who had retired as cashier in 1902 after working for the firm from the day it started.

The announcement of all these changes coincided with news of the death of Lady Pirrie, the president of the Company, in London on 17 June 1935. Throughout her declining years her sister, Agnes Carlisle, had been her constant companion as she had been for nearly all of Lady Pirrie's married life, acting as her secretary, housekeeper and nurse. Although the supply of gifts and letters to the senior managers came to a halt shortly after her husband's death, Lady Pirrie had remained deeply committed to the Company. She had kept in regular touch through John Craig, who remained her most stalwart friend. Occasionally she had visited the yard, being entertained by either William Tawse or Charles Payne whom she christened 'Charlie Blue-eyes Payne' after his award of the CBE. In her final years she was bemused and troubled by the lack of orders, praying constantly for a recovery. She was buried with her husband in Belfast's City Cemetery.

The takeover of Workman Clark's assets on Queen's Island was linked in the press with persistent rumours that Harland & Wolff was about to re-enter the airframe-building business, using part of the Victoria Shipyard for this purpose. The speculation stemmed from the publication of a Defence White Paper on 16 March 1935 recommending the opening of new 'shadow' aircraft factories as far north-west of London as possible. Rebbeck, encouraged by the Northern Ireland Government, was keen to press ahead. An official from the Westminster Air Ministry was invited to inspect the facilities at Queen's Island, which had been constructed during the First World War. He was impressed with what he saw and commended the Company's plans to build 'large seaplanes rather than smaller types of aircraft'. However the Air Ministry decided not to place any of the contracts authorised in the White Paper with new establishments because of protests from the existing airframe builders.

Undaunted, Rebbeck opened discussions with established builders in the London area with a view to setting up a new jointly owned company. These talks were given added impetus in November when the Belfast Harbour Commissioners obtained powers from the Northern Ireland Government to build a new airport at Sydenham alongside the Musgrave Shipyard.

By April 1936 outline agreement had been reached between Harland & Wolff and the aircraft-makers Short Brothers of Rochester for the construction of seaplanes and aeroplanes at Belfast. The Harbour Commissioners had given their consent to the new company leasing thirty-six acres of vacant ground formerly leased by Harland & Wolff but given up in 1933. Hyde of the Midland Bank sounded a note of caution when he warned Rebbeck not to tie up £100,000 in the company without assurances from the Air Ministry that a sufficient volume of orders would be forthcoming. The Ministry replied that the contracts would be placed with Short Brothers who, if it wished, could subcontract the work to its Belfast subsidiary which in turn could subcontract the manufacture of details and subassemblies to Harland & Wolff. It was to be a condition that Short Brothers held a controlling interest in the new firm. Accordingly when Short & Harland Limited was registered in June 1936, Short Brothers was allocated 60 per cent of the shares. The first orders were for 50 Bristol 'Bombay' aircraft and 150 twin-engined Handley Page 'Hereford' bombers. Work began at once on driving the piles for the new factory and by August 1937 the first aircraft components were being produced.[26] Rebbeck, calculating that shadow factories would be opened in Glasgow, which like Belfast was considered out of range of enemy bombers, launched a scheme to re-equip the toolroom at Finnieston to allow the manufacture of jigs and precision gauges for aero engines and gun mountings.

Meanwhile the Midland Bank and Sir William McLintock, representing the interests of the other holders of deferred creditor's certificates, had turned their attention to the reconstruction of the Harland & Wolff balance sheet, spurred on by the revival in orders and the sale of unwanted plant to NSS. McLintock proposed the formation of a realisation company to sell all Harland & Wolff's assets, on the model of the two companies recently established under his guidance for realising the assets of the old Royal Mail and Elder Dempster companies. By June 1935 McLintock and his partner John Morison had devised a plan which, it was envisaged, would result in the splitting up of the enterprise. Their experience told them that it would take months of intense and detailed negotiations to achieve agreement on a scheme for presentation to the courts. Their plan was immediately criticised by Hyde at the Midland Bank who was unhappy at the drastic devaluation of the assets from almost £14,000,000 to £2,500,000, preferring a figure of £4,000,000. This was partly because Hyde was hopeful that Vickers could be persuaded to take over the Company and he did not wish to open the bidding from a position of weakness. Hyde, in great secrecy, instructed Rebbeck to start negotiations with the managing director, Sir Charles Craven, with a view to a merger. Rebbeck resisted the proposal, feeling his personal position and reputation in Ulster were in jeopardy. Craven expressed interest, but only if the Midland Bank was prepared to finance the deal. He gave Rebbeck a broad hint that he would prefer to deal direct with McKenna.

In Belfast serious rioting began in July 1935 and sectarian passions smouldered for months afterwards. In these circumstances the Northern Ireland Government postponed the realisation proposal for a year, fearful that the sale of the Queen's Island yard would result in further rationalisation and loss of jobs.[27] By the end of September, McLintock had made Craven fully aware of the major problems

confronting Harland & Wolff and the Vickers board had agreed to abandon any plans to bid for the Company.

The directors, who had only Rebbeck's rather partial account of these developments, were grappling with more immediate problems. The liquidation of D. & W. Henderson Limited in April had deprived Harland & Wolff of the Meadowside graving dock and fitting-out quays, across the river from the Company's Govan yard. This placed a large question mark against the viability of Govan. Neither Andrew McHarg, the liquidator of D. & W. Henderson, nor NSS was to be rushed into a quick sale of the graving dock and fitting-out quays. They delayed until the autumn of 1935 while possible purchasers were canvassed. By the end of October Alexander Stephen & Sons, the Blythswood Shipbuilding & Engineering Company and Cochrane Morgan & Company were all showing interest. The Harland & Wolff board, deeply disturbed, was prepared to up its bid from what was considered to be a reasonable price of £50,000 to £80,000 so as 'to consolidate Harland & Wolff's position at the head of the River' and was also ready to throw in the building rights at A. & J. Inglis's Pointhouse yard on the other side of the River Kelvin. In the spring of 1936 their offer of £63,000 was accepted and a new company, D. & W. Henderson Limited, was formed as a wholly-owned subsidiary of Harland & Wolff. This expenditure coincided with a pressing need to upgrade the Company's plant and

309

The Shaw Savill
refrigerated cargo liner
Wairangi, being towed ▮
the fitting-out basin at
Harland & Wolff's Gov
yard on the Clyde, just
after her launch on
9 October 1934.

machinery to reduce costs by taking advantage of new techniques. In the spring of 1935 the board had agreed to spend £8,000 on welding equipment for Belfast. New machine tools, capable of working to high tolerance, were also acquired to facilitate the construction of the latest generation of Harland & Wolff/Burmeister & Wain airless-injection diesels. These capital additions, along with further investments later in the year, were to be financed out of the sale of the Company's investment of 50,000 ordinary shares in John Brown.

During 1935 Harland & Wolff launched 127,312 gross tons of shipping, a world record for the year. The vessels included from Queen's Island HMS *Penelope*, the *Stirling Castle*, *Athlone Castle* and *Rothesay Castle*; and from Govan the *San Arcadio*, a tanker for the Eagle Oil and Shipping Company, and the *Sonavati* for the Bombay Steam Navigation Company. Altogether sixteen vessels were completed. The *Wairangi*, last of the three ships for Shaw Savill & Albion, left the Lagan towards the end of January. Like her sisters she was an immediate success. She logged a cargo ship record with a passage of 17 days, 20 hours from Liverpool to the Cape. Her sister, *Waiwera*, delivered the year before, replied with an incredible voyage of 15 days, 14 hours, 12 minutes. The *Wairangi* rejoined with a non-stop run of 15 days, 10 hours,

310

11 minutes from London to the Cape and then set a record of 30 days, 10 hours from London to Wellington by way of Panama.[28] The three Blue Star refrigerated ships, of an equally high technical standard, were delivered between the end of December, 1934 and April 1935. The *Roslin Castle* and *Rothesay Castle* were handed over to Union-Castle in May. The *Inventor*, the last ship to be constructed at the Meadowside yard of D. & W. Henderson Limited, was finished in September. There was a steady resurgence in repair work, with turnover at Southampton, Liverpool and London up by more than 18 per cent to nearly £1,230,000. Despite this volume of business the Company's profits were only £42,934, augmented by the payment of £24,000 of interest on the indebtedness of associated companies, following the expiry at the end of 1934 of the Royal Mail Group's debt moratorium. There were insufficient profits either to make provision for depreciation or to pay the interest on the deferred creditor's certificates. The lack of an adequate return again stemmed from the practice of taking contracts at a loss. Discouraged by their previous attempts to improve the method of allocating overheads, the Midland Bank remained silent, probably in the expectation that the formation of the proposed realisation company would be a better way of enforcing financial discipline. The bank simply requested estimates of the profits for the coming year and details of each quarter's results.

During the autumn of 1935 and into 1936 prospects brightened, reinforcing the successes of the formation of Short & Harland and the new D. & W. Henderson Limited. Between October 1935 and the end of 1936 contracts were placed for no fewer than thirty-four vessels. These included four 8,300-gross-ton tankers for the British Tanker Company; the motor liners *Capetown Castle* (27,002 gross tons) and *Durban Castle* (17,388 gross tons) for Union-Castle; and the cruiser HMS *Belfast* which was symbolically allotted ship no. 1000. During 1936 Harland & Wolff again turned out more tonnage than any other British yard. With extensive press coverage, the beautifully designed *Stirling Castle* and *Athlone Castle* were handed over to Union-Castle. They were powered by technically advanced ten-cylinder, double-acting, two-stroke, airless-injection Harland & Wolff/Burmeister & Wain engines and were claimed to be the fastest motor ships in service. The *Stirling Castle* proved this without doubt in August when she beat the record set forty-three years earlier for the passage from Southampton to Capetown.

HMS *Penelope* was completed in November, and the repair business continued to recover strongly. At Govan the value of repairs and refits rose from £110,927 in 1935 to £213,327 in 1936. At Southampton the number of repairs moved up from 531 to 564. A typical refit was that undertaken on the *Empress of Britain*, owned by Canadian Pacific which had a commission-basis repair contract – 'Drydocked and painted after 1935/36 world cruise and four propellers fitted, cruise fittings dismantled, general overhaul and survey subsequently carried out prior to 1936/37 world cruise, 1,500 boiler air tubes renewed, soot collectors fitted in funnels.' The building of small craft was resumed with success at London and electrical subcontracting extended. During the year the London works delivered the following:

11 hatched swim barges of 160 tons each to William Corry & Son Ltd
 2 grab dredger pontoons to Priestman Brothers Ltd
 3 open swim canal barges of 110 tons to Associated Portland Cement Manufacturers Ltd
 1 crane pontoon to Cowans Sheldon & Co.
 1 lightship for Bahrein Harbour India Store Department

The 'Arethusa'-class cruiser HMS *Penelope*, at Belfast, on trials in November 1936.

6	hatched swim barges of 160 tons each for Thames Steam Tug and Towing Co.
42	motor boats ⎤ for the Grand Union Canal Carrying Co.
42	butty boats ⎦
6	open swim barges of 110 tons each to C.A. Etheredge Ltd
1	open swim barge of 300 tons to Union Lighterage Co.
2	pontoons for the Metropolitan Police

The last contract was part of one for floating police stations on the Thames. Meanwhile the Scotstoun works was recommissioned as a gun-mounting plant in the spring to help fulfil the rearmament programme. The Government agreed, as it did with other armaments-manufacturers, to meet the cost of any capital expenditure pending a settlement at the end of the programme in 1938. An 'educational order' of six twin gun mountings was placed in April, followed by a contract for a further twenty in September.

By June 1936 Sir William McLintock judged it time to reactivate the proposal to form the Harland and Wolff Realisation Company. Three months earlier the shares of Colvilles Limited had been successfully issued to the public and Harland and Wolff had netted £1,715,000 for its holding. The Company had also earned an estimated £250,000 profit in the year to date. Early in June a copy of McLintock's scheme was sent to Harland & Wolff for consideration. The directors objected to the smallness of the working capital, fixed at £415,000, and to the valuation of the fixed assets at £6,000,000, a figure they considered too high. After Rebbeck had discussed these points on 12 June with Reginald McKenna, the chairman of the Midland Bank, Hyde, the managing director, invited him to a meeting on 2 July 1936. Hyde took a strong line, dismissing Harland & Wolff's objections out of hand and telling Rebbeck, 'It is desirable to make sure that there should be no need of borrowing for some time.' He confessed that he did not understand why the Company wanted more cash and 'he did not want Harland & Wolff to have so much free cash as would tempt them to look round and see how many more new industries they could enter'. After an intense cross-examination Hyde relented and sanctioned an increase of £100,000 in the working capital on the understanding that the Company was earning profits of £20,000 a month. The meeting ended with a stinging blow when Hyde told Rebbeck that the bank had given Sir James Lithgow an option to purchase its shares in Harland & Wolff. John Morison, Sir William McLintock's partner, who had been present, was impressed by the way Rebbeck had stood up to Hyde's assault. Morison and McLintock later assured Rebbeck that the Midland would accept any reasonable modifications. The accountants, with Rebbeck's support, then set to work to obtain consent to the scheme from all the holders of the deferred creditor's certificates. The Northern Ireland Government remained unenthusiastic because they feared that the Company's poor performance over the last five years might result in a sale at bargain-basement prices and the closure of plant in Belfast.[29]

Any chance the scheme had of acceptance evaporated in October 1936 when the Midland Bank learned that the Company was once more making losses, cancelling the gains made in the first half of the year. It ordered an immediate investigation, and Morison counselled Rebbeck to provide a convincing explanation. This he was unable to do. McKenna summoned Rebbeck to his office on 15 December and charged him with . . .

> living in a wrong atmosphere, and that the Northern Ireland Government was so obsessed with the idea of providing employment that they were exercising considerable pressure on Harland & Wolff to take ships at any sort of price if only they would provide employment and take the men at Belfast off the 'dole'.

This allegation was not without foundation: at the annual meeting in 1935 Rebbeck had told the shareholders that they were 'making no small contribution to the solution of the country's unemployment problem'. However, Rebbeck was not to be browbeaten by the bank and offered a spirited defence. McKenna rejoined by asking what action he proposed to stem the losses, and made it clear that the Midland 'had done all they were going to do'. Rebbeck counterattacked by stating that 'the orders had been taken at the best prices that could be obtained' and that 'the alternative was to take no work at all'. In answering all McKenna's questions Rebbeck showed himself a worthy successor to Pirrie and Kylsant. His replies were lengthy and evasive, blaming the Company's plight on the worldwide depression, rather than on any deficiencies in the management. Rebbeck refused to make any positive forecast of the likely return in 1937, explaining that the Company did not know whether a contract would make a profit until it was almost finished. Taken aback by this admission of the shortcomings in financial control, McKenna bluntly told Rebbeck that, although the Midland had now received consent to the realisation scheme from all the holders of deferred creditor's certificates, he was not prepared to put the plan into action until a detailed estimate of profits for 1937 had been prepared. He made it as clear as possible that Rebbeck could whistle for any increase in the Company's working margin from the Midland Bank:

> If Harland & Wolff was going to live, it had got to live on its own income. Mr Rebbeck was Harland & Wolff, Mr McKenna was not. Mr Rebbeck knew what he could do, Mr McKenna did not. Mr Rebbeck must tell him whether he thought the future was such that the Bank would be well advised to help in the manner Mr Rebbeck required.[30]

The final profit for 1936 was a mere £64,047, just £20,000 better than the year before. When, by February 1937, the Midland had received no news from Harland & Wolff about prospects for the coming year, the proposed formation of the Harland & Wolff Realisation Company was laid aside. The Midland and the other creditors favoured an alternative plan that would enable the Company's management to be radically overhauled. McLintock and Morison proposed a drastic reconstruction of the capital and also the appointment of voting trustees for the Company, with wide powers to sell surplus assets and to investigate its affairs.

The scheme, which was drafted and agreed at the gallop, was made public with perfect timing on Coronation Day, 10 May 1937, when the media's attention was otherwise engaged. The authorised capital was reduced from £12,100,000 to £1,796,082 and the paid-up capital from £10,340,394 to £36,476. This was achieved by writing 12s. (60p) off the value of each £1 first cumulative preference share, writing 19s. (95p) off the 'A' and 'B' preference shares and writing £985.10s. (£985.50) off each £1,000 ordinary share. Arrears of interest outstanding since January 1925 on the first 'A' and 'B' preference shares were cancelled. The preference and ordinary shares of 1s. (5p) were amalgamated and consolidated into 'B' ordinary shares of £1. This drastic operation left investors and unsecured creditors in no doubt about the Company's predicament. The capital was then increased to £12,100,000 by the issue of 5,200,000 £1 'A' ordinary shares and the creation of 5,103,918 £1 'B' ordinary shares which were not to be issued for the time being. The 'A' shares, which had voting rights, were to be pooled and held by trustees on behalf of the creditors with the first call on the assets – namely the Midland Bank, the Treasury, the Northern Ireland Government and the Bank of Ireland. The trustees were also to take over the deferred creditor's certificates issued by associated companies, with a view to selling them on behalf of the Harland & Wolff creditors. McLintock and Lord Kennet, a distinguished public servant, were nominated as voting trustees representing the Treasury, while Frank Charlton, formerly secretary of White Star, E.T. Parkes, a former general manager of the Midland Bank, and Sir John Keene, a director of the Bank of Ireland, represented the other creditors. In the general euphoria surrounding the Coronation the scheme won the grudging approval of the press and was passed by a series of meetings of shareholders and creditors on 3 June.[31]

Even before formal sanction, the voting trustees had started work. Rebbeck, who had scarcely been consulted before the scheme's publication, was left in no doubt as to what was intended. McLintock and Morison immediately enforced a balance-sheet policy 'to make allowances for every known or expected contingency', and the introduction of a system for comparing final costs with estimates. The estimates were to be broken down under separate headings for hull and machinery and submitted to the chairman and voting trustees as soon after the completion of a vessel as possible.[32] On 13 May the first comparative statement was submitted for ship no. 984, the *Ernebank*, built at Queen's Island for the Bank line. This suggested that a

The oil tanker *British Integrity*, built at Govan, on trials in the Firth of Clyde in September 1937.

loss of £26,472 could be largely attributed to excessive overheads, particularly in the engine works. At least twelve of the nineteen vessels delivered in 1937 lost money, including the 5,495-gross-ton Donaldson cargo liner *Salacia* (with a loss of £57,711) and two intermediate vessels for Union-Castle, *Rochester Castle* (£20,508) and *Roxburgh Castle* (£8,736). By the end of August 1937 the Company had produced a deficit of over £85,000.

When this became known in October the Harland & Wolff voting trustees – with the support of the Midland Bank and the Government of Northern Ireland – took action. Parkes told his colleagues at the Midland that he suspected the 'cause of the trouble' was the two engine works, where 'Rebbeck was for ever striving after the perfect engine, no doubt entailing what might be called research expenditure'. Parkes reckoned that there was 'no director who can really stand up to Rebbeck'. His fellow trustees concurred, turning down an application from Rebbeck for more executive directors and proposing the appointment of 'a person who can examine whether contracts are being obtained upon a reasonably profitable basis or whether (as is suspected) experiments in engineering practice are being carried to such lengths that they are running away with the profits, which should accrue from the work undertaken'.[33] The voting trustees could do nothing to influence the final outcome for 1937, which showed a tiny profit of £24,556. The outlook was not encouraging.

Only eleven ships had been ordered during the year, including the 25,000-gross-ton liner *Andes* for Royal Mail, the aircraft carrier HMS *Formidable* of 28,000 gross tons, and five 8,000-gross-ton oil tankers. In addition Union-Castle placed a contract for the re-engining of the *Arundel Castle*, *Windsor Castle*, *Carnarvon Castle* and *Warwick Castle* with the new generation of two-stroke, airless-injection diesels.

Worn out by the pressure of events in the long years since Pirrie's death, John Philp's health finally broke down during 1937 in the face of the fresh onslaught. He retired formally the following year, being succeeded as secretary by A.T. Marshall, who remained in Belfast. The London office was entrusted to the care of the assistant secretary, J.S. Baillie. Rebbeck hoped to use this opportunity to appoint a number of executive directors and to establish two executive boards – one in Belfast and one in Glasgow. These suggestions were firmly squashed by McLintock.

The voting trustees' ambitions to cut costs were frustrated in January and February 1938 by the Stormont elections and the record unemployment figures for Northern Ireland which were fast approaching 100,000: the average level of unemployment for 1938 was 26.1 per cent. After the election and armed with the provisional results for 1937, Lord Kennet was commissioned by the Treasury to carry out a penetrating investigation. In May he confirmed the impression already gained by the voting trustees that the Queen's Island engine works were the biggest drain on the Company's resources. He reported that the new-generation airless-injection engines had required extensive modifications during their guaranteed period in service and that in one case they had failed to match the specifications. He was so shocked by the unfavourable comparison of the performances in 1937 of Swan Hunter, Cammell-Laird and Harland & Wolff that he advocated direct control of the Harland & Wolff board by the trustees. Parkes and McLintock immediately carried out their own inquiry. They were horrified 'at the weight and extent of establishment charges that had to be carried' and were disturbed to learn that the Admiralty was unhappy with the late delivery of HMS *Penelope*.[34] The high establishment charges stemmed from the physical size of the business and the failure of the management, despite all the warnings, to come to grips with the problem.

Although the voting trustees had correctly identified the Engine Works as being the biggest drain on the Company's resources, they were unjust in apportioning all the censure to Rebbeck. Until the development of the new generation of two-stroke, airless-injection engines, following the building of the *Ulster Monarch* in 1929, all the engines built in Belfast were true diesel engines where the fuel was blasted into the cylinder by air pressure at one thousand pounds per square inch. This made for a most complicated and expensive engine. Shipowners' demands for high power could be met only by making the largest engines double acting. The last massive engine of this type had been installed on the *Georgic*. All these engines had to be built with great precision and to high tolerances, and Rebbeck and Pounder knew that there was little hope of cutting overheads in the Engine Works until the new two-stroke, airless-injection models had been put into production. They realised, however, that they had little chance of convincing the voting trustees of this and that time was not on their side. Rebbeck cannot be blamed entirely for faults that these new designs developed in service. As in so much else, he was the victim of the system created by Pirrie. There had never been a research department at Queen's Island nor a test engine to investigate performance. The design office had never been allowed to experiment on engines on the testbed and the financial constraints since 1930 had prevented Rebbeck from changing this policy. The chief diesel designer, the Dane Vilhelm

316

Mickelson, is reported to have said that he felt like an astronomer conducting an experiment: he could observe, but not interfere with, the course of events.[35]

On 8 June 1938 the trustees, along with Clarence Sadd of the Midland Bank, interrogated Rebbeck for three and a half hours. They were disappointed to receive 'no satisfactory explanation' of the losses and were alarmed that there was 'very little new business coming along'. Kennet formed the impression that Rebbeck was ineffective – 'He has great abilities; but they need to be steadied and kept with his feet on the ground.' The trustees concluded that the senior management gave 'too much attention to technical aspects and insufficient attention to financial aspects'. It was proposed that the board should be strengthened by the appointment of Sir James Lithgow or of James Robb, chairman of the east-of-Scotland shipbuilders, Robb Caledon & Company. These nominations were impractical, however. Lithgow had more than enough to occupy him in the management of his own group and the overseeing of the reconstruction of William Beardmore & Company and the Fairfield Shipbuilding & Engineering Company. He detested Rebbeck, and also Harland & Wolff which he believed had escaped lightly in his efforts to rationalise the shipbuilding and marine engineering industries over the previous eight years.[36] Henry Pollock of the Bank of Ireland made it clear that for these reasons his appointment would be unacceptable and the Midland Bank dropped a proposal to offer Lithgow an option over its shares if he agreed to join the board. In the event it proved impossible to find anyone with sufficient experience and standing in the industry who was willing to join the board, and the trustees had to fall back on the policy preferred by McLintock and Morison of themselves supervising reforms in the internal financial discipline. In desperation Rebbeck tried to resurrect the Vickers merger proposal, but McLintock would not hear of it until the Company was in better condition. Rebbeck and Craig, appalled at the prospect of yet another round of investigation into establishment charges, co-operated willingly with McLintock and Morison 'to lay this ghost once for all'.

Unknown to the trustees and in great secrecy, Rebbeck had been striving to bring more rearmament work to Belfast. With encouragement from the Admiralty, he had approached the Harbour Commissioners and the Government of Northern Ireland in October 1937 with a proposal for the erection of a 250–300-ton crane and the deepening of the Victoria channel so that the yard would be able to build and, perhaps more importantly, refit battleships. Although Sir Ernest Henderson of the Northern Ireland Ministry of Finance was 'anxious to help in any way', he was daunted by the estimated cost of almost £500,000. At the Harland & Wolff board meeting on 8 June 1938 the directors agreed to find £75,000 towards the cost of the crane. Agreement was reached in February 1939 when the Company undertook to contribute £20,000 to the cost of the harbour improvement scheme. The bulk of the finance was provided by the Government of Northern Ireland, the Harbour Commissioners and the Admiralty. The work – which involved amalgamating no. 1 and no. 2 wharves in the Musgrave channel into a new fitting-out quay – began at once. It was hoped that the crane, which the contractors Sir William Arrol & Company had started building in 1938, would be installed by the time HMS *Formidable* was launched in the autumn. In the meantime Rebbeck had been negotiating with the War Office and the Air Ministry in London. During June 1938 he had finalised an arrangement for the War Office to erect, at a cost of £250,000, an armaments works in nos 1, 2 and 3 shops in the Abercorn Works, in which it had been intended to build a steel foundry. This plant was to be operated by the Company, which was instructed to co-ordinate all subcontracted munitions work in Northern Ireland. Later in the summer Harland & Wolff sublet about five acres of the Musgrave Shipyard to the Air Ministry for the construction of a factory to manufacture aircraft components, to be managed by Short & Harland Limited. This plant was to act as a 'shadow factory' should works elsewhere in Britain be bombed. The embellishment of the toolroom at Finnieston bore fruit with a mass of orders for rearmament work. Scotstoun was exclusively occupied in manufacturing naval gun mountings.

Despite these encouraging developments during the second half of 1938, there were few signs that the close examination Rebbeck had received from the Midland Bank, and more recently the voting trustees, was having an effect. The majority of contracts continued to yield losses. The *Delane* and *Devis* for Lamport & Holt together lost £26,963 on a price of £332,762 and the tankers *Donax* and *Dromus* for Anglo-Saxon Petroleum lost £11,350 on £462,750. There were some successes: the *Capetown Castle* yielded a profit of £44,861 on a contract price of £1,280,592 and the *Durban Castle* earned £75,243 on a price of £940,958. Total output of vessels and machinery for the year was again the largest for any shipyard in the United Kingdom. The failure to achieve a return on new building was more than offset by a dramatic improvement in the profitability of the repair works and by the gun-mounting contracts at Scotstoun. Profits for the year totalled £654,815 and for the first time since the collapse of the Royal Mail Group it was possible to make provision for depreciation of the fixed capital by the allocation of £500,000.

The annual report emphasised that, despite this healthier result, the Company's

The Musgrave yard, Belfast, almost fully occupied in 1936, with *Durban Castle* (left) and *Waimarama* (right) under construction.

The Union-Castle liner *Capetown Castle* leaving Queen's Island in March 1938. In 1942 she was requisitioned by the Admiralty for conversion into an aircraft carrier.

plant had not been operating at full capacity. During the first half of the year just eleven vessels had been ordered. With the exception of the order of a further two 12,382-gross-ton refrigerated cargo ships for Blue Star, they were all under 8,000 gross tons. The only contract to be placed between July 1938 and the end of February 1939 was for a tiny vessel for the Government of Fiji, to be built at Pointhouse and shipped in sections. On 14 February 1939 the assistant Company secretary, J.S. Baillie, confessed to the Midland Bank that thirteen of the eighteen slips at Belfast and seven of those at Govan were vacant. His only good news was that small orders for anti-aircraft mountings and 'Cruiser' tanks had been placed with the new armaments factory at Queen's Island as an experiment. He reported that the only contract in view was for the submarine base ship HMS *Adamant* (ship no. 1023). By June 1939 contracts for a further fourteen ships were placed, including four vessels of 5,400 gross tons for Royal Mail; HMS *Unicorn*, an aircraft depot ship; two ships of 7,200 gross tons for Andrew Weir; and the *Lavington Court*, of 5,372 gross tons, for the Court line. Delighted, Rebbeck decided to reopen the old Workman Clark Victoria Shipyard. The four berths were numbered 16 to 19, and £50,000 was set aside to reinstate the yard and build a shop for prefabricating hull sections, on similar lines to the one in the Musgrave Shipyard. To save expense the tower cranes in the other old Workman Clark yard on the Co. Antrim side of the Lagan were dismantled and moved across. The Midland Bank refused to help finance this new business as, understandably, they 'were not desirous of getting into the old position'.[37]

319

By midsummer 1939, as Europe drifted inexorably towards war, Harland & Wolff's
yards at Belfast suddenly took on a vital importance. The prospect of a steady flow
of Admiralty work and merchant contracts, supported by Government funds, made
it much more difficult for the voting trustees to do more to improve the management.
Although the sale of unwanted assets and investments had yielded over £1,130,000
for the creditors in 1938, there were still outstanding liabilities of £7,727,806. During
August the voting trustees hurriedly proposed a further reconstruction and the sale
of the assets to a new holding company, almost certainly because they were reluctant
to commit themselves to continued surveillance in the troubled times ahead.[38] This
scheme was to be overwhelmed by the declaration of war on 3 September. Since the
second week in June a stream of war contracts had poured into Harland & Wolff.
As a consequence of the urgent air-raid precautions being undertaken by firms and
individuals to comply with the Civil Defence Act, the London works alone was fitting
148 shutters to Port of London Authority warehouses, and manufacturing 224 Air
Ministry watchtowers, 3,052 ARP underground garden shelters, and 150 ARP garden
huts. Scotstoun, flooded with contracts for naval mountings, was working round
the clock to perfect its own design of anti-aircraft guns and Finnieston was
overwhelmed with orders for anti-aircraft gun cradles, carriage slides and axles.

As war loomed, Frederick Rebbeck had been at the helm of the Company for nine

HMS *Belfast*, a
'Southampton'-class
cruiser symbolically
located ship no. 1000, on
ials in August 1939. This
ship is now preserved in
the Pool of London.

years. Despite constant buffeting, he had brought Harland & Wolff almost intact
through the foulest conditions that the shipbuilding industry had ever experienced.
The physical strain he had endured to secure this triumph was enormous, constantly
travelling backwards and forwards to London by boat and train. His commanding
presence and his powers of oratory had won him the confidence of the shareholders
and creditors and even the grudging respect of McLintock and Morison. His
autocratic behaviour was reminiscent of his former master and patron, Lord Pirrie.
His shortcomings as chairman can be attributed to Pirrie's failure to share with any
of his managers the skills and vital financial information which he used to control
the Company. Rebbeck's concentration on excellence in engine design is hardly
surprising since he had never been trained in other aspects of shipyard management,
and in his formative years at Queen's Island, before the First World War, overheads
had scarcely been relevant. When the shipping press marvelled at the quality of the
liners constructed by Harland & Wolff in the 1930s and at the quality of their engines,
Rebbeck found it difficult to grasp the seriousness of the creditors' campaign to
impose financial discipline. Despite their efforts, the Midland Bank and the voting
trustees had achieved very little more than Kylsant in their attempts to reform the
almost impregnable system created by Lord Pirrie to control the business, but in the
immediate future it was for others, in the Admiralty and the Treasury, to shoulder
the burden. The Government, unlike its predecessor in 1914, was prepared. Montagu
Norman, as Governor of the Bank of England, and the economist John Maynard
Keynes, at the Treasury, were determined that profit margins throughout industry

were to be kept down to about 3 per cent and, however grave the crisis, war production would be efficient even if management had to be removed. The coming months would show whether Frederick Rebbeck was equal to the greatest challenge of his career. He could take comfort from the loyal support of the workforce throughout the tempest: the demarcation agreement list negotiated in 1914 had held secure and had been reaffirmed as recently as June 1935.

11
CORVETTES AND CARRIERS
1939–45

The integration – for it was nothing short of that – of Harland & Wolff with the rest of the United Kingdom war machine was well under way by the summer of 1939. The initiatives taken by Rebbeck to secure all kinds of military and naval work for Queen's Island have already been outlined. Their success was, as suggested, due in part to Belfast's favourable location far to the north west of the likely battle zones. It also owed much to the large pool of unemployed men in Belfast, many of whom had the skills required for munitions work.[1] The large contracts for the submarine base ship HMS *Adamant* and the aircraft depot vessel HMS *Unicorn* were the spectacular front, but behind the scenes aircraft manufacture was building up, and the munitions factory in the Abercorn Works was beginning to come on stream. The first product, searchlights known as 'War Office Projectors', was well established by June 1939, and work on trial orders, for gun conversions, cruiser tanks and 3.7-inch anti-aircraft guns, placed in November 1938, was under way. The first two tanks were delivered in June. An important contract completed in the summer of 1939 was the 'Southampton'-class heavy cruiser HMS *Belfast*, at 10,173 gross tons the largest cruiser in the Royal Navy. With the yard number 1000, the vessel was of great symbolic importance to Queen's Island.

The last ship to be launched before the declaration of war was the 'Illustrious'-class aircraft carrier HMS *Formidable*, ordered in 1937. On being asked by the assistant secretary, J.S. Baillie, to name a 'lady sponsor' for the launch ceremony, the Controller of the Navy, Admiral Bruce Fraser, paused, gazed at the ceiling and, knowing the deep antipathy between Rebbeck and Sir James Lithgow, said with impish fun: 'I've got it, Baillie – Lady Lithgow!'[2] The *Formidable*, in fact, went down the ways without warning a few minutes before the launch was due to take place on 17 August 1939. The fore poppets (the cradle supporting the bow of the ship) collapsed: the vessel itself was undamaged but a woman spectator was killed by a flying bolt.

Several small warships were ordered from Govan and Pointhouse in July. For A. & J. Inglis at Pointhouse these were the first Admiralty contracts since 1918 – for two of a series of twenty trawlers of the 'Tree' class; while Govan received an order for two 'Bangor'-class minesweepers. In August two 'Flower'-class corvettes were ordered from Pointhouse, part of an initial series of twenty-six of this new class of escort vessel ordered from various builders. The design of the class was developed rapidly during the first half of 1939, in anticipation of war breaking out in 1940, and was based on that of a modern whale-catcher built by Smith's Dock Company of Middlesbrough. Steam-reciprocating machinery and Scotch-type boilers were chosen for simplicity and speed of construction, and the vessels were fitted with sophisticated anti-submarine and basic anti-aircraft armament.[3]

Put together, these moves indicated that Rebbeck was succeeding in his efforts to revitalise the whole Harland & Wolff empire, and was doing so in a way that bypassed the voting trustees. The only one of his major schemes which failed to succeed was

the equipping of the Belfast yard with heavy cranes to handle battleship-building. Four prewar orders for battleships from established builders were indeed cancelled in 1940, and only one battleship – HMS *Vanguard* – was actually ordered during the war. There was thus no incentive for Harland & Wolff to go ahead with an expensive scheme.

Following the declaration of war on 3 September all ship ordering came under state control, as planned by the Admiralty in consultation with the Shipbuilding Conference. Naturally, the Admiralty itself ordered Royal Navy craft, but it also handled orders from the Ministry of Supply for merchant ships. The few vessels allocated to civilian shipping lines had to be licensed by the Admiralty, and licences were generally granted only for vessels replacing those sunk by enemy action. From the beginning of the war, orders for merchant-style vessels were for standard types.[4] As the war at sea was to be fought with oil-fired or diesel-engined ships, tankers featured largely in orders placed not only with Govan, which had specialised in tanker building in the interwar years, but also with Belfast. The first wartime orders for Govan were for two 8,000-gross-ton tankers, one each for the Admiralty and for the Ministry of Supply (*Dingledale* and *Empire Gem*) and for three smaller fleet oil carriers, the HMS *Black Ranger*, HMS *Blue Ranger* and HMS *Brown Ranger*. Belfast

The aircraft carrier HMS *Formidable*, prematurely launching herself from the east yard on 17 August 193 with the wreckage of the supporting cradle (fore poppets) for the on the left.

324

received orders for four 466-foot tankers, two each for the Admiralty and the Ministry of Supply, and for two refrigerated cargo vessels. One of the tankers, the *Derwentdale*, was eventually completed as a landing-ship carrier.

The most remarkable order for Belfast was, however, originated personally by Winston Churchill, First Lord of the Admiralty as he had been in the First World War. Shortly after war broke out he telephoned Rebbeck, from the offices of the Controller of the Navy at the Admiralty, asking him to make immediate preparations to build a large number of corvettes at Belfast. Rebbeck replied that the Admiralty had already made arrangements with the shipbuilders, through the Shipbuilding Conference, for a programme of wartime construction. Churchill's response was that the corvettes must take priority. The order, confirmed on 26 September, was for twenty vessels of the 'Flower' class. At 724 gross tons each, they were much smaller than the normal Belfast-built ship, and their steam-reciprocating engines were also unusual for Queen's Island by that time. The first ship of the order, HMS *Arabis*, was completed

on 5 April 1940, less than seven months after the placing of the contract and five months after the laying of the keel. The first eight vessels were laid down in batches of four, and the remainder in pairs. The last of the twenty was completed on 9 January 1941, and on average one corvette was handed over each fortnight, a striking tribute to the capability of Harland & Wolff.[5]

The rest of 1939 saw further orders for standard 466-foot tankers placed with Govan and Belfast, and a single 'Dido'-class light cruiser, HMS *Black Prince*, was ordered from Queen's Island. This vessel was not completed until the end of 1943, as resources were diverted to give priority to the corvettes. To cope with the expanding order book the modernisation of the Victoria Shipyard was undertaken in 1939/40, to allow prefabrication of subassemblies. Other capital works included a large shop for the steel construction department, intended to supply structural steelwork for the Company and for outside customers. The workforce grew substantially: by the end of 1939 there were nearly 18,000 employed at Belfast and about 5,500 in the four Glasgow works (Govan, the Clyde Foundry, Scotstoun and Finnieston). The corresponding numbers at the end of 1938 had been 14,000 and 3,000.

Ship-repair also boomed. From September 1939 onwards the task of arming

The 'Dido'-class cruiser HMS *Black Prince* was launched in August 19 the only vessel of her t built by Harland & Wo during the war.
Transferred to the Roy New Zealand Navy in 1948, she lasted until 1

merchant vessels with anti-aircraft guns provided a steady stream of business, while routine wear and tear and minor collision damage increased as vessels were used more intensively and as the convoy system brought ships into closer proximity. Conversions also formed an important part of the work of the repair yards. In August 1939, for example, ten trawlers arrived at Belfast for conversion to inspection vessels, followed in September by a further fifteen.

The most unusual conversion contracts came to Belfast on the initiative of Churchill. Mindful of the success of the Special Service Squadron in the First World War, he instructed the head of the Admiralty's Trade Division to acquire three merchant ships for conversion to dummy warships. The vessels chosen were three old Shaw Savill refrigerated cargo steamers, the *Pakeha*, *Waimana* and *Mamari*, which had been laid up on the Clyde. Two of them were transformed into fake battleships of the 'Royal Sovereign' class: *Pakeha* into HMS *Revenge* and *Waimana* into HMS *Royal Sovereign*. The third ship became the dummy aircraft carrier HMS *Hermes*. Bogus guns were made out of wood, the vessels were ballasted with stones to float low in the water, and steel drums were packed into the remaining space to give flotation in the event of attack. The two 'battleships' left Belfast on 22 November and the 'aircraft carrier' departed in December. They were referred to as 'fleet tenders', and were moved from port to port, acting as decoys for the *Luftwaffe* and as a means

327

diesel coastal tankers, the *Empire Shoal* and *Empire Deep*; and two 460-foot tankers. Originally intended for the British Tanker Company, one of the tankers was transferred to the Ministry of Shipping and delivered as the *Empire Vigilance*. Pointhouse took on the *Empire Gat* and the *Empire Spinney*, of the same design as the Govan coastal tankers; two 'Shakespearian'-class Admiralty trawlers, HMS *Romeo* and HMS *Rosalind*; and at the end of the year HMS *Stronsay* and HMS *Switha*, 'Isles'-class large trawlers, intended for fishery protection duty.[10] Less conspicuously, the London works at North Woolwich completed twelve narrow boats, six of them tankers for service on English canals; three pontoons; and a floating dock for the Admiralty.

The repair works were making a very substantial contribution to the war effort. Southampton dealt with 729 ships during 1940, of which 119 had to be dry-docked. Liverpool took 567 ships and London 785. Work included the conversion of merchant vessels for Admiralty purposes and the mounting of anti-aircraft guns on merchant ships. Much of Liverpool's work involved refitting liners as troopships, thus creating work for Heaton, Tabb & Company (formerly Aldam Heaton), the wholly-owned subsidiary normally occupied in fitting out liners. The Southampton works also turned its attention to canvas products, making 950 pairs of overshoes, 200 gymnasium mattress covers and 1,750 gun turret covers for 'Blenheim' bombers.

Throughout the year the engine works at Belfast were kept busy with munitions

HMS *Algerine*, the nar ship of her class of minesweepers, compl at Belfast in March 194 She had a short life, be sunk by an Italian submarine in November 1942.

orders, as well as with diesel, steam-reciprocating and steam-turbine machinery. Tanks and gun barrels, liners, mountings and breeches were the staples. The autofrettage process, whereby previously machined liners were expanded into barrels by internal hydraulic pressure, allowed large numbers of guns to be produced.[11] The first batch of a new type of tank, designated Mark IV Infantry, was ordered during the year. Propelling machinery with a total horsepower of 125,750 was turned out from Belfast and a further 20,400 horsepower was delivered from Finnieston. The Scotstoun works continued to specialise in the manufacture of gun mountings.

Short & Harland and the aircraft department at Harland & Wolff increased their levels of activity during 1940. In October the first Belfast-designed plane, and Britain's first heavy bomber, the Short 'Stirling', made a successful first flight and by the end of the year Short & Harland had delivered six of these important aircraft. With the completion of the order for 'Hereford' bombers in sight, it was possible to build up production of the 'Stirling', with major subassemblies being built by Harland & Wolff in the Queen's Island aircraft department. The new 'Sunderland' flying boats, which were intended for anti-submarine patrol work, began to take shape. These were developed from the prewar 'Empire' flying boats built by Short Brothers at Rochester for Imperial Airways. Two of these civilian craft were brought to Belfast in July 1940 for conversion to war planes and, as the Short & Harland slipway was at that stage unfinished, they were lifted out of the Musgrave channel by a Harland & Wolff floating crane.[12] The London works at North Woolwich also contributed to the expansion of aircraft production by fabricating the structural steelwork for a large extension to Short Brothers' Rochester works.

Another effect of the war was the development of Londonderry as a strategic naval base in 1940, a measure necessitated by the Republic of Ireland's refusal to allow the United Kingdom to use Cobh (Queenstown), Berehaven and Lough Swilly, ports which had all played a very valuable role during the First World War. By basing convoy escorts at Londonderry in Lough Foyle it was possible to add another hundred miles to the protected part of the Atlantic crossing. The wear and tear on destroyers during the autumn of 1940 completely swamped the capacity of local engineering firms and, as a result, the Admiralty asked Harland & Wolff to reopen Swan Hunter's former Londonderry shipyard as a repair works.[13] The Company was heavily committed elsewhere but, at a meeting on 8 November, agreed with some reluctance to take on the scheme. Physically the project involved enlarging the existing dry dock and building new machine and fitting shops. Over the next eighteen months Londonderry became the most important harbour for escorts in the Western Approaches command, with more than eighty vessels allocated to it.

The increased volume of production throughout the Company's shipyards and associated works was reflected in the rising number of employees. During 1940 Harland & Wolff's labour force in Belfast increased by 36 per cent to 24,361 and in the Glasgow works it grew by 41 per cent to 5,169. The associated companies, principally the Pointhouse yard of A. & J. Inglis and D. & W. Henderson's repair yard, expanded employment by 74 per cent to 2,248. Part of the increase in the Queen's Island workforce was accounted for by the higher proportion of welding required by war contracts. At the beginning of 1940 only 400 welders were employed; a new welding school was then set up and an agreement was reached with the unions for the training of 'dilutees' – men who were not time-served steelworkers. The recruits to this scheme were mainly men from the building trades, the employment of outside workers being necessitated partly by the reluctance of traditional craftsmen

The standard merchant ship *Empire Falkland*, completed at Belfast in February 1945.

to retrain.[14] During 1940 and 1941 more than 750 new welders were trained. The repair works at Southampton, Liverpool and London, which had not been as badly affected as the other plants by the depression of the prewar years, showed a more modest rise in numbers employed, from 8,233 to 9,751. Short & Harland, on the other hand, was employing fewer people (8,217) at the end of the year than at the beginning (8,497), probably as a consequence of more mechanised production lines.

It was during 1940 that the German blitzkrieg began to affect Harland & Wolff. Heavy bombing of the City of London during the Battle of Britain threatened the Company's London office, but the staff preferred the risks of a central location near the Admiralty to the inconvenience of dispersal. The main London works at North Woolwich and the Southampton works were hit, but not seriously damaged. To help combat the German aerial offensive, the *Belfast Telegraph*, emulating organisations in other parts of the UK, organised a Northern Ireland Spitfire Fund. The Queen's Island workers and the Company made the largest contribution to that fund, and in recognition one of the planes was named *Harlandic*.

War demand had an immediate effect on the profitability of all Harland & Wolff's operations. Although the prewar merchant-ship contracts completed in 1939/40 were all executed at a loss, with the exception of the *Andes* for Royal Mail, the balance was more than restored by the guaranteed 5 per cent on costs paid for Admiralty contracts, and 8 per cent for War Department work. As the increased throughput also reduced the burden of overheads, gross profits before tax and depreciation

The aircraft carrier
HMS *Campania*, ordered
as a merchant ship by
Shaw Savill & Albion,
but delivered in
March 1944 as an
escort aircraft carrier.

reached £804,210 in 1939 and £1,129,234 in 1940. The overall increase, however, concealed marked differences in profitability. Pointhouse and Meadowside performed well and there were sharp rises in receipts from ship-repair and conversion at Liverpool, Southampton and London. In contrast, the working profits for both the Queen's Island shipyard and for the main engine works fell. These poor results reflected the very high overheads at Belfast. The balance of profit came from munitions work, including aircraft subcontracts, though no dividends came from the Company's investment in Short & Harland. Higher profits allowed proper provision to be made for depreciation for the second year running and permitted the creation of reserves for losses on contracts, for income tax, excess profits tax (levied on profits over an agreed standard) and for contingencies. The financial reconstruction of the 1930s was at last beginning to bear fruit.

The year 1941 saw a shift in the pattern of ordering away from Admiralty contracts. These were overtaken by orders from established civilian shipping lines, licensed by the Admiralty to replace tonnage sunk by the German U-boat offensive. Some of these vessels were built to standard designs, others were to customers' specification. Ship no. 1091, HMS *Campania*, was started in January 1941 to an order from Shaw Savill & Albion, but eventually, like the Cunarder of the same name in the First World War, converted to an aircraft carrier, and delivered in 1944. Royal Mail ordered three vessels, the Pacific Steam Navigation Company and Union-Castle two each. Standard tankers were ordered in pairs by Eagle Oil, the British Tanker

Company and the Anglo-Saxon Petroleum Company. The Ministry of War Transport ordered six standard tankers and one 'X' and two 'Y'-type standard merchant vessels.[15] Four of the twenty-two ships ordered were built at Govan, and the remainder in Belfast. To help meet the need for fighter coverage for convoys one of the Govan-built tankers, *Empire Mackay*, entered service in 1943 as a merchant aircraft carrier, with a flight deck over the oil tanks. As before, the Pointhouse yard of A. & J. Inglis had a share of smaller vessels. Three 'Empire Cadet'- class diesel coastal tankers were ordered, as well as three 'River'-class twin-screw escort vessels. The only warship orders for Belfast were three tank carriers, HMS *Thruster*, HMS *Bruiser* and HMS *Boxer*, and the cruiser HMS *Minotaur*. The *Minotaur* was the name ship of her class, but was not completed until the end of the war, when she became the HMCS *Ontario* of the Canadian Navy. The army tank carriers were the first purpose-built bow-loading ferries and came to be known as landing ship tanks (LSTs). On the whole the pattern of the order book better suited

HMS *Thruster*, one of of tank-landing craft equipped with bow d and folding ramps. Bu Belfast and completed March 1943, she is she on test at the yard.

334

the capabilities of the various yards than did the large-batch ordering of 1939/40.

To cope with pressure on existing capacity in Belfast large extensions to the Victoria Works (the old Workman Clark engine works) and to the boiler shop were authorised. With the possibility of bombing in mind, a new office block was approved, with fireproof storage for records. Before this could be completed, the theory that the Clyde and Belfast yards were immune from aerial bombardment was suddenly and devastatingly destroyed. It had been believed that these areas were too far from Germany and France for effective bombing, and therefore they were not covered by Air Raid Protection legislation passed in 1938. The invasion of Norway in 1941 posed a new threat to the northern cities – though when attack did come it was from France.[16]

First to suffer was Glasgow, in March 1941, when the Harland & Wolff plants at Govan, Finnieston and Scotstoun suffered some damage. There was a narrow escape for the Govan and Pointhouse yards when a bomb went right through the fully ammunitioned cruiser HMS *Sussex*, awaiting repair in the Yorkhill basin, next to Pointhouse and opposite Govan. Had the bomb exploded and detonated the ammunition in HMS *Sussex* and her sistership HMS *Suffolk* lying alongside, the whole area would have been devastated.

It was Belfast's turn in April and May. Harland & Wolff had recognised the threat of blitzkrieg in 1940 and the board had authorised substantial expenditure on air-raid precautions at all its works. The Northern Ireland Government, however, had not taken the same precautions, and the city of Belfast remained underequipped with both shelters and anti-aircraft guns. It had been reckoned that for its size it was the worst-defended city in the United Kingdom. The Stormont Ministry of Public Security began to plan for the possibility of attack early in 1941 following the invasion of Norway, but the city was basically ill prepared, both physically and psychologically, for the onslaught.[17]

The first raid on Belfast was on the night of 7/8 April, when six bombers attacked. A single parachute oil bomb hit Harland & Wolff's aeroplane-fuselage factory, destroying the 4½-acre shed, the main assembly jigs, machine tools and parts for about fifty fuselages for 'Stirling' bombers. This was a crippling blow, not just to the Company but to Short & Harland which relied entirely on the factory for its fuselages. Just over a week later, on the night of 15 April, north Belfast was horrifyingly bombed. On this occasion almost 200 bombers attacked. Over 700 people were killed, 1,600 houses destroyed, 28,000 dwellings damaged and many public and commercial buildings severely hit. It transpired, after the war, that the German aircrews had mistaken the reservoirs of the Belfast Waterworks, in the Antrim Road area of north Belfast, for the commercial docks and thus had bombed a mainly residential part of the city instead of the Queen's Island works. Apart from material damage, the morale of the workers was seriously affected, absenteeism grew and production fell.[18]

It was the turn of the industrial areas on 4 May 1941. Queen's Island was the prime target and nearly two thirds of Harland & Wolff's premises were devastated. The death toll throughout the city was 150. At the yard, several vessels under construction were damaged, especially three corvettes. Few parts of the plant escaped damage, but the most serious losses were the electrical department, the main stores office, and vital records. Since early in the war, night working had been standard and staff had been designated as firewatchers and first-aiders. Francis Lowry, who was in charge of first-aid in the area round the main office, recalls that night just before the raid. William Strachan, director in charge of air-raid precautions, was presenting first-

including the aircraft department, was slight, almost flimsy, thrown up during the rapid expansion of the yard before and during the First World War. Rebbeck (who was created Sir Frederick Rebbeck for his services to the war effort in the summer of 1941) insisted on solidly built, steel-framed replacements, intended not only to suit a return to full-scale production but also to be easily adaptable to peacetime needs. Rebuilding in this fashion placed a great strain on the Company's finances. The overdraft with the Midland Bank soared to its limit of £2,500,000, incurring £100,000-a-year interest. Meantime the Government proved reluctant to pay compensation, despite the agreement of the Admiralty, Ministry of Aircraft Production and Ministry of Supply 'that maximum output must be maintained, and that the works be rehabilitated for that purpose'. By July 1941 the Company's claim to the War Damage Commission had been formulated, although the amount payable took many months to settle, further hindering a return to full production.

In September 1941 the reformation of Harland & Wolff's capital was again considered by the voting trustees. Substantial wartime profits, the elimination of older buildings and machinery and their replacement by solid modern structures and equipment made the Company a more attractive investment. Cazenove Akroyd & Greenwood, the London stockbrokers, were approached to market all the 'A' shares held by the voting trustees. A syndicate was formed by Cazenoves to buy all the shares, at discounts ranging from 10.5 to 20 per cent, and the Stock Exchange agreed to the marketing of these shares on 24 October. The outbreak of war with Japan in 1941, followed by the invasion of Burma and Malaya, caused a sharp decline on the stock market and prevented the sale of the Harland & Wolff shares.[21]

Not surprisingly the air raids took their toll on profitability for 1941. Nevertheless, the shipbuilding side at Belfast produced an increased profit, probably due to the higher proportion of Admiralty vessels delivered. The Queen's Engine Works (now known simply as the Engine Works) and Victoria Engine Works were badly affected, with profits down by a third. The Clyde Foundry, supplier of castings to the two engine works, had its operating profit nearly halved as fewer diesel engines were being built. However, better results elsewhere plus lower overheads ensured that net profit was not reduced disastrously, though the fall – from just under £700,000 to £517,716 – was serious in war conditions.

The Company's financial problems, however, should not overshadow recognition of the contribution it was making to the war effort. Although progress was not always as rapid as owners might have wanted, and costs had a tendency to be high, there was no other shipbuilding company that could undertake such a wide range of contracts, equipping them almost exclusively from within its own workshops. It was against this background that a great many new orders were directed to the yard in 1942, in a pattern not dissimilar to that of 1941. Civilian customers were allowed to place orders for eleven vessels. Royal Mail took three, one of them from Govan, and Lamport & Holt and Union-Castle were allocated a pair of ships apiece. Shaw Savill & Albion contracted for a replacement for the *Waiwera*. Eagle Oil placed an order for a standard tanker with Govan; Anglo-Saxon Petroleum took two tankers from Belfast and the Admiralty had one. Another large contract for small warships came to Queen's Island when a further eighteen 'Algerine'-class minesweepers were ordered (though the last seven were eventually cancelled). Those completed were all laid down in 1943, nine of them in threes. The first two were built with remarkable speed, probably as a result of the extensive replacement of riveting by welding. The first minesweeper was completed in only two and a half months from the keel-laying.

338

Later, delivery times stretched as labour was diverted to more urgent work.

The most extraordinary series of contracts – for a total of five aircraft carriers – represented a marked change in the direction of the war and in Admiralty policy towards Harland & Wolff. The first carrier, HMS *Glory* of the light 'Colossus' class, was ordered in March 1942; the second, the much larger HMS *Eagle* of the 'Ark Royal' class, in June; HMS *Warrior* of the 'Colossus' class in August; and, most remarkably, two ships of the 'Majestic' class, HMS *Magnificent* and HMS *Powerful*, together in October. These were all intended for the war in the Pacific, which was heavily dependent on carrier-borne aircraft. Only the *Glory* was completed before the end of the war against Japan. To expedite work on these contracts tank production was phased out during the autumn of 1943.

Other Admiralty contracts came to Pointhouse, Govan and Belfast. Four modified 'Flower'-class corvettes and two 'Empire Cadet' diesel coastal tankers were ordered from Pointhouse. Two fleet oil carriers went to Govan and a single Ministry of War Transport standard motor ship, *Empire Outpost*, was ordered from Belfast. The London works received orders for twelve tank-landing craft which were completed during 1942 and 1943.

Although 1942 was a good year for orders, it was a disastrous one financially. This can be attributed very largely to the after-effects of bomb damage, but it was suggested at the time that, as in the 1930s, costs on Queen's Island were not being kept under control. The working profit for the Belfast shipyard was a mere £117,317, only a third of the poor 1941 figure. The Engine Works fared little better. In contrast, most other departments, with the exception of the London works, performed well. Losses at Belfast were incurred on merchant-ship contracts and on the aircraft maintenance ship HMS*Unicorn*, ordered in 1938 before cost-plus contracts had been introduced. It was only the cost-plus ('time and lime') contracts for the Admiralty and the Ministry of Shipping that prevented the Belfast shipyard from sliding into loss.

It may well have been the financial problems at Belfast which prompted the strengthening of the board at the end of 1942. Charles Payne retired after forty-six years of service to the Company, and the opportunity was taken to appoint four new directors: Atholl Blair, engine works manager at Queen's Island; L.V. Dunlop, in charge of Govan; John Morrison, Queen's Island shipyard manager; and Frederick V. Spark, the chief accountant. The appointment of Spark – who was also a director of two Belfast shipping companies, G. Heyn & Sons Limited and the Ulster Steamship Company Limited – was particularly significant. For the first time in Harland & Wolff's history the chief accountant was to be allowed to share in directing the Company. Sir Frederick had now achieved what he had long wanted – a board composed largely of executive directors whom he could dominate. Sir William McLintock had resisted such appointments but in the circumstances he and his fellow voting trustees could not object.

Although the financial problems of the Company continued into 1943, Harland & Wolff's uniquely large capacity continued to be vital to the war effort. There were two further orders for aircraft carriers, HMS *Centaur* and HMS *Bulwark* of the 'Hermes' class, which were only partly completed at the end of the war. Most of the Admiralty orders, however, were for small warships including nine 'Castle'-class escorts ordered from Pointhouse and Belfast. These vessels were twin-screw developments from the 'Flower'-class corvettes, offering better accommodation, larger fuel tanks and better armament. Fifty-nine of them were ordered from British yards in 1943, but the success of the Allies in the Battle of the Atlantic led to cancellations, which included three of the Pointhouse vessels. Instead, the Inglis yard received orders for coastal oil tankers. A more interesting order was one for thirty 'Loch'-class frigates, placed with Belfast. These ships were developed from the 'River'-class escorts, five of which had been built by Inglis. They were designed for more efficient large-scale production, 80 per cent of the hull and superstructure being composed of prefabricated sections, for which a new prefabricating shop had to be built at Belfast. After the placing of the order, seven vessels were modified to 'Bay'-class anti-aircraft frigates, intended to accompany the British Pacific Fleet into Japanese waters, and nineteen were cancelled. The remaining four 'Loch'-class ships were towed to other yards for completion: two to Clydebank, one to Liverpool and one to Renfrew.[22]

The story of the 'Loch' class indicates the problems which faced both Admiralty and builders in matching demand to production in a rapidly changing war. Similar problems faced customers for merchant ships, as the submarine threat was effectively countered. The sequence of order numbers shows that vessels provisionally ordered were not started immediately, as licences were not issued by the Admiralty. The *Empire Wessex* for the Port line and the *Santander* and *Salaverry*, for the Pacific Steam Navigation Company, were obviously planned in 1942 but were not proceeded with until 1943. The *Riebeeck Castle* and *Rustenburg Castle*, for Union-Castle, and the tanker *Neothyris*, for the Anglo-Saxon Petroleum Company, were contemplated in 1943, but orders for ten tank-landing craft delayed starting times on the other ships. Like the 'Loch' class, the landing craft were not all completed by Harland & Wolff. Two of the eight vessels ordered from Belfast were towed to Vickers's yard at Barrow

e of the 'Bay'-class anti-
ircraft frigates designed
r batch production from
welded subassemblies,
HMS *Start Bay* was
delivered in
September 1945.

for completion and the two Govan craft were finished at Dalmuir.

A most unusual and interesting ship-repair contract started in 1943 was for the complete refitting of the White Star motor ship *Georgic*. She was requisitioned in March 1940 as a troopship and was bombed later the same year in Port Tewfik at the south end of the Suez Canal. Set on fire by the bombing, she was completely burned out and sank in shallow water. Salvage experts raised her and found that her main propelling machinery could be cleaned and brought back into service. With minimal patching, she made the voyage to Bombay in two thousand-mile stages. After some further work, but with her strength deck 'like a piece of corrugated iron', she returned to Belfast via the Cape of Good Hope, under her own power. Sir Frederick Rebbeck protested at being instructed by Sir James Lithgow, as Controller of Merchant Shipbuilding and Repair, to carry out such a major piece of reconstruction on top of all the other work in hand, but Sir James turned a deaf ear to his protest, saying that there was nowhere else for the ship to go.[23]

Financial results improved markedly in 1943 as Queen's Island recovered from the blitz, with a working profit up to pre-1941 level. The better overall performance allowed the depreciation allocation to be raised from £400,000 to £600,000. The reasons for the improvement at Belfast certainly included settlement of claims against the Admiralty for vessels completed. The good results concealed continuing financial problems for the Company. The level of debt to the Midland Bank, necessary to finance work in hand and the rehabilitation of Queen's Island, continued at a high level. By January 1943 the overdraft was £3,381,055, as against a limit of £3,500,000. There seem to have been two important reasons for concern on the part of the Midland Bank. One was the delay by the Admiralty in settling claims for work completed, a problem which affected many Government contractors at that time. It was exacerbated in the case of Harland & Wolff by the costs incurred at Belfast – higher than those at other yards carrying out identical work – and by delays in completion of contracts. Sir James Lithgow, who disliked Sir Frederick Rebbeck intensely, commented in a private letter to Sir Charles Craven, of Vickers, that Harland & Wolff was 'the most inefficient of all'.[24] The other reason for the Midland's anxiety was the determination of Sir Frederick Rebbeck to replace damaged buildings by solid structures rather than flimsy sheds. In the second half of 1942 Sir Frederick authorised £647,155 of capital expenditure, approved by the board in January 1943. It was at this time that Sir Frederick was dubbed by a Queen's Island wag 'King Concrete' because he insisted that all the roadways in the works should be made of concrete. Legend has it that a notice appeared at the entrance to the works: 'The wages of sin are death. The wages of Harland & Wolff are horrible. Ask King Concrete.'[25] Short & Harland also faced difficulties, including failure to meet production targets, and its problems were tackled by a Government takeover of the management in May 1943.

Sir Frederick was by that time under very severe pressure. The strain of bringing the yard and engine works into full production after the recession; the continued pressure from the voting trustees to improve the Company's financial management; the trauma of the blitz and its aftermath; coping with widely varying contracts; managing a munitions works and a subcontract aircraft factory; introducing new technology, including welding; as well as the overseeing of operations in Glasgow, London, Southampton, Liverpool and Londonderry: all this made for a very heavy burden. Small wonder that Sir Frederick felt himself pushed into a corner by Sir James Lithgow, by the Rt. Hon. Sir Basil Brooke, representative of the Ministry of Production for Northern Ireland and Prime Minister of the Province from June 1943, and by F.H. Cooper, appointed by the Government to head the Northern Ireland Civil Service. Contemporaries remember these three as 'always pin-pricking' at Sir Frederick. He feared a takeover by the Government – as had happened to Short & Harland – in which he would lose his position. Such a takeover was favoured by Ernest Bevin, the Minister of Labour, and might well have occurred had it not been for an approach made in April 1943 by J.S. Baillie to Sir Charles Craven of Vickers. Craven, Industrial Advisor to the Ministry of Production and an old friend of Sir Frederick's, advised Baillie to see Clarence Sadd, chief general manager of the Midland Bank, who had earlier agreed to Baillie's proposal to increase Harland & Wolff's overdraft to £3½ million. Sadd was sympathetic to the case presented by Baillie, and telephoned A.V. Alexander, First Lord of the Admiralty, who agreed to a proposal involving the replacement of Sir Frederick as chairman of the Company to allow him to concentrate on the management of Belfast. The new chairman was to be Charles Palmour, an accountant from Whinney Murray, the Midland Bank's auditor. With a promise of more effective financial control, Sadd agreed to raise the overdraft limit to £4 million to finance rehabilitation and work in progress, and sent Baillie and Spark to see the chairman of the Emergency War Damage Commission who doubled as Director-General (Finance and Contracts) at the Ministry of Supply – none other than John Morison, Sir William McLintock's partner. He

342

Table 11.1

Capital 1939-45

	'A' Ordinary shares £	'B' Ordinary stock £
1939-43	5,200,000	1,796,082
	4½ per cent cumulative preference stock £	Ordinary stock £
1944-5	2,600,000	4,396,082

Table 11.2

Profit and loss 1939-45

	Gross profit/(loss) for year before tax and depreciation £	Net profit/(loss) per published accounts after tax and depreciation £	Distribution (transfers to/from reserves and dividends) £	Balance carried to following year £
1939	804,210	393,566	341,902	96,891
1940	1,129,234	297,825	296,282	98,434
1941	972,484	187,716	211,882	74,268
1942	993,074	224,680	211,882	87,066
1943	1,517,939	421,224	414,133	94,157
1944	1,544,101	428,521	387,363	135,315
1945	1,621,653	546,497	531,749	150,063

proved willing to lend the money for rebuilding, subject to the approval of the Admiralty as the sponsoring department. Baillie and Spark then immediately motored to Bath where they saw the Admiralty's Director of Naval Construction, Edwin Jubb, who agreed to the release of funds and wrote accordingly to Morison. On the following day Baillie and Spark again met Morison who agreed that the War Damage Commission would make arrangements for interim payments on account as work progressed on the repair of Queen's Island. The outcome was that Sir Frederick's position as managing director was secured.[26]

That Rebbeck's dislike of Lithgow was not without foundation is indicated in a note made by Rebbeck after lunch with Sir Charles Craven in January 1944 – 'Sir Charles repeated in very precise terms exactly what Mr McKenna's last words were, "Keep in your mind for the rest of your life – never trust Lithgow." '

Reinstatement after the air raids swallowed up more money than had been anticipated. At a board meeting on 28 May 1943 it was resolved 'to curtail spending on capital account to such items as are absolutely essential for the prosecution of the programme of work in hand'. The overdraft continued at a high level. On 27 July it was still over £3 million, despite a special advance of £1 million from the Admiralty, and it was not until the end of the year that matters improved. Settlement by the

Table 11.2a (cont. on p. 345)
Profit and loss before depreciation: by cost centre 1939-45

	Shipyard	Engine Works	Victoria Works	Londonderry	Govan
	BELFAST				
	£	£	£	£	£
1939	534,182	344,866	72,015	—	59,279
1940	295,600	274,265	96,067	—	72,173
1941	329,227	172,478	58,822	—	86,108
1942	117,318	116,372	75,275	—	174,110
1943	399,864	228,609	97,293	—	276,735
1944	778,893	245,073	102,240	17,462	122,521
1945	924,321	159,887	115,414	11,468	133,747

Note
( ) = Loss

Admiralty for twenty-one vessels, and advances on merchant-ship contracts by Union-Castle and Lamport & Holt allowed the overdraft to be reduced to just over £2 million in November. It was estimated at that time that the Admiralty was more than £3 million in arrears on payment for work completed or in progress. Despite the serious cash-flow problems facing the Company, Charles Palmour, with the strong support of Sir John Craig – knighted that year – was able to push through a staff pensions scheme, reviving an attempt which had come to grief in 1939.

The orders placed with Harland & Wolff in 1943 were quite different in both character and number from those of the earlier war years. The tide of the conflict had turned and orders for warships ended. Instead, the prospect of an invasion of Europe led to the ordering of ten 'transport ferries' which were in fact tank-landing craft. Eight of these orders went to Belfast in two batches and the other pair to Govan. Two of the Belfast vessels were completed at Vickers's Barrow yard and the Govan ships were finished by John Brown at Dalmuir. Harland & Wolff's Southampton works was involved in building the Mulberry Harbours, trial-assembled in the Solent before they were towed across to Normandy to service the D-Day invasion. The only other Ministry of War Transport orders were for one 'standard fast' tanker, *Empire Edgehill*, from Govan; a refrigerated motor ship, *Empire Star*, from Belfast; and four coastal tankers from Pointhouse, designed for use in the Pacific war. The remaining five vessels ordered were for civilian owners: two of them, which had first been contemplated in 1943, were for Union-Castle. The others were tankers: one, postponed from 1943, for the Anglo-Saxon Petroleum Company; and the *Lyria* and *Linga*, smaller craft for the same owners. The number of orders was substantially down on the previous year. This may well have been deliberate policy on the part of the Government to concentrate effort on completing major contracts, especially the aircraft carriers already in hand.

The relatively good returns for 1943 allowed a 6 per cent dividend to be paid on the Company's ordinary stock. With the tide of the European war turning in the Allies' favour, an improvement on the stock market began in the spring of 1944. This encouraged the voting trustees and their brokers, Cazenove Akroyd & Greenwood, to revive the idea of recouping their debt. Cazenoves suggested that instead of

Table 11.2a (cont.)
Profit and loss before depreciation: by cost centre 1939-45

Finnieston	Clyde Foundry	Scotstoun	Liverpool	Southampton	London
£	£	£	£	£	£
48,236	24,287	60,450	108,727	28,913	62,924
60,888	64,782	57,620	206,956	98,979	182,059
54,685	34,853	48,829	206,262	70,953	154,221
179,095	44,395	44,239	264,310	71,903	121,584
162,611	47,378	55,181	262,321	93,328	131,041
74,456	(6,869)	50,809	209,583	93,914	199,418
32,365	(9,939)	62,100	171,823	96,455	147,043

Table 11.3
Fixed assets 1939-45

FREEHOLD AND LEASEHOLD LAND, PROPERTY AND BUILDINGS

	Additions	Depreciation and sales	Total
	£	£	£
1939	103,681	36,715	3,283,966
1940	121,269	159,154	3,248,491
1941	80,716	104,199	3,224,942
1942	544,091	76,862	3,683,377
1943	264,347	83,913	3,863,812
1944	82,974	160,114	3,786,672
1945	101,355	188,875	3,701,652

MACHINERY, PLANT AND TOOLS

	Additions	Depreciation and sales	Total
	£	£	£
1939	270,213	463,285	2,939,707
1940	369,079	240,846	3,065,255
1941	178,504	295,800	2,947,471
1942	678,776	323,137	3,301,869
1943	467,800	316,087	3,452,400
1944	180,001	439,886	3,190,743
1945	121,654	411,126	2,899,890

Note

Depreciation excludes sums transferred from 'Reserve for writing down fixed assets', generally small.

Table 11.4
Reserves 1939-45

	Capital expenditure reserve	General reserve
	£	£
1939	76,980	100,000
1940	78,613	200,000
1941	78,058	300,000
1942	68,023	300,000
1943	66,841	300,000
1944	65,069	300,000
1945	66,187	400,000

Table 11.5
Bank balances 1939-45

	Midland Bank	Belfast Banking Co.	Clydesdale Bank	Bank of Ireland	National Bank of Scotland	Royal Bank of Scotland	Total
	£	£	£	£	£	£	£
1939	128,584	26,298	673	59,282	2,921	328	218,086
1940	(1,575,503)	46,065	6,554	115,595	30,709	2,402	(1,374,178)
1941	(2,892,534)	2,335	24,645	90,102	7,616	1,984	(2,765,852)
1942	(3,257,675)	17,375	6,225	101,888	20,834	441	(3,110,912)
1943	(1,903,799)	14,747	11,526	6,142	16,413	1,159	(1,853,812)
1944	(1,058,669)	14,814	5,050	18,129	12,746	7,670	(1,000,260)
1945	222,535	20,089	7,347	40,171	9,697	8,681	308,520

Note

( ) = Overdraft

Table 11.6
Investments 1939-45

	Investments in subsidiary companies	General investments
	£	£
1939	207,549	100,575
1940	207,249	100,576
1941	207,249	100,576
1942	207,249	100,576
1943	207,249	104,576
1944	207,249	54,576[1]
1945	207,249	54,076

Note

1   £50,000 written off Short & Harland shares

Table 11.7
Number of employees 1939-45[1]

	Belfast	Glasgow	Associated companies[2]	Repair branches
1939	17,850	5,451	1,290	8,233
1940	24,361	7,697	2,248	9,751
1941	25,509	8,498	2,393	10,651
1942	29,971	8,333	2,284	10,698
1943	29,244	8,083	2,413	11,241
1944	30,801	7,706	2,177	10,702
1945	26,393	7,585	2,281	10,585

Notes
1 At December in each year
2 The wholly owned subsidiaries A. & J. Inglis and D. & W. Henderson

Table 11.7a
Numbers employed in aircraft construction in Belfast 1939-45

	Short & Harland	Harland & Wolff
1939	8,451	n/a
1940	8,217	n/a
1941	11,319	n/a
1942	n/a	n/a
1943	n/a	1,485
1944	n/a	1,364
1945	n/a	91

Note
n/a = Not available

marketing the 'A' shares – representing the debt – on their own, there should be a complete reconstruction of the Company's capital. They proposed that each of the 5,200,000 £1 'A' shares should be divided into one ordinary and one preference share, and that the new preference shares should be bought by a syndicate at 12s. (60p) a share. The Midland Bank objected to this proposal, but after lengthy discussions with the Bank of England the scheme was approved. The effect was that the 1,796,028 'B' ordinary shares already issued were designated ordinary stock; the 5,103,918 unissued 'B' ordinary shares were classed as ordinary shares; the 5,200,000 'A' ordinary shares were divided into two shares of 10s. (50p), one ordinary and one preference. The voting trustees, their task completed, stood down.[27] After fourteen difficult years Harland & Wolff's involvement with the Royal Mail Group reconstruction was at an end and Sir Frederick, for the first time since becoming chairman in 1930, was released from Sir William McLintock's tight rein.

The issue of shares was well-timed from the Company's point of view, since the operating profit for 1944 – not available until after the issue – turned out to be about a third lower than that for 1943. The fall was accounted for largely by a rise in overheads at Belfast and by poor returns from the Clyde operations and the Liverpool repair works. The London works, however, was very successful, with a

profit increase of nearly a third. The most striking success was the Belfast shipyard whose profit almost doubled, reaching £778,893 as payments were made for contracts completed earlier. The main Engine Works and the Victoria Engine Works also performed satisfactorily, as did Southampton and the Scotstoun works, which were mainly engaged in making gun mountings. By calling on reserves it was possible to boost the Company's overall profit as published in the balance sheet.

The last few months of the war and the rest of 1945 saw a continuation of the trend in ordering established in 1944. No more warships were booked, but contracts for fourteen tankers known as 'Tedships' – 'tankers, eastern, diesel' – were placed with Govan and Pointhouse. As these were intended for the Pacific war, its ending resulted in the cancellation of six vessels. The only other Admiralty order was for nine 'L'-class tugs from Pointhouse, the last new Government order for a number of years, though work continued on aircraft carriers which had been started during the war. The gap left by the cessation of war work was more than filled by the pent-up demand for merchant vessels, and both old and new customers placed orders for a wide range of ships. Before the end of the war in Europe the British Tanker Company had ordered a standard tanker from Govan and Anglo-Saxon had ordered another, of a slightly smaller type, from Belfast. Shaw Savill was licensed by the Admiralty to order the *Athenic* and Royal Mail took the *Loch Garth* and *Loch Avon*. The most unusual contract for the year was the *Balaena*, a whale factory ship for United Whalers, intended to take advantage of the expected high level of demand for oil and protein during the period of postwar reconstruction. After Victory in Europe on 8 May the amalgamated Cunard-White Star line placed its first order with Harland & Wolff

The *Empire Tesland*, on a class of steam-power coastal tankers designe for service in the Far Ea and completed at Gova in September 1945.

348

HMS *Kent,* a 'County'-class guided-
missile destroyer and first of her type,
delivered to the Admiralty
in August 1963.

The *Edenfield,* launched in
March 1965 for Hunting
(Eden) Tankers Limited. At
59,000 tons deadweight, she
reflected the trend towards
orders for oil tankers of
increasingly massive
proportions.

The cargo ship *Gowanbank,* the las
eighty-five vessels built by Harlan
Wolff for Andrew Weir's Bank line, v
delivered in January 19

Balaena, the first whale factory ship built by Harland & Wolff, completed for United Whalers Ltd in 1946. She was the last Belfast-built ship to be fitted with steam-reciprocating main propelling engines.

for the *Parthia*, and this was followed in August by a contract from Union-Castle for two large turbine liners, the *Pretoria Castle* and *Edinburgh Castle*, of 28,705 gross tons each. Sir Frederick and Sir Vernon Thomson, chairman of Union-Castle, were close associates.

After the surrender of Japan and the consequent relaxation of the licensing restrictions on new shipbuilding, the London & North Eastern Railway was able to order from Pointhouse the paddle steamer *Waverley*, as a replacement for the vessel of the same name lost in 1940 while serving as a coastal minesweeper. Anglo-Saxon ordered two tankers, the *Lingula* and *Lepton*, from Belfast. French owners contracted with Govan to build three small motor ships, and diesel engines were built for vessels of the same class constructed in other yards. Lastly, in December, Blue Star ordered the *Imperial Star* and *Melbourne Star*, refrigerated motor ships, and Coast Lines placed orders for the *Munster* and *Leinster*, cross-channel passenger/cargo vessels. By the end of the year, forty-one orders had been placed and the Company was returning rapidly to peacetime conditions. There were still several warships to be completed, notably most of the aircraft carriers. With some of the urgency for rapid delivery disappearing, the workforce in Belfast was reduced from 30,801 in December 1944 to 26,393 in December 1945. This was in part a consequence of the rundown of the aircraft department during 1945. At its peak in November 1943 this section had employed 1,517, and at the beginning of 1945 there were still 1,343 employees.

By the end of the year, when the department closed down completely, there were just ninety-one working. There was only a small reduction in the numbers employed in the Clyde works.

Overall, results for 1945 were not dissimilar to those for 1944, with a working profit of £1,621,653, but this concealed widely varying fortunes in each department. The Belfast shipyard did particularly well, with an operating profit of £924,321, nearly 20 per cent up on 1944. The Engine Works, however, had a poor year, as had Finnieston, the London repair works and the Clyde Foundry. With overheads at Belfast down, due to higher throughput, the general position was satisfactory. By February agreement had been reached with the War Damage Commission as to the 'proper cost' of restoring the buildings in Belfast. This amounted to £2,032,344. If claims already settled are taken into account, the sums received in compensation for damage to buildings, plant and stock amounted to about £3.5 million. Final settlement allowed the board to authorise the construction of new offices and so permit staff, who had been dispersed to the suburbs, to return to Queen's Island.

Borrowing too was reduced during the year. By February the overdraft was down to £973,332, and in July there was actually a credit of £62,004 with the Midland Bank for the first time since the First World War. Pending payments due for contracts not completed, this apparent transformation had been achieved only through a loan of £2.5 million from the Admiralty and an advance of £716,320 from Union-Castle against two large liners. With the overdraft wiped out, the Midland Bank saw no necessity for Charles Palmour to remain as chairman, and Sir Frederick resumed his dual position as chairman and managing director from the July board meeting. The feeling of change in the summer of 1945 was reinforced by the death of Henry P. Harland on 10 August. The last member of the Harland family to retain a connection with the Company, he had for many years been in charge of the London office and represented the interests of the subsidiary ship-finishers Heaton, Tabb & Company on the board, though since his election as a Member of Parliament in 1940 he had been less involved in the management of the Company, and J.S. Baillie had assumed his London duties.

As it had been impossible to maintain contact with Burmeister & Wain in Copenhagen after the German occupation of Denmark, the design team of the Queen's Island Engine Works had been working in isolation for most of the war. They were indeed physically separated from the works itself, having been 'dispersed' after the Belfast blitz. With the degree of antipathy that existed between C.C. Pounder, head of the Engine Works' design and drawing offices, and Sir Frederick, direction of research seems to have been notably absent. A new type of slow-speed diesel engine with cylinders 740 mm in diameter, operating at 115 revolutions per minute, was designed under Pounder's direction, and was put into production for tanker propulsion after 1945. Relations with Burmeister & Wain were resumed during 1945 and a six-year extension of licences was negotiated, to run from 31 December 1945.

With the war at last over, the management and workers of Harland & Wolff could take stock. It had not been an easy period. The most traumatic time had been the Belfast blitz, although the London works had remained in the front line throughout the war, enduring altogether 1,386 air raids, totalling 2,383 hours and 53 minutes. Six men had died and 156 had been injured. Bombardment continued right up to the end of hostilities, with flying-bomb raids in the summer and autumn of 1944 and V2 rocket attacks in April 1945. The last of the V2 rockets fell just outside the main building into the lock that linked the Royal system of docks to the Thames. All the

350

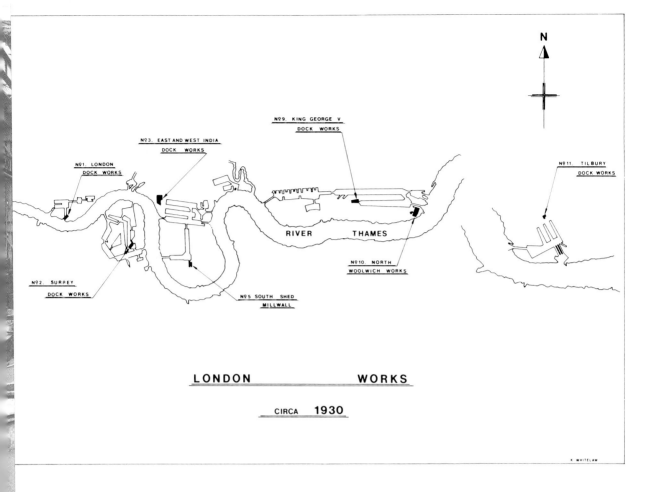

N

Nº9. KING GEORGE V
DOCK WORKS

Nº3. EAST AND WEST INDIA
DOCK WORKS

Nº1. LONDON
DOCK WORKS

Nº11. TILBURY
DOCK WORKS

RIVER   THAMES

Nº2. SURREY
DOCK WORKS

Nº10. NORTH
WOOLWICH WORKS

Nº5 SOUTH SHED
MILLWALL

LONDON   WORKS

CIRCA 1930

K WHITELAW

windows in the works were shattered.[28]

Apart from the physical damage, the Company had also suffered from a high level of strain and disruption, with Sir Frederick and Company officials constantly travelling back and forth from London. Nonetheless there had been positive effects from the war. The Company's finances had been transformed and it had gained independence from its bankers. Queen's Island had been largely rebuilt, in a solid and enduring way. Electric welding, first introduced in 1934, had become a routine technique on a limited scale, and fabrication of hull sections off the berth was now commonplace.[29] Expertise had been gained in the construction of marine steam turbines for warships. Less obviously, the war had been a period of 'working up' for all the Company's facilities, when men – and women – learned to work together under pressure. Weaknesses, concealed by low levels of throughput in the prewar years, had been exposed at various levels and had, in large measure, been eliminated. The Company's management – particularly in costing and financial control – had been toughened and valuable experience had been gained in working with the Admiralty, a critical customer in every sense. With a slow rundown of Admiralty orders for warships, the transition to peacetime production had been eased and the Company was well placed to meet the expected high level of demand for ships to replace those sunk or worn out during the war.

The immediate feeling was, however, consciousness of a difficult job well done. According to the official résumé of the Company's wartime activities, issued on 9 July 1945, the output of naval vessels from Belfast, Govan and Pointhouse between 1939 and 1944 was 139, including four aircraft carriers, two cruisers, two large depot ships,

351

After the end of hostilities United Kingdom shipbuilders were favourably placed to secure orders. Japan and Germany had, at least for the time being, been neutralised as competitors. Replacement of ships destroyed during the war and of worn-out older vessels provided a basic level of demand, which was supplemented as world trade expanded and the short-term effects of the war were overcome. The prospect of this increased demand had led Sir Frederick Rebbeck, in 1944, to resist strongly a proposal from the Prime Minister of Northern Ireland that a permanent naval dockyard be established at Belfast. Instead Sir Frederick placed his faith in merchant-ship contracts, and indeed he had berth bookings to back his position. Like other UK shipbuilders, he was, however, acutely aware of the experience of the post-1918 period when the growth of building capacity had proved ill timed. It was that experience that enabled him to resist any temptation to expand production capacity.

Immediately after the war new Admiralty orders ceased and work was stopped on the aircraft carrier HMS *Powerful*, but there were notable compensations: contracts for HMS *Eagle*, HMS *Centaur* and HMS *Bulwark* were still creating work, and constant modification resulted in extended delivery times for these ships. The *Eagle*, the Royal Navy's largest warship, was actually called the 'iron lung' of Queen's Island: some of her compartments are said to have been refitted twenty times. A former managing director, Alan Watt, recalls that, after her launch by Princess Elizabeth, beside the vessel's berth at the Thompson wharf, some bright lad inscribed on a board the first verse of a hymn: 'O God our help in ages past, Our hope for years to come, Our shelter from the stormy blast, And our eternal home'.

As expected, the postwar boom produced a stream of orders, with no fewer than twenty contracts placed in 1946. Apart from two high-speed motor ferries for the London, Midland and Scottish Railway, orders were placed for eight sizeable passenger and cargo vessels, and three tankers. The largest ship ordered was the turbine-powered passenger steamer *Magdalena* of 17,547 tons, for Royal Mail. The only other large vessel was the *Thorshavet*, a 17,000-ton diesel-engined whale factory ship for A/S Thor Dahl, similar to, though larger than, the reciprocating steam-engined *Balaena* ordered in 1945. J.S. Baillie and William Strachan were on very friendly terms with A/S Thor Dahl but the ordering of a second factory ship was frustrated when the British Labour Government rationed steel. The restriction on the supply of steel was due to dollar shortages which curbed the importation of iron ore, and to constraints imposed by Government on the steel industry.[1] For a time permits for the supply of steel to build tankers were issued only if the owners were willing to charter the ships to the British Petroleum Company or to the Anglo-Saxon Petroleum Company, part of the Shell group. As the proposed factory ship would have been used to carry whale oil from the Antarctic for part of the year, a permit was refused, much to the annoyance of both owners and builders.[2] The remaining orders in 1946 went to Pointhouse: two were for little pilot cutters for the lighthouse and pilotage administrators Trinity House, and the others were for small motor ships

for the China Navigation Company.

Apart from new orders, Harland & Wolff also secured contracts for the reconversion of passenger liners which had been engaged in trooping during the war. Belfast handled the Union-Castle ships *Capetown Castle*, *Warwick Castle* and *Athlone Castle*, and the North Woolwich works took on the Royal Mail liners *Highland Brigade* and *Highland Chieftain*; all five vessels had been built by the Company. Payment flowed in from the Admiralty for work completed during the war, allowing bank lending to be eliminated, the Admiralty loan of £2.5 million to be repaid and a £250,000 advance from Union-Castle to be returned. By May 1946 there was £1.6 million at credit with the banks. This dramatic turnaround in liquidity, coupled with good working results, made it possible to begin a phased programme of improvement of the Company's facilities, an approach dear to the heart of Sir Frederick, now freed from the control of the voting trustees. Early priorities were a new managerial dining room, including facilities for launching ceremony luncheons and other business functions, new stores for the Thompson wharf and new shops at Govan. The function-room facilities might have seemed extravagant at a time of national austerity, but probably reflected the need to court owners: gone were the days of tied contracts when formal launches had been the exception and not the rule.

The death of Henry Harland on 10 August 1945 had ended the Harland connection with the Company after more than eighty years. Henry Harland had been the London office manager and a director of the Company since 1929. He was Member of Parliament for East Belfast from 1940 to 1945, and an excellent ambassador for Harland & Wolff. His death created a vacancy on the board and in the London office.

On the recommendation of Sir John Craig, Denis Rebbeck was appointed to succeed Harland on the board. Denis, son of Sir Frederick, had joined the Company in 1935 after graduating in Mechanical Sciences at Cambridge, the first of a number of graduates appointed to the board. He had been actively involved in the war effort, especially as manager of the Abercorn ordnance factory, and in the development of welding.[3] J.S. Baillie, who had played a key role in wartime negotiations with the Admiralty, the banks and the shipowners, succeeded to Harland's post in London. The London office had an important function at that time, serving as the main point of contact with owners and potential customers, and, under the direction of F.G. Dunlop, was the centre for the administration of the repair branches. The management of the Company was further strengthened by the appointment to the board of A.T. Marshall, Company secretary, who had been private secretary to Lord Pirrie.

Not all postwar developments were beneficial. The high costs that had plagued the Belfast yard during the war continued to give concern and a further problem emerged with the threat of an increase in the freight rates on steel for Belfast,

An aerial view of the Queen's Island establishment about 1 with some thirty-six vessels under constru and repair. This show yard as rebuilt after th blitz of 1941.

jeopardising the arrangement whereby steel was supplied to Queen's Island at the same price as it was delivered to yards on the British mainland. This difficulty was resolved with Colvilles Limited and Burns & Laird Lines Limited through the offices of Sir John Craig, chairman of Colvilles and a director of Harland & Wolff. Steel rationing also proved a general problem as it restricted output.

Harland & Wolff's connection with Short & Harland also came under review in postwar conditions. To cope with the reduction in demand for aircraft, the Ministry of Supply and Aircraft Production decided to amalgamate Short Brothers' Rochester and Bedford plants with the Queen's Island factory, concentrating aircraft-building in Belfast and forming a new company. The Harland & Wolff board was consulted as to whether the Company wished to retain a share in the new enterprise. It agreed to continue its involvement, while recognising that its 40 per cent shareholding would be reduced. The new company, known as Short Brothers & Harland Limited, was jointly owned by the Government and Harland & Wolff, the latter being allocated a 15 per cent shareholding.

An inquiry from the London, Midland and Scottish Railway for two 21-knot motor ships for its Irish Sea services posed the problem of developing a new type of main diesel propelling engine and it was agreed to quote a price for the vessels discounting the cost of development work, in order to remain competitive in building Irish Sea ferries. The move worked: after a series of exacting speed trials the vessels were delivered in 1949 as the *Hibernia* and *Cambria* and became highly successful in service between Holyhead and Dun Laoghaire with Board of Trade certificates for the carriage of 2,000 passengers.

The working results for 1946 were, on the whole, good. The return from the Queen's Island shipyard was down, but the Engine Works' profit was more than double that for 1945. The Victoria Works (specialising in stationary engines and ship-repair) and Finnieston did poorly, but the Clyde Foundry did exceptionally well, with a profit of more than £100,000 after two years of losses. Liverpool, London and Southampton all improved on their 1945 results. Overall profit before depreciation amounted to £1,054,198.

New vessels ordered in 1947 included no fewer than seventeen tankers. This flood of orders was a response to the high level of demand for oil in the fuel-starved postwar world. The biggest customer was the British Tanker Company which ordered eight standard vessels of 12,500 tons deadweight (carrying capacity), five of which were built at Govan. Anglo-Saxon took two smaller tankers and the Tanker Corporation and Common Brothers ordered the *Vikingen* and the *Kurdistan* respectively, wartime standard ships of 12,000 tons deadweight. The remaining tanker orders came from Norwegian owners. In March A/S Bulls Tankrederi ordered the standard tanker *Jalta*, and Fred Olsen, Thor Thoresen, Viriks Rederi A/S and Borgestad A/S all followed with orders for identical vessels. Workman Clark had built vessels for Norwegian owners before its collapse in 1934: Strachan, a former director of that company, developed this connection for Harland & Wolff after the war, working with Baillie from the London office. They laid the ground for what was to become a very substantial market for the Company.[4]

Of the other orders in 1947 six were for steam whale-catchers to be built at Pointhouse. The Bombay Steam Navigation Company ordered the *Sarasvati* and *Sabarmati*, steam-turbine-powered passenger vessels of 3,750 tons, with the curious distinction of having two funnels where only one was required, to satisfy their owner's idea of what a ship should look like. Two turbine steamers and one motor

Work in progress in 194█
on refitting the *Reina de█
Pacifico* for peacetime
service, showing the h█
corrosion that had take█
place during the war.

ship were ordered by the Ocean Steamship Company, and two motor ships by Moss
Hutchison.

Further contracts for the refurbishment of liners built by the Company were also
secured. In 1947 Belfast handled the *Durban Castle* and *Stirling Castle*, Govan the
Llangibby Castle, and London the *Highland Monarch*. In addition, the Pacific Steam
Navigation Company's Belfast-built motor ship *Reina del Pacifico* was taken in hand
at Queen's Island. When the refit had been carried out the liner crossed to the Clyde
for speed trials which were completed satisfactorily on 11 September, though slight
overheating was observed in one of the four twelve-cylinder, blast-injection, trunk-
piston diesel engines which had been installed when the vessel was built in 1931.
During the return voyage to Belfast, while speed was being increased, all four engines
exploded without warning. In an instant the engine room was a shambles, the lighting
extinguished, ladders and access platforms destroyed and the atmosphere thick with
smoke. When rescuers entered the engine room they found fires breaking out and
bodies lying everywhere. The appalling result was that twenty-eight people died,
either instantly or from their injuries, and a further twenty-three were hurt. A public
inquiry into the disaster concluded that overheating in one of the cylinders had ignited
gases in the crankcase of one engine, causing an explosion which had detonated the
other engines. As the vessel was in the hands of the repairers, almost all those killed

358

The Union-Castle motor ship *Llangibby Castle* at Southampton in May 1944, when in service as a 'landing ship infantry'. This shows the extent of the external work needed to return liners to peacetime conditions.

and injured were Queen's Island men. Among the dead was Leonard S. Brew, the Victoria Works manager in charge of the engines. He had been manager of the Londonderry repair works during the war. The injured included Alan Watt, at that time a shipyard manager.[5]

The programme of diesel-engine development initiated in 1946 continued in 1947, when it was agreed that a prototype of the new Harland & Wolff/Burmeister & Wain propelling engine, being designed for the LMS ferries, be installed in Queen's Island's main generating station. The primary motivation for this decision was the reluctance of shipowners to take the first of a new type of engine. Developed during the war under the direction of C.C. Pounder, the engine was of the 'coverless' type with a cylinder bore of 530 mm. Its installation in the generating station would allow extensive experimental and developmental work to take place. The board's agreement was ultimately obtained on the basis that the engine would probably be sold to a shipowner before completion. In fact this prospect did not materialise, though this type of engine was fitted and performed successfully on the *Hibernia* and *Cambria* and was widely used for power-generation and pumping duties in the Middle East and elsewhere.[6]

An important new customer for Scotstoun came through the Labour Government's programme of expanding the electricity supply industry. Both hydroelectric and steam-powered generating equipment were required on an unprecedented scale, and prime suppliers were forced to subcontract much of the work. The Secretary of State for Scotland, Tom Johnston, insisted that the equipment for the North of Scotland Hydro-Electric Board – his 'baby' – should be made in Scotland. As Admiralty gun-mounting manufacture was phased out due to reduction in demand, Scotstoun had

359

the capacity for high-precision machining of the large components necessary for electrical work. An agreement was therefore made through Sir George Nelson, chairman of the English Electric Company, for Scotstoun to undertake subcontract work on hydroelectric plant for a period of five years. Sir George had worked at the drawing board next to Sir Frederick before the First World War when they were colleagues in the drawing office at the Metropolitan Amalgamated Railway Carriage & Wagon Company, later to become part of British Westinghouse.[7] In order to carry out the subcontract work it was necessary to take over the buildings and machinery installed by the Admiralty at Scotstoun for gun-mounting manufacture. At Belfast and Liverpool other Admiralty investments were also proving useful and their acquisition was considered. Of the Belfast installations the most important was the welding shop built at a cost of £317,508 for prefabricating sections for 'Loch' and 'Bay'-class frigates, which was used in building sections of the whale factory ship *Thorshavet*, the first merchant vessel built by Harland & Wolff to incorporate a large proportion of welding. Butt welding for the hull-plating on this ship was initially adopted after Christen Fred Christensen, consultant to the Norwegian owners, brought pressure to bear on Strachan and Baillie during their visits to Norway.[8]

Another acquisition in 1947 was the works of Napier Brothers in Hydepark Street, Glasgow. This abutted the Finnieston engine works and was acquired to provide storage for that works. Napier Brothers' establishment was of considerable historical interest: built in the late 1830s by Mitchell & Neilson as a foundry and engine works, it became Glasgow's first specialist locomotive-building works. Harland & Wolff's acquisition of the plant was the first in a series of moves in 1947 to expand production capacity in order to cope with a growing order book. In Belfast a laboratory and offices were planned for the Queen's Works, and, to keep up with demand for electroplated fittings and light electrical equipment, the former Sunderland Forge & Engineering Company's property in Sydenham Road was purchased. Further improvements included the construction of a concrete apron and caisson at the foot of no. 3 slip in the Queen's Shipyard, to allow larger vessels to be built there. At Govan, no. 7 berth was eliminated: this had been at the east end of the yard, at right angles to the other berths, and was capable of holding only small vessels. The stimulus for its elimination, which created more working space, was probably the order for five tankers secured for Govan from the British Tanker Company.

Also in Glasgow, James and George Inglis, the last two members of the family on the board of A. & J. Inglis, retired at the end of 1947. The possibility of amalgamating Inglis with D. & W. Henderson was discussed, but it was decided that there was no advantage to be gained by the move. Instead Sir John Craig was appointed chairman of Inglises as well as of Hendersons; Denis Rebbeck was made a director of both companies; two directors of Hendersons were appointed to the Inglis board; and one Inglis director came onto the Henderson board – thus making the two boards the same.

Two notable launches in 1947 were those of the Union-Castle liners *Pretoria Castle* and *Edinburgh Castle*, the former launched by Sybella Smuts, wife of the South African Premier. She was unable to travel to Belfast, so Sir Frederick arranged a link with her home in Pretoria so that she was able, by electrical impulse, to release the trigger holding the ship on the ways. She made the sponsor's naming speech by means of a complicated radio-telephone link devised with the assistance of the BBC and other broadcasting authorities. The attenuated voice of the sponsor, travelling 6,000 miles over the airwaves, against a background of crackling static, fascinated the listeners

The Union-Castle liner *Pretoria Castle* in the dry dock at the Company's Southampton repair establishment in 1948 a her delivery voyage from Belfast.

The *Pretoria Castle* as completed in July 1948. She was one of a pair o[f] vessels of 28,705 gross [tons] built for Union-Castle [and] she shows how the traditional elegance of [the] design was retained ev[en] in a period of austerity

in Belfast.[9] This attention to detail was entirely characteristic of Sir Frederick.

With no break in the boom conditions, the Company continued in 1948 to follow the course set in the immediate postwar period. The modernisation and re-equipment of Queen's Island went ahead. The acquisition of Admiralty-financed buildings and equipment was taken further and plans were made to convert the Admiralty stores into an electrical manufacturing shop for alternating-current equipment. In a more far-reaching move, negotiations began with the Belfast Harbour Commissioners for the closure of the Abercorn Road to allow the main Engine Works to be extended. There was a high level of activity in engine-building, not only for marine purposes but also for land installations. Contracts were announced during 1948 for stationary diesel-generating sets for East Africa, Malaya, Iraq and the Potteries, and for pumping sets for Iran and Wales. These orders, secured by Norman McCallum, sales manager in the London office for stationary diesel engines, reflected Sir Frederick's enthusiasm for diesel engines as prime movers, and made it necessary to expand capacity in the Victoria Works.[10]

The pattern of orders secured in 1948 was not dissimilar to that for 1947. Contracts were placed for eleven tankers, eight of them for Norwegian owners: only three were for the 12,000-ton-deadweight type which had been standard since the war; the other five were 24,000-ton-deadweight vessels. Four of the larger vessels were ordered on

The Royal Mail ship *Andes* as she entered peacetime service in January 1948. This vessel had been completed in 1939 but had been converted to a troopship without entering normal service.

the same day – 16 January – by Fred Olsen, Martin Mosvold, Sigurd Herlofsen and Lorentzen; and Olsen placed a repeat order in September. An even larger tanker, the *Verena* of 28,000 tons deadweight, the first of a new line of standard ships, was ordered by Anglo-Saxon in March and a vessel of the same type was booked by the British Tanker Company in November. The eleventh tanker ordered was one of the 12,000-ton-deadweight class, for Hunting & Son Limited. With oil shipments expanding, the increased size of vessels allowed economies to be made in manning and in fuel costs. The economy in fuel offered at that time by Harland & Wolff/Burmeister & Wain diesel engines was vividly illustrated to shipowners in the dictum that on a thimbleful of diesel oil an owner could carry a ton of cargo a distance of one mile.[11]

Seven other merchant ships were ordered during 1948 and three of these were large liners: the diesel-engined *Bloemfontein Castle* of 18,400 tons, for Union-Castle; and the sister ships *Runic* and *Suevic*, turbine steamers of 13,587 tons, with a refrigerated cargo capacity of 0.5 million cubic feet, for Shaw Savill & Albion. The other merchant vessels were the *Ascanius* and *Ixion* for the Ocean Steamship Company. In typical shipyard fashion the *Ixion* was nicknamed 'Nine to one on'.[12] The other orders for Belfast were a further two small turbine steamers for India and a large diesel whale factory ship, the *Juan Peron*, of 24,569 tons, for the Compania Argentina de Pesca. Pointhouse received orders for two whale-catchers for the Union Whaling Company and one steam-propelled fishery survey vessel for South Africa.

Further liner reconversion contracts kept the repair departments busy. The *Andes* was a fast and luxurious vessel of 25,688 gross tons, built for the centenary of the Royal Mail Steam Packet Company in 1939 and intended for its South-American service. She was completed, with magnificent furnishings, just after the outbreak of war. After a brief period laid up on the Clyde she was returned to Belfast and converted into a troopship. The furnishings removed from the vessel were stored in the joiners' shop on Queen's Island and were destroyed in the blitz. The *Andes* operated as a trooper until 1947 and was reconverted for passenger service and delivered to Royal Mail in January 1948. Later in the same month the London works completed the refit of the *Highland Prince*. Govan was responsible for the *Mataroa*, completed in April, and later in the year the *Reina del Pacifico* and *Mooltan* were delivered from Belfast, the *Britannic* from Liverpool, the *Alcantara* from Southampton, and the *Ranchi* from London. The question of who was to blame for the *Reina del Pacifico* engine-room explosion was not conclusively settled by the public inquiry so the costs of compensation and reinstatement were shared equally by the Pacific Steam Navigation Company and Harland & Wolff. On a less serious note, Dr Denis Rebbeck tells an amusing story of a launch from Pointhouse in 1948. The vessel involved was the lightship tender *Granuaile* for the Commissioners of Irish Lights. The former chairman recalls: 'The sponsor was a veritable amazon of a woman (appropriately named Miss Guinness!) who literally hurled the bottle of champagne from the stand at the poor unsuspecting little ship, whereupon Sir John Craig leaned over to me and said, "Dr Rebbeck, someone should have warned yon lassie that the hull plating is only mild steel." '[13]

The steady progress, which seems in retrospect to have characterised 1948, was challenged by two setbacks. The work secured from English Electric for Scotstoun was threatened by a shortage of skilled labour, and this brought criticism from Sir George Nelson, chairman of English Electric, who stressed the priority attached by the Government to expanding the generating capacity of the North of Scotland Hydro-Electric Board. The problem of scarcity in skilled labour was a serious one in the west of Scotland and was a legacy from the rundown of heavy engineering in the 1920s and 1930s, resulting in a lack of apprenticeships and in the migration of trained men to England or overseas. The other setback for the Company involved the double-acting, two-stroke, airless-injection diesel engines evolved just before the war, which were plagued with breakage of piston rods, leading Burmeister & Wain, Harland & Wolff and Union-Castle to launch a joint investigation. These failures compounded the problems being faced by the Belfast and Finnieston works in competing with the Doxford opposed-piston engine and the well-known Sulzer poppet-valve type, which were in the same market for slow-speed diesels as the Harland & Wolff/Burmeister & Wain designs.[14]

The continuity that can be traced through 1946, 1947 and 1948 ended in 1949, when only one ship order was placed – with A. & J. Inglis of Pointhouse for a whale-catcher for the Australian Whaling Commission. Fortunately there was enough work in hand to keep Belfast and Govan fully occupied but Finnieston's loss in 1948 was repeated in 1949, and towards the end of the year Sir John Craig reported that repair work at D. & W. Henderson had fallen off rapidly because of the limited size of the private dry dock. The shortage of work was attributed largely to increasing competition from Continental builders and repairers, especially in Germany which had rapidly recovered from war damage. Contracts for liner reconversions and stationary engine sets, however, continued to be placed, orders for the latter coming from East Africa, Cyprus and England. Belfast received contracts for the refitting of four vessels and Liverpool, Govan and London had one refit each. Despite the adverse trading conditions, the board pressed on with expansion. The remaining Admiralty buildings and plant in Belfast were acquired, ending direct Admiralty involvement on Queen's Island. With the closure of the Abercorn Road approved, authorisation was given for the Engine Works extension – the first stage being the consolidation of the ground by piling. The Victoria Works was partly re-equipped to build smaller engines and other machinery, and at Scotstoun new machinery was installed for the English Electric work. At Liverpool, however, the consistently unprofitable carpenters' shops and part of the timber yard were sold to Littlewoods, the football-pools proprietor. In an attempt to secure more orders for the Victoria Works at Belfast, negotiations were opened with the Cooper-Bessemer Corporation, an American company, for a licence to build reciprocating gas compressors for the petro-chemical industry.

One of the contracts completed in 1949 was the Royal Mail passenger/cargo liner *Magdalena*, intended for the company's South-American service. This 17,547-ton vessel ran aground off Rio de Janeiro in April while on her maiden voyage to Argentina with more than 350 passengers on board and a crew of 100. All the passengers were safely disembarked, but the ship broke in two while an attempt was being made to refloat her.

The Company fared better for orders in 1950. The outbreak of the Korean War in June raised freight rates generally and resulted in the resumption of work on three of the aircraft-carrier hulls – HMS *Eagle*, HMS *Centaur* and HMS *Bulwark* – lying at Belfast. Major capital investments were made in the engine works and in the former Admiralty shops, named King's Works, which had been converted to manufacture alternators. Only four petroleum tankers were ordered and the upward trend in tanker size had been temporarily halted: none of the new vessels were of more than 19,000 tons deadweight. Eighteen cargo/passenger ships were booked, the largest being three steam-turbine-powered 17,000-ton liners for Union-Castle, the *Rhodesia Castle*, *Kenya Castle* and *Braemar Castle*. Most of the remaining orders came from traditional customers. Andrew Weir & Company ordered three of their standard motor ships, and Royal Mail, Shaw Savill & Albion, Elder Dempster and the King line each took pairs of vessels, all of moderate size. The Ulster Steamship Company, the Port line, the Australia-China Line Limited and Lamport & Holt all ordered single vessels, and Coast Lines Limited booked the cross-channel motor ship *Irish Coast* for the Liverpool – Belfast service. The remaining orders were all for whaling companies. The Spermacet Whaling Company ordered two 12,700-ton tankers, and four whale-catchers were ordered singly from Pointhouse. The large passenger liner conversion contracts were coming to an end: only *Carnarvon Castle* and *Arundel Castle* were completed during the year.

Among the vessels launched in 1950 was the whale factory ship *Juan Peron*. It was intended that she should be launched by Eva Peron, wife of the Argentinian dictator, but owing to political ferment in Argentina which led to the downfall of Peron, Eva could not attend the ceremony. At very short notice it was arranged for one of the shipyard secretaries, Irene McClurg, who was considered to look suitably Latin-American, to stand in, and she duly performed the duties of sponsor![15]

Land-engine business boomed. By November 1950 there were twenty-five stationary sets and two turbines in hand. During the year orders were placed for engines for Singapore, Nigeria, East Africa, and Zanzibar. The largest order was for a 40,000 kw steam turbine for Blackburn Power Station, and a 30,000 kw turbine was ordered for a Finnish power station. The licence agreement with the Cooper-Bessemer Corporation was completed, and the first compressors ordered were for Trinidad, and for the Grangemouth and Llandarcy refineries of the Anglo-Iranian Oil Company.

Overall, the year was a good one financially, with the best working results since the war. The Queen's Island shipyard turned round the poor results of 1948 and 1949, returning a profit of £561,168, a fourfold increase on 1949. This was, however, counteracted by a decline in engine works' profitability both in Belfast and Finnieston, and the Clyde Foundry had its worst year since the war. Ship-repair at Southampton and London recovered somewhat from the reverses of 1949, though profits continued to slide at Liverpool, probably because liner-reconversion work had come to an end. As in all previous postwar years, the Company had the largest output of new tonnage in the United Kingdom.

There were several changes in the composition of the board during the year. Following the resignation of Company secretary A.T. Marshall, F.V. Spark, chief accountant since the Kylsant crash in 1930, was appointed to the post. In August three new executive directors were appointed. These were Henry Rees Humphreys, Norman McCallum and C.C. Pounder, head of the design and drawing offices in the Engine Works. It could be argued that this recognition of Pounder's capabilities was belated, due to some ill feeling between him and Sir Frederick. Pounder was well read and took delight in company, unlike Rebbeck who had brought Pounder forward. It was unfortunate for the Company that these two distinguished men were unable to see eye to eye on most matters. Humphreys had come from Cammell-Laird in 1948, leaving that company when the chairman, Sir Robert Johnson, himself an Ulsterman, appointed his own son as his deputy, blocking Humphreys's path to the top.[16] On the death of F.G. Dunlop, Humphreys succeeded him as general manager of Harland & Wolff's repair works. Norman McCallum, a fine engineer and a good salesman, was in charge of stationary-engine manufacture and was based in the London office.

The generally good conditions of 1950 persisted throughout 1951, the Festival of Britain year, which saw the return of the first postwar Conservative Government. The relaxation of war-induced rationing encouraged international trade, and the continuation of the Korean War helped to keep freight rates high. Never had the Company's yards been so fully occupied. In June 1951 there were no fewer than sixty-eight vessels either under construction or on order at Belfast, Govan and Pointhouse.

The tanker market revived during 1951, with eleven firm orders: a further two were rescheduled to 1952 and two were cancelled. The postponed and cancelled contracts were for Norwegian owners, who also took four 19,500-ton-deadweight tankers. The other tanker orders were all for British owners. The British Tanker Company placed contracts for four vessels, three of 13,800 tons deadweight and one, the *British Engineer*, of 31,600 tons deadweight, the largest tanker yet built by the Company. Anglo-Saxon initially ordered three 18,000-ton-deadweight tankers, one of which was transferred to the Hadley Shipping Company before completion. Anglo-Saxon replaced this vessel with another of the same class. There were eleven orders for merchant vessels of orthodox types: two each for Ocean Steamship and Union-Castle, and one each for the King line, the Ulster Steamship Company, the Port line, Elder Dempster, Royal Mail and Andrew Weir. In addition to these moderately sized vessels, P & O ordered the *Iberia* of 29,614 gross tons, the largest merchant ship built by the Company since the war,[17] and Shaw Savill & Albion started negotiations for

The Clyde motor ferry
Maid of Argyll about to be
launched from the
Pointhouse yard of
A. & J. Inglis in 1953.

the *Southern Cross*, a 20,204-gross-ton liner not formally ordered until 1952. The other merchant orders were remarkably varied: a phosphate carrier for the British Phosphate Commissioners; an oil tanker for the Hvalfangerselskapet Pelagos A/S; and, for Pointhouse, two small motor ships, the *Maid of Argyll* and *Maid of Skelmorlie*, for steamer services on the Clyde. Pointhouse also received an order for a paddle steamer for service on Loch Lomond. This vessel, the *Maid of the Loch*, was trial-assembled at Pointhouse, partly dismantled, then built up on the patent slip at Balloch on Loch Lomond. She was the last paddle steamer built in the United Kingdom.

The most striking change in the pattern of ordering was, however, the resumption of new Royal Navy work, after a lapse of six years. This was a consequence of the 'Cold War' between the Communist and non-Communist worlds rather than an effect of the immediate conflict in Korea. Belfast received orders for two frigates of the 'Whitby' class, HMS *Torquay* and HMS *Blackpool*. The class was developed to counter improved Soviet submarines, and incorporated features designed to resist ice forming on the superstructure in Arctic conditions.[18] In addition, Pointhouse received orders for HMS *Brayford* and HMS *Bryansford*, Admiralty seaward defence vessels. The variety of work undertaken by the Company indicates its flexibility, though the product range was not conducive to economy.

Between May and November 1951 no fewer than fourteen stationary generating

The paddle steamer *Maid of the Loch* prefabricated by A. & J. Inglis for service on Loch Lomond, and assembled and launched at Balloch in 1953.

sets were ordered, three of which were built at Finnieston, and orders were also placed for three Cooper-Bessemer gas compressor sets. Work on a set of marine auxiliary diesels also went to Finnieston, as well as an order for one main propelling engine – all in an attempt to move the works out of loss.

The trend towards increased profitability in the Belfast shipyard, which had started in 1950, continued in 1951, with working profit rising by 17 per cent to £656,477, the best figure since 1946. Overall, however, it was a poor year for the Company, with profits before depreciation down to £1,472,184, the worst result since the war. The order famine of 1949 certainly contributed to this disappointing performance. Investment continued at a fairly high level, especially in the main Engine Works' extension, in the new alternator shop in the King's Works and at Scotstoun. Significantly, electric welding plant was ordered for Belfast and for the London works: the long-standing commitment to riveted construction was beginning to be weakened.

On 31 January 1951 tragedy struck again at Queen's Island. The vessel involved was the whale factory ship *Juan Peron*, which was being fitted out alongside no. 2 quay in the Musgrave channel. The accident happened at the end of the working day. The manager who would normally have assembled the men on deck before signalling for them to cross the gangway had been taken ill during the afternoon. In his absence the workers gathered on the gangway itself. It collapsed, throwing men into the water and onto a fender floating between the ship and the quay. Eighteen men were killed and fifty-nine were seriously injured. A public inquiry established that the immediate cause of the accident was a flaw in one of the wooden longitudinals of the gangway, which had caused the part to break under an excessive load. The inquiry tribunal found that there were no design criteria for gangways and no procedures for testing them. Although no blame was assigned to anyone in the Company, the chairman of the tribunal proposed a set of gangway regulations to prevent the recurrence of such a disaster.[19]

A notable event in 1951 was the retirement of Atholl Blair as a director and as head of the Engine Works. Blair had joined the Company as an apprentice at the turn of the century and had earned a formidable reputation both within and outside Harland & Wolff. He is said to have been an excellent diagnostic engineer, and he had a farsighted policy of purchasing large high-quality machine tools, some of them the largest in the world at the time, which served the Company well. Like his contemporaries in senior management, he was a stern disciplinarian, especially with his management team, and he has been called 'the terror of the management', though his nickname in the yard was 'The Whippet', probably on account of his appearance. He was, behind the stern facade, a kindly and cultured man who did much good by stealth, and he was much loved by his workforce. Outside the yard his great interest was technical education.[20]

Though 1952, like 1951, was a good year in terms of volume of work and new orders, there were worrying undercurrents. The dominant position of United Kingdom shipbuilders between 1945 and 1950 was being seriously challenged by foreign competitors.[21] Losses were being incurred on some fixed-price contracts and the value of work in progress was, in some instances, written down.

The orders placed with the Company during 1952 reflected this situation. Only five tankers were ordered, though all were large. The trend toward larger tankers was due in part to the growing use of oil for fuel, in place of coal. With rising wages for seamen and heightened competition, the incentives to build large ships were powerful. Clearly illustrating this trend was the *Solfonn*, originally ordered on 10 October 1951 as a 530-foot vessel, 69 feet 3 inches wide, with a depth of 39 feet – a ship of 18,000 tons deadweight. As rescheduled in June 1952 it became a 615-foot vessel, 83 feet wide, with a depth of 45 feet, and before completion it was further increased in size to a width of 84 feet and a depth of 49 feet, giving a total deadweight of 29,600 tons. Knut Knutsen's *Elin Knudsen*, also postponed from 1951, underwent a similar transformation, ending up as a vessel of 31,600 tons deadweight, and the other vessels ordered, Anglo-Saxon's *Vibex* and *Vitrina* and the British Tanker Company's *British Honour*, were all of comparable size.

Two large passenger ships were also ordered. The more conventional was the *Reina del Mar*, a 20,225-gross-ton liner for the Pacific Steam Navigation Company. The *Southern Cross*, of 20,204 gross tons, for Shaw Savill & Albion, was entirely novel in conception, with its propelling machinery aft, as in a tanker, giving short propeller shafts and more space for passengers in the midship area. Shaw Savill's first approach was for a vessel of conventional design, but during negotiations the owners raised the possibility of moving the machinery aft. The detailed investigation and final design were carried out by Harland & Wolff, under the supervision of Rupert Cameron, the Company's assistant naval architect.[22]

The other merchant ship orders in 1952 were more modest. Two small motor ships were booked by the Prince line and one by Johnston Warren. Andrew Weir & Company ordered two standard motor ships, and the Port line took one vessel from Govan. Pointhouse secured orders for a collier for the Belfast firm of John Kelly Limited, and for two whale-catchers. The remaining vessels ordered in 1952 were for the Admiralty. The largest was the fleet auxiliary tanker RAFA *Tide Austral*, of 13,165 tons, which entered service with the Royal Australian Navy, but the biggest single order, reminiscent of the Second World War, was for twelve coastal minesweepers of the 'Ton' (later 'Coniston') class with a total contract value of approximately £3 million. The design of these little vessels was conditioned by experience of contact with magnetic and acoustic mines during the Korean War. Their construction involved double-diagonally planked mahogany hulls, aluminium superstructures and other components of materials with low magnetic content. The building technique required that a constant temperature be maintained. Accordingly a specially designed covered shop, containing three slips, was built opposite Queen's Island, on the north side of the Victoria channel. Construction of the minesweepers and of the building shop was directed throughout by W.H. Park, who showed great ingenuity in adapting existing machinery to build these novel vessels.[23] The other contracts, which went to Pointhouse, were for a barge, and for the first two of the 'Confiance' class of coastal tugs.

A problem emerged in 1952 which was to prove increasingly intractable. Since the war and the abandonment of the Northern Ireland Loans Guarantee Act, which had allowed financial guarantees to be given to the Company,[24] it had been difficult to finance occasional large contracts for liners. Now tankers were moving into the same league. A Weir cargo vessel, the *Foylebank*, cost £734,000, and a small tanker cost £686,250. In contrast, a 30,000-ton tanker could cost more than £1.7 million. Only contracts like the *Southern Cross* (£3.5 million) and *Reina del Mar* (£3.1 million) substantially exceeded these figures. The trend towards smaller numbers of larger ships, with more thought given to the placing of individual orders, was beginning to pose serious difficulties for builders like Harland & Wolff whose plant was geared to producing large numbers of what had become medium-sized vessels.

Twenty-one orders for stationary engines were placed during the year, four of which went to Finnieston, though a large contract for thirty-five engines for the Middle East, under negotiation since 1950, was cancelled. Four diesel engines of the locomotive type, built at Finnieston without specific orders, were sent to the North British Locomotive Company to be installed in diesel-mechanical locomotives for Colvilles – an instance of Sir John Craig providing practical help to Harland & Wolff. Even this level of successful diversification could not, of course, make much impact on the problems being encountered in shipbuilding and main machinery manufacture.

The relatively poor financial results of 1951 were repeated in 1952. The problem divisions were the shipyards and engine works. At Belfast, shipyard profits were more than halved and the Engine Works' returns fell by 40 per cent. Govan and Finnieston both made losses, though the other divisions did comparatively well. Total profit before depreciation was down by £389,674. Despite these problems, there was substantial investment in the Engine Works, Victoria Works, and King's Works at Belfast. The most important new project was the upgrading of the Govan shipyard.

The year 1953 was one of mixed fortunes for Harland & Wolff: good financial results, but few new orders. The end of the Korean War on 27 July brought a depression in freight rates, and foreign competition continued unabated. The

Company's liquidity slumped to a low level. In April 1953 the bank balance was £162,539, but a total of £2,149,663 had been extended in credit – mainly to Norwegian customers – over periods of three to five years from delivery. By November the overdraft was £1,846,604 and a new limit of £3.5 million had been negotiated, taking into account a revolving credit of £1.5 million to Sigval Bergesen (an ongoing loan to finance production of a series of ships).

Even the expedient of giving credit did not boost orders. Only seven were placed and four of these – all Norwegian – were later cancelled. The cancellations included two vessels for Bechs Tankrederi A/S and Moltzaus Tankrederi A/S; the value of these two contracts alone was £1.86 million. The effective orders were for a cargo vessel for the Port line, a cargo liner for Royal Mail, and a coaster, ordered from Pointhouse, for the Belfast Steamship Company.

For the Company it was a time of consolidation. Two new directors, W.H. Park and H.C. MacEwan, were appointed in April, one of them taking the seat on the board vacated by John Morrison in 1952. Park's appointment was popular and well deserved. In 1935 he had created the steel construction department and he had managed it successfully for many years, initiating, among other things, the design and construction of a building for Short & Harland with an entrance capable of taking a complete 'Sunderland' flying boat. This design was adopted by the Ministry of Aircraft Production and was widely built during the war. In 1940 he opened up the old Workman Clark south yard as the Victoria Shipyard, and he added the Queen's and Abercorn yards to his responsibility in 1945/6. After the war he and Rowley McKinney, founder of a well established Ulster firm of structural engineers, practically cornered the market for structural steel in Northern Ireland at a time of great activity in large building construction.[25] Park was a sound practical engineer, often consulted by Sir Frederick Rebbeck, and was a good delegator of duties. MacEwan was electrical director.

In 1953, Sir Frederick Rebbeck also announced his intention to continue as chairman and managing director after his seventy-fifth birthday. Dr Denis Rebbeck was appointed deputy managing director, on Sir John Craig's recommendation. Below board level an important appointment was that of Rupert Cameron as naval architect. He succeeded T.C. Tobin, a clever abstract mathematician and designer whose name is associated with the 'Tobin Bow', a feature of the Union-Castle liners of the 1930s. Tobin was also responsible for the striking 'chunky' look of passenger ships built at Belfast in the late 1920s and early 1930s, such as the *Georgic*. Later in his career he seems to have been disregarded by Sir Frederick and was not drawn into negotiations with owners, probably because of his poor health.[26] Cameron, who had joined Harland & Wolff as an apprentice in the drawing office in 1920 and was appointed assistant to the naval architect in 1934, was largely responsible for the fine appearance of the Union-Castle liners built by the Company from the 1940s onwards. Certainly throughout his career he was interested in the aesthetics of ship design.[27]

Working results for 1953 were good, as contracts entered into at an unrealistic fixed price were succeeded by more flexibly priced orders. The Belfast shipyard increased its profit to £665,232, the best figure since 1946. The Engine Works' returns were up by 70 per cent, and only the Victoria Works, producing smaller units and thus quicker to respond to adverse trading conditions, saw a drop in its profits. Elsewhere, Govan and Finnieston turned losses into profits. The overall position was an increase of almost 80 per cent in profits before depreciation, despite a marked rise in overheads.

The pattern of investment by the Company in 1953 was in line with earlier policy.

The last tram from Que
Road on 27 February 1

One of the largest projects was the continuation of the modernisation of Govan, including the creation of a new welding shop and the re-erection of five tower cranes bought second hand from Fairfield. Substantial investment, mainly in machine tools, also took place at the Victoria Works, the Abercorn Works, the main Engine Works and at Scotstoun.

The order famine ended in 1954, the first indication of improvement being the signing of a contract for the tanker *Storfonn*, of 36,000 tons deadweight, for Sigval Bergesen, largely financed by his revolving credit with the Company. This vessel was the largest then projected by Harland & Wolff. The only other tanker orders were for two vessels of 27,800 tons deadweight for the Texas Company (Panama), later Texaco (Panama), contracts secured on a sales trip to New York by J.S. Baillie and W. Strachan. There they met the general manager of the marine department of the Texas company, T.E. Buchanan, and his assistant, J.V.C. Malcolmson, a former Workman Clark employee and friend of Harry Campbell, chief of the Queen's Island ship design office. They came away with the contract signed. Malcolmson had previously paid apparently casual visits to both Belfast and the London office.[28] The other contracts were all for passenger/cargo vessels. Royal Mail took two cargo motor ships, as did Elder Dempster, and the ever faithful Andrew Weir & Company placed a six-ship order. The remaining contracts were for Irish Sea ferries: the British Transport Commission ordered the steam-turbine-powered *Duke of Lancaster* and *Duke of Argyll* for the Belfast – Heysham route; and Coast Lines booked the motor ship *Scottish Coast* for the Belfast – Glasgow service, as a near sister of the *Irish*

372

Coast, completed in 1952. Only one of these orders went to Govan, and there was none for Pointhouse.

A notable completion in 1954 was the twin-screw turbine steamer *Iberia* built for P & O, the largest passenger liner constructed at Belfast since the war. A note by C.C. Pounder indicated that at this time the owners, too, held conservative views on certain aspects of ship construction. 'Owners do not want a "welded box", they expect plenty of riveting.' Attitudes were to change later.

The results for 1954 were undeniably good. Both the Queen's Island shipyard and the Engine Works substantially improved their profitability, producing their best returns since the war. Despite mixed fortunes elsewhere, overall profits before depreciation were £2,699,608, up by 41 per cent on 1953. After a gap of one year the Company again had the highest output of new tonnage in the United Kingdom. Capital programmes continued along the same lines as in 1953, with the most substantial expenditure being on the Engine Works at Belfast. The only change on the board was the appointment of shipyard manager James McCuaig as shipyard director. McCuaig was a tough man, a necessity in a hard age. He was nicknamed, in Queen's Island fashion, 'Air Raid' because on the day he was made an assistant manager a horse called 'Air Raid' won the Derby. His assistant, David Hunter, who wore a brown overall coat, was known as the 'Brown Bomber', the name given to the then heavyweight boxing champion of the world, Joe Louis, but in Hunter's case referring also to his habit of sudden attack.[29]

If 1954 was a good year, in some ways 1955 was even better. Although profits were down, largely on account of the order famine of 1953, liquidity was well maintained and non-shipbuilding work was fairly plentiful and reasonably profitable. Orders for ships were numerous and varied, and the mix was well suited to the capability of the Company. Four tankers were ordered, two each by British Petroleum and Shell. The BP vessels were the largest yet ordered, 710 feet long overall, with a deadweight tonnage of 42,000: but they were outstripped by the Shell vessels, over 750 feet long, with a deadweight tonnage of 47,000. Named *William Wheelwright* and *Edward Stevinson*, the Shell ships were transferred to other owners before completion, the former to the Pacific Steam Navigation Company and the latter to Stevinson Hardy & Company for charter back to Shell. These vessels were the biggest that could then be built in the Queen's Shipyard. Each of the four large tankers cost over £2 million. Other important contracts included the *Pendennis Castle*, a 28,582-gross-ton passenger and cargo liner for Union-Castle and the last vessel ordered from Harland & Wolff by that old-established customer. For well over half a century Union-Castle had ordered all its ships, with one exception, from the Company, and this link was reflected in the close friendship between Sir Frederick and Sir Vernon Thomson, chairman of Union-Castle. The Admiralty, on behalf of the Indian Navy, ordered a frigate of the 'Whitby' class which was commissioned as the INS *Trishul*. Most of the other orders were for cargo vessels for traditional customers. Royal Mail took four motor ships, of which one was built at Govan. The King line ordered two 6,000-ton vessels, and Shaw Savill and the Ulster Steamship Company took one ship each. British Phosphate Commissioners ordered the *Tri-Ellis*, a cargo carrier for the phosphate trade. Of particular interest were two ships built at Govan, the *Afghanistan* and the *Iron Age*, 16,000-ton-deadweight bulk carriers, the first vessels of the type built by Harland & Wolff. They were ordered initially by the Hindustan Steam Shipping Company but transferred to other owners before completion. Pointhouse picked up orders for two pairs of tugs for Clyde Shipping and for the

Admiralty. The latter two were of the 'Confiance' class, as previously ordered in 1952.

The most important vessel completed in 1955 was Shaw Savill's *Southern Cross*, delivered in February only six months after she had been launched by Her Majesty the Queen on a pouring wet day, the first merchant vessel to be launched by a reigning monarch.[30] This was a remarkably quick delivery for a large passenger liner, and illustrated the extent to which Sir Frederick had created an effective machine for building ships.

The agreement with Colvilles Limited, which guaranteed that the prices of steel delivered at Belfast were the same as those on the British mainland, was renewed for ten years. Agreement was also reached with Danly Machine Specialities Incorporated, of Chicago, for the manufacture at Scotstoun of twenty-two steel presses for the motor industry. This was a most important development, as hydro-electric work was running down and motor manufacturing was a growth industry throughout Europe. Scotstoun was in a good location for making this product, as finished presses could be loaded onto coasters in the works dock.

The retirement of F.V. Spark as director, secretary and chief accountant marked the end of an era: he had been chief accountant since 1930 and had thus been through all the turmoil of the reconstruction of the Company. Spark was succeeded as chief accountant by W.T. Underwood and as secretary by G.H. Patton, who had been with the Company since 1911. Unhappily, soon after his appointment Patton had to retire on account of ill health. He was succeeded by T.E. Murphy who had started his career as a civil servant and had moved to Harland & Wolff in 1935.[31]

The financial results for 1955 were patchy. The Belfast shipyard profits dropped by a quarter and the Engine Works' and Victoria Works' results were also poor. Govan did badly too, but the Clyde Foundry's profits were up. On the ship repair side, London and Liverpool returned increased profits but at Southampton profits dropped by nearly a third. Overall profit before depreciation was 17 per cent lower than in the previous year.

During the five-year period 1951/5 world output of merchant tonnage rose dramatically, from the annual average for the previous five years of 2,624,000 gross tons to 4,739,000. The United Kingdom output rose only marginally, with German and Japanese yards accounting for much of the increase. United Kingdom shipbuilders, still mindful of the overcapacity that had bedevilled them in the interwar years, seem to have been reluctant to expand output. The view held in progressive economic circles that shipbuilding was an 'old' industry also deterred investment, as did the relatively low profitability of shipbuilding. Harland & Wolff under Sir Frederick was conservatively managed, which in effect meant that no speculative investment decisions were taken. While this may have made sense between 1945 and 1955, the consequences of the policy in the longer term were at least debatable. In particular, reluctance to introduce modern production techniques resulted in low levels of productivity.[32]

There were, however, few immediate external influences to disturb the pattern established in the first half of the 1950s. The event which had the most significant effect on the Company was the Suez crisis in 1956, with the accompanying closure of the canal in November.

Although there were fewer orders than in 1955, had all intentions been fulfilled 1956 would have been a boom year. Thirteen orders were placed for tankers, but in the event nine of these were either cancelled or postponed. Of the four orders that were confirmed in 1956 two were for vessels of 15,000 tons deadweight for the BP Tanker Company, one built at Govan. The others were the *Vestfonn*, of 19,000 tons deadweight, for Sigval Bergesen, a vessel postponed from 1955; and the *Eskfield* for Hunting & Son, of 28,500 tons deadweight. Of those contracts postponed eight were a group order by the BP Tanker Company for three large and five smaller vessels. It was the Suez crisis that caused them to be temporarily abandoned. The largest single order taken at the time was for three diesel-powered 20,000-gross-ton passenger/cargo liners for Royal Mail. Named *Amazon*, *Aragon*, and *Arlanza*, these were the biggest vessels built for Royal Mail since the war. The contract price was estimated at £4.2 million each. The British India Steam Navigation Company placed a five-ship order for cargo vessels of 6,750 tons, all of which were built at Govan. Andrew Weir & Company ordered two of its smaller standard ships; the King line and Manchester Liners each took a single motor ship; and Blue Star ordered the *Ulster Star*, a refrigerated cargo vessel. The order book was completed by Admiralty contracts for five vessels: two of these were frigates, HMS *Berwick* of the 'Rothesay' class, an improvement on the pioneering 'Whitby' class, and HMS *Leander*, the name ship of a new class of improved 'Rothesay's. The Admiralty also ordered three more wooden minesweepers of the 'Ton' class which were subsequently allocated to the South African Navy as the SAS *Port Elizabeth*, SAS *Mosselbaai* and SAS *Walvisbaai*, probably to keep shipping lanes round the Cape of Good Hope free of mines as they assumed a new importance with the closure of the Suez Canal.

Financial results were affected during 1956 by a prolonged dispute with the Queen's Island riveters over wages. It was the first major dispute in the Company since the war, a fact which reflected well on industrial relations during previous years, when a mutual respect had been established between senior managers and shop-floor workers. Riveters were generally paid on piecework, with a fall-back rate for work

in areas where the number of rivets to be inserted in a given time did not guarantee a reasonable take-home pay. The dispute was about both piecework rates and the fall-back rate, as well as the riveters' underlying concern over continuity of employment. Industrial action began in March 1956 with an overtime embargo and developed in August into a general ban on piece and overtime working throughout the yard. After a series of offers to increase the rates were rejected by the men, the offers were withdrawn at the end of September, and twelve squads were paid off 'for idling'. In response, the men took strike action and remained out until 29 October. The dispute was finally resolved on 5 November.[33]

The industrial action resulted in the postponement of several launches into 1957, and was partly responsible for a reduction in profit at the Belfast shipyard and the Engine Works. Apart from Govan, Finnieston and Scotstoun, where hydroelectric work was running down, other divisions did well. The Victoria Works' profits were more than doubled, and ship repair did handsomely. Overall profit before depreciation was marginally down, to £2,215,968. Continuing prosperity permitted a high level of capital investment, of which the largest share went to Belfast for new machinery in the Engine Works and Victoria Works. The other substantial

376

Queen Elizabeth II launching the Shaw liner *Southern Cross* on 17 August 1954. This the first occasion on which a reigning monarch launched a merchant

investment was in equipment for Scotstoun. The physical amalgamation of A. & J. Inglis and D. & W. Henderson was again proposed, using the Meadowside offices of the latter. As National Shipbuilders Security had sterilised Henderson's berths during the reduction of shipbuilding capacity in the 1930s, the permission of NSS for the amalgamation had to be sought, and this was granted. The only other important organisational development was the introduction of a scheme for the recruitment and training of apprentices. That this was thought necessary suggests both a need to compete for labour, and a higher level of technical awareness among management. An apprenticeship manager was appointed and plans were drawn up for the construction of offices and a training centre.

Costs arising from the industrial unrest of 1956 were carried over into 1957 and the number of new orders fell to thirteen, though a further ten vessels were seriously considered. Six of these were postponed – two to 1959 and the rest to 1960 – and the remainder were cancelled. Two of the cancelled ships were to have been bulk ore carriers and the others tankers. The uncertainties in the tanker market after the Korean War had been heightened by the Suez conflict. The closure of the canal, necessitating a longer journey from the Persian Gulf to Europe and North America, created a demand for more tankers. At the same time, the dimensions of tankers no

longer had to be restricted to suit the canal, and once the Egyptians had taken control of the waterway they continued to enlarge it. Shipowners realised that, when this work was completed and the canal reopened, very large vessels would be able to pass through unladen on the east-bound voyage, returning laden via the Cape and thus escaping the high freight rates payable if they used the canal. Robert Gillespie, managing director of the BP Tanker Company, and Sigval Bergesen were both very helpful to Harland & Wolff in planning for the larger vessels.[34]

Of the contracts proceeded with in 1957, the outstanding vessel was the P & O liner *Canberra*. With an estimated cost of £11.73 million, this was the most valuable contract ever awarded to the Company. In traditional manner, it was negotiated by the chairmen of P & O and Harland & Wolff, with the expectation that costs over and above contract price would be amicably settled. The *Canberra*, at 45,270 gross tons, with a speed of 26.5 knots, was the largest liner built in Britain since the *Queen Elizabeth*. She incorporated the machinery-aft layout pioneered in the *Southern Cross* of 1955, and had her lifeboats recessed, giving more space on the sun deck. To reduce weight, 1,200 tons of the superstructure was of aluminium, the largest quantity of this metal used on a ship by any builder at the time. It is a tribute to Harland & Wolff that the design still looks modern in the 1980s, and new cruise liners still being built have features in common with the *Canberra*. A paradox lies in the not immediately obvious point that her hull had riveted frames and three riveted seams: she was, indeed, the last large vessel built to incorporate significant amounts of riveting. This use of riveting reflected the view which had been held in Belfast and by some owners

The Royal Mail liner *Amazon*, one of a class three vessels of just ov 20,000 gross tons, was for the company's Sou American service. See here on trials, she was delivered on the last d of 1959.

The Royal Mail ship *Aragon*, another of the three 'A's being built a Musgrave yard, show the traditional construction of the hu and the use of wooden staging. This was shipbuilding as Sir Frederick Rebbeck love

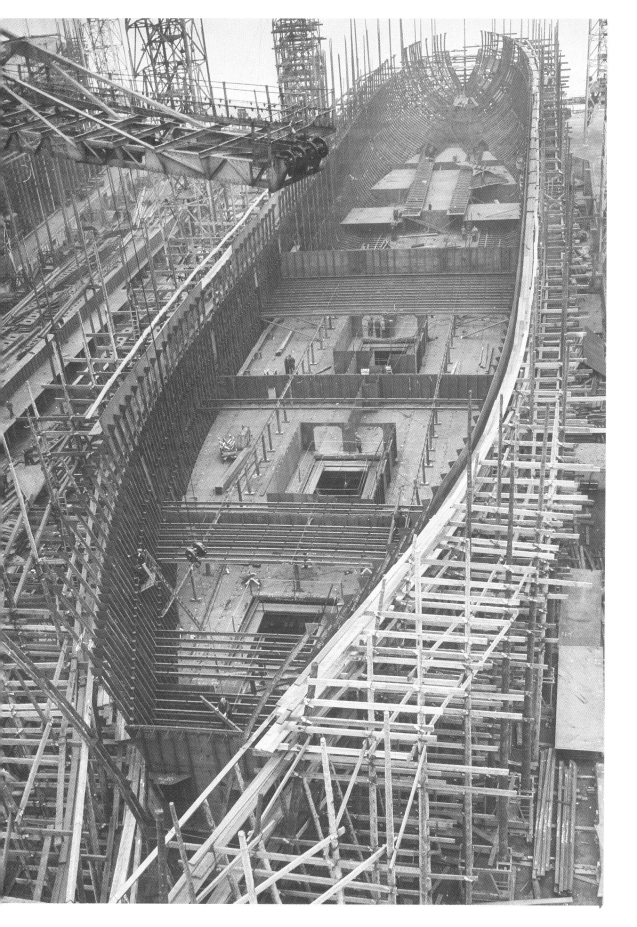

that riveted ships were superior to welded vessels, a belief which delayed total commitment to welding at a time when emerging shipbuilding countries, such as Japan, Sweden and Germany, were producing all-welded vessels. Another factor preventing the adoption of welding at Belfast was the inadequacy of the cranage, which dated from wartime reconstruction.[35] Sir Frederick discouraged contact with other shipbuilders in Britain or abroad, and new initiatives from within the Company were likely to meet with rebuffs.[36] The effect of this conservatism – to the annoyance of P & O – was that there were not enough welders on Queen's Island to allow the *Canberra*'s hull to be fully welded. By the time the challenge from foreign yards became compelling, in 1957/8, it was almost too late to make the necessary changes in thinking to compete effectively. There were people in the Company who saw the need for change, but when reasonable profits were being made using largely traditional methods, incentives to modernise were simply not strong enough.

The other contracts secured in 1957 were varied. The Admiralty ordered HMS *Kent*, a 'County'-class guided missile destroyer. These were the first vessels of their type in the British Navy. With a displacement of 5,200 tons, the *Kent* was more than twice the size of a 'Leander' frigate, and the value of the contract – £5.5 million – was proportionate. Only three tankers were ordered, two of which had been postponed from 1956 by Sigval Bergesen and another Norwegian owner. The third vessel was for the Pacific Steam Navigation Company. Significantly, Sigval Bergesen also ordered a bulk carrier – the 13,471-gross-ton *Tresfonn* – the first vessel of its type to be built at Belfast. The remaining orders were mainly for cargo liners of conventional types. The Pacific Steam Navigation Company took two ships, Andrew Weir & Company booked the first two of an intended six-ship order, and Shaw Savill & Albion ordered one vessel. The engines fitted to the Weir vessels were of the opposed-piston type, on which development work continued. Pointhouse secured orders for three coasters for the Hull & Netherlands Steamship Company, and a major defence contract was received for the completion of a 'Majestic'-class aircraft carrier for the Indian Navy. This vessel had been launched in 1945 as HMS *Hercules* by Vickers-Armstrong on the Tyne, but the hull had been mothballed. At Queen's Island, work on the ship, renamed INS *Vikrant*, continued until February 1961.

The Belfast yard's great flexibility was demonstrated during 1957 when – while the *Pendennis Castle* was being built – Union-Castle was taken over by Cayzer, Irvine & Company, owners of the Clan line and other shipping companies. At a meeting in London the new owners asked Harland & Wolff if it would be possible to add ten feet to the length of the vessel and to increase the speed on trial by two knots. Under W.H. Park's direction the already completed double-bottom was cut, the after portion pulled ten feet down the ways and a new section inserted. C.C. Pounder found no difficulty in giving the vessel the additional speed.[37]

The financial results for 1957 were very mixed. At Belfast, the shipyard and Engine Works profits were halved, and only the Victoria Works redeemed the position, with a record postwar profit. On the other side of the water, the Clyde did very much better, but the ship-repairing branches all had reduced profits, though none performed disastrously. The profit for the Company as a whole, before depreciation, was £1,735,711, down by 22 per cent on that for 1956.

The pattern of capital investment during 1957 followed established lines. The biggest project was the reorganisation of the Govan yard but substantial amounts were also spent on new machinery at Scotstoun, Finnieston and at Belfast, where the Company began re-equipping the Musgrave Shipyard to cope with larger vessels.

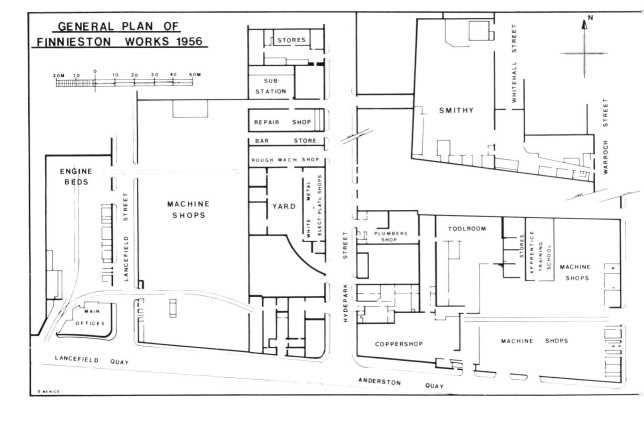

GENERAL PLAN OF FINNIESTON WORKS 1956

Harland & Wolff also contributed to a major scheme devised by the Belfast Harbour Commissioners to widen and deepen the Victoria channel and turning basin. This Government-aided project was essential to accommodate the larger ships which were to be built in the Musgrave yard.

Despite the poor order position and reduced profit, 1957 was by no means a bad year for Harland & Wolff. It was, in a sense, the last of the 'Rebbeck years', with the balance of power in the Company beginning to shift. A sign of this was the death of Sir John Craig who had been on the board since 1924. Remembered with affection by those who knew him – 'a perfect gentleman' is the phrase commonly used of him – Sir John had been effective head of the Inglis and Henderson yards on the Clyde and, as one of the architects of Colvilles Limited, had been deeply committed to the price agreement between that company and Harland & Wolff. He had been the friend and confidant of Pirrie, Kylsant, Rebbeck and McLintock and his wide-ranging industrial and commercial interests had been of great value to the Company. Gently but firmly pushing Harland & Wolff in the right direction, he was the only person who could manage Sir Frederick, and he tried to ensure that Denis Rebbeck had the opportunities his abilities deserved.[38] Sir John, who had been like Sir Frederick an old man, was replaced on the board by Sir Andrew McCance, the technical brain behind Colvilles Limited and a man with a penetrating intellect and extensive business interests. Sir Andrew and the experienced and knowledgeable T.E. Murphy seem to have been responsible for the rather fuller board minutes which ensued from 1957. On 6 December of that year William Strachan died. He had come to Harland & Wolff, with a seat on the board, on the closure of Workman Clark & Company. Throughout his service with Harland & Wolff he had been an exceptionally able and devoted director, held in high esteem by the chairman. He had reshaped the tendering and estimating departments, and after the war he and

382

J.S. Baillie together had made many successful trips abroad seeking orders. His personal links with Norwegian shipowners, formed during his time as a director of Workman Clark, were of great value to the Company in securing contracts after 1945.

The year 1957 proved to be the last of the good years for orders. By 1958 United Kingdom shipbuilders were facing an entirely changed set of circumstances. Demand for passenger and passenger/cargo liners was beginning to be eroded seriously by the development of jet airliners, which were both faster and cheaper to operate than their predecessors, and on the whole more attractive to passengers than ocean liners. For freight, the closure of the Suez Canal meant that owners wanted larger tankers and general cargo vessels. Coastal shipping was hit by improvements in roads and road vehicles. These trends were effectively eroding the product mix which had been the rationale of many yards, including Queen's Island. Compounding the dislocating effects of these developments was the rise of the new shipyards in mainland Europe and in Japan. The new builders used welding, prefabrication and a high degree of mechanisation, in yards laid out for flow-line production, to achieve better productivity, with low costs and good delivery dates. Unlike United Kingdom shipbuilders, they had none of the labour problems associated with demarcation disputes over the threat to old skills from new techniques. Specialising in tankers and bulk carriers, these foreign yards had captured most of the orders for the types of vessel chiefly in demand, quoting prices and construction times which United Kingdom builders were quite unable to match. This threat to Harland & Wolff's position was recognised by senior management of the Company, but, due to Sir Frederick's conservatism, little action was taken. With average annual world output up to nearly double that of the earlier 1950s, demand clearly existed, but Harland & Wolff and other United Kingdom companies were proving increasingly unable to compete.

The short-term effect was a decline in both the number and value of orders placed with the Company. All except one of the orders placed in 1958 had first been considered in 1956 but, for reasons outlined earlier, had not been confirmed. Five were tankers for the BP Tanker Company, four of them sister ships, of just over 15,000 tons deadweight, of which two were allocated to Govan. The fifth tanker was a much larger vessel, *British Lancer*, of 52,000 tons deadweight, one of three large tankers postponed in 1956, and the biggest tanker yet ordered from Harland & Wolff. The other two orders were for bulk carriers. One was a sister ship to the vessel ordered by Sigval Bergesen in the previous year and the other was the *Daghestan*, an ore carrier for the Hindustan Steam Shipping Company, sister to the *Afghanistan* of 1955 and, like her, built at Govan. Significantly, there were no orders for traditional cargo vessels, passenger liners or warships. The first of a series of contracts for the modernisation of three P & O liners was taken in hand in December 1958 when the *Orcades* arrived in Belfast. The contract for the refit of the *Orcades*, which included the installation of air conditioning, required delivery within thirteen weeks, with severe penalties for failure to meet the deadline. It was secured in the face of international competition. Harland & Wolff's management and workforce rose to the occasion and the ship was handed over with a day to spare.[39] The *Arcadia* and *Chusan* were similarly refitted at Belfast and the *Orsova* at Liverpool.

At the end-of-year board meeting in 1957, the chief accountant, W.T. Underwood, had sounded a warning note. Emphasising the need for economy and increased vigilance over production costs during 1958, he had pointed out that the 1958 profit after depreciation and taxation was likely to be substantially lower than in 1957. The

383

pressure for economy was a continuing theme throughout the year.

To remain in the forefront of diesel-engine manufacture, the Company developed the design of a direct-coupled engine of 20,000-brake horsepower, of the latest pressure-charged, single-acting, two-stroke type. This was intended to power a bigger class of vessel than any yet ordered – the largest engine built up to that date was of 10,300 horsepower – but, clearly, it was seen that the established trend towards smaller numbers of larger vessels would persist. In November 1958 it was decided to design and build at Belfast a twelve-cylinder, medium-speed 'V' engine, intended as a development engine for land-based power stations.[40] Subsequently, sixteen-cylinder engines were sold to the Channel Islands and Bermuda.

Financially Harland & Wolff did reasonably well in 1958, with overall profit before depreciation up to £2,023,203, a 16 per cent increase on 1957. All the Belfast departments performed well and Govan was fairly profitable, although the other Clyde works returned poor results, as did the ship-repairing branches at Southampton and Liverpool. Despite the desire for economy, capital investment continued at a high level, with the intention of reducing production costs. The re-equipment of the Musgrave Shipyard, begun in 1957, continued, as did the Govan reorganisation. Substantial sums were also spent on machinery for the Belfast Engine Works, the Victoria Works, Finnieston and Scotstoun. Capital expenditure on welding equipment was a feature of this investment, probably encouraged by Sir

Tankers fitting out in th Musgrave channel in October 1958 with the cranes of the Musgrave yard on the right. The *New Mexico* was built for Texaco (Panam Incorporated.

Andrew McCance who was a director of the British Welding Research Association.

The updating of the capital equipment was parallelled by the strengthening of the board. Underwood, the chief accountant, was made a director and a member of the finance committee which then consisted of Sir Frederick, J.S. Baillie and Dr Denis Rebbeck. J.H. Crossey, head of the electrical department, was appointed a director in November, in succession to H.C. MacEwan, recently retired after forty-six years with the Company. The other change in senior management was the appointment of Baillie as deputy chairman of the Company. Apart from recognising the key role Baillie had played, as head of the London office, in securing orders, in negotiation with the banks and in other high-level business affecting the Company, this appointment was also an acceptance that the ageing chairman, Sir Frederick, needed more support.

The changed circumstances in which the Company was operating, in common with other British shipbuilders, became abundantly clear in 1959. While there was still plenty of work from existing contracts, new orders became very scarce as freight rates were low and yards throughout the world were chasing work in a poor market.[41] Only two ships were booked, making 1959 the worst year for orders since 1949. The vessels ordered were cargo motor ships of about 10,000 tons for the Port line, both first contemplated in 1957. Such cyclical depressions were familiar, and the Company's response was typical: in November it was agreed in principle to take the modernisation of the Musgrave Shipyard much further than had previously been contemplated, in belated recognition of the methods of building being devised in Europe and Japan. A new welding shop was proposed, for building subassemblies up to about 60 tons, and eight of the 10-ton tower cranes installed in the 1920s were to be dismantled and replaced by four electric travelling cranes, two with 60-ton capacity and two with 40-ton capacity. During the year, however, there was a cautious holding-back on investment, the only large sums being spent on machinery for the main Engine Works and for Scotstoun. Despite the gloomy outlook, 1959 was not too bad financially. Shipbuilding at Queen's Island made a postwar record profit, though the Engine Works' and the Victoria Works' profits were halved. The Glasgow works did particularly badly. Ship-repairing had mixed fortunes: Southampton's profit more than doubled, but returns from Liverpool and London were markedly lower than in 1958. In the circumstances the overall profit of £1,682,242 was creditable.

Nevertheless, the trends towards increased competition, lower prices, fewer orders and larger vessels were already well established. It became increasingly clear during 1960 that, so far as smaller vessels were concerned, there was substantial overcapacity in the Company's yards, and that for larger vessels Belfast was not competitive. This was demonstrated when the Company tendered for a repeat of the highly successful *Southern Cross* for Shaw Savill, and Vickers-Armstrong, the successful bidder, quoted a price which 'would not cover wages and materials at Belfast', let alone overheads. This was a return to the conditions of the 1930s. Another sign of uncompetitiveness was the mounting loss on the *Canberra*, estimated at £1.2 million in November 1960. The financial problems encountered with the *Canberra*, however, should not be allowed to overshadow the considerable achievement of her construction. Her launch on 16 March 1960 was a splendid occasion and attracted mass media attention. Dame Pattie Menzies, wife of Australia's Prime Minister, was the sponsor, and guests included many distinguished representatives of shipping and commercial interests and of Government, amongst them the Governor and Prime

The merchant ship *Avonbank*, delivered to Andrew Weir & Company's Bank line in January 1961. She was typical of the standard motor ships built by Harland & Wolff throughout the 1950s and [ear]ly 1960s for this old and valued customer.

[Th]e P & O liner *Canberra* [be]ing launched from the Musgrave yard on [M]arch 1960. The shining [alu]minium superstructure has yet to be painted.

Minister of Northern Ireland. A testimony to the soundness of the *Canberra*'s design and construction is her survival in service a quarter of a century after her launch.

A trickle of new orders came in during 1960. Andrew Weir & Company again came to the rescue, with an order for four standard motor ships, first booked provisionally in 1957. Among the other orders was the *Regent Liverpool*, a tanker of 49,000 tons deadweight for Texaco, originally ordered in 1956 but postponed as a result of the Suez Canal closure. The only other ocean-going vessel ordered was a cargo motor ship for the Port line. The rest of the contracts were for Pointhouse: a diesel launch for the Clyde Navigation Trust and a dredger and hopper for the British Transport Commission. The diesel launch was of some historic interest, for it was the successor to a steam-powered vessel built in 1906, which was in turn the replacement for a paddle steamer whose engine was built in 1851 by A. & J. Inglis at Warroch Street, later part of the Finnieston works. Major ship-repair contracts included the partial air-conditioning of the *Rhodesia Castle*, *Kenya Castle* and *Braemar Castle*.

Despite the clouds on the horizon, 1960 was not a disastrous year, though by November W.T. Underwood was reporting that the surplus would be hardly adequate to cover taxation, depreciation at normal rate, dividends and directors' fees. He proclaimed the need for rigorous economies, in the light of rising costs generally. The capital expenditure programme, cut in 1959, rose again in 1960, though the money spent was concentrated mainly on the modernisation of the Musgrave yard. The new welding shop there was planned on an ambitious scale, with two bays each 560 feet long, 84 feet in span and 84 feet to the underside of the roof members. The concrete floor was constructed on piled foundations, always a necessity for heavy shops on Queen's Island.

One possible way ahead for Harland & Wolff emerged during the year as a result of a visit made by J.S. Baillie to Scandinavia at the invitation of Jorgen Lorentzen. It transpired that Lorentzen wanted to discuss the building of future tanker tonnage,

with credit terms. As only one slip at Belfast – no. 4 in the Musgrave yard – could have taken a vessel of the size Lorentzen contemplated, Baillie returned advocating Government-backed revitalisation of Queen's Island.[42] This proposition did not find favour with Sir Frederick, whose experience of Government involvement in the Company's affairs was none too happy.

The team to face up to the rigours of shipbuilding life in the 1960s was strengthened by the retirement of Humphreys and Park from the board and their replacement by Alan Watt and Rupert Cameron. 'Billy' Park, who had become a very effective shipbuilder, had been a good servant of the Company, as had Henry Humphreys, who had been in charge of the ship-repair establishments since 1948, operating from the London office. Of the new men, Alan Watt was a survivor of the *Reina del Pacifico* explosion. He had been in charge of the Southampton repair works, but was brought back to Belfast to replace McCuaig and strengthen shipyard management. He supported the idea of creating new facilities at Belfast, though he found it difficult, as others had, to persuade Sir Frederick of the need for action. Rupert Cameron was Harland & Wolff's chief naval architect. Both men brought keen minds to the problems facing the Company.

Financially, there was a drastic reduction in working results during 1960. The Belfast shipyard was only marginally profitable, while the Engine Works' and

HMS *Fearless*, one of a of assault ships conspicuous by their staggered funnels. Completed in Novem 1965, the *Fearless* is remembered as the ba for the abortive talks on the future of Southern Rhodesia he October 1968. She ga sterling service in the Falklands War.

388

Victoria Works' returns were substantially down. On the Clyde, Govan did well but losses at Finnieston and the Clyde Foundry were again serious. Most disappointingly, Scotstoun returned its first loss since before the war. The only encouraging figures were those for ship-repair, with profits up at the three branches.

Another difficult year for United Kingdom shipbuilding followed in 1961, with Harland & Wolff's overdraft rising to finance contracts. Working results were slightly better, but trading conditions generally continued to be poor and contracts scarce. Only five orders for new vessels were placed during 1961, two of them for standard motor ships for Andrew Weir & Company. Govan received orders for two bulk carriers for Norwegian owners: these were sister ships, of 15,000 tons deadweight, and proved to be the last vessels built at Govan. The fifth order was for HMS *Fearless*, to be built at Belfast, an 11,060-gross-ton commando assault ship, capable of carrying four landing craft and helicopters. A contract was secured for the modernisation of the Furness Withy liner *Queen of Bermuda*, involving the installation of air conditioning and the fitting of new boilers which allowed the vessel's three funnels to be replaced by one. This work took place at Belfast over two winters.

To allow larger vessels to be built capital investment continued at a high level, though in other areas of the Company's operations rigorous economy was practised. Most money was invested in the Musgrave yard modernisation project. With the first phase of this scheme well under way, J.S. Baillie's recommendation led to the approval in principle of a second phase, at a specially called board meeting on 25 May 1961. The three-year project involved the amalgamation of nos 10 and 11 slipways, with the piling of the strip between them, the erection of concrete causeways to take four 60-ton Arrol travelling cranes, and the resiting of stores and offices at the heads of the slipways. Finance was a problem, as the Company's internal resources were fully committed. Nor could the Midland Bank overdraft be used, as it too was needed to finance work in hand. An informal approach to the Ministry of Finance for Northern Ireland resulted in a firm assurance that a guarantee for £1 million over seven years would be available.

Financially, 1961 was similar to 1960. Belfast shipyard profits recovered, though the Engine Works recorded its first loss since before the war. In Glasgow, Govan had an excellent year, as did Scotstoun, but the Clyde Foundry's result was even worse than in 1960, largely due to lack of demand. Not only were few orders being placed for marine engines, but steel fabrications were taking the place of castings for engine bedplates and frames. The ship-repair branches had mixed fortunes. Overall profit before depreciation was £958,366, almost exactly the same as that for 1960.

J.H. McCuaig, the last of the old-style shipyard directors, resigned from the board on 30 June 1961. The expertise developed by McCuaig and his former colleague Park was invaluable in the production of high-grade riveted ships which they continued to favour until their retirement: but, with the new emphasis on welded ships and cost-cutting, new skills were required. McCuaig's hard-line attitudes to work were also becoming outmoded. Wives of Queen's Island men are said to have threatened their children, 'If you don't go to your bed I'll get Mr McCuaig to you.' Those who knew him suggest that he 'steamrollered' his way through difficulties, with little concern for the effect on his staff, though others hint that he had his kindly side.[43] McCuaig was succeeded on the board by A.O. Milne, who replaced Henry Humphreys as general manager of the repair works.

The difficulties with the *Canberra* contract entered another phase in the autumn of 1961, with P & O owing over £1.5 million to Harland & Wolff at a time when the

Company's overdraft was £3.3 million. P & O countered requests for payment with the claim that the *Canberra* was not up to the standard agreed, as excessive after-draft would restrict the vessel's use of harbours on her route. P & O wanted compensation for the losses they expected to accumulate during the life of the vessel. Harland & Wolff counterclaimed that the vessel's draft and trim were to specification and that the excessive draft aft was largely due to the absence of a planned 1,000 tons of cargo which was to have been stowed in the forward end, but which proved unavailable, through lack of demand. The problem was largely resolved by the removal, where possible, of excess weight aft, and by the provision of additional fuel tanks at the forward end to compensate for the absence of cargo.[44] Had the *Canberra* not proved such a loss-maker, the Musgrave yard schemes could have been financed internally.

Towards the end of 1961 Sir Frederick fell ill and was unable to take an active part in the management of the Company. In his absence, Baillie, as deputy chairman, and Dr Denis Rebbeck, as deputy managing director, assumed responsibility.

In retrospect, the period 1946/61 was one of relative stability for Harland & Wolff. For most of the time, despite fluctuations in orders and in profitability, the Company was operating in a sellers' market, dealing largely with established customers, slowly modifying what had become traditional techniques and designs, and adapting capital assets without radical change. The most important new customers, the Norwegians, were assimilated into the established pattern of building. There was a slow tendency for the size and the cost of ships to increase, but at no time was there a very marked change. These were conditions that helped to breed complacency, not just in Harland & Wolff, but in United Kingdom yards generally. Harland & Wolff, however, had a tradition of autocratic management which was maintained by Sir Frederick and his senior colleagues and, furthermore, the Company had been accustomed to building on commission for many years, with customers more concerned about the quality of the product than about the price. Managers had been discouraged from taking an interest in costs, though the best of them did so; and, as long as year-to-year profitability was maintained, the board does not seem to have taken very decisive action.

Harland & Wolff aged with Sir Frederick, who proved increasingly resistant to change, remembering the traumas of the 1920s and 1930s. Throughout his association with the Company he had been dedicated to its success, but after his wife's death on 2 January 1955 it became virtually his only interest.[45] Surrounding himself with men who were disinclined to mount an effective challenge to his authority, he became convinced that he was the sole person able to run the Company, and it was only his failing health that forced him to step down from his controlling position. Dr Denis Rebbeck, deputy managing director and well informed on developing production techniques, and Alan Watt, the most determined senior shipbuilding manager, attempted to tighten up the management and to improve facilities, but were prevented from having any marked effect on policy. The delay in making such changes was of critical significance to the Company and, indeed, to Northern Ireland. Not until Sir Frederick's retirement was senior management able to begin to bring the Company's facilities into line with those of more progressive shipyards elsewhere. It is worth pointing out, however, that until the late 1950s Harland & Wolff's Belfast yard was as modern as any in the United Kingdom, and the only serious deficiency was in crane capacity. The cranes in the Musgrave yard, which had been extensively damaged in the May 1941 bombing, had been replaced with cranes of similar capacity and type, because these were readily available to meet wartime needs. Although the choice of new cranes had been in conflict with the Company's desire to modernise the facilities in that yard, the need to minimise disruption to wartime production had been paramount.[46]

It is easy to be critical of Sir Frederick's regime, but in many ways it was a successful one. He had good relationships with owners and was respected by the unions. He took a close – almost too close – personal interest in the Queen's Island establishment and earned the loyalty of many of his associates. The personality conflict which he had with C.C. Pounder, however, did nothing to improve the performance of the yard, and, rather than curb Pounder's excesses, he left the Engine Works largely under the command of that strange figure, and of Atholl Blair, who had control of production. Under these two, the works continued to build on its established reputation as a major designer and constructor of very large diesel engines, though commercially it proved less successful.

For most of the period, the peripheral works of the Company contributed notably to profit, as they had done since 1920. The ship-repair yards at London, Liverpool and Southampton were effectively run, as were the Clyde works. Only Finnieston proved a problem, as it was difficult to programme enough work through it to ensure consistency. The Govan yard, so long as suitable demand continued, was an efficient unit, generally building at a lower cost than Belfast. The wholly owned subsidiaries D. & W. Henderson and A. & J. Inglis were also effective units.

It was commonly believed that the *Canberra* was Queen's Island's knockout blow. As a ship – graceful in appearance, up-to-date in concept, soundly built – she represented the best traditions of the Company. The building agreement signed by the respective chairmen of the builders and the owners was also traditional – in its lack of precision. It proved an inadequate contractual base for a vessel so advanced in overall concept and with so many innovative features. The loss on what should have been a profitable contract was bad enough, but just as serious was the dead end that the *Canberra* represented, for the era of the great passenger liner was coming to a close.

It should be remembered that Harland & Wolff was not alone in its problems after 1957. Yards that had been fully occupied did not have the opportunity, or indeed the incentive, to undertake modernisation on an extensive scale before that date, and low profit margins did not, on the whole, encourage new investment in subsequent years. Successive Conservative governments tended to follow the line that shipbuilding and marine engineering were old, declining industries, and to offer incentives to 'new industries', such as synthetic materials manufacture and light engineering, rather than encouraging established companies to meet growing foreign competition. There was, too, a generation of both politicians and senior managers who could recall the part that borrowing had played in the business crises of the late 1920s, and who were most reluctant to use borrowed money for new facilities.

Sir Frederick's withdrawal from active management not only marked the end of the prosperous postwar years, it also symbolised the demise of a whole shipyard culture, the disintegration of a social and technical system based on high standards of personal skill and judgement, and its replacement by an organisation in which skill was built into machines, and judgement passed from the craftsman to the manager. The old system was apparently rigid and strictly hierarchical, but it had a basis of mutual respect between managers and workers, with strong loyalty to the Company and to the department within the Company. The life of workers at all levels, especially

in the shipyard had become more 'urbanised' as rural roots were severed by generations of town life. Everywhere conditions in the home improved – the greatest single benefit was electricity which gradually transformed the lives of shipyard wives. By the end of the 1950s the affluent society was emerging, in the guise of Continental holidays and family motor cars – and, in the 1960s, traffic jams were to replace the torrent of bicycles that had poured from Queen's Island into the city centre at the end of each working day.

Despite all this, older ways persisted. The 'grannyarchy', for instance, survived. In its heyday it had depended on closely-built terraces where branches of families lived within a short distance of one another; in the 1960s it expressed itself in two-way traffic between young couples in the suburbs and their older relatives in the Victorian streets.[48]

The hierarchical structure of Harland & Wolff until the 1960s was typical of a period symbolised by bowler-hatted directors, management and foremen. The day-to-day running of the Company was in the hands of a key group of middle managers on whose organisational ability its reputation depended. They had a power over the shop-floor worker which is today inconceivable, and wielded it to build good ships, engines and structural steel quickly and effectively. Sir Frederick's success was due in large measure to his ability to recognise managerial talent at Belfast and to reward it with responsibility, in stark contrast to his attitude to the appointment of directors.

Rush-hour traffic leavi\
Queen's Island along\
Hamilton Road in 195\
The ships, *Raeburn* an\
Pontia, are in the Musg\
channel – now the site\
the building dock.

394

By selecting managers of character and decisiveness he ensured that his values of hard work, attention to detail and pursuit of quality permeated the Company. The existence of a fine team of middle managers and senior foremen was a source of great strength to the Company during the Rebbeck years.

Any assessment of the postwar years must take into account the fact that Harland & Wolff, throughout the period, maintained its reputation for quality and built a steady stream not only of high-class liners, but also of handsome cargo vessels and tankers, which demonstrated the virtues of the Company on the world's seaways. For more than half the period Harland & Wolff produced a greater tonnage of vessels annually than any other British company and in the three years 1946, 1947 and 1948 the Company headed the world league of shipyard output.

Table 12.1
Issued capital 1946-61

	4½ per cent cumulative preference stock	Ordinary stock
	£	£
1946-61	2,600,000	4,396,082

Table 12.2
Profit and loss 1946-61

	Gross profit/(loss) for year before tax and depreciation	Net profit/(loss) per published accounts after tax and depreciation	Distribution (transfers to/from reserves and dividends)	Balance carried to following year
	£	£	£	£
1946	1,798,156	454,198	437,681	166,580
1947	2,107,307	673,258	637,849	201,989
1948	1,628,142	452,126	417,976	236,139
1949	1,673,793	619,171	587,849	267,461
1950	1,673,553	934,334	887,866	313,929
1951	1,472,184	470,366	427,731	356,564
1952	1,082,510	342,008	335,299	363,273
1953	1,916,243	1,087,966	1,060,876	390,363
1954	2,699,608	1,151,143	1,054,059	487,447
1955	2,228,569	878,359	854,962	510,844
1956	2,215,968	871,549	855,050	527,343
1957	1,735,711	436,527	424,597	539,273
1958	2,023,203	633,250	621,319	551,204
1959	1,682,242	508,833	496,172	563,865
1960	958,605	210,018	206,292	567,591
1961	958,366	140,501	138,977	569,115

Table 12.2a
Profit and loss before depreciation: by cost centre 1946-61

	BELFAST				
	Shipyard	Engine Works	Victoria Works	Londonderry	Govan
	£	£	£	£	£
1946	763,423	359,875	38,210	9,752	118,184
1947	552,329	371,794	118,802	—	256,240
1948	56,619	215,184	133,566	—	270,632
1949	140,908	577,332	86,592	—	150,531
1950	561,168	356,137	78,679	—	185,470
1951	656,477	251,708	84,245	—	15,923
1952	264,172	151,671	180,964	—	(127,346)
1953	665,232	257,833	104,261	—	143,464
1954	745,496	546,748	144,783	—	58,064
1955	563,925	476,131	91,022	—	23,083
1956	506,579	431,945	184,495	—	(60,209)
1957	248,605	228,703	196,841	—	128,815
1958	399,558	739,452	377,537	—	199,096
1959	833,308	401,386	133,167	—	(44,852)
1960	83,986	330,819	109,236	—	30,850
1961	440,558	(109,864)	53,174	—	380,835

Table 12.2a (cont.)
Profit and loss before depreciation: by cost centre 1946-61

Finnieston	Clyde Foundry	Scotstoun	Liverpool	Southampton	London
£	£	£	£	£	£
21,904	102,987	45,182	238,943	111,955	180,500
79,296	98,044	35,185	343,849	159,209	280,916
(43,877)	105,968	46,645	345,470	364,408	291,592
71,862	71,849	53,855	273,348	124,453	158,585
44,256	28,925	67,337	203,820	162,502	191,348
(18,988)	63,913	36,284	239,351	126,736	190,879
(220,829)	115,722	84,189	235,996	173,467	224,878
57,944	99,066	96,186	172,921	176,511	276,922
73,690	27,597	184,360	254,358	256,353	229,066
65,383	115,381	158,527	278,173	180,611	312,538
34,378	49,409	106,061	461,132	198,502	336,982
65,827	136,513	124,854	364,205	157,177	291,465
(38,880)	29,472	81,881	258,189	54,870	265,288
(172,648)	(53,936)	138,555	118,755	123,747	162,031
(127,078)	(57,670)	(30,112)	206,433	138,267	177,230
16,598	(64,847)	78,743	75,842	162,808	107,543

Note
( ) = Loss

Table 12.3
Fixed assets 1946-61

FREEHOLD AND LEASEHOLD LAND, PROPERTY AND BUILDINGS

	Additions	Depreciation and sales	Total
	£	£	£
1946	246,215	96,424	3,851,827
1947	117,417	163,329	3,806,367
1948	161,371	239,946	3,726,367
1949	107,926	87,384	3,746,908
1950	165,656	1,772	3,910,792
1951	127,523	1,868	4,035,427
1952	159,914	74,020	4,121,324
1953	242,444	79,128	4,278,448
1954	159,213	101,233	4,334,810
1955	62,131	103,356	4,293,112
1956	103,223	95,798	4,300,432
1957	369,543	133,897	4,531,756
1958	266,816	215,772	4,581,114
1959	94,817	175,024	4,500,127
1960	173,482	173,613	4,502,843
1961	336,043	157,859	4,685,669

MACHINERY, PLANT AND TOOLS

	Additions	Depreciation and sales	Total
	£	£	£
1946	279,907	503,576	2,675,754
1947	312,566	436,671	2,552,820
1948	352,425	360,054	2,547,140
1949	374,293	412,616	2,513,311
1950	224,817	10,769	2,738,390
1951	366,417	219,969	2,885,512
1952	412,635	285,840	3,017,819
1953	368,816	320,872	3,065,967
1954	332,724	398,767	2,998,769
1955	430,426	396,823	3,033,746
1956	653,264	404,202	3,278,434
1957	755,301	466,103	3,578,040
1958	882,865	484,228	3,976,562
1959	485,182	525,924	3,936,731
1960	887,910	530,435	4,297,949
1961	894,586	542,141	4,662,393

Table 12.4
Reserves 1946-61

	Capital reserve	Capital expenditure reserve	General reserve
	£	£	£
1946	—	66,105	600,000
1947	—	67,726	800,000
1948	—	1,100,000	1,250,000
1949	—	1,368,000	1,400,000
1950	—	1,618,000	1,800,000
1951	—	1,818,000	1,800,000
1952	—	1,918,000	1,800,000
1953	—	2,218,000	2,250,000
1954	71,600	2,500,000	2,700,000
1955	1,479,289	1,480,000	2,950,000
1956	1,803,646	1,530,000	3,200,000
1957	2,348,192	1,240,000	3,200,000
1958	2,997,294	890,000[1]	3,350,000
1959	3,647,838	500,000[2]	3,350,000
1960	4,193,862	220,000[3]	3,350,000
1961	4,772,752	—	3,350,000

Notes
1 £480,000 transferred to Capital reserve as estimated excess cost of fixed-asset replacement during 1957
2 £540,000 transferred to Capital reserve as estimated excess cost of fixed-asset replacement during 1958
3 £280,000 transferred to Capital reserve as estimated excess cost of fixed-asset replacement during 1959

Table 12.5
Bank balances 1946-61

	Midland Bank	Belfast Banking Co.	Clydesdale Bank	Bank of Ireland	National Bank of Scotland	Royal Bank of Scotland	Hambros	Total
	£	£	£	£	£	£	£	£
1946	1,851,673	546,670	55,174	510,085	32,600	16,991	—	3,013,193
1947	704,041	378,322	38,660	248,633	25,623	42,706	—	1,437,985
1948	542,600	18,500	10,614	78,440	25,220	2,309	—	677,683
1949	906,586	94,669	21,146	190,761	11,349	7,907	—	1,232,418
1950	1,464,541	57,906	40,156	169,839	10,335	965	—	1,743,742
1951	429,442	5,068	26,308	203,756	15,381	19,568	—	699,523
1952	627,265	89,760	27,148	151,175	21,048	4,172	—	920,568
1953	358,477	84,693	2,752	147,284	8,391	1,889	—	603,486
1954	553,333	852,110	16,829	848,239	9,296	8,858	—	2,288,665
1955	1,624,443	150,947	23,318	292,391	31,755	93	447,000	2,569,947
1956	57,494	1,998	3,518	35,382	25,053	—	32,095	155,540
1957	1,663,899	59,942	3,945	280,221	33,208	—	40,420	2,081,635
1958	306,442	3,498	10,983	273,041	28,704	—	44,062	666,730
1959	945,650	4,389	14,337	429,784	9,956	—	296,223	1,700,339
1960	306,155	26,146	5,613	76,116	9,298	—	12,193	435,521
1961	(3,795,288)	6,895	6,260	3,935	8,129	—	13,478	(3,756,591)

Note
( ) = Overdraft

Table 12.6

Bills receivable discounted 1946-61[1]

	£
1946	226,000
1947	452,000
1948	574,500
1949	890,100
1950	882,453
1951	1,259,000
1952	1,376,400
1953	476,500
1954	725,000
1955	1,365,500
1956	1,273,000
1957	—
1958	981,100
1959	3,767,400
1960	2,870,000
1961	4,218,000

Note

1 Bills to the value of £978,450 had been discounted in 1939, but apparently no bills had been discounted in the years 1940-45.

Table 12.7

Investments 1946-61

	Investments in subsidiary companies	General investments	Investments in government securities
	£	£	£
1946	204,101	54,076	1,040,442
1947	204,230	134,076[1]	1,015,442
1948	204,230	131,550	—
1949	204,230	127,750	—
1950	204,230	47,750[2]	—
1951	204,230	46,750	—
1952	204,230	46,750	—
1953	204,230	46,750	—
1954	204,230	226,750	—
1955	204,230	226,750	—
1956	204,230	226,750	—
1957	204,230	226,750	—
1958	204,230	226,750	—
1959	204,230	349,649[3]	—
1960	204,230	280,272	—
1961	204,230	280,272	—

Notes

1 Addition of 80,000 £1 shares in Short Brothers & Harland
2 Writing down of Short Brothers & Harland
3 Purchase of shares in Brown Brothers

13
CONTRACTION AND CONSOLIDATION
1962–71

Sir Frederick Rebbeck's illness led to his retirement in March 1962 after thirty-two years as sole managing director and twenty-nine as chairman of Harland & Wolff. In this remarkable period of service he had taken the Company through a horrific collapse, a major war and a period of consolidation and expansion. In his last years, however, it had become increasingly clear that in changed market conditions the Company, like many British shipbuilders, was not competitive with foreign yards – though it is likely that the board was unaware of the true extent of the problems facing it until 1962 when profits fell sharply. Sir Frederick was succeeded as chairman by J.S. Baillie and as managing director by Dr Denis Rebbeck: both men had in effect been filling these posts since the autumn of 1961. At the same time the Company secretary, T.E. Murphy, was appointed to the board. Towards the end of his time in office Sir Frederick had relied increasingly on Murphy to deal with important correspondence, and Murphy's skill had done much to retain shipowners' confidence in the Company. His experience was now invaluable.

The new management, with access to more detailed financial information than had previously been available, and freed from the conservative attitudes which Sir Frederick had accumulated over his lifetime, quickly faced up to the 'impossible task of floating a stranded whale', as the Company's plight was described in the *Sunday Times*. The key issues were high costs, a perennial problem never mastered by Sir Frederick; capacity in excess of any likely demand; and an impending cash-flow crisis. The parallels with 1931 were striking. The problem of high costs, always a burden on Belfast in comparison with the best of the British yards, was being compounded by a trading atmosphere of fierce competition for few orders. It seemed to Harland & Wolff that other companies were taking contracts at a loss, simply to secure continuity of work – a practice which was contrary to the directives of the Shipbuilding Conference. At a specially convened board meeting on 4 September 1962 J.S. Baillie warned that the Company was heading towards a deficit on the year's trading, before provision for depreciation. He stressed the immediate need to cut costs in order to achieve a profit before depreciation. Measures taken to make savings included the adoption of a programme to reduce manning levels by retiring employees over sixty-five – a policy difficult to implement when the chairman had been nearing the age of eighty-four.

The problem of excess shipbuilding capacity was tackled vigorously during 1962. Denis Rebbeck made a thorough examination of the physical assets both of Harland & Wolff and of its subsidiaries, in the light of the changing market for ships and ship-repair. His father, on the instruction of the voting trustees, had carried out just such an exercise in 1930. As a result of Denis Rebbeck's investigation it was decided to close down A. & J. Inglis and D. & W. Henderson as soon as possible. Inglis's plant was out of date; modernisation would cost about £200,000 and, even if this investment was made, demand for the type of vessel which Inglis was capable of building did not look like picking up. D. & W. Henderson's dry dock was too small

...ueen Elizabeth II touring the Engine Works on 8 August 1961, accompanied by Dr Denis Rebbeck, then deputy managing director.

for much of the repair work available and its position on the upper reaches of the Clyde further restricted its market. To bring the dry dock up to date would cost an estimated £1 million, an expenditure which could not be justified. It was therefore decided not to tender for any more shipbuilding or repair work at Pointhouse and Meadowside. Heaton, Tabb & Company, the ship decorating subsidiary, was still trading profitably but its future was threatened by the continued absence of contracts for the construction of passenger liners in British yards.

In Belfast the rundown in work had already led to the closure of the Victoria Shipyard and it was agreed to close slipways 4, 5 and 6 in the Abercorn yard, leaving slipways 7 and 8 which had cranes with a lifting capacity of up to twenty tons. The immediate target was to reduce the number of berths at Belfast from eighteen to seven, and to equip the remaining berths to modern standards. In Glasgow a proposal to put the Govan yard on a care-and-maintenance footing was temporarily shelved as Govan was in a position to take over some of the repair work formerly carried out by D. & W. Henderson. Finnieston, on the other hand, 'which continued to be a heavy drag on the Company', was partly closed, and its future was uncertain, as a progressive withdrawal of orders to Belfast did not leave Finnieston with enough of

401

a basic workload to justify carrying on.

The cash-flow crisis of 1962 was, as J.S. Baillie put it, 'mainly the result of the heavy loss which had arisen from the *Canberra* contract', although the situation was exacerbated by difficulties in obtaining repayment of loans to shipowners. As a result of action by Sir Frederick the worst of the crisis in 1961 had been averted, and more recently additional borrowing facilities had been agreed with the Midland Bank. An overdraft limit of £3.5 million had again been arranged, after a period when Government credit control had reduced it to £2.5 million. In addition the bank had agreed to finance the construction of ship no. 1653, the first methane carrier to be completed in Britain, which would not be paid for until delivery. The overall limit on bank lending would be £7 million at any one time.

By the end of November 1962 the modernisation of the Belfast shipyard was progressing well. The first of the 60-ton travelling cranes for the new enlarged slipway in the Musgrave Shipyard had been erected, and the second was well under way. In pursuance of rationalisation, slipways 4, 5 and 6 in the Abercorn yard had been closed and the cranes dismantled, apart from one which was retained to service the Hamilton dry dock. Numbers 7 and 8 slipways, however, were being retained for possible

The large floating crane with one of the liquefied petroleum gas tanks for the *Methane Progress*. The first gas carrier built by Company, she was delivered in May 1964.

future use in constructing frigates or other suitable naval tonnage. In the Victoria Shipyard the cranes were being dismantled, except for one which was to serve the steel constructional department now using the platers' shed. In the Queen's yard the hydraulic gantry on no. 3 slipway – which had been installed for the construction of the second *Oceanic* in 1899 – had been sold for scrap. The disappearance of this remarkable piece of nineteenth-century engineering was symbolic of the radical changes taking place on Queen's Island.

Attempts to develop ship-repair capacity at Belfast, to cope with the larger vessels now being built, were hampered by the lack of dry-docking space. The issue was raised with the Ministry of Commerce, with a view to obtaining Government support for an additional large repair dry dock, and the Company revived schemes first mooted early in the Second World War and repeatedly rejected in the intervening years.

The shortage of new orders continued during 1962. Andrew Weir, which had a clear policy of building in British yards and a long-standing and good relationship with Harland & Wolff, placed orders for three vessels. These brought to twenty-five the total number of Bank line vessels built at Belfast since 1953. The other two orders placed in 1962 were secured by the provision of extended credit, a sign of the rising cost of building new ships in relation to the trading receipts of both shipbuilders and shipowners. One of these orders was for a conventional but large tanker, *Rimfonn*, for Sigval Bergesen. This vessel had first been considered in 1956, but as planned in 1962 she was an 86,760-ton-deadweight ship, by far the largest tanker yet built at Belfast, and larger than any tanker previously launched from a British yard. She was the first vessel laid down on the modernised slip in the Musgrave Shipyard. The other new order, entirely novel in concept, was a 24,115-ton-deadweight ship, designed to carry liquefied methane gas from Algeria to Britain. Named *Methane Progress*, she was ordered by Methane Tanker Finance Limited, for operation by Shell, and was built with a cargo containment system licensed by Conch International Methane Limited. This pioneering vessel and her sister ship *Methane Princess*, built by Vickers-Armstrong, represented a significant advance in the long-distance carriage of liquid gas.

The results for 1962 were down on those for 1961, but were not discreditable given the conditions in which the Company was operating. The shipbuilding division at Belfast made a small profit, although the Engine Works' perfomance was poor owing to shortage of work. Govan and Scotstoun returned profits, but Finnieston and the Clyde Foundry made serious losses. The ship-repair branches had mixed fortunes, but all made profits, Southampton's returns – boosted by the Cunard repair contract – more than doubling.

The tightening-up of Company organisation continued during 1963, and the cash-flow problem envisaged in 1962 did not materialise, thanks to 'persistent and sustained efforts'. The modernisation of the Musgrave yard continued and showed good results. The only other slips still operable were two in the Queen's yard, which remained in use, and the two in the Abercorn yard retained for possible Admiralty contracts. A review of engineering capacity at Belfast confirmed that, like shipbuilding, this area suffered from inadequate demand and that a radical approach was necessary here too. The appointment of R.S. Punt to succeed C.C. Pounder as chief engine designer paved the way for new thinking. Pounder, as head of engine design, had developed during and after the war the 'coverless', single-acting, two-cycle engine with which his name was particularly linked. In the 1950s this had proved

very successful, but the power output per cylinder had been expanded to the point where it overstressed the materials available, and failure of cylinder liners became commonplace. Towards the end of his career Pounder had refused to accept the trend to poppet-valve engines and he resented his replacement by Punt, which coincided with the introduction of this detested new development. As a man concerned with originality of design, he disliked the new cost-conscious age.[1]

The rundown of the Victoria Works began early in 1963, with the closure of the smithy and the plant drawing office, and finished in the early autumn. The rationalisation of the electrical department was completed in April when the Sydenham Road factory closed, and, as a further economy measure in that department, female labour was introduced, with union approval.

In September 1963 it was decided to close Govan, Finnieston and the Clyde Foundry. The immediate reason was that the three establishments were making substantial losses. The longer-term view of Govan was that it was equipped to

Women working on wi for the stator of a large alternator in the electri works, soon after the practice of employing women on this type of work had started.

404

produce three medium-sized ships a year, and that, with no shipbuilding work in hand, it was most unlikely that profitable contracts could be obtained without modernisation, which was put at an estimated cost of £0.9 million. If needed, additional shipbuilding capacity could be provided more cheaply at Belfast, particularly as Government grants were available in Northern Ireland: it was calculated that no. 3 slip in the Queen's Shipyard at Belfast could be modernised with heavy lift cranes for £370,000 and that this project would be eligible for grant aid. Finnieston had been running at a loss for several years and if Govan were closed there would be no hope of building up general engineering work to fill the gap. At the Clyde Foundry losses had been considerable, owing to low throughput, and the best option seemed to be to transfer the existing work to Belfast where the foundry could be modernised. The Clyde Foundry had been the largest iron foundry in Europe at the time of its completion after the First World War. Its closure meant that Scotstoun – still operating profitably – was now the only remaining part of the organisation built up on the Clyde by Lord Pirrie between 1911 and 1924.

There was a certain inevitability in the closure of Govan in 1963, though it was characteristic of the yard that it made profits on its last two ships. It was really sited too far up the Clyde and its market was sagging in the early 1960s. Its land was potentially saleable, and a housing estate has since been built there. Govan had, in its day, been a highly efficient unit: it was the only Clyde yard with cofferdam gates to the berths; it had a good run into the river; and it had both able men and efficient office staff. The manager for many years, L.V. Dunlop, had been very effective and one of the most respected shipbuilders on the Clyde. He had been succeeded by 'Charlie' Simpson, a man of considerable character, an autocrat and a perfectionist, who chose as his subordinates 'men who would not pose a challenge to him, and who would relay gossip to him'. Like the Queen's Island managers, he had had a great fondness for riveting, and he had delayed the introduction of welding as long as he could. When the closure of the yard was agreed it was not publicised; instead the last manager, Angus Carrick, kept yard maintenance going and continued work on the limited-scale conversion of the yard to welding. At the very end there were favourable severance payments, reflecting employees' length of service, and the Company was successful in placing many workers, including apprentices, with other yards and works on the Clyde. The death of Govan was as becoming as its life, a proper tribute to its origin as Robert Napier's pioneering iron-shipbuilding yard in 1843.[2]

Attempts to alleviate the shortage of new construction work at Belfast by expanding ship-repair proved successful. Contracts were secured for the insertion of a new midship section in the *Santos Star* and for conversion work on the *Ocean Monarch*. Negotiations continued for the construction of a new dry dock by the Belfast Harbour Commissioners, and the hope was expressed that it would be available early in 1968.

Baillie stressed throughout 1963 the need for economy, in particular the reduction of overheads. Harland & Wolff's controlling interest in the ship furnishers and decorators Heaton, Tabb & Company was sold to Ashby Tabb Limited for £199,250: this reflected the continuing absence of new passenger liner work, as well as the need for cash. Part of the Finnieston works was also sold.

The director in charge of the Engine Works at Belfast, Ronald Newell, resigned from the board in September. Further board members appointed in November 1963 were S.H. Dunlop, general manager of the Belfast engineering works, and James

The launch party for the tanker *Texaco Maracaibo* 6 August 1964 with (left-right) Henry Moore (apprentice), J.I. Mingay, Sir Edward Beetham, Sir Andrew McCance, J.S. Baillie, Lady Beetham, J.V.C. Malcolmson, Elinora Mingay (sponsor), Lady O'Neill, Captain Terence O'Neill, Prime Minister of Northern Ireland, Eileen Baillie, Dr Denis Rebbeck, Lady McCance and Rosamond Rebbeck.

Crawford who was manager of Scotstoun. Dunlop took charge of reorganising the Engine Works.

After the lean times, 1963 proved to be a relatively good year for orders, with a Government-financed credit scheme in operation. Of four tankers ordered from Harland & Wolff two were for the BP Tanker Company and had originally been contemplated in 1956. One was a vessel of 19,989 tons deadweight, but the other, *British Centaur*, was a 64,300-ton-deadweight ship, significantly larger than had first been envisaged. Of the other two, *Edenfield* for Hunting (Eden) Tankers was of 59,000 tons deadweight, while *Texaco Maracaibo* for Texaco (Panama) Incorporated, at 88,000 tons deadweight, was even bigger than Sigval Bergesen's *Rimfonn*, and became in her turn the largest tanker built in Britain. These contracts indicated clearly that the recovery in shipping was not producing orders for the traditional cargo liners that had been the core of production in the 1950s. The trend to larger vessels was confirmed by the other two merchant-ship orders placed during the year, two bulk carriers of 41,000 tons deadweight for Buries Markes Limited, *La Estancia* and *La Sierra*. These were more than double the size of previous bulk carriers and were partly financed by Government credit.

The other two new orders were for Admiralty vessels, HMNZS *Waikato*, a 'Leander'-class frigate for the Royal New Zealand Navy, and the RFA *Regent*, of 19,000 gross tons, a large fleet replenishment ship. The order for the *Waikato* justified the decision to retain berths in the Abercorn yard.

The financial results for 1963 were also quite reassuring. The shipbuilding division at Belfast increased its profitability fourfold and the Engine Works substantially reduced its loss. During their rundown period Govan, Finnieston and the Clyde Foundry all made substantial losses, though Scotstoun increased its profit. The ship-repair establishments continued to be profitable.

The endeavours made to place the Company on a sound practical and commercial

the Musgrave yard on 11 October 1966, during the construction of the *Myrina*, with the 150-ton floating one. On the far left, work in progress on the superstructure of the *Ulster Prince*. This view shows the yard as redeveloped in the early 1960s to build large tankers.

footing continued during 1964. By March the modernisation of the Musgrave yard had almost been completed, with no. 7 slipway available for production and the last of the 80-ton Arrol travelling cranes (upgraded from the 60 tons originally envisaged) well under way. The stockyard was being reorganised and a collocator, a special type of crane for distributing plates, was being fitted in the steel preparation shop along with a horizontal shot-blasting machine. Further piling on no. 8 slipway was being carried out to enable the maximum width of vessel to be increased to 106 feet 6 inches. The Engine Works' reorganisation was under way, with the aim of providing capacity to produce fourteen diesel-engine and four steam-turbine sets annually. Cooper-Bessemer compressor production was being transferred to Scotstoun for a trial period, as that works needed a new product. Because recent contracts for generating sets and other stationary installations had been completed at a loss, this side of the Company's activities was reviewed. In the absence of a programme of design development, it was found that competition in this field had left Harland & Wolff behind, and the board resolved to abandon stationary-engine manufacture. Harland & Wolff's stationary engines had a name for sound design and first-class construction and many are still in service. The Bank of England, which installed Belfast-built engines in the generating station at its Threadneedle Street head office in the 1930s, returned to Harland & Wolff in 1965 for a new engine after the official end of

407

and on the difficulty of maintaining working tempo in the Musgrave yard if a different ship was introduced. The weight of the argument was, however, clearly in favour of cancellation, and Shell agreed. Thus, the last merchant-ship launch from the Queen's Shipyard was that of ship no. 1661, *La Sierra*, on 24 November 1965.

As the Abercorn yard had been closed after the launch of HMNZS *Waikato* on 18 February 1965, the closure of the Queen's yard finally reduced the Company's operation at Belfast to the one, modernised Musgrave yard – though the site of the Queen's yard was retained in case rebuilding became feasible. Lord Pirrie's expansionist philosophy and Sir Frederick Rebbeck's wartime investments allowed Harland & Wolff to make the transition to the new world of the 1960s fairly painlessly by comparison with other companies. It was possible to stage an orderly rundown of production to a sensibly organised unit. This was not much consolation to the men in Govan, Pointhouse and Belfast who lost their jobs, but it did ensure that the Company remained alive. The retreat from the Clyde continued during 1965. The tidal fitting-out basin at Govan was sold to Alexander Stephen & Sons, the *Daily Record* newspaper bought property at Finnieston as a site for a new printing works, and negotiations were started for the sale of the main yard at Govan and the Clyde Foundry to Glasgow Corporation.

There was more rationalisation and modernisation at Belfast, affecting both plant and workers. The ratio of helpers to tradesmen was higher at Queen's Island than in other United Kingdom yards – a legacy from the days of building on commission, when cost-control had been lax – and a reduction was now needed in order to make savings.[5] During 1965 an agreement on this move was reached with the unions after long and hard negotiations. Also at Belfast a unified plant department was set up with the aim of effecting economies in maintenance, and the replanning of the Engine Works was put in hand. In an effort to counter competition the electrical department developed new products, including brushless alternators and thermistor-controlled motors. New workshops for the ship-repair department were created in the Victoria Engine Works, in the production space left when the construction of stationary engines ceased. The shops were intended in part to service the new dry dock at the east end of Queen's Island. The Belfast Harbour Commissioners celebrated the placing of the construction contract for the dock by a ceremonial driving of the first pile, carried out by the Northern Ireland Premier. In his speech Captain O'Neill referred to Denis Rebbeck as having 'chased [him] persistently through the corridors of Stormont' to secure consent to the project. The dock was constructed by the civil engineering contractors Charles Brand and is still referred to locally as 'Brand's dock',[6] although it is chiefly known as the 'Belfast' dry dock.

Also during 1965 the all-important Burmeister & Wain diesel-engine licence agreement was renegotiated and the territorial rights for Commonwealth and Empire countries were withdrawn, leaving the sole rights for the United Kingdom and the Republic of Ireland in Harland & Wolff's hands, with J.G. Kincaid of Greenock as sublicensee. The new agreement was signed on 3 August for a term of ten years.

So far as orders were concerned, 1965 was a successful year. Through the close relationship between Harland & Wolff and John Kirby, chairman of Shell Tankers (UK), Deutsche Shell AG of Hamburg was persuaded to take over ship no. 1666, a massive oil tanker originally ordered by a Norwegian owner, then cancelled. The Shell takeover was extremely important for Harland & Wolff because the cancellation had left some 6,000 tons of worked steel on the premier berth in the Musgrave Shipyard. The ship was designed to have a deadweight capacity of 140,000 tons, but

410

The launch of the frig
HMNZS *Waikato* by
Princess Alexandra fr
the Abercorn Shipyar
18 February 1965. Thi
the last vessel to be bu
that yard.

the new owners wished to enlarge it to 190,060 tons. This could be accomplished only by sliding the completed after part of the vessel down the ways, to create more building space on the berth. The operation involved pulling the section down the slipway with drag weights, rather than allowing it to move freely under gravity. The necessary calculations were undertaken by the research department in the Engine Works design office, headed by Desmond Parker. To monitor the ship's slide, electronic instruments were used in a manner very advanced for the time. Robert Harkness, then in the research department and later an engineering director, recalls: 'I remember Desmond Parker being asked what to do if the vessel did not stop at the required position, and his answer – "Run!"' The successful completion of the operation, on 26 February 1967, was a technical triumph, but not one which it was desired to repeat.[7]

When she slid down the ways on 6 September 1967, the *Myrina*, as she was named, was the largest vessel launched in Europe and the first 'very large crude carrier' (VLCC) built in the UK. When she arrived in Hamburg for dry-docking prior to hand-over she was the largest ship ever to enter that port under the German flag. The

412

The berth ends in the Musgrave yard in Ma*
1967 with, on the righ*
hull of the tanker *Myr*
after it had been move
down the berth. On th*
is one of the five bulk
carriers ordered in 19(
the Norwegian Bulk
Carriers consortium.

The launch of the *Myr*
from the Musgrave ya*
6 September 1967. At
190,000 deadweight t*
she was the largest
European-built tanke*
her day.

Harland & Wolff employees on board were greeted by the city's mayor and bands, and were given a festive welcome. As ordered in 1965, the *Myrina* was at the upper end of the capacity of the yard, and, with the trend to larger ships seeming bound to continue, the Company for the first time seriously considered the possibility of constructing a building dry dock at Belfast. The other substantial order placed in 1965 was for five large bulk carriers for Norwegian owners, originally intended to be sister ships of 67,750 tons deadweight. This important contract, described by the *Belfast Telegraph* as 'Dr Rebbeck's Five Great Goals' and won in the face of keen international competition, was, at the time, one of the largest export orders ever secured. It was agreed after three weeks of tough negotiations in Oslo. The series production of the five large vessels proved to be ideal work for the modernised Musgrave Shipyard.

During 1965 all the main Belfast departments made serious losses, though that on the shipyard was halved. Other branches of the Company had a fairly good year. Despite intense competition, the steel construction department was fully employed and secured a valuable contract for the steelwork for Ballylumford 'B' Power Station in Co. Antrim. At Scotstoun a new order for gun mountings was received, work on Danly presses for the motor industry continued to come in and manufacture of Cooper-Bessemer compressors had started. The London works maintained its turnover and the Southampton branch improved its working results, mainly because it was carrying out the routine maintenance and annual survey work on all Cunard

The new mid-ships sec being floated into place the jumbo-ising of the cargo ship
Niceto de Larrinaga,
in the Thompson dock.
In the background is th gantry in the Queen's constructed for the *Oly* and the *Titanic*
in the early 1900s.

414

vessels based in the port. Southampton also secured contracts for modernising the Union-Castle ships *Pretoria Castle* and *Edinburgh Castle*. Between October and December 1965 the Cunard line's *Caronia* was extensively refitted at Belfast, and another notable ship-repair contract there was that for lengthening the tanker *Eskfield*. The lengthening involved using a berth in the redundant Queen's Shipyard to construct a new 70-foot midship section and inserting it into the vessel in the Thompson dock. The fitting of the new section, which increased the deadweight tonnage of the tanker by 5,200, kept the vessel out of service for only twenty-eight days. Of the ship-repair branches only Liverpool showed a decline in trade. In spite of the contributions made by non-shipbuilding activities, the Company's overall loss before depreciation rose in 1965.

The end, for the time being, of passenger-ship construction at Belfast reduced the workload for both men and machines in the woodworking department. To utilise these resources an 'industrial building department' was set up in a workshop adjacent to the Company's main generating station, with the intention of making prefabricated wood-framed houses. In 1965/6 contracts were secured from the Greater London Council for 359 wood-framed homes to be erected in three East Anglian towns. A further 307 houses of the same type were supplied to Andover in 1967 and twelve houses of a different type were despatched to the Bahamas in 1966. By 1969 the department had ceased to be viable and it was closed in a rationalisation move in that year.

There were important changes in the management of the Company during 1965. J.S. Baillie resigned as chairman on 30 June. He was succeeded by Rebbeck, who retained his managing directorship; Alan Watt was appointed joint managing director; and R.S. Punt, head of the Engine Works design and drawing offices, was at the same time made a director. With the departure of Baillie the end of an era had come. He had started work with the Company in 1913 and had worked in the London office in Lord Pirrie's time. His financial, diplomatic and selling skills had been of inestimable value to the Company, especially during the Second World War and in seeking new customers after the war. Sir Andrew McCance, who had been taking a progressively smaller part in board meetings, resigned in December 1965. With his resignation the board-level link with Colvilles Limited came to an end after nearly thirty years.[8] Because of the untimely death of Samuel Gibb, the senior shipyard manager, and Alan Watt's absence through illness, the shipyard management had to be strengthened. To achieve this, Sir Andrew's place on the board was taken from 1 January 1966 by Derek Kimber, former deputy managing director of the Clyde shipbuilders Fairfield. He also became shipyard director.

The year 1965 had been a bad one financially, but 1966 was worse. The Company, trapped by contracts which were proving unprofitable, and with serious cash-flow problems, was fighting for its existence, certainly as an independent concern and possibly as a shipbuilder. The year started off with a degree of optimism, however, when Andrew Weir placed a contract for two vessels. Ship-repair work at Belfast was expanding, with the prospect of further 'jumbo-ising' contracts, involving the insertion of new midship sections into ships to increase their capacity. This prospect temporarily justified the retention of the out-of-date Arrol gantry in the Queen's Shipyard, as the Musgrave yard berths were fully committed.

During 1966 an important concern for the Company was the possibility of a takeover by Aristotle Onassis who already had a substantial shareholding and was at the height of his power as a shipowner. Another major worry was the implication of the Geddes Report for the Company.[9] The board was also acutely conscious that the financial position was likely to worsen. Onassis had been building up an ordinary stockholding in the Company since the early 1960s, using the covers of Credit Suisse Zurich Nominees Limited and Barings Nominees Limited. These acquisitions had been carefully monitored in the Company secretary's office. By the end of 1965 the Greek tycoon's stockholding had reached a total of £1,180,032 out of £4,396,082, representing a 26.8 per cent holding of the issued ordinary capital. It had crept up to £1,241,900 by March 1966, a 28 per cent holding. The implications of the Geddes Report, clear even before its publication, were that there would be pressure on yards to amalgamate, to reduce duplication of facilities, and that failure to comply would be likely to result in the withholding of substantial Government aid to finance unprofitable contracts and to invest in new facilities. Anticipation of the report had led Cammell-Laird to approach Harland & Wolff late in 1965 about a possible merger, but options were still open in 1966.

By March 1966 the cash-flow problem had become serious. The failure of operating profit to reach expected levels had increased bank borrowing to about £2.4 million. It was not until May 1966 that the gravity of the situation – both immediately and in the medium term – became apparent. Discussing the implications of the Geddes Report and its reception by the Shipbuilding Conference, the Harland & Wolff directors decided that amalgamation with Cammell-Laird was unlikely to afford the Company any positive advantage, particularly in view of Harland & Wolff's geographical isolation. As the report itself, in paragraph 319(c), referred to the Company's special circumstances and to the support it received from the Northern Ireland Government, the board resolved to consult the Minister of Commerce for Northern Ireland, the Rt. Hon. Brian Faulkner, to ascertain what support the Company could expect if it decided to continue independently. Other implications of the report were that the industry would have to segregate product lines, and that the building of slow-speed diesels, steam turbines and machinery spares would be concentrated at four main units in the United Kingdom.[10] If Harland & Wolff could secure the position of building at Belfast all Burmeister & Wain-type engines for the UK, this could result in additional engineering employment in Northern Ireland, to the advantage of the Northern Ireland Government. The Minister of Commerce was approached and exploratory negotiations were opened with J.G. Kincaid, the Company's sublicensee.

A meeting with the Minister of Commerce and the Permanent Secretary to the Ministry was held on 3 May 1966. It was preceded by an *ad hoc* board meeting at which Rebbeck informed the directors of meetings he had had with Aristotle Onassis on 15 April, and with Terence O'Neill on 19 April. At the first meeting Onassis had said that he would be prepared to sell his holdings in Harland & Wolff at the average purchase price, in the region of 20s.3d. per £1 unit of ordinary stock. He had suggested, however, that it might not be a bad thing if he himself were to take over the Company, a move which he estimated would cost £1.5 million. He said it would be his intention to keep the present board and that he would expect a prior claim on the Company's larger building berths. At the meeting with the Prime Minister, Rebbeck had referred not only to Onassis's position, but also to the cash problems expected at the end of 1966 and the beginning of 1967. At the *ad hoc* board meeting the directors agreed as a priority to press the Northern Ireland Government to acquire the Onassis holding. In pursuance of this objective, Price Waterhouse & Company, Harland & Wolff's auditor, was commissioned to investigate the current financial

416

position and to make proposals for the consideration of board and Government.

The Price Waterhouse report, received on 28 June 1966, highlighted the possibility of the directors' incurring personal liability if they entered into contracts knowing that the Company might become insolvent. It also pointed out the basic situation, 'that the Company was unable to put its financial house in order from its own internal resources'. The report assumed that there was confidence in the long-term future of the United Kingdom shipbuilding industry: if this were not the case, then 'more radical action would have to be taken'. The board took the view that the first call for assistance should be to the Northern Ireland Government, but that a loan could at best be a palliative and would not solve the problems of reducing production costs and cutting overheads. The Price Waterhouse report made suggestions for internal action to help the immediate problem. The option of selling Scotstoun and the repair works was put forward, but the board agreed that the repair business, currently the most profitable part of the Company's operations, should not be sold to subsidise unprofitable activities.

The future of Scotstoun was then raised as a separate issue. The works was suffering from low throughput, being heavily dependent on Danly presses and Cooper-Bessemer compressors. In some respects, though, it was better equipped than the Belfast Engine Works and had better buildings. It would, in theory, have been possible to construct the new Burmeister & Wain 980-type engines there at lower capital cost than at Belfast. On the other hand, the shortage of skilled labour in Scotland was particularly acute. On balance, and especially given the poor conditions for selling an engineering works on the Clyde, it was reckoned better to hold on to Scotstoun.

The auditor's report also looked at the possibility of cancelling any contracts not contributing at least 30 per cent to establishment charges. This meant primarily the five Norwegian bulk carriers, but it was agreed that cancellation of any of these would have 'a calamitous effect on the Company's substantial association with the Norwegian market' where its standing was high, in contrast with that of other British firms. The central problem with the Norwegian vessels was the low level of productivity at Belfast, caused for the most part by labour difficulties associated with the rundown of employment. It was estimated that by the end of 1966 about 36,000 tons of steel would have been fabricated, against a target of 44,000 tons. This would make the achievement of contract dates difficult, and when the contracts had been obtained it had actually been expected that some of the ships would be completed early, bringing welcome relief for the Company's cash flow. New agreements with the Boilermakers Society and with other unions were expected to bring a reduction in the number of unskilled workers. The agreement with the Boilermakers, comparable with moves by Fairfield (Glasgow) Limited – formed to take over the Fairfield yard at Govan in January 1966 – gave the 1,500 Belfast steelworkers security of employment for a fixed period and a revised wage structure, in return for an end to demarcation between boilermakers, shipwrights, blacksmiths and structural steelworkers. A similar initiative in the Engine Works was having limited effects: the problem there was shortage of skilled workers, which was affecting the output of spare parts and thus creating difficulties with owners.

It was proving increasingly hard for all the departments to obtain skilled labour. This was partly due to the poor public image of the shipbuilding industry, but also to the Northern Ireland Government's successful policy of introducing new industries to the Belfast area: as Harland & Wolff had traditionally provided most of the skilled

engineering labour for the area, this policy drained manpower from the Company. The problem of shortage of skilled labour was a general one throughout the United Kingdom in the 1960s when diversification was being actively practised in regional economies. It has been claimed that the shortage of skilled workers was the factor which limited the achievement of high growth rates in the Scottish economy at that time.[11]

Price Waterhouse also recognised Harland & Wolff's need to reduce establishment charges and proposed the closure of areas not absolutely essential – for example the Victoria Shipyard, which was being used by the steel construction department – in order to eliminate duplicated facilities and to reduce staff.

While negotiations with the Northern Ireland Government and with Onassis were in progress, and the Price Waterhouse report was being prepared and considered, talks were held with Cammell-Laird and Vickers-Armstrong on the feasibility of amalgamation on the lines recommended by the Geddes Report. The subcommittee from Harland & Wolff, consisting of Alan Watt and W.T. Underwood, came to the conclusion that the only advantage in joining with Cammell-Laird would be for the financial assistance that might be forthcoming under the Geddes recommendations.

Aristotle Onassis (centr on a visit to Queen's Island. He is being introduced to John McCullough, a painter, shipbuilding manager Stewart Tennant. Behir Onassis is Amos Sutcli then shipbuilding direc and behind Stewart Tennant is Colin Simps Onassis's nominee on the board.

418

Rebbeck and Watt had had a meeting with representatives of Vickers-Armstrong, who envisaged the possibility of collaboration without Cammell-Laird. This seemed a more promising option, but further negotiation was deferred until a response had been received from the Northern Ireland Government.

There was a partial clarification of the situation at a meeting between Onassis, Faulkner and the Permanent Secretary of the Northern Ireland Ministry of Commerce, held in London at the end of May 1966. It was made clear that the Northern Ireland Government was not interested in acquiring Onassis's stockholding. Onassis's response was to propose a more active interest in the Company, suggesting that his London representative, C.C. Simpson, should be appointed to the board. At a subsequent board meeting Rebbeck said he felt that the influence of Onassis and his knowledge of world shipping could be of assistance to the Company, and it was agreed that Simpson should be invited to join the board, subject to the outcome of the meeting with the Northern Ireland Government.

Another issue, the possibility of an amalgamation with Kincaids, as suggested in the Geddes Report, was resolved by a meeting between Rebbeck and G.R. Rickman, chairman of Kincaids and son-in-law of the late Sir James Lithgow. Rickman was of the view that his company's future lay in alignment with the Scotts' yards and Lithgow yards on the lower Clyde, rather than in integration with Harland & Wolff. This attitude was endorsed by Harland & Wolff and negotiations were allowed to lapse.

Events did not move particularly quickly thereafter. Not until 17 August 1966 was it reported that the board's request for financial assistance had been put to the Northern Ireland Minister of Commerce and the Permanent Secretary on 30 June. Since then the Permanent Secretary had met the Board of Trade, the Treasury and the manager of the Midland Bank's Threadneedle Street office. Three options were being explored. The first was that William Swallow, recently designated chairman of the Geddes-inspired Shipbuilding Industry Board, would investigate the Company's affairs with a view to an amalgamation with Cammell-Laird and/or Vickers-Armstrong: this proposal was open to the criticism that premature disclosure of the Company's financial position would be prejudicial to a merger, and that Swallow's response could not be quick enough to save the Company. The Northern Ireland Government's view was clear, however: that to obtain a Government guarantee of, say, £3 million the Company would have to accept the need for reorganisation, and that an independent person must be able to state positively that a merger was in principle feasible. The second option was an arrangement similar to that applied in the case of Short Brothers & Harland – a straight Government takeover – but in the Permanent Secretary's view this would have been virtually impossible. The third option was that of help from Onassis. C.C. Simpson had informed Rebbeck of a message from Onassis to the Ministry of Commerce to the effect that he was prepared to make available a loan of $5 million for two years at 7 per cent interest, to be backed by a bank guarantee, on condition that he was allowed to buy the repair works of his choice and to pay for it in Harland & Wolff stock. This was quite unacceptable to the board.

As the first option, or some version of it, seemed the only practicable one, its implications were explored. Reorganisation was likely to mean partial reconstruction of the board, with a shift in control away from the existing directors. Because of the Government's credit squeeze, there would be problems in additional borrowing from the Midland Bank – necessary to allow legal trading to continue – unless, as seemed unlikely, the Treasury was to grant a dispensation. Though the decision of the Minister of Commerce on a financial guarantee could not be forecast, negotiations about a basis for amalgamation with Vickers-Armstrong and Cammell-Laird continued. The two English-based companies wished to begin by instituting a complete sharing of information and projections for joint policy. Harland & Wolff's view was that the form of physical integration should have priority over financial and other matters.

Into this already complex situation a further variable had been introduced through a visit to Belfast on 27 July 1966 by David Brown, chairman and managing director of the David Brown Corporation, and John Rix, managing director of Vosper Limited, a member of the David Brown group. Though the intention was to talk about the Southampton works, which Brown offered to buy, he had informally floated the idea of taking over the whole Harland & Wolff organisation, and a further meeting was planned.

Though most of the time at the board meeting of 17 August 1966 was taken up with these major policy issues, the board also accepted the resignation of S.H. Dunlop as a director, and appointed C.C. Simpson, Onassis's nominee, to take his place. The management consultants P-E Consulting Group had reported on the Engine Works and were commissioned to report on establishment charges. R.S. Punt, who had been the director responsible for the Engine Works design and drawing offices since June 1965, became engineering director, taking on the additional responsibility of engineering production.

The uncertainties which had dominated corporate thinking since the spring were resolved in September 1966 when an offer of financial assistance was received from the Ministry of Commerce. The gist of the offer, as accepted by the board, was that the Ministry of Finance would guarantee a loan of £1.5 million to be provided jointly by the Northern Bank and the Belfast Banking Company, for up to nine months. This was to be secured by a floating charge on all Harland & Wolff's assets. The Company agreed to appoint a nominee of the Minister of Commerce as financial controller, with the position of deputy chairman. In addition the Ministry was to control membership of the board, and, to this end, all directors with service contracts had to relinquish them without compensation. The Company was also to produce proposals for reconstruction which might involve a merger with other shipbuilders. The temporary loan would be replaced, as soon as legislation would permit, by a longer-term loan of up to £3.5 million: the first £1.5 million of this would be used to redeem the initial loan and the remaining £2 million would be advanced in instalments.

The provision of the temporary loan gave the board respite from its immediate worry about the legality of continuing to trade, but it was still necessary to explore methods of 'reconstruction'. On 5 October 1966 the board discussed the views of the Ministry of Commerce on the implementation of the Price Waterhouse report and on plans for reconstruction, and a joint committee with the Ministry was set up to make specific proposals. On the same day Rebbeck reported on a further informal talk he had had with David Brown. Brown wanted to engage in merger discussions, with a view to creating a repair monopoly at Southampton involving the David Brown group's interest in Thornycrofts and Vospers. The possibility of a David Brown takeover of Harland & Wolff had again been raised, but it still seemed nebulous. Another possibility was the use of part of the Queen's Island works for expanding production of David Brown tractors. Brown intended to put forward his

420

formal proposals on 14 October 1966.

Further moves by the David Brown Corporation were considered at a board meeting on 25 October 1966. By then Brown had consulted the Ministry of Commerce and had indicated that his corporation was thinking seriously of bidding for control of Harland & Wolff. The board decided to engage J. Henry Schroder Wagg & Company as financial advisers and further negotiations with Brown were to be conducted through this firm and the Company's solicitors. Meanwhile Vickers-Armstrong had come to the view that the possibility of a merger with Harland & Wolff should be pursued without the agreement of Cammell-Laird, though no further firm progress had been made.

In November 1966 Norman McCallum, formerly director in charge of land-engine sales, and manager of the London office since July 1965, retired from the board in order to make way for the financial controller required by the Ministry of Commerce. The full implications of this appointment became apparent on 16 November when the Minister of Commerce notified the Company that J.F. Mallabar was his nominee as financial controller. As Mallabar insisted that he could not exercise proper financial control without being chairman, Rebbeck was required to stand down and became deputy chairman. This very forcibly brought home the effective transfer of control from the board to the Ministry. Mallabar was the senior partner of J.F. Mallabar & Company, chartered accountants: he had been on the board of Plessey from 1946

Sir John Mallabar, chairman of the Company from 1966 to 1970, talking Jimmy Easton, a retired plumber.

to 1962 and in 1964 had been brought into Ruston & Hornsby, the Lincoln-based engineering concern, to rationalise that company's operations. It was his success in this role which recommended him particularly as 'company doctor' for Harland & Wolff. He was the chairman of Davey, Paxman & Company, the Bergius-Kelvin Company and British Indestructo Glass, and a director of several other companies.

Mallabar faced a difficult problem when he took over the chairmanship and the financial direction of Harland & Wolff. There was, despite the efforts of Baillie, Rebbeck and their colleagues, a legacy of conservative, inward-looking management. Financial control, never a strong point, had been tightened but still lagged behind good practice of the time. Losses were mounting and productivity, though improving, was poor. Mallabar found that on the first nine months of 1966 there was a trading loss of £1.6 million before depreciation. The total debt to the banks was about £3.6 million and there were accounts for about £2.5 million due for payment. The P-E Consulting Group's report on establishment charges indicated that a significant reduction in the payroll was needed. The report commented, 'If there should be any difficulties with the unions at that stage, the Company must be prepared to face up to the consequences, since it was essential that the "pruning" exercise, which was fully accepted as a prerequisite of the securing of the Company's future, should be carried out as quickly as possible.'

As a sign of the change of control, the last board meeting for 1966 was held in the offices of Ruston & Hornsby in London, where the new chairman demonstrated his style. He opened by saying that the discussions at the previous meeting 'had lacked a sense of urgency and had failed to get down to bedrock'. He stressed that the situation facing the Company was so serious that, in view of the strictly limited time available, it must be tackled at once with 'energy, ruthlessness and even violence'. He proposed restructuring senior management and recommended that executive directors should take a 10 per cent reduction in their salaries, as a bargaining counter with the unions. Other moves which he suggested included the establishment of work-study methods in the Engine Works and the imposition of tighter budgetary control. Shipyard director Derek Kimber advised that more effective supervision was needed and that ineffective managers and foremen would have to go. Mallabar commented that he was in favour of a labour force short of actual needs – and having to work overtime – on the grounds that this produced a sense of urgency and purpose.

The need for the directors to take action became even clearer in December 1966 when Price Waterhouse showed that an increase in losses for 1966/7 of about £1.6 million would create a cash requirement of £2 million in addition to the £3.5 million Government loan and the Midland Bank overdraft. Against this, the paying-off of about 800 employees, which was in progress and would save at least £700,000 in a full year, seemed rather ineffective. Other ways of raising money were still being pursued. Claims were being made against the Admiralty for *Fearless*, *Waikato* and *Regent*, on the basis that their specifications had increased in complexity; and the disposal of Scotstoun and of the Abercorn Works in Belfast was being actively considered.

The financial trauma of 1966 and the gloomy forecasts for 1967 were in contrast with the solid technical achievement. On 7 January 1966 the drilling rig *Sea Quest*, of American design, was successfully launched, the first time a rig structure had been launched complete. Each of her three legs rested on separate slipways, making the launch a nerve-wracking occasion. *Sea Quest* was one of the largest rigs then built and her launch was a real triumph, especially for the staff of the ship-design office

422

headed by the Company's naval architect, Rupert Cameron, and including future chairman John Parker. It was also a great occasion for Belfast, and those who were among the spectators, lining in their thousands along the banks of the Musgrave channel, remember the excitement and expectation beforehand, the heart-stopping wobble as the rig slid down the ways and the jubilation when she was safely in the water. It had been hoped that the successful completion of the *Sea Quest* would lead to other orders, but, as had been the case with a similar rig built by John Brown at Clydebank, it proved difficult to integrate rig-building with shipbuilding. The rolling of steel plates for the legs disrupted production of steelwork for ships, and the balance of work between trades was markedly different to that in conventional shipbuilding.[12]

A less spectacular, but equally important, achievement during the year was that of a record throughput of steel. This was made possible by better management and by the sense of urgency which the threat to the yard engendered, and was accomplished in spite of relatively poor steel-handling facilities.

423

important contract undertaken during the year was the conversion of the *Anita Dan*, a 2,641-ton cargo ship strengthened for use in ice, into an ice-patrol ship for the Royal Navy. The complete refit of this vessel took fifteen months, from the end of March 1967. This vessel, renamed HMS *Endurance*, is still in service, and played a prominent part in the Falklands War of 1982.

Apart from the successful negotiations on the Esso vessels and the building dock, which had the most profound implications for the Company, Mallabar and his board could congratulate themselves on having contained the operating losses for 1967 in all divisions. The loss on shipbuilding was down only marginally, but losses on the electrical department, the Engine Works and Scotstoun were substantially lower. Ship-repair was again the most profitable side of the Company's activities. The trading loss before depreciation was down to £619,833, almost a sixth of that in 1966.

The building-dock project dominated the Company's activities and thinking during 1968. Although commitment to the scheme was now complete, it was still necessary to arrange Harland & Wolff's share of the necessary capital. By March an agreement had been reached in principle with the Ministry of Technology and the Shipbuilding Industry Board that a loan would be granted on certain conditions: that engine-building be separated from shipbuilding; that the management structure be strengthened; and that the Company accept the idea of merging or associating with

An early stage in the construction of the building dock on 5 Au 1968. In the backgroun excavation of the bed o Musgrave channel un way, and, in the foreground, the placin underfloor drainage material.

other shipbuilding firms. These conditions were accepted, with the proviso, made
clear to the Ministry of Technology, that a merger would make sense only if benefits,
rather than burdens, would accrue. The loan was finally approved in June 1968, when
a temporary sum of £3 million was obtained from the Shipbuilding Industry Board,
on the basis that the Company would create loan capital of £8 million which would
be issued to the Shipbuilding Industry Board, to be secured by a floating charge on
Harland & Wolff's assets. The final conditions of the long-term loan were not agreed
until 1969.

In the meantime, however, work on the building dock and the steelworking
facilities was progressing. Wimpey was the main contractor for the dock structure,
but the intermediate dock gate and the steelwork of the block assembly shop were
fabricated and erected by Harland & Wolff. The Company also built some of the
steelwork – including the cross-span – for the Goliath crane, the prime contractor
for which was Krupp-Ardelt, the most experienced company in the field. J.H.
Crossey, the director responsible for the electrical department, was put in charge of
the project from 1 March 1968. In August 1968, even before the first section of the
dock was available for use, fabrication of steelwork for the first Esso tanker began,
and completed weldments (steelwork subassemblies) had to be stored at several
locations in the yard. During 1968 work on the dock itself was concentrated on

427

excavation, piling and concreting.[16]

The strengthening of management stipulated by the Shipbuilding Industry Board was taken further during 1968. Edward McKelvey, brought by Mallabar from British Indestructo Glass, was appointed financial director in May. In October J.R. Edwards was also made a director, replacing G.C. Kennedy. Edwards was an experienced industrialist, a former managing director of the British Motor Corporation and a member of the board of Joseph Lucas (Industries) Limited. He had played a major part in the merger of the Pressed Steel Company with the British Motor Corporation in 1965 and had also been actively involved in the negotiations leading to the formation of British Leyland. C.C. Simpson was appointed joint deputy chairman along with Edwards – a sign of the growing influence of the Onassis connection. Another indication of this influence was the appointment of Simpson to the board of Short Brothers & Harland on the resignation of J.S. Baillie from the Shorts board in March 1968. Simpson joined Mallabar on the Shorts board, the latter having been appointed a director in December 1967. Watt and Rebbeck, joint managing directors of Harland & Wolff, had their positions formalised, with Watt assuming full responsibility for production and Rebbeck for marketing.

A limited amount of rationalisation was carried out during the year. The last part of Finnieston was sold and the liquidation of D. & W. Henderson and A. & J. Inglis was completed.

During 1968 the world demand for shipping was buoyant, owing to the continued closure of the Suez Canal, and United Kingdom shipbuilders were able to capitalise on the situation, following the devaluation of the pound in 1967. For Harland & Wolff this resulted in the receipt of four orders for bulk carriers in 1968, a pattern of ordering which not only reflected the general trend in shipbuilding, but also confirmed Alan Watt's view that specialisation was the way to reduce costs. Of the four vessels, two were relatively modest in size, *La Pampa*, for Buries Markes, and *Bulk Eagle* for the Kriship Shipping Company, of 24,800 tons deadweight each. The other two ships were larger: the *Sydney Bridge*, for the Bowring Steamship Company, was of 58,600 tons deadweight and the *Rudby*, for the Ropner Shipping Company, was a bulk ore carrier of 105,500 tons deadweight, of the same dimensions as the enlarged Norwegian bulk carriers *Skaufast* and *Aino* (two of 'Dr Rebbeck's Five Great Goals'). *Rudby* was intended for long-term time charter with Norwegian Bulk Carriers. During the year a letter of intent was also received from the Onassis group for three tankers of 255,000 tons deadweight, one of which was subsequently cancelled. These vessels were of similar dimensions to the Esso tankers but were totally redesigned and became the first vessels for which the metric system was adopted for dimensions, calculations and measurement. Thereafter this practice became standard for all shipbuilding work making Harland & Wolff the first major yard in the United Kingdom to go fully metric. Two of the Norwegian bulk carriers, *Thara* and *Skaufast*, were launched ahead of schedule, *Thara* on 14 May, six weeks in advance, and *Skaufast* three weeks early on 9 August. At the signing of the contract for these vessels in 1965 the Harland & Wolff sales team had been presented with a Japanese ceremonial sword, accompanied by a comment on what was to be done in the event of late completion! *Skaufast* was completed two months ahead of delivery date, on 29 October 1968, and, in her finishing stages, was the first vessel to use the new 'Belfast' dry dock. She was the largest dry bulk carrier built in Europe at that time. 1968 also saw the last launch from the Queen's Shipyard when HMS *Charybdis* went down the ways on 28 February.

There was a further improvement in working results during the year. The loss incurred on the shipyard was reduced to £899,948, although that on the Engine Works almost doubled, due largely to shortage of work. Of the repair works, only Southampton did well. The poor results for Liverpool and London were attributable chiefly to the decline in the trade of these ports. The Company's overall loss before depreciation was down by almost a third.

One of the most significant factors affecting Harland & Wolff in the late 1960s had little to do with internal problems. This was a time when communal division in Northern Ireland seemed to be declining: the new industries which were attracting skilled labour away from the Company were bringing to Belfast a prosperity that reduced the economic basis of tensions between Protestants and Catholics. Terence O'Neill's Government, pledged to ease sectarian bitterness, attracted criticism both from ultra Unionists and from Nationalists who felt that promised reforms, particularly of the electoral system, were not being implemented. In 1967 the Northern Ireland Civil Rights Association began a campaign to seek universal, instead of ratepayer, suffrage in local elections. At first the civil rights movement and reaction to it was relatively low key, but tension escalated during 1968. On 5 October that year police broke up a banned civil rights protest march in Londonderry and rioting followed. Later that month there were further protests in Belfast and a pattern began to emerge of civil rights protests and angry reaction from ultra loyalists. The heightened tensions created by these developments were disquieting.[17]

Civil unrest was one of the factors that made 1969 a year of mixed fortunes for Queen's Island and was probably the reason for increased absenteeism. The completion of the building dock was a major preoccupation and, as might have been expected with such a large project, problems did occur. In February 1969 difficulties were being encountered with the anchorage of piles in what was, after all, reclaimed land. The completion of the Goliath crane fell behind schedule and this delayed work on the Esso vessels. It had been intended to place the first fabrications for ship no. 1676 in the dock at the beginning of March, but it was not until 1 May that the first weldment was in position. Even then a temporary gantry had to be built and the cumbersome procedure was adopted of jacking weldments off a trailer onto the temporary gantry, off the gantry onto a trailer in the dock, and off that trailer into position. The first 500 feet of the bottom of the ship were put together in this way before the first 60-ton cantilever crane was available in late May. Before assembly of the vessel had begun, about 16,000 tons of steel had been fabricated and stored in the yard. After the Goliath crane was commissioned, at the end of June, weldments were assembled at the head of the dock into blocks weighing up to 750 tons for bottom sections and 450 tons for deck sections. Because the yard had no previous experience in lifting such heavy assemblies, the sections had to be tested against model experiments to gauge the effect of the stresses of lifting, and extra stiffening had to be built in. With experience, it proved possible to design sections which did not need extra stiffening.[18]

At the end of 1969 the building dock was still unfinished, though the second 60-ton crane was commissioned in November. Not only were construction deadlines slipping, but costs were rising: in October 1969 it was reckoned that the cost of the dock would be almost £16 million, some £2.5 million in excess of the estimate. The difficulties encountered in keeping to schedule in the construction of the dock and its support systems had direct repercussions on the shipbuilding programme. The delay in starting to build the first of the Esso tankers, with the accompanying

stockpiling of weldments, was a cause for concern. Perhaps more important factors
in reducing productivity were bans on overtime working and a degree of 'working
without enthusiasm', especially among steelworkers. Tensions in Belfast due to civil
disturbances were also influencing performance. By October 1969 the net loss for
the year was running at £970,000 over budget and the completion dates for ships nos
1676, 1678 and 1679 had been deferred, causing the Company to incur financial
penalties.

Now that Harland & Wolff had capacity – both in the Musgrave yard and in the
building dock – to construct larger vessels on an unprecedented scale, the Company
attracted great interest from potential customers. United Kingdom shipbuilding was
booming, with world demand for shipping at a high level. The world order book
increased by 57 per cent between 1967 and 1969. The orders actually booked with
the Company during 1969 were for five large bulk carriers and for two supertankers.
Three of the bulk carriers were of 108,000 tons deadweight, similar to the *Aino* and
Skaufast. Two of them, for Norwegian owner Arthur H. Mathiesen, subsequently
had their depth increased to give them a deadweight tonnage of 116,000. The third

carrier, *Iron Somersby*, was for the Ropner Shipping Company. During 1969 discussions continued with the Onassis group on the details of the contract for VLCCs. There were frustrating delays in obtaining agreement from Onassis on subcontract components, including the main turbines, the choice of which rested with the owner. As time went on Harland & Wolff realised that, in the light of experience with the Esso tankers, the prices quoted for the Onassis vessels were no longer realistic. Although the prices were revised before the contracts were signed on 19 December 1969, they inadequately reflected rising costs and, as a result, Harland & Wolff made substantial losses on both vessels.[19]

During 1969 there were many other approaches about possible orders. In October, Sir John Mallabar – knighted in the New Year's Honours list – wrote to Barry Barker, director of the Shipbuilding Industry Board, to tell him that there had been thirty-three inquiries about large ships between May and September. In this heady atmosphere of burgeoning demand, the Company, in collaboration with the Ministry of Technology, initiated a design study for tankers of 400,000 to 1,000,000 tons. Sir John informed Barker that a number of 'highly profitable contracts for newbuildings,

431

particularly of tankers' were having to be turned away owing to shortage of space in the yard. He then went on to suggest that the building dock's steelworking capacity of 120,000 tons of steel a year would be inadequate by 1973, and that facilities for fabricating 200,000 tons of steel would then be required. In such a concept there were certainly echoes of Lord Pirrie's pre-First-World-War expansionist projects. The current situation differed, however, in the major respects that there was no tied market for ships, and that competition was keeping profit margins low.[20]

It was not only shipbuilding that suffered from uncertainties. A strike in the steel construction department, affecting the delivery of steelwork for the building-dock project, also damaged the profitability of that department. Its poor performance was compounded by competition from Great Britain for the limited Northern Ireland market and by the slowing-down of new investment in the Province – partly

The Canadian Pacific liner *Empress of England*, being repaired by Harland & Wolff at Liverpool in October 1969. A new bow section is being hoisted into position.

because of the political unrest. In consequence, the Company decided to close down the department, though this decision could not be implemented until the work for the dock project had been completed. Scotstoun showed no immediate prospect of a return to profitability, so, on receipt of a purchase offer of £800,000, it was resolved to close this works too. Scotstoun shut down in September, with a loss of £183,000 on the year to the end of August.

The structure of the senior management changed relatively little during 1969. Derek Kimber left the board in October to become director general of the Chemical Industries Association and in November the Shipbuilding Industry Board nominated as a new director H.E. Jones, former Permanent Secretary to the Ministry of Commerce for Northern Ireland. The intention was that he would monitor the use of the Shipbuilding Industry Board's loan. Jones had been involved in the negotiations leading to the first loan of £1.5 million in 1966 and to the appointment of Mallabar, and so he was thoroughly familiar with the problems of the yard. At the time of his appointment he was industrial development adviser to the Ministry of Commerce.

The results for 1969 were most discouraging, although in making a judgement on them account should be taken of the difficulties associated with the construction of the building dock. The shipyard's losses returned to the 1967 level, at just over £2 million, and the Engine Works lost nearly £0.5 million, due to a failure to achieve a satisfactory throughput. Elsewhere the position was equally bleak. Of the repair branches, London made a loss, and profits at Liverpool and Southampton were down: all three works were suffering not only from the decline of traditional shipping, but from the effects of a prolonged seamen's strike. The overall working loss before depreciation, including estimated prospective losses, was over £8 million: it had become clear that rising costs would result in substantial losses on fixed-price contracts.

In the summer of 1969 after fierce street battles in parts of west Belfast the Prime Minister of Northern Ireland requested Westminster to deploy troops in the city. This was done but sporadic rioting and shooting continued in both loyalist and republican areas. In June 1970 a new element in the conflict emerged when the Provisional IRA launched a bombing campaign. Violent incidents increased steadily throughout 1970 and were to reach a pitch in 1971. Apart from the trauma and pressures of the 'Troubles', there was also an unhelpful belief among the workforce that the Northern Ireland and Westminster Governments could not afford to let Harland & Wolff close. At a board meeting in March 1970 Sir John Mallabar cited the failure to implement productivity agreements as a major reason for mounting losses, but the influence of external factors should not be disregarded. In January the new fabrication facilities were four to six weeks behind schedule. The price of bought-in ship components was also rising rapidly. In his statement to the annual general meeting the chairman referred to the need for increased throughput; to the necessity of finding ways of encouraging people to work harder and longer; but also to the need to renegotiate contract prices.

At that annual meeting Sir John resigned as chairman: the reason given was that he had 'now disposed of the matters which called for his personal attention'. His chairmanship was regarded, within the Company, as a controversial one. As a non-shipbuilder, he had appeared to threaten the ethos of Queen's Island, and as a Government nominee he had represented a loss of face to some board members: nonetheless his contribution was important. He introduced better accounting systems, saw through the construction of the building dock and prepared the way for expanding the steelworking facilities to match the capacity of the dock. He had, however, been unable to solve the continuing problems of Queen's Island which were, arguably, insoluble at that time. He was replaced as chairman by J.R. Edwards.

On 5 March 1970 Amos Sutcliffe became shipbuilding director in succession to Derek Kimber. Sutcliffe, who had started his career at Queen's Island in 1936, came to the board from the Ministry of Technology, where his responsibilities had included commissioning designs of large vessels. On 31 May 1970 Rebbeck resigned as joint managing director, to devote himself to his other business interests, which were substantial. He was chairman of John Kelly Limited, the Belfast firm of coal importers; vice-chairman of the Iron Trades Employers Insurance Association Limited and of the Iron Trades Mutual Insurance Company; and a director of the Royal Bank of Scotland and of the Shipbuilding Corporation Limited, as well as other concerns. His contribution to Harland & Wolff has been somewhat overshadowed by the image of his father, and by the financial problems which overtook United Kingdom shipbuilders during the 1960s. Nevertheless, his period in office as managing director and later also as chairman saw the development of the facilities at Queen's Island to build large vessels. His technical knowledge and personal charm made him many friends among shipowners, creating valuable connections for Harland & Wolff.[21] Excluded by his father from high-level decision-making within the Company, he had spent much of his time serving as Harland & Wolff's representative on technical and industrial committees. He was, in particular, a Belfast Harbour Commissioner and with his departure from the Company the long-established representation of Harland & Wolff on the Commission came to an end. Rebbeck continued in his role as a Commissioner until September 1985 and his period in office combined with that of his father totalled fifty-one years of uninterrupted family service to the harbour authority. Following his resignation from Harland & Wolff, the organisational structure of the Company was revised. Rebbeck's post of managing director (marketing) was eliminated and Alan Watt became sole managing director. Four new divisions, each with a sales organisation, were set up from July: these were shipbuilding, marine engineering, ship-repairing and electrical. Personnel management, formerly dispersed, was assigned to a central department, as was estimating. Ship-design, research and development were put under Rupert Cameron, the chief naval architect, and J.H. Crossey was confirmed in his position as director in charge of new shipyard facilities. These changes reflected the approach to shipyard organisation favoured by the Geddes Report. In an effort to improve throughput and morale in the yard, Edwards, as the new chairman, proposed 'communications' meetings, a shift system for steelworkers and an improved pay structure for foremen.

Such initiatives, welcome though they were in many respects, were overshadowed by continuing problems. The building dock was completed on 23 March 1970 but the new steelworking facilities fell behind schedule, retarding the efforts to build up steel throughput. In spite of these setbacks, the first vessel to be constructed in the new dock, the *Esso Ulidia*, was floated out successfully on 11 May 1970 in an operation which took several hours – in contrast to the dramatic and tension-filled moments of the conventional slipway launch.

The worldwide sellers' market for ships which had characterised 1969 continued during 1970. The Company received an inquiry from the Onassis group for fifteen Liberty-ship-replacement general cargo vessels of 15,000 tons, ten ore carriers of 38,000 tons, and four tankers of 80,000 tons, and the Admiralty invited Harland & Wolff to tender for a type-42 'Sheffield'-class destroyer. Alan Watt, however, recommended that the Company confine its output to tankers of the 250,000–300,000-ton class and bulk carriers of the 100,000–125,000-ton class, 'as our facilities are specially designed for this type of work. Series building is, in my opinion, the surest method of getting a return for our money.' The logic behind this concept was that a mix of ships slowed down output, with a resultant escalation in costs; specialisation avoided this problem and had the additional benefit of streamlining ship design and the preparation of tenders. As Watt put it, 'This is not a change of policy, it quite simply is a policy. We have never had a policy before.' Given the nature of the market and the limited number of berths available, this certainly made sense at the time.

The backing of the Labour Government, which had been generously forthcoming through the Shipbuilding Industry Board and the Northern Ireland Government, had given the Company a first-rate facility in the form of the building dock, but, as anticipated, the financial results during the period of its construction proved poor, and in 1970 a cash-flow problem emerged. To counter this the board adopted a wide range of measures. The Company's claim for additional work on the RFA *Regent* was settled by the Admiralty, but approaches to Esso, Onassis and Bowring for increased payments on fixed-price contracts were only marginally successful. The Northern Ireland Government helped by agreeing in June 1970 to postpone repayment of the loan capital, but not of the interest. In July 1970, however, the Ministry of Commerce agreed not only to defer interest payment, but also to advance payment of an investment grant of £900,000.

Orders for two more VLCCs were received during 1970. These were tankers of 268,450 tonnes deadweight, for Y.K. Pao's Worldwide Shipping Company, of Hong Kong. It was intended that they would be operated by single-ship companies, the Hendale Navigation Company and Broughton Navigation Company, but the Broughton Company was subsequently bought by Shell Tankers (UK) Limited before the construction of the second tanker had started.

The reasonably assured supply of capital made available to the Company by the Labour Government at Westminster was jeopardised when the Conservatives won the general election of June 1970. The new Government, headed by Edward Heath, adopted a policy of withdrawing support from what it considered to be 'lame ducks' – a label for industries suffering from cash-flow problems and having no identifiable medium-term future. The new strategy was outlined to the Company at a meeting with Nicholas Ridley, Joint Parliamentary Secretary at the Ministry of Technology, who made it clear 'that it was not the Government's intention to continue to support British shipbuilding and any assistance offered to Harland & Wolff must therefore be regarded as temporary'. Despite this, a second grant payment of £3.5 million was agreed in August 1970, together with a programme of further assistance covering the period up to 1974. These measures were taken in recognition of the view that 'because of the local difficulties, Harland & Wolff was a special case'. Nevertheless, the Government explicitly wished to be relieved of continued responsibility for financing the yard.

The most immediate alternative to the continuation of direct Government support appeared to be the leasing of the yard to other interests. Two serious lease offers had emerged by the beginning of September 1970. The major party involved was Aristotle Onassis, whose new interest in a takeover had arisen after a visit by Roy Bradford, Minister of Commerce for Northern Ireland, to the shipping tycoon's New York office. It was reported that Bradford had expressed the view to one of Onassis's assistants

C.C. Simpson, the Onassis nominee, to resign. No more was heard of the proposed Onassis takeover. Indeed, after January 1971 the proposals to amalgamate the Company with other yards recommended by the Shipbuilding Industry Board also ceased. From this point onwards Harland & Wolff's existence as an independent unit and a 'special case' was tacitly accepted.

Amid the turmoil there was still room for humour. Shortly after Edwards had departed, Watt, as acting chairman, was presiding over a naming ceremony function at a time when the media was giving some prominence to James Martin, an Ulsterman who had invented the ejector seat. Before Watt began his address to the assembly of invited guests, he stood up, looked at his chair, then commented that he just wanted to check that he had not been sitting in an ejector seat.[23] Such were the uncertainties of life at the top.

In operating terms 1970 showed a distinct downturn on 1969, mainly accounted for by the shipyard, whose losses rose substantially. The Engine Works and ship-repair departments at Belfast improved their position, while the Liverpool, Southampton and London establishments recorded their usual mixed results. During the year it was finally decided that these three works should be sold off.

The politico-economic uncertainties of 1970 were not repeated in 1971. With the Northern Ireland Government and the Shipbuilding Industry Board providing substantial financial support, the directors' freedom of manoeuvre was severely circumscribed. Restructuring of the board was a high priority, as Alan Watt was in his sixty-fifth year and Herbert Crossey and Rupert Cameron were to retire at the end of February 1971.

With the departure of Crossey the Company lost a loyal and devoted servant. As manager of the electrical department he had been responsible for its modernisation and then for its rationalisation, and more recently he had been in charge of the building-dock project. He is still remembered at Queen's Island as a great character, a hard man with a heart of gold. He was very well organised and conscientious and spoke his mind to colleagues and to unions: both took it well, recognising his fundamental honesty and kindness. Though trained as an electrical engineer, he was able to turn his hand to almost anything.[24]

Rupert Cameron had been responsible for the design of some of the yard's most striking and beautiful ships. He broke away from the chunky look of Harland & Wolff vessels in the 1920s and early 1930s, and introduced a more streamlined hull form.[25] Throughout the Company's serious financial problems there was never any doubt that vessels designed by Harland & Wolff were good, economical and had their own aesthetic integrity.

The decade 1962 to 1971 was a traumatic one, not just for Harland & Wolff but for British and world shipbuilding as a whole. During the 1950s Britain's share of the world output of merchant-ship tonnage had declined from over 40 per cent to only 16 per cent: by 1970 this was down to just over 6 per cent. The period had been characterised by intense competition from Sweden, Japan and West Germany. Demand for passenger liners and cargo liners, already tailing off at the end of the 1950s, dried up almost completely and the most rapidly expanding markets were for tankers and for bulk dry-cargo vessels, all of increasing size. The total tonnage of oil shipments expanded annually by 10 per cent between 1960 and 1970, and bulk carrier shipments rose from 73 million tonnes in 1960 to 508 million tonnes in 1970. The development of such trading patterns favoured shipyards which were experienced in series production of standard ships, and new yards purpose-built for

BULK CARRIERS BUILT AT BELFAST
1958–84

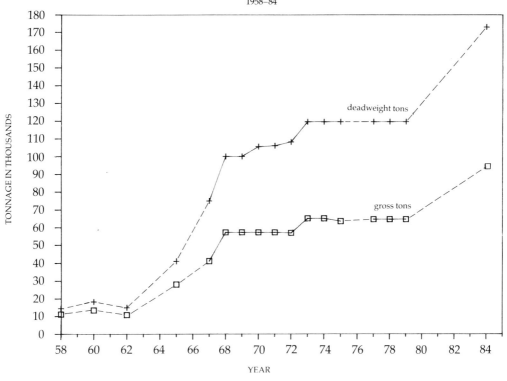

TONNAGE IN THOUSANDS

deadweight tons

gross tons

YEAR

TANKERS BUILT AT BELFAST
1941–77

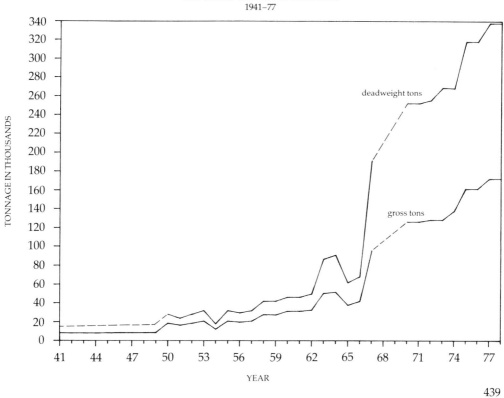

TONNAGE IN THOUSANDS

deadweight tons

gross tons

YEAR

such production. In the case of yards of the first type, such as Kockums in Sweden, existing management structures and labour relations agreements were readily adaptable to the construction of larger vessels. New yards, especially in Japan, were able to profit from the experience of others, and established from the outset administrative structures and ideally laid-out facilities for the rapid production of large, basically simple vessels.[26]

As was the case with other major British shipbuilders, Harland & Wolff, restricted by the physical layout and facilities at Queen's Island and by the lack of finance for capital investment, found itself in intense competition for orders. The limited amount of modernisation possible had to be scheduled so as to allow continuity of production. The skills of management and workforce and the administrative structures suited to 'traditional' shipbuilding were not always appropriate to the series production of large vessels. The conventional economic wisdom that shipbuilding was an 'old' industry, due to be phased out in favour of new, light industry, was a commonplace fallacy in Britain and a belief not conducive to investment in major capital projects.[27]

At first Harland & Wolff, like the rest of the industry, had to tailor its response to changed circumstances to suit its limited finance and the physical restriction of berth size. Under the guidance of men like J.S. Baillie, Denis Rebbeck and Alan Watt, the Belfast yard became the leading British builder of large vessels, an achievement that formed a basis for the major Government-funded creation of the Queen's Island building dock, the only one of its size in the United Kingdom and the largest in the world at the time of its construction.

Government support for shipbuilding was slow to develop to meet the crisis of the early 1960s, but in 1963 the Shipbuilding Credit Scheme was introduced, and the Labour Government, elected in 1964, favoured assistance to shipbuilders, largely as a means of sustaining employment. The Geddes Report, commissioned in 1964, was published in 1966 and its recommendation that companies should be merged on a regional basis, with substantial Government aid, was crystallised in the Shipbuilding Industry Act of 1967. The thinking embodied in the Geddes Report was that Government-aided modernisation of the industry would allow it to become competitive without further assistance.[28] This was the logic behind the Northern Ireland Government's aid to Harland & Wolff from 1966 onwards, and the appointment of J.F. Mallabar was made, in the first place, to monitor the use of that aid, and to ensure the management changes deemed necessary for it to be effective. The Mallabar era saw not only the creation of the dock but also the laying of foundations for expanding steel throughput to realise the yard's full potential.

By 1971, however, it was clear that Geddes had only partly worked. Mergers on the Tyne and Wear, the upper and lower Clyde and in east Scotland had mixed success. An order boom in the industry in the second half of 1968 caused a degree of complacency amongst management and men. As most of these orders were taken on a fixed-contract-price basis, inflation in materials and wages costs led, through uncontrollable losses, to the liquidation of Upper Clyde Shipbuilders in 1971. Harland & Wolff also suffered on this count. The Conservative Government, which took office in 1970, was markedly less sympathetic to shipbuilding than its predecessor, but was committed to the maintenance of employment in Northern Ireland: had it not been, Harland & Wolff could have suffered the same fate as Upper Clyde Shipbuilders. The appointment of a new chairman and chief executive was a priority consideration in the drive towards the elusive goal of profitability, with

An aerial view of the building dock (foreground) on [De]cember 1970, with the [b]uild-up shop, the low [buil]dings of the panel line the new stockyard, on the right.

the hope of reaping some reward for all the investment made since 1966.

If the 1960s had been difficult for the management of Harland & Wolff, they had also been traumatic for the workforce, who had seen their workplaces transformed or indeed removed altogether, and had watched traditional skills fall out of favour and jobs disappear. The challenge to ingenuity involved in designing and constructing large numbers of small vessels was considerable, and the work varied: welded bulk carriers and tankers were, by contrast, dull and comparatively unlovely. Yet there could still be pride in building large vessels, as exemplified by the *Myrina*, and in embracing new technology, as in the *Methane Progress* and the *Sea Quest*. The traditionally good labour relations in the yard stood up well to the strains of changing conditions and not least to the civil unrest in the Province. Throughout this very testing time the attitude of the workforce was creditable.

Table 13.1
Issued capital 1962-70

	4½ per cent cumulative preference stock	Ordinary stock
	£	£
1962-70	2,600,000	4,396,082

Table 13.2
Profit and loss 1962-70

	Gross profit/(loss) for year before tax and depreciation	Net profit/(loss) per published accounts after tax and depreciation	Distribution (transfers to/from reserves and dividends)	Balance carried to following year
	£	£	£	£
1962	837,330	123,595	138,977	553,732
1963	905,506	144,800	138,977	559,555
1964	(118,361)	(327,516)	136,229	95,810
1965	(1,353,798)	(1,932,909)	(1,881,262)[1]	44,163
1966	(3,560,766)	(4,146,152)	(4,101,989)[2]	—
1967	(619,833)	(1,156,391)	(1,063,046)[3]	(93,345)
1968	(450,628)	(755,024)	—	(848,369)
1969	(8,031,351)	(8,329,770)	—	(9,178,139)
1970	164,431	(181,227)	—	(9,359,366)

Notes
1 £1,950,000 transferred from General reserve
2 £4,160,489 transferred from General reserve
3 £1,063,046 transferred from General reserve

Table 13.2a (cont. on p. 443)
Profit and loss before depreciation: by cost centre 1962-70

	BELFAST						
	Shipyard	Engine Works	Victoria Works	Ship-repair dept[1]	Structural steel dept[1]	Electrical dept[1]	Industrial housing dept
	£	£	£	£	£	£	£
1962	152,915	(765,673)	14,370	—	—	—	—
1963	660,059	(75,286)	4,924	56,297	69,396	—	—
1964	(887,417)	202,389	—	34,116	84,949	—	—
1965	(381,294)	(345,156)	(8,415)	119,584	101,341	(64,693)	—
1966	(2,035,055)	(321,152)	—	89,736	141,851	(162,252)	(52,882)
1967	(2,067,532)	(60,426)	—	43,196	(79,283)	(73,156)	18,091
1968	(899,948)	115,185	—	114,041	(118,052)	(21,560)	(116,778)
1969	(2,066,389)	(494,963)	—	(20)	30,303	(56,717)	(8,199)
1970	(3,282,895)	(378,332)	—	303,181	18,715	(31,386)	(117)

Notes
1 Before 1963 profit and loss for some cost centres was not shown in the detailed balance sheet.
( ) = Loss

Table 13.2a (cont.)

Profit and loss before depreciation: by cost centre 1962-70

Govan	Finnieston	Clyde Foundry	Scotstoun	Liverpool	Southampton	London
£	£	£	£	£	£	£
223,615	(75,951)	(115,652)	47,327	42,367	379,383	18,565
(72,622)	(64,103)	(144,144)	80,822	111,698	246,305	181,290
(6,205)	(14,823)	(54,971)	(547)	88,023	342,120	185,009
(8,810)	16,603	(32,672)	39,847	99,037	223,068	94,790
(1,470)	(7,545)	(10,247)	(139,388)	110,444	202,615	140,380
—	—	—	(47,209)	91,507	208,275	91,759
—	—	—	(366,279)	47,630	170,021	(86,574)
—	—	—	(214,355)	38,719	42,664	(173,626)
—	—	—	(6,635)	(13,228)	119,941	(80,334)

Table 13.3

Fixed assets 1962-70

FREEHOLD AND LEASEHOLD LAND, PROPERTY AND BUILDINGS

	Additions	Depreciation and sales	Total
	£	£	£
1962	226,749	164,307	4,741,187
1963	72,561[1]	174,085[1]	4,679,485
1964			4,093,110
1965			3,804,497
1966			3,070,008
1967			2,914,729
1968			5,678,297
1969			8,799,004
1970			10,905,843

MACHINERY, PLANT AND TOOLS

	Additions	Depreciation and sales	Total
	£	£	£
1962	1,091,859	556,240	5,208,963
1963	684,132[1]	556,621[1]	5,351,385
1964			3,754,988
1965			3,629,541
1966			3,562,893
1967			3,219,244
1968			2,973,604
1969			2,509,319
1970			2,576,284

Note

1   In 1964 and subsequent years the accounts are presented in a way that vitiates comparison with earlier years.

Table 13.4
Reserves 1962-70

	Capital reserve		General reserve
	£		£
1962	5,190,658		3,350,000
1963	5,631,968		3,350,000
1964	3,656,523[1]		3,350,000
1965	3,779,372[1]		1,400,000[2]
1966	—		1,063,046[3]
		£	
1967		(93,345)[4]	
1968		(848,369)[4]	
1969		(9,178,139)[4]	
1970		(9,359,366)[4]	

Notes
1 After deducting statutory grants
2 £1,950,000 transferred to profit and loss account
3 Balance in Capital reserve transferred to General reserve, then adverse balance on profit and loss account deducted
4 Adverse balance on profit and loss account

Table 13.5
Overdrafts and loans 1962-71

	Overdraft with Midland Bank	Government loans	Shipbuilding Industry Board loans
	£	£	£
1962	2,563,022	—	—
1963	1,307,818	—	—
1964	1,859,942	—	—
1965	2,333,308	—	—
1966	2,235,135	500,000	—
1967	1,459,522	3,500,000	—
1968	437,155	3,500,000	2,100,000
1969	—	3,500,000	8,000,000
1970	—	3,500,000	8,000,000
1971	—	3,500,000	8,691,000

Note
In addition, smaller accounts were operated for day-to-day needs.

Table 13.6
Bills receivable discounted 1962-70

	£
1962	3,176,000
1963	2,450,000
1964	2,285,000
1965	300,000
1966	50,000
1967	—
1968	—
1969	—
1970	—

Table 13.7
Investments 1962-70

	Investments in subsidiary companies	General investments
	£	£
1962	204,230	280,272
1963	16,775[1]	280,272
1964	173,363[2]	280,272
1965	2,161	280,272
1966	986	100,000
1967	1,799	183,333
1968	1,799	50,000[3]
1969	1,799	50,000
1970	2,000	50,000

Notes
1 Writing off debts
2 Net assets after realisation of larger part of subsidiaries
3 Nominal value of Short Brothers & Harland shares

Table 13.8
Number of employees at Belfast 1962-70

1962	12,582
1963	11,372
1964	11,681
1965	13,019
1966	11,454
1967	10,049
1968	9,007
1969	9,274
1970	10,007

14
CHANGING HANDS AT THE TILLER
1971–85

The timing of the appointment of a new chairman and a new managing director was determined by the passing of legislation by the Northern Ireland Government in June 1971, enabling it to provide additional support to Harland & Wolff.[1] Much care was taken in the choice of suitable people. The man chosen to be chairman, Viscount Rochdale, had chaired both the National Ports Council and the Government Committee of Inquiry into the shipping industry which had produced a thorough and perceptive report in May 1970. He had extensive experience in other industries and, at the time of his appointment to Harland & Wolff, was deputy chairman of West Riding Worsted & Woollen Mills Limited and a director of Williams & Glyns Bank.

Even before Lord Rochdale had been chosen, however, a new managing director had been selected. Given the relatively poor performance of British shipbuilding since the mid-1950s, it was not altogether surprising that the Government should look abroad for a chief executive, employing as head hunters the London-based firm of Heidrick & Struggles. The man chosen, Iver Hoppe, was the managing director of Odense Staalskibsvaerft A/S shipyard in Odense, Denmark. A lawyer by training, he had come to shipbuilding late and had applied his penetrating logic to an industry ready at that time for an analytical approach. Hoppe, like Lord Rochdale, had become a banker, and he was a director of Den Danske Landmansbank and the Danmarks Nationalbank. On the appointment of Lord Rochdale and Hoppe in August 1971, Alan Watt became deputy chairman, a post he retained until his retirement in September 1975. Two new board members appointed in 1971 were Christopher Gladstone and John G. Robinson. Gladstone, a chartered accountant, was a partner in J. Henry Schroder Wagg & Company. His appointment coincided with the departure of D.H. Templeton, who had been appointed financial controller in December 1970, and the post of financial controller disappeared. John G. Robinson was the nominee of the Shipbuilding Industry Board, and, as ex-technical director of Shell International Marine, had acquired an invaluable knowledge of shipping. The final board change, at the end of the year, was the appointment of Douglas L. Cooper, the Company's chief accountant, as financial director, to replace E.J. McKelvey, financial director since 1968. These changes to the board broadened the base of the Company's administration.

The new regime took over as the building-dock project neared completion. The coming-on-stream of the new steelworking facilities was expected to eliminate the accumulated delays on the ship-construction programme. However, this aim was not realised, partly because of an overtime ban imposed by the 1,800 steelworkers in May 1971 in pursuance of a wage claim. The action was stepped up in June when the steelworkers voted for a 'withdrawal of co-operation'. Hoppe took office in the middle of this dispute and regarded it as a very serious threat to the Company's recovery efforts. It cast a shadow over his first few months in office and it was 27 September before normal working was resumed.

Even before the building dock had been completed, however, Hoppe had revived

Iver Hoppe standing in front of the building dock in November 1973.

the proposal, envisaged in 1969 under Sir John Mallabar, to expand steelworking capacity from the nominal 120,000 tonnes a year of the building-dock project to 200,000 tonnes. The intention was firstly to make the Company viable and secondly to maintain, and if possible to expand, employment. The estimated increase in the labour force, of up to 2,000, was certainly likely to appeal to the Northern Ireland Government. The initial development of the expansion idea was entrusted to AB Svenska MEC, a firm of Swedish consultants whose preliminary report estimated that the net cost of the scheme to the Company would be about £20 million, allowing for Government grants, and would in fact lead to the creation of an extra 4,200 jobs. On the strength of this report the board commissioned a detailed study from the consultants.

447

Pouring molten iron into mould in the foundry at Queen's Island in the mid-1970s.

As the Company expected losses to continue for several years ahead, the fact that it could even contemplate raising capital on this scale is an indication that there had been a radical change in political attitudes. This change had been apparent also in the Northern Ireland Government's June 1971 legislation.[2] The purpose of the change in law, as outlined by the Ministry of Commerce, was 'to put the Company in a position of commercial viability . . . Once this has been done there will be no question of either the United Kingdom Government or the Northern Ireland Government accepting responsibility for making good any deficiency in the Company's resources should it get into financial difficulties in the future.' The mechanism for the provision of aid was complex. A Government shareholding of £4 million was to be taken, representing 47.6 per cent of the enlarged issue of ordinary capital, with the objective of preventing a takeover of the Company after substantial expenditure of Government money. The remainder of the share capital was held by various private and institutional investors. A grant of £300,000 was to be made, together with funding to cover losses of around £10 million as assessed in October 1970. Repayment of the existing £3.5 million loan was to be rescheduled. No clearer statement could have been made of the importance attached to the retention of the Queen's Island shipyard as a major sector of the Northern Ireland economy.

Another very welcome development for the Company was the conclusion of negotiations with Shell International Marine for a series of very large crude carriers (VLCCs). When the contract was signed on 12 May 1971 the order was for five vessels, each of 256,000 tonnes deadweight. Even at that stage, however, a change in size was contemplated, and in October 1971 the size of the individual ships was raised to 313,000 tonnes deadweight and the number reduced to four. This was by far the largest order ever placed with the Company.

After the resolution of the steelworkers' dispute productivity improved rapidly. In an effort to increase output still further, the former production manager of the highly successful Swedish yard of Kockums, Eric Hellström, was brought into the consultants' team for the first quarter of 1972. Hellström had been at Kockums from

1945 to 1969 and had helped to create the facilities which enabled that yard to float out a VLCC every forty working days in 1972. In May 1972 Hoppe dismissed Amos Sutcliffe, director in charge of ship production, and appointed in his place Ronald Punt, who had been in charge of the Engine Works. At the same time Eric Hellström was recruited from the consultants onto the Company's staff to take charge of the programme to expand the yard's production facilities. In November Hellström was appointed to the board, in place of John G. Robinson. Though Sutcliffe had failed in the short term to improve productivity, the good groundwork he had laid made it possible to build up production after his departure.

As the tempo of activity quickened at Queen's Island, the winding down of the repair branches continued. Part of the London works was sold to the ship-repairers Green & Silley Weir. The North Woolwich works was closed on 30 June 1972 and its machinery and plant were auctioned. Prolonged negotiations took place on the disposal of Liverpool, though no firm agreement was reached during the year. Meanwhile, in Northern Ireland the political 'Troubles' had reached a new height, and in world headlines Belfast meant violence. It was hardly surprising that shipowners, seeing media reports of trouble in the city, were reluctant to place ship-repair contracts with the yard, and this resulted in a serious loss of work.

In March 1972 the continuing political problems of the Province, and in particular Nationalist concern about the eight-month-old policy of internment without trial, led Edward Heath's Conservative Government to present Brian Faulkner, Prime Minister of Northern Ireland, with an ultimatum. Among other terms, the Government demanded the phasing-out of internment and the transfer of responsibility for law and order to Westminster. Faulkner was unable to accept these demands, so on 24 March the Northern Ireland Parliament was prorogued by Westminster and all its legislative and executive powers were transferred to the United Kingdom Parliament. William Whitelaw, then leader of the House of Commons, was appointed to the newly created office of Secretary of State for Northern Ireland.[3] For the first time in fifty years Harland & Wolff would not have a provincial government to deal with or to look to for support.

The vigorous initiatives taken by Hoppe began to show results during 1972. Productivity began to climb: in the week ended 24 June 2,441 tonnes of steel were prepared for fabrication, an achievement which was in line with the planned throughput of 120,000 tonnes a year. This rate of steel preparation, however, created problems at the fabrication stage, owing to a shortage of steelworkers. An adult training scheme, for men from outside the yard, began feeding new steelworkers into the production line, and by the end of September 1972 about 100 were at work. By November there were over 900 employees in training. This injection of new labour helped to increase the weekly steel-fabrication throughput to over 2,000 tonnes.

A dock strike and delays in deliveries of steel from the British Steel Corporation, combined with the internal industrial disputes already mentioned, prevented the full effect of the expansion drive being realised. It was estimated that during the year more than twenty-five full production days were lost, half of them because of the dock strike: this loss of production, it was suggested, was equivalent to more than half of a 260,000-tonne tanker. Stoppages of work arising from Company employees' taking part in organised political marches and rallies, both inside and outside Queen's Island, accounted for about a quarter of the time lost and, as Hoppe stated, 'had it not been for the restraining influence of the majority of shop stewards the total time lost would have been substantially more'. In the nature of things, the workforce in the shipyard could be neither indifferent to nor apart from the politics of the community in which it lived, but there was no recurrence of the sectarian violence of the 1920s on the shipyard premises, and a voice of moderation was heard from Northern Ireland trade-union officials and leading shop stewards such as Sandy Scott of the Boilermakers Society. Violence did strike at the yard itself in November 1972 when the IRA planted two bombs. One caused minor damage to the offices, destroying part of the photographic collection and other documents. The second bomb was placed under one leg of the Goliath crane. The weight of the crane confined the effects of the explosion, preventing the collapse of the dock wall, though blast damage restricted the movement of the crane at the seaward end of the dock, causing two weeks' delay in the hull-building programme of ship no. 1686, one of the Onassis VLCCs.[4]

Despite the problems encountered in stepping up production, the project to increase steelworking capacity to 200,000 tonnes a year went ahead. The programme, named P200, was scrutinised by a second firm of consultants, who agreed that it made sense. The estimated cost rose to £39 million, but the potential benefit both to the Company and to Northern Ireland was such that the project speedily received Government approval in principle from Westminster, confirmed by Secretary of State William Whitelaw on 4 May 1972. The Government's financial package to fund the scheme provided for a grant of 30 per cent of expenditure, together with an initial loan of £5 million and a further loan not exceeding £8 million. The first loan was to be repayable over thirty-three years, with each instalment free of interest for five years. These favourable terms were made on conditions that showed clearly the Government's thinking . . .

> The Company shall take all reasonable steps consistent with the efficient conduct of the Company's business and undertaking to ensure that its entire business and undertaking will be carried on in such manner as may best be calculated to promote and maintain employment in Northern Ireland; in particular, the Company shall use its best endeavours, to the satisfaction of the Ministry, to employ at its undertaking in Belfast not fewer than 13,000 employees at 31 December 1973 [when the project was to be complete] and to maintain such level of employment thereafter.

The positive effect of this substantial Government support was countered by two unexpected adverse developments. Firstly, the reorganisation of the nationalised British Steel Corporation by Sir Monty Finniston was causing further serious delays in the delivery of steel. By October 1972 there was a shortage of 9,500 tonnes, forcing importation of steel from Sweden and Japan. Even more importantly, before Harland & Wolff had concluded pay negotiations with its workforce, at a time when shipbuilding wage rates were advancing all over the United Kingdom, the Government imposed a wages standstill, thus preventing the Company awarding a sought-for bonus to its employees, and stimulating unrest in a labour force which had been working hard to meet new production targets. The problems arising from the pay freeze, which seriously affected progress on P200, were still unsettled by the end of 1972. This situation was particularly unfortunate in view of the efforts of management to ensure good labour relations at a time of social tension. It emerged during 1972 that the Company's record for industrial disputes 'compared very favourably' with the records of other large UK shipyards, and absenteeism, a growing problem, was also lower in Belfast than in mainland Britain, running at just over half

the industry's average.

With the prospect of a substantial increase in the Company's labour force, following the approval of P200, and realising that the traditional hinterland of east Belfast was unlikely to be able to supply the number of workers needed, the board decided to restate the Company policy of non-discrimination on sectarian grounds. This was endorsed by shop stewards in the yard.

Throughout 1972 intensive effort was put into securing profitable new work for the yard. World demand for ships continued at a high level, with the market most active in container ships, refined-products tankers and VLCCs. The upward trend in the size of VLCCs was continuing, but at a slower rate. Vessels of about 330,000 tons deadweight were the largest being contemplated. Though it became clear during the year that Harland & Wolff's prices were higher than those of Japanese yards, the combination of investment grants and favourable credit terms in the financial packages devised by the Company offered attractive incentives to shipowners. Contracts for two bulk carriers of 117,850 tonnes deadweight were placed by two members of the Norwegian Bulk Carriers consortium. These vessels were identical to ship no. 1691, *Mount Newman*, for Furness Withy, ordered in 1969. Of a number of inquiries for VLCCs, one very significant order was firmed up during 1972: this was for six steam-turbine-driven tankers, each of 333,000 tonnes deadweight, for Maritime Fruit Carriers, for delivery over the period 1975/7 and to be owned nominally by single-ship partnerships. These vessels were extended versions of the Shell tankers already under construction at Belfast. With a total value of about £150 million, the Maritime contract was believed at the time to be one of the largest merchant marine orders ever placed in the world. It was made possible through a Government guarantee, via the Ship Mortgage Finance Company, under the 1972 Industry Act.[5] This was just the kind of order which made P200 realistic, rather than a pipe dream; though, because it was a fixed-price contract, it was a hostage to fortune.

If 1972 was a year of optimistic planning and good relations with Government, a honeymoon period for the new management, 1973 was something of a nightmare. Perhaps the most serious of the many difficulties Hoppe had to face was the fact that pay levels for the Belfast labour force continued to lag behind those of comparable workers in mainland British shipyards. This problem stemmed from the imposition of the Government pay freeze before Harland & Wolff wages settlements had caught up with those in other yards. In pursuit of a pay increase, steelworkers imposed an overtime ban, reducing productivity below target levels. The continuation of the pay freeze,[○] part of Government anti-inflationary policy, made this a long-drawn-out dispute. Under the Government's Price and Pay Code, the only way to give the workforce an increase in wages was through a productivity deal, but the steelworkers' leaders refused to discuss such a proposal or to pass it on to their members. Hoppe's response was to threaten the closure of the yard unless the steelworkers resumed normal working by 30 March 1973. The deadline passed and, loath to implement the threat, Company representatives met officials of the Boilermakers Society at the office of the Shipbuilders' and Repairers' National Association in London. The general secretary of the union tried to persuade the Harland & Wolff employees to return to normal working, but without success. Even an order from the national executive council of the union was ignored. For Hoppe this was the last straw. He reckoned that since 1968 the steelworkers had lost a whole working year, and £1 million in wages. 'No shipyard could progress or even survive under such a handicap,' he declared.

Notices of termination of employment were given to all steelworkers on 6 April 1973. Over 600 left on 13 April, 300 went on 20 April and the remaining 1,400 on 4 May. The dispute dragged on through May – despite the intervention of William Whitelaw – causing the Company to consider subcontracting VLCC hull sections to other yards. Not until 11 June 1973 did the steelworkers return, on the basis of an agreement that involved the application of work-study methods, the recruitment of more apprentices and the employment of more 'dilutees' – men who had not served their time in the steel trades. However, still faced with the inflexibility of the Pay Board, appointed by the Government to adjudicate on wage agreements, the yard's workforce remained discontented. By August 1973 the seriousness of the situation was beginning to become more obvious. Not only had there been a loss of production, but the workforce had declined by 150 as a direct result of the dispute, and no dilutees had been recruited since February.

At the beginning of September 1973 it was still hoped that a build-up to normal working patterns could be achieved by the end of the month. During discussions it was evident that the Secretary of State fully appreciated that the pay policy was continuing to prevent the restoration of reasonable equality between earnings at

Belfast and those in Great Britain. But, instead of offering to rectify the wages disparity, the approach adopted was to try to impress upon the steelworkers the critical position of the Company. Dan McGarvey, general secretary of the Boilermakers, was approached and the Government spoke to the Confederation of Shipbuilding and Engineering Unions, making the point that, at the present rate of production, the Company could not meet its contractual commitments and that jobs were genuinely at risk.

The financial situation was in fact deteriorating to the point where, according to the Companies Act and Stock Exchange rules, the Company might not be able to continue to trade. Whitelaw's view was that 'we were all in it together' and he said he would do what he could to help, though it was essential that he should be given time. He asked for a practical report, 'tending towards pessimism rather than optimism'. In the meantime the position worsened, as a second-stage payment promised by Hoppe to the outfitting trades was ruled out by the Pay Board. The unions were naturally unhappy, and imposed an overtime ban.

There was no improvement in the pay anomaly position before the end of 1973, but, probably in recognition of the serious position of the yard, the work rate did begin to improve. The Boilermakers Society proved more co-operative, agreeing to the introduction in September 1973 of dilutees and in October of two-year, late-start apprenticeships for eighteen-year-olds. A new problem now surfaced, however – that of a labour shortage in Belfast. In November the managing director reported that the workforce was about 800 below target and that other companies in the Belfast area were having difficulty in recruiting skilled engineering workers. As Harland & Wolff's plan for a return to profitability was based on expansion of the workforce and throughput, this shortfall was a matter of some concern. It was compounded by the high proportion – 70 per cent – of adult trainees who had left the Company before entering full employment. Though there seemed no clear way to improve this position, a working party was set up, involving officials of the Department of Manpower Services, to determine the true availability of labour in the Belfast area.

The fear that it might become impossible to trade legally hung over the Company from early September 1973. The view emerged that if the Government agreed to make finance available in 1975/6, when current contracts would be completed, the Company would be entitled to continue trading, despite the negative net worth (excess of loans over assets) in the balance sheet. With Whitelaw's support, the Government approved in principle the provision of finance, conditional on an independent review of the Company's capital investment programme, on some response from the labour force – with a recognition of what was at stake – and on a review of the Company's plans for dealing with labour relations. The Government's package, put forward in December 1973, consisted of replacing the accumulated debt of £10,262,000 by an issue of £8.1 million of preference shares, convertible at par into £1 ordinary stock units, and a guarantee of £10 million as needed for not less than three years from the second half of 1974. On this basis the Department of Trade and Industry was able to issue letters of offer of finance to Maritime Fruit Carriers for the VLCCs – for which conditional agreements had been signed on 1 December 1972 and the yard's internal instruction to commence work had been issued in February 1973. The delay in reaching a satisfactory deal was a consequence partly of the very large amount of credit which had to be provided against financial and charter-hire agreements, but also of the effects of the continuing dispute. The only new order placed during 1973 was for another standard 117,850-tonne-deadweight bulk carrier for a Norwegian owner. The failure of other orders to materialise was, in some respects, a consequence of the lack of confidence engendered by the steelworkers' dispute, but was also an indication of the problems of financing contracts for very large, high-value vessels. The shortage of orders did not augur well for the P200 programme, which required a steady, large throughput to justify the capital investment.

Though not apparent in firm orders for Harland & Wolff, the world market for large vessels continued buoyant for most of 1973.[7] Against this background, the yard began design work on a series of VLCCs of 500,000–750,000 tonnes deadweight and on smaller vessels, partly or wholly owned by the Company, of 50,000–80,000 tonnes deadweight, including black-products tankers for heavier refined oils. Hoppe's analysis of the market was that as the United States' dependence on imported crude oil increased, offshore oil terminals would be created, accelerating the ordering of VLCCs. As the oil companies were channelling investment into new refineries and terminals, they would tend to leave transportation more and more to 'independents' like Maritime Fruit Carriers. By the autumn of 1973, however, the prospect of orders for vessels of 500,000 tonnes and upwards had receded and the Company's marketing effort was geared to VLCCs of up to 330,000 tonnes, bulk carriers of 118,000 tonnes and black-products carriers of 63,000 tonnes. Onassis was interested in four 333,000-tonne VLCCs but 'negotiations could not be concluded until current production problems looked like being resolved'.

In October 1973 the Company was considering converting the Belfast dock – the Belfast Harbour Commissioners' dry dock, built for ship-repair work – into a building dock for black-products carriers. That it was possible to contemplate this was a consequence of shipowners' reluctance to send vessels for repair so long as civil unrest persisted in Belfast. As the year ended, it became apparent that demand for oil tankers had peaked. The raising of oil prices by the Arab oil producers in 1973, which had a dramatic effect on all major oil consumers, inevitably hit the demand for large crude carriers. At first there was a pause in ordering, but by December 1973 the harsh reality had to be faced. Hoppe's report to the board emphasised that product carriers of 60,000–70,000 tonnes deadweight would be most in demand in the next decade, suggesting again that part-ownership by Harland & Wolff would attract finance for about a dozen vessels. As for VLCCs, he cautiously commented that, 'although following a settlement of the Arab oil dispute by perhaps April 1974 the VLCC market could gradually recover, it was unlikely that it would return to its recent "dizzy" heights. There could even be cancellation of some of the existing VLCC orders placed abroad.' In other words, the bubble had burst.

Concern about labour relations, finance and orders dominated corporate thinking throughout 1973, but other developments were proceeding. Work on P200 began to show results. The erection of a new shop to manufacture boilers for the Maritime Fruit Carriers vessels was started. Another scheme discussed at some length was the establishment of a factory for the production of medium-speed diesel engines of Sulzer design, with predominantly Catholic west Belfast as its likely location. Discussions on this possibility continued for some time but the idea was eventually dropped. The Southampton works was sold to Vosper Thornycroft as a going concern and negotiations on selling the lease of the London works were begun. Mallabar's aim of concentrating all Harland & Wolff operations in Belfast was close to realisation.

The year 1973 saw little change in the composition of the board. Christopher Gladstone, of Schroder Wagg, left in May and was replaced by Niall Charlton, a

former finance director of the Mond Division of ICI. In July personnel director James
Crawford resigned his post. Crawford was a fine engineer and had worked hard
through a particularly difficult period to maintain good industrial relations in the
Company. The confrontation with the steelworkers – which, for Hoppe and the
union leaders, also took on the character of a personal conflict – had, however,
escalated to a level beyond Crawford's control. In May 1972 Ronald Punt was
appointed assistant managing director, in an effort to lighten the load on Hoppe, to
whom virtually all departmental heads reported; and further load-sharing was
introduced in September 1973 with the appointments of Douglas Cooper and Eric
Hellström as assistant managing directors, responsible respectively for the
commercial and facilities areas. In October 1973 Leo Curran, the head of the
engineering division, was appointed a director. Below board level, an interesting
move in the light of later developments was the temporary transfer of John Parker,
then general manager, sales and projects, to a position as a 'trouble shooter',
investigating problem areas in ship production.

The winter of 1973/4 has gone down in history as the 'winter of discontent', when
Edward Heath's Conservative Government took on the National Union of
Mineworkers in a prolonged struggle over what was seen as an inflationary wage
claim.[8] This conflict resulted in power cuts and a three-day working week for much
of British industry. Though Harland & Wolff was not affected directly by power cuts,

455

delays in the delivery of bought-in materials did cause disruption both to ship production and to the P200 programme. Shortage of steel, a problem in 1973, continued to give concern in 1974. Although there was some improvement in labour relations, the wage disparity with mainland shipyards continued, affecting staff as well as blue-collar workers. Draughtsmen in particular were leaving in significant numbers – fifty-nine had left during 1973 and only ten had been recruited – and the consequent delay in the supply of working drawings further reduced productivity. The difference in pay between foremen and the men they supervised was also a cause for concern: in many cases foremen were paid less.

The shortage of manpower became acute in the spring of 1974. The continuing low level of wages in the yard encouraged men to move to other firms in the Belfast area, including Government-sponsored businesses. It became increasingly clear that the Government had been too optimistic about the effects of introducing new industry into the area. It proved virtually impossible for Harland & Wolff to recruit labour from west Belfast, and east Belfast was quite incapable of supplying more workers to the yard. As the production facilities created by P200 were dependent on an increased workforce, this manpower deficiency posed a serious problem and bit deeply into the morale of the managers who were making strenuous efforts to pull the Company out of its difficulties.

Iver Hoppe, whose commitment to the modernisation of the yard was absolute, spent much of his time trying to find orders to fill the berths in the Musgrave yard and to secure continuity of work after the Maritime Fruit Carriers contract had been completed. VLCCs were not in demand, but in January 1974 Hoppe was able to announce an order from Furness Withy for two products carriers of about 66,000 tonnes deadweight, and to reveal that negotiations were in hand for two similar vessels for Scandinavian shipowners. Other owners were also interested in joint-venture ships of the same type. During this period of new-found optimism John Parker – who had, with Hoppe, been actively involved in seeking orders worldwide – was appointed managing director of Austin & Pickersgill, the Sunderland shipbuilders, from June 1974. He was succeeded in the critical post of general manager, sales and projects, by Kenneth W.J. Ruddock.

Before the interest of shipowners in products carriers could be developed further the fortunes of the Company again became entangled in politics. The immediate cause was the General Election called by Edward Heath in February 1974 to secure a mandate for his policy of opposing the wage claims of the miners and others. The resulting situation at Westminster, in which neither major party had an overall majority and the Liberals held the balance, was resolved by the formation of a Labour government under Harold Wilson after Heath failed to negotiate an alliance with the Liberals. These events had no immediate impact on the Company because on 1 January 1974 power in Northern Ireland had been handed over to an elected Assembly and an Executive at Stormont. The transition had come about following agreement on power-sharing between Unionists and Nationalists and the establishment, through the Sunningdale agreement, of a new 'Council of Ireland'. However, on 28 May 1974, the Executive was forced to resign after an upsurge of political unrest and a fortnight-long provincewide stoppage of work, organised mainly by the Ulster Workers' Council, an alliance of loyalist organisations which had rejected Sunningdale. The Westminster Government resumed direct rule, with Merlyn Rees as Secretary of State and Stanley Orme as Minister of State.[9] Merlyn Rees's support for the Company was to prove vital in securing continuity of

Government assistance.

The UWC strike and its aftermath brought problems for Harland & Wolff. Although the involvement of the Company's workforce in the stoppage was sporadic, the political manoeuvres before the fall of the Executive produced a Government statement, published on 22 May 1974, to the effect that a committee of Ministers chaired by Prime Minister Harold Wilson had decided to make no further financial aid available to the Company while the strike in Northern Ireland continued. The statement said that the Government would not let the shipyard go under, but that it felt 'now was the wrong time to be giving it taxpayers' money'. Fortunately, the labour force did not react to the statement. As the Company minutes record, 'Most employees were apparently more concerned with their own private and domestic difficulties, including travelling to and from work, arising from the current political strike.' The general response to the Government's apparent threat was that it was a matter for the board, who obtained the legal opinion that if they could not get firm written assurances from Government they would have to petition for the winding-up of the Company. On 24 May, four days before the fall of the Stormont Executive, Lord Rochdale, Hoppe and the Company's legal adviser met Stanley Orme and John Hume, Minister of Commerce for Northern Ireland in the power-sharing administration. At this meeting Orme 'expressed a high regard for the Company and said he wanted to see it flourish', but no written assurances were given at this stage. When an official letter did arrive, on 13 June, some parts of it proved most unsatisfactory from the Company's point of view. Because existing contracts were already loss-making, the Government was imposing a twelve-month moratorium on new ship orders, to allow for a reappraisal of the Company's activities generally. During this period only Government-approved capital expenditure was to be allowed, and the Company was required to work out a sound system of labour relations. The Company would have to plan on the assumption that there would be no significant expansion of the labour force, and that increased output would be dependent on improved productivity. Attracting labour from other employers was ruled out but it was resolved that existing efforts to facilitate recruitment and to upgrade the unskilled unemployed from areas such as west Belfast would be vigorously pursued.

The Company's response to the Government's letter was to assert that the basic problem affecting labour relations and productivity was the restriction on wages imposed by the Pay Board. Merlyn Rees replied in turn that the Government would look favourably on a Company request for relaxation of pay control. He added that Government, the workforce and the Company's management were all in trouble. The immediate consequence of these discussions was a Government assurance on 20 June 1974 that Harland & Wolff could continue to trade normally, but just six days later Orme restated the Government's position of 13 June. The twelve-month stipulation was not to be publicised, but Hoppe pointed out that shipowners already involved in contract negotiations would have to be informed of the restrictions; that to secure improvement in productivity there would have to be freedom to negotiate wages; and that the steelworkers would have to be persuaded to accept modern working practices. It emerged in July 1974 that the Government's stated position had been the outcome of a Cabinet decision, so there were difficulties in revising it; Orme did, however, give an assurance that if the Government decided not to continue to support the Company the rundown would be conducted responsibly. He also stated cryptically that, in the context of proposals to nationalise shipbuilding, the Secretary

457

of State for Industry had given him an assurance that there was 'a ring round Harland & Wolff'.

The situation facing the Company was critical. Owing to slippage in the building programme, the forecast losses for 1974/9 had risen substantially from the February 1974 estimates. Contracts which in total had been expected to make a profit of £10 million had now become unprofitable, and it was reckoned that the negative net worth of the Company was nearly £32 million. Further losses would be incurred if, as seemed possible, the British Steel Corporation exercised its right to amend its fixed-price supply contracts because of the reduction in the Company's requirements for steel. The board agreed that 'in the present situation the board of a normal company would have only one course open to it, but as the Government did not regard the present situation as normal it should be asked how it proposed to tackle it'. The options appeared to be the appointment of a receiver, nationalisation or a massive injection of permanent capital. Douglas Cooper, the finance director, advised Hoppe on 2 July that it was essential that the Government give guarantees to existing creditors, otherwise the Company would be trading unlawfully. On the same day a deputation from the board met the Permanent Secretary of the Northern Ireland Office at Stormont and clarified the steps necessary to relieve the directors from the possibility of fraudulent trading.

It was agreed that the Government's decision on whether or not to provide financial support for the Company, and if so on what terms, would be communicated in a letter to be delivered to the board in London by 11 am on 18 July. In anticipation of the possibility that the terms offered would prove unacceptable, the board had prepared a resolution petitioning for the winding-up of the Company. By noon on the appointed day no letter had been received. At 12.30 pm the directors adjourned for lunch with the clear understanding that if the letter were not received within the hour they would pass a resolution to initiate the winding-up of the Company. Fortunately the letter arrived during lunch.[10]

To some extent it was a restatement of existing policy: the labour force could not be increased by recruitment from other companies, and wage rises had to be linked to productivity. The new and significant points were that the Government required a very substantial majority of the equity to be in its hands; that the Company should appoint a senior executive, responsible directly to the managing director, to organise labour relations and specifically to improve consultation with the workforce; and that discussions should take place with a view to cancellation and rescheduling of contracts. Government thinking was probably influenced by the Booz-Allen Report on British Shipbuilding, published in 1973, which painted a gloomy picture of the prospects for the industry into the 1980s.[11] After much discussion at the reconvened board meeting, the Government's terms were accepted.

The next Government move was swift. Hoppe had been abroad, and on his return, at a meeting in London on 5 August, Lord Rochdale and deputy chairman Alan Watt handed him a letter from the Permanent Secretary at the Northern Ireland Office, breaking the news that 'in accordance with Article 83(F) of the Articles of Association of Harland & Wolff you are hereby requested to resign the office of a director in that Company'. With effect from 5 August 1974 Hoppe ceased to be a director and managing director. In retrospect it might seem that the way in which he was removed from office was somewhat insensitive, but given the critical situation of the Company and the highly charged circumstances there was perhaps no alternative. Shortly after his dismissal Hoppe was recalled urgently to Denmark to attend the funeral of an old friend. Whilst in Denmark he suffered the first of several strokes which ultimately resulted in the complete collapse of his health.

Looking back on his time in Belfast, it is said that he had difficulty in relating to the Northern Ireland workforce, that his autocratic behaviour made him enemies and that his policy of widespread introduction of Scandinavians to senior management positions, without prior board discussion, created ill will. Others say that both staff and men found his accent difficult to understand, so creating problems of communication. In fairness to him, much of his time in office was bedevilled by the effects of inflexible Government pay policy. It is tragic that an appointment that augured so well at the start should have ended in this way.

On the day of Hoppe's removal, and as an immediate step to improve labour relations, David Tinkler was made personnel director. Formerly industrial relations manager and local director with Swan Hunter & Tyne Shipbuilders Limited, Tinkler had joined Harland & Wolff in September 1973 as general manager, employee relations. The chairman had been anxious that a new managing director should also be appointed at a very early date and had urged the Government to approve Ronald Punt who was already responsible for ship production. This was not accepted, and as a temporary arrangement an executive committee of the board was nominated to manage the day-to-day business of the Company. A Government project team was also created with the intention of assesssing the financial implications of the order book and of monitoring progress thereafter.

The appointment of a permanent managing director could not be long delayed, but in order to demonstrate its democratic principles the Government insisted on an appointment procedure which proved to be both cumbersome and time-consuming. There were almost 100 applicants and it took over a year to come to a decision to appoint none other than Ronald Punt. Thus a whole year had been lost in the alleged interests of industrial democracy. To contemplate such a delay in the appointment of a managing director was surely no way to conduct the affairs of a company which was passing through such critical times, when the livelihood of thousands of workers was at stake.

Now began the melancholy task of minimising the ill effects of the situation created by the combination of external and internal problems. With the labour force of around 10,000 unlikely to grow significantly and the prospect looming of progressive losses due to late completion of vessels, the cancellation of hard-won contracts was now essential in order to contain the financial slide. The first casualties were the products tankers: potential contracts for five vessels had reached the stage of letters of intent, and these were not taken further. The possibility of cancelling two of the Shell tankers was balanced against cancellation of two of the Maritime Fruit Carriers vessels, and it was decided that it would be better to eliminate the latter from the programme, especially as the contracts gave the owners the right to reject the ships on late delivery. With the VLCC trading market increasingly depressed, MFC agreed to the cancellation of three of the six vessels originally ordered – ships nos 1702, 1703 and 1707. Another casualty of the retrenchment was the Sulzer medium-speed diesel-engine project, and the planned unit shop was eliminated from P200, though work continued on the rest of the scheme. Progress was made on wage claims and on flexibility of working, with steelworkers transferred to part-time welding. A joint consultative council was established with nine staff members, three management representatives and eight manual workers, together with the managing director and personnel director. This proved a useful and constructive move. Analysis of the effect of industrial disputes was later to show that less than 1 per cent of the time lost in 1974 had arisen from internal industrial disputes and that the percentage for 1975 was even less. Both figures were well below the national average and proved a tribute both to the Queen's Island workforce and to the new industrial relations regime.

Amid all the sober rethinking of the late summer and autumn of 1974 there was a piece of good news, though even that could not be received without some reservation. After prolonged negotiations involving Leo Curran, the director of the Engine Works, twelve main propelling engines were ordered by the Hyundai shipyard of South Korea. This was a welcome boost to the Engine Works, which had been suffering from a shortage of diesel-engine work, as the VLCCs were all steam-turbine-driven vessels. However, the coming-on-stream of the Hyundai yard, which was intended to be the largest shipyard in the world, was a cause for concern, especially as the engines ordered from Harland & Wolff were for a series of medium-sized vessels – just the sort of ships that Iver Hoppe had been hoping to build at Belfast.

Nevertheless, the Company had survived the 1974 crisis and the Labour Government had effectively agreed to support it through the difficult loss-making years ahead. Unlike the previous Conservative Government's commitment of the early 1970s, which had led to the appointment of Hoppe, State support was now being given with little indication of a profitable period ahead. What was abundantly clear, however, was that the value of Harland & Wolff as an employer in Northern Ireland was immense in political terms, and that a contented, productive labour force would be an important stabilising influence in a political situation where feelings, particularly among loyalists, were still running high.

The Government's emphasis on improving industrial relations continued into 1975, and a radically new approach was heralded in a statement by Stanley Orme to the House of Commons on 26 March. Announcing Government-funded provision for losses on Harland & Wolff's current contracts, he referred to the P200 modernisation programme, entirely financed by Government, which was making the yard one of the best equipped in Europe for large vessels. On this basis, he said, and taking into account the Company's status at the time as the largest employer in Northern Ireland, its traditions of technical excellence and its substantial order book, the Government had decided that it had no alternative but to give Harland & Wolff a chance of survival. To this end he announced that the Government, by an Order in Council under the Northern Ireland Act of 1974, would acquire all the share capital of the Company.[12] The timing of this move was perhaps significant, as the board meeting of 20 March 1975 had noted 'with regret' the death of Aristotle Onassis, by far the largest private shareholder in the Company. 'No Government could go on supporting the yard indefinitely,' said Orme, 'unless it can obtain orders which can be completed without loss, a halt must be called.' He concluded his statement with the assertion that 'in the future the yard will in a real sense be owned by Northern Ireland. Those working in the yard will no longer be working for private shareholders, or for themselves alone, but for Northern Ireland. It is their responsibility to ensure that, in the interests of Northern Ireland, the yard will survive.'

Government aid to Harland & Wolff became available after the takeover of the Company had been approved, and the indebtedness of the Company to the Shipbuilding Industry Board was repaid from Government loan facilities. The terms of compensation were advised to shareholders by the Department of Commerce in August 1975: ordinary shareholders received 9p for each £1 of ordinary stock and

he Lampas, delivered in November
75, the first of four 313,000-tonne-
adweight supertankers for Shell, built
the order of Airlease International.

(opposite)

The *British Steel,* a bulk carrier of 170,000
tonnes deadweight, delivered to
Lombard Finance on 19 October 1984 for
charter to the British Steel Corporation.

The *Auckland Star,* third in a series of four
refrigerated cargo ships for the Blue Star
Line, on trials off the west coast of
Scotland in January 1986.

preference shareholders 8p. The transfer of control was effective from 13 August 1975, when the Shipbuilding Industry (No. 2) (Northern Ireland) Order 1975 took effect.

Within a few weeks of Stanley Orme's statement, discussions on worker participation had begun, with the initial suggestion of a two-tier board system, as was common practice in West Germany.[13] As a basis for opening the dialogue a paper entitled 'The Next Step' was prepared by Frank Stephen, of Strathclyde University, for the Joint Liaison Committee of the Irish Congress of Trade Unions (Northern Ireland Committee) and the Confederation of Shipbuilding and Engineering Unions (Northern Ireland District). What in due course emerged was a proposal for a far-reaching reconstruction of the board, which, in addition to the chairman, was to consist of five executive directors, five non-executive directors and five worker directors to be appointed by trade-union members.

Lord Rochdale had earlier been approached by the Government on the question of having worker directors and had welcomed the idea. Indeed he had proposed a scheme of his own which he confidently believed could be put into useful effect immediately, but evidently it did not go far enough. His term as chairman was due to end in the summer of 1976, and he was invited by the Secretary of State to retire earlier in order that his successor could start from the outset with the new style board, as from 1 November 1975.

Thus at the end of October 1975 Lord Rochdale left the Company, though at the expressed wish of the Secretary of State he remained on the books until his scheduled retiring date the following summer. His period as chairman had been one of the most critical in the history of the Company. He was appointed after the decision had been taken to make Hoppe managing director and he found it difficult to communicate to Hoppe the distinction between the roles of chairman and managing director in the management of an United Kingdom company. Despite this difficulty, he was able to hold the board together and he is remembered with affection and respect by those who served under him. He did much to secure a continued existence for the Company.[14]

The new chairman, Sir Brian Morton, was a prominent local businessman. From 1969 to 1973 he had been chairman of the Londonderry Development Commission, for which service he had received a knighthood. The experience gained in that role, which brought him into contact with both sides of industry and all sections of the community, was seen as being particularly beneficial in the transition to employee participation in the Company's decision-making process.

Alan Watt retired on 31 October 1975. It had previously been his wish to retire at the time of Hoppe's appointment but he had been asked to stay on as deputy chairman until Hoppe found his feet. Watt's contribution to the Company had been a notable one. In his first senior position, as manager of the Southampton repair works, he had demonstrated his managerial ability, and when recalled to Belfast by Sir Frederick Rebbeck in 1958 he immediately began to attempt to modernise the facilities in the yard. After Sir Frederick retired he played a major role in the rebuilding of the Musgrave yard, and later in the building-dock project. It was his concept that Queen's Island should concentrate on building large vessels. During the serious financial crises of the mid and late 1960s he had been a source of strength to the Company, and in his acquired role of elder statesman he provided a much-needed element of continuity during Hoppe's period as managing director. His dry humour and his directness of approach are still remembered in the yard.

461

As regards the new board, Dr Bill McCarthy, Alan Fisher and William Downey were appointed non-executive directors. McCarthy, created a life peer in 1975, was a fellow of Nuffield College, Oxford, chairman of the Railway Staff National Tribunal and author of *In Place of Strife*, a book on a new system of labour relations. Fisher was general secretary of the National Union of Public Employees. These two replaced Eric Hellström and Niall Charlton who had been asked to relinquish their directorships. Downey had been a member of the Government working party on the viability of contracts. The other non-executive directors were Cliff Baylis and Alec Cooke.

As T.E. Murphy, a director and Company secretary, had retired at his own request in September 1975, the remaining five executive directors were thus Ronald Punt, Douglas Cooper, Leo Curran (Engine Works), David Tinkler (personnel) and Stewart Tennant (shipbuilding). Tennant had returned to Belfast on 15 December 1975 after two-and-a-half years at Robb-Caledon, the Scottish shipbuilding combine. Before moving to Scotland he had been shipbuilding manager at Queen's Island under Derek Kimber and had been involved in the development of the yard's production facilities. The position of Company secretary, vacated by Murphy, was filled by the appointment of David Geary. Although Eric Hellström was no longer a director, he was invited to attend board meetings because of his responsibilities for the P200 project. The nomination of the planned five worker directors proved more difficult than had been anticipated and it became clear that it might take some time for this idea to be realised.

The building programme proceeded relatively smoothly during 1975, although problems arose from shortages of materials, particularly pipes which were required in large quantities for the VLCCs. As a matter of policy, the Government had directed the British Steel Corporation to give priority to oil firms working in the North Sea and this meant that some 90 per cent of the Corporation's output of tubes was going to the oil industry. The *Lampas*, the first of the four 313,000-tonne-deadweight supertankers for Shell, was floated out of the building dock in July 1975 and delivered in November of that year. These vessels were built to the order of a leasing company, Airlease International, which put together credit facilities to finance their construction. On completion the ships were chartered to Shell. This method of financing contracts has since become common practice.

The renegotiation of contracts, cancellations and the possibility of new orders continued to be major preoccupations during 1975. Maritime Fruit Carriers proposed the cancellation of the first two of the three remaining VLCCs, but in fact the contracts for the first two were confirmed in November 1975, leaving only the third in doubt. Shell at one stage considered cancelling three of their four VLCCs and Furness Withy proposed the cancellation of their two products carriers, a proposition rejected by Harland & Wolff, although the ensuing renegotiations of the contract terms were not advantageous to the Company. In view of the uncertainties surrounding Harland & Wolff's position, and the extremely depressed world market for new tonnage,[15] it is not surprising that no ships were ordered during 1975 despite intensive marketing efforts to sell large bulk carriers, products carriers, Panamax bulk carriers (vessels of the largest size that could use the Panama Canal), 25,000-tonne, multi-purpose cargo liners and liquefied-natural-gas tankers to a design by Conch International Methane. By October 1975 the market for new merchant tonnage was virtually dead. The only firm order of the year for the Engine Works was for a main propelling engine for the Cochin shipyard in India, secured after protracted negotiations in the face of severe international competition. In the absence of ship orders during 1975 and 1976, there was no demand for main propelling engines from within the Company. During 1975 the decision was taken to phase out the foundry, due to its excessive operating costs. In its day it had been the largest foundry in Ireland, employing over 800 workpeople at its peak.

In 1976 the Company did not face crises of the severity that had assailed it in 1974 and 1975. It had to come to terms, however, with the likelihood of a prolonged downturn in demand, with the implementation of full-scale worker participation and with extended and complex negotiations with owners. The chairman, Sir Brian Morton, had to put in hand an orderly rundown of the level of activity at Queen's Island, with closure of the yard being a possible outcome. In January 1976 the board undertook to make a five-year financial forecast, and, rather than envisaging shutdown, the directors made the basic assumption that the Company would continue to trade, with a labour force considerably reduced but adequate to keep the assets functioning and to form a nucleus on which to build when the market improved. The options presented to Government were as follows: rundown leading to closure; continuation of work at the current level; building ships for stock after completion of the existing order book; or continuation at a reduced level, with a minimum of two vessels a year and the prospect of naval repair and refit work. The directors stressed the effect of possible closure on the Northern Ireland economy as a whole, and the social costs of the unemployment which would be caused directly and indirectly.

The submission had the desired effect: in March 1976 the Government indicated that it was sympathetic to continuing support for the yard, and by June 1976 its attitude had firmed up. The Company was expected to plan for operation on a reduced scale if orders were not obtained: the Government was not prepared to support speculative building of ships, but would consider financing the construction of vessels for which there was an identifiable owner. On the strength of these assurances a new loan agreement was completed with the Department of Commerce, increasing the borrowing limit, and negotiations began with the British Steel Corporation, Shell and P & O regarding vessels for which Government-supported leasing schemes would be required.

The ideal on which the Labour Government's support had been founded, that of improved labour relations based on worker participation in decision-making, received a good deal of consideration. The intention of appointing workers to the board was restated in January 1976. It was at first envisaged that elections for the five board positions would take place in August 1976 and that they would be followed by a period of training for elected worker directors. The problems involved in reconciling the interests of union members with board responsibility soon became evident. The only union to put forward a candidate was the white-collar union APEX (Association of Professional, Executive, Clerical and Computer Staff); and despite pressure from the Department of Manpower Services other unions did not make nominations. As late as October 1976 no date had been fixed for the election. It was apparent that there was no substantial grass-roots demand from the trade unions generally for the kind of worker directors' role envisaged by the Westminster Government. As it emerged, they had reservations about possible conflict between their responsibilities as trade unionists and as directors. Because no real progress was being made toward elections, the board was concerned to develop participative structures below board level. To comply with the Government's initial conditions for aid, the management continued to have talks with the trade unions in an attempt to set up productivity committees, departmental joint councils and, eventually, a 'joint implementation council'. The only part of the participative organisation that was seen to function was the joint consultative committee, which was used as a forum by management for getting union reaction to new ideas.

While attempts were being made to modernise existing administrative structures, work on the P200 scheme continued, and in August 1976 the impressive new facilities were nearly complete. Costs had been kept well under control: the original 1972 estimate had been £36.5 million and this was only marginally exceeded. Considering the high rate of inflation during the intervening period, this was a highly commendable performance, much to the credit of Eric Hellström, who of all the Scandinavians introduced by Iver Hoppe became the most involved and respected at Queen's Island. It was tragic that the completion of the modernisation of the shipyard should coincide with the financial crisis and the depressed state of world shipping which prevented the impressive new facilities being used to their full capacity.

The state of the order book remained very worrying throughout 1976. The cancellations of 1975 had gone as far as was desirable; attempts to remove further vessels from the order book were resisted strenuously. The most worrying contracts were those for the three vessels left in the Maritime Fruit Carriers VLCC order and for the Furness Withy products carriers. MFC managed to persuade the Coastal States Gas Corporation, of Houston, to take over the first two vessels, nos 1704 and 1705, in March 1976, but the position of no. 1706 remained in balance. By May 1976 it had been offered unsuccessfully to Shell and Coastal States, and MFC was virtually bankrupt. The problems thrown up by MFC's financial position dragged on without settlement until 1977, though it became increasingly clear that, despite the costs which would be incurred, cancellation of ship no. 1706 would prove inevitable. After prolonged discussions the Furness Withy contract was renegotiated on price and delivery, as were contracts for the bulk carriers nos 1701 for Ropner Shipping and 1708 for Golden West.

In the context of the continuing very low worldwide demand for new tonnage, talks were held in September 1976 between the Shipbuilding Association of Japan and the Association of West European Shipbuilders on reduction in shipbuilding capacity. These broke down, as the Japanese would agree neither to limit capacity nor to curb price reduction. It was estimated that United Kingdom yards would obtain orders totalling only 0.25 million gross tonnes a year, against an estimated world demand of 13 million gross tonnes and a UK output in the best years of 1.25 million gross tonnes. This forecast had serious implications for the Belfast shipyard, which on its own had the capability of producing about 1 million gross tonnes of large bulk carriers and tankers a year. Apart from the low prices being quoted by Japanese yards, the major problem facing British builders was the current credit terms which could be offered to owners. The OECD (Organisation for European Co-operation and Development) had stipulated that 30 per cent of the cost of a ship had to be paid in cash and that credit could be given on only 70 per cent for seven years at 7.5 per cent – terms unattractive to shipowners at a time of low freight rates. It appeared that other countries were offering better terms, but in the absence of concrete evidence it was difficult for the Government to improve credit packages. This affected the placing of a contract for a large bulk carrier which the British Steel Corporation wished to lease, and on which negotiations began in

October 1976. The other serious prospects were for liquefied petroleum gas (LPG) carriers for Shell and a series of cargo vessels and ferries for P & O. Harland & Wolff was one of twenty-nine companies asked to tender for the LPG ships. The outcome of negotiations on both these possibilities was still not clear at the end of 1976, so for the second year running there were no orders at all for new vessels.

As in earlier depressions, it appeared that one way of tiding the Company over was to diversify into non-shipbuilding activities. Accordingly in August 1976 the board endorsed the view that 'it was important that strenuous efforts be made to divert a high proportion, as much as 40–50 per cent, of the Company's labour force in the long term to activities other than shipbuilding'. Three avenues appeared worth exploring, the most speculative being the possibility of co-operation with a United States company in the building of floating factories. By September 1976 the possibility of forming a consortium with other Northern Ireland concerns to build floating factories was being investigated. In a departure from the policy of building large vessels, the Company also considered the possibility of building warships, small roll-on-roll-off ferries for Saudi Arabia and small cargo vessels for Andrew Weir & Company. The possibility of the Engine Works' taking on outside contracts with a high steelwork content was also investigated. The Engine Works, operating profitably on the Hyundai contract, negotiated a contract for a further six engines from the South Korean yard and began to investigate the possibility of acquiring a licence to build Stork-Werkspoor medium-speed engines, suitable for smaller vessels and for land applications. The Company was also offered the possibility of taking over the experimental Seahorse medium-speed diesel engine, the development of which had been discontinued by Hawthorn Leslie, the Tyneside engine-builders. The Seahorse was an intriguing design, based on the opposed-piston layout, but design problems had cropped up, and early in 1977 the decision was taken for technical reasons not to go ahead with the project.

The generally gloomy position of Harland & Wolff's financial forecasts and accumulating losses was in marked contrast to its public face which was that of a busy company with a record output of tonnage. Three of the Shell tankers, representing a total of 954,000 deadweight tonnes, were floated out during 1976. At that time the vessels were the largest ever built in the United Kingdom. The yard's total tonnage output was up by 45 per cent on the previous record, set in 1974, and represented more than a third of the total United Kingdom output. The Engine Works also had a good year, with an output of sixteen sets of machinery totalling 273,600 brake horsepower, only slightly below the previous best output in 1967. Nine of the sets of machinery were for export, a record for United Kingdom marine engine-builders in that year. These record figures were believed by some to be creating an attitude of complacency in the yard, hindering progress to more cost-effective working. Ronald Punt commented that the output was encouraging, but added that he 'would not like the figures to give people inside or outside the industry the impression that all our troubles are over'.

One of the imponderables which the Company was facing, in addition to inflation and the shipbuilding slump, was the position of the rest of the British shipbuilding industry. The nationalisation of shipbuilding, forecast in the Queen's speech at the opening of Parliament in 1975, was in fact taking longer than expected. Harland & Wolff was planning in a vacuum, though the Government had given assurances that the Company would not be treated any less favourably than the new nationalised concern.

The depression dragged on during 1977, affecting both management and workers. The effect on the workers could be seen in small-scale industrial grumbles, a response to the threat of redundancies as the level of activity in the yard declined. No more was heard about worker directors after September 1977, and in the run-up to a general election the Government developed other preoccupations. In addition to the continuing internal problems the Company was seriously affected by two events which were due to circumstances outside its control. One was a political strike called by the Ulster Unionist Action Committee in May 1977,[16] which resulted in delays of ten to fourteen days on the last of the Shell VLCCs and the Ropner bulk carrier. The other problem was a dispute in the British Oxygen Company, which cut off supplies of oxygen gas for cutting steel plate and led to the lay off of 3,500 men at the end of October. These two external disputes cost the Company about £1 million.

With the rundown in VLCC construction, a reduction in the workforce was essential, but the statutory redundancy payments required would make this a costly move. Paradoxically this consideration created an incentive to allocate finance to new contracts rather than incur redundancy payments. To reduce the workforce with the minimum disruption, retirement of workpeople aged over sixty-five was negotiated, followed by compulsory retirement at sixty-five. At the other end of the employment cycle, difficulty was experienced in recruiting and training suitable young people, who could command higher wages and better conditions in service industries.

A new problem facing the Company in 1977 was that of claims for industrial deafness, a legacy, in part, from the days of riveted ship construction. A legal ruling that deafness was admitted as an industrial injury brought claims immediately from about 1,000 employees. This was about a third of the United Kingdom total for all industries in 1977, and negotiations on the settlement of claims proved a continuing burden on the Company. Claims on this scale would bear very hard on the insurers and there was a distinct possibility that underwriters would not renew the normal employers' liability cover. It was initially extremely difficult and costly to achieve continuity of employers' liability insurance.

It proved very hard to secure orders to follow the Furness Withy products-carrier contracts. Negotiations on the promising inquiry for a bulk carrier for British Steel, initiated in 1976, continued during 1977, though agreement with British Steel, the Treasury and financiers remained elusive. British Steel wanted the ship and Harland & Wolff needed the order, but no conclusion was reached during the year. The most significant orders received were for a passenger and car ferry for British Rail and for two liquefied petroleum gas tankers for Shell. In the case of the Shell vessels, singularly complicated financial discussions took place between Shell and the Government. Although the internal instructions to start work on these two complex vessels were issued on 5 May 1977, the final contract terms were not agreed until December 1978.

Interest in diversification continued throughout 1977. The medium-speed diesel engine project was revived, this time with Maschinenfabrik Augsburg Nuremberg (MAN), of Augsburg, as the licensor. A licence agreement was subsequently signed introducing a new product line to the Engine Works, thus making it less reliant on slow-speed diesel engines. This was particularly important because Hyundai, the Engine Works' best customer in the last few years, was setting up its own engine works. Harland-MAN Engines Limited was to be incorporated in July 1978 as a subsidiary company of Harland & Wolff, with MAN holding a minority share interest. The need to find other products for the Engine Works was reinforced by discussions taking place at that time on the renewal of the licence agreement with Burmeister & Wain for slow-speed diesel engines. A condition imposed by the licensor was that the exclusive licence held by Harland & Wolff for the United Kingdom be withdrawn and that J.G. Kincaid be given a direct licence instead of acting as a sublicensee of Harland & Wolff. The impending formation of British Shipbuilders, which would include the Burmeister & Wain engine-building facilities at Kincaids in Greenock, as well as the Sulzer engine-building operation on the north-east coast of England, but would exclude Harland & Wolff, provided the opportunity for Burmeister & Wain to impose the change of terms, achieving the long-desired objective of increasing the licensor's financial returns. A more unusual move to diversify was the establishment of a subsidiary company, Hawk Products, to make motorcycle accessories, utilising the existing fibre-glass production facilities in the Kings Works and the electroplating plant. Other diversification was less radical, in the form of an order obtained for two loading ramps for the Larne harbour ferry terminal in Northern Ireland.

Changes were taking place in the Company's relationships with other United Kingdom shipbuilders through the creation of the nationalised British Shipbuilders; and with western European shipbuilders through the shared experience of depression and Japanese competition. As not all ship-repairing was nationalised, and a few shipbuilders remained outside the net, the disbanding in 1976 of the Shipbuilders' and Repairers' National Association left a gap. This was partially filled in 1977 by the formation of the Shiprepairers' and Shipbuilders' Independent Association (SSIA). Harland & Wolff became a member of this association primarily to protect its commercial interests in the ship-repair sector, but the Company specifically divorced itself from SSIA industrial-relations and pressure-group activities. The Company secured representation on the Association of West European Shipbuilders through the Belfast Shipbuilders' Association – of which, since the demise of Workman Clark, Harland & Wolff was the only member. It was particularly crucial that the Company's interests be represented in this forum, which was discussing such matters as a projected decline of up to 40 per cent in the output of European yards over a five-year period. A proposal that the British Ship Research Association might be merged with British Shipbuilders led to concern that Harland & Wolff's involvement in the research body might be brought to an end at a time when access to a research facility might be vital. In November 1977 Harland & Wolff's chairman, Sir Brian Morton, had his initial two-year appointment extended by three years, a tribute to his diplomacy.

Though the output of ships and engines in 1977 did not match the record set in the previous year it was, nonetheless, very respectable. Two vessels were floated out, the bulk carrier *Lackenby* for Ropner Shipping, of 119,500 tonnes deadweight, and the *Coastal Corpus Christi*, the first of the former MFC ships, of 333,000 tonnes deadweight, which, with her sister ship, remains one of the two largest vessels ever built in the United Kingdom. The Engine Works turned out the main diesel propelling engine for the *Lackenby*, the steam-turbine set for the *Coastal Corpus Christi* and seven smaller diesel engines for export, six of them to Hyundai.

There was no significant relief during 1978 from the problems which faced the Company. In some respects this was the worst year of the recession so far, with the full effects of the rundown from peak production being felt. The Coastal States Gas VLCCs, which had taken so much trouble to secure, proved equally troublesome to hand over; when the *Coastal Corpus Christi* was tendered for delivery on 13 February 1978 the owner's representative did not appear at the hand-over meeting. It transpired that Coastal States was referring alleged defects in the vessel to arbitration, with the apparent intention of delaying acceptance to the point where, according to the contract, it would have the right to reject the ship. Harland & Wolff's response could have been to sue the owner for breach of contract arising from the refusal to accept a 'valid tender' of the vessel. Instead, the immediate course of action decided upon by the yard was to tender the vessel again on 1 March 1978, but once more this was unsuccessful. The dispute dragged on, and because the ship was occupying valuable berth space at the outfitting quay it was proposed to move her in June to Loch Striven in Scotland to be laid up. By that time her sister ship, *Coastal Hercules*, was ready for sea trials, and when these were completed the same delivery difficulties were encountered as with the *Coastal Corpus Christi*. Arbitration of the *Coastal Corpus Christi* started in July and by 10 August 1978, when the *Coastal Hercules* was tendered for delivery, no settlement had been reached. The arbitration hearings continued in London throughout 1979 and into early 1980, in the process tying up several members of the yard's senior technical and management staff for prolonged periods. The underlying reason for this turn of events was the depression in demand for bulk oil transportation, caused in part by the increase in oil prices but also by a glut of shipping due to the almost universally over-optimistic market projections of the early 1970s.

The stress which the arbitration imposed on senior management was compounded by the prolongation of negotiations for new contracts and the complexity of the financial packages necessary to secure orders in a highly competitive market. The extended negotiations for the British Steel Corporation bulk carrier were eventually concluded in August 1978. The persistence of Cooper and Ruddock played a large part in the Company's securing of this much needed order. The other contracts placed in 1978 were for a further two ferries for British Rail for the Dover-Calais Sealink service. These were similar to the *Galloway Princess* ordered in 1977. A fourth vessel, for the Fishguard-Rosslare service, was not booked formally until 1979. An unusual contract was that for the steelwork for a new bridge over the River Foyle at Londonderry, awarded by the main contractor, a consortium formed by Redpath Dorman Long and the Northern Ireland firm of Graham Contracts.

Despite the recession, the Company's public profile remained high during 1978. Three vessels, with a total deadweight tonnage of 523,500, were floated out. These were the *Coastal Hercules*, the Ropner bulk carrier *Appleby* (ordered as *Golden Master*) and the first of the Furness Withy products tankers, *Hornby Grange*. The engines for these vessels, one steam-turbine and two diesel, were the only main propulsion sets produced by the Engine Works, which was seriously underemployed.

Industrial relations were difficult during 1978, largely because the Labour Government's anti-inflationary pay policy made it impossible to achieve reasonable wage and salary levels. Unlike the Heath Government's action in 1972/3 this affected employees of all grades and there was general dissatisfaction. The inclusion in the British Rail contracts of the statutory 'fair wages' clause provided the opportunity for the unions to put in claims for parity with British yards. These were not heard at the Industrial Court until December 1978 and January 1979 when the issues were resolved. Even then, the phasing of wage and salary awards caused some difficulties in the yard. As a move to remedy these problems and to motivate the workforce, personnel director David Tinkler was appointed to take charge also of the ship

The VLCC *Coastal Herc* being floated out of the building dock on 27 January 1978, with bulk carrier *Appleby* ur construction at the far of the dock.

production and facilities departments on a temporary basis. This multiple responsibility lasted until 1983.

Pay policy faded into the background with the election in May 1979 of a Conservative Government, led by Margaret Thatcher, with a policy of reducing State expenditure and encouraging private enterprise. This promised some relief from such constraints as legal pay limitation, but entailed instead other restrictions. In particular the imposition of cash limits – limits of the total amount of debt a company could incur – as a means of controlling public spending, and Government reluctance to accept financial packages requiring a high degree of State subsidy or contingent liability hindered the process of securing orders to provide a reasonable flow of work.

The first direct contact with the new administration was in June 1979, when board representatives met Giles Shaw, the Parliamentary Under-Secretary responsible for the Northern Ireland Department of Commerce, who warned that strict cash limits were likely to be imposed. He stated that a plan had to be prepared for Government, showing how improvements in performance could be achieved and that the Company was capable of becoming viable at some future date in improved market conditions. An immediate measure to contain costs was agreement on a new redundancy

A rare instance of both 'Goliath' cranes being on the same lift. The occasion is the loading the main girders for th Foyle Bridge at Londonderry. Blockin, together of the fabrica weldments was done along the east side of t building dock.

470

A flotation collar built for Highland Fabricators for use in placing an oil-roduction platform in the North Sea, seen after its launch on 22 March 1978.

programme. As a first stage, over 600 employees were made redundant during the summer of 1979; a second stage involved the cancellation of the dilutee agreement of 1971/2 and the redundancy of the dilutees.

By October 1979 it looked as though the forecast loss to 31 March 1980 would be in excess of the limit approved by Government, whose response was again to propose diversification. Giles Shaw envisaged Harland & Wolff as a holding company for a conglomerate of small companies with diverse activities based on Queen's Island: a parallel here was with the British Steel Corporation's attempts to provide alternative employment for redundant steelworkers. The Company was reluctant to take up this idea, as previous experience with diversification had been unsatisfactory. The over-optimistic views of the Minister were clearly expressed in his statement that 'the heavy industry activities of the Company needed to become profitable within the next year'.

The first response to the demand for diversification was a meeting with the Department of Commerce and the Northern Ireland Development Agency (NIDA), at which it was agreed that Harland & Wolff would take the lead in initiating what were termed 'old style' projects, related to existing facilities, manpower and skills. NIDA was to take the lead in 'new style' projects such as hydrofoil-building. It was agreed to seek shipbuilding contracts, which seemed to be available given a measure

471

shipbuilder, the Government placed its faith in diversification. Parliamentary Under-Secretary Giles Shaw set up an independent 'diversification review team' for the Company. The chairman was industrialist Patrick Meaney and the other members were Alec Cooke, David Berriman and Sir Gordon Booth. The team had a remit to take initiatives as well as to respond to them, and was certainly better placed than the Company's overworked executive directors to explore possibilities in depth.

The vigorous approach adopted by Alec Cooke to the Company's problems was presumably a major factor in his appointment. Sir Brian Morton had presided over the difficult period of running down the level of activity in the yard from the almost frenetic days of P200 and VLCCs to modestly sized, relatively sophisticated vessels, without any significant new changes to the yard's facilities. Cooke, who had been interested in the Company since the mid-1950s and who was one of the most experienced of Northern Ireland industrialists, was a good choice. The other board changes were the appointment of Robert Harkness and Ken Ruddock as directors in December 1980. Harkness was engineering director, with responsibility for the Engine Works and the electrical department, and Ruddock was appointed as ship marketing director.

Redundancy and wage negotiations were continuing problems for both workforce and management during 1980. In January notice of 400 redundancies was given, and it was expected that this would moderate wage claims. In February British Shipbuilders concluded an 11.5 per cent increase, including a 5 per cent 'self-financing' element. This became the basis for negotiation at Harland & Wolff, but the Company wanted to make the whole of its offer of 15 per cent dependent on improved productivity. By the end of September 1980 all trades had accepted the new agreement. The impact of the redundancies, however, not only affected wage negotiations but also reduced confidence in the future of the Company, and there was a drift of employees to new companies and to other established employers. This trend was already a feature of the Company's position as the largest and most structured employer in Northern Ireland, but it gave increasing concern during the year.

Relationships with British Shipbuilders, which had not been altogether happy, began to improve during 1980. By this time John Parker had become deputy chief executive of British Shipbuilders, and he and Derek Kimber, chairman of the medium-sized yards in British Shipbuilders, helped to smooth the way. After more than a year of negotiation Harland & Wolff secured continued membership of British Shipbuilding Research Association committees. There was also some collaboration on the BP tanker contracts. More substantially, two orders for a new type of Burmeister & Wain engine came from Govan Shipbuilders, a welcome addition to a thin order book, and Scott Lithgow subcontracted some of the design work on its BP 'emergency support' vessel to the Belfast drawing office. British Shipbuilders also indicated its willingness to put its marketing resources at the disposal of Harland & Wolff, to further the sale of large vessels which were beyond the capacity of British Shipbuilders to build.

The only firm orders during 1980 were for the two BP tankers, though there was considerable interest in the Company's bulk-carrier range. Cooke suggested that a builder/owner joint-venture sales package be prepared, aimed at the bulk-carrier market. It was a sign of the times that only two vessels were launched during 1980. These were the British Rail ferries *St Christopher* and *St David*. Their total gross tonnage of 14,000 was the smallest output from Belfast since the 1930s' depression.

474

The *St Christopher* was launched by Tina Heath of the BBC *Blue Peter* children's television programme and the vessel was adopted by the programme, which ran a competition to produce a picture to hang in the ship. The launch of the *St David* on 25 September 1980 was the last from the Musgrave yard which was then put on a care-and-maintenance basis. Output from the Engine Works was also at a desperately low ebb, with only one main propelling engine completed, the first of the order for Govan Shipbuilders. The rest of the engines built were Harland-MAN medium-speed diesels, some for power generators in the British Rail ferries. Small wonder that many feared for the continued existence of the yard and that the confidence of the Government in its future appeared to be faltering.

The uncertainties persisted into 1981, although at first the Government's attitude seemed to be more helpful. In January a new Minister of State was appointed to the Northern Ireland Office: Adam Butler took a lively interest in the Company's affairs and promised Government support for the policy of building large ships. This reversal of attitude was prompted by market trends: 80 per cent of orders placed worldwide in late 1980 were for tankers and bulk carriers. Cash limits continued, however, to threaten seriously the Company's ability to operate. Early in the year there was still uncertainty about the level for 1981/2. When in March 1981 the limit was announced it was £4.4 million lower than the anticipated figure, and this implied 'calamitous financial repercussions' if the building programme were retarded to contain cash requirements.

With the revival in the world market for ships, negotiations for a large bulk carrier were begun with a Norwegian owner. It proved impossible to put together a suitable financial package, though such an order was desperately needed to avoid a surplus of steelworkers. A high level of Government support would have been required to secure this contract and hopes of such Government assistance persisted throughout the summer and autumn. With work in the yard running out, the board was acutely aware of the danger that the Company's continued existence could again be threatened. Despite assurances from Government in August 1981 that the Company should act on the assumption that its policy of building large ships had been accepted, the board was not convinced that Government fully understood the major implication of such a decision – 'that the alternatives which resulted in the least cost to Government, and which at the same time gave the Company the best chances to achieve stability and long-term viability were those which were based on an early order for a 170,000-tonne-deadweight bulk carrier'. The Norwegian owner's interest had died by November 1981, but in June 1982, after lengthy negotiations, the British Steel Corporation placed an order for the same type of vessel, ship no. 1720. The delay in finalising such a contract, however, substantially increased the Company's operating loss.

To help cope with the serious financial problems, the Northern Ireland Office appointed a new chairman in May 1981 to succeed Alec Cooke whose agreed six-month term of appointment was coming to an end. Vivian Wadsworth, the man selected, was director and chief executive of Tanks Consolidated Investments, a mining-finance and industrial holdings group. The only other appointment to the board in 1981 was that of John M. Williams, a director of Stone-Platt Industries, who joined the Company in November. To harmonise with the Government accounting year, the Company's financial year was altered to run from 1 April to 31 March. As a consequence the accounts for 1981 were included in a fifteen-month accounting period ending on 31 March 1982.

The problems of reconciling the needs of the Company with the aims of Government had once again surfaced. With a Government committed to reducing public expenditure and at the same time to maintaining the position of Northern Ireland, there was clearly a dilemma. As earlier governments had found, it was not politically possible to engage in the kind of expensive radical surgery that the British Steel Corporation had been encouraged to undertake. At the same time – based on the experience of the early 1970s – there was a fear that to endorse large-ship construction would be to sign a blank cheque. This attitude, however understandable, affected the judgement of the board, with serious consequences throughout the senior management structure.

In this period of gloom a certain light relief was had from an inquiry for three repeats of the *Titanic*. The board felt that the proposal 'seemed unrealistic', but that it could not be ignored, if only because of the possibility of adverse publicity. Inquiries into the status of the American would-be owner revealed that his financial prospects were 'somewhat dubious'.

The Government-sponsored diversification review team reported in May 1981 and its findings backed up the original views of management that there was little chance of diversifying on any sizeable scale and that the Company's energies should be directed to improving its effectiveness in the construction of ships and marine engines.

The low morale engendered by the state of uncertainty persisted into 1982 and was evident in problems encountered in recruiting senior executives, and in a number of demarcation disputes. There was little sign of a high level of Government commitment to the Company, and this produced adverse comment within the board on the 'drip-feed' method of keeping the yard alive, especially in the light of the positive attitudes taken by other nations to their shipbuilding industries.

Having led the Company since 1975 through the aftermath of the slump in the VLCC market, Ronald Punt decided to retire at the end of May 1982. Punt, who had had to contend earlier in his career with the extreme hostility of Pounder, had been through some of the most difficult years of the Company's existence. His appointment as managing director had been the result of a long-drawn-out consultative procedure, and the manner of the departure of his predecessor, Iver Hoppe, was hardly a happy omen. Following Hoppe's dismissal the Scandinavian management team he had established in the yard soon began to fragment and the early part of Punt's term of office presented the challenge and opportunity of restructuring management. Later he had to contend with the prolonged arbitration on the Coastal States Gas tankers *Coastal Corpus Christi* and *Coastal Hercules* and with the rundown in the yard's activity against the background of pressure by the EEC authorities to reduce the shipbuilding industry in the United Kingdom. Throughout all these testing times Punt demonstrated qualities of diplomacy and commitment of a high order.[19]

After Punt's retirement Douglas Cooper, deputy managing director, was made acting managing director, pending a new appointment. During this period some progress was made in gaining Government support for the Company, as James Prior, Secretary of State for Northern Ireland, showed a keen interest in the yard and in particular in an inquiry for six refrigerated cargo vessels for the Blue Star line.

In an atmosphere of cautious optimism the physical and organisational rationalisation of the Company was tackled. Before Punt's retirement PA Management Consultants had been appointed to examine overhead costs, and A & P Appledore continued an investigation of the restructuring of the yard's physical facilities. While this work was in progress, however, changes in the market for ships

476

Painting the funnel of c of the Shell liquefied petroleum gas tankers the paint hall in 1981.

had invalidated the underlying assumption that the Company would engage in series production of tankers and bulk carriers, and had thus rendered obsolete the systems which the consultants had envisaged. The presence in the yard of consultants and the absence of definite new orders, coupled with the issue in April 1982 of redundancy notices to 170 steelworkers and 30 staff, not surprisingly, affected the morale of the workforce and reduced productivity. The total labour force was now just under 7,000.

Behind the scenes, however, definite progress was being made. In October 1982 Prior, who had been involved actively in the negotiations, announced that the Government would back the contracts for the Blue Star ships only on three conditions: the Company had to accept the consultants' reports; the workforce had to agree to the elimination of restrictive working practices; and a 'tough and low' wage and salary settlement for 1983/4 had to be reached. The Secretary of State warned that 'failure to honour any such undertaking would result in the loss of Government support for any future orders'.

In November 1982 the Government announced the appointment of a new chief executive for Harland & Wolff. John Parker, who came from the prestigious position of deputy chief executive of British Shipbuilders and was a former Company employee, was appointed to the dual role of chairman and chief executive. His nomination was of the highest significance. Vivian Wadsworth, in the grip of forces beyond his control, had been able to do little more than keep the yard ticking over; his successor was clearly intended to justify the continuance of Government support. The consequences of failure were not stated, but were evident to all. However, John Parker's appointment was more than a reflection of the Government's wish to have value for money; it was also a recognition of the worth of the modern facilities in the yard, of the sophistication of its design systems, and of its well earned reputation for quality products. Two new non-executive directors were appointed during 1982. The first of these, nominated by Wadsworth, was John Boyer, chairman of Antony Gibbs Holdings and former deputy chairman of the Hong Kong & Shanghai Banking Corporation. The second was Dr Roelof Schierbeek who had previously been associated with the former British Enkalon plant at Antrim in Northern Ireland.

During the year the order for the British Steel Corporation bulk carrier, ship no. 1720, was confirmed. There were a number of inquiries about other vessels, but against the background of low prices in Korean yards little progress was made in following them up. Apart from the Blue Star project, the only major inquiry being taken forward at the end of 1982 was for large container ships for Lykes Lines, a United States company. The ship-repair division secured a number of contracts. These included refits of two of the Sealink ferries built for cross-channel service, *St Anselm* and *St Christopher*, which were brought to Belfast for modifications including the installation of a duty-free supermarket at the stern of each ship. A bulk carrier damaged during its launch at Govan Shipbuilders' yard was also repaired by the Company, a major operation involving replacement of the stern frame. After successfully completing intensive commissioning programmes, the two Shell LPG carriers *Isomeria* and *Isocardia* were delivered during 1982; these were the most complex merchant ships built by the Company.

John Parker attended, as an observer, the first board meeting of 1983 when a gloomy picture was painted. Low morale, due to the failure to announce contracts, was causing the building programme to slip, and the engineering division was short

The first of the Shell liquefied petroleum gas carriers, *Isomeria*, being ed out at the Thompson wharf in 1981.

of work. Negotiations on the Blue Star vessels were still dragging on. Clearly the new chairman and chief executive, who took office on 1 February 1983, had a major task on his hands. To assist him, Eric Hellström, who had left the yard in 1976 and had spent some years as managing director of a Swedish company, came back to Belfast as ship production director. Within a week of taking office Parker had issued a statement of intent to managers, foremen, supervisory staff and union representatives, outlining his strategy for improving the management of the yard, laying great stress on accountability, planning, and the application of new technology and management systems to increase productivity. Agreement had been reached with the Department of Economic Development, the former Department of Commerce, to place advance orders for certain key components and materials for the Blue Star vessels. In the search for new orders for the engineering division, the board discussed the possibility of joint ventures with a suitable partner to supply diesel engines for land-based power-plant installations. Sales teams were despatched to the Far East and to Greece and efforts were being made to secure a share of Ministry of Defence orders for fleet auxiliary vessels. The preparation of a corporate plan was started, with the intention that it should be submitted to Government by the end of May 1983.

479

To concentrate thought on the future, a 'product development planning group' and a 'new technology committee' were set up.

Parker's prime objectives were to meet delivery dates and to become more competitive. In achieving these ends he was hindered by the continuing delay in finalising the Blue Star contracts, to say nothing of orders to succeed them – essential to prevent underemployment of the workforce. Negotiations on the Blue Star ships dragged on until the end of September 1983 when the contracts for the first two vessels were signed, and it was not until 30 November 1983 that Government approval for the second two was forthcoming. The delay in concluding these contracts caused serious production problems.

In worsening market conditions it proved difficult to attract the vital follow-on orders necessary to make forward planning meaningful. However, orders were gradually won, though not for conventional ships. A contract for a floating harbour for Port Stanley in the Falkland Islands generated work throughout the Company. This was intended to serve the 'Fortress Falklands' created by Government after the war with Argentina in 1982. The main contractor to the Ministry of Defence was ITM (Offshore) of Middlesbrough, which subcontracted the bulk of the work, worth £6 million, to Harland & Wolff. The project involved alterations to six large offshore-oil barges, including the construction of superstructures and the building of a linking causeway. The 'Flexiport' was produced to a very tight schedule and completed in just over thirteen weeks in the winter of 1983/4, a remarkable achievement. Two inquiries being followed up were for a repeat of *British Steel*, ship no. 1720, and for the Lykes Lines container ships first discussed in 1982.

Despite the absence of any firm guarantee of future work, the task of tailoring the yard to changing conditions went on. The rationalisation of facilities continued and a programme of redundancy cut the workforce by 750 to around 5,500. A start was made on a new automated pipe shop planned in 1982, within the shell of the former Engine Works boiler shop, and a new computer graphics system for pipe design was installed. Parker began reorganising management structures to achieve a greater level of accountability. The most significant change was the switch from the traditional system of managing ship construction, by trade or function, to a zone system in which the vessel was split, for management purposes, into sections, with managers given responsibility for their individual zones, rather than for the work of specific trades throughout the vessel. This new approach fitted into the pattern of increasing 'preoutfitting', the incorporation of equipment and fittings in hull sections before assembly in the building dock, and had the potential to improve the effectiveness of both management and workers. By the end of the year zone management was also extended to the technical department. Two new non-executive directors were appointed during 1983, Robert Huskisson in August, and the Duke of Westminster in October. John Boyer resigned in November.

New initiatives were taken to establish technical contacts with foreign shipyards. To broaden the Company's range of preferred products, negotiations for a sublicence were commenced with the Japanese IHI shipyard, licensee of a multi-purpose cargo vessel known as the 'Friendship', designed by G.T.R. Campbell. The chairman, accompanied by Ken Ruddock, visited Japan and reached agreement on a licence package for the 'Friendship'. Although the Company preferred series production of standard ships, it entered into negotiations on some one-off contracts including a helicopter support-ship conversion for the Ministry of Defence and two large barges for ITM. A more unorthodox inquiry came from British Petroleum, for a new type of vessel for exploiting marginal offshore oilfields, termed a SWOPS vessel. 'SWOPS' stood for 'single-well oil-production system', although in service the vessel will actually move from one sub-sea oil well to another, collecting oil as a bee collects nectar.

After the uncertainties of the previous three years, 1984 was a year of positive developments, with every evidence of renewed confidence in the Company by owners and Government. Early in the year firm orders were placed by ITM for the two barges, and the prolonged negotiations with Lykes Lines resulted in the issue of a letter of intent for two container vessels, part of a projected six-ship order, the others going to Japan. Discussions continued with British Petroleum on the technically advanced SWOPS vessel; the Company was placed on the shortlist of six tenderers in April 1984, and on a final list of three in May, along with a French and a Japanese yard. On 7 August 1984 a letter of intent was signed by Harland & Wolff and British Petroleum on the basis of a joint venture, the two companies co-operating in the construction of the vessel and sharing operating profits. The SWOPS vessel was designed jointly by the two companies with Matthew Hall Engineering assisting in the design of the oil-processing plant. It is intended to extract oil from marginal offshore fields which would be uneconomic to develop with conventional recovery methods. Unlike conventional oil-extracting plants, it will be self-propelled, with a processing plant to separate the oil from gas and water, and it has storage capacity for 42,000 tonnes of oil. Positioned over each oil well by seven propellers, the *Seillean* (Gaelic for 'bee') will be powered, when collecting oil, by gas turbines running on gas recovered from the oil being processed on board, and by diesel generators. The first steel plate for the hull was cut on 6 November 1985. The decision to tender for this innovative vessel – said to be the world's most sophisticated merchant ship – prompted John Parker and his colleagues to begin to introduce the idea of dedicated project management. Under this system each major contract is allocated its own 'dedicated' management team, responsible across all the Company functions from the signing of the contract to delivery of the vessel. The project manager is also the contact point for the customer. Such an approach is essential for highly complex contracts like the SWOPS vessel, but it has also been applied to give the same degree of increased control in the production of conventional ships.

The securing of the prestigious SWOPS order ended the Company's negotiations with Lykes Lines, as the revised delivery dates offered for these ships did not suit the owner's programme. Negotiations with the British Steel Corporation on a second bulk carrier, similar to *British Steel*, resulted in the conclusion of a provisional agreement in August 1984. These orders for new vessels were complemented by a Ministry of Defence contract for the conversion of a container ship into an aviation training ship (ATS) suitable for training helicopter pilots and for transporting Harrier 'jump jet' fighters. This was the first major defence contract placed directly with the Company for more than fifteen years and represented a breakthrough. The preparation of the bid package for the contract was unusual in that, apart from the very tight tender submission schedule set by the Ministry of Defence, the responsibility for selecting and actually purchasing a suitable vessel for conversion rested solely with the tenderers. In the event the Italian-built container ship *Contender Bezant*, which had formed part of the Task Force Support Group in the Falklands conflict, was the vessel chosen and the sale transaction took place on 14 March 1984 when the ship was in passage from the Gulf of Mexico to northern Europe, thereby enabling the Company to close the deal. For the Ministry of Defence the conversion

of an existing vessel, as opposed to the construction of a purpose-built ship, was significantly cost-effective. In her new role the ship will be renamed RFA *Argus*. For a short time in the early part of 1985 the building dock contained two of the Blue Star refrigerated cargo vessels, the two ITM barges and the *Contender Bezant*, a graphic illustration of the capacity of the dock and of the variety of work which Harland & Wolff could undertake.

The flexibility of the Company's facilities was further demonstrated in February 1984 when agreement was reached with Abex Denison Limited Jetway U.K. on the construction of fifteen aircraft boarding bridges for the new Terminal Four at London's Heathrow Airport. These were to be built in the Engine Works. The engineering division also introduced a new product in the form of simulator modules for training power-station operators. The securing of the SWOPS vessel contract was also a source of important new work for the Engine Works.

In the autumn of 1984 Alan Fisher, a non-executive director since 1975, retired and Charles Perrin, a director of Hambros Bank, and Alex Ferry, general secretary of the Confederation of Shipbuilding and Engineering Unions, were appointed to the board as non-executive directors. Below board level a noteworthy event was the retirement of David Geary, Company secretary since 1975. To comply formally with the Companies (Northern Ireland) Order 1982, the word 'Limited' was deleted from the name of the Company with effect from September 1984 and replaced by 'plc', standing for 'public limited company'.

Two vessels were completed in 1984: *British Success*, the second of the two

An artist's impression of the BP SWOPS vessel superimposed on a view of a VLCC under construction in the building dock. The derrick for lowering the collecting pipe to the sea-bed well-head is in the centre of the SWOPS vessel, the flare stack at the bow and the power plant at the stern.

482

109,000-tonne-deadweight tankers for British Petroleum, and the BSC's bulk carrier *British Steel*. With a deadweight tonnage of just over 173,000, *British Steel* is the largest bulk carrier to be built in Europe, and she is fitted with a new type of fuel-efficient main propelling engine. Painted rust red, she was a spectacular sight when she was delivered in October 1984. On 16 December, a few weeks before the first of the Blue Star vessels, ship no. 1721, *English Star*, was due to be delivered, she was damaged by a serious fire which broke out in the engine room when sparks from a welding torch ignited rags and a section of pipe insulation which had become saturated with oil. The fire spread rapidly, fuelled by plastic sheeting, insulation and staging materials. Fortunately there were only minor casualties, but the engine room was completely gutted. This incident, which caused serious disruption to the building programme of the Blue Star vessels, was the first major fire on board a ship in Harland & Wolff's hand's at Belfast since the *Reina del Pacifico* incident in 1947.

With the fire being mainly confined to the engine room, the vessel's naming ceremony proceeded as programmed and on 23 January 1985 HRH the Duchess of Kent arrived to a snow-covered yard to perform the ceremony. Ken Ruddock, the sales director, was unable to attend the ceremony due to a sudden illness, and on 24 January a shocked workforce learned of his untimely death. A contemporary and friend of John Parker, Ruddock was in his early forties and had established himself as an excellent ambassador for the Company in the British and international shipping markets. His warm personality, energy and enthusiasm have been greatly missed by his colleagues. On a happier note, the 1985 New Year's Honours list saw the award of the CBE to Douglas Cooper, a fitting reward for his services to the Company and the community. In February 1985 William Gallagher, a former manager with the Company, who had since been working for Govan Shipbuilders, was brought back to Harland & Wolff as ship production director. Only six months later he returned to Govan to take up a more senior position. In August 1985 Stuart Hunter joined the board as director responsible for the project management teams covering the Company's major contracts. With a background in project management in the offshore oil industry, he was well placed to strengthen the Company's position in the oil-related market.

The 1970s and early 1980s was a traumatic period for United Kingdom, and indeed European, shipbuilders. Yards in countries such as Sweden and Germany, which had been very successful during the previous twenty years, came under severe pressure from Japan and Korea, especially after the collapse of the market for VLCCs in 1974. The United Kingdom share of world output fell from 4 per cent to 3.42 per cent between 1972 and 1975, and by 1980 was down to 3.26 per cent. The effect of such intense competition was to bring ship prices down to what were by European standards ridiculously unrealistic levels. The survival of merchant shipbuilding could be assured only by Government assistance to shipbuilders. In Britain support was given at first in the hope of securing 'viability' or 'correcting distortions in the world markets'. More recently Government policy has been, so far as possible, to allow market forces to prevail, tempered by the implications of unemployment in the regions.[20]

Harland & Wolff's experience fits into this general framework, with the added complication of the political problems of Northern Ireland. On the one hand, the troubles proved a deterrent to the placing of contracts, especially for ship-repair, and affected the morale of the Queen's Island workpeople both collectively and individually. On the other hand, the 'Northern Ireland factor' encouraged the

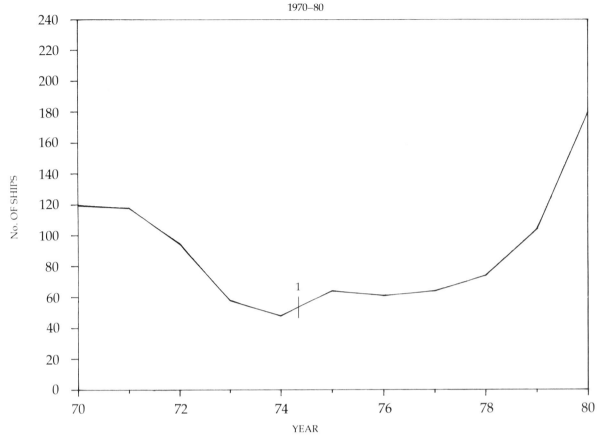

SHIPS REPAIRED AT BELFAST
1970–80

1 Closure of Alexandra graving dock

Westminster Government to support substantial investment in new facilities and to exclude Harland & Wolff from the general scheme of nationalising shipbuilding. This has ensured that the Company remains a cornerstone of the Northern Ireland economy and that a large measure of decision-making is retained within the Province. The different perspectives of Company management and Government departments have sometimes caused frustrations on both sides, but in general relations have been good, with a common objective of obtaining value for money in hard times. The close interest taken by most of the Ministers and civil servants responsible for the Company has seen Harland & Wolff through some of its worst moments.[21]

Some features of the period 1971/85 particularly stand out, notably the number of changes at the top of the Company, in contrast to the long periods of office of Lord Pirrie and Sir Frederick Rebbeck. Indeed, since 1965 the Company has had ten chairmen, six managing directors and no fewer than forty directors. The frequent changes on the board have arisen largely from the transfer of control, then ownership, to government. Under Lord Rochdale and Iver Hoppe expansion of capacity continued to make Queen's Island more productive, in tonnage terms, then ever before. It is a tragedy that the new facilities could not, in the event, achieve their designed throughput. The P200 project, however, provided the advanced environment in which the business of shipbuilding is still carried out.[22] The existence of the building dock and its support shops has been vitally important to the survival of the Company. The succeeding regime of Sir Brian Morton and Ronald Punt effectively led an orderly retreat from the exposed position in which the 1974 recession left the Company. It is ironic that the new pattern of industrial relations developed after Hoppe's departure found its main test in contraction rather than in the intensive use of the building dock. Most recently the management team has had to think more of containing losses and cash requirements, and this too has been done with a considerable measure of success.

Because of the complexities of the critical events in Harland & Wolff's history since 1971 it has not been possible to say much about the workforce. It should be recorded, however, that the Queen's Island employees have stood up remarkably well to pressures both of expansion and contraction and the Company's labour-relations record is good. The old Queen's Island spirit of good humour and comradeship is not dead, though it has been buffeted by changes in technology, by the political problems of the Province and by the shrinkage of the workforce. The success of the independent social clubs – Welders and Staff – speaks of cohesion outside as well as inside the Company, and pride in its name.

At the very end of the period signs of quickening life appear. The role of European shipbuilding has changed radically since 1971, but not necessarily permanently. Ships will be required in substantial numbers for the foreseeable future, and countries reliant on maritime trade should have a substantial stake in their provision. At times this involves, in the cyclical nature of demand for shipping, physical retrenchment and painful reappraisal. Within the current framework of expectation there is every reason to believe that the Company, with a broadly based order book worth over £300 million, has achieved a tenable position. The maintenance of that position and advance from it will demand thought and resolution from all concerned with the future of Harland & Wolff.

Table 14.1
Capital 1971-85

	4½ per cent cumulative preference stock	Ordinary stock
	£	£
1971-4	2,600,000	8,396,082

	Ordinary shares
	£
1975-85	10,996,082

Table 14.2
Profit and loss 1971-85

	Gross profit/(loss) for year before tax and depreciation	Net profit/(loss) per published accounts after tax and depreciation	Distribution (transfers to/from reserves and dividends)	Balance carried to following year
	£	£	£	£
1971	860,000	(302,000)		(9,662,000)
1972	622,000	(513,000)		(10,175,000)
1973	(31,882,000)	(33,012,000)		(43,187,000)
1974	(15,286,000)	(16,711,000)		(59,898,000)
1975	(2,667,000)	(4,884,000)	(26,971,000)[2]	(37,811,000)
1976	5,569,000	2,591,000		(35,220,000)
1977	1,277,000	(1,907,000)		(37,127,000)
1978	(22,421,000)	(25,452,000)		(62,579,000)
1979	(40,115,000)	(43,296,000)		(105,875,000)
1980	(28,489,000)	(31,997,000)		(137,872,000)
1981-2	(22,109,000)[1]	(26,205,000)		(164,077,000)
1982-3	(37,850,000)	(42,822,000)		(206,899,000)
1983-4	(26,684,000)	(29,756,000)		(236,655,000)
1984-5	(32,248,000)	(35,819,000)		(272,474,000)

Notes
1   For fifteen months 1 January 1981 to 31 March 1982
2   Effect of cancellation and redemption of loans

Table 14.3
Fixed assets (at book value) 1971-85

	Freehold and leasehold land, property and buildings	Machinery, plant and tools
	£	£
1971	7,270,000	5,902,000
1972	8,357,000	5,854,000
1973	13,962,000	5,751,000
1974	17,574,000	8,950,000
1975	22,362,000	10,248,000
1976	20,700,000	12,724,000
1977	18,819,000	13,220,000
1978	17,896,000	12,573,000
1979	16,532,000	11,803,000
1980	15,168,000	10,444,000
1981-2	13,627,000[1]	9,220,000[1]
1982-3	10,480,000	8,493,000
1983-4	9,548,000	8,764,000
1984-5	8,843,000	9,532,000

Note
1   At 31 March 1982

Table 14.4
Investments 1971-85

	Investments in subsidiary companies	General investments
	£	£
1971	2,000	50,000[1]
1972	—	50,000
1973	—	50,000
1974	—	50,000
1975	—	50,000
1976	—	50,000
1977	—	20,000
1978	—	20,000
1979	74,000	—
1980	178,000	—
1981-2	162,000	—
1982-3	161,000	—
1983-4	—	—
1984-5	—	—

Note
1   Nominal value of shareholding in Short Brothers & Harland

Table 14.5
Number of employees at Belfast 1971-85

	Manual	Staff
1971	7,123	2,006
1972	7,708	2,242
1973	7,497	2,499
1974	7,429	2,518
1975	7,335	2,322
1976	7,117	2,119
1977	6,739	1,967
1978	6,292	1,920
1979	5,732	1,810
1980	5,700	1,670
1982[1]	5,412	1,622
1983	4,736	1,426
1984	4,064	1,388
1985	3,758	1,405

Note
1   Change in financial year: figures for 1982-5 are as at 31 March; earlier figures are as at 31 December. All figures are averages for the year.

An artist's impression
RFA *Fort Victoria*
(AOR 01), the first in a
generation of auxiliary
oiler replenishment
vessels of the 'Fort' class
for the Ministry of
Defence.

workforce. Agreements have been reached with the trade unions on flexible working practices, and the introduction of new technology has made a significant contribution to reducing work content right through from the tendering stage to delivery of the finished product. For many years the Company has been a user of advanced computer-based systems. Substantial investment continues to be made in CAD/CAM (computer-aided design and manufacturing systems) and in applying them to make far-reaching changes in ship production. Large sections of ship structure and associated outfit services, such as piping and ventilation, can now be produced directly on computer screen without the use of conventional drawings. In the yard's fabrication shops steel plates are profile-cut with the aid of computer-controlled burning machines, and in a new automated pipe shop opened in 1985 pipes can now be cut and bent under computer control. There are more than 200 computer terminals throughout the yard, communicating with a central data base, planning and controlling all movement of materials at each manufacturing stage.

At the time of writing, the remaining three of the four Blue Star refrigerated cargo ships – the order for which the Company fought so hard – have just been completed. Construction of the bulk carrier *Ironbridge*, the Mark II version of the *British Steel*, for charter to the British Steel Corporation, is well advanced and is targeted to be completed with a 22 per cent reduction in man hours compared to her predecessor. On completion the *Ironbridge* will be the largest bulk carrier to have been built in Europe. The first steel was cut for the hull of the BP SWOPS vessel in November 1985 and the Aviation Training Ship conversion for the Ministry of Defence is well under way, with the superstructure lifted into position in December

1985. Together the contracts for the bulk carrier, the SWOPS vessel and the ATS are valued at nearly £200 million – no mean achievement in depressed market conditions.

Flexibility in the marketplace is a cornerstone in the new corporate strategy, and the follow-up effort to secure orders has been unremitting. Platforms had already been established from which this sales drive could be launched: the technical and organisational abilities of the shipyard had been demonstrated in the efficient demilitarisation and refurbishment of the *Atlantic Causeway* and the *Rangatira* after Falklands service, and in the successful completion of the subcontracted 'Falklands Flexiport' for use at Port Stanley. In many respects these were 'pathfinder' contracts and, as events were later to prove, the high level of commitment from shopfloor upwards to the achievement of target delivery dates, despite the original workload being nearly doubled on the 'Flexiport', was a prudent investment in the Company's future relationship with the Ministry of Defence. Harland & Wolff's inclusion in the Ministry's list of approved contractors was to follow, together with the award of the breakthrough ATS conversion contract.

Of even greater significance, however, was the announcement in April 1986 – after one of the most fiercely contested public battles for a Ministry of Defence contract – that the Company was to design and build the first in a new generation of highly sophisticated 'auxiliary oiler replenishment' vessels of the 'Fort' class. With a contract value in excess of £120 million, AOR 01 is the largest single-ship order, in cash terms, which the Company has secured. The placing of the contract followed more than eighteen months of design development and detailed technical and contractual negotiations with the Ministry. To be named RFA *Fort Victoria*, with a displacement in excess of 30,000 tonnes, ship no. 1727 will take Harland & Wolff into the next decade, lifting the value of the current order book to over £300 million and placing the Company in a strong position to secure further orders in the potential six-ship series of the 'Fort' class.

After intensive research in the merchant-shipping market, key types of vessel have been identified for sales exploitation, namely large bulk carriers, smaller crude-oil tankers, products carriers and liquefied petroleum gas carriers; and the Company has promoted new product lines which include the IHI 'Friendship' and other types of multi-purpose dry-cargo vessels. The unique capabilities of the Belfast yard are convincing selling points in a wide range of markets, assisting the Company to compete effectively in construction and repair contracts of unusual complexity.

The competitive and technically demanding offshore-oil market is another area which the Company is energetically exploring, and an important asset here is Harland & Wolff's experience in building gas carriers and the complex and innovative SWOPS vessel.

The 'three legged' structure of the Company's current marketing strategy, concentrating on advanced merchant-ship, quasi-naval and offshore-oil contracts, has placed new demands on the management of the yard. The improved techniques of design and manufacture, and the increased application of management information services have made it both necessary and possible to introduce new management systems. Of these the most notable are zone and project management – already discussed in Chapter 14.

It is taking time for the full potential of all these initiatives to be realised. Prolonged contract negotiations have from time to time affected morale and have resulted in periods of imbalance in the workload of the various trades in the yard. This has led

T. John Parker, chairman
of the Company, 1986.

to under-usage of human and capital resources with a resultant under-recovery of
overheads, a particularly serious problem when Government has set stringent targets
for the reduction of external funding. With considerable progress being made towards
achieving these targets, it would be misleading to see aid from Government as being
an entirely one-way transaction. The Company has been a demonstrably peaceable
symbol of British commitment to Northern Ireland, generating a significant proportion of all employment in the Province's manufacturing sector. It has also been a leader
in United Kingdom shipbuilding, producing, in the largest construction yard in
Europe, the biggest, the best and the most technically advanced products. Queen's
Island has been a training ground not only for first-class shipbuilders and marine
engineers but also for skilled workers and managers for the whole of Northern
Ireland. The Company's purchases of materials and components – amounting to
almost two-thirds of the price of a ship – provide a market for hundreds of United
Kingdom suppliers. The purchasing power of Harland & Wolff employees is of vital
importance to the city of Belfast and to Northern Ireland as a whole.

The Company has a dedicated, highly competent and increasingly youthful
management team and a responsible and skilled workforce. The Queen's Island
complex, offering the physical integration of engineering with shipbuilding and ship-
repairing facilities, provides an industrial platform unrivalled in the UK, while the
building dock and the advanced steelworking facilities, including a massive paint
hall, firmly establish Harland & Wolff in the front line of European yards.

The dominant attitude throughout the Company is a will to win, to innovate, to
produce a quality product on time, and above all to sell. The 125th anniversary of
the partnership, in 1986, is not an occasion for complacency, but an opportunity to
look back on the resolution to survive through the bad times, and on prosperity in
the good times symbolised by the years when the Company headed the world tonnage
league. A past as distinguished as that of Harland & Wolff, with its traditions of
excellence in design, craftsmanship and human relations, is a sound and stimulating
basis for moving into the future.

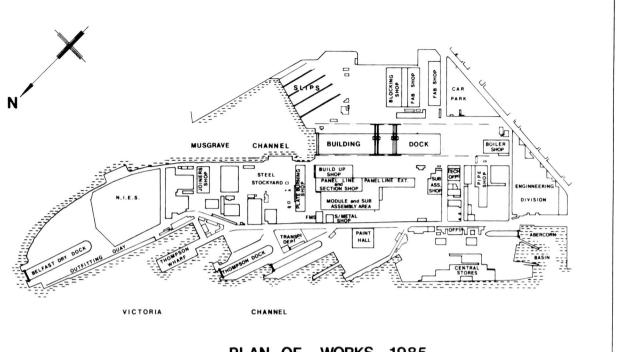

N

MUSGRAVE   CHANNEL

SLIPS

BLOCKING SHOP

FAB SHOP

FAB SHOP

CAR PARK

BUILDING   DOCK

BOILER SHOP

JOINERS SHOP

STEEL STOCKYARD

PLATE BURNING SHOP

BUILD UP SHOP

PANEL LINE and SECTION SHOP

PANEL LINE EXT.

SUB ASS. SHOP

TECH OFF.

PIPE SHOP

ENGINNEERING DIVISION

N.I.E.S.

MODULE and SUB ASSEMBLY AREA

FMS

S/METAL SHOP

OFFICE

ABERCORN

BASIN

BELFAST DRY DOCK

OUTFITTING   QUAY

THOMPSON WHARF

THOMPSON DOCK

TRANSPT DEPT

PAINT HALL

CENTRAL STORES

VICTORIA   CHANNEL

PLAN OF WORKS 1985

100   0   200 m   400 m

K. WHITELAW

493

REFERENCES

References to Harland & Wolff's records have not been endnoted. In 1903 W.J. Pirrie imposed a severe records management procedure whereby all the correspondence of the Company was destroyed after seven years. This was revised in 1919 when Pirrie instructed that the only records to be retained after ten years were the private journal and ledger, the general ledger and 'private letter books and letters constituting contracts, kept in safe, also letter books and letters on labour affairs, and management papers in Secretary's Office'. Subsequently the private letters and contract letters were also destroyed. As a result the private ledgers from 1863, which also contain details of ship costs, are the only continuous series of corporate records to survive. From 1900 these are elaborated by annual detailed balance sheets and working papers. From the formation of the limited company in 1885 there are board and general meeting minutes. When the posts of managing directors were created in 1907 minutes of managing directors' committee meetings were recorded in a new series of books which run to 1928. In 1917 works committees were inaugurated but the only minutes to survive are those for the Belfast organisation from 1917 to 1931. Lord Kylsant formed a finance committee in 1924 and its minutes are continuous to the present. The minutes and corporate financial records of the sister company and later subsidiary, Ocean Transport Company, survive from 1894. These are the core records used to research the history of the Company. The source of information is usually made obvious from the context and the period. There are a few files containing policy information dating from 1932, which support the board minutes, and detailed labour relations files dating from 1910. These, along with all the Company's other corporate records, are in the process of being transferred to the Public Record Office of Northern Ireland, 66 Balmoral Avenue, Belfast BT9 6NY. The collection reference is D2805.

References to sources outside the Company's records have been endnoted. Individual documents and letters in files have not been itemised. Piece numbers only have been given.

Key to abbreviations

B of E	Bank of England
Bel Tel	*Belfast Telegraph*
BHC	Belfast Harbour Commissioners
BNL	*Belfast News-Letter*
GUA	Glasgow University Archives
H & W	Harland & Wolff
HMSO	Her Majesty's Stationery Office
MB	Minute Book
MBA	Midland Bank Archive
NMM	National Maritime Museum, London
PRO	Public Record Office
PRONI	Public Record Office of Northern Ireland
RMSP	Royal Mail Steam Packet Company
RMT	Royal Mail Trustees
TRINA	Transactions of the Royal Institute of Naval Architects

CHAPTER 1

1 George Benn, *A History of the Town of Belfast from the Earliest Times to the Close of the Eighteenth Century* (Marcus Ward, 1877), p. 65.

2 D.J. Owen, *A Short History of the Port of Belfast* (Mayne, Boyd & Son, 1917), chs. 1, 2.

3 John Sinclair, *Statistical Account of Scotland* (William Creech, 1793), vol. 7, pp. 21-2.

4 S. Shannon Millin, *Sidelights on Belfast History* (Baird, 1932), p. 101. Ballast Board accounts, 1791.

5 *BNL* 10 July 1792.

6 Owen, pp. 20, 25.

7 Shannon Millin, p. 102.

8 Quoted in Denis Rebbeck, *Presidential Address on Belfast Shipyards 1791-1947* (Belfast Association of Engineers, 1947), pp. 5-6.

9 *BNL* 21 March 1820.

10 *Bel Tel* 13 June 1941. Historical note on Charles Connell & Sons.

11 *BNL* 9 October 1838.

12 Indenture in possession of H & W.

13 Rebbeck, p. 8.

14 *BNL* 11 December 1838.

15 Owen, ch. 3. R. Sweetnam, 'The development of the port' in J.C. Beckett *et al*, *Belfast: The Making of the City* (Appletree Press, 1983), pp. 61-3.

16 H. Jefferson, *Viscount Pirrie of Belfast* (Mullan, 1948), pp. 11-19. Information supplied by Innes Macleod and Dr G.D. Pirrie.

17 Owen, ch. 3. Sweetnam in Beckett, pp. 61-3.

18 Owen, ch. 3. Sweetnam in Beckett, pp. 61-3.

19 Ballast Board minutes vol. 8. BHC annual and engineers' reports, 1849.

20 BHC engineers' memo book, 1849. BHC annual and engineers' reports, 1849/52. Cathal O'Byrne, *As I Roved Out* (Irish News, 1946), pp. 286-9.

CHAPTER 2

1 BHC annual report, 1853. *BNL* 7 September 1853.

2 *BNL* 3 December 1851. BHC MB no. 3. PRONI D1905/2/22.

3 BHC MB no. 4. BHC engineers' memo book, 1853, 1854.

4 *BNL* 29 September 1834. Denis Rebbeck, 'The history of iron shipbuilding on the Queen's Island up to July, 1874' (Unpublished Ph.D. thesis, Queen's University, Belfast, 1950), pp. 71-85.

5 J.B. Baker, *History of Scarborough* (Longmans, 1882), pp. 453-5. E.J. Harland, 'Shipbuilding in Belfast – its origin and progress' in S. Smiles (ed.), *Men of Invention and Industry* (John Murray, 1884), pp. 288-90.

6 Harland in Smiles, pp. 291-2.

7 *Ibid*. pp. 292-3.

8 *Ibid*. pp. 293-5.

9 *Ibid*. pp. 297-8.

10 Sir Bernard Burke and Ashworth P. Burke, *A Genealogical and Historical History of the Peerage and Baronetage* (Harrison & Sons, 1885). Information supplied by Douglas Carson (see 'The shipyard family', p. 93), and Staatsarchiv Hamburg.

11 Abstracted from B of E agents' letter books, held in the bank archives, London, and supplied by Dr Stanley Chapman, University of Nottingham.

12 Information supplied by Staatsarchiv Hamburg.

13 *Gore's Directory of Liverpool*, 1880/1900. *Liverpool Courier* 13 January 1897.

14 Abstracted from B of E agents' letter books, held in the bank archives, London, and supplied by Dr Stanley Chapman, University of Nottingham.

15 *Ibid*. E.W. Paget-Tomlinson, *Bibby Line: 175 Years of Achievement* (Privately published, 1982), p. 7.

16 Harland in Smiles, pp. 298-300.

17 *Ibid*. pp. 300-3.

18 James Douglas, 'The romance of self-made men, no. II, Lord Pirrie', *Strand Magazine*, vol. 58, no. 347 (1919), pp. 423-8.

19 Harland in Smiles, pp. 302-3.

20 PRONI D1905/2/22.

21 BHC engineers' memo book, 1855. Harland in Smiles, p. 303.

22 Harland in Smiles, p. 303.

23 *Ibid*. pp. 303-4. Harland misspelled William Houston's name as William Hanston.

24 *BNL* 5 October 1855.

25 C.R. Vernon Gibbs, *Passenger Liners of the Western Ocean* (Putnam, 1952), p. 243. *BNL* 19 May 1859.

26 Harland in Smiles, p. 304.

27 *Ibid*. p. 305. Jefferson, pp. 54-5.

28 Jefferson, pp. 62-3.

29 Harland in Smiles, p. 304.

30 Letter in possession of H & W.

31 GUA UCS1/11/1.

32 Harland in Smiles, p. 307.

33 *Ibid*. p. 305. *Belfast and Province of Ulster Directory for 1858-9* (Henderson, 1859), vol. IV.

34 Harland in Smiles, p. 310. *BNL* 5 September 1860.

35 Harland in Smiles, pp. 306-7.

36 Paget-Tomlinson, p. 8.

37 'Agreement for partnership' in possession of H & W.

38 Jefferson, pp. 1-3. *The Register Book* held at the Customs House, Belfast. *Henderson's Belfast Directory and Northern Repository* (Henderson, 1850).

39 *BNL* 12 June 1858.

40 Information supplied by Douglas Carson. Pirrie family obituary notices at Liverpool City Libraries, Record Office and Local History Department.

41 Jefferson, pp. 4-5.

42 Rebbeck, 'The history of iron shipbuilding on the Queen's Island', ch. 7.

43 Douglas, *Strand Magazine*, vol. 58, no. 347 (1919), pp. 424-5. *Report of the Belfast Riots Commission, with Evidence and Appendices*, Cmd. 4925 (HMSO, 1887), q7595, 7648. Evidence of Sir E.J. Harland. D.J. Owen, *History of Belfast* (Baird, 1921), p. 304.

44 Harland in Smiles, p. 311.

45 BHC engineers' report, 1867.

46 GUA DC90/4/35.

47 W.J. Oldham, *The Ismay Line* (Journal of Commerce of Liverpool, 1961), p. 29.

48 Harland in Smiles, p. 318. 'Shipbuilding at Belfast', *Engineering*, vol. 8 (1869), p. 266.

49 Jefferson, pp. 8-9.

50 Oldham, p. 29.

51 E.J. Harland's private ledger, 1875/84, in possession of H & W.

52 Harland in Smiles, p. 316.

53 BHC MB 1870/1.

54 Jefferson, p. 98.

55 Original apprenticeship indenture in possession of David Comeskey, Bangor.

56 Henry Fry, *The History of North Atlantic Steam Navigation with Some Account of Early Ships and Shipowners* (Sampson Low, Marston, 1896), pp. 162-5. Harland in Smiles, p. 314.

57 Harland in Smiles, pp. 314-5.

58 PRONI D2889/1/1.

59 West Yorkshire Archive Service, Leeds District Archives SS/A/I/39.

60 Jefferson, pp. 73-4.

61 Paget-Tomlinson, p. 10.

62 Jefferson, p. 58.

CHAPTER 3

1 E.J. Harland's private ledger, 1875/84, in possession of H & W. Memoir of A.B. Wilson, *Proceedings of the Institute of Mechanical Engineers* (1913), p. 984.

2 Harland in Smiles, p. 320.

3 D. Pollock, 'The work of ship lengthening', *Shipbuilder*, vol. 3, no. 9 (1908), p. 5.

4 NMM, Asiatic Steam Navigation Company MB no. 1, Memorandumed Articles of Association, 1878.

5 *BNL* 25 April 1913.

6 BHC engineers' report, 1867.

7 J. Caughey, *Seize then the Hour: A History of James P. Corry & Co. Ltd and of the Corry Family 1123-1974* (Privately published, 1979), p. 76.

8 BHC MB 1878/9.

9 Memoir of W.J. Pratten, *Proceedings of the Institute of Mechanical Engineers* (1928), pp. 516-7.

10 NMM, Asiatic Steam Navigation Company MB no. 1, 16 September 1879.

11 Jefferson, pp. 84-91. R.S. Allison, *The Seeds of Time: Being a Short History of the Belfast General and Royal Hospital 1850-1903* (Brough, Cox & Dunn, 1972), p. 187.

12 GUA UGD3/25/1.

13 J.F. Clarke and F. Storr, *The Introduction of the Use of Mild Steel into the Shipbuilding and Marine Engine Industries*, Occasional Papers in the History of Science and Technology, no. 1 (Newcastle upon Tyne Polytechnic, 1983). *TRINA*, vol. 9 (1868), p. 24. E.J. Harland's question on the treatment of steel plates in the shipbuilder's yard.

14 Douglas, *Strand Magazine*, vol. 58, no. 347 (1919), p. 427.

15 Patent no. 4637, 1882. Jefferson, p. 63.

16 Harland in Smiles, p. 321.

17 Alec Wilson, 'The shipbuilding industry in Belfast', *Proceedings of Belfast Natural History and Philosophical Society* (1915/16).

18 E.J. Harland's private ledger, 1875/84, in possession of H & W.

19 NMM, Asiatic Steam Navigation Company MB no. 1, October, 1883.

20 P.L. Cottrell and D.M. Aldcroft, *Shipping Trade and Commerce: Essays in Memory of Ralph Davis* (Leicester University Press, 1981), p. 144.

21 BHC MB 1881/4.

22 BHC 'Harbour Commissioners' plan of Belfast harbour, 1882'.

23 *Lloyd's Register of Shipping*, 1884/5.

24 *The Times* 21 April and 10 July 1885.

25 Articles of Association of Queen's Island Shipbuilding & Engineering Company Limited in possession of H & W.

26 Memoir of James Jack, *Proceedings of the Institute of Mechanical Engineers* (1886), p. 462.

CHAPTER 4

1 Jonathan Bardon, *Belfast: An Illustrated History* (Blackstaff Press, 1982), pp. 147-9.

2 *Report of the Belfast Riots Commission, with Evidence and Appendices*, Cmd. 4925 (HMSO, 1887), q7586-648. Evidence of Sir E.J. Harland.

3 *Ibid.* q7594.

4 *Royal Commission on the Depression of Trade*, Cmd. 4715 (HMSO, 1886), vol. XXII, p. 7.

5 NMM ADM138/36.

6 Oldham, pp. 105-6.

7 'Messrs. Harland & Wolff's works at Belfast', *Engineering*, vol. 94 (1912), p. 4.

8 'Harland & Wolff's shipyard and engine works', *Engineering*, vol. 46 (1888), pp. 103-5. 'Shipbuilding

and marine engineering works of Harland and Wolff', *Engineer*, vol. 66 (1888), pp. 142-3.

9 G.F.L. Giles, 'Belfast harbour', *Proceedings of the Institute of Mechanical Engineers* (1896), pp. 425-7.

10 PRONI D2190.

11 PRONI VAL12B/17/2D.

12 Oldham, p. 101.

13 NMM, Asiatic Steam Navigation Company MB no. 1, 16 September 1879.

14 'Shipbuilding and marine engine works, Belfast', *Proceedings of the Institute of Mechanical Engineers* (1888), pp. 418-19. *Engineer*, vol. 66 (1888), pp. 142-4.

15 Fry, pp. 175-7.

16 BHC engineers' annual report, 1890.

17 GUA UCS1/3/5.

18 D. Lyon, *Denny List* (National Maritime Museum, 1975), p. 357.

19 B. Huldermann, *Albert Ballin* (Cassell, 1922), p. 112.

20 Jefferson, p. 66.

21 *Ibid*. p. 133.

22 Minutes of the Mersey Dock and Harbour Board shipbuilding yards, 1879/1906, item 70, held at Merseyside County Archives Service.

23 Jefferson, pp. 133-4.

24 BHC rent book no. 1, p. 45.

25 'Wages dispute on the Clyde', *Engineer*, vol. 80 (1895), pp. 356-7. 'The lockout in the Clyde shipbuilding trade', *Engineer*, vol. 80 (1895), p. 456. 'The strike on the Clyde', *Engineer*, vol. 80 (1895), p. 619. 'Free labour on the Clyde', *Engineer*, vol. 81 (1896), p. 8.

26 Baring Brothers' archives MC3.35, 1895.

27 *BNL* 27 and 28 July 1896.

28 *BNL* 28 December 1895.

29 Jefferson, pp. 117-18.

30 *Ibid*. p. 59.

31 'Travelling gantry at Messrs. Harland and Wolff's shipyard, Belfast', *Engineering*, vol. 65 (1898), p. 111.

32 BHC MB 1898/9. Jefferson, pp. 107-8.

33 Strathclyde Regional Archives, Glasgow, TD 145/90. Jefferson, pp. 200-1.

34 Oldham, pp. 133-4.

35 Pollock, *Shipbuilder*, vol. 3, no. 9 (1908), pp. 7-9.

36 Jefferson, pp. 266-82.

37 Oldham, p. 134.

38 J. McGoldrick, 'Trade unions and industrial relations in the British shipbuilding industry' in F.M. Walker and A. Slaven (eds.), *European Shipbuilding: One Hundred Years of Change* (Marine Publications International, 1984), p. 179.

39 Douglas, *Strand Magazine*, vol. 58, no. 347 (1919), p. 424.

CHAPTER 5

1 L. Hannah, *The Rise of the Corporate Economy* (Methuen, 1978), p. 21.

2 J.D. Scott, *Vickers: A History* (Weidenfeld & Nicholson, 1962). A. Grant, *Steel & Ships: The History of John Brown's* (Privately published, 1919).

3 GUA UGD3/2. Denny private ledgers, 1844/1910.

4 F.E. Hyde, *Cunard and the North Atlantic 1840-1973: A History of Shipping and Financial Management* (MacMillan, 1975), pp. 100-9.

5 J. Taylor, *Ellermans: A Wealth of Shipping* (Wilson House Gentry, 1976), pp. 15-20.

6 Hyde, p. 102. Huldermann, p. 44.

7 Huldermann, pp. 44-5.

8 Arthur Bibby's letter book in possession of Bibby Brothers & Company, Liverpool.

9 Taylor, pp. 16-17.

10 'Chamber of Shipping of the United Kingdom – annual meeting and dinner', *Shipping World*, vol. 23 (1901), pp. 325-8.

11 Oldham, pp. 136-7.

12 *Ibid*. pp. 137-8.

13 BHC MB 1899/1900.

14 Eng. Captain Edgar C. Smith, *A Short History of Naval and Marine Engineering* (Babock & Wilcox, 1937), pp. 251-3, 262, 282-4.

15 P.N. Davies, *The Trade Makers. Elder Dempster in West Africa 1852-1972* (Allen & Unwin, 1973), p. 28.

16 Huldermann, pp. 48-9.

17 *Ibid*. pp. 46-7.

18 Oldham, p. 140. PRO 30/60/48.

19 PRO 30/60/48.

20 *Ibid*. Ocean Transport Company Limited board minute book, 5 September 1894 – 18 July 1935.

21 'The shipping trust agreements', *Shipping World*, vol. 24 (1902), p. 493.

22 Hyde, pp. 109, 118. V. Vale, 'The government and the Cunard contracts 1903', *Journal of Transport History*, NS vol. 5 (1979), pp. 36-45.

23 *Report from the Select Committee on Steamship Subsidies*, Cmd. 300 (HMSO, 1901) and Cmd. 385 (HMSO, 1902). Evidence of W.J. Pirrie.

24 Information supplied by Dr Freda Harcourt, Queen Mary College, London, from P & O archives.

25 Jefferson, pp. 63-4.

26 'Mr Kempster's retirement', *Shipbuilding and Shipping Record*, vol. 40 (1932), p. 286.

27 Information supplied by J.S. Baillie.

28 BHC MB 1902/3.

29 MBA diary, 1902/3.

30 Edwin Green and Michael Moss, *A Business of National Importance – The Royal Mail Shipping Group, 1902-1937* (Methuen, 1982), ch. 2.

31 RMSP MB no. 14, 2 December 1903.
32 Oldham, pp. 160-1.
33 *Ibid*. p. 151.
34 Information supplied by J.S. Baillie.

CHAPTER 6

1 John Boyle, 'The Belfast Protestant Association and the Independent Orange Order, 1901-10', *Irish Historical Studies*, vol. 13 (1962/3), pp. 117-52.
2 Jefferson, pp. 92-7, 135-6.
3 'Harland & Wolff's works at Belfast', *Engineer*, vol. 105 (1908), pp. 607-8.
4 'Harland & Wolff's works at Southampton', *Engineer*, vol. 106 (1908), pp. 61-4.
5 Pollock, *Shipbuilder*, vol. 3, no. 9 (1908), pp. 3-4.
6 Douglas, *Strand Magazine*, vol. 58, no. 347 (1919), p. 424. Information supplied by Helen W. Taylor.
7 Information supplied by J.S. Baillie.
8 Jefferson, pp. 169-70.
9 John Brown & Company board minutes, 1904/5.
10 John Brown & Company AGM and board minutes, 1907.
11 Jefferson, pp. 182-5.
12 *Ibid*. pp. 217-23.
13 Green and Moss, pp. 29-30.
14 Information supplied by Helen W. Taylor, J.S. Baillie and Colonel V.S. Laurie.
15 John Brown & Company AGM minutes, 1910.
16 Allison, p. 255. *BNL* 21 October 1910.
17 *BNL* 2 April 1910. Jefferson, p. 76.
18 Jefferson, pp. 76-7.
19 Oldham, p. 173.
20 Jefferson, pp. 98-9.
21 *Ibid*. p. 137.
22 BHC MB 1911/12.
23 *The Times* 16 January and 23 February 1912.
24 'Harland & Wolff on the Tyne', *Shipbuilding and Shipping Record*, vol. 3 (1914), p. 498.
25 'Clyde and Tyne shipyard extensions', *Engineer*, vol. 111 (1911), p. 159.
26 Green and Moss, p. 31.
27 C.C. Pounder, 'The history of Harland & Wolff's Finnieston Works, Glasgow, and its association with Burmeister & Wain', (Unpublished, 1978), in possession of H & W.
28 Jefferson, p. 156.
29 *Ibid*. pp. 144-5.
30 *The Times* 12 February 1912.
31 *The Times* 23, 24, 27, 28, 29 February and 16 March 1912.
32 Jefferson, p. 157.
33 S.F. Bulloch, 'A Titanic Hero' Thomas Andrews Shipbuilder* (Mansell & Company, 1912). Andrews family papers in possession of Thomas M. Andrews, Comber.

34 Oldham, pp. 185-218. GUA DC90/1/40, *Titanic* inquiry paper and reports.
35 *Official Journal of Patents* (Patent Office, 1912/15).
36 MBA 30/38/40.
37 GUA UGD4/1/53.
38 PRONI D2805/132/6.
39 PRONI D2805/130/5.
40 *Ibid*.
41 *Ibid*.
42 McGoldrick in Walker and Slaven, p. 180.
43 Demarcation list in possession of personnel department, H & W.
44 MBA 13/17.
45 Oldham, pp. 177-84. E.A. Subiers, 'Some financial aspects of the International Mercantile Marine Company', *Journal of Political Economy*, vol. 23 (1915), p. 921.
46 Information supplied by J.S. Baillie.
47 *Ibid*.
48 Information supplied by Cecil Slator.

CHAPTER 7

1 A.C. Hampshire, *The Phantom Fleet* (White Lion, 1930).
2 Ian Buxton, *Big Gun Monitors: The History of the Design, Construction and Operation of the Royal Navy's Monitors* (Naval Institute Press, 1978), pp. 12-13, 15-25.
3 *Ibid*. pp. 41-5.
4 *History of the Ministry of Munitions*, vol. 1, part II (London, 1922), 'Treasury agreement'.
5 Buxton, pp. 15-25, 41-5.
6 *Ibid*. p. 69.
7 *Ibid*. pp. 39, 67.
8 Oldham, p. 225.
9 P.L. Payne, *Colvilles and the Scottish Steel Industry* (Oxford University Press, 1979), p. 135.
10 *Merchant Shipbuilding Under Government Control from May 1917 up to the Cessation of Hostilities* (Privately published, 1918), pp. 12-13. Copy held in GUA DC35/71, papers of Sir James Lithgow.
11 *Ibid*. p. 14.
12 GUA DC35/7.
13 'The first standard ship', *Shipbuilding and Shipping Record*, vol. 10 (1917), p. 217. 'Trial trip of the first standard ship', *Shipbuilding and Shipping Record*, vol. 10 (1917), p. 230.
14 PRONI D2805/134/14.
15 *Merchant Shipbuilding*, pp. 34-7.
16 GUA DC35/71.
17 Sholto Douglas, *Years of Combat* (Collins, 1963), pp. 355-6. J. Corlett, *Aviation in Ulster* (Blackstaff Press, 1981), ch. 3.
18 Green and Moss, p. 38.

19 Jefferson, p. 255. Information supplied by J.S. Baillie.

20 Information supplied by Dr T.R. Craig, a former chairman of Colvilles Limited.

21 *Merchant Shipbuilding*, pp. 12-13.

22 *BNL* 23 August 1919.

23 John Brown & Company board minutes, 1918.

24 *Merchant Shipbuilding*, p. 41.

25 Douglas, *Strand Magazine*, vol. 58, no. 347 (1919), p. 425.

CHAPTER 8

1 Lamport & Holt general meeting minutes, 11 April 1919.

2 C.E. Fayle, *The War and the Shipping Industry* (Oxford University Press, 1927), p. 243.

3 S.G. Sturmey, *British Shipping and World Competition* (Athlone Press, 1962), pp. 56-7. 'The private work of shipbuilding and ship repairing firms', *Shipbuilding and Shipping Record*, vol. 13 (1919), p. 77.

4 Henry Patterson, *Class Conflict and Sectarianism: The Protestant Working Class and the Belfast Labour Movement 1868-1920* (Blackstaff Press, 1980) pp. 92-114.

5 'Greenock shipyard extension', *Shipbuilding and Shipping Record*, vol. 13 (1919), p. 386.

6 'Industrial expansion at Greenock', *Shipbuilding and Shipping Record*, vol. 14 (1919), p. 529.

7 GUA UCS1/5/18.

8 *Seventy Adventurous Years: The Story of the Bank Line 1885-1955* (Privately published, 1955), pp. 65-6. Jefferson, pp. 145-6.

9 Payne, pp. 135-6.

10 'A new shipyard for Belfast', *Modern Transport*, vol. 2, no. 38 (1919), pp. 14-15.

11 John Brown & Company AGM minutes, 1920.

12 Patterson, pp. 119-20.

13 *Ibid.* pp. 135-42. The problems of H & W seem to have been less than those at Workman Clark.

14 Oldham, p. 233.

15 Information supplied by J.S. Baillie.

16 *Parliamentary Debates, Commons, 1921*, vol. 147 (HMSO, 1921), pp. 75-98.

17 PRO T190/96, T190/97.

18 MBA diary, 1922.

19 Information supplied by Cecil Slator.

20 Information supplied by Helen W. Taylor.

21 *TFA Statements of Guarantees*, (61) XIII (HMSO, 1927), p. 529.

22 Payne, p. 158.

23 GUA UCS1/5/22.

24 Information supplied by J.S. Baillie.

25 Letter from Lady Pirrie to W. Slator, 24 October 1923, in possession of Cecil Slator.

26 Jefferson, pp. 283-4.

27 'The late Viscount Pirrie: the man and his work', *Syren and Shipping Illustrated*, vol. 3, no. 1450 (1924), pp. 1-8.

28 Information supplied by D.H. Alexander.

CHAPTER 9

1 Information supplied by J.S. Baillie.

2 Will of Lord Pirrie in possession of J.S. Baillie.

3 Information supplied by J.S. Baillie.

4 GUA UGD104/33/8. Correspondence of Sir John Craig.

5 PRONI FIN18/3/234.

6 'Harland & Wolff', *Shipbuilding and Shipping Record*, vol. 24 (1924), p. 100.

7 Information supplied by J.S. Baillie.

8 GUA UGD104/33/8.

9 Green and Moss, pp. 67-9.

10 'New White Star liner – *Laurentic*', *Shipbuilding and Shipping Record*, vol. 30 (1927), pp. 495-9.

11 PRO T190/97. Green and Moss, p. 78.

12 PRO T190/97. Green and Moss, p. 85.

13 PRO T190/97. Green and Moss, p. 86.

14 PRO T190/97. Green and Moss, p. 86.

15 Information supplied by D.H. Alexander.

16 '*Llangibby Castle*', *Shipbuilding and Shipping Record*, vol. 34 (1929), p. 654.

17 PRO T190/97. Green and Moss, p. 96.

18 Green and Moss, pp. 99-100.

19 *Ibid.* pp. 106-7.

20 Payne, pp. 183-6.

21 NMM RMT 205.

22 PRO T190/97.

23 Green and Moss, pp. 100-4.

24 *Ibid.* pp. 115-17.

25 'A special passenger liner and "Britannic" number', *Motor Ship*, vol. 11, no. 122 (1930), p. 62.

26 *BNL* 11 August 1930.

CHAPTER 10

1 Green and Moss, ch. 7.

2 B of E SMT2/280.

3 MBA 30/58.

4 B of E SMT2/82.

5 NMM RMT 11.

6 *Ibid.*

7 *BNL* 11 August 1930.

8 Green and Moss, pp. 121-2.

9 NMM RMT 11.

10 *Ibid.*

11 *Ibid.*

12 NMM RMT 12. MBA, F. Hyde's diary no. 8.

13 NMM RMT 12. MBA, F. Hyde's diary no. 8.

14 NMM RMT 12. MBA, F. Hyde's diary no. 8.

15 Green and Moss, pp. 140-3.

16 *Ibid.* pp. 148-9. NMM RMT 12.

17 NMM RMT 12.

18 *Ibid.*

19 *Ibid.* Information supplied by Sir Archibald Forbes.

20 'Confidence in the *Georgic', Shipbuilding and Shipping Record*, vol. 39 (1932), p. 629.

21 MBA, R. Buchanan's diary.

22 MBA 30/109/110.

23 MBA 30/109/111.

24 'D. & W. Henderson & Co.', *Shipbuilding and Shipping Record*, vol. 45 (1935), pp. 342, 365. 'Financing the owners', *Shipbuilding and Shipping Record*, vol. 45 (1935), p. 375.

25 *BNL* 20 April 1935 and press cuttings in possession of H & W.

26 Corlett, ch. 7.

27 MBA 30/109/111.

28 Frank C. Bowers, *The Flag of the Southern Cross* (Shaw,Savill & Albion, 1946), p. 115.

29 MBA 30/109/111.

30 *Ibid.*

31 John Philp, 'Harland & Wolff Ltd', *Fairplay Weekly Shipping Journal*, vol. 143, no. 2818 (1937), pp. 298-9.

32 MBA 30/109/111.

33 *Ibid.* PRO T190/101.

34 PRO T190/107.

35 Information supplied by D.H. Alexander.

36 Information supplied by J.S. Baillie.

37 MBA 30/109/111.

38 PRO T190/100.

CHAPTER 11

1 J.W. Blake, *Northern Ireland in the Second World War* (HMSO, 1956), p. 77.

2 Information supplied by J.S. Baillie.

3 Antony Preston and Alan Raven, *Man o' War 7: Flower Class Corvettes* (Arms and Armour Press, 1982), pp. 1-2.

4 W.H. Mitchell and L.A. Sawyer, *Empire Ships of World War II* (Journal of Commerce & Shipping Telegraph, 1965), pp. 3-29.

5 Preston and Raven, p. 56.

6 A.C. Hampshire, *The Phantom Fleet*, 2nd edn (Kimber, 1960), pp. 78-9.

7 Corlett, pp. 63-6.

8 Green and Moss, pp. 193-4.

9 Information supplied by J.S. Baillie.

10 H.T. Lenton and J.J. Colledge, *Warships of World War II*, 2nd edn (Ian Allan, 1973), pp. 450-6.

11 Information supplied by Denis Rebbeck.

12 Corlett, pp. 72-5, 77.

13 Black, pp. 316-20.

14 E. Cuthbert and D. Rebbeck, 'British shipbuilding: the Harland and Wolff yards, Belfast', *Welding*, vol. 15, no. 9 (1947), pp. 429-40.

15 Mitchell and Sawyer, p. 3.

16 Blake, pp. 226-9.

17 *Ibid.* pp. 225-6.

18 *Ibid.* pp. 229-35. C.D. McGimpsey (ed.), *Bombs on Belfast: The Blitz 1941* (Pretani Press, 1984). Bardon, pp. 236-40.

19 Blake, pp. 235-8. Information supplied by Francis Lowry.

20 Blake, p. 399.

21 Green and Moss, p. 194.

22 Leo Marriott, *Royal Navy Frigates 1945-1983* (Ian Allan, 1983), pp. 22-32.

23 Information supplied by J.S. Baillie.

24 Letter from Lithgow to Craven.

25 Information supplied by J.S. Baillie.

26 Information supplied by J.S. Baillie.

27 Green and Moss, pp. 194-5.

28 Information supplied by J.S. Baillie.

29 Cuthbert and Rebbeck, *Welding*, vol. 15, no. 9 (1947), pp. 429-40.

CHAPTER 12

1 A. Cairncross, *Years of Recovery: British Economic Policy 1945-51* (Methuen, 1985), pp. 106, 470.

2 Information supplied by J.S. Baillie.

3 Information supplied by Denis Rebbeck.

4 Information supplied by J.S. Baillie.

5 *Ministry of Transport, Formal Investigation into a casualty by explosion in the engine room of the British Motor Ship 'Reina Del Pacifico' on 11th September 1947 off the Belfast Lough* (HMSO, 1948). Information supplied by Alan Watt.

6 Information supplied by Alan Brew.

7 Information supplied by Denis Rebbeck.

8 Information supplied by J.S. Baillie.

9 Information supplied by J.S. Baillie and Denis Rebbeck.

10 Information supplied by J. Smith and E. Moller.

11 Information supplied by Denis Rebbeck.

12 Information supplied by David Geary.

13 Quoted in Libby Purvis (ed.), *All at Sea* (Fontana, 1984), p. 132.

14 Information supplied by Alan Brew.

15 Information supplied by J.S. Baillie.

16 Information supplied by J.S. Baillie, Alan Brew and Denis Rebbeck.

17 Information supplied by Denis Rebbeck.

18 Leo Marriott, pp. 54-5.

19 *Report by the Tribunal of the Public Inquiry into the Accident at the Gangway on the Whale Factory Ship 'Juan Peron' on 31st January 1951* (HMSO, 1951).

20 Information supplied by Alan Brew and others. *Engineering*, vol. 184, no. 4772 (1957), p. 229. Atholl Blair's obituary.

21 Anthony Slaven, 'Growth and stagnation in British/Scottish shipbuilding' in Jan Kuuse and Anthony Slaven (eds.), *Scottish and Scandinavian Shipbuilding Seminar: Development Problems in Historical Perspective* (University of Glasgow, 1980), pp. 27-30.

22 Information supplied by Denis Rebbeck.

23 Information supplied by Denis Rebbeck, Jack Kirkpatrick and others. Jack Worth, *British Warships Since 1945. Part 4: Minesweepers* (Maritime Books, 1984), p. 5.

24 Northern Ireland Loans Guarantee Act, 1922.

25 Information supplied by J.S. Baillie, Denis Rebbeck, Robin Cameron and others.

26 Information supplied by Denis Rebbeck.

27 Information supplied by Robin Cameron.

28 Information supplied by J.S. Baillie.

29 Information supplied by Jack Kirkpatrick and others.

30 *BNL* 17 August 1954.

31 Information supplied by Ewart Murphy.

32 Slaven in Kuuse and Slaven, pp. 27-30.

33 Information supplied by Denis Rebbeck.

34 Information supplied by Denis Rebbeck.

35 Information supplied by Denis Rebbeck.

36 Information supplied by Alan Watt.

37 Information supplied by Alan Watt.

38 Information supplied by J.S. Baillie and others.

39 Information supplied by Denis Rebbeck.

40 Information supplied by Alan Brew.

41 Slaven in Kuuse and Slaven, p. 32.

42 Information supplied by J.S. Baillie.

43 Information supplied by Billy Baxter and others.

44 Information supplied by Billy Harrison.

45 Information supplied by Denis Rebbeck.

46 Information supplied by Denis Rebbeck.

47 *Northern Whig* 20 March 1946.

48 Information supplied by Douglas Carson.

CHAPTER 13

1 Information supplied by Alan Brew.

2 Information supplied by Angus Carrick.

3 Information supplied' by J. Smith.

4 Anthony Slaven, 'Management policy and the eclipse of British shipbuilding' in F.M. Walker and Anthony Slaven (eds.), *European Shipbuilding: One Hundred Years of Change* (Marine Publications International, 1983), pp. 832-3.

5 Information supplied by Alan Watt.

6 Information supplied by Denis Rebbeck.

7 R.R.G. Cameron, 'The sliding of a large tanker on the slipway', *TRINA*, vol. 3 (1969), pp. 141-8.

8 Colvilles Ltd was incorporated in 1936, including David Colville & Sons, owned by Harland & Wolff since 1920.

9 *Report of the Shipbuilding Inquiry Committee 1965-1966*, Cmd. 2937 (HMSO, 1966).

10 *Ibid.*

11 Information supplied by Sir Alec Cairncross, the economist.

12 Information supplied by Malcolm Mackenzie.

13 Information supplied by Denis Rebbeck.

14 Booz-Allen & Hamilton International BV, *British Shipbuilding 1972* (HMSO, 1972), pp. 210-12. Lists European berths for VLCCs.

15 Information supplied by E. Greer.

16 R.R.G. Cameron and S.M. Tennant, 'The building dock and new steelworking facilities at Queen's Island, Belfast', *Transactions of the North East Association of Engineers and Shipbuilders*, vol. 87 (1971), pp. 153-68, Discussion D31-3.

17 W.D. Flackes, *Northern Ireland: A Political Directory* (Gill & Macmillan, 1980), pp. 95-6, and Bardon, pp. 278-81 give a summary of events.

18 Cameron and Tennant, *Transactions of the North East Association of Engineers and Shipbuilders*, vol. 87 (1971), pp. 153-68.

19 Information supplied by Alan Watt.

20 Slaven in Walker and Slaven, pp. 82-4.

21 Information supplied by Denis Rebbeck, J.S. Baillie and others.

22 Flackes, pp. 112-13. Bardon, pp. 283-4.

23 Information supplied by Alan Watt.

24 Information supplied by Alan Watt.

25 Information supplied by Robin Cameron.

26 Slaven in Walker and Slaven, pp. 83-4.

27 *Ibid.*

28 *Report of the Shipbuilding Inquiry Committee 1965-1966*, Cmd. 2937 (HMSO, 1966). Shipbuilding Industry Act 1967, 15 & 16 Eliz II, c40.

CHAPTER 14

1 Clause 2.2 of the Shipbuilding Industry Act 1971, 19 & 20 Eliz II, c46 extended the provisions of the Shipbuilding Industry Act 1967 to Northern Ireland.

2 *Ibid.*

3 Merlyn Rees, *Northern Ireland: A Personal Perspective* (Methuen, 1985), p. 16.

4 Flackes, pp. 5, 7, 147 and Brian Faulkner, *Memoirs of a Statesman* (Weidenfeld and Nicholson, 1978), pp. 260-71 give a summary of the events of 1972.

5 Industry Act 1972, 20 & 21 Eliz II, c63.

6 Counter-Inflation Act 1973, 21 & 22 Eliz II, c9 authorised the 'pay-freeze'.

7 Slaven in Kuuse and Slaven, p. 43.

8 Alan Sked and Chris Cook, *Post War Britain* (Penguin, 1979), pp. 318-24 gives a brief summary of the 'winter of discontent'.

9 Flackes, pp. 132-4, Faulkner, pp. 226-38 and Rees, pp. 65-107 give a summary of the Sunningdale Agreement.

10 Information supplied by Lord Rochdale and Douglas Cooper.

11 Booz-Allen & Hamilton International BV, pp. 4-9.

12 Northern Ireland Act 1974, 22 & 23 Eliz II, c28 provided for United Kingdom administration by Orders in Council in the absence of a Northern Ireland Government.

13 Information supplied by R.S. Punt.

14 Information supplied by Ewart Murphy, Douglas Cooper and others.

15 Slaven in Kuuse and Slaven, pp. 43-4.

16 Flackes, pp. 8, 9, 148 gives a summary of the May 1977 strike and its context.

17 Information supplied by John Parker.

18 Council Directive 81/363/EEC, 28 April 1981, on aid to shipbuilding.

19 Information supplied by Lord Rochdale, Alec Cooke and others.

20 Slaven in Walker and Slaven, pp. 78-85.

21 Rees, pp. 23, 96, 288 refers to support by Whitelaw, Rees and Orme.

22 T. John Parker, 'Harland & Wolff – towards 125 years of shipbuilding' in Walker and Slaven, pp. 153-77, gives a recent summary of facilities.

SELECT BIBLIOGRAPHY

PERIODICALS

Belfast News-Letter
Economist
Evening Standard
Fairplay
Financial News
Glasgow Herald
Hansard
Lloyd's Register of Shipping

Motor Ship
Proceedings of the Institute of Mechanical Engineers
Shipbuilding and Shipping Record
Statist
Stock Exchange Year Book
Syren and Shipping Illustrated
The Times
TRINA

BOOKS, ARTICLES, REPORTS AND THESES

Aberconway, Lord. *The Basic Industries of Great Britain: Coal, Iron, Steel, Engineering, Ships – An Historic and Economic Survey*, London, Ernest Benn, 1927

Aldcroft, D.H. 'The depression in British shipping 1901-1911', *Journal of Transport History*, vol. 7 (1965/6)

see Cottrell, P.L. and D.H. Aldcroft

see Slaven, Anthony and D.H. Aldcroft (eds.)

Allison, R.S. *The Seeds of Time: Being a Short History of the Belfast General and Royal Hospital 1850-1903*, Belfast, Brough, Cox & Dunn, 1972

Anderson, R. *White Star*, Prescot, Stephenson & Sons, 1964

Bardon, Jonathan. *Belfast: An Illustrated History*, Belfast, Blackstaff Press, 1982

Beckett, J.C. *et al. Belfast: The Making of the City*, Belfast, Appletree Press, 1983

Belfast Harbour Commissioners Centenary 1847-1947, Belfast, Privately published, 1947

'Belfast works', *Proceedings of the Institute of Mechanical Engineers*, London, 1896

Bell, A.M.B. see Mallett, A.S. and A.M.B. Bell

Blake, J.W. *Northern Ireland in the Second World War*, Belfast, HMSO, 1956

Booz-Allen & Hamilton International BV. *British Shipbuilding 1972*, London, HMSO, 1973

Bourn, A.M. see Davies, P.N. and A.M. Bourn

Boyle, John. 'The Belfast Protestant Association and Independent Orange Order, 1901-10', *Irish Historical Studies*, vol. 13 (1962/3)

Bridges, Structural Steel Work, and Mechanical Engineering Productions by Sir William Arrol and Company Ltd, Dalmarnock Iron Works, Glasgow, London, Engineering, 1909

Brooks, C. *The Royal Mail Case*, London, Hodge, 1933

Bulloch, S.F. *'A Titanic Hero' Thomas Andrews Shipbuilder*, Dublin, Mansell & Company, 1912

Buxton, Ian. *Big Gun Monitors: The History of the Design, Construction and Operation of the Royal Navy's Monitors*, Annapolis, Maryland, Naval Institute Press, 1978

Cairncross, A. *Years of Recovery: British Economic Policy 1945-51*, London, Methuen, 1985

Caughey, J. *Seize then the Hour: A History of James P. Corry & Co. Ltd and of the Corry Family 1123-1974*, Belfast, Privately published, 1979

Chambers, George. *Faces of Change: The Belfast and Northern Ireland Chambers of Commerce and Industry 1783-1983*, Belfast, Privately published, 1983

Coe, W.E. *The Engineering Industry of Northern Ireland*, Newton Abbot, David & Charles, 1969

Colledge, J.J. *see* Lenton, H.T. and J.J. Colledge

Cook, Chris. *see* Sked, Alan and Chris Cook

Corlett, John. *Aviation in Ulster*, Belfast, Blackstaff Press, 1981

Cottrell, P.L. and D.H. Aldcroft. *Shipping Trade and Commerce: Essays in Memory of Ralph Davis*, Leicester, Leicester University Press, 1981

Cuthbert, N. *see* Isles, K.S. and N. Cuthbert

Davies, P.N. 'Business success and the role of chance: the extraordinary Philipps brothers', *Business History*, vol. 23 (1981)

  Sir Alfred Jones, Shipping Entrepreneur Par Excellence, London, Europa, 1978

  The Trade Makers. Elder Dempster in West Africa 1852-1972, London, Allen & Unwin, 1973

  see Marriner, Sheila

Davies, P.N. and A.M. Bourn. 'Lord Kylsant and the Royal Mail', *Business History*, vol. 14 (1972)

Ervine, St J. *Craigavon – Ulsterman*, London, Allen & Unwin, 1949

Faulkner, Brian. *Memoirs of a Statesman*, London, Weidenfeld & Nicholson, 1978

Fayle, C.E. *The War and the Shipping Industry*, Oxford, Oxford University Press, 1927

Flackes, W.D. *Northern Ireland: A Political Directory*, Dublin, Gill & Macmillan, 1980

Fry, Henry. *The History of North Atlantic Steam Navigation with Some Account of Early Ships and Shipowners*, London, Sampson Low, Marston, 1896

Gibson, J.F. *Brocklebanks 1770-1950*, Liverpool, Young, 1953

Giles, G.F.L. 'Belfast harbour', *Proceedings of the Institute of Mechanical Engineers*, London, 1896

  'Belfast harbour and its development', *TRINA*, vol. 45 (1903)

Grant, A. *Steel & Ships: The History of John Brown's*, Privately published, 1919

Green, E. *The Making of a Modern Banking Group: A History of the Midland Bank Since 1900*, London, St George's Press, 1979

Green, Edwin and Michael Moss. *A Business of National Importance – The Royal Mail Shipping Group, 1902-1937*, London, Methuen, 1982

Green, E.E.R. *The Lagan Valley, 1800-50*, London, Faber & Faber, 1949

Gribbon, Sybil. *Edwardian Belfast: A Social Profile*, Belfast, Appletree Press, 1982

Hampshire, A.C. *The Phantom Fleet*, London, Kimber, 1960

Hannah, L. *The Rise of the Corporate Economy*, London, Methuen, 1976

Harkness, D. and M. O'Dowd (eds.). *The Town in Ireland: Historical Studies XIII*, Belfast, Appletree Press, 1979

Hardy, A.C. *History of Motorshipping*, London, Whitehall Technical Press, 1955

Harland, E.J. *see* Smiles, S.

Huldermann, B. *Albert Ballin*, London, Cassell, 1922

Hume, J.R. and M.S. Moss. *Beardmore: The History of a Scottish Industrial Giant*, London, Heinemann, 1979

Hyde, F.E. *Cunard and the North Atlantic 1840-1973: A History of Shipping and Financial Management*, London, Macmillan, 1975

503

Isles, K.S. and N. Cuthbert. *An Economic Survey of Northern Ireland*, London, HMSO, 1957

Jameson, J. *The History of the Royal Belfast Academical Institution 1810-1960*, Belfast, Mullan, 1959

Jefferson, H. *Viscount Pirrie of Belfast*, Belfast, Mullan, 1948

Jones, L. *Shipbuilding in Britain Mainly Between the Two World Wars*, Cardiff, University of Wales Press, 1957

Kuuse, Jan and Anthony Slaven (eds). *Scottish and Scandinavian Shipbuilding Seminar: Development Problems in Historical Perspectives*, Glasgow, University of Glasgow, 1980

Lee, T.A. and R.H. Parker (eds.). *The Evolution of Corporate Financial Reporting*, Oxford, Nelson, 1979

Lenton, H.T. and J.J. Colledge. *Warships of World War II*, 2nd edn, Shepperton, Ian Allan, 1973

McGimpsey, Christopher D. (ed.). *Bombs on Belfast: The Blitz 1941*, Belfast, Pretani Press, 1984

McCutcheon, W.A. *The Industrial Archaeology of Northern Ireland*, Belfast, HMSO, 1980

McGoldrick, J. *see* Walker, F.M. and Anthony Slaven

Mackay, R.F. *Fisher of Kilverstone*, Oxford, Clarendon Press, 1973

Maguire, W.A. *Living Like a Lord: The Second Marquis of Donegall 1769-1844*, Belfast, Appletree Press, 1984

Mallett, A.S. and A.M.B. Bell. *The Pirrie-Kylsant Motorships 1915-1952*, Norwich, Mallett & Bell Publications, 1984

Marriner, Sheila (ed.). *Business and Businessmen: Studies in Business, Economic and Accounting History*, Liverpool, Liverpool University Press, 1978

Marriott, Leo. *Royal Navy Frigates 1945-83*, Shepperton, Ian Allan, 1983

Millin, S. Shannon. *Sidelights on Belfast History*, Belfast, Baird, 1932

Ministry of Transport, Formal Investigation into a casualty by explosion in the engine room of the British Motor Ship 'Reina del Pacifico' on 11th September 1947 off the Belfast Lough, Belfast, HMSO, 1948

Mitchell, W.J. and L.A. Sawyer. *Empire Ships of World War II*, Liverpool, Journal of Commerce & Shipping Telegraph, 1965

Moss, Michael. *see* Green, Edwin and Michael Moss

  see Hume, J.R. and M.S. Moss

O'Brien, C.C. (ed.). *The Shaping of Modern Ireland*, London, Routledge & Kegan Paul, 1960

O'Byrne, Cathal. *As I Roved Out*, Belfast, Irish News, 1946

O'Dowd, M. *see* Harkness, D. and M. O'Dowd (eds.)

Oldham, W.J. *The Ismay Line*, Liverpool, Journal of Commerce of Liverpool, 1961

Owen, D.J. *A Short History of the Port of Belfast*, Belfast, Mayne, Boyd & Son, 1917

Paget-Tomlinson, E.W. *Bibby Line: 175 Years of Achievement*, Liverpool, Privately published, 1982

Parker, R.H. *see* Lee, T.A. and R.H. Parker (eds.)

Patterson, Henry. *Class Conflict and Sectarianism: The Protestant Working Class and the Belfast Labour Movement 1868-1920*, Belfast, Blackstaff Press, 1980

Payne, P.L. *Colvilles and the Scottish Steel Industry*, Oxford, Oxford University Press, 1979

Peirson, J.G. *Great Ship Builders or the Rise of Harland & Wolff*, London, Stockwell, 1935

Pollard, S. and P. Robertson. *The British Shipbuilding Industry 1870-1914*, Cambridge, Mass., Harvard University Press, 1979

Preston, Antony and Alan Raven. *Man o' War 7: Flower Class Corvettes*, London, Arms and Armour Press, 1983

Purvis, Libby (ed.). *All at Sea*, London, Fontana, 1984

Raven, Alan. *see* Preston, Antony and Alan Raven

Rebbeck, Denis. 'The history of iron shipbuilding on the Queen's Island up to July, 1874', Unpublished Ph.D. thesis, Queen's University, Belfast, 1950

Rees, Merlyn. *Northern Ireland: A Personal Perspective*, London, Methuen, 1985

Reid, J.M. *James Lithgow – Master of Work*, London, Hutchinson, 1964

Report by the Tribunal of the Public Inquiry into the Accident at the Gangway on the Whale Factory Ship 'Juan Peron' on 31st January 1951, Belfast, HMSO, 1951

Report from the Select Committee on Steamship Subsidies, Cmd. 300, London, HMSO, 1901

Report of the Belfast Riots Commission, with Evidence and Appendices, Cmd. 4925, London, HMSO, 1887

Report of the Commissioners of Inquiry 1864, Respecting the Magisterial and Police Jurisdiction, Arrangements and Establishment of the Borough of Belfast, Cmd. 3466, London, HMSO, 1865

Report of the Commissioners of Inquiry into the Origin and Character of the Riots in Belfast in July and September 1857, Cmd. 2309, London, HMSO, 1857/8

Report of the Shipbuilding Inquiry Committee 1965-1966, Cmd. 2937, London, HMSO, 1966. (Geddes Report)

Robertson, P. *see* Pollard, S. and P. Robertson

Roebuck, Peter (ed.). *Plantation to Partition: Essays in Ulster History in Honour of J.L. McCracken*, Belfast, Blackstaff Press, 1981

Rowland, K.T. *Steam and Sea: A History of Steam Navigation*, Newton Abbott, David & Charles, 1970

Salamand, T.R. 'On the Belfast harbour', *Report of the British Association for the Advancement of Science*, London, 1874

Sawyer, L.A. *see* Mitchell, W.J. and L.A. Sawyer

Sked, Alan and Chris Cook. *Post War Britain*, Harmondsworth, Penguin, 1979

Slaven, Anthony. 'A shipyard in depression: John Brown's of Clydebank 1919-1938', *Business History*, vol. 19, no. 2, 1977

see Kuuse, Jan and Anthony Slaven (eds.)

see Kuuse, Jan and Anthony Slaven

see Walker, F.M. and Anthony Slaven

Slaven, Anthony and D.H. Aldcroft (eds.). *Business, Banking and Urban History: Essays in Honour of S.G. Checkland*, Edinburgh, John Donald, 1982

Smellie, J. *Shipbuilding and Repairing in Dublin: A Record of Work Carried Out by the Dublin Dockyard Co. 1901-1923*, Glasgow, McCorquodale, 1923

Smiles, S. (ed.). *Men of Invention and Industry*, London, John Murray, 1884

Sturmey, S.G. *British Shipping and World Competition*, London, Athlone Press, 1962

Sweetnam, R. *see* Beckett, J.C.

Taylor, J. *Ellermans: A Wealth of Shipping*, London, Wilton House Gentry, 1976

Vale, V. 'The government and the Cunard contracts 1903', *Journal of Transport History*, NS vol. 5, no. 1 (1976)

Vernon Gibbs, C.R. *British Passenger Liners of the Five Oceans*, London, Putnam, 1957

Passenger Liners of the Western Ocean, London, Putnam, 1952

Walker, F.M. and Anthony Slaven (eds.). *European Shipbuilding: One Hundred Years of Change*, London, Marine Publications International, 1984

'Works in Belfast', *Proceedings of the Institute of Mechanical Engineers*, London, 1888

Worth, Jack. *British Warships Since 1945. Part 4: Minesweepers*, Liskeard, Maritime Books, 1984

SHIP LIST

This is a list of ships built by Harland & Wolff. Where no letter follows the ship number, the ship was constructed at Queen's Island. A letter indicates that the ship was built in one of the Company's other yards or subcontracted to a subsidiary, a related company or another shipbuilding concern. The list is not comprehensive, as some vessels subcontracted, for example to Hawthorn Leslie, were not given Harland & Wolff numbers.

Where more than one name appears for a ship, this indicates a change in name during construction. The last entry is the name at delivery. The same principle applies to cases in which more than one owner is given, except where the second owner appears in brackets, indicating an associated company or a managing company.

Where the ship's name entry is blank this normally indicates that the contract was cancelled before a name was allocated, although in the case of some small craft it was not always the practice to allocate a name.

Tonnages are normally expressed in gross tons, calculated on the volume of space within the vessel, but for Admiralty and Ministry of Defence ships the figures represent approximate standard displacement tonnage, i.e. the weight of water displaced by the ship.

At the end of the main list details are given of vessels whose numbers were, for various reasons, not part of the sequence. Items of small craft were also built at the Harland & Wolff shipyards, particularly at Belfast and London, but were not included in the Ship List – such as pontoons, motor boats, dry-dock gates, hull sections, linkspan bridges, dredgers and ships' lifeboats.

Every effort has been made to ensure the accuracy of this list but, given the age and extent of the records on which it is based, it is impossible to guarantee the data, particularly in the case of very early vessels.

Key to letters

BC	Barclay Curle & Company, Glasgow
C	Clydebank, John Brown Shipbuilding & Engineering Company
C/G	Built at Clydebank and engined at Govan
D	Dumbarton, Archibald MacMillan & Son
Dy	William Denny & Brothers, Dumbarton
G	Govan yard, Glasgow
G/B	Built at Govan and engined at Belfast
G/P	Built at Govan and engined at Pointhouse
Gk	Greenock yard
I	Irvine yard of Mackie & Thomson
M	Meadowside yard, Glasgow, of D.&W. Henderson
P	Pointhouse yard, Glasgow, of A.&J. Inglis
WC	Workman Clark, Belfast

Ship no.	Name	Vessel type	Launch date	Delivery date	Tonnage	Owner
1	*Venetian*	cargo ship	30 July 1859	14 August 1859	1508	J. Bibby Sons & Co.
2	*Sicilian*	cargo ship	12 November 1859	24 November 1859	1492	J. Bibby Sons & Co.
3	*Syrian*	cargo ship	26 March 1860	1 April 1860	1492	J. Bibby Sons & Co.
4	unnamed		cancelled			
5	*Jane Porter*	sailing ship	1 September 1860	15 September 1860	952	J.P. Corry & Co.
6	*Miranda*	yacht	21 June 1860	June 1860	34	T. Yates
7	*Grecian*	cargo ship	12 January 1861	30 January 1861	1854	J. Bibby Sons & Co.
8	*Italian*	cargo ship	27 March 1861	13 April 1861	1859	J. Bibby Sons & Co.
9	*Egyptian*	cargo ship	23 July 1861	11 August 1861	1986	J. Bibby Sons & Co.
10	*Ballymurtagh*	'Wherry' barge	25 September 1861	September 1860	41	Wicklow Mining Co.
11	*Dalmatian*	cargo ship	19 November 1861	December 1861	1989	J. Bibby Sons & Co.
12	*Arabian*	cargo ship	15 April 1862	2 May 1862	1994	J. Bibby Sons & Co.
13	*Persian*	cargo ship	21 January 1863	February 1863	2137	J. Bibby Sons & Co.
14	*Castilian*	cargo ship	10 May 1862	July 1862	607	J. Bibby Sons & Co.
15	*Catalonian*	cargo ship	15 July 1862	2 August 1862	607	J. Bibby Sons & Co.
16	*Star of Erin*	sailing ship	9 October 1862	31 October 1862	948	J.P. Corry & Co.
17	*Recife*	sailing ship	21 October 1862	November 1862	465	James Napier
18	*Worrall*	sailing ship	December 1862	December 1862	484	J. Worrall
19	*Alexandra*	sailing ship	7 April 1863	8 June 1863	1352	T.&J. Brocklebank
20	*Star of Denmark*	sailing ship	19 June 1863	June 1863	998	J.P. Corry & Co.
21	*Victoria Nyanza*	sailing ship	15 August 1863	August 1863	1022	Joshua Prouse & Co.
22	*Palestine*	sailing ship	13 October 1863	October 1863	623	W.H. Tindall
23	*Olano*	sailing ship	29 September 1863	September 1863	445	Larrinaga Steamship Co.
24	*Star of Scotia*	sailing ship	January 1864	January 1864	999	J.P. Corry & Co.
25	*Kitty of Coleraine*	river boat	7 October 1863	30 October 1863	24	Lower Bann Steamboat Co.
26	*Waipara*	cargo ship	October 1863	28 November 1863	90	J. Ritchie
27	*Baroda*	sailing ship	23 April 1864	April 1864	1364	T.&J. Brocklebank
28	*Volador*	sailing ship	April 1864	20 April 1864	174	G. Lomer
29	*Star of Albion*	sailing ship	20 July 1864	July 1864	999	J.P. Corry & Co.
30	*Dharwar*	sailing ship	3 September 1864	September 1864	1456	Iron Ship Co. Ltd
31	*Douro*	cargo ship	November 1864	21 November 1864	528	J. Bibby Sons & Co.
32	*British Peer*	sailing ship	31 January 1865	February 1865	1478	British Shipowners Ltd
33	*Sesostris*	cargo ship	27 May 1865	1865	2053	James Moss & Co.
34	unnamed	iron-ore barge	1865	1865		James Moss & Co.
35	unnamed	iron-ore barge	1865	1865		James Moss & Co.
36	unnamed	shearsfloat	8 August 1865	8 August 1865		Dublin Corporation
37	*Pilot*	schooner	1865	1865	34	
38	*Fairy Queen*	ferry (paddle steamer)	1865	1865	149	Rock Ferry Co.
39	*Gypsy Queen*	ferry (paddle steamer)	1865	1865	149	Rock Ferry Co.
40	*Boyne*	sailing ship	18 September 1865	September 1865	617	W.H. Tindall

Ship no.	Name	Vessel type	Launch date	Delivery date	Tonnage	Owner
41	*Annie Sharp*	sailing ship	November 1865	1865	584	R.G. Sharp
42	*Duddon*	paddle tug	1865	1865	106	New Steam Navigation Co. (Hodbarrow Mining Co.)
43	*Guarani*	cargo ship	1865	1865	320	J. Dalglish
44	*Broughton*	sailing ship	25 January 1868	January 1868	602	Ismay, Imrie & Co.
45	*Candahar*	sailing ship	1 May 1866	May 1866	1418	T.&J. Brocklebank
46	*Tenasserim*	sailing ship	30 August 1866	September 1866	1418	T.&J. Brocklebank
47	*Istrian*	cargo ship	9 March 1867	21 April 1867	2930	J. Bibby Sons & Co.
48	*Iberian*	cargo ship	4 June 1867	July 1867	2930	J. Bibby Sons & Co.
49	*Illyrian*	cargo ship	31 August 1867	25 September 1867	2931	J. Bibby Sons & Co.
50	unnamed	caisson for Hamilton dock	14 February 1867	5 July 1867		Belfast Harbour Commissioners
51	*Black Diamond*	steam collier	1867	1867	105	P. Evans & Co.
52	*Camel*					
53	*Corsanegetto*	steam collier	1867	1867	183	M.A. Corsanego
54	*HMS Lynx*	'Beacon'-class gun boat	25 April 1868	12 June 1868	603	Admiralty
55	*Hebe*	lighter	1868	1868	157	W.&J. Phillips
56	*Star of Persia*	sailing ship	23 June 1868	June 1868	1289	J.P. Corry & Co.
57	*Woodlawn*	schooner	1868	1868	63	S. Morland
58	*Star of Greece*	sailing ship	19 September 1868	September 1868	1288	J.P. Corry & Co.
59	*Juliet*	sailing ship	1 January 1869	January 1869	1301	C.T. Bowring & Co.
60	*Elaine*	coaster	16 February 1869	31 May 1869	544	F. Lervick & Co.
61	*Lady Cairns*	sailing ship	24 April 1869	April 1869	1311	Harland and Wolff
62	unnamed	iron dredger	13 May 1869	May 1869	60	Dublin Harbour Board
63	unnamed	iron dredger	13 May 1869	May 1869	60	Dublin Harbour Board
64	unnamed	iron dredger	13 May 1869	May 1869	60	Dublin Harbour Board
65	unnamed	iron dredger	17 May 1869	May 1869	60	Dublin Harbour Board
66	unnamed	iron dredger	17 May 1869	May 1869	60	Dublin Harbour Board
67	unnamed	iron dredger	17 May 1869	May 1869	60	Dublin Harbour Board
68	*Carry*	lighter	31 March 1869	April 1869	81	William Gossage & Sons
69	*Bavarian*	cargo ship	7 October 1869	5 November 1869	3111	J. Bibby Sons & Co.
70	*Historian*	cargo ship	5 January 1870	9 March 1870	1830	T.&J. Harrison
71	*Bulgarian*	cargo ship	17 February 1870	20 March 1870	3112	J. Bibby Sons & Co.
72	*Bohemian*	cargo ship	16 April 1870	29 May 1870	3113	J. Bibby Sons & Co.
	unnamed	floating dry dock	1870	1870		Lord Erne
73	*Oceanic*	passenger ship	27 August 1870	24 February 1871	3808	Oceanic Steam Navigation Co.
74	*Atlantic*	passenger ship	26 November 1870	3 June 1871	3708	Oceanic Steam Navigation Co.
75	*Pacific*	passenger ship	1870	1870		
	Baltic	passenger ship	8 March 1871	2 September 1871	3708	Oceanic Steam Navigation Co.
76	*Republic*	passenger ship	4 July 1871	21 January 1872	3708	Oceanic Steam Navigation Co.

Ship no.	Name	Vessel type	Launch date	Delivery date	Tonnage	Owner
77	*Adriatic*	passenger ship	17 October 1871	31 March 1872	3868	Oceanic Steam Navigation Co.
78	*Camel*	cargo ship	7 September 1870	17 September 1870	269	Harland and Wolff
	Arctic					
79	*Celtic*	passenger ship	8 June 1872	17 October 1872	3867	Oceanic Steam Navigation Co.
80	*Gaelic*	cargo ship	21 September 1872	7 January 1873	2651	Oceanic Steam Navigation Co.
81	*Belgic*	cargo ship	17 January 1873	29 March 1873	2651	Oceanic Steam Navigation Co.
82	*Star of Germany*	sailing ship	11 March 1872	20 May 1872	1337	J.P. Corry & Co.
	Hellenic					
83	*Britannic*	passenger ship	3 February 1874	6 June 1874	5004	Oceanic Steam Navigation Co.
84	*Ferry No. 1*	river ferry	27 June 1872	1 October 1872	9	Belfast Harbour Commissioners
85	*Germanic*	passenger ship	15 July 1874	24 April 1875	5008	Oceanic Steam Navigation Co.
86	*Star of Bengal*	sailing ship	3 January 1874	7 March 1874	1870	J.P. Corry & Co.
87	*Belfast*	sailing ship	15 August 1874	26 October 1874	1957	T.&J. Brocklebank
88	*Star of Russia*	sailing ship	12 December 1874	12 February 1875	1981	J.P. Corry & Co.
89	*Majestic*	sailing ship	5 May 1875	24 June 1875	1974	T.&J. Brocklebank
90	*Aglaia*	sailing ship	10 March 1875	13 April 1875	821	Workman Brothers
91	*East Croft*	sailing ship	23 June 1875	10 August 1875	1367	J. Gambles
92	*Connaught Ranger*	sailing ship	17 August 1875	23 October 1875	1200	J.G. McCormick
93	*Millie*	river steamer	1875	27 July 1875	107	William Gossage & Sons
94	*Katie*	river steamer	13 August 1875	1875	107	William Gossage & Sons
95	*Fiji*	sailing ship	21 September 1875	29 October 1875	1436	W.J. Myers
96	*Pizarro*	sailing ship	December 1875	20 December 1875	1439	W.J. Myers
97	unnamed	barge (Nile boat)	1875	1875		W. Henderson & Co.
98	unnamed	barge (Nile boat)	1875	1875		W. Henderson & Co.
99	unnamed	barge (Nile boat)	1875	1875		W. Henderson & Co.
100	*Princess Beatrice*	paddle steamer	4 November 1875	4 February 1876	556	Larne & Stranraer Steam Packet Co.
101	*Thursby*	cargo ship	19 February 1876	16 July 1876	497	W. Thursby
102	unnamed	hopper barge	4 December 1875	1876		Cork Harbour Commissioners
103	*Lord Cairns*	sailing ship	12 May 1877	1878	1372	T. Dixon Hughes & Co.
104	unnamed	barge (Nile boat)	1875	1875		
105	*Mousmie*	yacht	1876	1876		
106	*E.J. Harland*	sailing ship	20 April 1876	1 June 1876	1333	Samuel Lawther, Thomas Dixon & Sons
107	*Thurland Castle*	sailing ship	22 July 1876	20 September 1876	1301	Lancaster Shipowners Co.
108	*Steelfield*	sailing ship	2 December 1876	1 January 1877	1315	R.C. McNaughton & Co.
109	*Gladys*	schooner	11 May 1876	May 1876	52	N. Mathieson
110	*Slieve More*	jute clipper	10 February 1877	24 March 1877	1749	W.P. Sinclair & Co.
111	*Slieve Bawn*	jute clipper	31 March 1877	12 May 1877	1749	W.P. Sinclair & Co.
112	*The Lagan*	barge	12 February 1876	22 February 1876	55	A. Guinness & Sons
113	*Star of Italy*	sailing ship	26 July 1877	18 October 1877	1644	J.P. Corry & Co.

Ship no.	Name	Vessel type	Launch date	Delivery date	Tonnage	Owner
114	Star of France	sailing ship	21 November 1877	5 January 1878	1663	J.P. Corry & Co.
115	Slieve Roe	sailing ship	2 February 1878	16 March 1878	1749	W.P. Sinclair & Co.
116	River Lagan	sailing ship	30 June 1877	14 August 1877	895	R. Neill & Sons
117	British Empire	passenger/cargo ship	7 March 1878	24 August 1878	3360	British Shipowners Ltd
	HMS Hecla	torpedo depot ship				Admiralty
118	British Empire	passenger/cargo ship	18 May 1878	10 August 1878	3361	British Shipowners Ltd
119	Faugh-a-Ballagh	barge	22 May 1878	21 June 1878	500	Dublin Harbour Board
120	Cyprus					
	Aerolite					
121	G.W. Wolff	sailing ship	28 September 1878	25 October 1878	1663	S. Lawther
122	Nubia	cargo ship	9 November 1878	February 1879	1958	African Steamship Co.
123	Shahjehan	cargo ship	24 December 1878	22 February 1879	1650	Asiatic Steam Navigation Co.
124	Shahzada	cargo ship	29 January 1879	April 1879	1677	Asiatic Steam Navigation Co.
125	Maharaja	cargo ship	26 March 1879	3 May 1879	1666	Asiatic Steam Navigation Co.
126	Maharani	cargo ship	26 April 1879	5 June 1879	1667	Asiatic Steam Navigation Co.
127	Fair Head	cargo ship	24 May 1878	3 July 1879	1175	Ulster Steamship Co.
128	British Crown	passenger ship	2 August 1879	8 October 1879	3487	British Shipowners Ltd
129	Galgorm Castle	cargo ship	June 1879	21 August 1879	192	A. McMullin
130	Lord Dufferin	sailing ship	1 October 1879	14 November 1879	1697	T. Dixon & Sons
131	Dawpool	sailing ship	1 January 1880	24 January 1880	1697	North Western Shipping Co.
132	HMS Algerine	gun boat	6 November 1880	12 December 1880	835	Admiralty
133	Holmhurst	cargo ship	5 November 1879	12 December 1879	495	J.H. Thursley
	Winnebah					Asiatic Steam Navigation Co.
134	Peshwa	cargo ship	27 March 1880	9 June 1880	2159	Turner & Co.
	Rosetta	passenger ship	27 May 1880	27 August 1880	3457	Peninsular & Oriental Steam Navigation Co.
135	White Head	cargo ship	5 May 1880	1880	1192	Ulster Steamship Co.
136	Black Head	cargo ship	15 January 1881	14 March 1881	1191	Ulster Steamship Co.
137	British Merchant	sailing ship	25 August 1880	7 October 1880	1742	British Shipowners Ltd
138	British Queen	passenger ship	4 November 1880	15 January 1881	3558	British Shipowners Ltd
139	British King	passenger ship	22 January 1880	29 March 1881	3559	British Shipowners Ltd
140	Woodhopper	hopper barge	18 June 1880	1880		Oceanic Steam Navigation Co.
141	Asiatic					
	Arabic	cargo ship	30 April 1881	12 August 1881	4368	Oceanic Steam Navigation Co.
142	Coptic	cargo ship	10 August 1881	9 November 1881	4448	Oceanic Steam Navigation Co.
143	Minnehaha					
	Winnebah	cargo ship	16 April 1881	1 July 1881	1390	African Steamship Co.
144	Akassa	cargo ship	24 June 1881	17 August 1881	1389	African Steamship Co.
145	Shannon	passenger ship	6 October 1881	5 January 1882	4189	Peninsular and Oriental Steam Navigation Co.

Ship no.	Name	Vessel type	Launch date	Delivery date	Tonnage	Owner
146	*Garfield*	sailing ship	7 January 1882	19 February 1882	2317	North Western Shipping Co.
147	*British Prince*	passenger ship	4 February 1882	4 April 1882	3973	British Shipowners Ltd
148	*Lord Downshire*	sailing ship	29 April 1882	31 May 1882	2322	T. Dixon & Sons
149	*Mandingo*	cargo ship	18 March 1882	6 May 1882	1700	African Steamship Co.
150	*Walter H. Wilson*	sailing ship	6 July 1882	18 August 1882	2518	S. Lawther
151	*Yucatan*	cargo ship	15 June 1882	19 August 1882	2816	West India & Pacific Steam Navigation Co.
152	*Ionic*	cargo/passenger ship	11 January 1883	28 March 1883	4753	Oceanic Steam Navigation Co.
153	*Doric*	cargo/passenger ship	10 March 1883	4 July 1883	4744	Oceanic Steam Navigation Co.
154	*British Princess*	passenger ship	14 December 1882	19 April 1883	3994	British Shipowners Ltd
155	*W.J. Pirrie*	sailing ship	26 May 1883	29 July 1883	2576	S. Lawther
156	*Fingal*	sailing ship	11 April 1883	2 June 1883	2570	R. Martin & Co.
157	*Lord Wolseley*	sailing ship	21 July 1883	6 September 1883	2576	Irish Shipowners Co.
158	*Dundela*	cargo ship	4 August 1883	13 November 1883	876	Harland and Wolff
159	*Dunluce*	cargo ship	1 September 1883	3 November 1883	877	Harland and Wolff
160	*La Nevera*	cargo ship	10 February 1883	26 March 1884	359	River Plate Co.
161	*Niger*	cargo ship	23 June 1883	3 August 1883	2006	African Steamship Co.
162	*Dynamic*	cross-channel ship	19 September 1883	13 December 1883	879	Belfast Steamship Co. Ltd
163	*Guido*	cargo ship	17 October 1883	12 January 1884	3313	G.H. Fletcher
164	*Bay of Panama*	sailing ship	14 November 1883	12 January 1884	2365	J. Bullock
165	*Horn Head*	cargo ship	1 March 1884	24 May 1884	2496	Ulster Steamship Co.
166	*Lord O'Neill*	cargo ship	17 May 1884	12 July 1884	2753	Irish Shipowners Co.
167	*Texan*	cargo ship	29 December 1883	15 March 1884	3257	West India & Pacific Steam Navigation Co.
168	*Floridan*	cargo ship	12 April 1884	16 August 1884	3257	West India & Pacific Navigation Co.
169	*Benin*	cargo ship	7 June 1884	24 July 1884	2215	African Steamship Co.
170	*Lord Lansdowne*	cargo ship	26 July 1884	15 September 1884	2752	Irish Shipowners Co.
171	*Belgic*	cargo ship	3 January 1885	7 July 1885	4212	Oceanic Steam Navigation Co.
172	*Gaelic*	cargo ship	28 February 1885	18 July 1885	4205	Oceanic Steam Navigation Co.
173	*Nurjahan*	cargo ship	23 August 1884	27 September 1885	2967	Asiatic Steam Navigation Co.
174	*Kohinur*	cargo ship	8 October 1884	16 January 1885	2967	Asiatic Steam Navigation Co.
175	*Callao*	sailing ship	1 January 1885	26 January 1885	1016	Oceanic Steam Navigation Co.
176	*Santiago*	sailing ship	17 January 1885	4 March 1885	1017	Oceanic Steam Navigation Co.
177	*Eblana*	hopper barge	24 October 1885	1 November 1885	347	Dublin Corporation
178	*Teneriffe*	cargo ship	19 February 1885	16 April 1885	1799	British & African Steam Navigation Co.
179	*Elmina*	cargo ship	23 April 1885	28 June 1885	1764	African Steamship Co.
180	*Costa Rican*	cargo ship	16 June 1885	27 August 1885	3251	West India & Pacific Steam Navigation Co.

Ship no.	Name	Vessel type	Launch date	Delivery date	Tonnage	Owner
181	Irene	passenger ferry	10 July 1885	29 September 1885	897	London & North Western Railway Co.
182	Zemindar	sailing ship	30 June 1885	14 August 1885	2120	T.&J. Brocklebank
183	Talookdar	sailing ship	22 August 1885	24 September 1885	2120	T.&J. Brocklebank
184	Queen's Island	sailing ship	22 September 1885	29 September 1885	2093	S. Lawther
185	Iran	cargo ship	5 January 1886	16 March 1886	3530	Edward Bates & Son
186	Saint Fillans	cargo ship	25 February 1886	24 September 1886	3130	Rankin, Gilmour & Co.
187	Caloric	cross-channel ship	10 October 1885	21 December 1885	942	Belfast Steamship Co.
188	Optic	cross-channel ship	12 November 1885	29 January 1886	880	Belfast Steamship Co.
189	Inishowen Head	cargo ship	17 April 1886	30 June 1886	3050	Ulster Steamship Co.
190	HMS Lizard	'Bramblé'-class gun boat	27 November 1886	4 February 1887	715	Admiralty
191	HMS Bramble	'Bramblé'-class gun boat	11 December 1886	1 March 1887	715	Admiralty
192	Lord Templeton	sailing ship	5 May 1886	12 June 1886	2151	Irish Shipowners Co.
193	Ormiston	cargo ship	31 August 1886	30 October 1886	3158	Irish Shipowners Co.
194	Swanmore	sailing ship	22 June 1886	10 August 1886	1821	W.J. Myers Sons & Co.
195	Stanmore	sailing ship	14 August 1886	25 September 1886	1824	W.J. Myers Sons & Co.
196	Etolia	cargo ship	8 January 1887	9 April 1887	3211	D.&C. MacIver (City of Liverpool Steam Navigation Co.)
197	Minnesota	cargo ship	2 August 1887	22 November 1887	3143	Williams, Torrey & Feild
198	Lycia	cargo ship	5 November 1887	12 May 1888	3223	D.&C. MacIver (City of Liverpool Steam Navigation Co.)
199	Hercules	dredger	12 October 1886	8 March 1887	818	Londonderry Harbour Commissioners
200	Michigan	passenger ship	5 July 1887	15 October 1887	4979	White Diamond Steamship Co.
201	Oceana	passenger ship	17 September 1887	26 February 1888	6362	Peninsular and Oriental Steam Navigation Co.
202	Arcadia	passenger ship	17 December 1887	12 May 1888	6362	Peninsular and Oriental Steam Navigation Co.
203	Anglesey	cross-channel ship	20 August 1887	1 May 1888	887	London & North Western Railway Co.
204	Sindia	sailing ship	19 November 1887	6 February 1888	3067	T.&J. Brocklebank
205	Holkar	sailing ship	11 February 1888	30 April 1888	3072	T.&J. Brocklebank
206	Idar	cargo ship	14 April 1888	3 July 1888	4049	Edward Bates & Son
207	Bostonian	cargo ship	14 March 1888	11 August 1888	4472	F. Leyland & Co.
208	Teutonic	passenger ship	19 January 1889	25 July 1889	9685	Oceanic Steam Navigation Co.
209	Majestic	passenger ship	29 June 1889	22 March 1890	9861	Oceanic Steam Navigation Co.
210	Cufic	livestock carrier	10 October 1888	1 December 1888	4639	Oceanic Steam Navigation Co.
211	Runic	livestock carrier	1 January 1889	16 February 1889	4649	Oceanic Steam Navigation Co.
212	Palmas	cargo ship	24 July 1888	13 October 1888	2428	A.L. Jones (Sir)

Ship no.	Name	Vessel type	Launch date	Delivery date	Tonnage	Owner
213	Lord Londonderry	cargo ship	17 November 1888	6 December 1888	2409	Irish Shipowners Co.
214	British Empire	cargo ship	28 February 1889	13 April 1889	3020	British Shipowners Ltd
215	Queensmore	cargo ship	26 June 1889	26 July 1889	4195	William Johnstone
216	Lancashire	cargo ship	27 April 1889	10 August 1889	3870	Bibby Steamship Co.
217	Yorkshire	cargo ship	27 July 1889	5 October 1889	3870	Bibby Steamship Co.
218	Ameer	cargo ship	24 August 1889	17 October 1889	4014	T.&J. Brocklebank
219	Gaekwar	cargo ship	24 December 1889	15 March 1890	4202	T.&J. Brocklebank
220	Nawab	cargo ship	28 September 1889	23 November 1889	3142	Asiatic Steam Navigation Co.
221	Nadir	cargo ship	26 October 1889	24 December 1889	3142	Asiatic Steam Navigation Co.
222	Nizam	cargo ship	21 December 1889	26 February 1890	3142	Asiatic Steam Navigation Co.
223	Alexander Elder	cargo ship	23 January 1890	19 April 1890	4173	Elder Dempster & Co.
224	Saint Pancras	cargo ship	8 February 1890	13 May 1890	4283	Rankin Gilmour & Co.
225	California	sailing ship	22 February 1890	24 April 1890	3099	North Western Shipping Co.
226	Imaum	cargo ship	25 March 1890	31 May 1890	4129	Edward Bates & Son
227	Michigan	cargo ship	19 April 1890	21 June 1890	3722	Baltimore Storage & Lighterage Co.
228	Talavera	cargo ship			3176	T.&J. Brocklebank
	Plassey	cargo ship	22 May 1890	5 July 1890		African Steamship Co.
229	Columbian	cargo ship	5 July 1890	23 August 1890	5088	F. Leyland & Co.
230	Georgian	cargo ship	16 August 1890	27 September 1890	5088	F. Leyland & Co.
231	Mississippi	cargo ship	29 August 1890	18 October 1890	3731	Baltimore Storage & Lighterage Co.
232	Sobraon	cargo ship	17 September 1890	6 November 1890	3185	African Steamship Co.
233	Memphis	cargo ship	18 October 1890	27 November 1890	3190	Elder Dempster & Co.
234	Ernesto	cargo ship	1 November 1890	11 December 1890	2573	G.H. Fletcher & Co.
235	British Crown	passenger ship	29 November 1890	17 January 1891	3204	British Steamship Co.
236	Nomadic	livestock carrier	11 February 1891	14 April 1891	5749	Oceanic Steam Navigation Co.
237	Tauric	livestock carrier	12 March 1891	16 May 1891	5727	Oceanic Steam Navigation Co.
238	Labrador	passenger ship	11 April 1891	13 August 1891	4737	Dominion Steamship Co.
239	Assaye	cargo ship	9 May 1891	4 July 1891	4296	Elder Dempster & Co.
240	Cheshire	passenger ship	6 June 1891	3 September 1891	5656	Bibby Steamship Co.
241	Shropshire	passenger ship	27 July 1891	3 October 1891	5660	Bibby Steamship Co.
242	Ionia	cargo ship	31 October 1891	12 January 1892	6335	D.&C. MacIver (City of Liverpool Steam Navigation Co.)
243	Lancastrian	cargo ship	25 July 1891	17 October 1891	5120	F. Leyland & Co. Ltd
244	Philadelphian	cargo ship	20 August 1891	12 November 1891	5120	F. Leyland & Co. Ltd
245	Pindari	cargo ship	17 October 1891	5 December 1891	5674	T.&J. Brocklebank
246	Mahratta	cargo ship	19 November 1891	28 January 1892	5680	T.&J. Brocklebank
247	Massachusetts	passenger ship	17 December 1891	5 March 1892	5590	Baltimore Storage & Lighterage Co.

Ship no.	Name	Vessel type	Launch date	Delivery date	Tonnage	Owner
248	Manitoba	passenger ship	28 January 1892	9 April 1892	5591	Baltimore Storage & Lighterage Co.
249	Memnon					Atlantic Transport Line
	Mohawk	passenger ship	25 February 1892	7 May 1892	5575	Elder Dempster & Co.
250	Lord Erne	cargo ship	29 March 1892	28 May 1892	5828	Irish Shipowners Co.
251	Naronic	livestock carrier	26 May 1892	11 July 1892	6594	Oceanic Steam Navigation Co.
252	Bovic	livestock carrier	28 June 1892	22 August 1892	6583	Oceanic Steam Navigation Co.
253	Mobile	cargo ship	17 November 1892	27 July 1893	5779	African Steamship Co.
254	Nurani	cargo ship	9 July 1892	10 September 1892	4432	Asiatic Steam Navigation Co.
255	Nairung	cargo ship	6 October 1892	10 November 1892	4425	Asiatic Steam Navigation Co.
256	Sagamore	passenger ship	8 September 1892	30 November 1892	5036	George Warren & Co. (Sagamore Steamship Co.)
257	Islam	cargo ship	22 October 1892	15 December 1892	5402	Edward Bates & Son
258	Damson Hill	sailing ship	24 November 1892	18 January 1893	2087	W. J. Myers Son & Co.
259	Orellana	passenger ship	7 December 1892	23 February 1893	4822	Pacific Steam Navigation Co.
260	Antisana	cargo ship	22 December 1892	11 March 1893	3584	Pacific Steam Navigation Co.
261	Gaul	passenger ship	16 February 1893	6 May 1893	4745	Union Steamship Co.
262	Lord Templemore	sailing ship	27 February 1892	19 April 1892	3045	Irish Shipowners Co.
263	Goth	passenger ship	16 March 1893	8 June 1893	4738	Union Steamship Co.
264	Orcana	passenger ship	7 March 1893	8 July 1893	4821	Pacific Steam Navigation Co.
265	Sarmiento	passenger ship	1 April 1893	17 June 1893	3603	Pacific Steam Navigation Co.
266	Mystic	cross-channel ship	4 February 1893	1 April 1893	726	Belfast Steamship Co.
267	Gothic	passenger ship	28 June 1893	28 November 1893	7669	Oceanic Steam Navigation Co.
268	Greek	passenger ship	18 May 1893	26 August 1893	4744	Union Steamship Co.
269	Magnetic	passenger tender	28 March 1891	6 June 1891	619	Oceanic Steam Navigation Co.
270	Cevic	livestock carrier	23 September 1893	6 January 1894	8301	Oceanic Steam Navigation Co.
271	Magic	cross-channel ship	20 April 1893	10 August 1893	1630	Belfast Steamship Co.
272	Sachem	passenger ship	29 June 1893	28 October 1893	5203	George Warren & Co.
273	Magellan	cargo ship	3 August 1893	23 November 1893	3590	Pacific Steam Navigation Co.
274	Torr Head	cargo ship	20 January 1894	7 April 1894	5910	Ulster Steamship Co.
275	Inca	cargo ship	12 October 1893	28 December 1893	3593	Pacific Steam Navigation Co.
276	unnamed	dredger	19 April 1893	11 May 1893	60	Lower Bann Navigation Trustees
277	Templemore	cargo ship	9 November 1893	7 February 1894	6276	William Johnstone
278	Staffordshire	passenger/cargo ship	7 December 1893	2 April 1894	6005	Bibby Steamship Co.
279	Ikbal	cargo ship	22 February 1894	5 May 1894	5404	Edward Bates & Son
280	Norman	passenger ship	19 July 1894	13 October 1894	7392	Union Steamship Co.
281	Prussia	passenger ship	10 April 1894	31 May 1894	5840	Hamburg Amerika Line
282	Persia	passenger ship	8 May 1894	15 July 1894	5857	Hamburg Amerika Line
283	Pontic	baggage tender	3 February 1894	13 April 1894	395	Oceanic Steam Navigation Co.
284	Guelph	passenger ship	26 June 1894	8 September 1894	4917	Union Steamship Co.
285	Oropesa	passenger ship	29 November 1894	9 February 1895	5317	Pacific Steam Navigation Co.

Ship no.	Name	Vessel type	Launch date	Delivery date	Tonnage	Owner
286	Orissa	passenger ship	15 December 1894	30 March 1895	5317	Pacific Steam Navigation Co.
287	Blairmore	cargo ship	14 August 1894	17 October 1894	2286	William Johnstone
288	Ulstermore	cargo ship	16 October 1894	6 December 1894	6326	William Johnstone
289	Scotsman	passenger ship	13 December 1894	11 April 1895	6041	Richard Mills & Co.
290	Marino	cargo ship	10 November 1894	2 March 1895	5819	T. Dixon & Sons
291	Victorian	passenger/cargo ship	6 July 1895	31 August 1895	8767	F. Leyland & Co. Ltd
292	Armenian	passenger/cargo ship	25 July 1895	19 September 1895	8765	F. Leyland & Co. Ltd
293	Georgic	livestock carrier	22 June 1895	8 August 1895	10077	Oceanic Steam Navigation Co.
294	American	cargo ship	8 August 1895	8 October 1895	8196	West India & Pacific Steam Navigation Co.
295	Historian	cargo ship	7 September 1895	29 January 1896	6857	Charente Steamship Co.
296	Cestrian	passenger ship	21 September 1895	5 March 1896	8761	F. Leyland & Co. Ltd
297	Iran	cargo ship	29 February 1896	30 April 1896	6250	Edward Bates & Son
298	Vedamore	cargo ship	19 October 1895	28 March 1896	6329	William Johnstone
299	China	passenger ship	13 June 1896	28 November 1896	7899	Peninsular and Oriental Steam Navigation Co.
300	Canada	passenger ship	14 May 1896	26 September 1896	8800	Dominion Line
301	Istrar	cargo ship	14 March 1896	4 June 1896	4582	Edward Bates & Son
302	Pennsylvania	passenger/cargo ship	10 September 1896	30 January 1897	13726	Hamburg Amerika Line
303	European	cargo ship	9 July 1896	3 December 1896	8194	West India & Pacific Steam Navigation Co.
304	Gascon	passenger ship	25 August 1896	13 February 1897	6288	Union Steamship Co.
305	Gaika	passenger ship	22 September 1896	15 April 1897	6287	Union Steamship Co.
306	Comic	cross-channel ship	9 June 1896	25 September 1896	903	Belfast Steamship Co.
307	Arabia	cargo ship	21 November 1896	7 March 1897	5550	Hamburg Amerika Line
308	Arcadia	cargo ship	8 October 1896	2 April 1897	5551	Hamburg Amerika Line
309	Delphic	passenger/cargo ship	5 January 1897	15 May 1897	8273	Oceanic Steam Navigation Co.
310	Oravia	passenger ship	5 December 1896	12 June 1897	5320	Pacific Steam Navigation Co.
311	Goorkha	passenger ship	23 January 1897	28 August 1897	6286	Union Steamship Co.
312	Rotterdam	passenger ship	18 February 1897	29 July 1897	8301	Holland-America Line
313	Briton	passenger ship	5 June 1897	26 November 1897	10248	Union Steamship Co.
314	Derbyshire	passenger ship	21 July 1897	8 October 1897	6635	Bibby Steamship Co.
315	New England	passenger ship	7 April 1898	30 June 1898	11394	Richard Mills & Co.
316	Cymric	passenger ship	12 October 1897	5 February 1898	12551	Oceanic Steam Navigation Co.
317	Oceanic	passenger ship	14 January 1899	26 August 1899	17274	Oceanic Steam Navigation Co.
318	Brasilia	passenger ship	27 November 1897	21 March 1898	10961	Hamburg Amerika Line
319	Winifreda	passenger ship	11 September 1897	17 February 1898	6833	F. Leyland & Co. Ltd
320	Statendam	passenger ship	7 May 1898	18 August 1898	10319	Holland-America Line
321	Bay State	cargo ship	4 June 1898	31 August 1898	6824	George Warren & Co.
322	Afric	passenger/cargo ship	16 November 1898	2 February 1899	11948	Oceanic Steam Navigation Co.

Ship no.	Name	Vessel type	Launch date	Delivery date	Tonnage	Owner
323	*Medic*	passenger/cargo ship	15 December 1898	6 July 1899	11985	Oceanic Steam Navigation Co.
324	*Winifredian*	passenger ship	11 March 1899	8 July 1899	10404	F. Leyland & Co. Ltd
325	*Persic*	passenger/cargo ship	7 September 1899	16 November 1899	11973	Oceanic Steam Navigation Co.
326	*Saxon*	passenger ship	21 December 1899	9 June 1900	12385	Union Steamship Co.
327	*Michigan*	passenger ship	5 October 1899	14 December 1899	9494	Atlantic Transport Co.
328	*Minneapolis*	passenger ship	18 November 1899	29 March 1900	13401	Atlantic Transport Co.
329	*Minnehaha*	passenger ship	31 March 1900	7 July 1900	13714	Atlantic Transport Co.
330	*Commonwealth*	passenger ship	31 May 1900	22 September 1900	12096	Richard Mills & Co.
331	*Devonian*	passenger ship	28 June 1900	6 September 1900	10417	F. Leyland & Co. Ltd
332	*Runic*	passenger ship	25 October 1900	22 December 1900	12482	Oceanic Steam Navigation Co.
333	*Suevic*	passenger ship	8 December 1900	9 March 1901	12531	Oceanic Steam Navigation Co.
334	*German*	passenger ship	4 August 1898	10 November 1898	6763	Union Steamship Co.
335	*Celtic*	passenger ship	4 April 1901	11 July 1901	20904	Oceanic Steam Navigation Co.
336	*Ryndam*	passenger ship	18 May 1901	3 October 1901	12302	Holland-America Line
337	*Cedric*	passenger ship	21 August 1902	31 January 1903	21073	Oceanic Steam Navigation Co.
338	*Noordam*	passenger ship	28 September 1901	29 March 1902	12316	Holland-America Line
339	*Minnetonka*	passenger ship	12 December 1901	17 May 1902	13397	Atlantic Transport Co.
	Minnewaska					Atlantic Transport Co.
340	*Arabic*	passenger ship	18 December 1902	21 June 1903	15801	Oceanic Steam Navigation Co.
341	*Athenic*	passenger ship	17 August 1901	23 January 1902	12234	Oceanic Steam Navigation Co.
	Celt					Union Steamship Co.
342	*Walmer Castle*	passenger ship	6 July 1901	20 February 1902	12545	Union-Castle Mail Steamship Co.
343	*Corinthic*	passenger ship	10 April 1902	14 July 1902	12231	Oceanic Steam Navigation Co.
344	*Warwickshire*	passenger ship	28 November 1901	6 March 1902	7966	Bibby Steamship Co.
345	*Columbus*	passenger ship	26 February 1903	12 September 1903	15378	Richard Mills & Co.
346	*Ionic*	passenger ship	22 May 1902	15 December 1902	12232	Oceanic Steam Navigation Co.
347	*Galeka*	passenger ship	21 October 1899	23 December 1899	6767	Union Steamship Co.
348	*Galician*	passenger ship	20 September 1900	6 December 1900	6756	Union-Castle Mail Steamship Co.
349	*Iowa*	passenger ship	5 July 1902	11 November 1902	8369	George Warren & Co.
350	*Marmora*	passenger ship	9 April 1903	19 November 1903	10522	Peninsular and Oriental Steam Navigation Co.
351	*Orita*	passenger ship	15 November 1902	26 March 1903	9230	Pacific Steam Navigation Co.
352	*Baltic*	passenger ship	21 November 1903	23 June 1904	23875	Oceanic Steam Navigation Co.
	Servian					F. Leyland & Co. (1900) Ltd
353	*President Lincoln*	passenger ship	8 October 1903	14 May 1907	18073	Hamburg Amerika Line
	Scotian					F. Leyland & Co. (1900) Ltd
354	*President Grant*	passenger ship	19 December 1903	3 September 1907	18089	Hamburg Amerika Line
355	*Macedonia*	passenger ship	9 July 1903	28 January 1904	10511	Peninsular and Oriental Steam Navigation Co.
356	*Kenilworth Castle*	passenger ship	5 December 1903	14 May 1904	12975	Union-Castle Mail Steamship Co.

Ship no.	Name	Vessel type	Launch date	Delivery date	Tonnage	Owner
357	*Amerika*	passenger ship	20 April 1905	21 September 1905	22724	Hamburg Amerika Line
358	*Adriatic*	passenger ship	20 September 1906	25 April 1907	24540	Oceanic Steam Navigation Co.
359	*Worcestershire*	passenger ship	3 March 1904	17 September 1904	7160	Bibby Steamship Co.
360	*HMS Enchantress*	yacht	7 November 1903	11 June 1904	2514	Admiralty
361	*Dunluce Castle*	passenger ship	31 March 1904	15 September 1904	8113	Union-Castle Mail Steamship Co.
362	*Slievemore*	cross-channel ship	17 May 1904	17 October 1904	1138	London & North Western Railway Co.
363	*Pardo*	cargo ship	30 June 1904	1 October 1904	4365	Royal Mail Steam Packet Co.
364	*Potaro*	cargo ship	10 September 1904	8 December 1904	4378	Royal Mail Steam Packet Co.
365	*Mamari*	passenger ship	24 September 1904	3 December 1904	6689	Shaw Savill & Albion Co.
366	*Nieuw Amsterdam*	passenger ship	28 September 1905	22 February 1906	16913	Holland-America Line
367	*Aragon*	passenger ship	23 February 1905	22 June 1905	9441	Royal Mail Steam Packet Co.
368	*Bologna*	cargo ship	9 March 1905	25 May 1905	4603	Hamburg Amerika Line
369	*Mahronda*	cargo ship	17 June 1905	3 August 1905	7630	T. &J. Brocklebank
370	*Slieve Bawn*	cross-channel ship	6 July 1905	10 October 1905	1147	London & North Western Railway Co.
371	*Herefordshire*	passenger ship	31 August 1905	29 November 1905	7183	Bibby Steamship Co.
372	*Amazon*	passenger ship	24 February 1906	5 June 1906	10036	Royal Mail Steam Packet Co.
373	*Malakand*	cargo ship	11 November 1905	14 December 1905	7653	T. &J. Brocklebank
374	*Manipur*	cargo ship	14 December 1905	13 January 1906	7654	T. &J. Brocklebank
375	*Matheran*	cargo ship	12 April 1906	12 May 1906	7653	T. &J. Brocklebank
376	*Ortega*	cargo ship	22 March 1906	28 June 1906	7970	Pacific Steam Navigation Co.
377	*Oronsa*	cargo ship	24 May 1906	16 August 1906	7907	Pacific Steam Navigation Co.
378	*Heroic*	cross-channel ship	13 January 1906	23 April 1906	2016	Belfast Steamship Co.
379	*Graphic*	cross-channel ship	27 February 1906	19 May 1906	2016	Belfast Steamship Co.
380	*Salamanca*	cargo ship	5 July 1906	15 September 1906	5969	Hamburg Amerika Line
381	*Rohilla*	cargo ship	6 September 1906	17 November 1906	7143	British India Steam Navigation Co.
382	*Avon*	passenger/cargo ship	2 March 1907	15 June 1907	11072	Royal Mail Steam Packet Co.
383	*Aburi*	cargo ship	18 October 1906	2 January 1907	3730	Elder Dempster & Co.
384	*Sierra Leone*	cargo ship	15 November 1906	8 January 1907	3730	Elder Dempster & Co.
385	*Iroquois*	oil tanker	27 June 1907	19 October 1907	9201	Anglo-American Oil Co.
386	*Fulani*	cargo ship	31 January 1907	1 June 1907	3730	Elder Dempster & Co.
387	*Prahsu*	cargo ship	28 March 1907	29 June 1907	3755	Elder Dempster & Co.
388	*Asturias*	passenger ship	26 September 1907	8 January 1908	12001	Royal Mail Steam Packet Co.
389	*Navahoe*	sailing oil barge	10 October 1907	18 January 1908	7718	Anglo-American Oil Co.
390	*Rotterdam*	passenger ship	3 March 1908	3 June 1908	23980	Holland-America Line
391	*Europa*		cancelled			Hamburg Amerika Line
	Ceric		cancelled			Oceanic Steam Navigation Co.
	Belgenland					Red Star Line
	Belgic	passenger ship	31 December 1914	21 June 1917	24147	International Navigation Co.

Ship no.	Name	Vessel type	Launch date	Delivery date	Tonnage	Owner
392	Pericles	passenger ship	21 December 1907	4 June 1908	10924	George Thompson & Co.
393	Lapland	passenger ship	27 June 1908	27 March 1909	18565	Red Star Line
394	Alberta		cancelled			Hamburg Amerika Line
	Laurentic	passenger ship	10 September 1908	15 April 1909	14892	Oceanic Steam Navigation Co.
395	Median	cargo ship	5 December 1907	25 January 1908	6296	F. Leyland & Co. (1900) Ltd
396	Memphian	cargo ship	23 January 1908	20 February 1908	6305	F. Leyland & Co. (1900) Ltd
397	Minnewaska	passenger ship	12 November 1908	24 April 1909	14816	Atlantic Transport Co.
398	Mercian	cargo ship	16 April 1908	16 May 1908	6304	Wilson & Furness-Leyland Line
399	Megantic	passenger ship	10 December 1908	3 June 1909	14877	Oceanic Steam Navigation Co.
400	Olympic	passenger ship	20 October 1910	31 May 1911	45324	Oceanic Steam Navigation Co.
401	Titanic	passenger ship	31 May 1911	2 April 1912	46328	Oceanic Steam Navigation Co.
402	Leopoldville	passenger/cargo ship	13 August 1908	10 November 1908	5350	Compagne Belge Maritime du Congo (Elder Dempster & Co.)
403	Leicestershire	passenger/cargo ship	3 June 1909	11 September 1909	8339	Bibby Steamship Co.
404	Karoola	passenger/cargo ship	9 March 1909	8 July 1909	7390	McIlwraith McEachern & Co.
405	Berbice	cargo ship	6 May 1909	8 July 1909	2379	Royal Mail Steam Packet Co.
406	Balantia	cargo ship	28 October 1909	18 December 1909	2379	Royal Mail Steam Packet Co.
407	Mallina	cargo ship	25 March 1909	29 April 1909	3213	Australasian United Steam Navigation Co.
408	Meltonian	cargo ship	8 July 1909	17 August 1909	6306	Wilson & Furness-Leyland Line
409	Pakeha	passenger/cargo ship	26 May 1910	20 August 1910	7910	Shaw Savill & Albion Co.
410	Edinburgh Castle	passenger ship	27 January 1910	28 April 1910	13326	Union-Castle Mail Steamship Co.
411	Gloucestershire	passenger/cargo ship	7 July 1910	22 October 1910	8324	Bibby Steamship Co.
412	Themistocles	passenger/cargo ship	22 September 1910	12 January 1911	11231	George Thompson & Co.
413	Baron Wattenberg					
	Sachsen	passenger/cargo ship	17 November 1910	21 January 1911	7986	Hamburg Amerika Line
414	Maloja	passenger ship	17 December 1910	7 September 1911	12430	Peninsular and Oriental Steam Navigation Co.
415	Arlanza	passenger ship	23 November 1911	8 June 1912	15043	Royal Mail Steam Packet Co.
416	Bayern	passenger/cargo ship	15 December 1910	16 February 1911	7986	Hamburg Amerika Line
417C	Preussen	passenger/cargo ship	25 August 1910	13 December 1910	7986	Hamburg Amerika Line
418	Demosthenes	passenger/cargo ship	28 February 1911	5 August 1911	11223	George Thompson & Co.
419	Galway Castle	passenger ship	12 April 1911	9 October 1911	7987	Union-Castle Mail Steamship Co.
420	Deseado	passenger ship	26 October 1911	27 June 1912	11471	Royal Mail Steam Packet Co.
421	Zealandic	passenger/cargo ship	29 June 1911	12 October 1911	10897	Oceanic Steam Navigation Co.
422	Nomadic	passenger tender	25 April 1911	27 May 1911	1260	Oceanic Steam Navigation Co.
423	Traffic	passenger tender	27 April 1911	27 May 1911	639	Oceanic Steam Navigation Co.
424	Patriotic	passenger ferry	7 September 1911	28 March 1912	2254	Belfast Steamship Co.
425	Demerara	passenger ship	21 December 1911	8 August 1912	11484	Royal Mail Steam Packet Co.

Ship no.	Name	Vessel type	Launch date	Delivery date	Tonnage	Owner
426	Desna	passenger ship	2 March 1912	3 October 1912	11483	Royal Mail Steam Packet Co.
427	Darro	passenger ship	16 May 1912	31 October 1912	11484	Royal Mail Steam Packet Co.
428	Drina	passenger ship	29 June 1912	16 January 1913	11483	Royal Mail Steam Packet Co.
429	Oxfordshire	passenger/cargo ship	15 June 1912	17 September 1912	8623	Bibby Steamship Co.
430	Abosso	cargo ship	15 August 1912	19 December 1912	7782	African Steamship Co.
431	Appam	passenger/cargo ship	10 October 1912	27 February 1913	7781	British & African Steam Navigation Co.
432	Ceramic	passenger ship	11 December 1912	5 July 1913	18481	Oceanic Steam Navigation Co.
433	Gigantic / Britannic	passenger ship	26 February 1914	8 December 1915	48158	Oceanic Steam Navigation Co.
434	Andes	passenger ship	8 May 1913	12 September 1913	15620	Pacific Steam Navigation Co.
435G/B	Alcantara	passenger ship	30 October 1913	28 May 1914	15831	Royal Mail Steam Packet Co.
436	Statendam / Justicia	passenger ship	9 July 1914	7 April 1917	32234	Holland-America Line / Oceanic Steam Navigation Co.
437	Katoomba	passenger ship	10 April 1913	10 July 1913	9424	McIlwraith McEachern & Co.
438	Ormeda / Orduna	passenger/cargo ship	2 October 1913	22 January 1914	15499	Pacific Steam Navigation Co.
439	Euripides	passenger/cargo ship	29 January 1914	6 June 1914	14947	George Thompson & Co.
440	Orduna / Orbita	passenger/cargo ship	7 July 1914	31 July 1915	15678	Pacific Steam Navigation Co.
441	Almanzora	passenger ship	19 November 1914	7 October 1915	16034	Royal Mail Steam Packet Co.
442	Orca	passenger/cargo ship	5 April 1917	25 May 1918	15120	Pacific Steam Navigation Co.
443G/B	Apapa	passenger ship	30 September 1914	4 March 1915	7832	Elder Dempster & Co.
444G	Egba	cargo ship	17 December 1913	5 April 1914	4989	African Steamship Co. / Elder Dempster & Co.
445G	Egori	cargo ship	22 April 1914	21 June 1914	4995	African Steamship Co. / Elder Dempster & Co. / British & African Steam Navigation Co.
446	Minnekahda	passenger ship	8 March 1917	21 March 1918	17220	Atlantic Transport Co.
447G	Attendant	passenger tender	10 July 1913	21 August 1913	317	Elder Dempster & Co.
448I	Maryland	passenger ship	4 September 1913	1 November 1913	4731	Atlantic Transport Co.
449I	Missouri	passenger ship	27 November 1913	28 February 1914	4707	Atlantic Transport Co.
450G	Mississippi	passenger ship	11 February 1914	5 November 1914	4717	Atlantic Transport Co.
451I	Falstria	cargo ship	12 March 1914	31 March 1915	4344	East Asiatic Co.
452I	Lalandia	cargo ship	9 July 1914	22 October 1915	4348	East Asiatic Co.
	Kangaroo	cargo ship				Western Australian Government
453	Brecknockshire	cargo ship	12 September 1916	11 January 1917	8422	Royal Mail Steam Packet Co.
454G/B	Pittsburgh / Regina	passenger ship	19 April 1917	26 October 1918	16313	International Mercantile Marine / Dominion Line

Ship no.	Name	Vessel type	Launch date	Delivery date	Tonnage	Owner
455	Amroth Castle	passenger ship	11 September 1919	8 April 1921	19500	Union-Castle Mail Steamship Co.
456C	Arundel Castle	passenger ship	9 March 1921	11 March 1922	19022	Union-Castle Mail Steamship Co.
457	Windsor Castle	passenger ship	11 November 1920	25 May 1922	16322	International Mercantile Marine
	Regina					International Navigation Co. (American Line)
	Pittsburgh					
458G/B	Rimouski	cargo ship	30 August 1917	11 July 1918	9281	Dominion Line
459	Lancashire	passenger/cargo ship	11 January 1917	9 August 1917	9445	Bibby Steamship Co.
460G/B	Millais	cargo ship	8 November 1916	18 September 1917	7300	Lamport & Holt Ltd
461G/B	Vedic	cargo ship	18 December 1917	10 July 1918	9332	Oceanic Steam Navigation Co.
462G/B	Marconi	cargo ship	19 April 1916	1 February 1917	7402	Lamport & Holt Ltd
463BC	Melita	passenger ship	21 April 1917	12 January 1918	13967	Canadian Pacific Railway Co.
464BC	Medora	passenger ship				
465G	Minnedosa	passenger ship	17 November 1917	21 November 1918	13972	Canadian Pacific Railway Co.
	Lobos	cargo ship				Pacific Steam Navigation Co.
466G	Glenavy	cargo ship	17 May 1917	1 September 1917	5075	Glen Line Ltd
	Bostonian	cargo ship				F. Leyland & Co. (1900) Ltd
467I	Glengyle	cargo ship	19 January 1915	7 December 1915	6225	Glen Line Ltd
	Montezuma	cargo ship				Elder Dempster & Co.
468I	Glenartney	cargo ship	14 April 1915	16 May 1916	7237	Glen Line Ltd
	Glenamoy	cargo ship				Elder Dempster & Co.
469	Nederland	cargo ship	2 May 1916	22 September 1916	7269	Red Star Line
470	Germanic	passenger ship	cancelled		26500	
	Homeric					
471	Laurentic	passenger ship	16 June 1927	1 November 1927	18724	Oceanic Steam Navigation Co.
	Narkunda	passenger ship	25 April 1918	30 March 1920	16118	Peninsular and Oriental Steam Navigation Co.
472	HMS Admiral Farragut	monitor	15 April 1915	29 May 1915	6180	Admiralty
473	HMS Abercrombie	monitor	29 April 1915	29 May 1915	6180	Admiralty
	HMS General Grant	monitor				
	HMS Havelock	monitor				
474		cargo ship	cancelled			Holland-America Line
475		cargo ship	cancelled			Holland-America Line
476G/B	HMS Robert E. Lee	monitor	29 April 1915	24 June 1915	6180	Admiralty
	HMS Raglan	monitor				
477G/B	HMS Prince Eugene	monitor	14 July 1915	2 September 1915	5920	Admiralty
478	HMS Lord Clive	monitor	10 June 1915	10 July 1915	5920	Admiralty
479	HMS General Craufurd	monitor	8 July 1915	26 August 1915	5920	Admiralty
480	HMS Earl of Peterborough	monitor	26 August 1915	23 September 1915	5920	Admiralty

Ship no.	Name	Vessel type	Launch date	Delivery date	Tonnage	Owner
481	HMS Sir Thomas Picton	monitor	30 September 1915	4 November 1915	5920	Admiralty
482/3/4	HMS Glorious	light battle cruiser	20 April 1916	31 December 1916	22354	Admiralty
485	HMS M29	coastal monitor	22 May 1915	20 June 1915	360	Admiralty
486	HMS M30	coastal monitor	23 June 1915	9 July 1915	360	Admiralty
487	HMS M31	coastal monitor	24 June 1915	9 July 1915	360	Admiralty
488WC	HMS M32	coastal monitor	22 May 1915	20 June 1915	360	Admiralty
489WC	HMS M33	coastal monitor	22 May 1915	26 June 1915	360	Admiralty
490G/B	HMS P24	patrol boat	24 November 1915	21 January 1916	616	Admiralty
491G/B	HMS P25	patrol boat	15 January 1916	17 March 1916	616	Admiralty
492G/B	HMS M35					
	HMS Erebus	monitor	19 June 1916	2 September 1916	8022	Admiralty
493	HMS M36					
	HMS Terror	monitor	18 May 1916	6 August 1916	8022	Admiralty
494G/B	HMS Salmon	'R'-class destroyer	7 October 1916	20 December 1916	1121	Admiralty
495G/B	HMS Sylph	'R'-class destroyer	15 November 1916	10 February 1917	1121	Admiralty
496G/B	HMS Skilful	'R'-class destroyer	3 February 1917	26 March 1917	1121	Admiralty
497G/B	HMS Springbok	'R'-class destroyer	9 March 1917	30 April 1917	1036	Admiralty
498G/B	HMS Tenacious	'R'-class destroyer	21 May 1917	11 August 1917	1036	Admiralty
499G/B	HMS Tetrarch	'R'-class destroyer	20 April 1917	2 June 1917	1036	Admiralty
500	HMS Cavendish	cruiser				
	HMS Vindictive	seaplane carrier	17 January 1918	19 October 1918	7764	Admiralty
501G/B	HMS P62					
	HMS PC62	patrol boat	7 June 1917	31 August 1917	682	Admiralty
502G	Glenogle	cargo ship	15 April 1920	19 August 1920	9513	Glen Line Ltd
503G	Glengarry	cargo ship	30 September 1920	23 February 1922	9460	Glen Line Ltd
504G	Glenfarne					
505G	Glenapp	cargo ship	14 July 1920	14 December 1920	9503	Glen Line Ltd
	Glenbeg	cargo ship	25 December 1920	20 April 1922	9461	Glen Line Ltd
506	Orova	passenger/cargo ship	16 December 1920	22 March 1923	12257	Pacific Steam Navigation Co.
507	unnamed					Union-Castle Mail Steamship Co.
	Asturias	passenger/cargo ship	7 July 1925	6 February 1926	22048	RMSP Meat Transports Ltd
508C/G	Lochkatrine	passenger ship	5 August 1921	18 January 1922	10183	Royal Mail Steam Packet Co.
509	Yorkshire	cargo/passenger ship	29 May 1919	2 September 1920	10184	Bibby Steamship Co.
510G/P	Coney	coaster	14 February 1918	27 April 1918	697	G. & J. Burns Ltd
511G	Loreta					Elder Dempster & Co.
	Glenade	cargo ship	15 April 1919	16 July 1919	6802	Glen Line Ltd
512G	Loriga					Elder Dempster & Co.
	Glenariffe	cargo ship	10 July 1919	23 October 1919	6795	Glen Line Ltd
513G	Salamanda					Elder Dempster & Co.
	Glentara	cargo ship	25 December 1919	13 April 1920	6754	Glen Line Ltd

Ship no.	Name	Vessel type	Launch date	Delivery date	Tonnage	Owner
514G	Glenluce	cargo ship	25 September 1919	14 January 1920	6755	Elder Dempster & Co.
515G	Dinteldyk	cargo ship	1 September 1921	10 February 1922	9388	Glen Line Ltd
516G	Lochgoil	passenger/cargo ship	24 August 1922	14 December 1922	9462	Holland-America Line
517	Lochmonar	passenger/cargo ship	8 December 1923	26 June 1924	9463	Royal Mail Steam Packet Co.
518C/G	unnamed	cargo ship	cancelled			RMSP Meat Transports Ltd
519C	Ekari	passenger/cargo ship	12 January 1920	13 April 1920	6741	RMSP Meat Transports Ltd
520	War Shamrock	'A'-type cargo ship	21 June 1917	20 August 1917	5174	Elder Dempster & Co.
521	War Clover	'A'-type cargo ship	16 August 1917	20 September 1917	5174	Shipping Controller (Thomas Dixon & Son)
522	War Trefoil	'A'-type cargo ship	15 September 1917	16 October 1917	5166	Shipping Controller (Thomas Dixon & Son)
523G	War Legate	'AO'-type tanker	25 May 1918	28 June 1918	5188	Shipping Controller (Thomas Dixon & Son)
524G	War Envoy	'AO'-type tanker	27 July 1918	5 September 1918	5197	Shipping Controller (Anglo-Saxon Petroleum Co.)
525G	War Hostage	'AO'-type tanker	16 October 1917	22 December 1917	5181	Shipping Controller (Anglo-Saxon Petroleum Co.)
526G	War Expert	'AO'-type tanker	29 December 1917	18 March 1918	5198	Shipping Controller (Anglo-Saxon Petroleum Co.)
527G	War African	'AO'-type tanker	28 March 1918	15 May 1918	5218	Shipping Controller (Anglo-Saxon Petroleum Co.)
528G	War Airman / War Aryan	'AO'-type tanker	24 September 1918	7 November 1918	5392	Shipping Controller (Anglo-Saxon Petroleum Co.)
529G	War Cowslip	'A'-type cargo ship	22 November 1918	13 December 1918	5292	Shipping Controller (Andrew Weir & Co.)
530G	War Maple / Treverbyn	'AO'-type tanker	22 November 1919	29 January 1920	5281	Shipping Controller (Anglo-American Oil Co.); Shipping Controller (J. Temperley & Co.); Shipping Controller; Hain Steamship Co.
531	War Viper	'B'-type cargo ship	14 February 1918	14 March 1918	5160	Shipping Controller (G. Heyn & Sons)
532	War Lemur	'B'-type cargo ship	9 May 1918	28 May 1918	5185	Shipping Controller (G. Heyn & Sons)
533	War Cobra	'B'-type cargo ship	15 November 1917	20 December 1917	5155	Shipping Controller (G. Heyn & Sons)
534	War Python	'B'-type cargo ship	29 December 1917	24 January 1918	5155	Shipping Controller (G. Heyn & Sons)
535	War Bittern	'B'-type cargo ship	14 March 1918	11 April 1918	5178	Shipping Controller (Anchor Line)

Ship no.	Name	Vessel type	Launch date	Delivery date	Tonnage	Owner
536	War Buckler	'D'-type cargo ship	28 March 1918	30 May 1918	2357	Shipping Controller (J.&J. Denholm)
537	War Tabard	'D'-type cargo ship	28 March 1918	15 June 1918	2357	Shipping Controller (J.&J. Denholm)
538	War Snake	'B'-type cargo ship	22 August 1918	29 August 1918	5222	Shipping Controller (G. Heyn & Sons)
539Gk	War Poplar Dromore Castle	'B'-type cargo ship	28 August 1919	25 November 1919	5242	Shipping Controller (Union-Castle Mail Steamship Co.)
540	War Icarus	'G'-type cargo ship	19 September 1918	31 October 1918	8002	Shipping Controller (British Steamship Co. Ltd)
541	War Paris Otira	'G'-type cargo ship	5 March 1919	17 April 1919	7995	Shipping Controller Shaw Savill & Albion Co.
542	War Priam Bardic	'G'-type cargo ship	19 December 1918	13 March 1919	8010	Shipping Controller Oceanic Steam Navigation Co.
543	War Melody	'N'-type cargo ship	19 October 1918	7 November 1918	6533	Shipping Controller
544	War Music	'N'-type cargo ship	2 November 1918	5 December 1918	6498	Shipping Controller (Clyde Shipping Co. Ltd)
545	War Dream	'N'-type cargo ship	5 December 1918	9 January 1919	6498	Shipping Controller (Clyde Shipping Co. Ltd)
546	War Vision Nasmyth	'N'-type cargo ship	3 April 1919	8 May 1919	6509	Shipping Controller Lamport & Holt Ltd Liverpool Brazil & River Plate Steam Navigation Co Ltd
547	War Triumph Bonheur	'A'-type cargo ship	17 June 1920	7 October 1920	5326	Shipping Controller Lamport & Holt Ltd
548G	War Jasmine	'A'-type cargo ship	17 December 1918	31 December 1918	5263	Shipping Controller
549G	War Jonquil Treveal	'A'-type cargo ship	11 June 1919	9 September 1919	5242	Shipping Controller Hain Steamship Co.
550	War Bamboo Boswell	'A'-type cargo ship	1 July 1920	19 November 1920	5327	Shipping Controller Lamport & Holt Ltd
551	War Pampas Trelissick	'A'-type cargo ship	29 April 1919	13 June 1919	5265	Shipping Controller Hain Steamship Co.
552G	HMS St Aubin	tug	27 June 1918	21 August 1918	468	Admiralty
553G	HMS St Bees	tug	5 September 1918	24 October 1918	422	Admiralty
554	War Justice Newton	'N'-type cargo ship	30 April 1919	27 May 1919	6509	Shipping Controller Lamport & Holt Ltd Liverpool Brazil & River Plate Steam Navigation Co Ltd

Ship no.	Name	Vessel type	Launch date	Delivery date	Tonnage	Owner
555	*War Liberty*	'N'-type cargo ship	15 May 1919	26 June 1919	6529	Shipping Controller
	New Toronto					Elder Dempster & Co.
	New Brunswick					Shipping Controller
556	unnamed	'N'-type cargo ship	12 June 1919	14 August 1919	6566	Elder Dempster & Co.
	New Georgia					Shipping Controller
557	unnamed	'N'-type cargo ship	26 June 1919	28 August 1919	6566	Elder Dempster & Co.
	New Mexico					Shipping Controller
558	unnamed	'N'-type cargo ship	28 August 1919	9 October 1919	6568	Elder Dempster & Co.
	New Brunswick					Shipping Controller
	New Toronto					Elder Dempster & Co.
559	unnamed	'N'-type cargo ship	14 August 1919	18 September 1919	6568	Shipping Controller
	New Texas					Elder Dempster & Co.
560	unnamed	'N'-type cargo ship				Shipping Controller
	Bompata	'B'-type cargo ship	28 October 1920	16 January 1923	5570	Elder Dempster & Co.
561G	unnamed					Elder Dempster & Co.
	Boma	'B'-type cargo ship	23 October 1919	26 February 1920	5407	British & African Steam Navigation Co. Ltd
562G	*Banda*	lighter	24 August 1926	27 August 1926	70	Elder Dempster & Co. New York & West Africa Steam Navigation Co.
563G	HMS *St Mellons*	tug	30 November 1918	30 December 1918	421	Admiralty
564G	HMS *St Olaves*	tug	27 December 1918	4 March 1919	468	Admiralty
565	*War Riddle*	'N'-type cargo ship	27 November 1919	4 March 1920	6600	Shipping Controller
566	*Maine*					Atlantic Transport Co.
	War Romance					Shipping Controller
	New Brooklyn	'N'-type cargo ship	11 December 1919	31 March 1920	6545	Elder Dempster & Co.
567	*War Pageant*					Shipping Controller
	New Columbia	'N'-type cargo ship	25 March 1920	30 June 1920	6573	Elder Dempster & Co.
568G	*War Passion*	'N'-type cargo ship				African Steamship Co. Shipping Controller (Elder Dempster & Co.)
	Berma	barge	24 August 1926	27 August 1926	70	New York & West Africa Steam Navigation Co.
569G	*La Paz*	cargo ship	6 May 1920	23 September 1920	6548	Pacific Steam Navigation Co.
570Gk	*War Dahlia*					Shipping Controller Elder Dempster & Co.
	Biafra	'B'-type cargo ship	29 April 1919	19 June 1919	5327	African Steamship Co.
571Gk	*War Geum*					Shipping Controller
	Siris	'B'-type cargo ship	26 June 1919	25 September 1919	5242	Royal Mail Steam Packet Co.

Ship no.	Name	Vessel type	Launch date	Delivery date	Tonnage	Owner
572Gk	War Oak	'B'-type cargo ship	23 October 1919	31 December 1919	5242	Shipping Controller
	Dundrum Castle					Union-Castle Mail Steamship Co.
573	Calgary					International Mercantile Marine Co.
574	Doric	passenger ship	8 August 1922	29 May 1923	16484	Oceanic Steam Navigation Co.
	Patagonian					
575	Philadelphian	'N'-type cargo ship	11 October 1919	19 February 1920	6585	F. Leyland & Co. (1900) Ltd
576	Sophocles	passenger ship	22 September1921	2 February 1922	12361	George Thompson & Co.
577	Diogenes	passenger ship	2 March 1922	4 July 1922	12341	George Thompson & Co.
	New Brighton					F. Leyland & Co. (1900) Ltd
						Elder Dempster & Co.
578	Dorsetshire	'N'-type cargo ship	6 November 1919	31 January 1920	6538	African Steamship Co.
579	Somersetshire	cargo ship	22 April 1920	14 August 1920	7445	Bibby Steamship Co.
580Gk	Lobos	cargo ship	24 February 1921	9 June 1921	7456	Bibby Steamship Co.
581G	Losada	cargo ship	14 October 1920	14 October 1921	6479	Pacific Steam Navigation Co.
582G	Ediba	cargo ship	10 March 1921	1 November 1921	6520	Pacific Steam Navigation Co.
						Elder Dempster & Co.
583	Baradine	passenger/cargo ship	7 December 1922	18 April 1923	6919	African Steamship Co.
		passenger ship	27 November 1920	18 August 1921	13143	Peninsular and Oriental Steam Navigation Co.
584	Barrabool	passenger ship	3 November 1921	30 March 1922	13143	Peninsular and Oriental Steam Navigation Co.
585Gk	Bendigo	passenger ship	26 January 1922	9 August 1922	13039	Peninsular and Oriental Steam Navigation Co.
586	Amazon					
587	Alcantara	passenger ship	23 September 1926	18 February 1927	22181	Royal Mail Steam Packet Co.
	Mooltan	passenger ship	15 February 1923	22 September 1923	20847	Peninsular and Oriental Steam Navigation Co.
588	Maloja	passenger ship	19 April 1923	25 October 1923	20837	Peninsular and Oriental Steam Navigation Co.
589	Inverleith	'N'-type oil tanker	26 August 1920	3 March 1921	6957	British Mexican Petroleum Co.
590	Inverurie	'N'-type oil tanker	9 June 1921	23 November 1922	6907	British Mexican Petroleum Co.
591	Inveravon	'N'-type oil tanker	18 January 1923	27 March 1923	6906	British Mexican Petroleum Co.
592G	Somerset Coast	coaster	27 December 1919	25 March 1920	1352	Coast Lines Ltd
593Gk	Drechytk	passenger/cargo ship	24 October 1922	22 March 1923	9324	Holland-America Line
594	Glencree					
	Glenshiel	cargo ship	24 January 1924	22 May 1924	9415	Glen Line Ltd
595	Glenlochy					Glen Line Ltd
	Carnarvon Castle	passenger ship	14 January 1926	26 June 1926	20063	Union-Castle Mail Steamship Co.
596C	Calgary	refrigerated cargo ship	27 August 1920	3 February 1921	7206	Elder Dempster & Co.
597C	Cochrane	refrigerated cargo ship	28 December 1920	8 March 1923	7203	Elder Dempster & Co.

Ship no.	Name	Vessel type	Launch date	Delivery date	Tonnage	Owner
598C	*Calumet*	refrigerated cargo ship	1 July 1922	15 March 1923	7268	Elder Dempster & Co.
599C	*Cavally*					
	Cariboo	refrigerated cargo ship	22 March 1924	16 August 1924	7275	Elder Dempster & Co.
600P	*Ayrshire Coast*					
	Northern Coast					
	Lady Valentia	coaster	29 November 1920	16 November 1921	1211	Coast Lines Ltd
601P	*Scottish Coast*					
	Eastern Coast	coaster	10 March 1922	1 June 1922	1223	Coast Lines Ltd
602G	*Princess Caroline*					
	Redbreast	coaster	14 October 1920	11 February 1921	772	Coast Lines Ltd
603D	*Leighton*	cargo ship	11 January 1921	13 October 1921	7412	Lamport & Holt Ltd
604D	*Linnell*	cargo ship	4 October 1921	27 December 1921	7424	Lamport & Holt Ltd
605D	*Lassell*	cargo ship	15 March 1922	22 June 1922	7417	Lamport & Holt Ltd
606P	*Lady Limerick*	coaster	cancelled			Coast Lines Ltd
606G	*Francunion*	oil barge	14 April 1921	3 May 1921	737	British Union Oil Co.
607P	*Lady Olive*					
	Ayrshire Coast	coaster	22 August 1922	5 October 1922	773	Coast Lines Ltd
608Gk	*Ancobra*					
	Adda	passenger/cargo ship	25 May 1922	14 November 1922	7816	Elder Dempster & Co.
609	*Invergarry*	'N'-type oil tanker	8 November 1923	17 April 1924	6907	British Mexican Petroleum Co.
610G	unnamed					King Line Ltd
	Gujarat	passenger/cargo ship	11 October 1923	20 December 1923	4148	Andrew Weir & Co.
611G	*Kathiawar*	passenger/cargo ship	22 November 1923	15 February 1924	4150	Andrew Weir & Co.
612	*Statendam*	passenger ship	11 September 1924	13 April 1927	28130	Holland-America Line
613	*Minnewaska*	passenger ship	22 March 1923	25 August 1923	21716	Atlantic Transport Co.
614	*Minnetonka*	passenger ship	10 January 1924	24 April 1924	21998	Atlantic Transport Co.
615	*Laurentic*		cancelled			Oceanic Steam Navigation Co.
615D	*Oakton*	cargo ship	30 April 1923	31 May 1923	1727	Matthews Steamship Co.
616	*Accra*	passenger ship	18 March 1926	17 August 1926	9337	Elder Dempster & Co.
617	*Britmex No. 2*	dumb oil barge	15 April 1920	16 June 1920	474	Andrew Weir & Co.
618	*Britmex No. 3*	dumb oil barge	15 April 1920	17 June 1920	474	Andrew Weir & Co.
619	*Britmex No. 4*	dumb oil barge	29 April 1920	4 June 1920	474	Andrew Weir & Co.
620	*Britmex No. 5*	dumb oil barge	29 April 1920	1 July 1920	475	Andrew Weir & Co.
621G	*Britmex No. 6*	dumb oil barge	7 April 1920	28 May 1920	475	Andrew Weir & Co.
622G	*Britmex No. 7*	dumb oil barge	7 April 1920	3 June 1920	475	Andrew Weir & Co.
623G	*Britmex No. 8*	dumb oil barge	22 April 1920	8 June 1920	475	Andrew Weir & Co.
624G	*Inveritchen*	coastal tanker	13 July 1920	1 October 1920	708	British Mexican Petroleum Co.
625G	*Inverampton*	coastal tanker	9 September 1920	1 November 1920	708	British Mexican Petroleum Co.
626G	*Princess Dagmar*					
	Gorilla	coaster	29 December 1920	7 February 1922	772	Coast Lines Ltd

Ship no.	Name	Vessel type	Launch date	Delivery date	Tonnage	Owner
627M	*Dorelian*	cargo ship	4 April 1923	15 May 1923	6300	F. Leyland & Co. (1900) Ltd
628M	*Delilian*	See D.&W. Henderson ship list, no. 512, page 564				
629M	*Davisian*	See D.&W. Henderson ship list, no. 511, page 564				
630D	*Araby*	cargo ship	1 February 1923	16 March 1923	4936	David MacIver & Co.
631D	*Cedarton*	cargo ship	22 January 1924	5 April 1924	899	Matthews Steamship Co.
632G	*Laguna*	cargo ship	19 April 1923	3 July 1923	6469	Pacific Steam Navigation Co.
633M	*Tonbridge*	cross-channel ship	3 June 1924	21 July 1924	682	Southern Railway Co.
634M	*Minster*	cross-channel ship	17 June 1924	18 August 1924	682	Southern Railway Co.
635	*Ulster Monarch*	cross-channel ship	24 January 1929	10 June 1929	3851	Belfast Steamship Co.
636D	*Elmworth*	cargo ship	3 September 1924	13 November 1924	4963	R.S. Dalgleish Ltd
637D	*Oakworth*	cargo ship	26 November 1924	12 February 1925	4963	R.S. Dalgleish Ltd
638G	unnamed					Ocean Transport Co.
639G	*Ferry No. 6*	river ferry	7 November 1922	7 November 1922	16	Clyde Navigation Trustees
	unnamed					Ocean Transport Co.
640Dy	*Ferry No. 7*	river ferry	7 November 1922	7 November 1922	16	Clyde Navigation Trustees
641	*Inverglass*	oil tanker	30 September 1924	25 November 1924	6901	British Mexican Petroleum Co.
642G	*Invergoil*	oil tanker	21 September 1922	9 November 1922	6966	British Mexican Petroleum Co.
643G	*Luxmi*	passenger/cargo ship	19 January 1924	25 March 1924	4148	Andrew Weir & Co.
	Boveric	cargo ship	24 March 1924	29 May 1924	5149	Andrew Weir & Co.
644C	*Inverbank*	oil tanker	20 January 1923	5 April 1923	6921	British Mexican Petroleum Co.
645G	*Invergordon*	oil tanker				British Mexican Petroleum Co.
646Gk	unnamed	floating dock	5 April 1923	12 April 1923		Harland & Wolff Ltd
647D	*Grantleyhall*	'N'-type cargo ship	16 June 1927	16 August 1927	4761	West Hartlepool Steam Navigation Co.
648P	*Birchton*	cargo ship	21 February 1924	12 April 1924	1732	Matthews Steamship Co.
649G	*Cable Enterprise*	cable layer	8 February 1924	20 May 1924	943	Western Telegraph Co.
650G	*Volendam*	passenger ship	6 July 1922	12 October 1922	15440	Holland-America Line
651G	*Veendam*	passenger ship	18 November 1922	29 March 1923	15450	Holland-America Line
652G	*Britmex No. 1*	dumb oil barge	30 October 1920	26 November 1920	472	British Mexican Petroleum Co.
653G	*Britmex No. 9*	dumb oil barge	30 October 1920	23 December 1920	471	British Mexican Petroleum Co.
654G	*Britmex No. 10*	dumb oil barge	16 December 1920	7 March 1921	475	British Mexican Petroleum Co.
655G	*Britmex No. 11*	dumb oil barge	28 December 1920	8 March 1921	475	British Mexican Petroleum Co.
	Inveric					Andrew Weir & Co.
656G	*Glenbank*	cargo ship	23 April 1924	27 June 1924	5150	British Mexican Petroleum Co.
657P	*Foreric*	cargo ship	2 June 1924	4 September 1924	5150	Andrew Weir & Co.
	Birchbank					
	Scottish Coast					Coast Lines Ltd
	Lurcher	coaster	20 September 1922	11 November 1922	774	Burns & Laird
658M	*Asuka Maru*	cargo ship	2 July 1924	12 November 1924	7488	Nippon Yusen Kaisha
659Gk	*Razmak*	passenger/cargo ship	16 October 1924	26 February 1925	10602	Peninsular and Oriental Steam Navigation Co.

Ship no.	Name	Vessel type	Launch date	Delivery date	Tonnage	Owner
660Gk	Rawalpindi	passenger/cargo ship	26 March 1925	3 September 1925	16618	Peninsular and Oriental Steam Navigation Co.
661Gk	Rajputana	passenger/cargo ship	6 August 1925	30 December 1925	16568	Peninsular and Oriental Steam Navigation Co.
662G	Cedarbank	cargo ship	7 July 1924	16 October 1924	5151	Andrew Weir & Co.
663G	Comliebank	cargo ship	3 September 1924	6 December 1924	5149	Andrew Weir & Co.
664G	Clydebank	cargo ship	13 October 1924	22 January 1925	5156	Andrew Weir & Co.
665G	unnamed	ore-carrying barge	21 August 1923	25 August 1923	50	Elder Dempster & Co.
666G	unnamed	ore-carrying barge	21 August 1923	25 August 1923	50	Elder Dempster & Co.
667G	unnamed	ore-carrying barge	21 August 1923	25 August 1923	50	Elder Dempster & Co.
668G	unnamed	ore-carrying barge	27 September 1923	30 September 1923	50	Elder Dempster & Co.
669G	unnamed	ore-carrying barge	27 September 1923	30 September 1923	50	Elder Dempster & Co.
670G	unnamed	ore-carrying barge	27 September 1923	30 September 1923	50	Elder Dempster & Co.
671G	unnamed	lighter	15 September 1923	21 September 1923	50	Elder Dempster & Co.
672G	Itu II	lighter	15 September 1923	21 September 1923	50	Elder Dempster & Co.
673G	unnamed	lighter	15 September 1923	21 September 1923	50	Elder Dempster & Co.
674G	unnamed	lighter	shipped in sections to Sudan	4 December 1923	25	W.H. Allen & Sons Ltd
675M	Thistleros	cargo ship	9 December 1924	19 March 1925	4615	Allan Black & Co.
676G	Alyntbank	cargo ship	15 January 1925	26 March 1925	5151	Bank Line Ltd
677G	Elmbank	cargo ship	12 February 1925	23 April 1925	5155	Bank Line Ltd
678G	Fernbank					
679G	Forresbank Forthbank	cargo ship	8 April 1925	11 June 1925	5155	Bank Line Ltd
680G	Nairmbank Hazelbank Weirbank	cargo ship	21 May 1925	7 July 1925	5155	Bank Line Ltd
681G	Larchbank	cargo ship	18 June 1925	9 September 1925	5150	Bank Line Ltd
682G	Levernbank	cargo ship	14 July 1925	1 October 1925	5150	Bank Line Ltd
683G	Myrtlebank	cargo ship	24 September 1925	23 November 1925	5150	Bank Line Ltd
684G	Olivebank	cargo ship	29 October 1925	29 December 1925	5150	Bank Line Ltd
685G	Oakbank	cargo ship	3 December 1925	9 February 1926	5154	Bank Line Ltd
686G	Speybank	cargo ship	18 January 1926	11 March 1926	5154	Bank Line Ltd
687G	Springbank	cargo ship	25 February 1926	20 April 1926	5155	Bank Line Ltd
		cargo ship	13 April 1926	26 May 1926	5155	Bank Line Ltd
688P	Procris	cargo ship	26 September 1924	27 November 1924	1320	J.&P. Hutchison Ltd
689P	Fendris	cargo ship	25 November 1924	5 February 1925	1320	J.&P. Hutchison Ltd
690G	Papuan Chief	cargo ship	1 July 1924	24 September 1924	255	Steamship Trading Co.
691M	River Ottawa King James	cargo ship	8 May 1925	28 November 1925	5065	British Motorship Co. King Line Ltd
692M	River St Lawrence King Malcolm	cargo ship	7 July 1925	29 December 1925	5064	British Motorship Co. King Line Ltd

Ship no.	Name	Vessel type	Launch date	Delivery date	Tonnage	Owner
693G	*Temuco*	tug tender	1 September 1925	22 September 1925	125	Pacific Steam Navigation Co.
694G		pontoon		27 May 1926		Cowans Sheldon & Co.
695	*Apapa*	passenger ship	26 August 1926	28 January 1927	9350	Elder Dempster & Co.
696	*Ulster Queen*	cross-channel ship	28 March 1929	11 February 1930	3756	Belfast Steamship Co.
697	*Ulster Prince*	cross-channel ship	25 April 1929	3 March 1930	3756	Belfast Steamship Co.
698G	*Redline No. 1*	coastal tanker	13 October 1924	5 November 1924	272	British Mexican Petroleum Co.
699	*Inverlago*	shallow-draft tanker	26 February 1925	24 March 1925	2372	Lago Shipping Co.
700	*Inverrosa*	shallow-draft tanker	26 March 1925	24 April 1925	2372	Lago Shipping Co.
701	*Invercaibo*	shallow-draft tanker	23 April 1925	9 June 1925	2372	Lago Shipping Co.
702	*Inverruba*	shallow-draft tanker	26 May 1925	30 June 1925	2372	Lago Shipping Co.
703G	unnamed	water carrier		21 January 1925		Andrew Weir & Co.
704P	*Madrid*	cargo ship	28 October 1925	30 December 1925	1453	Argentine Navigation Co.
705P	*Roma*	cargo ship	29 December 1925	24 February 1926	1455	Argentine Navigation Co.
706M	*Hythe*	cross-channel ship	24 April 1925	5 June 1925	685	Southern Railway Co.
707M	*Whitstable*	cross-channel ship	23 June 1925	17 August 1925	685	Southern Railway Co.
708G	*Inverpool*	tanker	6 April 1925	20 May 1925	680	British Mexican Petroleum Co.
709M	*Marthara*	cargo ship	28 November 1925	16 January 1926	4999	Maclay & McIntyre
710G	unnamed	oil-carrying barge	10 March 1925	13 March 1925		Elder Dempster & Co.
711G	unnamed	oil-carrying barge	10 March 1925	13 March 1925		Elder Dempster & Co.
712G	unnamed	oil-carrying barge	10 March 1925	13 March 1925		Elder Dempster & Co.
713G	unnamed	oil-carrying barge	20 April 1925	23 April 1925		Elder Dempster & Co.
714G	unnamed	oil-carrying barge	20 April 1925	23 April 1925		Elder Dempster & Co.
715G	unnamed	oil-carrying barge	20 April 1925	23 April 1925		Elder Dempster & Co.
716D	*Gascony*	cargo ship	2 September 1925	25 November 1925	4716	David MacIver & Co.
717G	unnamed	barge		17 March 1925	80	Andrew Weir & Co.
718G	unnamed	barge		17 March 1925	80	Andrew Weir & Co.
719M	*Haslemere*	cross-channel ship	22 May 1925	6 July 1925	756	Southern Railway Co.
720M	*Fratton*	cross-channel ship	18 August 1925	28 September 1925	757	Southern Railway Co.
721M	*Colonial*	cargo ship	19 December 1925	19 February 1926	5108	T. &J. Harrison
722M	*Director*	cargo ship	12 February 1926	8 March 1926	5107	T. &J. Harrison
723G	unnamed	lighter	25 September 1925	28 September 1925		Elder Dempster & Co.
724G	unnamed	lighter	25 September 1925	28 September 1925		Elder Dempster & Co.
725P	*Dolores de Urquiza*	train ferry	10 August 1926	2 October 1926	2217	Entre Rios Railways Co.
726G	unnamed	barge		29 October 1925		Andrew Weir & Co.
727G	unnamed	barge		29 October 1925		Andrew Weir & Co.
728G	*Koolinda*	cargo ship	26 August 1926	23 December 1926	4372	Government of Western Australia
729M	*Maidstone*	cross-channel ship	16 March 1926	30 April 1926	688	Southern Railway Co.
730M	*Ringwood*	cross-channel ship	13 April 1926	14 June 1926	755	Southern Railway Co.
731G	*London Mammoth*	floating crane pontoon	9 September 1926	16 July 1927	1580	Port of London Authority
732D	*Begonia*	barge	15 April 1926	26 April 1926	814	Argentine Navigation Co.

Ship no.	Name	Vessel type	Launch date	Delivery date	Tonnage	Owner
733D	Boltonia	barge	28 April 1926	28 April 1926	814	Argentine Navigation Co.
734G	George Livesey	tug	20 May 1926	12 May 1928	107	South Metropolitan Gas Co.
735D	Dunkwa	cargo ship	15 June 1927	24 August 1927	3789	Elder Dempster & Co.
736D	Duala					Elder Dempster & Co.
	Dixcove	cargo ship	25 August 1927	21 October 1927	3789	Elder Dempster & Co.
737D	Daru	cargo ship	28 October 1927	20 December 1927	3838	Elder Dempster & Co.
738D	Dagomba	cargo ship	24 January 1928	15 March 1928	3845	Elder Dempster & Co.
739	San Nicolas	shallow-draft tanker	15 April 1926	20 May 1926	2391	Lago Shipping Co.
740G	Papudo	tug	20 May 1926	2 June 1926	47	Pacific Steam Navigation Co.
741G	Palacio	cargo ship	8 September 1927	19 October 1927	1346	MacAndrews & Co.
742G	Pelayo	cargo ship	12 October 1927	1 December 1927	1346	MacAndrews & Co.
743G	Pelajo					
	Pacheco	cargo ship	10 November 1927	22 December 1927	1346	MacAndrews & Co.
744G	Pinto	cargo ship	24 November 1927	2 February 1928	1346	MacAndrews & Co.
745G	Ponzano	cargo ship	21 December 1927	28 February 1928	1346	MacAndrews & Co.
746	Ambrosio	shallow-draft tanker	3 June 1926	7 July 1926	2391	Lago Shipping Co.
747G	Petronella	shallow-draft tanker	12 July 1927	11 October 1927	2770	Nederlandsch Indische Tank Stoomboot Mij
748G	Paula	shallow-draft tanker	22 September 1927	22 November 1927	2770	Nederlandsch Indische Tank Stoomboot Mij
749G	Agatha	shallow-draft tanker	16 June 1927	8 September 1927	3126	Nederlandsch Indische Tank Stoomboot Mij
750G	Paua	shallow-draft tanker	14 April 1927	9 June 1927	1260	Nederlandsch Indische Tank Stoomboot Mij
751	Highland Monarch	passenger/cargo ship	3 May 1928	2 October 1928	14137	H.&.W. Nelson Ltd
752G	Sin Kheng Seng	coaster	17 February 1927	2 April 1927	200	McKie & Baxter Ltd
753G		floating dock		2 December 1926		Entre Rios Railways Co.
754P	La Falaise	yacht	28 June 1927	13 July 1927	119	James Allan
755G		caisson		12 February 1927		Montevideo Gas & Drydock Co.
756M	Minmi	collier	31 May 1927	30 June 1927	1455	James & Alexander Brown
757	King Edgar	cargo ship	15 September 1927	30 November 1927	4536	King Line Ltd
758	King Edwin	cargo ship	29 September 1927	20 December 1927	4536	King Line Ltd
759	King Egbert	cargo ship	27 October 1927	17 January 1928	4535	King Line Ltd
760	King John	cargo ship	24 November 1927	16 February 1928	5228	King Line Ltd
761	King Lud	cargo ship	22 December 1927	15 March 1928	5224	King Line Ltd
762	King Neptune	cargo ship	26 January 1928	17 April 1928	5224	King Line Ltd
763	King Arthur	cargo ship	22 March 1928	17 May 1928	5224	King Line Ltd
764	King Stephen	cargo ship	24 April 1928	14 June 1928	5274	King Line Ltd
765	King William	cargo ship	19 May 1928	5 July 1928	5274	King Line Ltd
766G	unnamed	barge		29 December 1926		Andrew Weir & Co.

Ship no.	Name	Vessel type	Launch date	Delivery date	Tonnage	Owner
767G	unnamed	barge		29 December 1926		Andrew Weir & Co.
768G	unnamed	barge		29 December 1926		Andrew Weir & Co.
769G	unnamed	barge		29 December 1926		Andrew Weir & Co.
770G	unnamed	barge		29 December 1926		Andrew Weir & Co.
771G	unnamed	barge		29 December 1926		Andrew Weir & Co.
772G	unnamed	barge		29 December 1926		Andrew Weir & Co.
773G	unnamed	barge		29 December 1926		Andrew Weir & Co.
774G	unnamed	barge		29 December 1926		Andrew Weir & Co.
775G	unnamed	barge		29 December 1926		Andrew Weir & Co.
776G	unnamed	barge		29 December 1926		Andrew Weir & Co.
777G	unnamed	barge		29 December 1926		Andrew Weir & Co.
778G	unnamed	barge		29 December 1926		Andrew Weir & Co.
779G	unnamed	barge		29 December 1926		Andrew Weir & Co.
780G	Encina	lighter	5 May 1927	9 May 1927	165	Argentine Navigation Co.
781G	Enea	lighter	5 May 1927	24 May 1927	165	Argentine Navigation Co.
782G	Erarta	lighter	14 June 1927	5 July 1927	165	Argentine Navigation Co.
783G	Erica	lighter	30 June 1927	5 July 1927	165	Argentine Navigation Co.
784G	unnamed	lighter	21 March 1927	8 April 1927		Elder Dempster & Co.
785G	unnamed	lighter	21 March 1927	21 April 1927.		Elder Dempster & Co.
786G	Portvey	tug	10 August 1927	28 April 1928	94	Portland & Weymouth Coaling Co.
787M	Eddystone	coaster	12 July 1927	15 September 1927	1550	Clyde Shipping Co.
788G	D1	barge	9 June 1927	16 July 1927	55	Elder Dempster & Co.
789G	D2	barge	9 June 1927	26 July 1927	56	Elder Dempster & Co.
790G	D3	barge	20 June 1927	13 July 1927	56	Elder Dempster & Co.
791M	Uganda	cargo ship	29 September 1927	4 November 1927	4966	Maclay & McIntyre Ltd
792	Lagunilla	shallow-draft tanker	26 May 1927	16 June 1927	2402	Lago Shipping Co.
793	Icotea	shallow-draft tanker	26 May 1927	17 June 1927	2402	Lago Shipping Co.
794	La Salina	shallow-draft tanker	31 May 1927	28 June 1927	2402	Lago Shipping Co.
795	San Carlos	shallow-draft tanker	28 June 1927	29 July 1927	2395	Lago Shipping Co.
796Gk	Lahej	tug	19 July 1927	16 October 1927	283	Peninsular and Oriental Steam Navigation Co.
797Gk	Tremayne Nimoda	cargo ship	24 November 1927	19 January 1928	4736	Hain Steamship Co.
798	Berta	shallow-draft tanker	30 June 1927	14 July 1927	2611	Anglo-Saxon Petroleum Co.
799	Brigida	shallow-draft tanker	11 August 1927	30 August 1927	2609	Anglo-Saxon Petroleum Co.
800Gk	Kheti	cargo ship	31 August 1927	25 October 1927	2650	James Moss & Co.
801Gk	Saugor	cargo ship	21 February 1928	29 March 1928	6303	James Nourse Ltd
802G	Cabo Espichel	tug/salvage steamer	29 November 1927	28 March 1928	304	McKie & Baxter (Lisbon Harbour Board)
803G	Cabo Raso	tug/salvage steamer	29 December 1927	2 August 1928	230	McKie & Baxter (Lisbon Harbour Board)

Ship no.	Name	Vessel type	Launch date	Delivery date	Tonnage	Owner
804G	*Cabo Sardao*	tug/salvage steamer	31 December 1927	17 August 1928	230	McKie & Baxter (Lisbon Harbour Board)
805P	*Iguazu*	shallow-draft passenger ship	12 October 1927	26 November 1927	523	Argentine Navigation Co.
806	*Highland Chieftain*	passenger/cargo ship	21 June 1928	26 January 1929	14130	H.&W. Nelson Ltd
807	*Britannic*	passenger ship	6 August 1929	21 June 1930	26943	Oceanic Steam Navigation Co.
808M	*Clydefield*	oil tanker	23 April 1928	12 July 1928	6758	Hunting & Son Ltd
809	*Oranjestad*	shallow-draft tanker	1 September 1927	23 September 1927	2396	Andrew Weir & Co.
810	*Sabaneta*	shallow-draft tanker	8 September 1927	30 September 1927	2396	Andrew Weir & Co.
811G	*Zahra*	tanker	5 October 1927	22 November 1927	821	Vacuum Oil Co.
812	*Highland Brigade*	passenger/cargo ship	1 November 1928	27 April 1929	14131	H.&W. Nelson Ltd
813G	*Highland Hope*	passenger/cargo ship	24 January 1929	26 January 1930	14129	H.&W. Nelson Ltd
814	*Highland Princess*	passenger/cargo ship	11 April 1929	25 February 1930	14128	H.&.W. Nelson Ltd
815P	*Delfina Mitre*	train ferry	19 April 1928	29 May 1928	2235	Entre Rios Railways Co.
816M	*Dafila*	cargo ship	8 December 1927	10 January 1928	1940	British & Continental Steamship Co.
817M	*Nyanza*	cargo ship	17 May 1928	4 July 1928	4974	Maclay & McIntyre Ltd
818M	*Deal*	cross-channel ship	10 February 1928	20 March 1928	688	Southern Railway Co.
819G	*JJ1*	tug	3 October 1927	6 October 1927	29	Lago Shipping Co.
820G	*JJ2*	tug	3 October 1927	6 October 1927	29	Lago Shipping Co.
821G	*JJ3*	tug	3 October 1927	6 October 1927	29	Lago Shipping Co.
822G	*JJ4*	tug	3 October 1927	6 October 1927	29	Lago Shipping Co.
823P	unnamed	oil barge	shipped in sections to Rangoon, Burma	1 November 1927	110	Burmah Oil Co. Ltd
824D	*Brittany*	cargo ship	17 May 1928	30 June 1928	4772	David MacIver & Co.
825	*Winchester Castle*	passenger ship	19 November 1929	11 October 1930	20108	Union-Castle Mail Steamship Co.
826M	*Designer*	cargo ship	3 July 1928	7 September 1928	5945	T.&J. Harrison
827G	*Sefui*	ore-carrying barge	28 November 1927	29 November 1927	57	Elder Dempster & Co.
828G	*Wala*	ore-carrying barge	28 November 1927	29 November 1927	57	Elder Dempster & Co.
829G	*Ciudad del Salto*	shallow-draft passenger ship	5 July 1928	21 September 1928	1952	Argentine Navigation Co.
830Gk	*Behar*	cargo ship	16 August 1928	7 November 1928	6100	Hain Steamship Co.
831M	*Kerma*	cargo ship	21 August 1928	20 September 1928	4333	Frank C. Strick & Co.
832	*Punta Benitez*	shallow-draft tanker	21 February 1928	16 March 1928	2394	Lago Shipping Co.
833	*Tia Juana*	shallow-draft tanker	8 March 1928	4 April 1928	2395	Lago Shipping Co.
834	*San Matias*					
	Hooiberg	shallow-draft tanker	27 March 1928	25 April 1928	2395	Lago Shipping Co.
835	*Punta Gorda*	shallow-draft tanker	23 April 1928	18 May 1928	2395	Lago Shipping Co.
836	*Bella Vista*					
	Yamanota	shallow-draft tanker	22 May 1928	13 June 1928	2395	Lago Shipping Co.
837M	*Celtic Monarch*	cargo ship	15 November 1928	7 January 1929	5822	Raeburn & Verel Ltd

Ship no.	Name	Vessel type	Launch date	Delivery date	Tonnage	Owner
838P	*Centaura*	dumb lighter	26 June 1928	12 July 1928	788	Argentine Navigation Co.
839P	unnamed	oil barge	shipped in sections to Rangoon, Burma	19 September 1928	110	Burmah Oil Co.
840	*Warwick Castle*	passenger ship	29 April 1930	16 January 1931	20444	Union-Castle Mail Steamship Co.
841G	*Llangibby Castle*	passenger ship	4 July 1929	21 November 1929	11951	Union-Castle Mail Steamship Co.
842G	*Bhutan*	cargo ship	12 December 1928	13 March 1929	6104	Hain Steamship Co.
843G	*Westralia*	refrigerated cargo ship	25 April 1929	15 August 1929	8107	Huddart Parker
844	*Oceanic*	passenger ship	cancelled		60000	Oceanic Steam Navigation Co.
845P	*Cardiff*	cargo ship	25 January 1929	7 March 1929	1483	Argentine Navigation Co.
846P	*Glasgow*	cargo ship	26 February 1929	24 April 1929	1483	Argentine Navigation Co.
847P	*Ciudad de Ascuncion*	passenger/cargo ship	22 August 1929	17 March 1930	2851	Argentine Navigation Co.
848P	*Ciudad de Corrientes*	passenger/cargo ship	10 June 1930	14 October 1930	2854	Argentine Navigation Co.
849	*Achimota*					British & African Steam Navigation Co.
850P	*Wanganella*	passenger ship	17 December 1929	29 November 1932	9576	Huddart Parker
851G	*Idomo*	lighter	21 December 1928	10 January 1929	55	Elder Dempster & Co.
852	*Dunbar Castle*	passenger ship	31 October 1929	20 May 1930	10002	Union-Castle Mail Steamship Co.
853	*Reina del Pacifico*	passenger ship	23 September 1930	24 March 1931	17707	Pacific Steam Navigation Co.
853D	*David Livingstone*	cargo ship	24 October 1929	20 March 1930	4022	British & African Steam Navigation Co.
854D	*Mary Slessor*	cargo ship	18 December 1929	23 April 1930	4016	British & African Steam Navigation Co.
855M	*William Wilberforce*	cargo ship	14 January 1930	10 May 1930	4013	African Steamship Co.
856M	*Baron Vernon*	cargo ship	23 April 1929	28 June 1929	3642	H. Hogarth & Sons
857M	*Baron Ramsay*	cargo ship	13 June 1929	12 July 1929	3650	H. Hogarth & Sons
858G	*Kufra*	cargo ship	21 August 1929	19 November 1929	2608	James Moss & Co.
859M	*Irwin*	passenger ferry	10 June 1929	2 September 1929	970	South Indian Railway Co.
860M	*Goschen*	passenger ferry	27 June 1929	20 September 1929	970	South Indian Railway Co.
861	*Tamare*	shallow-draft tanker	23 April 1929	7 May 1929	3046	Lago Shipping Co.
862	*Tasajeras*	shallow-draft tanker	30 April 1929	20 May 1929	3046	Lago Shipping Co.
863	*Ule*	shallow-draft tanker	9 May 1929	29 May 1929	3046	Lago Shipping Co.
	Surinam	shallow-draft tanker	19 June 1929	19 September 1929	3046	Lago Shipping Co.
864D	*Kavak*	cargo ship	22 August 1929	1 November 1929	2743	Moss Steamship Co.
865D	*Kana*	cargo ship	1 November 1929	13 December 1929	2743	Moss Steamship Co.
866P	*Carmen Avellaneda*	train ferry			2234	Entre Rios Railways Co.
867G	*Edward Blyden*	cargo ship	27 February 1930	29 May 1930	4022	British & African Steam Navigation Co.
868G	*Alfred Jones*	cargo ship	29 April 1930	20 August 1930	4022	British & African Steam Navigation Co.
869M	*Macgregor Laird*	cargo ship	28 February 1930	3 July 1930	4015	African Steamship Co.

Ship no.	Name	Vessel type	Launch date	Delivery date	Tonnage	Owner
870	*Innisfallen*	passenger ferry	4 March 1930	14 June 1930	3019	City of Cork Steam Packet Co.
871M	*Ardanbhan*	cargo ship	6 September 1929	7 November 1929	777	Clark & Service
872G	*Lochness*	passenger/cargo ferry	6 June 1929	9 July 1929	1497	David MacBrayne (1928) Ltd
873P	*Amberes*	cargo ship	24 October 1929	25 March 1930	1497	Argentine Navigation Co.
874G	*Barcelona*	cargo ship	19 December 1929	16 April 1930	1496	Argentine Navigation Co.
875G	*Genova*	cargo ship	28 January 1930	27 May 1930	1496	Argentine Navigation Co.
876P	*Hamburgo*	cargo ship	8 May 1930	17 September 1930	1496	Argentine Navigation Co.
877P	*Guayra*	passenger ferry	26 June 1930	14 November 1930	1496	Argentine Navigation Co.
878	*Foylebank*	cargo ship	12 June 1930	14 November 1930	5582	Andrew Weir & Co.
879	*Laganbank*	cargo ship	10 July 1930	11 December 1930	5582	Andrew Weir & Co.
880M	*Dorothy Rose*	cargo ship	31 October 1929	21 November 1929	1600	Richard Hughes & Co.
881M	*Dudley Rose*	cargo ship	4 December 1929	23 December 1929	1600	Richard Hughes & Co.
882	*Silvercypress*	cargo ship	18 February 1930	18 June 1930	6770	Silver Line Ltd
883	*Silverwalnut*	cargo ship	15 April 1930	23 July 1930	6770	Silver Line Ltd
884	*Silverteak*	cargo ship	29 May 1930	2 September 1930	6770	Silver Line Ltd
885	*Silversandal*	cargo ship	26 June 1930	19 September 1930	6770	Silver Line Ltd
886M	*Baron Napier*	cargo ship	12 February 1930	21 March 1930	3659	H. Hogarth & Sons
887M	*Baron Erskine*	cargo ship	17 March 1930	17 April 1930	3659	H. Hogarth & Sons
888	*San Antonio*	cargo ship	1 July 1930	24 September 1930	5986	Compagnie Générale Transatlantique
889	*San Diego*	cargo ship	14 August 1930	11 November 1930	5986	Compagnie Générale Transatlantique
890	*San Francisco*	cargo ship	11 September 1930	10 December 1930	5984	Compagnie Générale Transatlantique
891	*San Jose*	cargo ship	23 October 1930	23 January 1931	5982	Compagnie Générale Transatlantique
892	*San Mateo*	cargo ship	20 November 1930	6 March 1931	5935	Compagnie Générale Transatlantique
893	*San Pedro*	cargo ship	20 December 1930	17 April 1931	5935	Compagnie Générale Transatlantique
894P	*Ciudad de Concepcion*	passenger/cargo ferry	22 October 1930	25 January 1931	897	Argentine Navigation Co.
895D	unnamed	lighter	5 March 1930	25 March 1930	900	Argentine Navigation Co.
896	*Georgic*	passenger ship	12 November 1931	10 June 1932	27267	Oceanic Steam Navigation Co.
897G	*Ganges*	passenger/cargo ship	26 August 1930	29 October 1930	6253	James Nourse Ltd
898G	*Somali*	cargo ship	9 October 1930	18 December 1930	6809	Hain Steamship Co.
899	*Ebano*	liquid-asphalt carrier	27 May 1930	30 October 1930	2627	Ebano Oil Co.
900M	*Prestatyn Rose*	cargo ship	28 April 1930	20 May 1930	1151	Richard Hughes & Co.
901M	*Anglesea Rose*	cargo ship	12 May 1930	7 June 1930	1151	Richard Hughes & Co.
902M	*Medoc*	cargo ship	30 May 1930	26 June 1930	1166	Worms & Co.
903M	*Saint Emilion*					
	Pomerol	cargo ship	12 June 1930	8 July 1930	1167	Worms & Co.
904M	*Chateau Larose*	cargo ship	10 July 1930	23 August 1930	2047	Worms & Co.
905M	*Chateau Pavie*	cargo ship	11 August 1930	11 September 1930	2047	Worms & Co.
906M	*Maurice Rose*	cargo ship	25 September 1930	24 October 1930	1600	Richard Hughes & Co.
907M	*Dennis Rose*	cargo ship	14 October 1930	7 November 1930	1600	Richard Hughes & Co.
908	*Cliona*	oil tanker	14 May 1931	14 October 1931	8375	Anglo-Saxon Petroleum Co.

Ship no.	Name	Vessel type	Launch date	Delivery date	Tonnage	Owner
909	Conch	oil tanker	2 July 1931	22 December 1931	8376	Anglo-Saxon Petroleum Co.
910M	Rockabill	coaster	10 December 1930	29 January 1931	1392	Clyde Shipping Co.
911G	Troad					
	Triona	cargo ship	22 January 1931	21 March 1931	4413	British Phospate Commissioners
912M	Autocarrier	cross-channel car ferry	5 February 1931	26 March 1931	822	Southern Railway Co.
913G	Ogeni	stern-wheel steamer	5 March 1931	17 April 1931	47	Elder Dempster & Co.
914P	East Goodwin	lightship	23 December 1931	13 April 1932	260	Corporation of Trinity House
915	Maracay	shallow-draft tanker	21 May 1931	16 June 1931	3795	Lago Shipping Co.
916	Highland Patriot	passenger/cargo ship	10 December 1931	13 May 1932	14156	Nelson Steam Navigation Co.
917G	Floating Crane No. 2	crane pontoon	15 March 1932	20 August 1932	608	Cowan Sheldon & Co.
918G	Royal Iris II	river ferry	22 March 1932	12 May 1932	607	Corporation of Wallasey
919G	Baron Ardrossan	cargo ship	4 May 1932	4 June 1932	3896	H. Hogarth & Sons
920G	Duchess of Hamilton	Clyde passenger steamer	5 May 1932	24 June 1932	795	Caledonian Steam Packet Co.
921P	North Carr	lightship	2 December 1932	27 February 1933	268	Commissioners of Northern Lighthouses
922	Waiwera	refrigerated cargo ship	1 May 1934	29 August 1934	10781	Shaw Savill & Albion Co.
923	Waipawa	refrigerated cargo ship	28 June 1934	19 October 1934	10784	Shaw Savill & Albion Co.
924G	Wairangi	refrigerated cargo ship	9 October 1934	26 January 1935	10779	Shaw Savill & Albion Co.
925G	Bhadravati	passenger ferry	5 July 1932	10 September 1932	1306	Bombay Steam Navigation Co.
926G	Chandravati	passenger ferry	4 July 1933	31 August 1933	556	Bombay Steam Navigation Co.
927M	Baron Dunmore	cargo ship	9 August 1933	22 September 1933	3938	H. Hogarth & Sons
928M	Baron Elgin	cargo ship	6 September 1933	4 October 1933	3942	H. Hogarth & Sons
929G	Prabhavati	passenger ferry	17 August 1933	28 September 1933	556	Bombay Steam Navigation Co.
930	Idalia	yacht	29 May 1934	2 July 1934	147	Alan F. Craig
931M	Loch Lomond	cargo ship	16 August 1934	21 September 1934	5452	Maclay & McIntyre Ltd
932G	Anadara	oil tanker	19 December 1934	28 February 1935	8008	Anglo-Saxon Petroleum Co.
933	New Zealand Star	refrigerated cargo ship	9 October 1934	29 December 1934	10733	Blue Star Line Ltd
934	Imperial Star Australia Star	refrigerated cargo ship	22 November 1934	1 March 1935	10740	Blue Star Line Ltd
935G	New Zealand Star Sir Hastings Anderson	target towing ship	14 June 1934	12 September 1934	228	War Office
936G	John Dock	tug	26 July 1934	9 October 1934	551	South African Railways & Harbour Board
937G	W.H. Fuller	tug	28 August 1934	9 November 1934	551	South African Railways & Harbour Board
938G	San Arcadio	oil tanker	19 February 1935	10 April 1935	7419	Eagle Oil and Shipping Co.
939	Imperial Star Australia Star	refrigerated cargo ship	8 January 1935	17 April 1935	11122	Blue Star Line Ltd
940	HMS Penelope	'Arethusa'-class cruiser	15 October 1935	13 November 1936	5050	Admiralty
941	Stirling Castle	passenger ship	15 August 1935	29 January 1936	25594	Union-Castle Mail Steamship Co.

Ship no.	Name	Vessel type	Launch date	Delivery date	Tonnage	Owner
942	Athlone Castle	passenger ship	28 November 1935	13 May 1936	25567	Union-Castle Mail Steamship Co.
943	Roslin Castle	refrigerated cargo/passenger ship	20 December 1934	4 May 1935	7016	Union-Castle Mail Steamship Co.
944	Rothesay Castle	refrigerated cargo/passenger ship	21 February 1935	11 May 1935	7016	Union-Castle Mail Steamship Co.
945M	Henzada	cargo ship	11 October 1934	22 November 1934	4161	P. Henderson & Co.
946M	Martaban	cargo ship	8 November 1934	26 December 1934	4161	P. Henderson & Co.
947M	Baron Renfrew	cargo ship	6 February 1935	March 1935	3635	H. Hogarth & Sons
948M	Baron Cawdor	cargo ship	10 December 1934	16 January 1935	3638	H. Hogarth & Sons
949P	Flying Falcon	tug	20 August 1934	15 September 1934	283	Clyde Shipping Co.
950M	Saganaga	cargo ship	6 March 1935	15 April 1935	5454	Christian Salvesen
951	Duke of York	passenger ferry	7 March 1935	4 June 1935	3759	London Midland & Scottish Railway Co.
952P	Mpasa	coaster	shipped in sections to Nyasaland	1 February 1935	270	Nyasaland Railways
953M	Inventor	cargo ship	3 July 1935	11 September 1935	6210	T. &J. Harrison Ltd
954	Calabar	passenger/cargo ship	7 February 1935	19 March 1935	1932	Elder Dempster Lines Ltd
955	Kanimbla	passenger ship	12 December 1935	26 April 1936	10984	McIlwraith McEachern & Co.
956P	Talisman	paddle ferry	10 April 1935	12 June 1935	544	London & Northern Eastern Railway Co.
957	Sydney Star Empire Star	refrigerated cargo ship	26 September 1935	20 December 1935	11093	Blue Star Line Ltd
958	Melbourne Star Sydney Star	refrigerated cargo ship	11 January 1936	19 March 1936	11095	Blue Star Line Ltd
959	Dunnottar Castle	passenger ship	25 January 1936	27 June 1936	15007	Union-Castle Mail Steamship Co.
960	Dunvegan Castle	passenger ship	26 March 1936	27 August 1936	15007	Union-Castle Mail Steamship Co.
961G	Standella	oil tanker	9 January 1936	16 April 1936	6197	Anglo-Saxon Petroleum Co.
962G	Simnia	oil tanker	20 February 1936	14 May 1936	6197	Anglo-Saxon Petroleum Co.
963	Laird of Ulster Royal Ulsterman	passenger/cargo ferry	10 March 1936	13 June 1936	3290	Burns & Laird Lines Ltd
964	Laird of Scotia Royal Scotsman	passenger/cargo ferry	11 March 1936	29 May 1936	3244	Burns & Laird Lines Ltd
965G	Sonavati	passenger/cargo ferry	26 November 1935	21 February 1936	1663	Bombay Steam Navigation Co.
966	Eros	fruit carrier	9 January 1936	8 April 1936	5888	Erin Steamship Co.
967	Duchess of Abercorn	tug/tender	25 August 1936	17 March 1937	308	Belfast Harbour Commissioners
968G	British Power	oil tanker	16 September 1936	16 December 1936	8334	British Tanker Co.
969G	British Destiny	oil tanker	3 November 1936	21 January 1937	8334	British Tanker Co.
970G	Adelong	cargo ship	5 May 1936	18 July 1936	3576	Huddart Parker
971G	Boardale	oil tanker	22 April 1937	7 June 1937	8334	British Tanker Co.
972G	British Integrity	oil tanker	22 June 1937	8 September 1937	8334	British Tanker Co.

Ship no.	Name	Vessel type	Launch date	Delivery date	Tonnage	Owner
973G	*Broomdale*	oil tanker	2 September 1937	3 November 1937	8334	British Tanker Co.
974G	*British Security*	oil tanker	4 November 1937	29 December 1937	8334	British Tanker Co.
975P	*Charles MacIver*	trawler	27 May 1936	17 July 1936	500	Lancashire & Western Sea Fisheries Joint Co.
976	*Lairdswood*	cattle boat	21 July 1936	15 August 1936	789	Burns & Laird Lines Ltd
977	*Lairdscrest*	coaster	6 August 1936	26 August 1936	789	Burns & Laird Lines Ltd
978	*Lairdsbank*	coaster	3 September 1936	24 September 1936	789	Burns & Laird Lines Ltd
979P	*Cameo*	coaster	2 December 1936	3 February 1937	946	William Robertson
980	*Delius*	cargo ship	12 April 1937	6 July 1937	6065	Lamport & Holt Line Ltd
981G	*Sitala*	oil tanker	29 December 1936	10 March 1937	6218	Anglo-Saxon Petroleum Co.
982G	*Salacia*	cargo ship	11 March 1937	17 August 1937	5495	Donaldson Lines Ltd
983	*Walmer Castle*	cargo ship	17 September 1936	30 November 1936	905	Union-Castle Mail Steamship Co.
984	*Ernebank*	cargo ship	17 November 1936	18 February 1937	5388	Andrew Weir & Co.
985G	*Dipavati*	passenger ferry	14 July 1936	17 September 1936	840	Bombay Steam Navigation Co.
986	*Capetown Castle*	passenger ship	23 September 1937	31 March 1938	27002	Union-Castle Mail Steamship Co.
987	*Durban Castle*	passenger ship	14 June 1938	15 December 1938	17388	Union-Castle Mail Steamship Co.
988P	*Crossgar*	collier	6 October 1936	28 November 1936	661	John Kelly Ltd
989P	*Leonora*	tug	13 May 1936	15 July 1936	86	McKie & Baxter
990G	*Comara*	coaster	27 January 1937	7 April 1937	751	North Coast Steam Navigation Co.
991P	*May*	lighthouse tender	14 January 1937	30 March 1937	491	Commissioners of Northern Lighthouses
992	*Rochester Castle*	refrigerated cargo ship	11 February 1937	29 April 1937	7795	Union-Castle Mail Steamship Co.
993	*Roxburgh Castle*	refrigerated cargo ship	25 March 1937	26 June 1937	7800	Union-Castle Mail Steamship Co.
994	*Torr Head*	cargo ship	25 February 1937	10 April 1937	5021	Ulster Steamship Co.
995	*Leinster*	passenger ferry	24 June 1937	2 November 1937	4302	British & Irish Steam Packet Co.
996	*Munster*	passenger ferry	3 November 1937	22 February 1938	4302	British & Irish Steam Packet Co.
997P	*Lady Sylvia*	passenger ferry	16 March 1937	8 May 1937	199	Union Steamship Co. of British Columbia Ltd
998P	*Donaghadee*	collier	5 August 1937	9 September 1937	662	John Kelly Ltd
999G	*Lochavon*	cargo ship	3 March 1938	29 July 1938	9204	Royal Mail Lines Ltd
1000	*HMS Belfast*	'Southampton'-class cruiser	17 March 1938	3 August 1939	10173	Admiralty
1001	*Delane*	cargo ship	21 October 1937	17 January 1938	6054	Lamport & Holt Line Ltd
1002	*Devis*	cargo ship	21 December 1937	14 February 1938	6054	Lamport & Holt Line Ltd
1003G	*Koolama*	cargo ship	16 December 1937	2 April 1938	4026	Western Australian Government
1004	*Waimarama*	cargo ship	31 May 1938	6 October 1938	11091	Shaw Savill & Albion Co.
1005	*Andes*	passenger ship	7 March 1939	24 September 1939	25688	Royal Mail Lines Ltd
1006	*Pretoria Castle*	passenger ship	12 October 1938	18 April 1939	17382	Union-Castle Mail Steamship Co.
1007	*HMS Formidable*	'Illustrious'-class aircraft carrier	17 August 1939	24 November 1940	28094	Admiralty

Ship no.	Name	Vessel type	Launch date	Delivery date	Tonnage	Owner
1008G	Donax	oil tanker	28 April 1938	7 July 1938	8036	Anglo-Saxon Petroleum Co.
1009G	Dromus	oil tanker	28 June 1938	14 September 1938	8036	Anglo-Saxon Petroleum Co.
1010G	British Fidelity	oil tanker	25 August 1938	26 October 1938	8465	British Tanker Co.
1011G	British Trust	oil tanker	27 October 1938	19 January 1939	8466	British Tanker Co.
1012	Richmond Castle	refrigerated cargo ship	8 November 1938	11 February 1939	7798	Union-Castle Mail Steamship Co.
1013	Rowallan Castle	refrigerated cargo ship	8 December 1938	11 March 1939	7798	Union-Castle Mail Steamship Co.
1014	Erato	oil tanker	25 October 1938	26 January 1939	8129	Anglo-Saxon Petroleum Co.
1015G	Cairndale	oil tanker	20 December 1938	5 April 1939	8071	Admiralty
1016	San Emiliano		20 April 1939	24 August 1939		Eagle Oil and Shipping Co.
1017	Wellington Star	refrigerated cargo ship	20 June 1939	4 November 1939	12382	Blue Star Line Ltd
1018G	Auckland Star	refrigerated cargo ship	25 January 1939	15 March 1939	12382	Blue Star Line Ltd
1019	Bangalow	coaster	1 August 1939	24 November 1939	632	North Coast Steam Navigation Co.
1020P	Waiotira	passenger/cargo ship	23 May 1939	23 May 1939	11102	Shaw Savill & Albion Co.
1021P	Theodor Woker	tug	6 July 1939	1 November 1939	620	South African Government
1022P	Watermeyer	tug	shipped in sections to Fiji	18 April 1939	620	South African Government
1023	Degei	passenger ferry	30 November 1940	28 February 1942	205	Crown Agents for the Colonies (Government of Fiji)
1024P	HMS Adamant	submarine depot ship	27 April 1940	4 July 1941	12500	Admiralty
1025	Lincoln Castle	paddle passenger ship	21 May 1940	15 August 1940	598	London & North Eastern Railway Co.
1026	Pardo	refrigerated cargo ship	4 September 1940	19 November 1940	5400	Royal Mail Lines Ltd
1027	Potaro	refrigerated cargo ship	2 November 1940	23 January 1941	5409	Royal Mail Lines Ltd
1028	Pampas	refrigerated cargo ship			5415	Royal Mail Lines Ltd
1029	Pelotas	refrigerated cargo ship	14 January 1941	2 April 1941	5419	Royal Mail Lines Ltd
1030	Palma	refrigerated cargo ship	23 March 1940	23 May 1940	8104	Lamport & Holt Line Ltd
1031	Debrett	cargo ship	20 June 1940	30 August 1940	6245	Lamport & Holt Line Ltd
	Defoe	cargo ship	20 November 1941	12 March 1943	14750	Lamport & Holt Line Ltd
	HMS Unicorn	aircraft maintenance carrier				Admiralty
1032G	Lavington Court	cargo ship	21 March 1940	26 June 1940	5372	Court Line Ltd
1033G	Novelist	cargo ship	4 June 1940	8 August 1940	6133	T.&J. Harrison Ltd
1034	Araybank	cargo ship	6 June 1940	24 October 1940	7258	Andrew Weir & Co.
1035	Shirrabank	cargo ship	20 July 1940	5 December 1940	7274	Andrew Weir & Co.
1036	Fanad Head	cargo ship	3 September 1940	19 December 1940	5038	Ulster Steamship Co.
1037P	HMS Elm	'Tree'-class trawler	12 December 1939	9 March 1940	530	Admiralty
1038P	HMS Fir	'Tree'-class trawler	27 January 1940	30 April 1940	530	Admiralty
1039G	HMS Bangor	'Bangor'-class minesweeper	23 May 1940	4 November 1940	656	Admiralty
1040G	HMS Blackpool	'Bangor'-class minesweeper	4 July 1940	7 February 1941	656	Admiralty

Ship no.	Name	Vessel type	Launch date	Delivery date	Tonnage	Owner
1041P	HMS Coreopsis	'Flower'-class corvette	23 May 1940	17 August 1940	925	Admiralty
1042P	HMS Crocus	'Flower'-class corvette	26 June 1940	20 October 1940	925	Admiralty
1043P	Vipya	passenger/cargo ferry	shipped in sections to Nyasaland	23 October 1942	270	Nyasaland Railway Co.
1044G	Dingledale	replenishment tanker	27 March 1941	10 September 1941	8145	Admiralty
1045G	Empire Gem	'Ocean'-type tanker	29 May 1941	24 October 1941	8139	Ministry of Supply
1046G	HMS Black Ranger	'Ranger'-class tanker	22 August 1940	27 January 1941	3417	Admiralty
1047G	HMS Blue Ranger	'Ranger'-class tanker	29 January 1941	6 June 1941	3417	Admiralty
1048G	HMS Brown Ranger	'Ranger'-class tanker	12 December 1940	11 April 1941	3417	Admiralty
1049	HMS Black Prince	'Dido'-class cruiser	27 August 1942	20 November 1943	5950	Admiralty
1050	Empire Hope	refrigerated cargo ship	27 March 1941	22 October 1941	12688	Ministry of Supply (Shaw Savill & Albion Co.)
1051	Empire Grace	refrigerated cargo ship	25 August 1941	1 April 1942	13478	Ministry of Supply (Shaw Savill & Albion Co.)
1052	Derwentdale	landing-ship carrier	12 April 1941	30 August 1941	8398	Ministry of Supply
1053	Empire Diamond	'Ocean'-type tanker	10 July 1941	12 November 1941	8236	Ministry of Supply (Anglo-Saxon Petroleum Co.)
1054P	HMS Rumba	'Dance'-class trawler	31 July 1940	12 November 1940	530	Admiralty
1055P	HMS Sarabande	'Dance'-class trawler	29 August 1940	2 January 1941	530	Admiralty
1056P	HMS Spirea	'Flower'-class corvette	31 October 1940	27 February 1941	724	Admiralty
1057P	HMS Starwort	'Flower'-class corvette	12 February 1941	26 May 1941	724	Admiralty
1058	HMS Arabis	'Flower'-class corvette	14 February 1940	5 April 1940	724	Admiralty
1059	HMS Periwinkle	'Flower'-class corvette	24 February 1940	8 April 1940	724	Admiralty
1060	HMS Clarkia	'Flower'-class corvette	7 March 1940	22 April 1940	724	Admiralty
1061	HMS Calendula	'Flower'-class corvette	21 March 1940	6 May 1940	724	Admiralty
1062	HMS Hibiscus	'Flower'-class corvette	6 April 1940	21 May 1940	724	Admiralty
1063	HMS Heartsease	'Flower'-class corvette	20 April 1940	4 June 1940	724	Admiralty
1064	HMS Camellia	'Flower'-class corvette	4 May 1940	18 June 1940	724	Admiralty
1065	HMS Mallow	'Flower'-class corvette	22 May 1940	2 July 1940	722	Admiralty
1066	HMS Peony	'Flower'-class corvette	4 June 1940	2 August 1940	722	Admiralty
1067	HMS Erica	'Flower'-class corvette	18 June 1940	9 August 1940	722	Admiralty
1068	HMS Gloxinia	'Flower'-class corvette	2 July 1940	22 August 1940	722	Admiralty
1069	HMS Picotee	'Flower'-class corvette	19 July 1940	5 September 1940	724	Admiralty
1070	HMS Gentian	'Flower'-class corvette	6 August 1940	22 September 1940	723	Admiralty
1071	HMS Hyacinth	'Flower'-class corvette	19 August 1940	3 October 1940	723	Admiralty
1072	HMS Rhododendron	'Flower'-class corvette	2 September 1940	18 October 1940	724	Admiralty
1073	HMS Heather	'Flower'-class corvette	17 September 1940	1 November 1940	724	Admiralty
1074	HMS Freesia	'Flower'-class corvette	3 October 1940	19 November 1940	724	Admiralty
1075	HMS Orchis	'Flower'-class corvette	15 October 1940	29 November 1940	724	Admiralty

Ship no.	Name	Vessel type	Launch date	Delivery date	Tonnage	Owner
1076	HMS Kingcup	'Flower'-class corvette	31 October 1940	3 January 1941	724	Admiralty
1077	HMS Pimpernel	'Flower'-class corvette	16 November 1940	9 January 1941	724	Admiralty
1078	Empire Norseman					Ministry of Supply
	Dinsdale	'Ocean'-type tanker	21 October 1941	11 April 1942	8214	Admiralty
1079	Empire Spenser	'Ocean'-type tanker	17 February 1942	29 September 1942	8194	Ministry of Shipping (Anglo-Saxon Petroleum Co.)
1080	Empire Chapman	'Ocean'-type tanker	17 January 1942	25 June 1942	8194	Ministry of Shipping (Sir R. Ropner & Co.)
1081	Empire Fletcher	'Ocean'-type tanker	4 April 1942	31 July 1942	8194	Ministry of Shipping (Halden & Philipps Ltd)
1082	Deseado	refrigerated cargo ship	17 March 1942	28 November 1942	9641	Royal Mail Lines Ltd
1083G	Empire Onyx	'Ocean'-type tanker	21 August 1941	25 December 1941	8220	Ministry of Supply (British Tanker Co.)
1084P	HMS Romeo	'Shakespearian'-class trawler	20 March 1941	28 June 1941	545	Admiralty
1085P	HMS Rosalind	'Shakespearian'-class trawler	3 May 1941	20 October 1941	545	Admiralty
1086P	HMS Oxlip	'Flower'-class corvette	28 August 1941	27 December 1941	724	Admiralty
1087P	HMS Pennywort	'Flower'-class corvette	18 October 1941	5 March 1942	724	Admiralty
1088P	Empire Gat	'Tudor Queen'-type coaster	30 November 1940	2 April 1941	871	Ministry of Shipping (General Steam Navigation Co.)
1089P	Empire Spinney	'Tudor Queen'-type coaster	26 June 1941	23 September 1941	871	Ministry of Shipping (General Steam Navigation Co.)
1090	San Veronico	oil tanker	30 May 1942	31 December 1942	8189	Eagle Oil and Shipping Co.
1091	HMS Campania	escort aircraft carrier	17 June 1943	7 March 1944	12450	Admiralty
1092G	Empire Shoal	'Tudor Queen'-type coaster	13 February 1941	17 June 1941	878	Ministry of Shipping (W.A. Wilson)
1093G	Empire Ballantyne / Belgian Airman	standard 'X'-type cargo vessel	21 October 1941	25 February 1942	6960	Ministry of Shipping (W.A. Souter & Co.)
1094G	Empire Bede	standard 'X'-type cargo vessel	6 January 1942	31 March 1942	6959	Ministry of Shipping (Hain Steamship Co.)
1095	HMS Abelia	'Flower'-class corvette	28 November 1940	3 February 1941	724	Admiralty
1096	HMS Alisma	'Flower'-class corvette	17 December 1940	13 February 1941	724	Admiralty
1097	HMS Anchusa	'Flower'-class corvette	15 January 1941	1 March 1941	808	Admiralty
1098	HMS Armeria	'Flower'-class corvette	16 January 1941	28 March 1941	808	Admiralty
1099	HMS Aster	'Flower'-class corvette	12 February 1941	11 April 1941	808	Admiralty
1100	HMS Bergamot	'Flower'-class corvette	15 February 1941	9 May 1941	808	Admiralty
1101	HMS Broom					
	HMSVervain	'Flower'-class corvette	12 March 1941	9 June 1941	808	Admiralty

Ship no.	Name	Vessel type	Launch date	Delivery date	Tonnage	Owner
1102	HMS Bryony	'Flower'-class corvette	15 March 1941	16 June 1942	808	Admiralty
1103	HMS Buttercup	'Flower'-class corvette	10 April 1941	24 April 1942	808	Admiralty
1104	HMS Chrysanthemum					Admiralty
	FNFL Commandant Drogou	'Flower'-class corvette	11 April 1941	26 January 1942	808	French Navy
1105	HMS Cowslip	'Flower'-class corvette	28 May 1941	9 August 1941	811	Admiralty
1106	HMS Eglantine	'Flower'-class corvette	11 June 1941	27 August 1941	811	Admiralty
1107	HMS Fritillary	'Flower'-class corvette	22 July 1941	31 October 1941	811	Admiralty
1108	HMS Genista	'Flower'-class corvette	24 July 1941	18 December 1941	811	Admiralty
1109	HMS Gloriosa	'Flower'-class corvette	cancelled		811	Admiralty
1110	HMS Harebell	'Flower'-class corvette	cancelled		811	Admiralty
1111	HMS Hemlock	'Flower'-class corvette	cancelled		811	Admiralty
1112	HMS Ivy	'Flower'-class corvette	cancelled		811	Admiralty
1113	HMS Ling	'Flower'-class corvette	cancelled		811	Admiralty
1114	HMS Marjoram	'Flower'-class corvette	cancelled		811	Admiralty
1115G	Empire Deep	'Tudor Queen'-type coaster	9 September 1941	30 October 1941	878	Ministry of War Transport (Ald Shipping Co.)
1116G	British Vigilance	oil tanker	18 February 1942	23 May 1942	8093	British Tanker Co.
	Empire Vigilance	oil tanker	16 April 1942	9 July 1942	8093	Ministry of Shipping
1117G	British Merit	oil tanker				British Tanker Co.
1118	Empire Sidney	standard 'X'-type cargo vessel	4 September 1941	7 May 1942	6946	Ministry of War Transport (Morell Ltd)
1119	Empire Splendour	standard 'D'-type cargo vessel	18 December 1941	1 September 1942	7335	Ministry of War Transport (G. Heyn & Co.)
1120	Empire Strength	standard 'D'-type cargo vessel	28 May 1942	22 December 1942	7355	Ministry of War Transport (Blue Star Line Ltd)
1121	TLC 11	landing craft tank	9 December 1940	16 December 1940	229	Admiralty
1122	TLC 12	landing craft tank	9 December 1940	16 December 1940	229	Admiralty
1123P	HMS Stronsay	'Isles'-class trawler	4 March 1942	24 April 1942	545	Admiralty
1124P	HMS Switha	'Isles'-class trawler	3 April 1942	15 June 1942	545	Admiralty
1125	Empire Castle	standard 'D'-type cargo vessel	25 August 1942	31 January 1943	7356	Ministry of War Transport (Blue Star Line Ltd)
1126	TLC 25	landing craft tank	11 March 1941	25 March 1941	229	Admiralty
1127	TLC 26	landing craft tank	11 March 1941	25 March 1941	229	Admiralty
1128	TLC 100	landing craft tank	9 June 1941	29 June 1941	258	Admiralty
1129	TLC 101	landing craft tank	9 June 1941	11 July 1941	258	Admiralty
1130	TLC 102	landing craft tank	17 June 1941	31 August 1941	258	Admiralty
1131	TLC 103	landing craft tank	17 June 1941	16 September 1941	258	Admiralty
1132	HMS Algerine	'Algerine'-class minesweeper	22 December 1941	24 March 1942	1054	Admiralty

Ship no.	Name	Vessel type	Launch date	Delivery date	Tonnage	Owner
1133	HMS *Alarm*	'Algerine'-class minesweeper	5 February 1942	16 May 1942	1054	Admiralty
1134	HMS *Albacore*	'Algerine'-class minesweeper	2 April 1942	16 June 1942	1054	Admiralty
1135	HMS *Alert* HMS *Acute*	'Algerine'-class minesweeper	14 April 1942	30 July 1942	1054	Admiralty
1136	HMS *Cadmus*	'Algerine'-class minesweeper	27 May 1942	9 September 1942	1054	Admiralty
1137	HMS *Circe*	'Algerine'-class minesweeper	27 June 1942	16 October 1942	1053	Admiralty
1138	HMS *Espiegle*	'Algerine'-class minesweeper	12 August 1942	1 December 1942	1053	Admiralty
1139	HMS *Fantome*	'Algerine'-class minesweeper	22 September 1942	22 January 1943	1053	Admiralty
1140	HMS *Mutine*	'Algerine'-class minesweeper	10 October 1942	26 February 1943	1053	Admiralty
1141	HMS *Onyx*	'Algerine'-class minesweeper	27 October 1942	26 March 1943	1053	Admiralty
1142	HMS *Rattler*	'Algerine'-class minesweeper	9 December 1942	22 April 1943	1053	Admiralty
1143	HMS *Ready*	'Algerine'-class minesweeper	11 January 1943	21 May 1943	1053	Admiralty
1144	HMS *Rinaldo*	'Algerine'-class minesweeper	20 March 1943	18 June 1943	1053	Admiralty
1145	HMS *Rosario*	'Algerine'-class minesweeper	3 April 1943	9 July 1943	1053	Admiralty
1146	HMS *Spanker*	'Algerine'-class minesweeper	20 April 1943	20 August 1943	1053	Admiralty
1147	HMS *Vestal*	'Algerine'-class minesweeper	19 June 1943	10 September 1943	1053	Admiralty
1148	*Darro*	refrigerated cargo ship	21 November 1942	29 June 1943	9733	Royal Mail Lines Ltd
1149	*Parramatta* *Pampas*	cargo ship	25 September 1943	1 February 1944	8244	Royal Mail Lines Ltd
1150	*Rowallan Castle*	refrigerated cargo ship	23 December 1942	23 April 1943	7950	Union-Castle Mail Steamship Co.
1151P	*Empire Maiden*	'Cadet'-class coastal tanker	20 December 1941	10 March 1942	813	Ministry of War Transport
1152	*Paraguay*	cargo ship	8 February 1944	7 September 1944	5560	Royal Mail Lines Ltd
1153	HMS *Thruster*	landing ship tank	24 September 1942	14 March 1943	5593	Admiralty
1154	HMS *Bruiser*	landing ship tank	24 October 1942	2 April 1943	5596	Admiralty

Ship no.	Name	Vessel type	Launch date	Delivery date	Tonnage	Owner
1155	HMS *Boxer*	landing ship tank	12 December 1942	1 May 1943	5596	Admiralty
1156	*Samanco*	cargo ship	23 March 1943	9 August 1943	8336	Pacific Steam Navigation Co.
1157	*Sarmiento*	cargo ship	17 August 1943	28 October 1943	8335	Pacific Steam Navigation Co.
1158	*Empire Fusilier* / *Empire Bombardier*	'Ocean'-type tanker	8 August 1942	18 February 1943	8202	Ministry of War Transport (Dodd Thompson & Co.)
1159	*Empire Industry*	'Ocean'-type tanker	4 May 1943	16 September 1943	8203	Ministry of War Transport (Gow Harrison & Co.)
1160G	*Empire Metal*	'Ocean'-type tanker	30 June 1942	24 September 1942	8201	Ministry of War Transport (British Tanker Co.)
1161	*Waiwera*	refrigerated cargo ship	30 September 1943	29 October 1944	12028	Shaw Savill & Albion Co.
1162P	HMS *Kale*	'River'-class corvette	24 June 1942	4 December 1942	1370	Admiralty
1163G	*San Vulfrano*	oil tanker	23 September 1942	30 December 1942	8167	Eagle Oil and Shipping Co.
1164	*Empire Benefit*	'Ocean'-type tanker	24 November 1942	20 April 1943	8202	Ministry of War Transport (Dodd Thompson & Co.)
1165	*Empire Grange*	standard 'X'-type cargo ship	23 September 1942	17 March 1943	6981	Ministry of War Transport (Sir R. Ropner & Co.)
1166G	*British Patience*	oil tanker	23 March 1943	15 June 1943	8097	British Tanker Co.
1167G	*British Wisdom*	oil tanker				British Tanker Co.
	Empire Mackay	merchant aircraft carrier	17 June 1943	5 October 1943	8908	Admiralty
1168G	*Empire Torrent*	standard 'Y'-type cargo ship	29 October 1942	29 December 1942	7076	Ministry of War Transport (Counties Ship Management Co.)
1169G	*Empire Nerissa*	standard 'Y'-type cargo ship	23 December 1942	23 February 1943	7076	Ministry of War Transport (Chellew Navigation Co.)
1170P	HMS *Tweed*	'River'-class corvette	24 November 1942	28 April 1943	1370	Admiralty
1171	HMS *Minotaur* / HMCS *Ontario*	'Minotaur'-class cruiser	29 July 1943	25 May 1945	8800	Admiralty / Royal Canadian Navy
1172P	HMS *Oxna*	'Isles'-class trawler	26 January 1943	22 May 1943	545	Admiralty
1173	*Narica*	oil tanker	7 February 1943	28 May 1943	8213	Anglo-Saxon Petroleum Co.
1174G	*Neritina*	oil tanker	31 August 1943	3 December 1943	8228	Anglo-Saxon Petroleum Co.
1175P	*Empire Gypsy*	'Cadet'-class coastal tanker	31 August 1942	11 November 1942	813	Ministry of War Transport (Anglo-Saxon Petroleum Co.)
1176	*Drina*	refrigerated cargo ship	30 December 1943	25 July 1944	9789	Royal Mail Lines Ltd
1177	*Durango*	refrigerated cargo ship	5 September 1944	20 December 1944	9806	Royal Mail Lines Ltd
1178	*Richmond Castle*	refrigerated cargo ship	23 March 1944	28 September 1944	7971	Union-Castle Mail Steamship Co.
1179	unnamed	refrigerated cargo ship	cancelled			Blue Star Line Ltd
1180	unnamed	refrigerated cargo ship	cancelled			Blue Star Line Ltd
1181	*Devis*	cargo ship	12 April 1944	20 August 1944	8187	Lamport & Holt Line Ltd

Ship no.	Name	Vessel type	Launch date	Delivery date	Tonnage	Owner
1228	HMS *Magnificent*	'Majestic'-class aircraft carrier	16 November 1944	21 May 1948	14000	Admiralty
1229	HMS *Powerful* / HMCS *Bonaventure*	'Majestic'-class aircraft carrier	27 February 1945	21 January 1957	14000	Admiralty / Royal Canadian Navy
1230	*Empire Abercorn*	standard 'Fast'-type refrigerated cargo ship	30 December 1944	30 June 1945	8563	Ministry of War Transport (New Zealand Shipping Co.)
1231	*Empire Clarendon*	standard 'Fast'-type refrigerated cargo ship	14 May 1945	26 October 1945	8577	Ministry of War Transport (Peninsular & Oriental Steam Navigation Co.)
1232	HMS *Seabear*	'Algerine'-class minesweeper	cancelled		850	Admiralty
1233	HMS *Serene*	'Algerine'-class minesweeper	cancelled		850	Admiralty
1234	*Empire Rangoon*	standard 'X'-type cargo ship	25 January 1944	30 May 1944	6988	Ministry of War Transport (T. &J. Harrison Ltd)
1235P	HMS *Northam Castle*	'Castle'-class corvette	12 April 1944	20 September 1944	1100	Admiralty
1236P	HMS *Humberstone*	'Castle'-class corvette	20 July 1944	10 December 1944	1100	Admiralty
1237P	HMS *Oakham Castle*	'Castle'-class corvette	cancelled		1100	Admiralty
1238	HMS *Dover Castle*	'Castle'-class corvette	11 December 1943	10 March 1944	1100	Admiralty
1239	HMS *Oxford Castle*	'Castle'-class corvette	11 January 1944	10 June 1944	1100	Admiralty
1240	HMS *Pevesney Castle*	'Castle'-class corvette	8 February 1944	26 June 1944	1100	Admiralty
1241	HMCS *Arnprior*	'Castle'-class corvette	24 February 1944	14 July 1944	1100	Royal Canadian Navy
	HMS *Rising Castle*					Admiralty
	HMS *Sherborne Castle*	'Castle'-class corvette				Admiralty
	HMCS *Petrolia*					Royal Canadian Navy
1242	*Empire Saturn*	'Ocean'-type tanker	6 May 1944	20 September 1944	8224	Ministry of War Transport (Davies & Newman)
1243G	*Empire Jupiter*	'Ocean'-type tanker	21 September 1944	29 December 1944	8217	Ministry of War Transport (British Tanker Co.)
1244P	HMS *Calshot Castle*	'Castle'-class corvette	cancelled		1100	Admiralty
1245P	HMS *Dudley Castle*	'Castle'-class corvette	cancelled		1100	Admiralty
1246	HMS *Loch Craggie*	'Loch'-class frigate	23 May 1944	15 June 1944	1435	Admiralty
1247	HMS *Loch Gorm*	'Loch'-class frigate	8 June 1944	7 July 1944	1435	Admiralty
1248	HMS *Loch Killisport*	'Loch'-class frigate	6 July 1944	9 September 1945	1435	Admiralty
1249	HMS *Loch Lydoch*					
1250	HMS *St Austell Bay*	'Bay'-class frigate	18 November 1944	29 May 1945	1600	Admiralty
	HMS *Loch Achillty*					Admiralty
	HMS *St Brides Bay*	'Bay'-class frigate	16 January 1945	15 June 1945	1600	Admiralty
1251	HMS *Loch Ard* / SAS *Transvaal*	'Loch'-class frigate	2 August 1944	2 January 1945	1435	Admiralty / South African Navy

Ship no.	Name	Vessel type	Launch date	Delivery date	Tonnage	Owner
1252	HMS Loch Arkley	'Bay'-class frigate	15 February 1945	6 September 1945	1600	Admiralty
	HMS Start Bay					
1253	HMS Loch Arnish	'Bay'-class frigate	29 March 1945	11 October 1945	1600	Admiralty
	HMS Tremadoc Bay					
1254	HMS Loch Kirkaig	'Loch'-class frigate	cancelled		1435	Admiralty
1255	HMS Loch Hourn	'Loch'-class frigate	cancelled		1435	Admiralty
1256	HMS Loch Goil	'Loch'-class frigate	cancelled		1435	Admiralty
1257	HMS Loch Awe	'Loch'-class frigate	cancelled		1435	Admiralty
1258	HMS Loch Striven	'Loch'-class frigate	cancelled		1435	Admiralty
1259	HMS Loch Frisa	'Bay'-class frigate	19 October 1944	13 April 1945	1600	Admiralty
	HMS Widemouth Bay					
1260	HMS Loch Garasdale	'Bay'-class frigate	26 April 1945	19 January 1946	1600	Admiralty
	HMS Wigtown Bay					
1261	HMS Loch Lubnaig	'Bay'-class frigate	16 December 1944	30 July 1945	1600	Admiralty
	HMS Whitesand Bay					
1262	HMS Loch Ronald	'Loch'-class frigate	cancelled		1435	Admiralty
1263	HMS Loch Stemster	'Loch'-class frigate	cancelled		1435	Admiralty
1264	HMS Loch Tummell	'Loch'-class frigate	cancelled		1435	Admiralty
1265	HMS Loch Eye	'Loch'-class frigate	cancelled		1435	Admiralty
1266	HMS Loch Lurgain	'Loch'-class frigate	cancelled		1435	Admiralty
1267	HMS Loch Shell	'Loch'-class frigate	cancelled		1435	Admiralty
1268	HMS Loch Laro	'Loch'-class frigate	cancelled		1435	Admiralty
1269	HMS Loch Inchard	'Loch'-class frigate	cancelled		1435	Admiralty
1270	HMS Loch Vanavie	'Loch'-class frigate	cancelled		1435	Admiralty
1271	HMS Loch Swin	'Loch'-class frigate	cancelled		1435	Admiralty
1272	HMS Loch Enoch	'Loch'-class frigate	cancelled		1435	Admiralty
1273	HMS Loch Sunart	'Loch'-class frigate	cancelled		1435	Admiralty
1274	HMS Loch Sheallag	'Loch'-class frigate	cancelled		1435	Admiralty
1275	HMS Loch Eynort	'Loch'-class frigate	cancelled		1435	Admiralty
1276	Empire Falkland	standard 'X'-type cargo ship	2 September 1944	21 February 1945	7006	Ministry of War Transport (Blue Star Line Ltd)
1277	Riebeeck Castle	refrigerated cargo ship	23 October 1945	11 March 1946	8322	Union-Castle Mail Steamship Co.
1278	Rustenburg Castle	refrigerated cargo ship	5 March 1946	25 June 1946	8322	Union-Castle Mail Steamship Co.
1279G	Pilcomayo	cargo ship	21 August 1945	14 December 1945	5567	Royal Mail Lines Ltd
1280	HMS Centaur	'Hermes'-class aircraft carrier	22 April 1947	22 September 1953	22000	Admiralty
1281	HMS Bulwark	'Hermes'-class aircraft carrier	22 June 1948	2 November 1954	23300	Admiralty
1282P	Empire Jura	'Cadet'-class coastal tanker	28 August 1944	16 October 1944	813	Ministry of War Transport (Coastal Tankers Ltd)

Ship no.	Name	Vessel type	Launch date	Delivery date	Tonnage	Owner
1336P	*Linyon*	'L'-class tug	4 July 1946	2 August 1946	20	Ministry of War Transport
1337P	*Linno*	'L'-class tug	4 July 1946	2 August 1946	20	Ministry of War Transport
1338P	*Linda*	'L'-class tug	17 August 1946	18 September 1946	20	Ministry of War Transport
1339P	*Limpya*	'L'-class tug	17 August 1946	18 September 1946	20	Ministry of War Transport
1340P	unnamed	launch	1 July 1946	7 October 1946	20	Ministry of War Transport
1341P	unnamed	launch	8 August 1946	28 January 1947	20	Ministry of War Transport
1342P	unnamed	launch	15 August 1946	28 January 1947	20	Ministry of War Transport
1343G	*La Hague*	cargo ship	12 September 1946	4 June 1947	4027	French Line
1344G	*Franck Delmas*	cargo ship	21 November 1946	3 July 1947	4025	French Line
1345G	*Morbihan*	cargo ship	20 February 1947	17 September 1947	4027	French Line
1346	*La Heve*	cargo ship	26 September 1946	6 February 1947	6446	French Line
1347	*Lepton*	oil tanker	11 October 1946	25 March 1947	6445	Anglo-Saxon Petroleum Co.
1348	*Lingula*	oil tanker	19 June 1947	9 October 1947	17081	Anglo-Saxon Petroleum Co.
1349	*Thorshavet*	whale factory ship	25 March 1947	17 January 1948	4088	A/S Thor Dahl
1350G	*Munster*	passenger/cargo ferry	17 June 1947	12 March 1948	13181	Coast Lines Ltd
1351G	*Imperial Star*	refrigerated cargo ship	2 October 1947	14 July 1948	13179	Blue Star Line Ltd
1352	*Melbourne Star*	refrigerated cargo ship	20 May 1947	25 March 1948	4115	Blue Star Line Ltd
1353P	*Leinster*	passenger/cargo ferry	23 April 1947	18 December 1947	2950	Coast Lines Ltd
1354	*Soochow*	passenger/cargo ship	11 May 1948	18 February 1949	17547	China Navigation Co.
1355P	*Magdalena*	passenger/cargo ship	2 September 1947	28 January 1948	443	Royal Mail Lines Ltd
1356P	*Pelorus*	pilot tender	30 October 1947	7 April 1948	443	Corporation of Trinity House
1357	*Penlee*	pilot tender	7 March 1947	18 November 1947	6669	Corporation of Trinity House
1358	*Salinas*	cargo ship	29 August 1947	20 March 1948	6669	Pacific Steam Navigation Co.
1359	*Salamanca*	cargo ship	3 June 1947	19 November 1947	3213	Pacific Steam Navigation Co.
1360	*Kantara*	cargo ship	2 October 1947	30 January 1948	3198	Moss Hutchison Line Ltd
1361P	*Karnak*	cargo ship	11 February 1948	18 July 1948	1101	Moss Hutchison Line Ltd
1362G	*Granuaile*	lightship tender	11 December 1947	3 June 1948	8575	Commissioners of Irish Lights
1363	*British Ranger*	oil tanker	11 March 1948	14 October 1948	9592	British Tanker Co.
1364	*Soestdyk*	cargo ship	27 February 1948	7 July 1948	8583	Holland-America Line
1365	*British Security*	oil tanker	8 June 1948	12 November 1948	8580	British Tanker Co.
1366	*British Strength*	oil tanker	10 June 1948	19 February 1949	9592	British Tanker Co.
1367	*Schiedyk*	cargo ship	22 July 1948	5 April 1949	4972	Holland-America Line
1368	*Hibernia*	passenger/cargo ferry				London, Midland and Scottish Railway; British Railways, London, Midland Region
	Cambria	passenger/cargo ferry	21 September 1948	17 May 1949	4972	London, Midland and Scottish Railway; British Railways, London, Midland Region

Ship no.	Name	Vessel type	Launch date	Delivery date	Tonnage	Owner
1369G	*Liparus*	oil tanker	11 March 1948	7 September 1948	6473	Anglo-Saxon Petroleum Co.
1370	*Lotorium*	oil tanker	30 September 1947	30 December 1947	6490	Anglo-Saxon Petroleum Co.
1371	*Ramore Head*	cargo ship	25 May 1948	26 August 1948	6195	Ulster Steamship Co.
1372	*Antilochus*	cargo ship	2 November 1948	3 May 1949	8238	Alfred Holt & Co.
1373	*Jalta*	oil tanker	6 July 1948	17 September 1948	8247	A/S Bulls Tankrederi
1374	*Sarasvati*	passenger/cargo ferry	19 October 1948	20 June 1949	3750	Bombay Steam Navigation Co.
1375	*Sabarmati*	passenger/cargo ferry	19 October 1948	20 August 1949	3750	Bombay Steam Navigation Co.
1376	*Helenus*	passenger/cargo ship	13 April 1949	29 October 1949	10125	Ocean Steamship Co.
1377	*Hector*	passenger/cargo ship	27 July 1949	31 March 1950	10125	Ocean Steamship Co.
1378G	*British Mariner*	oil tanker	16 September 1948	29 December 1948	8576	British Tanker Co.
1379G	*British Workman*	oil tanker	16 November 1948	24 March 1949	8575	British Tanker Co.
1380	*Borgny*	oil tanker	4 November 1948	31 March 1949	8255	Fred Olsen & Co.
1381	*Vestfoss*	oil tanker	17 March 1949	27 June 1949	8250	A/S Thor Thoresen
1382	*Explorador*	oil tanker	15 February 1949	6 July 1949	6478	Anglo-Saxon Petroleum Co. / Estrella Maritima S.A.
1383	*Vikingen*	oil tanker	10 June 1949	7 October 1949	8263	Tanker Corporation of Panama City
1384	*Juan Peron*	whale factory ship	4 April 1950	15 October 1951	24569	Compania Argentina de Pesca S.A.
1385G	*Amarna*	cargo ship	29 March 1949	6 July 1949	3422	Moss Hutchison Line Ltd
1386	*Assiout*	cargo ship	31 May 1949	12 October 1949	3422	Moss Hutchison Line Ltd
1387	*Champavati*	passenger ferry	29 March 1949	20 October 1949	1288	Bombay Steam Navigation Co.
1388	*Rohidas*	passenger ferry	30 March 1949	20 October 1949	1288	Indian Co-operative Navigation and Trading Co.
1389G	*Cazador*	oil tanker	27 January 1949	15 June 1949	6441	Anglo-Saxon Petroleum Co. / Estrella Maritima S.A.
1390P	*Setter I*	whale catcher	26 May 1948	20 October 1948	599	United Whalers Ltd
1391P	*Setter II*	whale catcher	6 July 1948	8 November 1948	599	United Whalers Ltd
1392	*Ternoy*	oil tanker	22 September 1949	27 January 1950	8218	Viriks Rederi A/S / A/S Truma
1393P	*Setter III*	whale catcher	28 December 1948	18 August 1949	586	United Whalers Ltd
1394P	*Setter IV*	whale catcher	17 February 1949	2 September 1949	586	United Whalers Ltd
1395P	*Setter V*	whale catcher	24 May 1949	19 September 1949	586	United Whalers Ltd
1396P	*Setter VI*	whale catcher	28 June 1949	12 October 1949	586	United Whalers Ltd
1397G	*British Captain*	oil tanker	11 August 1949	25 November 1949	8700	British Tanker Co.
1398G	*British Commander*	oil tanker	21 November 1949	23 February 1950	8700	British Tanker Co.
1399G	*British Consul*	oil tanker	2 March 1950	9 June 1950	8655	British Tanker Co.
1400	*British Explorer*	oil tanker	21 March 1950	8 July 1950	8644	British Tanker Co.
1401	*British Prospector*	oil tanker	1 June 1950	28 September 1950	8655	British Tanker Co.
1402	*British Surveyor*	oil tanker	15 August 1950	8 December 1950	8655	British Tanker Co.
1403	*Verena*	oil tanker	29 June 1950	9 November 1950	18612	Anglo-Saxon Petroleum Co.

Ship no.	Name	Vessel type	Launch date	Delivery date	Tonnage	Owner
1404G	Bratsberg	oil tanker	14 June 1950	5 October 1950	8255	Borgestad A/S
1405G	Binta	oil tanker	28 September 1950	19 December 1950	8162	Per Gjerding
1406	Bolette	oil tanker	28 September 1950	17 January 1951	16394	Fred Olsen & Co.
1407	Dalfonn	oil tanker	12 January 1951	15 May 1951	16440	Martin Mosvold
1408	Kurdistan	oil tanker	26 October 1949	24 February 1950	8322	Common Brothers Ltd
1409P	Africana II	research trawler	10 October 1949	27 January 1950	882	Fisheries Division, Government of South Africa
1410	Tank King	oil tanker	22 May 1951	31 August 1951	16477	Sigurd Herlofsen A/S
1411	France Stove	oil tanker	2 July 1951	12 November 1951	16468	Lorentzen A/S
1412	Orkdal	oil tanker	8 February 1951	17 April 1951	8221	Moltzaus & Christensen
1413	Ringerd	oil tanker	12 December 1950	12 March 1951	8218	Olav Ringdal
1414	Runic	refrigerated cargo ship	21 October 1949	24 March 1950	13587	Shaw Savill & Albion Co.
1415	Suevic	refrigerated cargo ship	7 March 1950	5 July 1950	13587	Shaw Savill & Albion Co.
1416	Ascanius	passenger/cargo ship	15 June 1950	21 November 1950	7692	Ocean Steamship Co.
1417	Ixion	passenger/cargo ship	28 July 1950	5 January 1951	10125	Ocean Steamship Co.
1418	Laganfield	oil tanker	26 September 1950	29 December 1950	8196	Hunting & Son Ltd
1419G	Bollsta	oil tanker	5 May 1951	6 October 1951	16405	Fred Olsen & Co.
1420G	unnamed	oil tanker	cancelled		16000	A/S Thor Dahl
1421	Bloemfontein Castle	passenger/cargo ship	25 August 1949	25 March 1950	18400	Union-Castle Mail Steamship Co.
1422P	Ernst Larsen	whale catcher	28 July 1949	4 November 1949	598	Union Whaling Co.
1423P	Arnt Karlsen	whale catcher	16 August 1949	9 November 1949	598	Union Whaling Co.
1424G	unnamed	oil tanker	cancelled		12000	Eagle Oil and Shipping Co.
1425	British Skill	oil tanker	16 January 1952	12 June 1952	18550	British Tanker Co.
1426P	unnamed	lighter	cancelled			Admiralty
1427P	unnamed	lighter	cancelled			Admiralty
1428P	Carnarvon	whale catcher	6 February 1950	27 April 1950	598	Australian Whaling Commission
1429P	Simba	tug	12 March 1951	8 June 1951	359	East African Railways and Harbours Administration
1430P	Nyati	tug	23 May 1951	15 September 1951	359	East African Railways and Harbours Administration
1431	Rhodesia Castle	passenger/cargo ship	5 April 1951	6 October 1951	17041	Union-Castle Mail Steamship Co.
1432	Kenya Castle	passenger/cargo ship	21 June 1951	16 February 1952	17041	Union-Castle Mail Steamship Co.
1433	Roonagh Head	cargo ship	17 December 1951	20 March 1952	6153	Ulster Steamship Co.
1434P	Kvint	whale catcher	28 September 1950	27 November 1950	591	Falkland Shipowners Ltd
1435G	La Rochelle	oil tanker	11 October 1951	25 April 1952	12801	Societé Navale Delmas Vieljeux
1436	Clydefield	oil tanker	16 September 1952	21 January 1953	11163	Hunting & Son Ltd
1437	Port Nelson	refrigerated cargo ship	19 June 1951	31 October 1951	8375	Port Line Ltd
1438	Eastern Star	cargo ship	2 August 1951	20 December 1951	6523	Australia China Line Ltd

Ship no.	Name	Vessel type	Launch date	Delivery date	Tonnage	Owner
1439P	*Setter VII*	whale catcher	3 May 1951	14 September 1951	588	United Whalers Ltd
1440P	*Setter VIII*	whale catcher	7 June 1951	11 October 1951	588	United Whalers Ltd
1441P	*Star XI*	whale catcher	9 July 1951	30 October 1951	588	Hvalfanger A/S Rosshavet
1442G	*Tuscany*					
	Ebro	cargo ship	29 November 1951	12 June 1952	5855	Royal Mail Lines Ltd
1443	*Ianita*	oil tanker	25 March 1952	9 July 1952	12757	Spermacet Whaling S.A.
1444	*Raeburn*	cargo ship	6 August 1952	28 November 1952	8312	Lamport & Holt Line Ltd
1445	*Cedric*	refrigerated cargo ship	22 May 1952	11 November 1952	11232	Shaw Savill & Albion Co.
1446P	*J.K. Hansen*	whale catcher	3 August 1951	24 October 1951	742	Union Whaling Co.
1447G	*Essequibo*	cargo ship	25 March 1952	11 September 1952	5855	Royal Mail Lines Ltd
1448	*Onitsha*	cargo ship	29 January 1952	5 June 1952	5802	Elder Dempster Lines Ltd
1449	*Obuasi*	cargo ship	24 June 1952	12 November 1952	5883	Elder Dempster Lines Ltd
1450	*King Malcolm*	cargo ship	29 November 1951	29 February 1952	5883	King Line Ltd
1451	*King Alexander*	cargo ship	14 February 1952	6 May 1952	5883	King Line Ltd
1452	*Ianova*	oil tanker	8 July 1952	30 January 1953	12765	Spermacet Whaling S.A.
1453	*Cymric*	refrigerated cargo ship	5 November 1952	15 May 1953	11182	Shaw Savill & Albion Co.
1454G	*Blandford*	oil tanker	18 December 1952	14 May 1953	12514	Blandford Shipping Co.
1455P	*Anders Arvesen*	whale catcher	23 August 1951	15 November 1951	742	Union Whaling Co.
1456	*Beaverbank*	cargo ship	3 December 1952	26 February 1953	5690	Andrew Weir & Co.
1457	*Nessbank*	cargo ship	18 December 1952	24 June 1953	5690	Andrew Weir & Co.
1458	*Fleetbank*	cargo ship	29 June 1953	14 October 1953	5690	Andrew Weir & Co.
1459	*Braemar Castle*	passenger/cargo ship	24 April 1952	8 November 1952	17029	Union-Castle Mail Steamship Co.
1460	*Irex*	oil tanker	15 April 1953	8 July 1953	8280	A/S Fjeld
1461	*Irish Coast*	passenger/cargo ferry	8 May 1952	17 October 1952	3824	Coast Lines Ltd
1462	*King Arthur*	cargo ship	19 November 1952	19 March 1953	5883	King Line Ltd
1463G	*Britta*	oil tanker	12 May 1953	17 September 1953	12757	Arthur H. Mathiesen
1464	*British Engineer*	oil tanker	24 November 1953	30 April 1954	21077	British Tanker Co.
1465	*British Corporal*	oil tanker	9 December 1953	1 July 1954	10071	British Tanker Co.
1466G	*British Gunner*	oil tanker	22 December 1953	6 May 1954	10076	British Tanker Co.
1467G	*British Sergeant*	oil tanker	14 April 1954	20 August 1954	10073	British Tanker Co.
1468	*Harpa*	oil tanker	29 January 1953	11 June 1953	12202	Anglo-Saxon Petroleum Co.
1469	*Harvella*					Anglo-Saxon Petroleum Co.
1470	*Cerinthus*	oil tanker	26 April 1956	20 September 1956	12224	Shell Bermuda (Overseas) Ltd Anglo-Saxon Petroleum Co.
1471	*Jarena*	oil tanker	29 June 1954	9 November 1954	12194	Hadley Shipping Co.
1472	*HMS Torquay*	oil tanker	25 August 1953	20 November 1953	12706	A/S Kosmos
1473	*HMS Blackpool*	'Whitby'-class frigate	1 July 1954	10 May 1956	2150	Admiralty
1474P	*Maid of the Loch*	'Whitby'-class frigate	14 February 1957	14 August 1958	2150	Admiralty
		paddle steamer	5 March 1953	4 May 1953	555	British Railways, Scottish Region
		dismantled and re-erected at Loch Lomond				

Ship no.	Name	Vessel type	Launch date	Delivery date	Tonnage	Owner
1475	Rathlin Head	cargo ship	10 August 1953	4 November 1953	7439	Ulster Steamship Co.
1476	Iberia	passenger/cargo ship	21 January 1954	10 September 1954	29614	Peninsular and Oriental Steam Navigation Co.
1477	Elpenor	cargo ship	11 November 1953	22 April 1954	7757	Ocean Steamship Co.
1478	Jaranda	oil tanker	23 October 1953	9 January 1954	12776	Anders Jahre A/S
1479	Ouerri	cargo ship	14 October 1954	21 January 1955	6240	Elder Dempster Lines Ltd
1480	Loch Gowan	cargo ship	19 January 1954	27 June 1954	9718	Royal Mail Lines Ltd
1481	Cedarbank	cargo ship	29 September 1954	5 January 1955	5671	Andrew Weir & Co.
1482G	Port Montreal	refrigerated cargo ship	22 September 1953	4 February 1954	6843	Port Line Ltd
1483	Port Melbourne	refrigerated cargo ship	10 March 1955	7 July 1955	10470	Port Line Ltd
1484	Vibex	oil tanker	5 May 1955	20 October 1955	20787	Anglo-Saxon Petroleum Co.
1485	Harpula	oil tanker				Shell Bermuda (Overseas) Ltd
						Anglo-Saxon Petroleum Co.
1486G	Belfast	oil tanker	6 July 1955	21 December 1955	12258	Shell Tankers Ltd
1487	unnamed	oil tanker	28 September 1954	24 February 1955	12744	Belships Co.
			cancelled			Anders Jahre A/S
1488P	HMS Brayford	seaward defence boat	19 February 1954	8 May 1954	110	Admiralty
1489P	HMS Bryansford	seaward defence boat	2 April 1954	10 September 1954	110	Admiralty
1490G	unnamed	oil tanker	cancelled		12700	A.O. Anderson Shipping A/S
1491P	Maid of Argyll	passenger ferry	4 March 1953	1 June 1953	508	British Railways, Scottish Region
						Caledonian Steam Packet Co.
1492P	Maid of Skelmorlie	passenger ferry	2 April 1953	24 June 1953	508	British Railways, Scottish Region
						Caledonian Steam Packet Co.
1493	Solfonn	oil tanker	2 March 1956	13 June 1956	19810	Sigval Bergesen
1494	Pontia	oil tanker	2 June 1954	15 September 1954	8904	Hvalfangerselskapet Pelagos A/S
1495	unnamed	oil tanker	cancelled		7000	Moltzaus Tankrederi A/S
1496G	Triaster	cargo ship	21 April 1955	21 October 1955	9994	British Phosphate Commissioners
1497	Dolius	passenger/cargo ship	4 August 1955	5 January 1956	7964	Ocean Steamship Co.
1498	Southern Cross	passenger ship	17 August 1954	28 February 1955	20204	Shaw Savill & Albion Co.
1499	Tantallon Castle	cargo ship	22 October 1953	5 March 1954	7448	Union-Castle Mail Steamship Co.
1500	Tintagel Castle	cargo ship	4 February 1954	5 June 1954	7447	Union-Castle Mail Steamship Co.
1501P	YC327	lighter	19 March 1954	1 July 1954	561	Admiralty
1502	RAFA Tide Austral	fleet tanker	1 September 1954	17 May 1955	13165	Royal Australian Navy
1503P	Busen 5	whale catcher	10 June 1952	5 September 1952	588	Tonsbergs Hvalfangeri
1504P	Ballylumford	collier	3 February 1954	7 May 1954	1242	John Kelly Ltd
1505	unnamed	oil tanker	cancelled		12700	Spermacet Whaling S.A.
1506	unnamed	oil tanker	cancelled		7000	Olav Ringdal
1507P	Setter IX	whale catcher				United Whalers Ltd
1508G	Southern Prince		15 July 1953	19 November 1953	739	Hector Whaling Ltd
	Western Prince	cargo ship	9 December 1954	27 April 1955	7917	Prince Line Ltd

Ship no.	Name	Vessel type	Launch date	Delivery date	Tonnage	Owner
1509G	*Rowanmore*	cargo ship	27 March 1956	27 June 1956	8495	Prince Line Ltd
1510	unnamed	cargo ship	cancelled		20400	Johnston Warren Lines Ltd; Borgestad A/S
1511	*Elin Knudsen*	oil tanker	17 November 1955	11 April 1956	20492	Knut Knutsen OAS
1512	*Vitrina*	oil tanker	16 April 1957	4 July 1957	20802	Anglo-Saxon Petroleum Co.; Shell Bermuda (Overseas) Ltd
1513G	*Southern Prince*	cargo ship	16 November 1955	8 March 1956	7917	Tanker Finance Ltd; Johnston Warren Lines Ltd; Prince Line Ltd
1514	*Foylebank*	cargo ship	24 March 1955	4 August 1955	5671	Andrew Weir & Co.
1515	*Laganbank*	cargo ship	5 July 1955	27 October 1955	5671	Andrew Weir & Co.
1516	unnamed	cargo ship	cancelled		7000	Anders Jahre A/S
1517	HMS *Kemerton*	'Ton'-class minesweeper	27 November 1953	21 May 1954	360	Admiralty
1518	HMS *Kirkliston*	'Ton'-class minesweeper	18 February 1954	21 August 1954	360	Admiralty
1519	HMS *Laleston*	'Ton'-class minesweeper	18 May 1954	10 November 1954	360	Admiralty
1520	HMS *Lanton*	'Ton'-class minesweeper	30 July 1954	10 March 1955	360	Admiralty
1521	HMS *Letterston*	'Ton'-class minesweeper	26 October 1954	29 June 1955	360	Admiralty
1522	HMS *Leverton*	'Ton'-class minesweeper	2 March 1955	25 August 1955	360	Admiralty
1523	HMS *Liston* / HMS *Kildarton*	'Ton'-class minesweeper	23 May 1955	25 November 1955	360	Admiralty
1524	HMS *Lullington*	'Ton'-class minesweeper	31 August 1955	1 June 1956	360	Admiralty
1525	HMS *Maddiston*	'Ton'-class minesweeper	27 January 1956	8 November 1956	360	Admiralty
1526	HMS *Maxton*	'Ton'-class minesweeper	24 May 1956	19 February 1957	360	Admiralty
1527	HMS *Nurton*	'Ton'-class minesweeper	22 October 1956	21 August 1957	360	Admiralty
1528	HMS *Ossington* / HMS *Repton*	'Ton'-class minesweeper	1 May 1957	11 December 1957	360	Admiralty
1529P	HMS *Confiance*	'Confiance'-class tug	15 November 1955	29 March 1956	760	Admiralty
1530P	HMS *Confident*	'Confiance'-class tug	17 January 1956	6 September 1956	760	Admiralty

Ship no.	Name	Vessel type	Launch date	Delivery date	Tonnage	Owner
1531	British Honour	oil tanker	25 September 1957	31 January 1958	21031	British Tanker Co.
1532	unnamed	oil tanker	cancelled		7000	Anders Jahre A/S
1533	Reina del Mar	passenger ship	7 June 1955	8 April 1956	20225	Pacific Steam Navigation Co.
1534	Port Launceston	refrigerated cargo ship	21 November 1956	12 March 1957	8957	Port Line Ltd
1535	unnamed	oil tanker	cancelled			Bechs Rederi A/S
1536	unnamed	bulk carrier	cancelled			Moltzaus Tankrederi A/S
1537P	Ulster Premier	coaster	26 April 1955	20 September 1955	979	Belfast Steamship Co.
1538	Storfonn	oil tanker	20 November 1956	31 January 1957	24854	Sigval Bergesen
1539G	Escalante	cargo ship	5 July 1955	14 December 1955	7791	Royal Mail Lines Ltd
1540	Duke of Lancaster	passenger/cargo ferry	1 December 1955	22 August 1956	4797	British Transport Commission
1541	Duke of Argyll	passenger/cargo ferry	12 January 1956	22 September 1956	4797	British Transport Commission
1542	Missouri	oil tanker	7 August 1956	26 January 1957	18751	Texas Co. (Panama) Inc.
1543	New Mexico	oil tanker	20 March 1958	13 September 1958	18751	Texaco (Panama) Inc.
1544	Eden	refrigerated cargo ship	19 October 1955	1 February 1956	7791	Royal Mail Lines Ltd
1545G	Tuscany	refrigerated cargo ship	21 June 1956	25 October 1956	7455	Royal Mail Lines Ltd
1546	Oti	cargo ship	15 December 1955	26 April 1956	5485	Elder Dempster Lines Ltd
1547	Scottish Coast	passenger/cargo ship	21 August 1956	1 March 1957	3817	Coast Lines Ltd
1548	Cloverbank	cargo ship	21 December 1956	7 March 1957	6459	Andrew Weir & Co.
1549	Crestbank	cargo ship	15 February 1957	7 June 1957	6459	Andrew Weir & Co.
1550	Carronbank	cargo ship	30 May 1957	27 September 1957	6461	Andrew Weir & Co.
1551	Dartbank	cargo ship	28 August 1957	17 January 1958	6461	Andrew Weir & Co.
1552	Garrybank	cargo ship	27 December 1957	2 April 1958	8693	Andrew Weir & Co.
1553	Minchbank	cargo ship	19 June 1958	25 September 1958	8693	Andrew Weir & Co.
1554	Ondo	cargo ship	7 June 1956	24 October 1956	5435	Elder Dempster Lines Ltd
1555	INS Talwar	'Whitby'-class frigate				
	INS Trishul		18 June 1958	14 January 1960	2150	Indian Navy
1556	King Charles	cargo ship	15 March 1957	25 June 1957	5993	King Line Ltd
1557	King George	cargo ship	27 August 1957	19 December 1957	5989	King Line Ltd
1558	Pendennis Castle	passenger/cargo ship	24 December 1957	14 November 1958	28582	Union-Castle Mail Steamship Co.
1559G	Albany	refrigerated cargo ship	1 November 1956	13 February 1957	7299	Royal Mail Lines Ltd
1560	Picardy	refrigerated cargo ship	30 April 1957	22 August 1957	7306	Royal Mail Lines Ltd
1561G	Thessaly	cargo ship	29 May 1957	26 September 1957	7299	Royal Mail Lines Ltd
1562	Loch Loyal	refrigerated cargo ship	9 August 1957	30 December 1957	11035	Royal Mail Lines Ltd
1563P	Toucan	bulk lighter				
	Lappe		31 January 1956	23 March 1956	165	Shell Tankers Ltd
1564P	Flying Duck	tug	23 May 1956	29 October 1956	176	Clyde Shipping Co.
1565	Port Invercargill	refrigerated cargo ship	22 November 1957	26 March 1958	8847	Port Line Ltd
1566G	Attic	cargo ship				
	Alaric		8 October 1957	13 February 1958	6692	Shaw Savill & Albion Co.
1567G	Afghanistan	ore carrier	14 February 1957	20 June 1957	11188	Hindustan Steam Shipping Co. (Common Brothers Ltd)

Ship no.	Name	Vessel type	Launch date	Delivery date	Tonnage	Owner
1568	Ulster Star	refrigerated cargo ship	26 February 1959	3 July 1959	10413	Blue Star Line Ltd
1569	Esso Glasgow (midship section only)	oil tanker	14 March 1957	17 August 1957	10720	Esso Petroleum Co.
1570P	Flying Drake	tug	29 November 1956	17 May 1957	177	Clyde Shipping Co.
1571G	Eskfield	oil tanker	21 May 1959	22 December 1959	18851	Hunting & Son Ltd
1572	British Statesman	oil tanker	27 November 1958	18 April 1959	27586	BP Tanker Co.
1573	British Power	oil tanker	22 May 1959	15 November 1959	27586	BP Tanker Co.
1574	Ranella					Shell Tankers Ltd
	William Wheelwright	oil tanker	15 January 1960	1 July 1960	31320	Pacific Steam Navigation Co.
1575	Rhombus					Shell Tankers Ltd
	Edward Stevinson	oil tanker	24 August 1960	27 February 1961	31317	Stevinson Hardy & Co.
1576	Carrigan Head	cargo ship	2 July 1958	18 November 1958	8271	Ulster Steamship Co.
1577G	Iron Age	ore carrier	20 January 1958	22 May 1958	11188	Hindustan Steam Shipping Co. (Common Brothers Ltd)
1578	Vestfonn	oil tanker	7 March 1958	11 July 1958	13409	Sigval Bergesen
1579P	Accord	'Confiance'-class tug	10 September 1957	15 October 1958	640	Admiralty
1580P	Advice	'Confiance'-class tug	16 October 1958	17 June 1959	640	Admiralty
1581G	Tri-Ellis	phosphate carrier	15 May 1958	31 October 1958	11760	British Phosphate Commissioners
1582	Manchester Miller	cargo ship	12 December 1958	19 March 1959	9297	Manchester Liners Ltd
1583	HMS Dumbleton					Admiralty
	SAS Port Elizabeth	'Ton'-class minesweeper	8 November 1957	10 July 1958	360	South African Navy
1584	HMS Oakington					Admiralty
	SAS Mosselbaai	'Ton'-class minesweeper	3 July 1958	11 February 1959	360	South African Navy
1585	HMS Packington					Admiralty
	SAS Walvisbaai	'Ton'-class minesweeper	10 December 1958	21 May 1959	360	South African Navy
1586	unnamed	oil tanker	cancelled		18800	Hunting & Son
1587	King Henry	cargo ship	15 August 1958	5 December 1958	6133	King Line Ltd
1588	British Mallard	oil tanker	3 November 1959	6 May 1960	11174	BP Tanker Co.
1589G	British Seagull					
	British Gull	oil tanker	29 December 1959	29 April 1960	11156	BP Tanker Co.
1590	HMS Berwick	'Rothesay'-class frigate	15 December 1959	9 June 1961	2519	Admiralty
1591	HMS Weymouth					
	HMS Leander	'Leander'-class frigate	28 June 1961	28 March 1963	2450	Admiralty
1592	Ashbank	cargo ship	27 January 1959	2 May 1959	8694	Andrew Weir & Co.
1593	Rosebank	cargo ship	30 December 1958	3 April 1959	8693	Andrew Weir & Co.

Ship no.	Name	Vessel type	Launch date	Delivery date	Tonnage	Owner
1594	Amazon	passenger/cargo ship	7 July 1959	31 December 1959	20348	Royal Mail Lines Ltd
1595	Aragon	passenger/cargo ship	20 October 1959	12 April 1960	20362	Royal Mail Lines Ltd
1596	Arlanza	passenger/cargo ship	13 April 1960	23 September 1960	20362	Royal Mail Lines Ltd
1597	Tindfonn	oil tanker	31 January 1961	30 May 1961	31322	Sigval Bergesen
1598	Torr Head	cargo ship	cancelled		8000	Ulster Steamship Co.
1599	Tresfonn	bulk carrier	1 March 1960	11 June 1960	13471	Sigval Bergesen
1600	British Lancer	oil tanker	28 September 1962	28 June 1963	32547	BP Tanker Co.
1601	British Vine	oil tanker	23 September 1964	26 March 1965	13408	BP Tanker Co.
1602	British Centaur	oil tanker	15 June 1965	11 January 1966	37985	BP Tanker Co.
1603G	Norsk Drott	oil tanker	20 December 1960	28 April 1961	18483	Norsk Braendselolje A/S
1604	British Cormorant	oil tanker	19 January 1961	6 July 1961	11132	BP Tanker Co.
1605G	British Osprey	oil tanker	24 August 1961	12 January 1962	11132	BP Tanker Co.
1606G	British Merlin	oil tanker	23 November 1961	19 May 1962	11132	BP Tanker Co.
1607	British Cygnet	oil tanker	9 January 1962	7 June 1962	11131	BP Tanker Co.
1608G	unnamed	oil tanker	cancelled			Ringdals Rederi A/S
1609G	Bulimba	cargo ship	25 September 1958	26 March 1959	6796	British India Steam Navigation Co.
1610G	Bankura	cargo ship	22 January 1959	27 August 1959	6793	British India Steam Navigation Co.
1611G	Barpeta	cargo ship	10 March 1960	19 September 1960	6736	British India Steam Navigation Co.
1612G	Bamora	cargo ship	6 September 1960	30 January 1961	6744	British India Steam Navigation Co.
1613G	Bombala	cargo ship	29 March 1961	28 August 1961	6744	British India Steam Navigation Co.
1614	Regent Liverpool	oil tanker	5 April 1962	23 November 1962	30770	Regent Petroleum Tankship Co. (Texaco (Panama) Inc.)
1615P	Flying Dipper	tug	11 December 1957	27 March 1958	274	Clyde Shipping Co.
1616	unnamed	cargo ship	cancelled		5000	Belships Co.
1617G	unnamed	cargo ship	cancelled		10000	Belships Co.
1618	unnamed	oil tanker	cancelled		18330	Bernhard A/S
1619	Krossfonn	bulk carrier	23 November 1960	8 April 1961	13481	Sigval Bergesen
1620	Rimfonn	oil tanker	19 August 1963	18 December 1963	50677	Sigval Bergesen
1621	Canberra	passenger ship	16 March 1960	19 May 1961	45270	Peninsular and Oriental Steam Navigation Co.
1622	Somers Isle	cargo ship	9 April 1959	10 July 1959	5684	Pacific Steam Navigation Co.
1623P	York					Hull & Netherlands Steamship Co.
	Wakefield	coaster	19 May 1958	8 October 1958	1113	Associated Humber Lines
1624P	Leeds	coaster	2 December 1958	16 April 1959	1113	Hull & Netherlands Steamship Co.
1625P	Wakefield					Associated Humber Lines
	York	coaster	8 July 1959	14 November 1959	1095	Hull & Netherlands Steamship Co.
1626	George Peacock	oil tanker	17 March 1961	6 July 1961	18863	Pacific Steam Navigation Co.
1627	unnamed	bulk carrier	cancelled		7000	Lorentzens Skibs A/S
1628	unnamed	bulk carrier	cancelled		7000	Halfdan Ditlev-Simonsen & Co.

Ship no.	Name	Vessel type	Flotation/launch date	Delivery date	Tonnage	Owner
1629	unnamed	bulk carrier	cancelled		7000	Lorentzens Rederi A/S
1630	Port Alfred	refrigerated cargo ship	8 September 1960	1 March 1961	9044	Port Line Ltd
1631	Port St Lawrence	refrigerated cargo ship	31 May 1961	20 October 1961	9040	Port Line Ltd
1632	HMS Kent	'County'-class destroyer	27 September 1961	17 August 1963	5200	Admiralty
1633	Icenic	refrigerated cargo ship	23 June 1960	19 December 1960	11239	Shaw Savill & Albion Co.
1634	unnamed	oil tanker	cancelled		50000	Sigval Bergesen
1635	Pinebank	cargo ship	5 June 1959	24 September 1959	8694	Andrew Weir & Co.
1636	Elmbank	cargo ship	29 December 1959	28 April 1960	8694	Andrew Weir & Co.
1637	Avonbank	cargo ship	6 October 1960	13 January 1961	8694	Andrew Weir & Co.
1638	Levernbank	cargo ship	28 April 1961	11 August 1961	8694	Andrew Weir & Co.
1639	Springbank	cargo ship	26 October 1961	26 January 1962	8694	Andrew Weir & Co.
1640	Olivebank	cargo ship	21 December 1961	12 April 1962	8694	Andrew Weir & Co.
1641	unnamed	oil tanker	cancelled			Eagle Oil and Shipping Co.
1642G	Daghestan	ore carrier	25 May 1960	1 November 1960	11210	Hindustan Steam Shipping Co.
1643P	Clyde	launch	14 December 1960	13 March 1961	65	Clyde Navigation Trust
1644P	Cressington	grab-hopper dredger	24 August 1961	4 April 1962	1431	British Transport Commission
1645P	Aigburth	screw-hopper dredger	17 May 1962	29 March 1963	1037	British Transport Commission
1646	Port Nicholson	refrigerated cargo ship	4 May 1962	9 November 1962	13847	Port Line Ltd
1647	Roybank	cargo ship	21 June 1963	31 October 1963	6526	Andrew Weir & Co.
1648	Weybank	cargo ship	31 December 1963	26 March 1964	6527	Andrew Weir & Co.
1649G	Ringwood	cargo ship	31 May 1962	29 September 1962	10860	Ringdals Rederi A/S
1650G	Belisland	cargo ship	26 September 1962	23 January 1963	10862	Belships Co.
1651	HMS Fearless	commando assault ship	19 December 1963	27 November 1965	11060	Admiralty
1652	Lossiebank	cargo ship	25 January 1963	3 July 1963	8678	Andrew Weir & Co.
1653	Methane Progress	liquefied-gas carrier	19 September 1963	26 May 1964	21875	Methane Tanker Finance Ltd
1654	Hazelbank	cargo ship	27 January 1964	20 May 1964	10507	Andrew Weir & Co.
1655	Irisbank	cargo ship	25 June 1964	9 September 1964	10526	Andrew Weir & Co.
1656	Texaco Maracaibo	oil tanker	6 August 1964	14 January 1965	51774	Texaco (Panama) Inc.
1657	HMNZS Waikato	'Leander'-class frigate	18 February 1965	19 September 1966	2305	Royal New Zealand Navy
1658	RFA Regent	fleet replenishment ship	9 March 1966	6 June 1967	19000	Admiralty
1659	Edenfield	oil tanker	5 March 1965	2 July 1967	35805	Hunting (Eden) Tankers Ltd
1660	La Estancia	bulk carrier	30 June 1965	30 September 1965	28007	Buries Markes Ltd
1661	La Sierra	bulk carrier	24 November 1965	12 February 1966	28004	Buries Markes Ltd
1662	Orcoma	cargo ship	25 January 1966	30 March 1966	10509	Nile Steamship Co.
1663	Donax	oil tanker	5 July 1966	16 December 1966	42068	Shell International Marine Ltd
						Shell Tankers (UK) Ltd
1664	Doryssa	oil tanker	cancelled		41000	Shell International Marine Ltd
						Shell Tankers (UK) Ltd
1665	Nairnbank	cargo ship	6 May 1966	7 July 1966	10541	Andrew Weir & Co.

Ship no.	Name	Vessel type	Flotation/launch date	Delivery date	Tonnage	Owner
1666	Myrina	supertanker	6 September 1967	24 April 1968	95450	Deutsche Shell A.G.
1667	Ulster Prince	passenger/cargo ferry	13 October 1966	6 April 1967	4478	Coast Lines Ltd
1668	Fjordaas	bulk carrier	25 April 1967	29 August 1967	41079	Norwegian Bulk Carriers
1669	Essi Kristine	bulk carrier	21 November 1967	1 March 1968	41089	Norwegian Bulk Carriers
1670	Skaufast	bulk carrier	9 August 1968	29 October 1968	57204	Norwegian Bulk Carriers
1671	Thara	bulk carrier	14 May 1968	28 August 1968	41089	Norwegian Bulk Carriers
1672	Aino	bulk carrier	18 March 1969	16 May 1969	57204	C.H. Sorensen & Sonner
1673	Maplebank	cargo ship	24 May 1967	15 August 1967	10365	Andrew Weir & Co.
1674	Gowanbank	cargo ship	1 December 1967	30 January 1968	10365	Andrew Weir & Co.
1675	HMS Charybdis	'Leander'-class frigate	28 February 1968	6 June 1969	2450	Ministry of Defence
1676	Esso Ulidia	supertanker	11 May 1970	6 October 1970	126538	Esso Petroleum Co.
1677	Esso Caledonia	supertanker	29 May 1971	6 September 1971	126535	Esso Petroleum Co.
1678	La Pampa	bulk carrier	22 January 1970	13 May 1970	17180	Buries Markes Ltd
1679	Bulk Eagle	bulk carrier	6 May 1970	14 September 1970	17180	Kriship Shipping Co.
1680	Sydney Bridge	bulk carrier	2 June 1970	10 September 1970	35868	Bowring Steamship Co.
1681	unnamed	bulk carrier	cancelled		50000	Javelin Bulk Carriers Ltd
1682	unnamed	bulk carrier	cancelled		50000	Javelin Bulk Carriers Ltd
1683	unnamed	supertanker	cancelled		126100	Globtik Tankers Ltd
1684	Rudby	bulk carrier	11 December 1970	1 March 1971	57245	Ropner Shipping Co.
1685	Olympic Banner	supertanker	7 October 1972	24 November 1972	128561	Carlow Maritime Panama S.A. (an Onassis company)
1686	Olympic Brilliance	supertanker	4 August 1973	7 September 1973	128561	Lakeport Navigation Co. Panama S.A. (an Onassis company)
1687	unnamed	supertanker	cancelled		128500	Olympic Maritime S.A. (an Onassis company)
1688	Iron Somersby	bulk carrier	8 October 1971	7 December 1971	57250	Ropner Shipping Co.
1689	Barbro	bulk carrier	18 December 1971	18 February 1972	56915	Rederi A/S Mascot
1690	Belinda	bulk carrier	26 April 1972	30 June 1972	56915	Rederi A/S Mascot
1691	Winsford Bridge / Mount Newman	bulk carrier	1 October 1973	16 November 1973	65131	Pacific Maritime Services Ltd (Furness Withy & Co.)
1692	Canadian Bridge	bulk carrier	5 October 1974	29 November 1974	65135	Britain Steamship Co. (Bibby Brothers)
1693	World Cavalier	supertanker	23 March 1974	12 June 1974	138025	Hendale Navigation Co. Ltd (Worldwide Shipping Co.)
1694	Lotorium	supertanker	13 December 1974	27 February 1975	138037	Broughton Navigation Co. Ltd / Shell Tankers (UK) Ltd
1695	Lampas	supertanker	5 July 1975	17 November 1975	161632	Airlease International (Shell International)
1696	Lepeta	supertanker	27 January 1976	26 July 1976	161632	Airlease International (Shell International)

Ship no.	Name	Vessel type	Flotation/launch date	Delivery date	Tonnage	Owner
1697	*Leonia*	supertanker	2 July 1976	30 December 1976	161626	Airlease International (Shell International)
1698	*Lima*	supertanker	11 December 1976	3 June 1977	161632	Airlease International (Shell International)
1699	*Essi Camilla*	bulk carrier	8 October 1975	5 January 1976	63509	Bj Ruud-Pedersen
1700	unnamed	bulk carrier	cancelled		64000	Arnt J. Morland
1701	*Otterpool Lackenby*	bulk carrier	21 March 1977	5 July 1977	64640	Ropner Shipping Co.
1702	unnamed	supertanker	cancelled		172000	Kimberley Shipping Co. (Maritime Fruit Carriers)
1703	unnamed	supertanker	cancelled		172000	Malmesbury Shipping Co. (Maritime Fruit Carriers)
1704	*Coastal Texas Coastal Corpus Christi*	supertanker	18 June 1977	25 March 1980	172147	Woodstock Shipping Co. (Maritime Fruit Carriers) (Coastal States Gas Corporation)
1705	*Coastal Hercules*	supertanker	27 January 1978	25 March 1980	172147	Pomona Shipping Co. (Maritime Fruit Carriers) (Coastal States Gas Corporation)
1706	unnamed	supertanker	cancelled		172000	Wellsford Shipping Co. (Maritime Fruit Carriers)
1707	unnamed	supertanker	cancelled		172000	Kinross Shipping Co. (Maritime Fruit Carriers)
1708	*Golden Master Appleby*	bulk carrier	24 June 1978	31 October 1978	64641	Golden West & Fearnley & Egers Ropner Shipping Co.
1709	*Hornby Grange*	products carrier	6 October 1978	20 June 1979	39626	Alexander Shipping Co. (Furness, Withy & Co.)
1710	*Elstree Grange*	products carrier	27 January 1979	24 October 1979	39626	Alexander Shipping Co. (Furness, Withy & Co.)
1711	*Isomeria*	liquid petroleum gas carrier	21 March 1981	30 April 1982	42069	North Sea Marine Leasing Co. (Shell Tankers (UK) Ltd)
1712	*Isocardia*	liquid petroleum gas carrier	23 January 1982	29 October 1982	39932[1]	North Sea Marine Leasing Co. (Shell Tankers (UK) Ltd)
1713	*Galloway Princess*	passenger/car ferry	24 May 1979	22 April 1980	6268	Midland and Montagu Leasing Ltd (Sealink (UK) Ltd)
1714	*Ravenscraig*	bulk carrier	7 September 1979	14 December 1979	64651	Orion Leasing Ltd (British Steel Corporation)
1715	*St Anselm*	passenger/car ferry	5 December 1979	16 October 1980	7003.	Lloyds Leasing Ltd (Sealink (UK) Ltd)

Ship no.	Name	Vessel type	Flotation/launch date	Delivery date	Tonnage	Owner
1716	St Christopher	passenger/car ferry	20 March 1980	6 March 1981	6996	Barclays Mercantile Industrial Finance (Sealink (UK) Ltd)
1717	St David	passenger/car ferry	25 September 1980	24 July 1981	7109	Barclays Mercantile Industrial Finance (Sealink (UK) Ltd)
1718	British Skill	oil tanker	3 July 1982	26 April 1983	66034[1]	BP Thames Tanker Co.
1719	British Success	oil tanker	28 March 1983	14 February 1984	66034[1]	BP Thames Tanker Co.
1720	British Steel	bulk carrier	28 January 1984	19 October 1984	90831[1]	Lombard Finance (British Steel Corporation)
1721	English Star	refrigerated cargo ship	23 September 1984	7 January 1986	10291[1]	Lombard North Central (Blue Star Line Ltd)
1722	Scottish Star	refrigerated cargo ship	23 September 1984	2 April 1985	10291[1]	Lombard North Central (Blue Star Line Ltd)
1723	Auckland Star	refrigerated cargo ship	4 March 1985	21 January 1986	10291[1]	Investors in Industry (Blue Star Line Ltd)
1724	Canterbury Star	refrigerated cargo ship	1 July 1985	4 February 1986	10291[1]	Investors in Industry (Blue Star Line Ltd)
1725	Ironbridge	bulk carrier			90000[1,2]	Lloyds Equipment Leasing Ltd (British Steel Corporation)
1726	Seillean	SWOPS-type ship			51200[1,2]	BP Petroleum Development Ltd
1727	RFA Fort Victoria	Fort'-class auxiliary oiler replenishment ship			30000[3]	Ministry of Defence

Notes
1 Tonnage computed in accordance with International Convention on Tonnage Measurement of ships 1969
2 Estimated gross tonnage
3 Estimated displacement tonnage

Vessels under construction at Caird & Co. of Greenock when that yard was taken over by Harland & Wolff in 1916. Caird's ship numbers were retained for these vessels.

Ship no.	Name	Vessel type	Launch date	Delivery date	Tonnage	Owner
330	Naldera	passenger ship	29 December 1917	25 March 1920	15993	Peninsular and Oriental Steam Navigation Co.
348	Ballarat	passenger ship	14 September 1920	15 December 1921	13144	Peninsular and Oriental Steam Navigation Co.
349	Balranald	passenger ship	24 February 1921	5 April 1922	13144	Peninsular and Oriental Steam Navigation Co.
350	War Bracken	'A'-type cargo ship	31 October 1917	23 January 1918	5182	Shipping Controller (Lyle Shipping)
351	War Malayan	'AO'-type tanker	28 March 1918	27 June 1918	5223	Shipping Controller (Andrew Weir & Co.)
352	War Emu	'B'-type cargo ship	29 June 1918	28 August 1918	5244	Shipping Controller (Donaldson Brothers)
353	War Burman Burgondier	'AO'-type tanker	17 October 1918	10 May 1919	5292	Shipping Controller Lloyd Royal Belge
354	War Alyssum Bathurst	'A'-type cargo ship	20 February 1919	26 March 1919	5253	Shipping Controller Elder Dempster & Co.
355	War Anchusa	'A'-type cargo ship	7 December 1918	22 January 1919	5244	Shipping Controller

Vessels under construction at the yard of Archibald MacMillan & Son of Dumbarton in 1917 when Harland & Wolff took over the management of that yard. MacMillan's ship numbers were retained.

Ship no.	Name	Vessel type	Launch date	Delivery date	Tonnage	Owner
469	War Stock Dalworth	'A'-type cargo ship	18 February 1920	1 May 1920	4538	Shipping Controller Dalgleish & Co.
479	Lyghern	cargo ship	24 May 1920	6 July 1920	4896	Transatlantic & Co.
480	Torrey	cargo ship	30 August 1920	18 November 1920	4811	Heistein & Sons
481	War Marten Browning	'B'-type cargo ship	26 June 1919	28 August 1919	5332	Shipping Controller Lamport & Holt Line Ltd
482	War Mole Bonheur	'B'-type cargo ship	28 October 1919	16 December 1919	5335	Shipping Controller Lamport & Holt Line Ltd
	Bruyre					

574

GENERAL INDEX

Page numbers in italics denote illustrations or tables.

591

Ministry of Supply 324, 325, 338, 342, *see also* ship nos 1045G, 1050-51, 1053, 1078, 1083G
Ministry of Supply and Aircraft Production 357
Ministry of Technology 426, 427, 431, 434, 435
Ministry of War Transport 328, 334, 339, 344, *see also* ship nos 1115-16G, 1118-20, 1125, 1151P, 1158-9, 1160G, 1164-5, 1168-9G, 1175P, 1184P, 1188-9, 1190P, 1197G, 1219, 1225P, 1227P, 1230-31, 1234, 1242, 1243G, 1276, 1282P, 1286-8P, 1299-1302P, 1303, 1306G, 1311-14P, 1315G, 1317G, 1319-22P, 1323-4G, 1334-42P
Mississippi Dominion Steamship Co. 98
Mitchell & Co. 96
Mitchell & Neilson 360
Mitchell, P.G.M. 247
Moltzaus & Christensen ship no. 1412
Moltzaus Tankrederi A/S 371, *see also* ship nos 1495, 1536
Montevideo Gas & Drydock Co. ship no. 755G
Montgomery (of Dundesart), Alexander 24, *94-5*
Montgomery, Catherine *94-5*
Montgomery, Eliza Swan (Mrs J.A. Pirrie) 24, *94-5*
Montrose 84
Moore, Henry *406*
Morgan & Co., J.P. *125*, 138, 140, 149, 164
Morgan Grenfell & Co. *125*, 126, 164
Morgan, J. Pierpoint 106, 114, 117, 122, 125, 146
Morison, Elizabeth *see* Pirrie, Elizabeth
Morison, (Sir) John 278, 308, 313-14, 321, 342-3
Morison (of Sandyland), William 6
Morrison, John 340, 371
Morland, Arnt J. ship no. 1700
Morland, Harold 268, 272, 293
Morland, S. ship no. 56
Morrow, Dr J.S. 243
Morton, Sir Brian 461, 463, 467, 473, 474, 484-5
Moss & Co., James *271, see also* ship nos 33, 34, 35, 800Gk, 858G

Moss group *271*
Moss Hutchison Line Ltd 358, *see also* ship nos 1359-60, 1385G, 1386
Moss Steamship Co. 270, *271, see also* ship nos 864-5D
Mosvold, Martin 363, *see also* ship no. 1407
Motherwell 190
Mulberry Harbours 344
Munitions factory, Belfast 323, *352, 353*
Munitions of War Act 180
Murphy Ltd, Michael *271*
Murphy, MP, E.S. 299
Murphy, T.E. 374, 382, 400, 462
Musgrave channel 80, 81, 112, 113, 154, 188, 198, 222, 317, 331, 368-9, *384*, 394, *425, 426*
Musgrave yard *see* East yard
Myers, Son & Co., W.J. 36, 61, *see also* ship nos 95-6, 194-5, 258

Napier Bros 360
Napier, David 3
Napier, G.G. *214*
Napier, Isabella *214*
Napier, James ship no. 17
Napier, Robert 11, 29, 405
Napier & Sons, Robert 50, 92, 154
National Amalgamated Sheet Metal Workers and Braziers 172
National Amalgamated Society of Painters and Decorators 172
National Bank of Scotland *138*, 172, *184*, 185, 189, 205, *216, 256*, 263, *346, 398*
National Discount Co. 234
National line 28
National Ports Council 446
National Shipbuilders Security Ltd (NSS) 285, 292, 295, 298, 301, 306-309, 377
National Shipyards 197, 201, 202, *202*
National Society of Coppersmiths Braziers and Metal Workers 172
National Steamship Co. 72, 86
National Union of Mineworkers 455
National Union of Public Employees 462
National United Smiths and Hammermen 172

Navigation Syndicate *121*
Nederlandsch-Amerikaansche Stoomvart Maatschoppij *see* Holland-America line
Nederlandsch Indische Tank Stoomboot Mij 267, *see also* ship nos 747-50G
Neill & Sons, R. 40, *see also* ship no. 116
Nelson Ltd, H.&W. *183*, 205, *214*, 243, *254*, 263, *271*, 273, *see also* ship nos 751, 806, 812, 813G, 814
Nelson, Sir George 360, 364
Nelson Steam Navigation Co. *254, 271*, 277, 288, 294, *see also* ship no. 916
Netherlands Steamship Co. 102
Newcastle upon Tyne 13, 15, 149, 154
Newell, Ronald 405
Newport News shipyard 79
New South Wales Government 302
New Steam Navigation Co. ship no. 42
New York & West Africa Steam Navigation Co. ship nos 562G, 568G
New Zealand Shipping Co. ship no. 1230
Nigeria 365
Nile Steamship Co. 408, *see also* ship no. 1662
Nippon Yusen Kaisha 235, *see also* ship no. 658M
Nordat-Contischer Dampfer Linien Verband (NDLV) 96
Norddeutscher Lloyd 96, 106, 108, 230
Norman, Montagu 272, 278, 280, 283, 285, 320
Norsk Braendselolje A/S ship no. 1603G
North Atlantic Steam Navigation Co. *18*
North British Locomotive Co. 370
North Coast Steam Navigation Co. ship no. 990G
Northern Bank 420
Northern Ireland Act, 1974 460
Northern Ireland Civil Rights Association 429
Northern Ireland Development Association 471
Northern Ireland Government 224, 231, 235, 239, 248, 260, 288, 292-3, 297-8, 304-305, 307-308, 313-15, 317, 328, 335, 416-17, 418-19, 424, 425, 433, 435, 436, 437, 438,